# Kenya Handbook

**Lizzie Williams**

*Based on previous editions of the East Africa Handbook*
*by Michael Hodd and Angela Roche*

**" "**

**There is something about safari life that**
**makes you forget all your sorrows and feel as**
**if you had drunk half a bottle of champagne –**
**bubbling over with heartfelt gratitude for**
**being alive.**

*Karen Blixen (Isak Dinesen), Out of Africa.*

# Footprint story

### It was 1921

Ireland had just been partitioned, the British miners were striking for more pay and the federation of British industry had an idea. Exports were booming in South America – how about a handbook for businessmen trading in that far away continent? The Anglo-South American Handbook was born that year, written by W Koebel, the most prolific writer on Latin America of his day.

### 1924

Two editions later the book was 'privatized' and in 1924, in the hands of Royal Mail, the steamship company for South America, it became The South American Handbook, subtitled 'South America in a nutshell'. This annual publication became the 'bible' for generations of travellers to South America and remains so to this day. In the early days travel was by sea and the Handbook gave all the details needed for the long voyage from Europe. What to wear for dinner; how to arrange a cricket match with the Cable & Wireless staff on the Cape Verde Islands and a full account of the journey from Liverpool up the Amazon to Manaus: 5898 miles without changing cabin!

### 1939

As the continent opened up, The South American Handbook reported the new Pan Am flying boat services, and the fortnightly airship service from Rio to Europe on the Graf Zeppelin. For reasons still unclear but with extraordinary determination, the annual editions continued through the Second World War.

### 1970s

Many more people discovered South America and the backpacking trail started to develop. All the while the Handbook was gathering fans, including literary vagabonds such as Paul Theroux and Graham Greene (who once sent some updates addressed to "The publishers of the best travel guide in the world, Bath, England").

### 1990s

During the 1990s the company set about developing a new travel guide series using this legendary title as the flagship. By 1997 there were over a dozen guides in the series and the Footprint imprint was launched.

### 2000s

The series grew quickly and there were soon Footprint travel guides covering more than 150 countries. In 2004, Footprint launched its first thematic guide: *Surfing Europe*, packed with colour photographs, maps and charts. This was followed by further thematic guides such as *Diving the World*, *Snowboarding the World*, *Body and Soul escapes*, *Travel with Kids* and *European City Breaks*.

### 2009

Today we continue the traditions of the last 87 years that has served legions of travellers so well. We believe that these help to make Footprint guides different. Our policy is to use authors who are genuine experts who write for independent travellers; people possessing a spirit of adventure, looking to get off the beaten track.

**Title page**: Cheetah stalking from a hill in Larsek. **Above**: A flock of lesser flamingos (*Phoenicopterus minor*) take flight from Lake Bogoria.

Kenya's landscapes are diverse: from rolling savannah and mountain forests, to stony parched deserts and a tropical coastline. It is these habitats that harbour some of Africa's most incredible animal species and a safari, meaning 'journey' in Kiswahili, is a highlight for many visitors. Along the coast, coral reefs team with life and colour, while the Rift Valley lakes are home to thousands of flamingos. Kenya's is also known for its diversity of people: the majestic Masai and Samburu still stalk the plains dressed in their trademark red and purple robes; while the legacies of the European white settlers who came in search of pristine farming land and hunting trophies can still be seen. Kenya's two major cities – the high-altitude colonial-built capital Nairobi and the steamy trading port of Mombasa – have a vibrant urban feel, while on the coast Swahili culture has been much in evidence for hundreds of years.

NORTHERN KENYA

WESTERN KENYA

RIFT VALLEY

CENTRAL HIGHLANDS

Lake Victoria

NAIROBI

LAMU ARCHIPELAGO

SOUTHERN KENYA

THE COAST

Indian Ocean

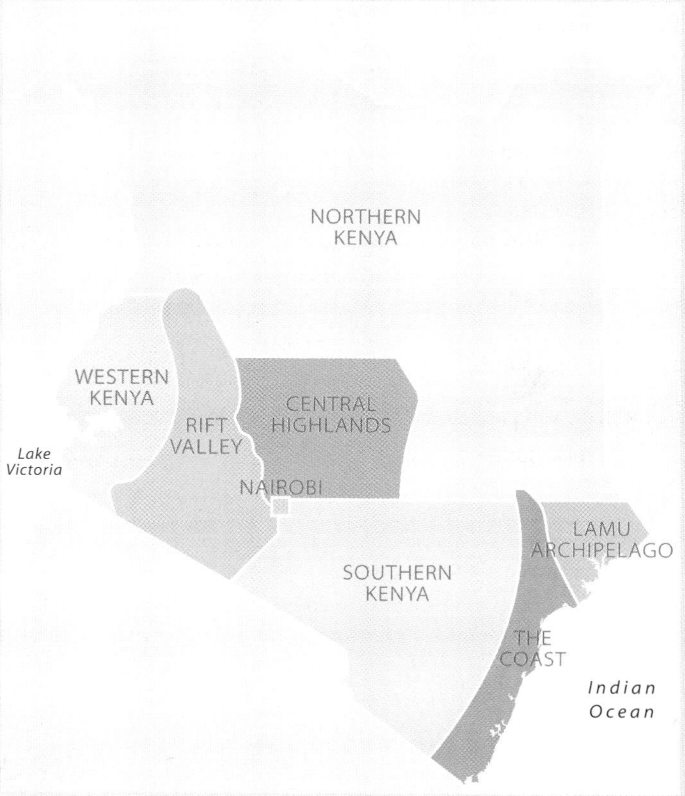

# Contents

# Planning your trip

PAUL BANTON/SHUTTERSTOCK

Wildebeest leap into the Mara River during migration.

# Where to go

Straddling the equator and with a temperate climate, most people travel to Kenya to visit one or several of the excellent game reserves and national parks in pursuit of the Big Five. Whilst the journey may be rough on the parks' bumpy and slippery roads, there is no denying that there is a wide range of locations in which to see game. Not so well known is Kenya's birdlife; the country has a huge number of species in the forests of the highlands and the Rift Valley lakes. Some of the game lodges are not as luxurious as in other regions of Africa, but they are improving, and some first-rate small establishments that match the luxury of lodges in southern Africa are beginning to appear on the safari circuit. In the Masai Mara alone there are almost 60 game lodges and tented camps, and in the other parks, such as Tsavo, tourism facilities are growing to match the demand of visitors.

Kenya's coastal attractions include palm-fringed, white sandy beaches and coral reefs surrounding the offshore islands, some of which drop away to form steep underwater cliffs that plunge to depths of more than 600 m. There are a number of marine national parks along the coast that form a veritable playground for a spectrum of marine species. Most visitors on package holidays combine time on the beach with a safari to see the animals. Independent visitors have the added opportunity to explore the areas away from the normal tourist circuit: the impossibly pretty forests and highlands in Western Kenya, the arid northern deserts, the stately Mount Kenya or the lively upcountry towns. Anyone with an interest in traditional Swahili culture should head to Lamu for the enchanting atmosphere of the ancient old town that has been there for thousands of years. Nairobi too has a growing clutch of attractions and is worth making time for. The animal welfare centres around its periphery offer unique opportunities for getting up close and personal to a number of animals; an experience children especially will enjoy, and Nairobi National Park probably offers the easiest safari options in the country.

Throughout Kenya there are a number of interesting museums, including the critically acclaimed and newly revamped Nairobi National Museum, which offers glimpses into the country's fascinating history and ethnicity. Nairobi is the obvious gateway not only to Kenya, but to the rest of East Africa, and safaris can be extended to Uganda to perhaps see the rare mountain gorillas, in the forests that straddle the borders with Rwanda and the Democratic Republic of Congo, or south to the parks and reserves in Tanzania, which can easily be combined with a safari to Kenya's southern parks.

HEMIS.FR/SUPERSTOCK

**Above:** One of Lamu Town's many mosques.
**Opposite page:** Lake Baringo is famous for its birdlife.

# Itineraries

None of the circuits below is a complete itinerary in itself, and they are not set in stone. Rather, they are regional suggestions for travellers wishing to explore a certain part of the country. Nairobi or Mombasa are the usual arrival points into Kenya for international travellers, so what you do rather depends on where you arrive.

## One week

If you arrive in Mombasa, you could easily spend a week by the beach at one of the affordable resorts, which have direct transfers from the airport. From the resorts you can take day trips along the coast to see attractions such as Wasini Island to the south, the old town of Mombasa itself, or the marine parks along the northern beaches. Not far away from the beach is the Shimba Hills National Reserve, a very popular day trip where there is an excellent chance of spotting elephant. Tsavo East and West national parks are also within striking distance of the coast, less than a two-hour drive away, and a beach holiday could be combined with one or two nights in a game lodge. There is also the possibility of heading north up the coast for a night or two to on the islands of Lamu, less than an hour's flight from Malindi, to experience a very different atmosphere from the beachside hotels. Lamu is yet to be developed for tourism and, in addition to beautiful beaches, there is the wonderfully friendly ancient stone town with its intriguing narrow alleyways, superb museum and Arabic houses.

If flying into Nairobi, there are parks and reserves just a few hours' drive away. The closest is Nairobi National Park, which has the city as its backdrop and can easily be visited on a half-day trip. Tour operators in Nairobi can organize safaris to the Masai Mara, Amboseli, Tsavo, the Aberdares, Lake Nakuru

HEMIS.FR/SUPERSTOCK

and the Rift Valley, and Mount Kenya. How many you visit and how long you stay depends on personal preference and there are any number of combinations. A popular circuit from Nairobi is two to three nights in the Masai Mara then one night to see Lake Naivasha, and one night to visit Nakuru National Park. Another option is to spend two to three nights in both Amboseli and Tsavo. The shortest safaris available from Nairobi are two nights in either Amboseli or the Masai Mara. Nairobi itself is worth allowing at least a day to explore as there are some very interesting wildlife centres and attractions on the edge of the city. These include the Langata Giraffe Centre, the David Sheldrick Wildlife Trust and the Karen Blixen Museum. In the city itself, it's well worth spending half a day at the newly revamped Nairobi National Museum to learn about Kenya's flora and fauna and its rich cultural history.

**Above**: Masai warriors in full regalia. **Opposite page left**: An ancient giant fig tree in the Kakamega Forest. **Opposite page right**: A white-bellied go-away bird in Tsavo.

## Two to three weeks

The above options can be combined as a two-week tour of Kenya allowing some time relaxing on the beach and some time watching the wildlife. Transport links between Nairobi and the coast are very good; there are several daily flights and buses and also there is the option of taking the overnight train. For those with more time, an interesting excursion from Nairobi, which shouldn't take more than three to four days, is to drive around Mount Kenya, with perhaps a night or two at the Aberdares National Park. The road is good and goes completely around the circumference of the mountain.

Here in the highlands are atmospheric colonial country hotels with the ever-present view of brooding Mount Kenya. If you want to climb the mountain allow four to five additional days. Another three- to four-day alternative is to explore the Rift Valley. Naivasha is a short drive from Nairobi where there is a fine selection of lakeshore accommodation to choose from and plenty of interesting things to do including walking or cycling in Hell's Gate National Park or visiting one of the new wildlife conservancies. From here, Nakuru and Nakuru National Park can easily be explored in half a day, and Lake Bogoria and Baringo, where you can see excellent bird life, are not far away.

## A month or more

From the Rift Valley you can head west into the Kenyan highlands towards Lake Victoria and the provincial towns of Kisumu, Kericho and Kitale. The towns themselves won't keep your interest for long but the countryside is extraordinarily pretty, especially at the Kakamega Forest and the verdant hillsides around Kericho, which are covered in tea plantations. This is also the region of the Mount Elgon and Saiwa Swamp national parks, which are very different to the southern reserves. In Mount Elgon there is the opportunity to see the unusual elephants that seek salt in the mountain's caves; Saiwa is home to the rare sitatunga antelope. North of the Aberdare Mountains is the newly established Laikipia Plateau, an applauded conservation effort by the ranch owners in this region to use their land for the protection of, and in many cases the breeding of, wildlife. This has been Kenya's greatest conservation success story in recent years and there are now some wonderful lodges and safari companies offering a huge range of safari activities. Here guests will receive more intimate and educational wildlife encounters than in the main parks (though at a price).

For those with a penchant for adventurous travel, Northern Kenya is a wild and untamed region of parched deserts, spectacular mountain ranges, and the turquoise waters of Kenya's largest lake, Turkana. Travel in this region is challenging and difficult, and has in recent years been marred by security problems. It is best to explore this region, where possible, on an organized tour.

ADRIAN ARBIB/ALAMY

STEFFEN FOERSTER PHOTOGRAPHY/SHUTTERSTOCK

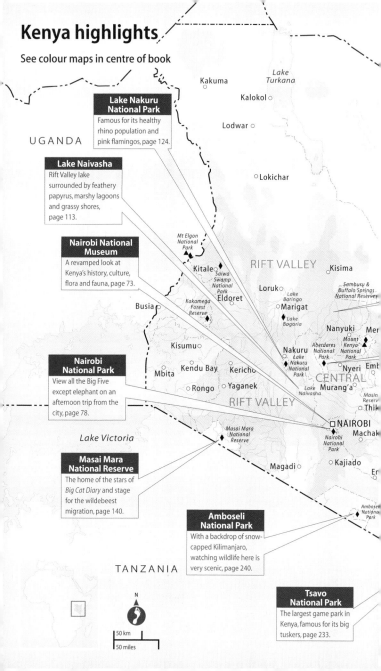

# Kenya highlights

See colour maps in centre of book

UGANDA

**Lake Nakuru National Park**
Famous for its healthy rhino population and pink flamingos, page 124.

**Lake Naivasha**
Rift Valley lake surrounded by feathery papyrus, marshy lagoons and grassy shores, page 113.

**Nairobi National Museum**
A revamped look at Kenya's history, culture, flora and fauna, page 73.

**Nairobi National Park**
View all the Big Five except elephant on an afternoon trip from the city, page 78.

**Masai Mara National Reserve**
The home of the stars of *Big Cat Diary* and stage for the wildebeest migration, page 140.

**Amboseli National Park**
With a backdrop of snow-capped Kilimanjaro, watching wildlife here is very scenic, page 240.

**Tsavo National Park**
The largest game park in Kenya, famous for its big tuskers, page 233.

Kakuma
Lake Turkana
Kalokol
Lodwar
Lokichar

Mt Elgon National Park
Kitale
Salwa Swamp National Park
Loruk
Kakamega Forest Reserve
Eldoret
Busia
Lake Baringo
Marigat
Lake Bogoria
Kisumu
Kendu Bay
Kericho
Mbita
Rongo
Yaganek
Nakuru
Lake Nakuru National Park
Lake Naivasha

RIFT VALLEY
Kisima
Samburu & Buffalo Springs National Reserve
Nanyuki
Mer
Aberdares National Park
Mount Kenya National Park
Nyeri
Emb
CENTRAL
Murang'a
Masin Reserv
Thik
NAIROBI
Nairobi National Park
Machak

Lake Victoria
Masai Mara National Reserve

Magadi
Kajiado
Er

Ambose National Park

TANZANIA

N

50 km
50 miles

ETHIOPIA

Ramu

Moyale

El Wak

**Samburu and Buffalo Springs national reserves**
Unusual wildlife in an arid environment, page 356.

SOMALIA

NORTH EASTERN

EASTERN

**Laikipia Plateau**
Kenya's newest wildlife destination and conservation success story, page 211.

**Aberdares National Park**
Treetops and The Ark are the famous park lodges, pages 195 and 198.

Garissa

Mwingi

**Lamu Old Town**
Steeped in Swahili history with intriguing alleyways and Arabian houses, page 325.

Mokowe   *Pate Island*

*Lamu    Manda
Island    Island*

Garsen

COAST

*Indian Ocean*

**Tamarind, Mombasa**
Eat delicious seafood on a romantic white-sailed *dhow*, page 260.

◆ *Tsavo
National Park*

Malindi

Voi

Kilifi

**Diani Beach**
One of the finest stretches of white-sand beach in the country, page 269.

*Shimba Hills
National Reserve* ◆   Mombasa

Lunga
Lunga   Shirazi

# Safaris and game reserves

Going on safari can be a most rewarding experience in Kenya. There are a number of national parks and game reserves, some owned by the government and administered by the Kenya Wildlife Services, and some in the private sector such as local ranches in local communities. The difference between a 'national park' and a 'national reserve' depends on the access given to local people. In national parks the animals have the parks to themselves. In national reserves the local people are allowed rights of grazing. Most people visit on an organized safari, which involves staying at a safari lodge or tented camp, or at the cheaper end of the scale at a campsite, and going out on game drives in a specially adapted vehicle, with a guide; although it's still a good idea to take along some wildlife and bird books. The best time of day to spot animals is early in the morning and late in the afternoon, as many animals sleep through the intense midday heat. Animals can most easily be seen during the dry season when the lack of surface water forces them to congregate around rivers and waterholes. However, the rainy seasons, from October to November and March to June, are when the animals are in the best condition – after feeding on the new shoots – and you might be lucky enough to see mating displays. The disadvantage of the wet season is that the thicker vegetation and the wider availability of water mean that the wildlife is more spread out and more difficult to spot; also, driving conditions are far harder in deep mud as none of the park roads are paved. However, prices for lodges can be up to a third lower during the rainy seasons.

Driving around endlessly searching for animals is not usually the best way to view animals. While speed limits are often 40 kph, the optimum speed for game viewing by car is around 15 kph. Drives can be broken up by stops at waterholes, picnic sites and hides. Time spent around a waterhole with your engine switched off gives you an opportunity to listen to the sounds of the bush and experience the rhythms of nature as game moves to and from the water.

Kenya's game parks and reserves are well organized; following the few park rules will ensure an enjoyable stay.

**Above**: A herd of elephants in Amboseli National Park in front of a snow-capped Mount Kilimanjaro.
**Opposite page**: Sunset over the Masai Mara's acacia-studded plains.

## Game-viewing rules

Keep on the well-marked roads and track; off-road driving is harmful because smoke, oil and destruction of the grass layer cause soil erosion.

▸▸ Do not drive through closed roads or park areas. It is mandatory to enter and exit the parks through the authorized gates.

▸▸ For your own safety, stay in your vehicle at all times. Your vehicle serves as a blind or hide, since animals will not usually identify it with humans. In all the parks that are visited by car it is forbidden to leave the vehicle except in designated places, such as picnic sites or walking trails.

▸▸ Stick to the parks' opening hours; it is usually forbidden to drive from dusk to dawn unless you are granted special authorization. At night you are requested to stay at your lodge or campsite.

▸▸ Never harass the animals. Make as little noise as possible; do not flash lights or make sudden movements to scare them away; never try and attract the animals' attention by calling out or whistling.

▸▸ Never chase the animals and remember that they always have right of way.

▸▸ Do not feed the animals; the food you provide might make them ill, and once animals such as elephants learn that food is available from humans they can become aggressive and dangerous when looking for more and will eventually have to be shot.

▸▸ If camping at night in the parks, ensure that the animals cannot gain access to any food you are carrying.

▸▸ Do not throw any litter, including used matches and cigarette butts; this not only increases fire risk in the dry season, but also some animals will eat whatever they find.

▸▸ Do not disturb other visitors. They have the same right as you to enjoy nature. If you discover a stationary vehicle and you want to check what they are looking at, never hinder their sight nor stop within their photographic field. If there is no room for another car, wait patiently for your turn, the others will finally leave and the animals will still be there. If there is a group of vehicles, most drivers will take it in turns to occupy the prime viewing spot.

▸▸ Always turn the engine off when you are watching game up close.

▸▸ Do not speed; the speed limit is usually 40 kph. Speeding damages road surfaces, increases noise and raises the risk of running over animals.

▸▸ Wild animals are dangerous; despite their beauty their reactions are unpredictable. Don't expose yourself to unnecessary risks; excessive confidence can lead to serious accidents.

STEFANIE VAN DEN VINDEN/SHUTTERSTOCK

# Diving in Kenya

## Scuba-diving

Undoubtedly one of Kenya's greatest tourism assets are the vast areas of coral reef that stretch south from the equator fringing the coastline and surrounding islands. These huge living coral formations, which in the past were a mariners' worst nightmare, have now become the playground for the tourist and house at least 3000 different species of marine animal and plant. The infamous El Niño has been to blame for much of the coral bleaching and damage to many top reefs of East Africa, but the positive signs of regrowth are definitely in place, and for divers the visible damage shouldn't detract from the splendour and abundance of the marine life. The best time to dive in Kenya is between October and April – before the long rains, which can cause subsequent river outflows that affect visibility.

Average visibility in the diving season ranges from 10 m to 30 m.

Most of the reefs and marine life along the coast are protected by national parks. The offshore reefs are alive with coral, myriad fish, sea turtles and dolphins. Both outer and inner reef walls offer world-class diving with spectacular coral gardens and drop-offs. None of the dive sites are more than a 30-minute boat ride away from the beaches. The marine parks include Kisite to the south of Mombasa around beautiful Wasini Island – an ideal day trip for divers and snorkellers – and Watamu and Malindi marine parks to the north of Mombasa. A wreck has been deliberately sunk off the coast just north of Mombasa, which is fast becoming a successful artificial reef (see box, page 290). There are many dive schools along the coast and almost every hotel and resort offers diving. Most schools

R GOMBARIK/SHUTTERSTOCK

AGE FOOTSTOCK/SUPERSTOCK

**Opposite page:** A starfish rests on a coral reef.
**Above:** Traditional outrigger canoe in Watamu.

offer single dives or diving courses, often in French, German and Italian, as well as English. Dive schools are listed in the relevant sections of the book and their websites are a very good resource for more information about diving in Kenya. Most resorts run PADI courses up to Dive Master level; BSAC, NAUI, CMAS and SSI centres also exist but are not as common. Costs average US$50-60 per dive, though if you book more than one dive at a time, costs come down. The beginner's PADI Open Water course takes four to five days and costs US$450-500 depending on marine park fees, day excursions including lunch, and whether you get to keep the expensive training manual after the course, but includes theory lessons, pool sessions and four or five ocean training dives. Medical questionnaires must be completed prior to a course and medical certificates might be required. Non-divers can also enjoy the reefs by snorkelling from the beach or a boat or, if you don't want to get wet, watching the fish through the floor of a glass-bottomed boat can be arranged at all of the coastal resorts.

## Diving tips

All divers should be aware of the potential threat they pose to the fragile underwater environment and should help to sustain this delicate ecosystem by taking a few simple precautions. These diving tips are adapted from the Marine Conservation Society's 'Coral Code'. For further information visit www.mcsuk.org or contact the Communications Officer, T+44 (0)1989-566 017.

▸▸ Review your skills. If you haven't dived for a while, practise in the pool or sandy patch before diving around the reef.
▸▸ Choose your dive operator wisely. Report irresponsible operators to relevant diving authorities (PADI, NAUI, SSI).
▸▸ Control your fins. Deep fin kicks around coral can cause damage, so move gently and smoothly.
▸▸ Practise buoyancy control. Through proper weighting and practice, you should not allow yourself or any item of your equipment to touch any living organism.
▸▸ Never stand on the reef. Corals can be damaged by the slightest touch. If you need to hold on to something, look for a piece of dead coral or rock.
▸▸ Avoid kicking up sand, which can smother corals and other reef life.
▸▸ Know your limits. Don't dive in conditions beyond your skills.
▸▸ Do not disturb or move things around (eg for photography).
▸▸ Do not collect or buy shells or any other marine curios (eg dried pufferfish).
▸▸ Do not feed fish.
▸▸ Do not ride turtles or hold on to any marine animal as this can easily cause heart attacks or severe shock to the creature.

# When to go

Kenya's daytime temperatures average between 20°C and 25°C, though it is cooler in the highlands and hotter along the coast. Humidity varies, being high along the coastal strip but much lower in the interior highlands. On the coast, high temperatures are cooled by ocean breezes so it is rarely overpoweringly hot. Away from the coast, it is much drier and the rains are a little kinder. On peaks above 1500 m the climate is cooler with permanent snow on the highest peaks, such as Mount Kenya where night-time temperatures drop to below zero.

There are two rainy seasons in the country: the long rains fall March to April and the short rains fall October to December. Even in these months, however, there is an average of four to six hours of sunshine each day. Bear in mind that malaria peaks during the rainy seasons, when mosquitoes are prolific. Travelling by road, especially in the more remote areas or through the national parks, is easier during the dry months, as road conditions deteriorate significantly in the rainy seasons.

High season along the coast is from September to January and it gets especially busy around the Christmas and New Year period. High season in the safari regions is July to November, especially in the Masai Mara as this is when the wildebeest have

**Above**: Traditional homesteads in Loyangalani, Lake Turkana. **Opposite page**: Tea plantations in Western Kenya.

arrived from the Serengeti in Tanzania on their annual migration.

For sheer numbers of birds the best time for birdwatching is October to April when over 120 migrant species arrive from the northern hemisphere, mostly from the Palearctic but with some African migrants too. The coast is particularly good during this period with large flocks of water birds congregating at Mida Creek and Sabaki Estuary, while the Rift Valley lakes and Amboseli attract a lot of waterfowl.

As Kenya is on the equator, the times of sunrise and sunset hardly change throughout the year – sunrise is generally and 0700-0800 and sunset 1800-1900.

## Kenya

| Activity | J | F | M | A | M | J | J | A | S | O | N | D |
|---|---|---|---|---|---|---|---|---|---|---|---|---|
| Glide over the wildebeest migration in a hot-air balloon | | | | | | | ★ | ★ | ★ | ★ | ★ | |
| Explore the dazzling coral reefs | ★ | ★ | ★ | ★ | | | | ★ | ★ | ★ | ★ | ★ |
| Twitchers will enjoy birdwatching over 1000 species | ★ | ★ | ★ | ★ | | | | ★ | ★ | ★ | ★ | ★ |
| Laze on tropical beaches lapped by the warm Indian Ocean | ★ | ★ | ★ | | | | ★ | ★ | ★ | | | ★ |
| Climb to the snow line on Mount Kenya | ★ | ★ | ★ | | | | ★ | ★ | | | | |
| Photograph elephants in front of Mount Kilimanjaro | ★ | ★ | | | ★ | ★ | ★ | ★ | ★ | ★ | ★ | ★ |

# Rainfall and climate charts

### Nairobi

| Month | Average temperature in °C max-min | Average rainfall in mm |
|---|---|---|
| Jan | 25 - 12 | 38 |
| Feb | 26 - 13 | 34 |
| Mar | 25 - 14 | 125 |
| Apr | 24 - 14 | 211 |
| May | 22 - 13 | 158 |
| Jun | 21 - 12 | 46 |
| Jul | 21 - 11 | 15 |
| Aug | 21 - 11 | 23 |
| Sep | 24 - 11 | 31 |
| Oct | 24 - 13 | 53 |
| Nov | 23 - 13 | 109 |
| Dec | 23 - 13 | 89 |

### Nakuru

| Month | Average temperature in °C max-min | Average rainfall in mm |
|---|---|---|
| Jan | 27 - 10 | 26 |
| Feb | 28 - 11 | 20 |
| Mar | 28 - 11 | 82 |
| Apr | 26 - 13 | 96 |
| May | 25 - 12 | 85 |
| Jun | 24 - 12 | 60 |
| Jul | 24 - 11 | 63 |
| Aug | 24 - 11 | 73 |
| Sep | 26 - 10 | 52 |
| Oct | 25 - 11 | 60 |
| Nov | 24 - 11 | 63 |
| Dec | 26 - 10 | 35 |

### Kisumu

| Month | Average temperature in °C max-min | Average rainfall in mm |
|---|---|---|
| Jan | 29 - 18 | 48 |
| Feb | 29 - 19 | 81 |
| Mar | 28 - 19 | 140 |
| Apr | 28 - 18 | 191 |
| May | 27 - 18 | 155 |
| Jun | 27 - 17 | 84 |
| Jul | 27 - 17 | 58 |
| Aug | 27 - 17 | 76 |
| Sep | 28 - 17 | 64 |
| Oct | 29 - 18 | 56 |
| Nov | 29 - 18 | 86 |
| Dec | 29 - 18 | 102 |

### Nyeri

| Month | Average temperature in °C max-min | Average rainfall in mm |
|---|---|---|
| Jan | 25 - 11 | 40 |
| Feb | 27 - 10 | 27 |
| Mar | 26 - 12 | 54 |
| Apr | 24 - 14 | 136 |
| May | 23 - 14 | 142 |
| Jun | 21 - 13 | 22 |
| Jul | 20 - 12 | 22 |
| Aug | 20 - 12 | 22 |
| Sep | 23 - 12 | 21 |
| Oct | 24 - 13 | 70 |
| Nov | 23 - 13 | 96 |
| Dec | 24 - 12 | 68 |

### Voi

| Month | Average temperature in °C max-min | Average rainfall in mm |
|---|---|---|
| Jan | 31 - 21 | 44 |
| Feb | 33 - 21 | 16 |
| Mar | 34 - 21 | 55 |
| Apr | 32 - 21 | 70 |
| May | 30 - 20 | 17 |
| Jun | 29 - 19 | 06 |
| Jul | 28 - 18 | 01 |
| Aug | 28 - 18 | 09 |
| Sep | 30 - 18 | 09 |
| Oct | 31 - 19 | 19 |
| Nov | 32 - 21 | 88 |
| Dec | 30 - 21 | 95 |

### Mombasa

| Month | Average temperature in °C max-min | Average rainfall in mm |
|---|---|---|
| Jan | 31 - 24 | 25 |
| Feb | 31 - 24 | 18 |
| Mar | 31 - 25 | 64 |
| Apr | 30 - 24 | 196 |
| May | 28 - 23 | 320 |
| Jun | 28 - 23 | 119 |
| Jul | 27 - 22 | 89 |
| Aug | 27 - 22 | 64 |
| Sep | 28 - 22 | 64 |
| Oct | 29 - 23 | 86 |
| Nov | 29 - 24 | 97 |
| Dec | 30 - 24t | 61 |

### Lamu

| Month | Average temperature in °C max-min | Average rainfall in mm |
|---|---|---|
| Jan | 31 - 24 | 08 |
| Feb | 31 - 24 | 02 |
| Mar | 32 - 25 | 33 |
| Apr | 31 - 25 | 110 |
| May | 29 - 24 | 180 |
| Jun | 28 - 23 | 96 |
| Jul | 27 - 22 | 68 |
| Aug | 27 - 22 | 40 |
| Sep | 28 - 22 | 36 |
| Oct | 29 - 23 | 57 |
| Nov | 30 - 24 | 43 |
| Dec | 31 - 24 | 26 |

### Lodwar

| Month | Average temperature in °C max-min | Average rainfall in mm |
|---|---|---|
| Jan | 36 - 22 | 03 |
| Feb | 37 - 23 | 02 |
| Mar | 37 - 24 | 18 |
| Apr | 35 - 25 | 27 |
| May | 35 - 25 | 22 |
| Jun | 34 - 25 | 06 |
| Jul | 33 - 24 | 11 |
| Aug | 34 - 24 | 07 |
| Sep | 35 - 25 | 04 |
| Oct | 36 - 25 | 08 |
| Nov | 35 - 24 | 13 |
| Dec | 35 - 23 | 05 |

### Marsabit

| Month | Average temperature in °C max-min | Average rainfall in mm |
|---|---|---|
| Jan | 25 - 17 | 28 |
| Feb | 26 - 17 | 15 |
| Mar | 26 - 17 | 34 |
| Apr | 25 - 17 | 163 |
| May | 24 - 16 | 60 |
| Jun | 24 - 15 | 09 |
| Jul | 23 - 14 | 06 |
| Aug | 24 - 14 | 06 |
| Sep | 25 - 15 | 04 |
| Oct | 25 - 16 | 54 |
| Nov | 24 - 17 | 94 |
| Dec | 24 - 16 | 50 |

# Sport and activities

## Ballooning

ⓘ Details of local operators are listed in the relevant chapters.

The Masai Mara is the top spot for a gentle float over the animals from a balloon and for many this excursion is the highlight of a visit to the reserve (albeit expensive). Most of the lodges and camps also offer this activity. Tourists are picked up around 0530 and driven to the site where the lift-off will take place. Watching the balloon inflate is part of the experience. Once the balloon rises, passengers can watch the dawn high above the plains when the sun comes up and turns the grasslands from blue to gold. This is a spectacular experience, especially during the autumn migration. Flights last 60-90 minutes.

PAUL BANTON/SHUTTERSTOCK

A hot-air balloon drifts over the Mara River in the Masai Mara.

## Birdwatching

ⓘ **Nature Kenya**, Nairobi, T020-749 957, www.naturekenya.org, runs regular birding trips from Nairobi. www.kenyabirds.org.uk, has checklists and species indexes.

Kenya is one of the world's top birding destinations, and has over 10% of the world's listed species. Serious twitchers should head for the lakes in the Rift Valley, the Arabuko Sokoke Forest on the coast, the Kakamega Forest National Reserve in the Western Highlands, Tsavo National Park, and the Ngong Forest just outside of Nairobi.

## Fishing

ⓘ Details of local operators are listed in the relevant chapters.

This is not a particularly popular pastime in Kenya's rivers, but very popular on the coast and Lake Victoria. The latter attracts big-game fisherman after the weighty Nile perch that reach up to 100 kg, though the fishing camps around the lake are only in the top price category. There is excellent deep-sea fishing on the coast. Marlin, tuna, sailfish, shark, swordfish and yellowfin are caught on a tag and release system. The best places to head for are Watamu, Shimoni, Malindi and Kilifi.

## Golf

ⓘ **Kenya Golf Union**, www.kgu.or.ke, has information on courses and events. Those heading to the coast can look forward to the completion of the 162-ha **Vipingo Ridge Golf Club**, between Mombasa and Malindi, www.vipingoridge.com, which will have two new 18-hole, 72-par golf courses.

Presumably because of Kenya's colonial legacy, there are over 35 golf courses in Kenya, some of a very high standard. Most permit temporary membership and allow visitors to play and some hire golf clubs. The most prestigious event in the year is the Kenya Open Golf Tournament held annually in February or March at the Karen Country Club in Nairobi.

## Kitesurfing

ⓘ Details of local operators are listed in the relevant chapters.

This is the latest craze on the coast, particularly at Diani Beach where most of the 12 km of smooth sand can be surfed.

## Mountain climbing

ⓘ **Mountain Club of Kenya**, Wilson Airport, Nairobi, T020-602 330, www.mck.or.ke, has lots of maps and books in its library; non-members can attend the open night on Tuesdays at the club house; the website is an excellent resource. Local tour operators are listed in the relevant chapters.

Mount Kenya is a popular climb although fairly technical. Tour operators and trekking companies will happily put together an itinerary that suits your preferences. Other treks include the Aberdares Mountains, Cherangani Hills, Mathew's Mountains, Hell's Gate and Rift Valley volcanoes.

## Riding

ⓘ **Ride Kenya Horse Safaris**, www.ridekenya.com.

There are many horse and camel treks on offer on the game ranches of the Laikipia Plateau and in Northern Kenya. Camels are usually used as pack animals off the beaten track into some real wilderness areas. These excursions mostly use local guides, especially in Samburu. It is possible to do multi-day horse safaris in Amboseli National Park and the Chyulu Hills with **Ride Kenya Horse Safaris**.

Mount Kenya, 5199 m high.

## Whitewater rafting

ⓘ **Savage Wilderness Safaris**, Sarit Centre, Nairobi, T020-521 590, www.whitewaterkenya.com,

The base for **Savage Wilderness Safaris** is on the Tana River just south of Sagana on the road around Mount Kenya. It offers whitewater rafting on the river; a one-day trip from Nairobi costs US$100, including transport from Nairobi. Longer three-day, 65-km rafting trips on the Athi River further south on the border of Tsavo National Park can be arranged for US$390: two nights are spent camping on sandbanks and rates include food and transfers to and from Nairobi. Most of the route is on fairly calm water, though there are some Grade II and III sections of rapids and two Grade IV drops. This is excellent for game-viewing and birdwatching.

## Watersports

ⓘ Details of local operators are listed in the relevant chapters.

Watersports are widely available at the coast and many hotels and resorts organize scuba-diving, windsurfing, kitesurfing, snorkelling, jet skiing, sailing and deep-sea fishing. For the less active the superb coral reefs can be explored by glass-bottomed boat. A recommended day excursion is to Wasini Island to the south of Diani Beach for snorkelling and a delicious seafood lunch, where there is also the opportunity to spot whales and dolphins.

# How big is your footprint?

Much has been written about the adverse impacts of tourism on the environment and local communities. It is usually assumed that this only applies to the more excessive end of the travel industry. However, travellers can have an impact at almost any density and this is especially true in areas 'off the beaten track', where local people may not be used to Western conventions and lifestyles and where natural environments are sensitive.

Of course, tourism can have a beneficial impact too, and this is something to which every traveller can contribute. The tourism industry in Kenya is very important for the country's economy, and creates many thousands of jobs. In recent years there has been a well-applauded effort to initiate projects that involve and benefit the local communities and wildlife. Both people and animals share and rely on Kenya's wide open spaces and Kenya really has embraced the age of ecotourism through effective community-run wildlife management.

## CITES

Environmental legislation, too, plays its role in protecting destinations. The Convention on International Trade in Endangered Species (CITES) aims to control the trade in live specimens of endangered plants and animals and also "recognizable parts or derivatives" of protected species such as seashells or coral. If you feel the need to purchase souvenirs and trinkets derived from wildlife in Kenya, it would be prudent to check whether they are protected. Importation of CITES-protected species can lead to heavy fines, confiscation of goods and even imprisonment.

Many national parks are part-funded by receipts from people who come to see exotic plants and animals. Similarly, travellers can promote protection of valuable archaeological and heritage sites through their interest and entrance fees. However, where visitor pressure is high and/or poorly regulated, damage can occur. In Kenya, many of the most popular destinations are in ecologically and culturally sensitive areas that are easily disturbed by extra human pressures.

It is worthwhile noting the major areas in which travellers can take a more responsible attitude to the countries they visit. These include changes to natural ecosystems (air, water, land, ecology and wildlife), cultural values (beliefs and behaviour) and the built environment (sites of antiquity and archaeological significance). At an individual level, travellers can reduce their impact if greater consideration is given to their activities. Canoe trips up the headwaters of obscure rivers make for great stories but how do local communities cope with the sudden invasive interest in their lives? Similarly, have the environmental implications of increased visitor pressure been considered? Where do the fresh fish that feed the trip come from? Hand caught by line is fine but dynamite fishing causes a great deal of damage and waste.

Some factors, such as the management and operation of a hotel chain, are beyond the direct control of individual travellers. However, it is possible to voice concern about damaging activities. An increasing number of hotels and travel operators are taking 'green concerns' seriously, even if it is only to protect their share of the market. Be wary of the 'eco' label, however; all too often companies use the word to refer to outdoor adventure activities, not environmentally protective practices.

## Responsible travel

▸ Where possible choose a destination, tour operator or hotel with a proven ethical and environmental commitment – if in doubt, ask.

▸ Spend money on locally produced (rather than imported) goods and services, buy directly from the producer or from a 'fair trade' shop, and use common sense when bargaining – the few dollars you save may be a week's salary to others.

▸ Use water and electricity carefully – travellers may receive preferential supply while the needs of local communities are overlooked.

▸ Learn about local etiquette and culture – consider local norms and behaviour and dress appropriately for local cultures and situations.

▸ Protect wildlife and other natural resources – don't buy souvenirs or goods unless they are clearly sustainably produced and are not protected under CITES legislation.

▸ Always ask before taking photographs or videos of people.

▸ Consider staying in local accommodation rather than foreign-owned hotels – the economic benefits for host communities are far greater and there are more opportunities to learn about local culture.

▸ Make a voluntary contribution to Climate Care, www.co2.org, to help counteract the pollution caused by tax-free fuel on your flight.

Modern times for a timeless people; Masai warrior with a digital watch.

# Kenya on screen and page

## Books to read

Probably the most famous book ever written about Kenya is *Out of Africa* by Karen Blixen (aka Isak Dinesen), published in 1937 about her life on her coffee plantation, which provides a vivid snapshot of African colonial life in the last decades of the British empire. *West with the Night* records the memoirs of Beryl Markham, who was brought up in Kenya and was the first woman to fly solo across the Atlantic from east to west. Elspeth Huxley's *Flame Trees of Thika* is her account of growing up on a Kenyan coffee farm, which she describes as "a bit of El Dorado my father had been fortunate enough to buy in the bar of the Norfolk hotel". John H Patterson's *Man Eaters of Tsavo* is the larger-than-life tale of finding and shooting two lions that killed over 100 workers on the Uganda Railway when it was being built in the early 20th century. In *White Mischief*, James Fox takes the reader into the world of Kenya's 1940s Happy Valley set and explores the unsolved murder of Josslyn Hay, 22nd Earl of Erroll.

## Films to watch

One of the greatest wildlife stories ever told was *Born Free* (1966) about Elsa the lioness who was rescued as a cub and rehabilitated back into the wild by Joy and George Adamson. *To Walk With Lions* (1999) follows George's later life and stars Richard Harris as the formidable man. The movie *I Dreamed of Africa* (2000) stars Kim Basinger in the leading role as former Italian socialite Kuki Gallmann's life on a ranch on the Laikipia Plateau and her subsequent work in conservation. *Out of Africa* (1985) is as much a story of Kenya's wildlife and scenic beauty, as it is of Karen Blixen's relationship with the aristocratic safari-goer Denys Finch Hatton; it stars Meryl Streep and Robert Redford and won seven Oscars. Adapted from John Le Carré's novel, *The Constant Gardener* (2005) revolves around a British diplomat in Nairobi whose wife is murdered in Northern Kenya while investigating a drugs trial scandal. Starring Ralph Fiennes and Rachael Weisz (who won Oscar for Best Supporting Actress) much of it was filmed in Nairobi's Kibera slum.

# Contents

## Footprint features

Essentials

# Getting there

## Air

Kenya is the cheapest country in East Africa to get to by air and consequently is a good place to start off a tour of the region. There are several airlines that fly into Kenya from various cities in the world and airfares are very competitively priced. The main point of arrival is Nairobi's **Jomo Kenyatta International Airport**, though there are also a substantial number of scheduled and charter flights from Europe to **Moi International Airport** in Mombasa. Airport information can be found at www.kenyaairports.co.ke, or see details of arriving at the airports in the Nairobi or Mombasa chapters. Nairobi is a nine-hour flight from London and Mombasa is about 11 hours. Because of the proximity of the Northern Circuit national parks in Tanzania, which are accessed from Europe, many visitors going on safari to Northern Tanzania also fly into Nairobi as it is closer than Tanzania's capital Dar es Salaam.

The cheapest plane tickets are in the 'off season', from February to June and again from October to early December. If you do have to go during peak times, book as far in advance as you can, particularly if you aim to get there in mid-December when flights get full very quickly. If you are short of time, a package holiday could well be a useful option, particularly if you go out of the peak season when you can get excellent deals. Beach holidays are far cheaper than safaris. It is a good idea to find out as much as you can about the hotel in the package deal before going, although you can always stay elsewhere if necessary. It is sometimes the case that a package trip to the coast will be cheaper than a flight alone. Once on the coast there is then the option to book a short overnight safari to one of the parks.

### From Europe

Airlines with daily direct services from Europe to Nairobi included the national carrier **Kenya Airways**, which flies from London, Amsterdam and Paris; **British Airways**; **KLM**; and **Virgin Atlantic**. Non-direct flights from Europe may work out economical and **Egypt Air** offers very good deals via Cairo, **Emirates**, via Dubai, and **Ethiopian Airlines** via Addis Ababa.

### From Africa

From southern Africa both **Kenya Airways** and **South African Airways** have daily flights between Johannesburg and Nairobi. Just about all of the African airlines serve Nairobi, so it's a good hub to travel onwards to other African cities.

### From North America

There are no direct flights from the USA to Kenya. Americans have to change flights in Europe or the Middle East depending on which carrier they choose. It is usual to fly via London, Amsterdam or Dubai if travelling from the USA. Alternatively, **Delta Airlines** has a code-share agreement with **South African Airways**, who run daily direct flights from Atlanta to Johannesburg, from where there are connections to Nairobi. By the time you read this, Delta might be flying directly from New York to Nairobi via Dakar in Senegal so it's worth enquiring.

### From Australia, New Zealand and Asia

Between them **Qantas** and **SAA**, on a code-share agreement, fly between Auckland, Sydney, Melbourne and Perth, and Johannesburg and there are several flights a week. **Singapore**

## Packing for Kenya

Before you leave home, send yourself an email to a web-based account with details of traveller's cheques, passport, driving licence, credit cards and travel insurance numbers. Be sure that someone at home also has access to this information. A good rule of thumb is to take half the clothes you think you'll need and double the money. Laundry services are generally cheap and speedy in Kenya and you shouldn't need to bring too many clothes. A backpack or travelpack (a hybrid backpack/suitcase) rather than a rigid suitcase covers most eventualities and survives the rigours of a variety of modes of travel. A lock for your luggage is strongly advised – there are cases of pilfering by airport baggage handlers the world over.

Light cotton clothing is best, with a fleece or woollen clothing for evenings. Also pack something to change into at dusk – long sleeves and trousers (particularly light coloured) help ward off mosquitoes, which are at their most active in the evening. During the day you will need a hat, sunglasses and high-factor sun cream for protection against the sun. Modest dress is advisable for women, particularly on the coast, where men too should avoid revealing shoulders. Kenya is a great place to buy sarongs – known in East Africa as *kikois*, which in Africa are worn by both men and women and are ideal to cover up when, say, leaving the beach. Footwear should be airy because of the heat: sandals or canvas trainers are ideal. Trekkers will need comfortable walking boots, and ones that have been worn in if you are climbing Mount Kenya. Those going on camping safaris will need a sleeping bag, towel and torch, and budget travellers may want to consider bringing a sleeping sheet in case the sheets don't look too clean in a budget hotel.

---

Airlines code share with **Air New Zealand**, and flights link Wellington with Johannesburg via Sydney and Singapore. **Malaysia Airlines** has regular flights from Perth, Melbourne, Sydney and Darwin in Australia and Auckland in New Zealand to Kuala Lumpur, connecting with a flight to Johannesburg three times a week. **Cathay Pacific** flies to Johannesburg from Hong Kong once a week. From Johannesburg there are daily connections to Nairobi on both **Kenya Airways** and **South African Airways**, as above.

## Airlines

**Air Malaysia**, T0603-7843 3000 (Malaysia), www.malaysia-airlines.com.
**Air New Zealand**, T0800-737 000 (NZ), www.airnewzealand.com.
**British Airways**, T0870-850 9850 (UK), www.britishairways.com.
**Cathy Pacific**, T0852-2747 1888 (Hong Kong), www.cathaypacific.com.
**Delta**, T1800-221 1212 (USA), www.delta.com.
**Emirates**, T0870-243 2222 (UK), www.emirates.com.

**Ethiopian Airlines**, T0208-987 7000, www.ethiopianairlines.com.
**Kenya Airways**, T0208-8283 1818, www.kenya-airways.com.
**Qantas**, T131313 (from anywhere in Australia), www.qantas.com.au.
**Singapore Airlines**, T065-6223 8888 (Singapore), www.singaporeair.com.
**South African Airways**, T0870-747 1111 (South Africa), www.flysaa.com.
**Virgin Atlantic**, T0870-574 7747 (UK), www.virgin-atlantic.com.

## Discount flight agents

### UK and Ireland
**Flightbookers**, T0871-223 5000,
www.ebookers.com.
**Flight Centre**, T0870-499 9931,
www.flightcentre.co.uk.
**STA Travel**, T0871-2300 0040,
www.statravel.co.uk.
**Trailfinders**, T0845-0585858,
www.trailfinders.com.
**Travelbag**, T0800-804 8911,
www.travelbag.co.uk.

### North America
**Air Brokers International**, T01-800
883-3273, www.airbrokers.com.
**STA Travel**, T1800-781 4040,
www.statravel.com.
**Travel Cuts**, T1866-246 9762 (Canada),
www.travelcuts.com.

### Australia and New Zealand
**Flight Centre**, T133-133 (Australia),
www.flightcentre.com.au.
**Skylinks**, T02-923 4277, www.skylink.com.au.
**STA Travel**, T134-782 (Australia),
www.statravel.com.au, T0800-474 400,
www.statravel.com.nz
**Travel.com.au**, T1300-130 482,
www.travel.com.au.

---

**Road →** *See opposite page for border crossing information.*

Border crossings between Kenya and its neighbours can be labourious or simple, depending on your preparation and the state of your vehicle's paperwork. If you are in your own vehicle you will require a Carnet de Passage issued by a body in your own country (such as the Automobile Association), vehicle registration, and you will also be required to take out third party insurance for Kenya from one of the insurance companies who have kiosks at the border posts. Most car hire companies will not allow you to take a rented vehicle out of the country, but some may consider it if you only want to go to Tanzania.

### Ethiopia
The crossing is at Moyale, between Marsabit and Addis Ababa, see page 372. The road from Isiolo up to the border is rough, particularly in the wet. Also, because of armed robberies in recent years, vehicles are required to travel in armed convoys on part of this road between Isiolo and Moyale. There is no public transport north of Isiolo so the only option is to hitch a lift from truck drivers on the route, but trucks are very infrequent.

### Somalia
In more tranquil times it has been possible to take a bus from Kismayo to the border at Liboi, and then on to Garissa, or from Mogadishu to Mandera, and then on to Wajir. These crossings are currently not an option for travellers as a result of the civil war in Somalia and public transport on this route has been largely suspended.

### Sudan
In principle it is possible to cross from Lokichokio to Juba, see page 349, although there is no public transport on this route, and it is a matter of hiring rides from truck drivers, many of whom are transporting aid into southern Sudan. During the civil war Lokichokio was the main United Nations base monitoring the situation in Southern Sudan. There's an immigration office north of town where you will have to get a Kenyan visa if coming from Sudan, and get stamped out of Kenya if going to Sudan. You'll need to have got a visa for

## Border crossings

**Kenya–Ethiopia**
Moyale, page 372.

**Kenya–Tanzania**
Isebania, page 165; **Namanga**, page 244; **Taveta**, page 244; **Lunga Lunga**, page 275.

**Kenya–Uganda**
Malaba, page 176; **Busia**, page 176.

Sudan before arrival here as they are not issued at the border. The road from the border to Juba was retarred and de-mined in 2008.

### Tanzania

The main road crossing is at Namanga, see page 244. As this border receives thousands of tourists on safari each week en route between the Kenyan and Tanzanian parks, it is reasonably quick and efficient. Other crossings are at Lunga Lunga, page 275, between Mombasa and Dar es Salaam on a recently improved road. There is also a crossing at Taveta, page 244 and Isebania, page 165. The border crossing from Masai Mara Park into the Serengeti is currently closed.

### Uganda

Buses run from Nairobi to Kampala, crossing at Malaba and Busia, see page 176.

# Getting around

Kenya has an efficient transport network linking its towns and cities. There are regular flights between Nairobi and the coast and Kisumu, and further afield to Tanzania and Zanzibar. There is an overnight train service between Nairobi and Mombasa that is a fairly enjoyable, if not slow experience, and in recent years there have been great improvements of standards of the bus and *matatu* (minibus) services. It is quite feasible for a visitor to move around by public transport, which is cheap and efficient, but be aware of petty theft not only on the vehicles but in the bus stands and stations.

## Air

**Kenya Airports Authority** ① *www.kenyaairports.co.ke*, established by the government in 1991, oversees the management and administration of the airports which include passenger services and freight services for horticultural and agricultural goods, for example the flowers and vegetables flown out of Eldoret International Airport daily headed for European supermarkets. Today internal travel in Kenya is regular and efficient and the introduction of 'no-frills' airlines have introduced competition and flights are very affordable. The following airlines offer daily scheduled flights. Specific schedules are detailed under each relevant chapter.

All tickets can also be bought directly from desks at the airports. **Kenya Airways** ① *5th floor, Barclays Plaza, Loita St, city centre, T020-327 4747, airport T020-642 2000, general enquiries T0208-283 1818, www.kenya-airways.com*, has daily flights from Jomo Kenyatta International Airport to Kisumu, Malindi, Lamu and Mombasa, plus regional destinations.

**Fly 540** ① *ABC Place, Westlands, T020-445 3252, airport T020-827 521, www.fly540.com*, has flights from Jomo Kenyatta International Airport to Eldoret, Kisumu, Lamu, Malindi, Masai Mara and Mombasa. It now also operates daily flights between Nairobi and Entebbe in Uganda.

**Air Kenya** ① *based at Wilson Airport, T020-605 745, www.airkenya.com*, has flights between Nairobi and Amboseli, Kilimanjaro, Lamu, Lewa Downs, Malindi, Masai Mara, Meru, Mombasa, Nanyuki and Samburu. It also code shares with **Regional Air** in Tanzania and offer flights from Nairobi to Kilimanjaro, Dar es Salaam and Zanzibar.

**Safarilink** ① *based at Wilson Airport, T020-600 777, www.safarilink-kenya.com*, has flights between Nairobi and Amboseli, Kiwayu, Lamu, Lewa Downs, Masai Mara, Nanyuki, Samburu and Tsavo. It code shares with **Air Excel** in Tanzania so have flights from Nairobi to Kilimanjaro.

In addition to scheduled flights there are many air charter services based at Wilson Airport, Nairobi, which can arrange private flights in small six- to eight-seater planes to over 150 airstrips spread all over the country. As well as ferrying tourists around, some of these companies have been involved in distributing food and medical aid in the Northern Kenya and southern Sudan and Somalia regions in recent years, as well as providing air access to the refugee camps for aid workers. These include **ALS** ① *Wilson Airport, T020-603 706, www.als.co.ke*; **Aero Kenya** ① *Wilson Airport, T020-601001, www.aerokenya.com*; **Capital Airlines** ① *Wilson Airport, T020-603 357, www.capitalairlines.biz*; and **Z-Boskovic Air Charters** ① *Wilson Airport, T020-602 026, www.boskovicaircharters.com*.

## Rail

**Nairobi Railway Station** ① *T020-221 211*, is to the south of Haile Selassie Avenue, at the very end of Moi Avenue. Despite Kenya's long association with what was the Uganda Railway, which effectively founded the colony, in recent years due to chronic under-investment the railway is close to collapse with dilapidated rolling stock, and frequent derailments and breakdowns. Added to this, part of the railway in the north of the country was ripped up during the post-2007 election violence so the service from Nairobi to Kisumu is no longer operational. For now, there's only the overnight train between Nairobi and Mombasa. This used to be an historic and authentic rail experience and an excellent way of getting to the coast, but these days and thanks to breakdowns of other freight trains using the same track, which subsequently block the line, this journey can be painfully slow. See under Transport for Nairobi (page 106) for fares and schedules.

## Road

The present road transport network comprises a variety of roads ranging from forest and farm tracks to multi-lane urban and suburban highways. The system is divided into classified and unclassified roads, with a total network of 151,000 km. Out of the classified network of 62,667 km, 7943 km are tarred (compared with 1811 km at Independence), 26,180 km are gravel and the rest are dirt.

## Bus and matatu

The most popular form of public transport in Kenya is the *matatu*, which has become a national icon and a large part of Kenyan modern culture. A *matatu* is a minibus, usually a Nissan, with a three-tonne capacity, hence the name *matatu – tatu* means 'three' in Kiswahili. Safety records for public transport have been pretty awful in the past with many road accidents involving overcrowded buses and *matatus* and some large derailments on the railways. However, since the government instigated new regulations in 2003, public transport in Kenya has undergone quite a transformation. While the vehicles introduced at the time are starting to show their age, overall they have contributed to positively getting the accident rate down. All buses, *matatus*, taxis and any vehicle carrying paying passengers must be licensed and have a yellow stripe around them, and *matatus*, which were once famously painted in lots of bright colours and murals, are now mostly uniformly white. Buses are still different colours, although each company has smartened up their image and many of the buses from the same fleet are in the same colour. **Metro** red buses have been introduced to Mombasa, and green **City Hoppers** in Nairobi, which are gradually taking over the old fleet of city buses. All public buses and *matatus* now have to be speed governed at 80 kph. Every vehicle has been fitted with seat belts and it is now law for every passenger in any vehicle to buckle up. Police issue on-the-spot fines to passengers who haven't got seat belts on. The number of passengers has been governed to stop the overcrowding. In *matatus* this has been restricted to 15 passengers, all with their own seat, with a seat belt. The police also frequently stop the vehicles and count how many people are on board. The same goes for larger buses where standing is no longer permitted and everyone gets their own seat. These regulations have improved safety and comfort, meaning that it is now reasonable for independent travellers to move around Kenya on buses and *matatus*. There are lots of private bus companies operating in Kenya, and the system is very good on the whole, being reliable, running on time and offering cheap fares. In addition, the accident rate on the roads has fallen dramatically in recent years. The larger buses cover the long-distance routes and you will be able to reserve a seat a day in advance, whilst the *matatus* do the shorter distances and link the major towns and usually go when full. If you have problems locating the bus station, alternatively called bus stand or bus stage in Kenya, or finding the right bus in the bus station, just ask around and someone will direct you. In Nairobi and Mombasa city buses operate on set routes with formal bus stops, while *matatus* follow the same routes and can be flagged down anywhere.

## Car

**Driving conditions**  The key roads are in good condition; away from the main highways the majority of roads are hazardous. The minor roads of unmade gravel with potholes can be rough going and they deteriorate further in the rainy season. Road conditions in the reserves and national parks of Kenya are extremely rough. During the rainy season, many roads are passable only with 4WD vehicles. Even some of the tarred roads are in poor shape: cracked, crumbling and littered with small and not-so-small potholes. There is little road maintenance and when re-tarring of the roads does occur, the new tar that is laid is so thin it deteriorates within months. On hills, heavy vehicles with hot tyres curve the tar into steep ridges, making the roads very bumpy. Added to this are Kenya's speed bumps (hardly necessary when the potholes do a fine job of slowing traffic down), which are in place every few metres wherever there is any kind of settlement and are prolific all over the towns. It is still possible to drive on Kenya's main roads in a normal saloon car, although the going is slow and you will have to take extra care to avoid the deeper potholes. A 4WD is recommended as the high clearance is better for the potholes, and is essential if you are going off the tarred roads or into the game parks. If you break down, it is common practice in Kenya to place a bundle of leaves 50 m or so in front and behind the vehicle to warn oncoming motorists. Note when parking in the towns, you pay a small fee to a parking official who will give you a ticket to display in the window.

Car hire  Renting a car has certain advantages over public transport, particularly if you intend visiting any of the national parks or remoter regions of the country, or there are at least four of you to share the costs. You should be able to rent either at a fixed price per day or by mileage. If you are organizing your own safari by hire car, it requires careful planning, and you need to be confident about driving on the poor roads. A 4WD is essential. Minimum engine size should be 1300cc, as anything smaller cannot cope with the rough roads in the game parks. Make sure that the car is not more than two years old. Driving is on the left side of the road.

To hire a car you generally need to be over 23, have a full driving licence (it does not have to be an international licence, your home country one will do – with English translation if necessary), and to leave a large deposit (or sign a blank credit card voucher). Always take out the collision damage waiver premium as even the smallest accident can be very expensive. Costs vary between the different car hire companies and are from around US$40-80 per day for a normal saloon car, rising to US$120-180 for a 4WD. Deals can be made for more than seven days' car hire. It is important to shop around to get the best-value rates. Things to consider include whether you take out a limited mileage package or unlimited mileage depending on how you many kilometres you think you will drive. For example, a company may offer a package for US$60 per day, with 200 km free per day, and any mileage after that at US$0.25 per km. If you think you are going to be driving for more than 200 km a day then a more expensive unlimited mileage package may be better. Also check the insurance policies. Some of the companies that offer the cheapest rates have no insurance policies at all where in the event of an accident, the hirer is responsible for costs, or, a costly option if the car gets stolen, reimbursement of the value of the vehicle. Alternatively it is best to take out an additional insurance of about US$10-25 per day on top of the car hire rates to cover these eventualities, although you'll still be liable of an excess of around US$500-1000. Finally, 16% VAT is added to all costs. It is essential to shop around and ask the companies about what is and what is not included in the rates. For car hire companies in Nairobi, see page 105. If you think you may not be that confident in driving in Kenya but still want the flexibility of your own vehicle, most companies can organize drivers for additional expense. However, for a group of four people, this option is going to be no cheaper than booking on an organized budget camping safari.

## Taxi

Hotels and town centres are well served by taxis, some good and some very run-down but serviceable. Hotel staff, even at the smallest locations, will rustle up a taxi even when there is not one waiting outside. If you visit an out-of-town location, it is wise to ask the taxi to wait – it will normally be happy to do so for the benefit of the return fare. Up to 1 km should cost US$1. Very few of the cabs have meters, and you should establish the fare (*bei gani?* – how much?) before you set off. Prices are generally fair as drivers simply won't take you if you offer a fare that's too low. A common practice is a driver will set off and then go and get petrol using part of your fare to pay for it, so often the first part of a journey is spent sitting in a petrol station. Also be aware that seemingly taxi drivers never have change, so try and accumulate some small notes for taxi rides.

**Tuk-tuks** A *tuk-tuk* is a motorized three-wheeled buggy; cheap and convenient, they are starting to feature in many Kenyan towns and cities. The driver sits in the front whilst two to three passengers can sit comfortably on the back seat. They are still quite a novelty and as yet there are few around, but the idea is catching on quickly and in the future they should offer a service that is at least half the price of regular taxis. They do not however, go very fast so for longer journeys stick to taxis.

**Boda boda** A *boda boda* is a bicycle taxi with one padded seat on the back, and so named as they were first popular in the border towns to transport people across no man's land between the border posts of East Africa and the cyclist would shout out '*boda boda*' offering his services. They are very popular along the coast and in the smaller towns, although not in Nairobi and Mombasa, and cost next to nothing. The driver/cyclist does an excellent job of cycling and keeping the bike balanced with you on the back of it, although you are still advised to hang on to the seat. A word of warning to the ladies, however, if you are wearing a skirt you will have to sit side saddle, which makes the bike far more wobbly.

## Trucks

Overland truck safaris are a popular way of exploring Kenya by road. They demand a little more fortitude and adventurous spirit from the traveller, but the compensation is usually the camaraderie and life-long friendships that result from what is invariably a real adventure, going to places the more luxurious travellers will never visit. The standard overland route most commercial trucks take through East Africa (in either direction) is from Nairobi: a two-week circuit into Uganda to see the mountain gorillas via some of the Kenya national parks, then crossing into Tanzania to Arusha for the Ngorongoro Crater and Serengeti, before heading south to Dar es Salaam, for Zanzibar. If you have more time, you can complete the full circuit that goes from Tanzania through Malawi and Zambia to Livingstone to see the Victoria Falls, and then another three weeks from there to Cape Town in South Africa via Botswana and Namibia. There are several overland companies and there are departures almost weekly from Nairobi, Livingstone and Cape Town throughout the year.

## Overland truck safari operators

### In the UK
**Dragoman**, T01728-861 133, www.dragoman.co.uk.
**Exodus Travels**, T020-8675 5550, www.exodus.co.uk.
**Explore**, T0845-0131 537, www.explore.co.uk.

**Kumuka Expeditions**, T0778-6201 144, www.kumuka.com.
**Oasis Overland**, T01963-363 400, www.oasisoverland.co.uk.

### In South Africa
**Africa Travel Co**, T021-385 1530, www.africatravelco.com.
**Wildlife Adventures**, T021-385 1530, www.wildlifeadventures.co.za.

## Maps

The best map and travel guide store in the UK is **Stanfords** ① *12-14 Longacre, Covent Garden, London WC2 9LP, T020-7836 1321, www.stanfords.co.uk,* with branches in Manchester and Bristol. In South Africa **The Map Studio** ① *T+27 (0)21-462 4360, www.mapstudio.co.za,* produces a wide range of maps covering much of Africa. The **Stanley Bookshop**, on Kenyatta Avenue in Nairobi, next to the Thorn Tree Café, has a good selection of maps, as do the book shops in the large shopping malls. Kenya Wildlife Services produce some maps for the parks, which are available at the park gates. Some of these are fairly simple and hand drawn, though there are exceptionally good ones such as the map for the Nairobi National Park that has numbered junctions which correspond to junction numbers on sign posts within the park.

# Sleeping

There is a wide range of accommodation on offer. At the top end are game lodges and tented camps that charge US$300-1000 per couple per day; mid-range safari lodges and beach resorts with self-contained double rooms with air conditioning charge around US$150-250 per room; standard and faded small town hotels used by local business people cost around US$50-100 per room; and basic board and lodgings used by local travellers are under US$10 a day. At the top end, Kenya now boasts some accommodation options that rival the luxurious camps in southern Africa – intimate safari camps with an amazing standard of comfort and service in stunning settings. The beach resorts too have improved considerably in recent years, and there are some luxurious and romantic beach lodges and hotels in commanding positions. At the budget end there's a fairly wide choice of cheap accommodation. A room often comprises a simple bed, shared toilet and washing facilities, and may have an irregular water supply; it is always a good idea to look at a room first, to ensure it's clean and everything works. It is also imperative to ensure that your luggage will be locked away securely for protection against petty theft especially in shared accommodation. For more expensive hotels, airlines, game park entrance and camping fees, a system operates whereby tourists are charged approximately double the rate locals are charged – resident and non-resident rates – although these can be paid in foreign currency as well as Kenyan Shillings. The word hotel (or in Kiswahili, *hoteli*) means food and drink, rather than lodging. It is better to use the word guesthouse (in Kiswahili, *guesti*).

Generally accommodation booked through a European agent will be more expensive than if you contact the hotel or lodge directly. Kenya's hoteliers are embracing the age of the internet, and an ever-increasing number can take a reservation by email or through their websites. Low season in East Africa is generally around the long rainy season from the beginning of April to the end of June, when most room rates drop considerably. Some establishments even close during this period.

### Hotels
There are roughly 75,000 hotel beds in over 2000 licensed hotels within the country. A large majority of these are found in the coastal region, thanks to the rapid development of tourism infrastructure and beach resorts in the late 1970s and early 1980s. Some of the beach hotels are resorts with a range of watersports and activities where guests stay for their entire holiday, and while they will appeal to those who enjoy the all-inclusive

## Accommodation price codes

| | | | |
|---|---|---|---|
| **L** | over US$450 | **A** | US$300-449 |
| **B** | US$175-299 | **C** | US$100-174 |
| **D** | US$50-99 | **E** | US$20-49 |
| **F** | under US$20 | | |

Unless otherwise stated, prices refer to the cost of a double room, not including service charge or meals.

package holiday experience; they may not appeal to more independent travellers. However, also on the coast are some small, simple beach cottage type of accommodation, which are mostly in good locations and are excellent value. A few international hotel chains, such as **Hilton International** and **Intercontinental Hotels** among others, have hotels in Nairobi. Most local town and city hotels tend to be bland with poor service, although there are a number of characterful hotels that have been around since the colonial days, such as Nairobi's **The Norfolk** or the **Country Club** in Naivasha. Prices of hotels are not always a good indication of their quality, and it is sensible to check what you will get before committing yourself, though prices are often negotiable, even in large hotels. On the coast and in the game parks, you can expect to pay more in the high season, particularly mid-December to mid-February. Low season in Kenya is generally 1 April-30 June (excluding Easter weekend). The town and city hotels tend to keep their rates the same year round.

### Self-catering and homestays

Renting a private property is a good way to gain a new perspective on Kenya and relax on your own. The real advantage of a Kenyan homestay is the opportunity to spend time with Kenyans and their families, and to share the benefit of their many years of local experience. These are often surprisingly good value if you intend to stay for a while. They vary from rustic cottages in the bush or historic Swahili mansions on the coast, to serviced city apartments. Many of the homes used as homestays are in the highland areas of Kenya, legacies of the pre-Independence settlers, and the coastal belt; very few are near the game parks. Homestays tend to be more expensive than hotels and are often built into the more expensive, individually tailored itineraries. Such properties can either be booked privately or through a travel agent or safari operator. There is also an increasing number of self-catering apartments for rental especially at the coast. Often assistance with cleaning and cooking is available. Whilst some of these facilities are custom built, many are holiday homes leased out when not in use by the owners. These range from quite simple and basic beach cottages to sophisticated villas. For more information contact **Kenya Holiday Villas** ⓘ www.kenyaholidayvillas.com, or **Kenya Safari Homes** ⓘ www.kenyasafarihomes.com. Each website has a full description, including photos of each property.

### Hostels

There are only a handful of hostels around the country, affiliated with the Youth Hostelling Association, YMCA and YWCA, and most are clean and safe and very cheap. Nevertheless they tend to be very spartan and generally cater for long-term residents such as students or church groups.

## Camping

There are many campsites all over Kenya. They are usually very cheap with basic amenities and some are very good. Camping is essential if you are on a tight budget but want to explore the national parks. You should always have your own tent and basic equipment as these cannot always be hired at the sites. You should also carry adequate supplies of fresh water, food, fuel and emergency supplies. Do not rely on local water supplies or rivers and streams for potable water. Any water taken from a stream should be filtered or boiled for several minutes before drinking. If you are trekking and planning to wild camp outside of official or designated campsites, seek local advice in advance. The land on which you are planning to camp may be privately owned or be traditional lands under the control of a nearby village. In some instances, advance permission and/or payment is required. If camping near a village, as you may be asked to do, remember to be culturally sensitive.

## Safari options

All safari companies offer basically the same safari but at different prices, which is reflective of what accommodation is booked. For example, you could choose a two-day safari of the Masai Mara and the options would be camping (the companies provide the equipment) or a lodge safari, making it considerably more expensive. For those that want to spend more, there is the option of adding flights between destinations or staying at one of the luxury private tented camps in the private concession areas on the edges of the parks. Everyone is likely to have the same sort of game-viewing experiences, but the level of comfort you want on safari depends on where you stay and how much you spend.

**Hotels and lodges** These vary and may be either typical hotels with rooms and facilities in one building or individual *bandas* or *rondavels* (small huts) with a central dining area. Standards vary from the rustic to the modern, from the simply appointed to the last word in luxury. Efforts are usually made to design lodges that blend into their environment, with an emphasis on natural local building materials and use of traditional art and decoration. Most lodges serve meals and have lounges and bars, often with excellent views or overlooking waterholes or salt licks that attract game. Many have resident naturalists, as well as guides for organized walks or game drives.

**Tented camps** A luxury tented camp is really the best of both worlds. They are usually built with a central dining area. Each tent will have a thatched roof to keep it cool inside, proper beds and a veranda and they will often have a small bathroom at the back with solar-heated hot water. But at the same time you will have the feeling of being in the heart of Africa and at night you will hear animals surprisingly close by. Tented camps can be found in many of Kenya's national parks and game reserves, as well as on private game ranches and sanctuaries.

**Campsites** There are campsites in most national parks. They are extensively used by camping safari companies. Vehicles, guides, tents and equipment, as well as food and a cook, are all provided. They are often most attractively sited, perhaps in the elbow of a river course but always with plenty of shade. Birds are plentiful and several hours can be whiled away birdwatching. Some campsites have attached to them a few *bandas* or huts run by the park where you may be able to shower. Toilet facilities can be primitive – the 'long drop', a basic hole in a concrete slab, being very common. Most camps are guarded but despite this you should be careful to ensure that valuables are not left unattended. If you are camping on your own, you will almost always need to be totally self-sufficient with all your own equipment. The campsites usually provide running water and firewood. Camping should always have minimal impact on the environment. All rubbish and waste matter should be buried, burnt, or taken away with you. Do not leave food scraps or containers where they may attract and harm animals. Campers should also take care of wildlife. Do not leave fruit or other food inside tents, it can attract monkeys, baboons, and even in some areas elephants, resulting in destruction.

# Eating and drinking

## Food

Kenyans are largely big meat eaters and a standard meal is *nyama choma* – roasted beef or goat meat, usually served with a spicy relish, although some like it with a mixture of raw peppers, onions and tomato known as *kachumbari*. This is usually prepared on simple charcoal grills outside in beer gardens. The main staple or starch in Kenya is *ugali*, a mealie meal porridge eaten all over Africa. In Kikuyu areas you will find *irio*: potatoes, peas and corn mashed together. A popular Luo dish is fried *tilapia* (fish) with a spicy tomato sauce and *ugali*. *Githeri* is a bean stew. Cuisine on mainland Kenya is not one of the country's main attractions. There is a legacy of uninspired British catering (soups, steaks, grilled chicken, chips, boiled vegetables, puddings, instant coffee). Small town hotels and restaurants tend to serve a limited amount of bland processed food, omelette or chicken and chips, and perhaps a meat stew but not much else. Asian food is extremely good in Kenya and cheap, and an important option for vegetarians travelling in the country. Many Indian restaurants have a lunchtime buffet where you can eat as much as you want for less than US$10 a head. Other cuisines include Italian, French, Chinese, Japanese and even Thai, though these can only be found in the upmarket Nairobi restaurants and coastal resorts. Also on the coast, the Swahili style of cooking features aromatic curries using coconut milk, fragrant steamed rice, grilled fish and calamari, and delicious bisques made from lobster and crab. Some of the larger beach resorts and safari lodges offer breakfast, lunch and dinner buffets for their all-inclusive guests, some of which can be excellent while others can be of a poor standard and there's no real way of knowing what you'll get. The most important thing is to avoid food sitting around for a long time on a buffet table, so ensure it has been freshly prepared and served. Restaurant prices are low; it is quite possible to get a plate of hot food in a basic restaurant for US$3 and even the most expensive places will often not be more than US$30 per person. The quality, standard and variety of food depends on where you are and what you intend to pay. Various Western-style fast foods are becoming ever more popular such as chips, hamburgers, sausages and fried chicken. Finally, the service in Kenyan restaurants can be somewhat slower than you are used to and it can take hours for something to materialize out of a kitchen. Rather than complain just enjoy the laid-back pace and order another beer.

A variety of items can be purchased from **street vendors** who prepare and cook over charcoal, which adds considerably to the flavour, at temporary roadside shelters (kiosks). Street cuisine is pretty safe despite hygiene methods being fairly basic. Most of the items are cooked or peeled, which deals with the health hazard. Savoury items include chips, omelettes, barbecued beef on skewers (*mishkaki*), roast maize (corn), samosas, kebabs, hard-boiled eggs and roast cassava (looks like white, peeled turnips) with red chilli-pepper garnish. Roadside stalls selling *mandazi* (a kind of sweet or savoury doughnut), roasted

# Restaurant price codes

| ♈♈♈ over US$30 | ♈♈ US$15-30 | ♈ under US$15 |

Prices refer to the cost of a main course with either a soft drink, a glass of wine or a beer.

maize, grilled, skewered meat, or samosas are popular and very cheap. Fruits include oranges (peeled and halved), grapes, pineapples, bananas, mangoes (slices scored and turned inside-out), paw-paw (papaya) and watermelon. These items are very cheap and are all worth trying, and when travelling, are indispensable.

Most food produce is purchased in open-air markets. In the larger towns and cities these are held daily and, as well as selling fresh fruit and vegetables, sell eggs, bread and meat. In the smaller villages, a market will be held on one day of the week when the farmers come to sell their wares. Markets are very colourful places to visit and just about any fruit or vegetable is available. Other locally produced food items are sold in supermarkets, often run by Asian traders, whilst imported products are sold in the few upmarket supermarkets in the larger cities such as Nakumatt.

## Drink

**Sodas** (soft drinks) are available everywhere and are very cheap, the bottles are refundable. Apart from the usual Cokes and Fantas look out for Krest bitter lemon and ginger ale, and the rather delicious Stoney's Ginger Beer. The other common drink throughout the country is *chai*, milky sweet tea, which is surprisingly refreshing. When available, fresh fruit juices are very good as they are freshly squeezed. Bottled water is fairly expensive, but is available in all but the smallest villages. Tap water is reputedly safe in many parts of the country, but is only really recommended if you have a fairly hardy traveller's stomach. If you don't have a strong stomach, do not use tap water to brush your teeth and avoid ice and washed salads and fruit if possible. Also see the health section for more information about food and water hygiene.

**Kenyan beer** is very good: *Tusker*, *White Cap* and *Pilsner* are the main brands sold in half-litre bottles. Fruit wines are also popular; they come in a variety of different flavours but tend to be sweet. Papaya wine is widely available, but is a little harsh.

**Spirits** tend to be extremely expensive and imported brands can be found in the supermarkets and in bars. Local alternatives that are sold in both bottles and sachets of one tot include *Kenya Cane*, a type of rum, and the sweet *Kenya Gold* coffee liqueur.

Traditional Kenyan drinks include *chang'aa*, a fierce spirit made from maize and sugar and then distilled. Sentences for distilling and possessing *chang'aa* are severe and it is sometimes contaminated. It has been known to kill so think twice before tasting any. Far more pleasant and more common are *pombe* (beer), brewed from sugar and millet or banana depending on the region. It is quite legal, tastes a bit like flat cider and is far more potent than it appears at first. **Palm wine** is drunk at the coast.

# Entertainment

Nairobi and the coast have a wide selection of bars, nightclubs, cinemas, casinos and live music venues. Much musical entertainment is performed in hotels where traditional dance programmes are staged for tourists, and there are live bands and discos.

## Bars and clubs

Kenyans themselves love to party and in Nairobi and Mombasa there are some raucous nightclubs, some of which can hold thousands of people. Prostitutes abound in many, and these girls aren't shy – it doesn't take much to work out what the term 'the Nairobi handshake' comes from! These places are fun and a real eye opener, but it is best to visit in a group and always take a taxi. Less visited areas tend to have more basic establishments, but even the smallest town will usually have a bar – the exception being Lamu, which is strongly Muslim and has few places to buy an alcoholic drink.

## Cinema

Modern cinema complexes can be found in Nairobi and Mombasa show up-to-date Hollywood and Bollywood movies.

## Music and dance

Displays of dancing are put on for the tourists all over the country including the **Bomas of Kenya** just outside Nairobi and many of the beach resorts and safari lodges. The best known are the **Masai** and **Samburu** dances. Traditional Kenyan music is most likely to be performed by the drummers of the **Akamba** and the **Mijinkenda** peoples.

**Congolese music** (*Lingala*) is extremely popular and the type you are most likely to hear on *matatus*, in the streets, in bars and clubs, in fact anywhere and everywhere. Many of the more upmarket discos and clubs play Western or reggae music.

# Shopping

Kenya has many types of souvenir on offer including wood carvings, soapstone carvings, musical instruments, basket ware and textiles. Also look out for fantastic women's hand-made leather sandals with Masai beading on them, especially at the coast. Other Masai crafts such as beaded jewellery, decorated gourds and spears are available to buy in southern Kenya as well as the distinctive red checked Masai blankets. Brightly coloured sarongs called *kangas* are worn by women all over Kenya and Tanzania; they're sold in pairs and emblazoned with a traditional proverb. Woven with vertical stripes, *kikois* are similar but are traditionally worn by the men of the Swahili Coast as wrap-around sarongs. There are many other items made from these clothes including trousers, tops and skirts, cushion covers and bags. Kenyan **baskets**, made from sisal and leather, are also popular and cheap.

Prices in tourist shops are largely fixed, though in the depths of the quiet low season, can be negotiable. Prices at roadside stalls or markets are always negotiable. See page 44 for tips on bargaining. There are generally no discounts for students in Kenya and student rates advertised for museums and parks will usually only apply to local residents. There are a few hostels affiliated to the YHA network, but you do not need to produce a card to either stay there or ask for a discount.

# Festivals and events

All along the coast and in the northeast the **Islamic calendar** is followed and festivals are celebrated. These include the beginning and end of **Ramadan** (variable); **Islamic New Year** (Jun) and **Prophet's birthday** (Aug). On Lamu the Islamic **Maulidi Festival** is held each year (see box, page 329).

## January
**New Year's Day Dhow Race**, Shela Beach on Lamu, is an important event on the island. Only 8 captains are invited to race, so winning the race is a great honour. *Dhows* are brightly decorated and festivities last well into the night. See box, page 332.

## June
**1 Jun Rhino Charge**. This is an off-road 4WD motor rally and fund-raising event to raise money for the fencing of the Aberdares National Park, which is almost complete, and provide solar power to electrify it. The winner is the car that visits all of the 10 control points along the course and has the lowest mileage within the allocated 10 hrs of driving time. Contact **Rhino Ark**, T020-213 6010, www.rhinoark.org.
**Safaricom Marathon**, at Lewa Wildlife Conservancy. A fundraising event to support the conservancy on the Laikipila Plateau amongst other good community causes. Both the half and full marathons attract runners from all over the world, including many world-class Kenyan long-distance runners. They are hard runs at altitude and the course is held within the game conservancy. Helicopters are used to keep an eye out for elephant and predators along the course. It is a unique experience! You can take part or watch. Contact **Lewa Wildlife Conservancy**, page 213, T064-31405, www.lewa.org.

## August
**1st weekend in Aug Maralal International Camel Derby**, operating since 1990, and from 1998 the event has been coupled with the **Kenya Amateur Cycling Association Race**. See box, page 363, or visit www.yaresafaris.com.

## October
**Nairobi Air Show**, held at Wilson Airport on Kenyan Aviation Career Day, features fly-bys by military and historical aircraft and helicopters, formation flying and parachuting displays. There's also plenty of on-the-ground entertainment and food and drink tents and it's a good family day out. See www.nairobiairshow.com.

## December
**Early Dec Craft Fair**, Ngong Racecourse, Nairobi, is a large craft fair with many home-made items from all over Kenya: curios, soaps, jams, furniture, toys, embroidery and quilted items.
**East African Safari Classic**, has been going since 1953 and was first car rally run to celebrate the queen's coronation. It runs for 3 days over a course of about 3000 km. It goes all over the country on some of the worst roads and often in appalling weather. Watching is exciting especially from a good vantage point in the Rift Valley where the cars go charging up and down the escarpments.
**Note** For the first time since 1972, the 2009 event will be run in Tanzania. Contact **East African Safari Classic**, Nairobi, T020-445 0030, www.eastafricansafarirally.com.

# Parks and safaris

## National parks and reserves

Kenya's wildlife is one of its greatest assets and many of the parks and reserves offer a glimpse of a totally unspoilt, peaceful world. Marine life is also excellent and is preserved in the marine national parks off Malindi, Watamu and Kisite. Along with the wildlife, some of the parks have been gazetted to preserve the vegetation and unique locations such as Mount Kenya or the Kakamega Forest. Some of the parks and reserves are world famous, such as the **Masai Mara** and **Amboseli**, and have excellent facilities and receive many visitors. Many others rarely see tourists and make little or no provision in the way of amenities for them.

It is essential to tour the parks by vehicle and walking is prohibited in most of the parks. The exceptions to this are Hell's Gate, parts of Nakuru and Saiwa Swamp National Park near Kitale, and walking safaris are on offer in many of the concession areas outside of the park boundaries where many of the safari lodges and tented camps are located. You will either have to join an organized tour by a safari company, or hire or have your own vehicle. Being with a guide is the best option as without one, you will miss a lot of game. There are a huge number of companies offering safaris, which are listed in the relevant chapters. Safaris can be booked either at home or once in Kenya. If you go for the latter it may be possible to obtain substantial discounts, but ensure that the company is properly licensed and is a member of the **Kenya Association of Tour Operators (KATO)** ① www.katokenya.org, which represents over 250 of Kenya's tour operators and is a good place to start when looking for a safari. Safaris do not run on every day of the week, and in the low season you may also find that they will be combined, meaning if you are on a six-day safari you could expect to be joined by another party say on a four-day safari. Safaris vary in cost and duration, but on the whole you get what you pay for. The costs will also vary enormously depending on where you stay and how many of you there are in a group. For an all-inclusive safari staying in the large safari lodges that offer twice daily game drives and buffet meals, expect to pay around US$150-250 per person per day (more if you opt for air transfers), and at the very top end of the scale, staying in the most **exclusive tented camps and lodges** and flying between destinations, expect to pay in excess of US$500 per day. At the lower end of the market, a **camping safari** using the basic national park campsites is about US$120-140 per person per day, which given that the park fees alone in some of the parks is US$60 per day, is not unreasonable. These rates include park entrance fees, cost of vehicle and driver, and food.

In total **Kenya Wildlife Services (KWS)** administers 30 national parks and five marine reserves. Some environmentally fragile parks with an overload of visitors, such as Amboseli and Lake Nakuru, charge higher park fees, while those parks with low tourist volume charge less, to encourage a wider spread of tourists around the parks. Entry fees to the most popular parks is by an electronic ticketing system known as Smartcard. If you are on an organized safari your tour operator will organize these, but if you are visiting the parks independently, you need to go to a 'point of sale' and load the card. Assess how much your park entry fees, vehicle costs and camping fees are going to be, depending on how long you will spend in the parks, and how many parks you want to visit, and load up the Smartcard with the relevant amount of money. Anyone over the age of 18 must have their own Smartcard, and under 18s can be paid for with a parent's Smartcard. At the main

## Parks and reserves: what's what?

**National parks** National parks are wildlife and botanical sanctuaries and form the mainstay of Kenya's tourist industry. They are conservation points for educational and recreational enjoyment and are managed by Kenya Wildlife Services.

**National reserves** National reserves are similar to national parks but under certain conditions the land may be used for purposes other than nature conservation. Some controlled agriculture or grazing may be permitted. In marine reserves there may be monitored fishing permitted.

**Biosphere reserves** These are protected environments that contain unique land-forms, landscapes and systems of land use. There are five in Kenya: Amboseli, Mount Kenya and Watamu-Malindi marine reserves, Mount Kalul and Kiungu Marine Reserve. Specific scientific research projects are attached to them.

**World Heritage Sites** World Heritage Sites are even more strictly protected. Kenya signed the convention in 1989; as yet only three sites have been inscribed: Mount Kenya, Sibiloi/Central Island national parks, and Lamu old town.

## Kenya Wildlife Services park entry fees

Prices as of 1 January 2009. Children's fees are from age 3-18; under 3s go free. Entry is per 24 hours. For further details contact Kenya Wildlife Service, Nairobi, T020-600 800, www.kws.org.

**Premier parks**
Amboseli and Lake Nakuru
US$60 adults; US$30 children.

**Wilderness parks**
Aberdares, Tsavo East, Tsavo West, Meru, Chyulu Hills
US$50 adults; US$25 children.

**Urban safaris**
Nairobi National Park
US$40 adults; US$20 children.
Nairobi Safari Walk
US$20 adults; US$5 children.
Nairobi Animal Orphanage and Kisumu Impala Sanctuary
US$15 adults; US$5 children.

**Nairobi combination ticket**
(Nairobi National Park, Nairobi Safari Walk and Nairobi Animal Orphanage)
US$65 adults; US$25 children.

**Mountain climbing**
Mount Kenya National Park
US$55 adults; US$20 children.
(Residents' rates apply to Kenyan porters and guides.)
Mount Kenya National Park (climbing for the first three days, includes accommodation in KWS mountain huts)
US$150 adults; US$70 children.

**Special-interest parks**
Mount Elgon, Hell's Gate, Shimba Hills, Arabuko Sokoke Forest, Kakamega Forest
US$25 adults; US$10 children.

**Marine parks and reserves**
Malindi, Watamu, Kisite, Kiunga
US$20 adults; US$10 children.

gates of the parks, you will slide the Smartcard through a machine that will deduct your entry fees, etc off the amount loaded on to the card. Smartcards can be obtained and loaded at: the KWS headquarters at the Main Gate of Nairobi National Park on Langata Road in Nairobi, where the Safari Walk and Animal Orphanage are located; the Main Gate at Lake Nakuru National Park; the Main Gate of the Aberdares National Park; and at the Voi Gate of Tsavo East National Park. They can also be reloaded (but not obtained) at the Mtito Andei Gate of Tsavo West. Money on the cards is not refundable.

National reserves, such as the Masai Mara and the Samburu-Buffalo Springs-Shaba complex, are not administered by KWS and are managed by local councils who set their own prices. These are paid for on arrival at the main gates or lodges in cash, or will be included in the price of an organized safari.

## Organizing your own safari
An alternative to going on an organized safari is to self-drive on a do-it-yourself safari. However, because of the entry fees for vehicles this does not necessarily work out cheaper but it is a good option if you are confident about driving on the poorly maintained tracks within the parks and are prepared to camp. Costs can be favourable compared to an organized safari for a family or group. Some of the parks are better for self-drive than others. For example, Lake Nakuru and Nairobi national parks are easily negotiable in a car and are a pleasure to drive around, whilst others, such as the Masai Mara or Tsavo, have rough roads and there are remote areas where you certainly do not want to get stuck in the event of a breakdown or emergency. On your own safari remember that you will need to budget for vehicle, camping and entry fees and load your Smartcard with the relevant costs. It is a good idea to discuss your itinerary with the staff at the Kenya Wildlife Services head office in Nairobi and they will advise on the fees. In the parks there is also the option to hire a guide from the park HQ for half or a full day to accompany you in your own vehicle.

## Special-interest safaris
There are a number of alternative safari options in Kenya. Whilst Kenya has always involved the local communities in park management, in recent years there have been some excellent conservation initiatives in Kenya that have involved and benefited local communities and have proved instrumental in the protection of the wildlife. An excellent example is the Laikipia Plateau where commercial ranches have turned their land into successful game farms and where new tourist lodges provide employment and other benefits to the local people. Many tour operators and lodges have also adopted cultural or environmental policies – worth thinking about when choosing a safari operator. There are a range of tours and establishments to visit away from the national parks that offer more unusual wildlife watching activities, such as tracking rhino and elephant, walking and trekking safaris with camels and Masai or Samburu guides, or horse- or mountain-bike safaris.

## Tipping
How much to tip the driver and guide is tricky. It is best to enquire from the company what the going rate is. As a rough guide you should allow about 10% of your safari cost. Always try to come to an agreement with other members of the group and put the tip into a kitty. Remember that wages are low and there can be long lay-offs during the low season. Despite this there is also the problem of over tipping, which can cause problems for future clients being asked to give more than they should. If you are on a camping safari and have a cook, give all the money to the guide and leave him to sort out the split.

# Kenya Wildlife Services

The Kenyan government has long been aware that the principal attraction of the country to tourists is its wildlife, and since 1989 has been keen to ensure it is available in abundance for tourists to see. During the 1970s and 1980s Kenya's parks suffered at the hands of poachers and whole populations of wildlife – particularly rhino and elephant – were all but wiped out. But thanks to gallant efforts by the well-organized Kenya Wildlife Services (KWS) and many private ranch owners, today the many species of animal, bird, marine life and plant are far better protected. When the country gained Independence in 1963, there were an estimated 170,000 elephants but by 1989 they numbered just 16,000. In 1989, 12 tons of confiscated ivory was burnt in Nairobi National Park, where today a mound of ash and an information board marks the spot. The fire was lit by then-president Moi and was a symbolic gesture that declared war on poachers and the mass slaughter of elephants in Kenya. The event, televised across the world, contributed to the CITIES international ban on ivory trading and the establishment of the KWS in 1990, headed up by Richard Leakey. Poaching patrols that were well trained and well equipped with Land Rovers and guns were put in place and extremely stiff penalties for anyone caught poaching were established. All employees of KWS are still armed. The present elephant population in Kenya is around 28,000, and thanks to the anti-poaching efforts by KWS employees, numbers of many more species of large animal have recovered significantly. If visiting the Nairobi National Park, in the car park at the main gate look out for the Conservation Heroes Monument, which lists all the names of KWS employees who have died in the line of duty since the KWS was established.

## Transport

It is worth emphasizing that most parks are some way from departure points, and obviously the longer you spend actually in the parks, rather than just driving to and from them, the better. If you go on a three-day safari by road, you will often find that at least one day is taken up with travelling to and from the park, often on bad bumpy and dusty roads – leaving you with a limited amount of time in the park itself. The easiest option, which is of course the most expensive, is to fly and most parks and reserves have a good network of airstrips and there are daily flights. This gives you the optimum time game viewing in the parks themselves.

# Essentials A-Z

## Accident and emergency

Police, fire and ambulance T999.

## Bargaining

Whilst most prices in the shops are set, the exception to this is shops selling typically tourist-related items such as curios, when a little good-natured bargaining is possible, especially if you are buying a number of things. Bargaining is very much expected in the street markets whether you are buying an apple or a Masai blanket. Generally traders will attempt to overcharge tourists who are unaware of local prices. Start lower than you would expect to pay, be polite and good humoured, and if the final price doesn't suit – walk away. You may be called back for more negotiation, or the trader may let you go, in which case your price was too low. Ask about the prices of taxis, excursions, souvenirs and so on at your hotel. Once you have gained confidence, try bargaining with taxi drivers and at hotels when negotiating a room.

## Begging

This is most common in Nairobi and Mombasa. Many Kenyans give money to beggars who are clearly destitute and or disabled and, in a country with no social welfare, have few alternative means of livelihood. A fairly recent phenomenon has been the rise of street children in Nairobi and Nakuru, and they can at times be fairly aggressive when it comes to begging. It's best not to give money or gifts like sweets directly to them as this only encourages begging; it's much better to give a donation to a local school or project – ask your hotel or tour operator how best to go about this.

## Children

Kenya has a great appeal to children because of the animals, and safaris are very exciting for children (and their parents) when they catch their first glimpse of an elephant or lion. However, small children may get bored driving around a hot game park or national park all day if there is no animal activity. Some game lodges do not permit children at all, whereas others are completely child-friendly and are aimed at families. If you travel in a group, think about the long hours inside the vehicle sharing little room with other people. Noisy and bickering children can annoy your travel mates and scare the animals away. Many travel agencies organize family safaris that are especially designed for couples

travelling with children. It's also a good idea to get children enthused about safaris by providing them with checklists for animals and birds and perhaps giving them their own binoculars and cameras. Pick one of the parks or reserves where animals are easily spotted; Nairobi or Amboseli National Parks are ideal. **Heritage Hotels** (www.heritage-east africa.com) runs the excellent Adventurer's Club for children aged 4 to 12 and have several family-orientated lodges in the parks. Fully trained guides take children out on educational game walks and in some cases to Masai villages. There are considerable discounts on accommodation at the beach for children, especially in the family-orientated resorts, when often children under 12 get a sizeable reduction and those under 6 go free. Many hotels have either specific family rooms or adjoining rooms suitable for families. This is always worth asking about when booking accommodation. Items such as disposable nappies, formula milk powders and puréed foods are only available in the major cities and they are expensive, so you may want to bring enough with you. It is important to remember that children have an increased risk of gastroenteritis, malaria and sunburn and are more likely to develop complications, so care must be taken to minimize risks. See the health section, page 47, for more details.

## Customs and duty free

There is no requirement to change currency on entry. A litre of spirits or wine and 200 cigarettes are permitted to be taken in duty free. There is no duty on any equipment for your own use (such as a laptop computers or cameras). Narcotics, pornography and firearms are prohibited. For more information visit www.revenue.go.ke. The CITIES convention was established to prevent trade in endangered species. Attempts to smuggle controlled products can result in confiscation, fines and imprisonment. International trade in elephant ivory, sea turtle products and the skins of wild cats, such as leopard, is illegal. Casual vendors and small stalls may offer prohibited products – sea-shells can be a particular problem. If you were to buy such items, you should always consider the environmental and social impact of your purchase. Removal of coral, shells from turtles or any other kind of marine animal also causes a tremendous upset to the balance of marine life which is often impossible to correct.

## Disabled travellers

Wheelchairs are very difficult to accommodate on public road transport, so Kenya would need to be visited on an organized tour or in a rented vehicle. Most operators are accommodating and being physically disabled should not deter you from visiting Kenya. With the exception of the most upmarket hotels and newer safari lodges, which have specially adapted rooms, there are few designated facilities for disabled travellers. However, a few of the game park lodges have ground-floor bedrooms, in contrast to most hotels where the bedrooms are upstairs and there are no lifts. Safaris should not pose too much of a problem given that most of the time is spent in the vehicle, and wheelchair-bound travellers may want to consider a camping or tented safari which provides easy access to a tent at ground level. One leading safari company that deals with disabled travel to Kenya is **Southern Cross Safaris**, Mombasa, T041-243 4600, www.southerncrosssafaris.com.

## Dress

Travellers are encouraged to show respect by adhering to a modest dress code in public places, especially in the predominantly Muslim areas like Mombasa or Lamu. In the evening at social functions there is no particular dress code although hosts will feel insulted if you arrive for dinner in shorts, sandals or bare feet, and you will be expected to dress up a little in the more upmarket lodges and hotels. On safari, clothes in muted brown and khaki colours are the best. This is certainly true of the more remote parks where seeing unexpected bright colours may startle the animals. But in the Masai Mara, the animals here are so used to seeing a hoards of tourists each day, it is not so important.

## Electricity

220-240 volts supply. Square 3-pin plugs in modern buildings. Great variety in older places. An adapter is advised.

## Embassies and consulates

**Australia**, 33 Ainstie Av, Civic Square, Canberra, ACT 2601, T026-247 4788, www.kenya.asn.au.
**Canada**, 415 Laurier Av East, Ottawa, K1N 6R4, T0613-563 1773, www.kenyahighcommission.ca.
**Democratic Republic of Congo**, 4002 Av De L'ouganda, Zone De Gombe, Kinshasa, T12-8170 08203.
**Ethiopia**, Hiher 16, Kebelle 01, Fikre Mariam Rd, Addis Ababa, T011-661 0033.
**European Union**, 3 Av de la Paix (1st floor), Geneva 1202, Switzerland, T022-906 4050.
**France**, 3 Rue Frey Cinet, Paris, T1-5662 2525, www.kenyaembassyparis.org.
**Germany**, Markgrafen Str 63, Berlin, T030-259 2660, www.embassy-of-kenya.de.
**Italy**, Via Archimede 164, Rome, T6-808 2714/17/18, www.embassyofkenya.it.
**Netherlands**, Nieuwe Park Laan 21, The Hague, T070-350 4215, kenre@dataweb.nl.
**Rwanda**, 1716 Kacyiru Av, De L'Umuganda, Kigali, T250-583 332.
**South Africa**, 302 Brooks St, Melo Park, Pretoria, T012-362 2249, www.kenya.org.za.

**Sudan**, Block 1 No 516, West Giraif, Street 60, Khartoum, T+249 155 772 801, www.kenembsud.org.
**Tanzania**, 127 Mafinga St, Kinondoni, Dar es Salaam, T022-266 8285, www.kenyahighcomtz.org.
**Uganda**, 60 Nakasero Rd, Kampala, T041-258 2325.
**UK**, 45 Portland Place, London W1A 1BS, T020-763 2371/5, www.kenyahighcommission.net.
**USA**, 2249 R St, Washington DC, T202-387 6101, www.kenyaembassy.com.

## Gay and lesbian travellers

Homosexuality is illegal in Kenya and is considered a criminal offence, so extreme discretion is advised and there are no specific gay clubs or bars. Nevertheless, Kenyans generally have the attitude that while being gay is considered 'un-African', they do accept that non-Africans may be gay, so you shouldn't receive any discrimination.

## Health

The health care in the region is varied. There are many excellent private and government clinics/hospitals. As with all medical care, first impressions count. If a facility is grubby then be wary of the general standard of medicine and hygiene. It's worth contacting your embassy or consulate on arrival and asking where the recommended clinics are. If you do get ill, and you have the opportunity, you should also ask your medical insurer whether they are satisfied that the medical centre or hospital that you have been referred to is of a suitable standard.

### Before you go
Ideally, you should see your GP or travel clinic at least 6 weeks before your departure for general advice on travel risks, antibiotics for travellers' bacterial diarrhoea, malaria and

vaccinations. Make sure you have travel insurance, get a dental check (especially if you are going to be away for more than a month), know your own blood group and if you suffer from a long-term condition such as diabetes or epilepsy make sure someone knows or that you have a Medic Alert bracelet/necklace with this information on it.

Basic vaccinations recommended include polio, tetanus, diphtheria, typhoid, and hepatitis A. If you are entering the country overland, you may well be asked for a yellow fever vaccination certificate, and most certainly if you are coming from Tanzania.

### A-Z of health risks
### Altitude sickness
Acute mountain sickness can strike from about 3000 m upwards and in general is more likely to affect those who ascend rapidly (for example by plane) and those who over-exert themselves. Teenagers are particularly prone. On reaching heights above 3000 m, heart pounding and shortness of breath are almost universal and a normal response to the lack of oxygen in the air. Acute mountain sickness takes a few hours or days to come on and presents with headache, lassitude, dizziness, loss of appetite, nausea and vomiting. Insomnia is common and often associated with a suffocating feeling when lying down. You may notice that your breathing tends to wax and wane at night and your face is puffy in the mornings – this is all part of the syndrome.

If the symptoms are mild, the treatment is rest, painkillers (preferably not aspirin-based) for the headaches and anti-sickness pills for vomiting. Should the symptoms be severe and prolonged it is best to descend to a lower altitude immediately and re-ascend, if necessary, slowly and in stages. The symptoms disappear very quickly with even a few 100 m of descent.

The best way of preventing acute mountain sickness is a relatively slow ascent. When trekking to high altitude, some time spent walking at medium altitude, getting fit and acclimatizing, is beneficial. On arrival at places over 3000 m a few hours' rest and the avoidance of alcohol, cigarettes and heavy food will help prevent acute mountain sickness. Other problems experienced at high altitude include sunburn, cracked skin, sore eyes (it may be wise to leave your contact lenses out) and sore nostrils. Treat the latter with Vaseline. Do not ascend to high altitude if you are suffering from a bad cold or chest infection and certainly not within 24 hrs after scuba diving.

## Bites and stings

Mosquitoes and other insects such as tsetse flies can administer a wicked bite and can carry diseases such as malaria. It is essential to wear long sleeves and trousers in the evening when mosquitoes are at their most prevalent and use a mosquito repellent (see under Malaria, below). Rooms with a/c or fans also help ward off mosquitoes at night.

It is a very rare event for travellers but if you are unlucky enough to be bitten by a venomous snake, spider, scorpion or sea creature, try to identify the creature, without putting yourself in further danger (do not try to catch a live snake). Snake bites in particular are very frightening, but in fact rarely poisonous. Victims should be taken to a hospital or a doctor without delay. Commercial snake bite and scorpion kits are available but are usually only useful for specific types of snake or scorpion. Most serum has to be given intravenously so it is not much good equipping yourself with it unless you are used to making injections into veins. It is best to rely on local practice in these cases, because the particular creatures will be known about locally and appropriate treatment can be given.

Certain tropical sea fish when trodden upon inject venom into bather's feet. This can be exceptionally painful. Wear plastic shoes if such creatures are reported. The pain can be relieved by immersing the foot in hot water (as hot as you can bear) for as long as the pain persists. The citric acid juice in fruits such as lemon can be useful.

Symptoms include swelling, pain and bruising around the bite and soreness of the regional lymph glands, perhaps nausea, vomiting and a fever. Symptoms of serious poisoning would be numbness and tingling of the face, muscular spasms, convulsions, shortness of breath or a failure of the blood to clot, causing generalized bleeding.

To treat a snake bite reassure and comfort the victim frequently. Immobilize the limb by a bandage or a splint and get the person to lie still. Do not slash the bite area and try to suck out the poison because this can do more harm than good, and the inexperienced should never apply a tourniquet.

Spiders and scorpions may be found in the more basic hotels. If stung, rest and take plenty of fluids and call a doctor. The best precaution is to keep beds away from the walls and look inside your shoes and under the toilet seat each morning.

## Dengue fever

There is no vaccine against this and the mosquitoes that carry it bite during the day. You will feel like a mule has kicked you for 2-3 days, you will then get better for a few days and then feel that the mule has kicked you again. It should all be over in 7-10 days. Heed all the anti-mosquito measures that you can.

## Diarrhoea and intestinal upset

It should be short lasting but persistence beyond 2 weeks, with blood or pain, requires specialist medical attention.

The key treatment with all diarrhoea is rehydration. Try to keep hydrated by taking the right mixture of salt and water. This is available as Oral Rehydration Salts (ORS) in ready-made sachets or can be made up by adding a teaspoon of sugar and a half teaspoon of salt to a litre of clean water. Drink at least 1 large cup of this for each loose stool. You can also use flat carbonated drinks as an alternative. Immodium and Pepto-Bismol provide symptomatic relief.

The standard advice to prevent problems is to be careful with water and ice for drinking. Ask yourself where the water came from. If you have any doubts then boil it or filter and treat it. Food can also transmit disease. Be wary of salads (what were they washed in, who handled them), re-heated foods or food that has been left out in the sun having been cooked earlier in the day. There is a simple adage that says wash it, peel it, boil it or forget it. Also be wary of unpasteurized dairy products as these can transmit a range of diseases.

## Diving

If you go diving make sure that you are fit do so. The **British Sub-Aqua Club (BSAC)**, Telford's Quay, South Pier Road, Ellesmere Port, Cheshire CH65 4FL, UK, T0151-350 6200, www.bsac.com, can put you in touch with doctors who do medical examinations.

Protect your feet from cuts, beach dog parasites and sea urchins. The latter are almost impossible to remove but can be dissolved with lime or vinegar. Watch for secondary infection, which you'll need antibiotics for. Serious diving injuries may require time in a decompression chamber.

Check that the dive company knows what it is doing, has appropriate certification from BSAC or **Professional Association of Diving Instructors (PADI)**, Unit 7, St Philips Central, Albert Rd, St Philips, Bristol, BS2 OTD, T0117-300 7234, www.padi.com, and that the equipment is well maintained.

## Hepatitis

Hepatitis means inflammation of the liver. Viral causes of the disease can be acquired anywhere in the world. The most obvious symptom is a yellowing of your skin or the whites of your eyes. However, prior to this all that you may notice is itching and tiredness. Pre-travel hepatitis A vaccine is the best bet. Hepatitis B (for which there is a vaccine) is spread through blood and unprotected sexual intercourse: both of these can be avoided. Unfortunately there is no vaccine for hepatitis C or the other hepatitis viruses.

## Malaria

Malaria can cause death within 24 hrs and can start as something just resembling an attack of flu. You may feel tired, lethargic, headachy, feverish; or, more seriously, develop fits, followed by coma and then death. Have a low index of suspicion because it is very easy to write off vague symptoms, which may actually be malaria. If you have a temperature, go to a doctor as soon as you can and ask for a malaria test. On your return home if you suffer any of these symptoms, get tested as soon as possible, even if any previous test proved negative, the test could save your life. Remember ABCD: Awareness (of whether the disease is present in the area), Bite avoidance, Chemoprohylaxis, Diagnosis.

To prevent mosquito bites wear clothes that cover arms and legs and use effective insect repellents in areas with known risks of insect-spread disease. Use a mosquito net treated with insecticide as both a physical and chemical barrier at night in the same areas. Guard against the contraction of malaria with the correct anti-malarials. Note that the Royal Homeopathic Hospital in the UK does not advocate homeopathic options for malaria prevention or treatment.

Repellents containing DEET (Di-ethyltoluamide) are the gold standard. Apply the repellent every 4-6 hrs but more often if you are sweating heavily. If a non-DEET product is used check who tested it. Validated products (tested at the London School of Hygiene and Tropical Medicine) include Mosiguard, Non-DEET Jungle formula and non-DEET Autan. If you want to use citronella remember that it must be applied very frequently (ie hourly) to be effective. If you are a popular target for insect bites or develop lumps quite soon after being bitten, carry an Aspivenin kit. This syringe suction device is available from many chemists and draws out some of the allergic materials and provides quick relief.

### Rabies

Avoid dogs and monkeys that are behaving strangely. Bats also carry rabies in Kenya. If you are bitten by a domestic or wild animal, do not leave things to chance: scrub the wound with soap and water and/or disinfectant, try to at least determine the animal's ownership, and seek medical assistance at once. The course of treatment depends on whether you have already been satisfactorily vaccinated against rabies. It is important to finish the course of treatment.

### Sun

Long-term sun damage can lead to a loss of elasticity of skin and the development of pre-cancerous lesions. Years later a mild or a very malignant form of cancer may develop.

To prevent burning, use sunscreen. The higher the SPF the greater the protection. However, do not use higher factors just to stay out in the sun longer. 'Flash frying' (bursts of excessive exposure), as it is called, is known to increase the risks of skin cancer. Follow the Australians with their Slip, Slap, Slop campaign: Slip on a shirt, Slap on a hat, Slop on sun screen.

### Ticks and fly larvae

Ticks usually attach themselves to the lower parts of the body often after walking in areas where cattle have grazed, and swell up as they suck blood. The important thing is to remove them gently, so that they do not leave their head in your skin because this can cause a nasty allergic reaction. Do not use petrol, Vaseline, lighted cigarettes, etc to remove the tick, but, with a pair of tweezers remove the beast gently by gripping it at the attached (head) end and rock it out in the same way that a tooth is extracted. Some tropical flies that lay their eggs under the skin of sheep and cattle also do the same thing to humans with the result that a maggot grows under the skin and pops up as a boil. The best way to remove these is to cover the boil with oil, Vaseline or nail varnish to stop the maggot breathing, then to squeeze it out gently the next day.

### Water

There are a number of ways of purifying water. Dirty water should first be strained through a filter and then boiled or treated. Bringing water to a rolling boil at sea level is sufficient to make the water safe for drinking, but at higher altitudes you have to boil the water for a few minutes longer to ensure all microbes are killed. There are sterilizing methods that can be used and there are proprietary preparations containing chlorine or iodine compounds. Chlorine compounds generally do not kill protozoa (eg giardia). There are a number of water filters now on the market. Make sure you take the spare parts or spare chemicals with you and do not believe everything the manufacturers say.

### Other diseases and risks

Fresh water can be a source of diseases such as bilharzia. Avoid infected waters, check the CDC, WHO websites and a travel clinic for up-to-date information. Lake Victoria and many smaller lakes are infected and it's always wise to ask locally about swimming.

Unprotected sex always carries a risk, with an awesome range of visible and invisible diseases including HIV, hepatitis B and C, gonorrhea, chlamydia, herpes, syphilis and warts, just to name a few. You can reduce the risk by using a condom, a femidom or avoiding sex altogether.

### Further information

**www.bloodcare.org.uk** The Blood Care Foundation (UK) will dispatch certified non-infected blood of the right type to your hospital/clinic.
**www.btha.org** British Travel Health Association (UK). This is the official website of an organization of travel health professionals.
**www.fitfortravel.scot.nhs.uk** Fit for Travel (UK). A-Z of vaccine and travel health advice requirements for each country.
**www.fco.gov.uk** Foreign and Common-wealth Office (FCO). This is a key travel advice site, with useful information on the country,

people and climate and lists of the UK embassies/consulates.

**www.masta.org** Medical Advisory Service for Travellers Abroad (MASTA). A-Z of vaccine and travel health advice and requirements.

**www.medicalert.co.uk** Medic Alert. Produces bracelets and necklaces for those with existing medical problems, where key medical details are engraved, so that if you collapse, a medical person can identify you.

**www.travelscreening.co.uk** Travel Screening Services). A private clinic that gives vaccine and travel health advice.

**www.who.int** World Health Organization. The WHO site has links to the WHO Blue Book on travel advice.

### Books

Lankester T, *Travellers' Good Health Guide* (2nd edition, Sheldon Press, 2006).

## Insurance

Before departure, it is vital to take out comprehensive travel insurance. There are a wide variety of policies to choose from, so shop around. At the very least, the policy should cover medical expenses, including repatriation to your home country in the event of a medical emergency. If you are going to be active in Kenya, ensure the policy covers trekking or diving for example. There is no substitute for suitable precautions against petty crime, but if you do have something stolen whilst in Kenya, report the incident to the nearest police station and ensure you get a police report and case number. You will need these to make any claim from your insurance company. Kenya is covered by the **Flying Doctors' Society of Africa**, based at Wilson Airport in Nairobi, T020-690 3000, www.amref.org. For an annual tourist fee of US$50, it offers free evacuation by air to a medical centre or hospital. This may be worth considering if you are visiting more remote regions, but

not necessary if visiting the more popular parks in the north as adequate provision is made in the case of an emergency.

## Internet

Internet cafés and email facilities are plentiful in the major towns, and range from the upmarket hotels, cybercafés with fast connections to small shops and business centres that may just have a single computer. The cost of access has fallen considerably over the last few years and is available from about US$1 per hr, although the use of faster non-dial-up connections may cost a little more. The **Kenya Post Office** now offers access in most of their branches even in the small towns. Wi-Fi is available at the **Jomo Kenyatta International Airport** and in some of the upmarket business hotels in Nairobi.

## Language

Kenya is a welcoming country and the first word that you will hear and come to know is the Kiswahili greeting *Jambo* – 'hello', often followed by *Hakuna matata* – 'no problem'! There are a number of local languages but most people in Kenya, as in all of East Africa, speak Kiswahili and some English. Kiswahili is the official language of Kenya and is taught in primary schools. English is generally used in business and is taught in secondary schools. Only in the remote rural regions will you find people that only speak in their local tongues. A little Kiswahili goes a long way, and most Kenyans will be thrilled to hear visitors attempt to use it. Although Kiswahili is a Bantu language in structure and origin, its vocabulary draws on a variety of sources including Arabic and English. The word for tea, *chai*, is the same in East Africa as it is in China and India for example. On the coast, Kiswahili is a little more grammatically developed. In other parts of the country, a more simplified version is spoken, known as 'kitchen swahili'. Since the language was originally written down by the British colonists, words are pronounced just as they are spelt. **▶** *For useful words and phrases in Kiswahili, see page 402.*

## Local customs and laws

Stand for the national anthem and show respect if the national flag is being raised or lowered. Do not take photographs of military or official buildings or personnel, especially the president. Always ask before photographing local people. In some regions, the Masai are so used to tourists wanting to take pictures of them a fee is definitely expected. Do not tear the local currency, and respect the currency laws of the country. Importing or possession of drugs and guns is prohibited and punished severely. The attitude to *bhangi* (cannabis) and *miraa* (a mild stimulant) is ambivalent: both are illegal but appear to be tolerated by the authorities. However, if you are caught your embassy is unlikely to be sympathetic. If you do get in trouble with the law or have to report to the police, always be exceptionally polite and relatively humble, even if you are reporting a crime against yourself. The Kenyan police generally enjoy their authoritative status; to rant and rave and demand attention will get you absolutely nowhere. Calling a policeman 'sir' is customary. Respect is accorded to elderly people, usually by the greeting *Shikamoo, mzee* to a man and *Shikamoo, mama* to a woman. In English, it is common for people to use the terms 'my sister' or 'aunt', 'my brother' or 'uncle' (depending on how old they think you are) as greetings. For anyone spending any length of time in Kenya, or returning after a long break, it is a sad day when you have reached the status of aunt or uncle – it means you are getting old!

## Media

### Newspapers and magazines

Kenya has several English-language newspapers. Generally, Kenyans are avid newspaper readers and each one has good online news. The most popular are the *Daily Nation* (www.nationaudio.com) and the *East African Standard* (www.eastandard.net). *The East African* (www.theeastafrican.co.ke) is a weekly newspaper sold throughout Kenya, Tanzania and Uganda. There is 1 daily newspaper written in Kiswahili, *Taifa Leo*. The *Kenya Times* (www.kenyatimesonline.com) is the government-owned paper. Of the international press, *Time* and *Newsweek* are regularly available, as is the International *Herald Tribune*. UK daily newspapers arrive a day or so late in larger towns. Most newspapers and magazines are available from street stalls, of which there is one on every street in Nairobi.

### Radio

Kenya Broadcasting Corporation (KBC) broadcasts in Kiswahili, English and some local languages. There are several popular FM stations that can be picked up in the cities such as **Capital FM** and **Kiss 100 FM**. **BBC World Service** is broadcast to Kenya; check www.bbc.co.uk/worldservice.

### Television

There are 3 television channels: **Kenya Broadcasting Corporation (KBC)**, broadcasts in Kiswahili and English with a considerable number of imported foreign programmes; **Nation TV**, which is the station of the newspaper of the same name and broadcasts news and imported shows from the US; and **Kenya Television News**, based on CNN material. Many hotels will have satellite TV. This is usually **DSTV** (Digital Satellite Television), South African satellite TV, with several channels. The most popular are the sports channels, especially **Supersport**, which provides coverage of European football.

## Money

### Currency

→ US$1=78KSh, £1=116.4KSh, euro1=104KSh (Jan 2009)

The currency in Kenya is the Kenyan shilling (the written abbreviation is either KSh or using /= after the amount, ie 500/=). Notes are 50, 100, 200, 500 and 1000KSh, coins are 5, 10 and 20KSh. As it is not a hard currency, it cannot be brought into or taken out of the country, however there are no restrictions on the amount of foreign currency that can be brought into Kenya. There are banks with ATMs and bureaux de change at both Nairobi and Mombasa airports. There are inevitable queues but at Nairobi it is marginally quicker to change your money after you go through customs. The easiest currencies to exchange are US dollars, UK pounds and euros. If you are bringing US dollars cash, try and bring newer notes – because of the prevalence of forgery, many banks and bureaux de changes do not accept bills printed before 2000. Sometimes lower denomination bills attract a lower exchange rate than higher denominations.

Departure taxes can be paid in local or foreign currency, but they are usually included in the price of an air ticket.

**Exchange** Visitors should change foreign currency at banks, bureaux de change or authorized hotels, and under no circumstances change money on the black market, which is illegal. All banks have a foreign exchange service. The government has authorized bureaux de change known as forex bureaux to set rates for buying foreign currency from the public. Forex bureaux are open longer hours and offer faster service than banks and, although the exchange rates are only nominally different, the bureaux usually offer a better rate on traveller's cheques.

### Credit cards and traveller's cheques

Traveller's cheques (TCs) are widely accepted, and many upmarket hotels, travel agencies, safari companies and restaurants accept credit cards. Most banks in Kenya are equipped to advance cash on credit cards, and increasingly most now have ATMs that accept Visa, Mastercard, Plus and Cirrus cards. Diners Club and American Express are, however, limited. Increasingly, many of the large petrol stations, such as Caltex and Mobil, are starting to install ATMs, especially in Nairobi and Mombasa. Your bank will probably charge a fee for withdrawing cash. It is quite feasible to travel around Kenya with just a credit or debit card, although it is always a good idea to bring some cash or TCs as a back-up.

### Cost of travelling

In upmarket luxury lodges and tented camps expect to pay in excess of US$150 per person per night for a double, rising to US$500 per night per person in the most exclusive establishments. There are a number of places aimed at the very top-of-the-range tourist or honeymooner that charge nearer US$1000 per person per night. For this you will get impeccable service, cuisine and decor in fantastic locations either in the parks or on the coast. In 4- and 5-star hotels and lodges expect to spend US$200-300 a day. Careful tourists can live reasonably comfortably on US$100 a day staying in the mid-range places, however, to stay in anything other than campsites on safaris, they will have to spend a little more for the cheapest accommodation in the national parks. Budget travellers can get by on US$40 utilizing the cheap guesthouses and going on a basic camping safari. However, with additional park entry fees and related costs, organized camping safari costs are at the bare minimum US$200 for a 3-day/2-night excursion to the Masai Mara for example. Commodities such as chocolate and toiletries are more expensive as they are imported but are readily available. Restaurants vary widely from side-of-the-road local eateries where a simple meal of chicken and chips will cost US$2-3 to the upmarket restaurants in the cities and tourists spots that charge in excess of US$60 for 2 people with drinks.

## Opening hours

**Banks** Mon-Fri 0830-1330, Sat 0830-1100.
**Embassies** Usually mornings only.
**Kiosks** Often open all hours, as the owner frequently lives on site. **Post offices** Mon-Fri 0800-1700, Sat 0900-1200. **Shops** Generally Mon-Sat 0800-1700 or 1800.

## Post

Sending post out of the country is cheap and efficient; it generally takes a week to Europe and about 10 days to Australia and the USA. There are post offices and post boxes in most towns. Many shops in tourist lodges and hotels sell stamps. Receiving post is also easy, but not parcels. All parcels need to be checked by officials for import duty and it is not uncommon for them to go astray unless they have been sent registered post or by courier. If you are sending things out of the country they must be wrapped in brown paper with string. There is no point doing this before getting to the post office as you will be asked to undo it to be checked for export duty. Parcels must not weigh more than 20 kg for seamail or 30 kg for airmail or be more than 100 cm long.

## Safety

The majority of the people you will meet are honest and ready to help you so there is no need to get paranoid about your safety. However, Nairobi and Mombasa do have reputations for crime, and the most popular national parks have their fair share of robberies. There is a high rate of street crime not just in Nairobi and Mombasa but also in Kisumu and the coastal beach resorts, especially bag-snatching. Basically, you just have to be sensible and not carry expensive cameras, open bags or valuable jewellery and be careful about carrying large sums of money. Waist pouches ('bum-bags' or 'moon-bags') are very vulnerable as the belt can be cut easily.

Day packs have also been known to be slashed, with their entire contents drifting out on to the street without the wearer knowing. Carry money and any valuables in a slim belt under clothing. Also, do not automatically expect your belongings to be safe in a tent. Avoid walking around after dusk, particularly in the more run-down urban areas – take a taxi – and walking alone at night, even on beaches, is dangerous. In built-up areas, lock your car, and if there is an *askari* (security guard) nearby, pay him a small sum to watch over it, although you should still be careful as con-artists have been known to impersonate hotel employees and even police officers. Also be wary of someone distracting a driver in a parked vehicle, whilst an accomplice gets into the car on the opposite side. Always keep car doors locked and windows wound up, and lock room doors at night as noisy fans and a/c can provide cover for sneak thieves. Crime and hazardous road conditions make travel by night dangerous.

Car-jacking occurs and is a particular problem in Nairobi. You also need to be vigilant of thieves on buses and trains and guard your possessions fiercely. For petty offences (driving without lights switched on, for example) police will often try to solicit a bribe, masked as an 'on-the-spot' fine. Establish the amount being requested, and then offer to go to the police station to pay, at which point you will usually be released with a warning. For any serious charges, immediately contact your embassy or consulate. The British High Commission strongly advise against travel in Northeast Kenya (Moyale, Mandera, Wajit and Garissa), because of difficulties with the Somalian unrest, and there is a problem with *Shiftas* (bandits) attacking vehicles on roads in Northern Kenya. See page 350 for more advice on this region.

It's not only crime that may affect your personal safety; you must also take safety precautions when visiting the game reserves and national parks. If camping, it is not advisable to leave your tent or *banda* during the night. Wild animals wander around the camps freely in the hours of darkness, and a protruding leg may seem like a tasty take-away to a hungry hyena. This is especially true at organized campsites, where the local animals have got so used to humans that they have lost much of their inherent fear. Exercise care during daylight hours too – remember wild animals can be unpredictable and potentially dangerous.

## Telephone

→ *Country code+254.*
Generally speaking, the telephone system is very good. You should be able to make international calls from public call boxes and the easiest way of doing this is with a phone card (available from most post offices). If this is not possible, make your call through post offices where you get your money back if you fail to get through. If you dial through the operator, there is a 3-min minimum charge. Most hotels and lodges offer international telephone and fax services, though they will usually charge double. In larger towns, private centres also offer international services. Calls from Kenya to Tanzania and Uganda are charged at long-distance tariffs rather than international. If you have a mobile phone with a roaming connection, you can make use of Kenya's cellular networks, which cover most larger towns, the length of the coast and the Mombasa to Uganda road and the tourist areas but not some of the parks and reserves or the north of Kenya away from the towns. Sim and top-up cards for pay-as-you-go mobile providers are available almost everywhere; in the towns and cities these often have their own shops, but you can buy cards from roadside vendors anywhere, even in the smallest of settlements. Mobile phones are now such a part of everyday life in Kenya that many establishments have abandoned the local landline services and use the mobile network instead. Quite remarkably, cell phone provider **Celtel**, operates a system

called **One Network**, the world's 1st borderless network. It covers 22 African countries from Zambia to Gabon and enables callers to use their phones without roaming and all calls across this vast region are at local (not international) rates. The network now has a staggering 25 million subscribers. If you are travelling on, say to Uganda or Tanzania, it's a good idea to opt for a Celtel Sim card. At the time of writing Celtel was rebranding itself under the Zain telecommunications umbrella so look out for both cards.

## Time

GMT+3.

## Tipping

It is customary to tip around 10% for good service, which is greatly appreciated by hotel and restaurant staff, most of whom receive very low pay. Some upmarket establishments may add a service charge to the bill. See page 43 for advice on tipping safari guides.

## Tour operators

If you plan to book an organized tour from your own country, the best bet is to locate a travel agent with a links to tour companies in Kenya as they will probably be able to get you the best deals. Within Kenya there is a bewildering array of tour operators offering safaris in Kenya and East Africa, with most having offices in Nairobi (see page 100) or Mombasa (see page 264). There is no reason why you cannot deal with them directly and they may often be cheaper and better informed than travel agents in your home country. Many companies offer tailor-made guided trips for small groups to the more remote parts of the country, which can be economical for families or groups of friends travelling together.

### Australia
**African Wildlife Safaris**, T+61 (0)3-9249 3777, www.africanwildlifesafaris.com.au.
**Classic Safari Company**, T+61 1 300-130218, www.classicsafaricompany.com.au.
**Peregrine Travel**, T+61 (0)3-8601 4444, www.peregrine.net.au.

### East Africa
**Bunyonyi Safaris Ltd**, Crusader House, 3 Portal Av, PO Box 26905, Kampala, Uganda, T+256 (0)41-434 7460, www.bunyonyi.com. Arranges tours throughout Uganda.
**Easy Travel & Tours Ltd**, Raha Tower, Bibi Titi Mohamed St, Dar-Es-Salaam, Tanzania, T+255 (0)22-212 3526, www.easytravel.co.tz.
**Predators Safari Club**, PO Box 2302 Arusha, Tanzania, T+255 (0)27-250 6471/T+255 7545 62254 (mob), www.predators-safari.com. Offers safaris in Kenya and Tanzania.

**Shoor Safaris**, T+254 20-374 5690, www.shoortravel.com.

### Germany
**Djoser Travel**, T+49 (0)21-920 1580, www.djoser.de.
**A & E Reiseteam**, T+49 (0)40-2787 8870, www.ae-reiseteam.de.
**Iwanowski's Individuelles Reisen GmbH**, T+49 (0)21-332 6030, www.afrika.de.

### North America
**Adventure Centre**, T1 800-228 8747, T+1 51-0654 1879, www.adventure-centre.com.
**Africa Adventure Company**, T+1 800-882 9453, T+1 954-491 8877, www.africa-adventure.com.
**Bushtracks**, T+1 707-433 4492, www.bushtracks.com.
**Menengai Holidays**, T+1 704-904 1081, www.menengaiholidays.com

**South Africa**
**Africa Travel Co**, T+27 (0)21-385 1390, www.africatravelco.com.
**Pulse Africa**, T+27 (0)11-325 2290, www.pulseafrica.com.
**Wild Frontiers**, T+27 (0)11-702 2035, www.wildfrontiers.com.

**United Kingdom**
**Aardvark Safaris**, T+44 (0)1980-849160, www.aardvarksafaris.com.
**Abercrombie & Kent**, T+44 (0)800-554 7016, www.abercrombiekent.com.
**Acacia Adventure Holidays**, lower ground floor, 23A Craven Terrace, London W2 3QH, T+44 (0)20-7706 4700, www.acacia-africa.com.
**Africa Travel Centre**, 3rd floor, New Premier House, 150 Southampton Row, London WC1B 5AL, T+44 (0)845-450 1520, www.africatravel.co.uk.

**Africa Travel Resource**, T+44 (0)1306-880 770, www.africatravelresource.com.
**Aim 4 Africa**, 21-23 Chelsea Rd, Sheffield, S11 9BQ, T+44 (0)114-255 2533, www.aim4africa.com.
**Audley Travel Ltd**, T+44 (0)1993-838 500, www.audleytravel.com.
**Footprint Adventures**, T+44 (0)1522-804 929, www.footprint-adventures.co.uk.
**Global Village**, 102 Islington High St, London N1 8EG, T+44 (0)844-844 2541, www.globalvillage-travel.com.
**Odyssey World**, T+44 (0)845-370 7733, www.odyssey-world.co.uk.
**Rainbow Tours**, T+44 (0)20-7226 1004, www.rainbowtours.co.uk.
**Safari Consultants**, T+44 (0)1787-888 590, www.safari-consultants.co.uk.
**Safari Drive**, Windy Hollow, Sheepdrove, Lambourn, Berkshire RH17 7XA, T+44 (0)1488-71140, www.safaridrive.com.

**Somak**, T+44 (0)20-8423 3000, www.somak.co.uk.
**Steppes Travel**, T+44 (0)1285-880 980, www.steppestravel.co.uk.
**Tim Best Travel**, T+44 (0)20-7591 0300, www.timbesttravel.com.
**Wildlife Worldwide**, T+44 (0)845-130 6982, www.wildlifeworldwide.com.

## Tourist information

The head office of the **Kenya Tourist Board** is on Ragati Rd in Nairobi, T020-271 1262, www.magicalkenya.com, but this is not a drop-in office. However, they will send you brochures on request and the website is excellent. Within Kenya the free publication *Tourist's Kenya* is published fortnightly and offers a rundown on things going on. There is another publication called *What's On*, which comes out monthly. **Kenya Tourism**

Federation, on Langata Road in the Kenya Wildlife Services Complex in Nairobi, offers a tourist helpline, T020-604 767, and a safety and communication centre, which advises tourists on most things including road conditions and emergency help. If you want to go off the beaten track, get advice from them first.

There is a wealth of information in print. The authoritative and inspirational *Travel Africa Magazine*, available in the UK, is well worth a read when planning a trip. See page 400 for background reading.

**Tourist offices overseas**
**France**, 11 Rue Blanche, Paris 75009, T+33 (0)1-5325 1207, kenya@interfacetourism.com.
**Germany**, Schwarz Bach Strasse 32, Mettman, T+49 (0)2-21048 32919, kenia@travelmarketing.de.
**Italy**, Via Monte Rosa 20, Milan 20149, T+39 (0)2 36561179, magicalkenya@aviareps.com.

**Netherlands**, Leliegracht 20, Amsterdam 1015, T+31 (0)20-638 4661, kenia@travelmc.com.
**UK**, Colethurch House, 1 London Bridge Walk, London SE1 2S6, T+44 (0)207-367 0900, kenya@hillsbalfoursynergy.com.
**USA**, 6422 City West Parkway, Minneapolis, 55344, T+1 866 445 3692, infousa@magiacalkenya.com.

## Useful websites

**www.africaonline.com** Comprehensive website of news, sport and travel over Africa.
**www.ecotourismkenya.org** Website for the Ecotourism Society of Kenya, a forum founded in 1996 to provide support for small community ecotourism projects.
**www.go2africa.com** Booking service for East Africa, with useful practical information.
**www.katokenya.org** Website for the Kenyan Association of Tour Operators.
**www.kenyalastminute.com** Bargain last-minute holidays to Kenya, excellent site and service.
**www.kenyalogy.com** General tourism information.
**www.kenyatravelideas.com** Comprehensive all-round information about Kenya and as the name suggest travel ideas.
**www.kenya.go.ke** Website for the Kenyan government.
**www.kws.org** Kenya Wildlife Services.
**www.magicalkenya.com** Official website of the Kenya Tourist Board, comprehensive and detailed information.
**www.mombasacoast.com** Tourist information, reservation service.
**www.overlandafrica.com** Sells a variety of overland tours throughout East Africa.
**www.shoortravel.com** Tour operator's website offering maps, hotel listings, safaris and general information.
**www.watamu.net** Information and booking services for coastal hotels.

## Visas and immigration

Almost all visitors require a visa, with the exception of some African countries. A transit visa valid for 7 days costs US$20 per person; a single-entry visa valid for 3 months costs US$50; a multi-entry visa valid for 12 months costs US$100. Visas are issued at the following entry points: Busia, Lunga Lunga, Malaba, Migori, Moyale, Namanga and Taveta border posts and at Jomo Kenyatta International Airport in Nairobi, Moi International Airport in Mombasa and Eldoret International Airport. Visas can be paid for in US dollars, euros or UK pounds sterling. Multi-entry visas are not available on arrival but only through embassies. As long as your single-entry visa remains valid you are allowed to move freely between Kenya, Tanzania and Uganda without the need for re-entry permits. If you want to get an extension you can stay a maximum of 6 months in the country fairly easily, but at extra cost. In Nairobi this can be done at Nyayo House, corner of Kenyatta Av and Uhuru Highway, T020-222 022, Mon-Fri 0830-1230 and 1400-1530; it can also be done at the Provincial Commissioner's Offices in Embu, Garissa, Kisumu, Mombasa and Nakuru. Do check your visitor's pass as it has been known for people who have overstayed their time in the country to be fined quite heavily. Your passport must be valid for a minimum of 6 months after your planned departure date from Kenya; this is a requirement whether you need a visa or not. For more information visit www.immigration.go.ke. Incidentally, if passengers are transiting through Nairobi and have a couple of hours to kill, they are allowed out of the airport on their transit visas, so there is no reason at all why they can't grab a taxi and go to Nairobi National Park for a game drive.

## Weights and measures

Metric. In country areas items are often sold by the piece.

## Women travellers

Women do have to be more wary than men, although Kenya seems to be a more pleasant place for lone women travellers than many other countries. If you are hassled, it is best to totally ignore the person, whatever you feel, as expressions of anger are often taken as acts of encouragement. Kenyan women will generally be very supportive if they see you are being harassed and may well intervene if they think you need help, but the situation is very rarely anything more than a nuisance. You are more likely to be approached at the coast, as the number of women coming to Kenya for sexual adventure has encouraged this type of pestering. The key is to keep patient and maintain a sense of humour. Women in Kenya dress very decorously, and it is wise to follow suit particularly in small towns and rural areas. In Lamu in particular, it is important for both men and women to dress modestly as it's a fairly conservative Muslim community.

## Working in Kenya

Whilst there is a fairly large expatriate community in Nairobi and Mombasa working in construction, telecommunications and the import/export industry, there are few opportunities for travellers to obtain casual paid employment in Kenya and it is illegal for a foreigner to work there without an official work permit. A number of NGOs and voluntary organizations can arrange placements for volunteers, especially teachers and HIV/Aids educators, for periods ranging from a few weeks to 6 months, see www.volunteerkenya.org or www.volunteerabroad.com/kenya. The **Kenya Voluntary and Community Development Project**, www.kvcdp.org, is a good grass-roots organization that puts volunteers in a number of placements, especially those involving Kenya's needy children.

# Contents

## Footprint features

# Nairobi

## At a glance

◓ **Getting around** On foot in the city centre; tours, bus or self-drive to the outlying attractions.

◉ **Time required** A minimum of 2 days to see the sights in the city centre and suburbs; half a day in Nairobi National Park.

☼ **Weather** Moderate temperatures year round of 15-25°C but often cloudy.

✖ **When not to go** Mar-May are the wettest months when the streets get flooded and muddy.

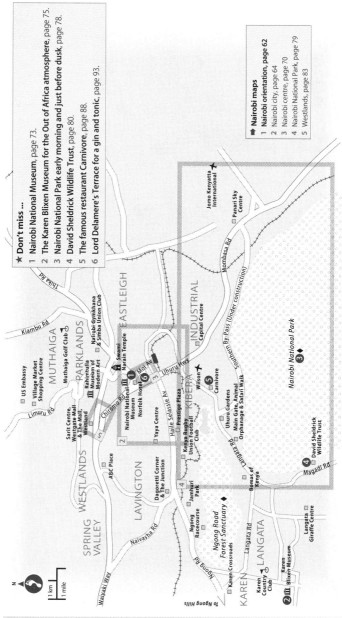

★ Don't miss ...

1 Nairobi National Museum, page 73.

2 The Karen Blixen Museum for the Out of Africa atmosphere, page 75.

3 Nairobi National Park early morning and just before dusk, page 78.

4 David Sheldrick Wildlife Trust, page 80.

5 The famous restaurant Carnivore, page 88.

6 Lord Delamere's Terrace for a gin and tonic, page 93.

➡ Nairobi maps

1 Nairobi orientation, page 62.
2 Nairobi city, page 64.
3 Nairobi centre, page 70.
4 Nairobi National Park, page 79.
5 Westlands, page 83.

N

1 km
1 mile

SPRING VALLEY

WESTLANDS

MUTHAIGA

PARKLANDS

EASTLEIGH

Waiyaki Way

US Embassy

Kiambu Rd

Thika Rd

Village Market Shopping Centre

Muthaiga Golf Club

Nairobi Gymkhana & Simba Union Club

Sarit Centre, Westgate Mall & The Mall, Westland

Limuru Rd

Rahimtulla Museum of Modern Art

Swami Narain Temple

Chiromo Rd

Nairobi National Museum

Norfolk Hotel

Moi Av

ABC Place

Yaya Centre

LAVINGTON

Naivasha Rd

Prestige Plaza

Halle Selassie Av

Uhuru Hwy

Wilson

Carnivore

Uhuru Hwy

Capital Centre

INDUSTRIAL

Panari Sky Centre

Jomo Kenyatta International

Mombasa Rd

Dagoretti Corner & The Junction

Jamhuri Park

Kenya Rugby Union Football Club

Ngong Rd

KIBERA

Uhuru Gardens

Main Gate, Animal Orphanage & Safari Walk

Southern By-Pass (Under construction)

Ngong Racecourse

Bomas of Kenya

Langata Rd

Nairobi National Park

Ngong Road Forest Sanctuary

Karen Crossroads

Magadi Rd

David Sheldrick Wildlife Trust

To Ngong Hills

KAREN

Karen Country Club

Karen Blixen Museum

LANGATA

Langata Giraffe Centre

Nairobi, capital of Kenya, is a lively, cosmopolitan and bustling city. The centre is modern and prosperous; services are well organized and efficient. Businessmen and women talking on mobile phones walk the pavements alongside Masai warriors with long, ochre-stained hair, tourists mingle with busy traders and commuters, markets sell traditional handicrafts in the shadow of office towers, and life goes on at a frenetic pace. The city never stops moving, and the streets throng with pedestrians, cars, *matatus* and *mkokoteni* (hand-drawn carts used to carry goods to market). However, the combination of Kenya's rising population and migration to the towns has resulted in the size of Nairobi increasing at an enormous rate. Housing and other facilities have failed to keep up and shanty towns in the outskirts are the inevitable result. The population is officially estimated at just under three million but, with a growth rate of 6.9 %, it is expected to reach around five million by 2015. Unfortunately Nairobi has also attracted fame for its high crime rate, and visitors should at all times exercise caution. Nevertheless, there are many interesting things to do and see. Nairobi National Park is in sight of the city, there are a number of other wildlife attractions within a stone's throw and Nairobi itself is home to some of the best restaurants and shops in East Africa. It's worthwhile making time for Nairobi at the beginning or end of a trip to Kenya. The city sits at 1870 m above sea level – from here it is a long and steady fall to the coast, 500 km away.

**Ins and outs** → *Colour map 1, A/B4. Phone code: 020. Population: 2.9 million.*

## Getting there

Nairobi is the most important air transport hub for East Africa, and international and domestic flights touch down at **Jomo Kenyatta International Airport** ① *15 km southeast of the city off the Mombasa Rd, T020-661 1000, www.kenyaairports.co.ke.* Although an untidy old building that is in desperate need of refurbishing, airport facilities are fully functional and include cafés, several banks (with longer banking hours than the rest of the country), ATMs, hotel booking, tour-operator and car-hire desks, and air-side, extensive duty free and souvenir shops and a branch of the excellent **Nairobi Java House** coffee shop, which also sells coffee beans for those wanting to take a lasting taste of Kenyan coffee home with them. Once through immigration and customs in the international arrivals hall, taxi drivers will start to badger you, but they are easy enough to deal with and move on to the next arrival if you say you are not interested or already have

**② Nairobi city**

Sleeping
Boulevard **1**
Fairview **2**
High Point **5**

Milimani Backpackers **3**
Nairobi Serena, Café
Maghreb & Aksum Bar **7**
Nairobi Youth Hostel **8**

Norfolk, Ibis Grill & Lord
Delamere Terrace **10**
Panafric **11**
Silver Springs **14**

Upper Hill Campsite **15**
YMCA **13**

arranged a transfer. If you do want a taxi, expect to bargain to around US$20-30 depending on the time of day (and traffic) for a ride into the city centre. Outside the domestic terminal (a short trolley push across the car park) is a desk for the **Airport Taxi Operators Association** and a taxi from the airport into the centre should cost around US$20. Pay at the desk, where they'll give you a receipt to show the driver. This is the better and slightly cheaper option, and by the time you read this, the association may have established a desk at the international terminal. Most hotels and tour operators also provide transport inclusive of a holiday package or at the very least can arrange a shuttle bus. There is also a bus service (0600-1800) to and from the airport, number 34 (to get on it ask for the bus stand at the airport), and to the airport, board outside the **Hilton Hotel** in the city, US$1.10, journey time 40 minutes depending on traffic and time of day, although this is best avoided if you have a lot of luggage as the buses get crowded nearer the city.

Nairobi's second airport is **Wilson Airport** ① *6 km south of the city on the Langata Rd, T020-603 260, www.kenya airports.com.* This airport is used for domestic scheduled and charter flights by the light aircraft airlines, as well as being the base for **AMREF** – the flying doctor service, and the annual host for the Nairobi International Air Show in November (see page 40). A taxi into the city centre should cost around US$8.

There are good road connections into the city from all directions. The long-distance bus station is on Landhies Road from where there are daily departures to most destinations. **Akamba Bus** is one of the better organized and safer of the many bus services travelling long distance within Kenya and to neighbouring countries. Their terminus is in Lagos Road. There are also several shuttle bus companies offering a daily service to/from Arusha and Moshi in Tanzania.

The railway station is at the southern end of Moi Avenue. It is easily spotted thanks to the coloured lights around the main entrance. There is currently only one passenger rail service from Nairobi to Mombasa, with the train travelling overnight through Tsavo National Park. Part of the railway in the north of the country was destroyed during the 2008 riots, so until it is repaired the service between Nairobi and Kisumu has been suspended. ▶▶ See Transport, page 103.

### Getting around

Central Nairobi is bounded by Uhuru Highway to the west, Nairobi River to the

Eating ⑦
China Plate **4**
Osteria del Chianti **1**
Railway **2**

Bars & clubs ⑪
Casablanca **3**

# Arriving at night

Jomo Kenyatta International Airport is very busy with a number of flights arriving and departing late in the evening or very early in the morning. If you arrive after dark the sensible option to get from the airport to the city safely is to take a taxi. Avoid the public bus. You will need KSh to pay for a taxi; you will be able to change money at the banks and bureaux de change in the airport.

north and east and the railway to the south. Across the Uhuru Highway is Uhuru Park and Central Park. In the southwest of this central triangle of about 5 sq km is the crop of high-rise buildings where most of the government buildings, offices, banks, hotels and shops are located. In the northern section the buildings are closer together and there are many less expensive shops and restaurants, while to the east of the triangle is the poorer section where there are cheaper hotels and restaurants, shops and markets. This is the area around River Road, which is very lively, full of character and has the authentic atmosphere of the African section of a great city (although it is an area in which visitors should take care over their safety).

Southeast of the city centre around the Mombasa Road is the concentrated industrial area that peters out near the airport. By contrast, to the south of here is the 117 sq km Nairobi National Park, which makes up about one fifth of the city's area. To the west of the city centre and hemmed in by the Langata and Ngong roads is the congested Kibera slum (see page 72), and beyond here and past the Main Gate to Nairobi National Park are the affluent suburbs of Langata and Karen where many of the sights are located. Much of this area was sold for development by Karen Blixen, the Danish authoress, when she left Kenya in 1931, and these leafy suburbs are isolated from the rest of Nairobi by the Ngong Road Forest Sanctuary. There is a semi-country status with seemingly more dogs and horses than human residents. This is changing however, as clusters of homes are being built on what were once large plots with single dwellings, and estates of houses occupy former farmland.

Walking around central Nairobi is relatively straightforward, as the city centre is small and accessible. Taxis are widely available, convenient and are parked on just about every street corner. Any make of car can serve as a taxi, although all Nairobi taxis are white and marked with a yellow line along each side. There is also a large fleet of London black taxis operating within the city. Taxis are not metered, and a price should be agreed with the driver before departure. Expect to pay in the region of US$5 for a short hop across the city centre rising to US$15-20 for a ride to outlying areas.

City buses are numbered and operate on set routes throughout the city, and can be boarded at any stop and tickets purchased on board. You can catch buses as far as Karen and beyond, and the main city bus terminal is located at the end of River Road. There are also main bus stops outside the **Hilton Hotel** on Moi Avenue, outside Nation House on Tom Mboya Street, outside the Railway Station at the end of Moi Avenue, and outside the General Post Office on Kenyatta Avenue. *Matatus* (minibuses) also operate on set routes and are the most popular form of local public transport. Again, like taxis most are white with a yellow stripe. Their destination is clearly written on the side. There are countless *matatu* stands throughout Nairobi, with continuous arrivals and departures throughout the day.

Most tour operators are able to arrange a tour of Nairobi, which is a very useful way of familiarizing yourself with the layout of the city, as well as seeing some of the sites that are further out. The tours will usually include a trip to the City Market, the Parliament buildings and the Nairobi National Museum. For tour operators, see page 100. You can also hire a car for a day or two to explore on your own, but only do so if you have had any experience of manic, congested traffic typical of an African city, although the suburbs like Karen, and the Nairobi National Park, are easy to negotiate by road. ▸▸ *See Transport, page 103.*

The best maps of Nairobi are the *City of Nairobi: Map and Guide*, published by the Survey of Kenya in English, German and French. If you want more detail or are staying a while it may be worth getting *A to Z Guide to Nairobi*, by RW Moss (Kenway Publications), which is clear and easy to use. There are several other maps on offer, so it's just a case of finding one that suits you. Try the bookshop in the **Stanley Hotel**, or the bookshops in the shopping malls, which all have a good selection.

## Best time to visit

Nairobi lies 145 km south of the equator but it's far from hot. The city is at 1870 m, so temperatures are a moderate 15-25°C year-round and rarely reach over 30°C. September to April are the hottest months, with maximum temperatures averaging 24°C, but falling at night to around 13°C. May to August is cooler, with a maximum average of 21°C, and minimum of 11°C at night. The main rainy seasons are March to May and October to December, when it gets slightly humid and the streets become flooded and muddy.

## Tourist information

There is no tourist information centre in Nairobi, but the tour operators will be able to help, see page 100. There are several useful publications for sale at the bookshops. These include the annual: *Visitors' Guide Kenya*, which is published by Yellow Pages Kenya and lists attractions, shops, restaurants and services, and the similar *Go Places*, which comes out bi-monthly. **Kenya Tourism Federation**, on Langata Road in the Kenya Wildlife Services (KWS) Complex, near to the Main Gate of Nairobi National Park, offers a **tourist help line** ① *T020-604 767*, which is staffed 24 hours, and a safety and communication centre, which advises tourists on most things including road conditions or emergency help. If you want to go off the beaten track, get advice from them first. **Kenya Wildlife Services (KWS)** ① *T020-600 800, www.kws.org*, also has a shop here that sells some useful brochures and maps on the national parks, and they are very helpful with advice about visiting the parks. For listings and restaurant and nightlife reviews, **Kenya Buzz** ① *www.kenyabuzz.com*, is a good source of information.

## Safety

Historically, crime in Nairobi has been well documented with frequent muggings, bag snatchings, car-jackings and robberies. These can certainly be a problem if you are not extremely sensible, and if you walk around with a camera hanging from your neck, an obviously expensive watch, jewellery or a money belt showing, then you are very vulnerable. If you are at all unsure take a taxi that you should lock from the inside if possible, and make it a rule to always do so at night. Places to definitely avoid walking around are River Road and its neighbouring streets; as a rule of thumb do not wander casually much farther west than Moi Avenue. Some thieves specialize in jostling, robbing and snatching from new arrivals on buses and *matatus* and on these **do not** take items to eat offered by strangers, as they may have been drugged to aid robbery. Despite all this, things have improved in central Nairobi since the mid-1990s. The Nairobi Central Business District Association (NCBDA) has worked with police to provide better policing of the streets and CCTV cameras have been installed, resulting in a marked decline in petty theft. Nevertheless it is always wise to exercise caution when walking around Nairobi, avoid walking around the city centre on Sundays as businesses are shut and the streets are virtually empty, and never walk around at night. If driving, be wary of car hijacking, especially at traffic lights in the suburbs. It's a good idea to travel with the windows closed and the doors locked. Remember, almost all car-jackers are armed and will use their weapons when faced with resistance.

## Background

The name Nairobi comes from the Masai *'enkare nyarobe'* meaning sweet (or cold) water, for originally this was a watering hole for the Masai and their cattle. Just 110 years ago Nairobi hardly existed. It began life in 1896 as a railway camp during the building of the Uganda Railway from the coast to the highlands. The location was chosen due to its central position between Mombasa and Kampala, just before the railway was to make its difficult descent and ascent of the walls of the Rift Valley. It was also chosen because its rivers could supply the camp with water. It grew steadily, and by 1907 had become a town sufficient in size to take over from Mombasa as capital of British East Africa. Its climate was considered healthier than that of the coast, as its temperature was too cool for the malaria mosquito to survive, and its position was ideal for developing into a trading centre for the settlers who farmed the fertile farmland around Nairobi and beyond into Western Kenya, referred to as the White Highlands, which attracted some 80,000 European settlers between the 1920s and 1950s. These 'intrepid adventurers' included Karen Blixen of *Out of Africa* fame – her house is now a museum on the outskirts of the city. Nairobi's famous **Norfolk Hotel** opened in 1904, and was once the social meeting place for this privileged community; today you can still enjoy a gin and tonic in the bar. The local Kikuyu who were losing their land to these white settlers and were dispersed further by the Mau Mau rebellion in the 1950s (see page 381), moved into Nairobi and the city swelled. It became a municipality in 1919, received city status in 1950, and after Independence in 1963 became capital of the republic.

The euphoria inspired by Independence brought with it a wave of construction in the city centre, which resulted in the many not terribly attractive 1960-1970s blocks that still stand today among the more modern gleaming skyscrapers. With 19 floors, the Hilton Hotel became the city's tallest building in 1969 before it was superceded by the Kenyatta International Conference centre with 33 floors in 1972, which in turn was overtaken by the New Central Bank Tower in 2000, which with 38 floors is currently the tallest building in Nairobi. Westlands pioneered the under-one-roof shopping mall when the Sarit Centre was built in 1983, and now modern shopping malls feature in almost every fairly affluent neighbourhood with more being built all the time.

Like many African cities, Nairobi today has bustling markets, alarming *matatu* drivers, potholed roads, shanty towns and leafy suburbs. As well as being the seat of government and commerce for Kenya, it is also the most important city in East Africa and is home to many diplomatic agencies, NGOs and multinationals and is an important base for the UN. Over the years it has also attracted many of Kenya's rural poor seeking employment in the big city, which has resulted in large slums developing around the city centre. Nevertheless it's a lively African city, which boasts a generally good infrastructure, amazingly friendly, interesting and intelligent people from all walks of life, and excellent facilities for tourists.

# Sights

Nairobi has an interesting cross section of sights that explore both its colonial past and Kenya's unique wildlife and cultural heritage, and at least a couple of days are warranted here before or after a longer safari. It's also the best place to buy souvenirs in the good curio shops and markets, or modern shopping malls. It has the best restaurants and nightlife in the country, and Kenyans themselves like to go out and socialize, especially at the weekends when nightclubs are pumping and families enjoy picnics in the parks or long lazy lunches around hotel swimming pools. ▸▸ *For listings, see pages 82-108.*

## Nairobi centre

### The Norfolk

Anyone with an interest in the growth of the city from its early colonial days should visit this hotel on Harry Thuku Road, a place that played a vital role in Nairobi's history. This was the city's first hotel, built to house new arrivals to the colony, and when it first opened on Christmas Day 1904, the Savoy Hotel in London was five years old and the London Ritz still a year away. The Norfolk became an important meeting point and watering hole for settlers, adventurers and travellers from all over the world, and American President Theodore Roosevelt, Lord Baden-Powell, the Earl of Warwick, Lord and Lady Cranworth, and the Baron and Baroness von Blixen have all been part of the hotel's history. It once looked out across sweeping plains and is now in the heart of the bustling city, but the mock Tudor façade and colonial opulence remains intact. The **Lord Delamere Terrace** is a good place for a drink and is the place where the early Nairobi colonial society enjoyed their gin and tonics in the evening. In 1980 a bomb went off and extensively damaged the hotel, which killed 20 people and injured more. At the time, responsibility for the attack was claimed by an Arab group that said it was seeking retaliation for Kenya allowing Israeli troops to refuel in Nairobi during the raid on Entebbe Airport in Uganda four years earlier to rescue hostages from a El-Al hijacked aircraft. The hotel consequently went through a major refit and it was refurbished again in 2008.

### Kenyatta Avenue

Kenyatta Avenue is the main multi-laned artery in the middle of the city centre, which is bordered by flowering trees and has a concrete 'island' in the middle it, which was originally designed to be wide enough for a full team of oxen to turn around in. At the eastern end, and now a tower block, another hotel with a place in history is the **Stanley** which started life as a boarding house on Victoria Street (later Tom Mboya street) in 1902, was built on its present site in 1913 and was named after the great African explorer. Some of its most revered guests have included authors Elspeth Huxley and Ernest Hemmingway and actor Stewart Granger. A central landmark on Kenyatta Avenue, its reputation as an important stopover for African travellers was cemented in 1961, with the creation of the famous **Thorn Three Café**. Here, a single acacia tree in the centre of the café became a noticeboard for travellers, who would leave notes, letters and messages for fellow travellers pinned to the trunk. This tradition became so popular that the thorn tree became an icon for African travel. Eventually notice boards were erected to protect the tree. The original tree died a natural death and has been replaced by a sapling, but the café remains popular, and these days there is an internet café for the passing-on of messages.

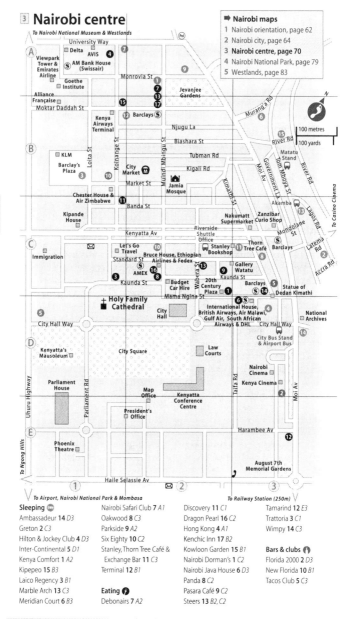

# ③ Nairobi centre

**Nairobi maps**
1 Nairobi orientation, page 62
2 Nairobi city, page 64
3 Nairobi centre, page 70
4 Nairobi National Park, page 79
5 Westlands, page 83

100 metres
100 yards

**Sleeping**
Ambassadeur 14 D3
Greton 2 C3
Hilton & Jockey Club 4 D3
Inter-Continental 5 D1
Kenya Comfort 1 A2
Kipepeo 15 B3
Laico Regency 3 B1
Marble Arch 13 C3
Meridian Court 6 B3

Nairobi Safari Club 7 A1
Oakwood 8 C3
Parkside 9 A2
Six Eighty 10 C2
Stanley, Thorn Tree Café &
  Exchange Bar 11 C3
Terminal 12 B1

**Eating**
Debonairs 7 A2

Discovery 11 C1
Dragon Pearl 16 C2
Hong Kong 4 A1
Kenchic 17 B2
Kowloon Garden 15 B1
Nairobi Dorman's 1 C2
Nairobi Java House 6 D3
Panda 8 C2
Pasara Café 9 C2
Steers 13 B2, C2

Tamarind 12 E3
Trattoria 3 C1
Wimpy 14 C3

**Bars & clubs**
Florida 2000 2 D3
New Florida 10 B1
Tacos Club 5 C3

Other colonial-era monuments include a pair of twin **War Memorials**, dedicated to the fallen members of the Carrier Corps and the King's African Rifles from the two World Wars. Opposite the post office is **Kipande House**, a historic building where Kenyans were once required to be registered and issued with identification cards known as *Kipand*.

## Jevanjee Gardens, Biashara Street and around

The small Jevanjee Gardens, off Moi Avenue north of the city market, were named after AM Jevanjee, one of Nairobi's first Indian businessmen. A railway contractor by trade, he was also a philanthropist and donated the land to the city after the small bazaar it housed was burned down. In 1906 a statue of Queen Victoria was unveiled here by her son, the Duke of Connaught. Today the park is a popular place with preachers and each lunchtime people come to sing evangelical hymns. This area is bordered by Biashara Street, still a stronghold of Asian enterprise. The influence of Nairobi's Indian community, the descendants of the original colonial railway labourers and merchants, is undeniable. They play a major role in the economic and social life of the city, and there are a number of Indian shops along this street, many of which sell Kenya's colourful textiles. There are several Hindu and Sikh temples throughout Nairobi, one of the most impressive being the **Swami Narain Temple** on Forest Road, a massive temple complex with fine statuary and an impressive interior of intricately carved wood, which was built in 1999 from 350 tonnes of stone mined near Rajasthan in India and shipped to Kenya. At the centre of the city on Banda Street near the market is the large **Jamia Mosque** with attractive twinned minarets and silver domes.

## National Archives

① *T020-228 959, www.kenyarchives.go.ke, Mon-Fri 0815-1615, Sat 0815-1300, US$2.70.*
This is much more interesting than it might sound. The building, built in 1906, originally served as the **Bank of India** and is located on Moi Avenue opposite the Hilton Hotel. On the ground floor it contains various exhibitions of arts and crafts, including some superb tribal artefacts gathered from across Africa, which were part of the private collection of avid art collector and former vice-president (1966-1997) Joseph Murumbi. His collection, which also included 8000 rare, pre-1900 books, was bequeathed to the National Archives after his death in 1990. Upstairs there's a fascinating gallery of photographs covering Kenya's history from the building of the Uganda Railway to the present day, as well as the library of archives housing hundreds of thousands of documents.

## Statue of Dedan Kimathi

On a triangle traffic island at the end of Kimathi Street and close to the Hilton Hotel is this new statue of Field Marshall Dedan Kimathi, one of the Mau Mau Rebellion's most influential leaders who was captured and executed by the British in 1957. The statue was unveiled in 2007, 50 years to the day of his death, by President Kibaki and Kimathi's widow, with some of the surviving Mau Mau soldiers attending the ceremony. The life-sized bronze statue features him in army fatigue sporting the famous Mau Mau dreadlocks, which were a feature of the Mau Mau fighters, and carrying a home-made gun and a sword.

## August 7th Memorial Gardens

① *Corner of Moi Av and Haile Selassie Av, T020-341 062, www.memorialparkkenya.org, daily 0630-1800, US$2.70.*
On 7 August 1998, Nairobi was rocked by a terrorist attack on the US Embassy, which resulted in the death of 213 people and seriously injured thousands more.

# Kibera

Driving out of the city centre southeast towards Langata and the Nairobi National Park, you cannot fail to miss the sight of the densely packed brown tin roofs of the Kibera slum, which is hemmed in between Langata and Ngong roads. Although no one really knows for sure how many people live here, it has a population of perhaps one million and covering just 2.5 sq km, is considered one of the densest slums in Africa. The site was first settled in 1918 by soldiers returning from the First World War, and has over time grown haphazardly and informally into a heaving, cramped grid of homemade shacks with few basic amenities or services. It is home to Nairobi's poorest people, many who come into the city looking for work from rural regions. The tightly packed community is multi-ethnic, which has at times sparked spats between the ethnic groups living within Kibera, including violence over the disputed 2007 elections. Aside from this there are many social problems of so many people living on top of each other as well as poor sanitation and health risks. The government, local NGOs, and the United Nations Human Settlements Programme (UN–HABITAT), which has its international HQ in Nairobi, are on a constant mission to improve the standard of life for Kibera's inhabitants.

Simultaneously, there was an attack on the US Embassy in Dar es Salam in Tanzania that killed 11 people. The attacks were linked to local members of Al Qaeda and brought the organization and its leader Osama bin Laden to international attention for the first time, resulting in the FBI placing Bin Laden on its 10-most-wanted list. On that fateful day in Nairobi, explosives were loaded on to the back of a truck, which was intended to be driven into the embassy's basement car park, but the vehicle was stopped at the gate, where the terrorists detonated the bombs. The explosion, which could be heard and felt 10 km away, ripped through the embassy and the building behind it and killed the 40 people inside the embassy including 12 Americans and many more ordinary Kenyans on the street. It was thought east Africa was chosen as a target by the terrorists because of its proximity to the US's activities in Sudan and because Nairobi was one of Africa's most important bases for both the CIA and FBI. In response to the bombings, on 20 August, the US implemented a series of cruise missile attacks on targets in Sudan and Afghanistan. After the attack the remainder of the buildings had to be demolished and the memorial gardens were opened on 7 August 2001. They feature a granite wall with a plaque of the names of all those who died, an information centre that documents what happened on the day, which includes some rather harrowing photographs, and a statue made up from debris collected after the attack. The gardens themselves are a peaceful green space where Kenyans still today come to contemplate and remember the loved ones that they lost. On 7 August 2008 Prime Minister Raila Odinga led a memorial service here to commemorate the 10-year anniversary of the attack.

## Minor Basilica Holy Family Cathedral

Nairobi's population is predominantly Christian, and there are countless churches throughout the city. In the city centre near the City Square is the large Catholic Minor Basilica Holy Family Cathedral, built in the 1960s. It doesn't have any particular architectural merit but is the largest church in Nairobi, with a capacity for 4000 people, and is the seat of the Archbishop of Nairobi. Also of interest is **All Saints' Cathedral**, on Kenyatta Avenue near the Nairobi Serena Hotel, a Gothic-style Anglican church that was founded in 1917 and consecrated in 1952.

## Parliament House and City Square

Parliament House on Parliament Road is recognizable by its clock tower and was built in the 1950s. When Parliament is in session you can watch the proceedings from the public gallery, otherwise you can usually arrange to be shown around the building – ask at the main entrance. Directly beside Parliament the republic's first president, Jomo Kenyatta, rests in a respectfully landscaped mausoleum. Along with other government buildings such as the law courts, President's office and City Hall, these flank the City Square, a popular place at lunchtime with office workers and dominated by a large statue of Jomo Kenyatta sitting regally in his gowns with his trademark fly swat in his hand.

## Kenyatta Conference Centre

ⓘ T020-2247 277, www.kicc.co.ke, US$5.

The Kenyatta International Conference Centre overlooks a large amphitheatre, built in the traditional shape of an African hut, with a central plenary hall that resembles the ancient Roman Senate. This building is the second tallest in the city with 33 floors and was built in 1972. You can usually go up to the viewing level during office hours from where you can take photos – ask at the information desk on the ground floor for the guide to take you up. There can be stunning views of Mounts Kenya and Kilimanjaro on a clear day.

## Nairobi National Museum

ⓘ On Museum Hill off Chiromo Rd, T020-374 2161-4, www.museums.or.ke, daily 0930-1800, US$11, children (under 18) US$5.50.

This museum presents an overview of Kenya's history, culture and natural history. Construction of the present site began in 1929 after the government set aside the land for it and in the 1950s the late Doctor Louis Leakey made a public appeal for funds to enlarge the Museum's galleries. The result was the construction of all the present galleries to the right of the main entrance. The Leakey Memorial building was opened in 1976 and houses the administration, archaeology and palaeontology departments. In 2005 the museum closed for an extensive refurbishment and re-opened again in early 2008 to critical acclaim. Outside, the grounds have been attractively landscaped and are now decorated with some interesting sculptures, including a map of Kenya and a mosaic garden made by Kitengela Glass (see page 97), and there's a new row of upmarket shops and cafés. Inside, the first gallery is the Kenya Hall, which has some interesting contemporary exhibits; the most spectacular of which is the gourd tower that is cleverly built from dozens of different sized gourds from Kenya's various ethnic groups and dominates the centre of the room. Gourds have a number of traditional uses such as to store water or grain, keep bees and are even used as suitcases. Also of note is the colourful map of Kenya made up of hundreds of butterflies. Beyond here are some stuffed animals and many thousands of East Africa's birds, a hall dedicated to the history of evolutionary finds in Kenya, which is particularly strong with exhibits of archaeological findings made so famous by the work of the Leakeys, and a display about the history of the museum itself that includes some old display cabinets and a larger-than-life bronze statue of Louis Leakey sitting on a rock. Upstairs are displays of traditional artefacts, a hall dedicated to ancient rock art all over Africa, and two excellent galleries of photographs; one on both Masai ceremonies and contemporary life in Nairobi taken by photographer Guillaume Bonn, and a striking collection of photographs of Kenya's animals taken by Masud Quraishy. The excellent museum shop stocks some fine upmarket Kenyan art and souvenirs and a comprehensive range of books on Kenya, and young guides – who are very enthusiastic about the new-look museum – are on hand throughout to talk visitors through the exhibits.

## Snake Park and Aquarium

ⓘ *Opening hours and charges are the same as the Nairobi National Museum (see above). At the time of writing, the snake park was closed for a complete renovation.*

Set within the grounds of the museum, this place houses examples of most of the snake species found in Kenya as well as crocodiles and tortoises. There are many live snakes including puff adders and black and green mambas. The staff here help with the removal of snakes from residential premises in Nairobi. To the right of the Snake Park follow the path down the hill through the pleasant gardens a short distance and you'll come across a view of the narrow Nairobi River as it tumbles over some rocks. The gardens are also a good spot for birdwatching and look out for sunbirds, flycatchers and bee-eaters.

## Nairobi Railway Museum

ⓘ *Near the railway station on Station Rd, in the rail compound at the corner of Haile Selassie and Uhuru Highway, T020-340 049, daily 0800-1645, US$5, children US$2.50.*

It can be seen from Uhuru Highway where the railway line crosses it but there's no access from this side and visitors should approach from the railway station. This is the best place to come and learn the history of the Uganda Railway, which effectively the colony of Kenya was founded on. Among the outside exhibits are a number of the old steam trains from the colonial era. One of the best known is the carriage that was used during the hunt for the Maneater of Kima in 1900. A lion halted the construction of the line with repeated attacks on the labour camps. A colonial officer, Captain Charles Ryall, and some other men positioned themselves in a rail carriage one night in an effort to shoot the man-eater. Unfortunately they all fell asleep, and the lion slipped into the carriage under cover of darkness, took Ryall into his mouth and sprang through a window. The inside of the museum is stuffed to the gills with railway memorabilia, original construction equipment, maps and old photographs. Look out for the bench seat that could be fitted to a locomotive's footplate at the front to allow distinguished travellers on the line, one of which was Theodore Roosevelt, unsurpassed views of the scenery and wildlife. There are also some marine exhibits including a model of *MV Liemba*, the German-built vessel that still plies Lake Tanganyika in Tanzania.

## Nairobi Arboretum

ⓘ *Arboretum Rd, off State House Rd and the Uhuru Highway, T020-272 5471, www.nature kenya.org, daily sunrise-sunset, free.*

Surrounded by buildings, the Nairobi Arboretum covers 32 ha and is home to many indigenous plant species, some 350 species of tree and over 100 species of bird, as well as Sykes and vervet monkeys and butterflies. There are picnic places, jogging trails and nature trails, and at the entrance you can buy a booklet on tree identification. It was originally established in 1907 as a trial area to see if fast growing non-indigenous trees (needed to fuel steam locomotives) could survive Nairobi's climate. Many did, and went on to be grown commercially, but there is also a sizeable collection of Kenya's indigenous trees here.

## Around the city

### Uhuru Gardens

Near Wilson Airport, on Langata Road, the Uhuru Gardens are Nairobi's largest memorial to the struggle for Independence and were built on the spot where freedom (*Uhuru*) from colonial rule was declared at midnight on 12 December 1963. The monument is a 24-m-high triumphal column, supporting a pair of clasped hands and the dove of peace, high over a statue of a group of freedom fighters raising the flag. Across the car park is a less interesting granite and black marble structure with a disused fountain put up in 1988 to mark 25 years of Independence. In 2005, the gardens were the site of a public burning of 3800 illegal firearms confiscated from criminals by the police to highlight a campaign to stamp out weapons in civil society.

### Karen Blixen Museum

ⓘ *T020-882 779, www.museums.or.ke, daily 0930-1800, US$11, children (under 18) US$5.50. From Nairobi take the No 24 bus from the front of the railway station, 1 hr, US$1.10. Guided tours are available and there is a museum shop offering handicrafts and books.*

The museum is in the house of Karen Blixen (Isak Dinesen), in the suburb of Karen, about 10 km from the city centre. Many people who have read her books or seen *Out of Africa* will want to savour the atmosphere. The house was originally a coffee plantation out in the country (she wrote, "I had a farm in Africa, at the foot of the Ngong Hills ...") but now finds itself on the outskirts of Nairobi. The quiet, tree-lined roads and older homes with large yards make this a pleasant place. The author lived in the house known as *Bogani* from 1914 until 1931. Efforts have been made to decorate all of the rooms of the house in their original style, and it is furnished with a mixture of original decor and props from the 1985 film production that was filmed here. Exhibits include many photographs of Karen Blixen, Denys Finch Hatton and various agricultural implements used to grade and roast coffee beans. The house was bought by the Danish government in 1959 and presented to the Kenyan government at Independence, along with the nearby agricultural college. The house is surprisingly small and dark but the gardens are quite special. **Karen Blixen Coffee Gardens** (see page 89) is just up the road, adjacent to an interesting old settler's house.

### Ngong Road Forest Sanctuary

ⓘ *Off Ngong Rd, 6 km from the city centre, the main gate is off Kibera Rd near the racecourse, T020-564 714, www.ngongforest.org.*

This sanctuary is a 620-ha piece of forest carved out of the larger Ngong forest characterized by indigenous trees interspersed with grassy patches, dams and streams. Here there are 120 bird species, 35 species of small mammal and numerous insects and reptiles. Because of its proximity to the Kibera slum (see box, page 72), there was a problem of trees being cut down by local people for firewood, but the sanctuary is now fenced with an electric fence and patrolled by KWS wardens. You can visit on one of the free guided group forest walks held on the first and third Saturday of each month, meet outside the restaurant at the Ngong Racecourse at 0900.

### Bomas of Kenya

ⓘ *Forest Edge Rd, off Langata Rd, 2 km past the Main Gate of Nairobi National Park on the right, T020-891 391, www.bomasofkenya.co.ke, shows Mon-Fri 1430-1600, Sat-Sun 1530-1715, US$8.60, children US$4.30. Take the No 24 bus towards Karen.*

# Planes, training and autobiographies

Beryl Markham was a champion horse trainer, record-breaking aviator, author and celebrated beauty, with two members of the British royal family among her lovers. Her style was formed by a childhood that embraced both traditional African and European ways of life.

Beryl was born in Leicestershire in 1902 and, when she was two, the family sold up and sailed for East Africa where her father took a job as dairy manager for Lord Delamere at Equator Ranch near Njoro in Kenya. Home was a rondavel – a mud hut with a thatched roof and sacking covering the windows.

Beryl grew up with local Nandi house servants and farm workers and their children with whom she formed a bond, going barefoot, eating with her hand and wearing a *shulen*, an African shirt. Kiswahili was Beryl's first language.

At nine she was sent to board at Nairobi European School, but ran away after less than a year, returning to Njoro, the stables and her Kipsigis companions.

Ten years later Beryl began training horses, first for a neighbour, Ben Birkbeck, and then for Delamere at his nearby estate, Soysambu.

In 1928, Kenyan society was in a frenzy of anticipation for the visit of Edward, Prince of Wales, and his younger brother Henry, Duke of Gloucester. Beryl and her then husband, the sophisticated, very well-off but rather frail Mansfield Markham, took up residence for the duration at the Muthaiga Club. In next to no time Beryl had secured both royal trophies.

When the royal tour ended at the end of November, cut short by the illness of King George V, Beryl, although six months pregnant, travelled to London where the Duke of Gloucester met her on the quay side and installed her in a suite at the Grosvenor Hotel, close to Buckingham Palace. When the Duke was out of town she would tryst with the Prince of Wales. Mansfield Markham came from Kenya for the birth of Gervaise Markham in February.

In the London of 1929 flying became a very fashionable pastime. Both of Beryl's royal lovers became aviators and Beryl took some flying lessons before returning to Kenya in 1930. Karen Blixen's coffee farm was failing and about to be sold, and Denys Finch-Hatton, adored lover of both Karen Blixen and Beryl, was killed when his plane crashed at Voi.

This tragedy did not deter Beryl, and under the tutelage of her instructor and lover, Tom Campbell-Black, she gained a pilot's licence in July 1931. In 1933 she got her 'B' licence, which allowed her to work as a commercial pilot – the first woman in Kenya to do so.

One evening in the bar of the White Rhino in Nyeri a wealthy local flying enthusiast JC Carberry dared Beryl to fly solo across the Atlantic from east to west, 'against the wind'. Carberry offered to bankroll the flight. The feat had never been achieved in 39 previous attempts. Beryl ordered the recently designed Percival Vega Gull, a single-engined monoplane, from De Havillands at Gravesend. At the end of 1935 she flew to London in her Leopard Moth, hopping across Africa and Europe with Bror Blixen, a former lover and white hunter husband of Karen, as passenger. *The Daily Express* bought exclusive rights to Beryl's story and the audacity of the attempt allied to Beryl's beauty created a fever of interest as she waited patiently for fair weather. On 4 September the winds had dropped. Beryl, in a white leather flying suit and helmet, squeezed into the cramped cockpit with five flasks of coffee, some cold meat, dried fruit, nuts and fruit pastilles and a hip flask of brandy. There was no room for a life jacket. Edgar Percival, the plane's designer, swung the propeller. With a wave, Beryl rumbled down the runway and climbed slowly into the air. It was close to twilight, just before 1900. Edgar Percival shook his head and observed to onlookers: "Well, that's the last we shall see of Beryl".

After a flight of over 21 hours Beryl saw land, but she was on the last tank of fuel and the engine began to splutter. She selected a landing field but ditched in a Nova Scotia bog.

The Atlantic flight made Beryl a sensation in America – a crowd of 5000 awaited her flight to New York – there were press conferences, radio interviews, banquets and guest spots on comedy shows. This was all cut short when she learned that Tom Campbell-Black, her flying instructor, had been killed in a flying accident. Beryl sailed back to England. She filled in time with an affair with Jack Doyle, the Irish heavyweight boxer.

In 1937 she returned to America to do some screen tests for a film of her epic flight – which were not a success. While in California she met Raoul Schumacher, five years younger than Beryl, tall, born in Minneapolis, comfortably off, and good company, who was working as a writer in Hollywood. They produced *West with the Night*, a memoir of Beryl's childhood and transatlantic flight. Although Beryl was credited as author, it seems clear that Raoul provided the structure and style. It was published in 1942 to excellent reviews and was on the best-seller lists. Ernest Hemingway judged it a 'bloody wonderful book'.

Raoul and Beryl married in 1942 but Beryl took a string of lovers and in 1946 Raoul moved out. Beryl continued to amuse herself in her accustomed manner, had a farewell fling with the singer Burl Ives, and in 1949 moved back to Kenya.

She stayed in the guest cottage of Forest Farm near Nanyuki, owned by the Norman family. Forest Farm was managed by a Dane, Jorgen Thrane, who became Beryl's lover. Beryl bought a small farm nearby and Jorgen managed that as well.

A trip to see her father in South Africa got her in the mood for training horses again. Back in Kenya she set to with a purpose, and over the next 15 years she was outstandingly successful, training winners for all the Kenyan Classic Races, and winning the Derby four times.

In 1965, the relationship with Jorgen waning, Beryl found a property in South Africa going for a song and she relocated her training stables there, but the move was not a success. Returning to Kenya in 1970, Beryl managed to get her trainer's licence back and she had some triumphs including a fifth Derby win. She carried on training until 1983, although the latter part of this period was marred by continual squabbles with jockeys, owners and the stewards.

The Jockey Club made her an honorary member and allocated her a cottage on the Ngong Racecourse. Interest in her book was revived and a reissue in 1983 sold over a million copies. Beryl enjoyed a revival of her fame as a celebrity and she was the subject of considerable television and newspaper interest. Greeting well-wishers with a cigarette in one hand and a tumbler of vodka in the other, however, she could be less than gracious to visitors.

Beryl died in 1986 and her ashes were scattered at Cemetery Corner on Ngong Racecourse.

A *boma* is a traditional homestead. Here programmes based on traditional dances of the different tribes of Kenya are presented. They are not in fact performed by people of the actual tribe but by a professional group called the **Harambee Dancers**. The dancers finish with a lively display of acrobatics and tumbling. The *bomas* form an open-air museum that shows the different lifestyles of each tribe. There is also a bar and a restaurant that serves *nyama choma* (grilled meat).

## Langata Giraffe Centre

ⓘ *Koitobus Rd, off South Langata Rd, Langata, T020-890 952, www.giraffecenter.org, 0900-1730, US$10, children (3-12) US$3.60. The No 24 bus drops at the top of the road then follow the signs; you may walk into a giraffe as they cross the road to get to the nature reserve.* Set in 6 ha of indigenous forest, this centre is 20 km out of the city near the **Hardy Estate Shopping Centre**. It is funded by the African Foundation for Endangered Wildlife and houses a number of Rothschild's giraffes. To date, the centre has rescued, hand-reared and released about 500 orphaned giraffes back into the wild. The Rothschild's giraffe is no longer threatened with imminent extinction, having tripled in number and been successfully reintroduced to four of Kenya's national parks. Money raised by ticket sales is used to fund an education centre promoting conservation, visited by school children from all over Kenya. There is information about the giraffes on display, designed to be interesting to children. The young visitors' artistic interpretations of East African wildlife adorn the walls. You can watch and feed the giraffes pellets from a raised wooden structure and children in particular will enjoy this experience. The centre is also an excellent spot for birdwatching.

## Nairobi National Park

**Ins and outs** The main point of entrance is through Main Gate, at the Safari Walk and Animal Orphanage on the Langata Rd, although there are 4 other gates through which visitors can access the park: East Gate on the northeast of the park on the Embakasi Plain; Cheetah Gate at the far eastern edge of the park; Banda Gate on the western edge of the park; and Masai Gate at the south of the park near the Oloonjua Ridge, T020-802 121, www.kws.org, daily 0600-1900, US$40, children (under 18) US$20; combination ticket for the national park, the animal orphanage and the safari walk, US$65 adults, US$25 children.

Facilities at the Main Gate include an information centre, an office where you can buy and load Smartcarts, a shop selling drinks, snacks, souvenirs and an excellent map that corresponds to the road markers within the park, as well as the headquarters of KWS and the office of the safety and communication centre (see page 67). Almost all roads are navigable in a normal car or see page 100 for details of guided tours from Nairobi. Staff at the gate will advise on where there has been recent animal activity, especially lion and cheetah, which are monitored closely, and it takes three to four hours to get around. There is a picnic site and nature trail at Hippo Pools in the southeast of the park, where you can get out of your vehicle as there is an armed KWS ranger stationed here. The Animal Orphanage and the Safari Walk at the Main Gate can both be visited independently from the park.

Nairobi National Park is so close to Kenya's capital city, it's not unusual to take a photo of a rhino browsing peacefully amongst the acacia thorn with a background of high-rise office buildings. The park covers 117 sq km, was established in 1946 and is the oldest in the country. It's only 7 km or a 20-minute drive from the city centre and most of its fences border Nairobi's suburbs with only the southern perimeter unfenced where some of the animals migrate into Masai grazing areas. Despite its proximity to the city, it is home to over 100 recorded species of mammal. Animals include the Big Five, except for elephant – the park is too small to sustain them, though you can see baby elephants at the David Sheldrick Wildlife Trust at the edge of the park (see page 81). You are also very likely to see zebra, giraffe, baboons, buffalo, ostrich, vultures, hippos and various antelope. This is one of the best parks for spotting black rhinos: the area is not remote enough for poachers, and the Park has proved to be one of the most successful rhino sanctuaries in Kenya.

The concentration of wildlife is greatest in the dry season when areas outside the park have dried up. Water sources are greater in the park as small dams have been built along the Mbagathi River. There are also many birds, up to 500 permanent and migratory species. To the south of the national park is the Kitengela Game Conservation Area and Migration Corridor leading to the Athi and Kaputiei plains. The herbivores disperse over these plains following the rains and return to the park during the dry season.

Apart from wildlife watching, the other point of interest is just a kilometre or two into the park from the Main Gate. The Ivory Burning Site is to the left of the road and is where on 18 July 1989 12 tons of confiscated ivory was burnt. A mound of ash and information board marks the spot. The fire was lit by then-president Moi and was a symbolic gesture that declared war on poachers and the mass slaughter of African elephants in Kenya. When the country gained Independence in 1963, there were an estimated 170,000 elephants but by 1989 they numbered just 16,000. The event, which was televised across the world, contributed to the CITIES international ban on ivory trading and the establishment of the Kenya Wildlife Services (KWS) in 1990. All employees were, and still are, armed and there's a shoot to kill policy against poachers. Today's elephant population in Kenya is put at around 28,000. Back at the Main Gate, in the car park, look out for the Conservation Heroes Monument, which lists all the names of KWS employees who have died in the line of duty since the KWS was established. Some died in accidents, when they were relocating animals for example, while others died during armed battles with poachers or bandits.

# 4 Nairobi National Park

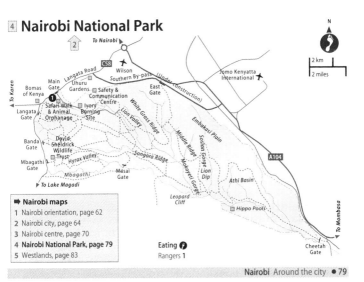

➡ **Nairobi maps**
1 Nairobi orientation, page 62
2 Nairobi city, page 64
3 Nairobi centre, page 70
4 Nairobi National Park, page 79
5 Westlands, page 83

**Eating** 🍴
Rangers 1

# Elephants never forget

David Sheldrick Wildlife Trust was set up in 1977 and was named after the late naturalist who created Kenya's vast Tsavo East National Park. It is administered by his pioneering wife Daphne who developed the first elephant formula milk (within 24 hours of becoming orphaned, a calf less than two years old will die without milk). It took years for Daphne to perfect the formula, which has proved to be a massive success and brought new hope for survival of Kenya's vulnerable milk-dependent calves. Most of the infants that are brought to the nursery are between a few days and three months old. It's not easy to hand-rear an elephant, they are complex feeders and it's difficult to duplicate a natural mother's nurturing and support. It takes endless patience by the keepers at the orphanage to teach a baby to suckle (the very young ones need to suckle every 12 minutes). These keepers become mother substitutes, providing all the care and attention a baby elephant needs whilst growing up. The calves are bottle-fed on demand, and the keeper provides a back or arm for the baby to rest its trunk while feeding. They also need to be taught how to use their trunks and ears, roll in the dust, bathe and cover their stools. (They have to learn to control their bowels, which can move up to 300 times a day!) In the wild the herd shelters the baby from the elements, but keepers provide hanging blankets for shade and as something warm to rub up against as if it was a mother's belly. They even apply sunscreen when necessary. The foster parents remain with the babies 24 hours a day and provide a close physical relationship and constant companionship. The extraordinary dedication and amount of time it takes to raise an elephant by these people is remarkable. A sense of family is crucial, as is mental stimulation – play and communication amongst the other orphans is encouraged. Keepers are employed for the full two years that it takes a calf to be weaned off milk and at one year the formula is changed. Skimmed milk, fat producing components, and antibodies needed to build up the immune system are added – stimulants for a stomach that will process

**Animal Orphanage** ① *at the Main Gate of the Nairobi National Park, T020-600 800, daily, US$15 adults, children (under 18) US$5.* Opened in 1963, this facility cares for orphaned and sick animals, which are brought from all over Kenya. Whenever possible they are re-released back into the wild, and if that's not possible relocated to the more spacious Safari Walk (see below), or if they are severely injured remain in the care of the orphanage for the rest of their lives. The centre is most popular at about 1430 when it is feeding time. There is also a **Wildlife Conservation Education Centre**, which has lectures and video shows about wildlife and guided park and orphanage tours, primarily but not exclusively to educate schools and local communities. When it was built, enclosures were quite cramped, but in response to criticism, the animals are now housed in more spacious accommodation in a more natural environment. If there are resident cheetah or lion cubs, visitors maybe be permitted to go into the enclosures for a close-up photograph.

**Safari Walk** ① *At the Main Gate of the Nairobi National Park, T020-600800, daily 0830-1730, US$20, children (under 18) US$5.* Opened in 2001 as an education centre for local school children, this is a lovely walk through 18 ha of indigenous trees and vegetation full of birds and butterflies. It's completely wheelchair friendly, everything is well labelled and a diet of greens later in life. Like humans, calves go through the upsetting and painful period of teething when their first molars appear at four months. When the calves are no longer dependent on milk they are transported to Tsavo National Park and gradually released back into the wild. (Nairobi National Park is too small to accommodate elephant.) In the beginning the keepers remain nearby, keeping a safe distance so the elephants can return to them at any time. Elephants are naturally sociable animals and integrate well both with the wild herds of Tsavo, and the ex-orphans who are led by a wild matriarch named Catherine. Since the project started, several of the orphans have given birth in Tsavo. Daphne Sheldrick has been involved in elephant conservation for over 30 years. Previous orphans of her nursery still recognize her decades later, and she has known some as long as her own children. Not only has she developed the milk formula, but recognized the sophisticated, almost human like, emotions and social needs of the calves. Some arrive at the trust severely traumatized and confused, having often witnessed their mother being killed by poachers or farmers, becoming irretrievably trapped, deserted by the herd, or suffering severely from drought or sunburn. They go through an intense period of grieving for many months, and are known to suffer depression and even cry. Survival depends on an individual's personality and willpower, but it is essential that the elephant is happy and feels safe and cared for – emotions necessary for the welfare of any baby. With her milk formulas and sensitivity for elephant's emotional needs, Daphne Sheldrick has contributed greatly towards conservation in Africa. All her elephants now in Tsavo retain a deep fondness for her and the keepers who acted as a foster family in their childhood. It seems that it is true when they say 'an elephant never forgets'.

*"Animals are indeed more ancient, more complex, and in many ways more sophisticated than man… perhaps the most respected and revered should be the elephant, for not only is it the largest land mammal on earth, but also the most emotionally human."*
– Daphne Sheldrick

there are a number of interesting boards about Kenya's flora and fauna, conservation issues, and the conflicts animals have with the environment and humans. The beginning of the walk begins on a concrete pathway, and this eventually rises on to an elevated boardwalk that goes to the edge of Nairobi National Park and overlooks a natural waterhole. Animals are housed not in cages, but on grassy mounds separated by moats so it's not zoo-like at all. Residents include lion, cheetah, leopard, pygmy hippo, rhino, plains game, hyena, ostrich, monkey, buffalo, two unusual albino zebras and the rare bongo antelope. Attached is the **Rangers Restaurant** (see Eating, page 90).

## David Sheldrick Wildlife Trust
ⓘ *Access via the Mbagathi Gate, Nairobi National Park (also signposted as staff/maintenance gate), Magadi Rd, T020-891 996, www.sheldrickwildlifetrust.org, daily 1100-1200, US$2.90.*
On the edge of the Nairobi National Park lies this remarkable rescue centre for lost, abandoned and orphaned elephants. Daphne Sheldrick lives in the national park on Magadi Road and set up this orphanage, see box above. The trust has constructed night stockades for orphaned elephants in Tsavo National Park, as part of their programme to reintroduce

them to wild herds and also plays an active role in de-snaring game in the national parks and in treating the injured animals. The morning trip involves visiting the sanctuary when the baby elephants are brought out into an enclosure for perhaps a bath or a play with each other and visitors can watch. It is an endearing experience and thoroughly recommended. It is a real treat to see a baby elephant trot along, trunk and ears flopping this way and that as they discover what they are supposed to do with them. It is like watching a playground full of kids – tearing around, chasing each other, playing, arguing and even standing in a corner and visibly sulking! Visitors are encouraged to adopt an elephant.

The Trust has also taken a primary role in protecting the remaining rhinos on private land and has coordinated a joint approach through the **Rhino Action Group**, comprising all the conservation groups in Kenya. The trust has played a pivotal role by financing initiatives, such as the construction of holding enclosures, travelling crates and a loading sledge, veterinary costs and equipping the Kenya Wildlife Services with radio communication. To date, several infant black rhino have also been re-released from the sanctuary. They are easier than elephants as they are only milk-dependent for one year and can take full-cream human-baby formula, but it takes longer to rehabilitate them in the wild.

## Ngong Hills

These undulating hills with four peaks, said to resemble knuckles, commonly numbered one to four (north to south) are located about 25 km to the southwest of Nairobi on the edge of the Great Rift Valley. Masai legend has it that the hills were created from a handful of earth that a giant clutched after falling over Mount Kilimanjaro. Partly wooded, the hills are no longer rich in animals, but zebra, giraffe and bush-buck remain in large numbers. Plan for at least a half-day round trip. It is advisable to go in a group and to take care over security as muggings have occurred here in the past. Take the Langata Road out through the suburbs of Langata and Karen until you reach the town of Ngong. Just after this town turn right up the Panorama Road, which should be well signposted. The road winds up fairly steeply in places, and to reach Lamwia, the highest peak (No 4), requires a 4WD vehicle. The route is about 100 km in all and you climb 1000 m. It is possible to walk along the four peaks, allow two to three hours for this. From the top you can look back from where you have come to see the skyline of Nairobi. The city centre with its skyscrapers is clearly visible and gradually peters out to the suburbs and farms. On a very clear day you can see Mount Kenya. Looking over in the other direction, towards the Great Rift Valley, you can see as far as 100 km.

## ⊙ Nairobi listings

**Hotel and guesthouse prices**
L over US$450  A  US$300-449  B  US$175-299
C US$100-174  D  US$50-99  E  US$20-49
F under US$20
**Restaurant prices**
♥♥♥ over US$30  ♥♥ US$15-30  ♥ under US$15

## ⊙ Sleeping

**Nairobi** p64, maps p64, p70, p79 and p83
There is an enormous range of hotels in Nairobi from luxury international chains to

the most basic board and lodgings. Although numerous and cheap, the latter are best avoided as they are mostly in insalubrious city-centre locations, are not wholly clean, and often double up as brothels. Nevertheless, there are a few good budget options in the city centre that are used to hosting international visitors and a number of backpackers' accommodation and campsites in the suburbs. Hotels at the top of the range have all the facilities that you would expect of any international 5-star hotel. The hotels out of town are more peaceful than those in the centre. At the time of writing a new large, 134-bed hotel was being built on the Mombasa Rd between the airport and city centre, which will have a view over a waterhole in the Nairobi National Park. It will be called **Ole Sereni Hotel**, check the website for progress (www.ole-serenihotel.com).

For long-term accommodation in Nairobi the main residential areas popular with ex-pats are Gigiri and Runda in the northwest, Westlands, Lavington, Kilimani, Hurlingham and Kileleshwa in the west and Karen and Langata to the southwest. Online sources for rental accommodation include www.prop ertykenya.com and www.estates.co.ke. There are also ads on community notice boards in the shopping centres – the biggest being in the **Sarit Centre** – and in newspapers.

**L Giraffe Manor**, Koitobos Rd, off South Langata Rd, Langata, T020-891 078, www.giraffemanor.com. This lovely red-brick, ivy-covered house is redolent of an English country manor house, and is set in beautiful woodland and gardens next to the Giraffe Centre (see page 78). A family home with 6 double bedrooms with bathrooms, and excellent food, it is perhaps the only place in the world that you can feed giraffe from your 2nd-floor bedroom window, over the lunch table, and at the front door. A double costs US$655 and includes all meals prepared by a gourmet chef, tea, wine and cocktails. Mick Jagger, Jerry Hall, Johnny Carson and Brooke Shields have all stayed here.

**L Karen Blixen Coffee Garden and Cottages**, 336 Karen Rd, Karen, T020-882 138, www.blixencoffeegarden.co.ke. Just up the road from the Karen Blixen Museum, and set in a gorgeous garden of indigenous trees and flowering bushes on an old settler's farm, these very comfortable cottages have high ceilings, fireplaces, stone floors, pretty verandas, satellite TV, internet, a pool, 2 gift shops, a restaurant and a garden bar. Guests can use facilities at the Karen Golf and Country Club.

**L Ngong House**, Induvo Lane, Karen, T020-891 856, www.ngonghouse.com. 5 beautifully decorated rooms in attractive treehouses in the forest, 1 cottage facing the swimming pool, 1 family cottage sleeping 6 and 1 room in the main house suitable for the elderly or disabled. Built wholly from wood, the treehouses are on 2 levels with a bedroom area upstairs and a living area on the lower floor, raised 5 m from the ground to gain an uninterrupted view of the Ngong Hills and feature hand-woven rugs and bedcovers,

## 5 Westlands

200 metres
200 yards

**Sleeping** 🛏
Holiday Inn **1**

Phoenician **8**
Tamambo **4**

**Eating** 🍴
Alan Bobbe's Bistro & Gardens **3**
Bangkok **7**
China Plate **6**
Haandi **4**
Pavement Club & Café **5**
Pepper's **1**

**Bars & clubs** 🍸
Gipsy **10**
Havana **12**
Hidden Agenda **9**
Klub House 1 **2**
Mercury Lounge **11**
Soho's **13**

stained-glass windows, paintings and other art. Superb 4-course dinners are on offer and eaten with the family and other guests or at the dining area in the treehouses. Penny Winter is an acclaimed fashion designer with a boutique in the garden.

**L The Norfolk**, Harry Thuku Rd, T020-221 6940, www.fairmont.com/norfolkhotel. Built in 1904 and one of Nairobi's original buildings, this is a world-famous hotel with a lot of history (see page 69) and as a result many people who cannot afford to stay drop in for a drink. It was completely refurbished in 2008, and now offers 168 luxury rooms, the **Lord Delamere's Terrace**, see page 93, which is a popular drinking spot, heated outdoor swimming pool, established tropical gardens, shops, 6 restaurants and bars and a ballroom.

**A House of Waine**, Masai Lane, Karen, T020-891 820, www.houseofwaine.com. A boutique hotel less than 2 km from the Karen Blixen Museum and set in 1 ha of gardens with heated swimming pool, with 11 elegantly furnished rooms complete with 4-poster beds, Persian rugs and marble bathrooms. Gourmet food includes rich afternoon teas, and well-presented set 3-course dinners, and there's a comfortable lounge and bar with fireplace.

**A Inter-Continental**, City Hall Way and Uhuru Highway, city centre, T020-320 0000, www.ichotelsgroup.com. A 5-star offering that was completely refurbished in 2007 with 387 rooms on 6 floors, with a/c, satellite TV and internet, and 4 restaurants, several bars, business/conference facilities, gym, sauna, jacuzzi and a 15-m swimming pool.

**A Nairobi Serena**, Kenyatta Av and Nyerere Rd, close to All Saints' Cathedral, city centre, T020-282 2000, www.serenahotels.com. Set in beautiful gardens the Serena has a good reputation and is generally considered the finest hotel in central Nairobi. It has wonderful views of the city, especially at sunset. 184 rooms including 10 suites, with Wi-Fi and a/c, a swimming pool, health club, meeting rooms, shops, 5 fine restaurants. New is the luxurious **Maisha Spa**, which has its own heated pool and a full range of beauty treatments.

**A The Tribe – The Village Market Hotel**, The Village Market, Limuru Rd, Gigiri, T020-712 4101, www.africanpridehotels.com. Opened in 2007 and adjacent to the **Village Market** shopping and entertainment complex, this is a new contemporary and very stylish addition to Nairobi with beautiful chic decor with African touches, and 142 rooms with Wi-Fi, mood lighting, floor-to-ceiling mirrors, beautiful wooden flooring, a/c, and power showers; some have free-standing baths. The restaurant serves continental cuisine, and there are very comfortable bars and lounges, and a spa.

**A Windsor Golf and Country Club**, 9 km north of the city centre on Garden Estate Rd, T020-856 2300, www.windsorgolfresort.com. Built in 1991, this has 130 luxury rooms with a/c, flat-screen TVs, 4-poster beds, Wi-Fi, and some have fireplaces. It is modelled on a Victorian-style English country hotel, with extensive facilities including a number of restaurants and bars, meeting rooms, a health club, an 18-hole golf course (in a forest), squash and tennis courts and horse riding.

**B Hilton**, Mama Ngina St, city centre, T020-250 000, www1.hilton.com. The 287-room Hilton is very centrally located and the circular building a landmark in the city centre. All rooms have a/c, satellite TV, internet access, electronic safes and mini bar and are soundproofed against the traffic noise. Facilities include 4 restaurants, 1 pub with live entertainment, a heated pool, gym, sauna, steam bath and massage.

**B Laico Regency**, Loita St, city centre, T020-221 1199, www.laicohotels.com. A profusion of marble and gilt, with 194 rooms in a 12-storey block, with a/c, satellite TV, internet access, several restaurants including the **Sitar** which is a very good Indian, cocktail lounges, bars, casino, ballroom, gym, swimming pool and a shopping arcade. Formerly the **Grand Regency**, this has recently been bought by the Libyan African Investment Company (LAICO).

**B Macushla House**, Nguruwe Rd, off Gogo Falls Rd, Langata, T020-891 987, www.macushla.biz. A small intimate and friendly guesthouse within walking distance of the **Giraffe Centre** with just 6 rooms nicely decorated with Afghan rugs and animal-print fabrics, some have 4-poster beds, set in pretty gardens with a pool and some interesting modern sculptures. Rates include breakfast and dinner is available for extra in the excellent restaurant.

**B Nairobi Safari Club**, Lillian Towers, University Way, city centre, T020-251 333, www.nairobisafariclub.com. The foyer is palatial with marble, fountains and lots of greenery, and there are 2 restaurants, a swimming pool, sauna, health centre, hairdresser and conference facilities. The furnishings are becoming slightly worn, but rooms are nevertheless comfortable with minibars, digital safes and satellite TV, and good city views from the top floors.

**B Panafric**, Kenyatta Av, Nairobi Hill, central, reservations, T020-271 4444, www.sarova.co.ke. A modern practical hotel, with 153 rooms and 43 apartments with satellite TV and Wi-Fi, but no atmosphere. An extensive range of conference facilities best suited for the local business traveller. Swimming pool, hairdressers, shop, a café by the pool and the popular **Flame Tree** restaurant.

**B Safari Park Hotel and Casino**, 15 km north of the city centre in Kasarani on the Thika Rd, T020-363 3000, www.safaripark-hotel.com. This was once a retreat for British army officers during the colonial period and now markets itself as an inland resort with 204 rooms, 7 restaurants, 3 bars, a swimming pool with an artificial beach, tennis and squash courts, a casino and meeting rooms, all set in 26 ha of lush gardens. All rooms have 4-poster beds, satellite TV, a/c and a balcony with a view.

**B Stanley**, corner of Kenyatta Av and Kimathi St, city centre, central reservations, T020-271 4444, www.sarova.co.ke. Today this is a modern tower block but it has a long history (see page 69). The celebrated outdoor **Thorn Tree Café** is found here, as is good **Stanley Bookshop**. The recently renovated 240 rooms have all mod cons and are attractively decorated. Facilities include meeting rooms, valet parking, gym, health club, shops, bars, and restaurants (see Eating, pages 90 and 91).

**C Boulevard**, Harry Thuku Rd, city centre, T020-227 567, www.hotelboulevard kenya.com. A popular mid-range option, though the decor is now very old-fashioned and it could do with a refit, but in a great location only 500 m from the city centre and near the museum and Norfolk Hotel. The 70 rooms have balconies, TV, and internet access, and there's a swimming pool, tennis courts, gardens, bar, restaurant and internet room. Virtually all the overland companies begin and end their tours here.

**C Fairview**, Bishops Rd, Nairobi Hill, T020-288 1000, www.fairviewkenya.com. A very peaceful, good value and family-run hotel set in 2 ha of well-kept and extensive tropical gardens that is extremely popular with overseas visitors and Kenyans alike and makes a change from the chain hotels. It caters both for business people and families and facilities include conference rooms, an excellent terrace restaurant, the new **Pango Brasserie** with its own underground winebar, swimming pool, health club, and a lounge for watching sports. Recommended.

**C Meridian Court Hotel**, Murang'a Rd, city centre, T020-231 3991, www.meridianhotel kenya.com. Good value, includes breakfast, 85 rooms with satellite TV, the more expensive suites have a small kitchen and a sitting room. The restaurant serves buffet meals, the **Khyber Restaurant** specializes in authentic Chinese and Indian cuisine, rooftop swimming pool with bar, gym with sauna, and a sports bar with widescreen TV and pool tables.

**C Silver Springs Hotel**, junction of Argwings Kodhek and Valley rds, Hurlingham, T020-272 2451, www.silversprings-hotel.com. Very nicely and brightly decorated, 124 rooms with satellite TV, internet access, electronic door locks and safes and room service. Restaurant with buffet meals, Indian and Chinese dishes from the **Flagship** restaurant, bar with satellite TV for sports, a new fully equipped modern gym and aerobics studio. Steam room, sauna, jacuzzi, massages, and pool. Recommended.

**C-D Utalii**, 8 km on the Thika Rd, T020-856 1201, www.utalii.co.ke. *Utalii* is the Kiswahili word for tourism and this is the government-run training centre for hotel and catering students (the service is very good). 50 plain but adequate rooms with TV, private bathroom and balcony. Swimming pool, lovely gardens, tennis courts, cocktail lounge and a restaurant.

**D High Point Hotel**, Lower Hill Rd, Nairobi Hill, T020-272 4312, www.highpoint court.com. Set in 1 ha with well-manicured gardens and exotic trees, there are 2 very modern blocks of apartments and hotel rooms around a large swimming pool (shaped like a fish), simply but comfortably furnished with satellite TV. There's a cocktail bar, laundry, internet café, beauty parlour and affordable restaurant.

**D Hotel Ambassadeur**, Moi Av, city centre, T020-246 615, www.hotelambassadeur kenya.com. Built in the 1960s, an old-fashioned block of 84 single, double and triple en suite rooms with TV and faded decor but nevertheless comfortable and in a central city centre position next to the **National Archives**. Mezzanine restaurant and bar for breakfast (US$10) and simple à la carte meals.

**D Marble Arch**, Lagos Rd, city centre, T020-246 114. In a pretty rough and ready area so the rooms that face the street can be very noisy, but next to the Akamba bus terminal so useful for early or late arrivals/departures for budget travellers. The 40 single, double and triple basic rooms are clean with TV, en suite shower and toilet. Breakfast is included and there's a bar and coffee shop with cakes.

**D Oakwood Hotel**, Kimathi St opposite the **Stanley Hotel**, city centre, T020-220 592, www.madahotels.com. Good value, just 20 well-furnished single, double and triple rooms with TVs and excellent en suite bathrooms, and price includes a full English breakfast. All the walls are wood panelled – hence the name. Bar, restaurant and a roof terrace and laundry service available.

**D-E Kenya Comfort Hotel**, corner of Muindi Mbingu/Monrovia streets, city centre, T722/733-608 866, www.kenyacomfort.com. Good location in one of the quieter sections of the centre opposite Jeevanjee Gardens, friendly set-up and well used to budget travellers, single, double, triple and quad rooms, 90 en suite rooms in total, more expensive ones have wardrobe and TV. 1st-floor restaurant, bar (excellent cappuccinos) and internet café. Rates are either with or without breakfast – go 'without'.

**D-E Six Eighty**, Muindi Mbingu St, T020-315 680, www.680-hotel.co.ke. Very central with an unprepossessing appearance with 370 tired-looking but clean rooms, those at the back of the hotel are the best option as the noise from a disco across the road can sometimes be heard. Underground car park, shops, 2 restaurants, a bar, casino, coffee shop and business centre. The staff are helpful and there are security guards on each floor.

**E Hotel Greton**, Tsavo Rd, T020-336 648/T020-331 865. Not in a great area, but handy for buses, good value and secure. A smart brick block with 52 rooms, with clean, decent-sized,

furnished rooms, hot water and breakfast is included in the tariff. Has a relaxed restaurant that is better for drinks than food.

**E Hotel Kipepeo**, River Rd, city centre, T020-313 571, www.hotelkipepeo.com. Brand new budget hotel, hence everything is very fresh. On the less busy part of River Rd, with 56 en suite rooms with nice modern furnishings, flat-screen satellite TVs, good hot showers, electronic door card keys, sound-proofed windows, and good security with panic buttons in the rooms and CCTV in the public areas. Given the facilities and the newness of the place, rates represent excellent value.

**E Parkside**, Monrovia St, city centre, T020-333 348. Overlooking the Jeevanjee Gardens in a relatively quiet part of the city, the 60 basic single, double and triple rooms have bathrooms and hot water and the price includes breakfast. There's a 1st-floor restaurant and bar for simple meals and beers. It's friendly and clean but there's no elevator so you may struggle with luggage up to the 3rd floor.

**E Terminal**, Moktar Daddah St, city centre, T020-228 817. Popular, although it has seen better days, but rooms are basic and clean with bathrooms and (sparodic) hot water, it is secure and has friendly, helpful staff. As it's just of Koinange St (Nairobi's red-light district), it can be noisy at night. Breakfast is not included.

**E-F Karen Camp**, Marula Lane, off Karen Rd, Karen, T020-883 3475, www.karencamp.com. Run by Dougie, an ex-overland driver, with a good and lively bar, home-cooked food, comfortable doubles in the main house with or without bathrooms, dorms with shared bathrooms in the outside buildings, plenty of grass for camping and overland vehicles in the gardens. Satellite TV and good music, excursions to local attractions.

**E-F Milimani Backpackers**, Milimani Rd, Nairobi Hill, T020-272 4827, www.milimani backpackers.com. Good and friendly set-up in an old 1940s stone house, with neat, clean dorms and doubles, good shared bathrooms, and parking and camping in the garden, where there are also a couple of permanent tents if you don't have your

own. Bar with open fire, BBQ area, meals available. The staff can book buses to Kampala and the Arusha shuttle, and organize Nairobi day tours. Also a good place to hook up with other travellers for budget safaris to the parks.

**E-F Nairobi Campsite**, Magadi Rd, Langata, T020-890 661, www.nairobi campsite.com. Excellent budget facilities, internet and email, pool table, bars and restaurant. Dorms are US$6, self-catering doubles are US$21, camping is US$4. Hot showers, laundry facilities, camping, parking for overland vehicles in a secure compound. Can organize airport pick-ups and tours to the local sights.

**F Nairobi Youth Hostel**, 3 km out of town on Ralph Bunche Rd (which runs between Ngong Rd and Valley Rd), buses 28, 36, 40, and 42 from the Hilton drop off at the traffic police headquarters on Ngong Rd, then cross over and walk down Ralph Bunche Rd for about 500 m, T020-723 012, www.yhak.org. You must be a member of the International Youth Hostels Association but can join here (120KSh per day). There are simple dorms or double bunk rooms and the shared bathrooms have sporadic hot water. Mostly used by Kenyan students, it's reasonably safe with parking, café, lounge with TV, lockers, luggage storage and communal kitchen, but not wholly clean.

**F Upper Hill Campsite**, Menengai Rd, Nairobi Hill, T020-675 0202, www.upperhillcamp site.com. Popular with European overlanders with 10 dorm bedrooms, 2 double rooms and 1 single room, plus tent space and tents for hire. It can get muddy. Good clean amenities, bar and restaurant, friendly staff and good security, and is reasonably central, only 30 mins' walk from city centre. They also offer long-term parking for overland vehicles.

**F YMCA**, State House Rd, T020-713 599, kenyaymca@net2000ke.com. Dorms and en suite rooms, women are permitted. Safe and reasonable value single rooms but overpriced shared rooms. It caters mostly for long-term visitors; many of the residents are

Kenyan students. Good sporting facilities including an excellent large swimming pool and tennis courts. Alcohol is not allowed.

## ⑦ Eating

**Nairobi** *p64, maps p64, p70, p79 and p83*
All the hotels have restaurants and bars, which are also very popular with non-guests. There are a number of superb individual restaurants but most of these tend to be out in the upmarket suburbs so you will need to take a taxi. Increasingly, many of the good restaurants have relocated from the city centre to the shopping malls on the outskirts. For cheap eats in the city centre there are numerous food kiosks around River Rd and Tom Mboya St selling African and Indian food and snacks, and around the business district of the city between Kenyatta Av and City Hall Way there are plenty of coffee bars. There are also branches of quality South African fast-food chains dotted around the city centre and at petrol stations in the suburbs. **Debonairs** serves pizza and salads, while **Steers** offers burgers, ribs and chips. There are also a number of **Wimpys** and several branches ofl local **Kenchic Inn**, for good chicken and chips costing around US$2.

Nairobi's tap water is not necessarily dysentery-inducing, but stick to bottled water (even to brush your teeth), and avoid ice and washed salads.

**††† Alan Bobbe's Bistro & Gardens**, 24 Riverside Dr, Westlands, T020-444 6325. Daily 1200-1500, Mon-Sat 1900-2200. Named after a chef who was once an apprentice at the London Savoy, who established the restaurant in 1962 and passed away at the age of 92 in 2006, this is a Nairobi institution and the likes of Pele, Richard Burton and Jackie Kennedy have eaten here. It recently moved from its original downtown location to Westlands. It specializes in gourmet French cuisine and very good wines, the food and atmosphere are both excellent, very personalized service, lovely garden terrace, reservations recommended.

**††† Café Maghreb**, Nairobi Serena Hotel, city centre, T020-282 2000. Daily 1230-1500, 1900-2400. A popular hotel restaurant serving buffet and à la carte menus with stunning Moroccan decor, tables next to the swimming pool, and good city views. It's particularly busy on Fri evenings for its seafood buffet, and other themed buffet evenings include Mongolian stir fries, Kenyan specialities and pasta. Coffee is poured from giant copper urns.

**††† Carnivore**, Langata Rd, about 20 mins out of town past Wilson Airport, T020-602 990, www.tamarind.co.ke/carnivore. Daily 1200-1430 and 1900-2230 for eating, much later for the bars. This is large complex of bars, restaurants and dance floors. It has been incredibly successful, has frequently appeared in listings as one of the world's top restaurants and is on most tourists' itineraries to Nairobi. It specializes in meat including game (warthog, antelope and crocodile), which is grilled over a huge charcoal fire. The waiters bring the skewer (a Masai spear) of meat to your table and keep carving the various meats until you say stop by lowering the little white flag of surrender that is placed on the table. There is also a vegetarian menu. In general portions are huge and it works out as fairly good value. It is also a drinking venue and a nightclub (see under Bars and clubs, page 94) and a Carnivore must-do is to try a *dawa* – vodka, crushed ice, sugar and lime served with a stick coated with honey.

**††† China Plate**, Chancery Building, Valley Rd, Nairobi Hill, T020-271 9194, and Mpaka Centre, Westlands, T020-444 6144. Daily 1230-1500, 1900-2230. Expensive but very good food, with authentic Chinese decor and attentive service and have been operating for almost 30 years. Best known for Szechwan cuisine and seafood such as crab, calamari, langoustine, lobster, scampi, and also does continental dishes like rotisserie chicken and steaks, and some Indian dishes. A varied winelist on offer.

**††† Haandi**, The Mall, Westlands, T020-444 8294, www.haandi-restaurants.com. Daily 1200-1430, 1900-2230. Excellent northern Indian cuisine, each dish is cooked to order and prepared with the utmost of attentiveness. One of the best Indian restaurants in Africa. Recommended.

**†††† Ibis Grill, The Norfolk Hotel**, city centre, T020-2216940, Mon-Fri 1230-1400. Daily 1930-2200. This elegant and atmospheric restaurant specializes in excellent nouvelle cuisine in a formal setting with chandeliers, with some shady garden tables and a pianist in the evenings. A great Nairobi experience and you'll need to dress up a little. Check that the current restaurant refurbishment has finished.

**†††† Karen Blixen Coffee Gardens**, up the road from the Karen Blixen Museum, 365 Karen Rd, T020-882 138, www.blixencoffee garden.co.ke. Daily 0700-2200. With an outstanding setting, this charming restaurant is set in what was Blixen's farm manager's house and it oozes with colonial atmosphere. There is a formal dining room and bar, and at lunchtime, tables are laid out in the pretty grounds next to the fish pond and water feature. Very good food and service, and there's accommodation in garden cottages, see Sleeping, page 83.

**†††† La Prugna D'oro, Intercontinental Hotel**, City Hall Way and Uhuru Highway, city centre, T020-320 0321, www.ichotelsgroup.com. Mon-Sat 1200-1500, 1900-2230. Superb Italian with Italian chefs and a small outdoor terrace with a pricey but full menu of pasta, meat, and seafood dishes. Lovely decor with drapes and paintings, white tablecloths and fine china. Not overly formal.

**†††† Lord Erroll**, 89 Ruaka Rd, off Limuru Rd, Runda Estate, T020-712 2433, www.lord-erroll.com. Tue-Sun 1200-1430, 1800-2100. Taking its name from the famous unsolved murder in colonial times of the 22nd Lord Erroll, this smart restaurant offers an exceptional garden setting and gourmet food such as Mongolian stir fry or BBQ prepared at your table, Italian and Oriental dishes, and the cheese fondue is a firm favourite. A pianist performs on Sun when there is a special and good-value buffet for US$23. Among the most atmospheric places to eat in Nairobi with fine champagnes,

wines and coffees, cranes stalk the grass, the bar is full of colonial memorabilia, very special and highly recommended.

**†††† Macushla House**, Nguruwe Rd, off Gogo Falls Rd, Langata, T020-891 987, www.macushla.biz. Daily 1230-1500, 1730-2130. The food here at this upmarket guest house will leave you in no doubt that you are in a private home, with a lovely terrace, gardens and pool. The continental dishes are prepared with very fresh ingredients with particular care to presentation.

**†††† Mediterraneo**, The Junction, Ngong Rd, Dagoretti Corner, T020-387 8608. Daily 0900-late. Fairly new with a growing reputation. Lovely modern decor, outside tables and good service from staff in bow ties. Imported parma ham and cheese, home-made pasta, pizzeria, seafood and meat, desserts.

**†††† Nyama Choma, Safari Park Hotel & Casino**, about 15 km north of the city centre in Kasarani on the Thika Rd, T020-363 3000, www.safaripark-hotel.com. Daily 1900-2300. A similar concept to **Carnivore** (see above), and popular with tour groups, this is an all-you-can-eat grilled meat buffet served at your table, including game meat, with African-inspired decor, and entertainment from the colourful **Safari Cats** band and a nightly acrobatic show at 2100.

**†††† Pampa Churrascarias**, Panari Sky Centre, Mombasa Rd, T020-828 132, www.pampa grillkenya.com. Daily 1200-1500, 1800-late. A Churrascaria is a meat-roasting house in southern Brazil, and this is a fairly new upmarket Brazilian restaurant with a menu of all-you-can-eat cuts of meat grilled over open flames plus a buffet of hot vegetables and salads, which is suitable for vegetarians. There's another branch in the **White Sands Hotel** in Mombasa. Brazilian wines are on offer.

**†††† Phoenician**, Karuna Rd, behind the Sarit Centre, Westlands, T020-374 4279. Daily 1130-late. Lebanese and continental dishes, pitta bread and pizzas cooked in a wood-burning oven, plenty of vegetarian options, mezzes, also has a delicatessen for olives, hummus and the like, inside and outside tables and children's play area in the garden. There's a live band on Fri evening.

**Rangers**, Main Gate, Nairobi National Park, Langata Rd, Langata, T020-235 7470, www.rangersnairobi.com. Daily 0700-2230. Set on the edge of the park in an ingenious wood and glass structure, this is a unique restaurant that offers diners the opportunity to spot animals in the Safari Walk (see page 80) as they eat. The **Twiga Terrace** overlooks a waterhole (floodlit in the evenings), while the **Oryx Terrace** overlooks the enclosure where the famous oryx that was rescued and mothered by a lioness in Samburu National Reserve in 2002 for 16 days now resides. Good *nyama choma* plus Western dishes and BBQs, and popular with tour groups.

**Tamambo**, The Mall, Westlands, T020-444 8064, www.tamarind.co.ke/tamambo. Mon-Fri 1030-2230, Sat 1200-2230, Sun 1100-2230. Part of the acclaimed Tamarind restaurant group, this has very high standards and is stylishly decorated in African antiques and warm, earthy colours. The bar features a wide choice of cocktails and wines, and there's very good gourmet food including baked local *tilapia* fish, seafood, and African dishes such as Moroccan tajines and Swahili curries. The lighter lunch menu offers salads, wraps and gooey chocolate desserts.

**The Tamarind**, National Bank building on Harambee Av, city centre, T020-251 811, www.tamarind.co.ke/nairobi. Mon-Sat 1200-1400, 1830-2200. Nairobi's finest seafood restaurant where seafood is flown up from the coast daily and best known for its lobster and giant crab claws and prawns, but fish like red snapper is also a good bet. Non-seafood eaters can opt for the steaks, duck, ostrich or quail. Set in a beautiful formal dining room with high ceilings and stained glass, and popular with Kenyan business people, with excellent ambience and service. Highly recommended. Reservations required.

**Thai-Chi**, **Stanley Hotel**, city centre, T020-228 830, www.sarovahotels.com. Daily 1230-1400, 1900-2200. One of the city's newest and best Thai restaurants with traditional decor of sculptures, Buddhas and Asian art, on the first floor of the Stanley. The authentic food is prepared by a Thai chef and features hot and sour flavours, lemongrass and coconut milk.

**Bangkok**, Amee Arcade, Parklands Rd, Westlands, T020-375 1312. Daily 1100-1500, 1800-2230. Very authentic Chinese, not Thai as the name suggests, specializing in seafood, the ginger garlic crab and pepper sautéed prawns are especially good. There's a full bar and takeaway service and it's deservedly popular.

**Blanco's**, Timau Plaza, just off Argwings Khodek Rd, Hurlingham, T020-386 4670, www.blancos.co.ke. Mon-Sat 1200-1500, 1700-2300. Smart modern decor and popular with local business people for lunch, the menu here is traditionally Kenyan but with a modern twist, such as *tilapia* fish cooked in coconut sauce, chicken casseroles, oxtail or char-grilled lamb chops with mint sauce, served with chapattis, cassava, and maize meal and relishes like *kachumbari*. There's a good choice of imported wine.

**Café Latino**, Village Market, Limaru Rd, Gigiri, T020-712 2661. Tue-Sun 1130-2200. High-quality Italian and continental food, such as home-made pastas and some seafood, and new are the Swiss cheese, meat, fish and chocolate fondues, which are great to share. The attractive outside terrace has large umbrellas and is decorated with flowering plants. There's also a good choice of wines.

**Dragon Pearl**, Bruce House, Kenyatta Av/Standard St, city centre, T020-338 863. Daily 1200-1430, 1830-2230. Rightly popular and one of the oldest Chinese restaurants in Nairobi with a full range of dishes including seafood, duck, lamb and pork, and attentive chefs who make requests. The hot and sour soup is very good.

**Haveli Restaurant**, Capital Centre, Mombasa Rd, T020-531 607. Daily 1200-1430, 1800-2200. A large venue with some outside seating and plenty of parking, offering excellent quality and very authentic food, all cooked from scratch by Indian chefs.

**❦ Horseman**, Karen Crossroads shopping centre, Ngong Rd, Karen, T020-882 033. Daily 1000-2300. A varied menu of steaks, pizza and some Chinese dishes. You can eat burgers and other cheaper light snacks outside in the garden for considerably less than the cost of a meal in the restaurant. The bar here is quite intriguing with broken bits of mirror embedded into the floor, swaths of fabric slung from the ceiling, and couches piled high with cushions.

**❦ Mister Wok**, Capital Centre, Mombasa Rd, T020-318 885. Daily 1200-2200. Stylish with black and red simple decor and Chinese lanterns. Good food that you can watched being cooked in woks in the open kitchen; try the fish in hot garlic sauce or very good beef with green pepper.

**❦ Osteria del Chianti**, Nyangumi Rd, off Lenana Rd, Hurlingham, T020-272 3173. Daily 1200-1600, 1900-2400. Cosy and intimate Italian with a friendly atmosphere, some outside tables under umbrellas, elegant decor, a vast range of food from melon and parma ham or fish carpaccio to start, followed by pasta or pizza, and big slices of creamy tiramisu.

**❦ Panda**, 1st floor, Fedha Towers, Kaunda St, T020-213 018. Mon-Sat 1200-1500, 1800-2200. Good food especially the Peking duck, lots of vegetarian options, Chinese chefs and friendly staff.

**❦ Pavement Club & Café**, Westview Centre, off the ring road, Westlands, T020-441 711. Daily 1200-1600, 1900-2300. A light and airy pavement-style café with bright blue and purple modern decor, and a varied menu of Thai, Japanese and Italian dishes or just steak and chips. Popular with Kenyans and expats and there's a nightclub in the basement (see under Bars and clubs, page 94).

**❦ Pepper's**, Parklands Rd, opposite the **Holiday Inn**, Westlands, T020-375 5267. Mon-Sat 1200-1500, 1800-2300, Sat-Sun 1200-2300. Specializes in Indian Tawa and Tandoor cuisine, but also has a chicken rotisserie and *shwarma* machine, and continental and Chinese dishes on the menu. There's also an excellent and affordable range of wines and cocktails. Stylish decor in a big house, you can eat inside or outside, there's a great family option with a kids menu, indoor crèche and outdoor playground and sandpit. Recommended.

**❦ Pool Garden**, Panafric Hotel, Kenyatta Av, city centre, T020-272 0822, www.sarova hotels.com. Daily 0900-2000. Varied Kenyan buffet of traditional local food such as grilled tilapia fish, beef and *matoke*, offal and *kachumbari*, sautéd spinach and sweet potatoes. International dishes also available, next to the swimming pool, popular with families especially for Sun lunch.

**❦ Salumeria**, Valley Arcade, Lavington, T020-387 5226. Sun-Fri 1200-late, Sat 1700-late. A small place with a dark wood interior and tables outside that serves very good home-made pasta and antipasta, excellent reputation, Italian wines.

**❦ Thorn Tree Café**, Stanley Hotel, city centre, T020-228 830, www.sarova hotels.com. Daily 0630-2200. Pavement bistro-style café and a very popular place to meet people although the service is notoriously slow. Famous for its message tree (see page 69). Varied menu with trendy coffees, sandwiches, pizzas, pastas and continental dishes, sometimes has live music in the evenings. Valet parking.

**❦ Trattoria**, Kaunda St, city centre, T020-340 855, www.trattoria.co.ke. Daily 0730-2400. Long-established Italian spread over 2 spacious floors, with traditional decor, checked tablecloths, buzzing atmosphere and quick, professional service. The menu of antipasti, soups, salads, grills, pasta, pizza, and gooey desserts is huge, its takes at least 30 mins to get through it, and there's a good selection of Italian wine and a deli counter. Delicious food, affordable and informal. Recommended.

**❦ Absolute Juice**, Yaya Centre, Hurlingham, T020-201 0372. Mon-Sat 0900-1800, Sun 1100-1500. Healthy eating, with a selection of freshly squeezed fruit and vegetable juices, crunchy salads and good sandwiches.

**❦ Discovery**, Corner of Koinange and Banda streets, above Kobil petrol station, city centre,

T020-241 120. Excellent new sandwich and coffee bar with bright modern decor and friendly staff. Sandwiches made from items in the display cabinet, freshly baked bread, salads, light meals and freshly squeezed juice.

† **Hong Kong**, College House, Koinange St, city centre, T020-288 612. Mon-Sat 1200-1500, 1800-2200. Chinese lanterns and bright red walls, specializes in Cantonese dishes and good and filling noodle soups and spring rolls at lunchtime. Nothing fancy but it's the cheapest Chinese around.

† **Kariokor Market**, Racecourse Rd. Good and cheap African local food can be found at numerous stalls here, you eat with your hands, although utensils are provided on request. A specimen menu is goats' ribs, *ugali*, chopped spinach, *irio* made with peas, potatoes and sweetcorn.

† **Kowloon Garden**, 2nd floor, Nginyo Towers, Koinange St, city centre, T020-318 885. Daily 1100-1530, 1800-2230. Typical decor of hanging lanterns, round tables, and fake flowers, standard but authentic food, good service, try the Peking duck or steamed chicken, some wines and spirits in the bar, also does takeaway and delivery.

† **Nairobi Dorman's**, www.dorman.co.ke. Great coffee shop chain with branches in the Jubilee Exchange building on Mama Ngina St, downtown, and at the Yaya Centre, Sarit Centre, Village market, Karen Crossroads, and The Junction. Modern interiors and serves an excellent range of Kenyan and Tanzanian coffee, plus smoothies, shakes, sodas, sandwiches and pastries.

† **Nairobi Java House**, T020-445 2273, www.nairobijavahouse.com. Daily 0700-2100. Similar to **Dorman's** (see above), this is a friendly, alcohol-free chain of coffee houses with 9 branches around the city in the shopping malls, at the airport, and a downtown branch on Mama Ninga St, serving excellent Java brand Kenyan coffee and tea in a modern bistro atmosphere. The menu offers generous portions of chilli con carne and other Mexican dishes, salads, omelettes and burgers, and the breakfasts of bagels, pancakes and French toast are excellent.

† **Pasara Café**, Kaunda St, ground floor of Lonrho House, city centre, T020-338 247. Mon-Fri 0730-1800. Although the decor is very worn now, this is a good downtown venue for lunch where you can build your own sandwiches from baguettes, French bread and pittas, plus pastries, coffee, soups, and some hot meals. Newspapers and magazines are available, and there are movie posters on the wall.

† **Railway Restaurant**, at the station. Cheap African food and basics like chicken and chips but the setting is everything, decor as it always has been, and the atmosphere when a train is getting ready to depart is fantastic.

## Bars and clubs

**Nairobi** *p64, maps p64, p70, p79 and p83*
Eating, drinking and dancing are the most popular evening entertainments in Nairobi. There are a number of popular bars and clubs, many of which serve food if they're open during the day or in the early evenings, and a number of casinos, but single men should expect a lot of attention from girls and prostitutes. There are numerous and very dodgy 'all day and night bars' around the River Road area where *miraa* chewing is common to liven up hard-core drinkers and fights are frequent. For sleeker and more sophisticated nightlife, head to Westlands. As with most establishments in Kenya, dress is casual with the exception of bars in the upmarket hotels.

**Aksum Bar**, Nairobi Serena Hotel, Kenyatta Av, city centre, T020-282 2000, www.serenahotels.com. Daily 0800-2400. Expensive but atmospheric, upmarket cocktail bar with stunning Ethiopian decor and soothing lighting, offering savoury snacks and pastries, cocktails and specialist coffees, salsa sessions on Sat night and live jazz on Thu evening. Suited to a quieter, older crowd.

**Casablanca**, Nyangumi Rd, off Lenana Rd, Hurlingham, T020-272 3173. Daily 1700-late.

Cocktail bar and club with Moroccan-inspired decor with whitewashed walls and hookah pipes. Pricey but excellent cocktails including a good margarita, large dance floor that teems at the weekends, good music. Outside the ground is covered in sand and there's a large bonfire. Cover charge US$3-7.

**The Exchange Bar**, Stanley Hotel, corner of Kenyatta Av and Kimathi St, city centre, T020-228 830, www.sarova.co.ke. Daily 0930-late. Comfortable lounge with leather sofas and elaborate drapes, plasma TVs, and a wide range of drinks. The Nairobi Stock Exchange operated from here for 37 years from 1954 and there are early photos and memorabilia on the walls.

**Gipsy Bar**, Woodvale Grove, opposite Barclays Bank, Westlands, T020-444 0964. Daily 1200-1500, 1800-late. There are 3 back-to-back bars here, decorated in a Spanish theme, which are consistently popular, especially with expats. Lots of atmosphere, infectious Latin and flamenco music, delicious tapas, packed on weekend nights, a DJ plays on Fri.

**Havana Bar**, Woodvale Grove, Westlands, T020-445 0653, www.havana.co.ke. Daily 1200-late. Lively bar and restaurant with a bright red interior and Latin theme, with Latin and Brazilian music, snacks and cigars, occasional live bands, and long cocktail menu including a good *mojito* – rum, sugar, lime and fresh mint.

**Hidden Agenda**, Sarit Centre, Westlands, T020-374 3872. Daily 1000-late. Cosy laid-back bar with comfortable lounge areas, the menu features continental dishes and grills including good flame-grilled steaks, and there's an extensive choice of drinks.

**Jockey Club**, Hilton Hotel, Mama Ngina St, city centre, T020-250 000. Mon-Sat 1200-2400, Sun 1600-2400. Very popular British-style pub with dark wood, booths, paintings of jockeys and horses on the walls, beer on tap, and a pub menu of sandwiches, steaks, burgers and savoury snacks.

**Klub House 1**, Ojijo Rd, Parklands, T020-375 1310, www.klubhouse.co.ke. Daily from 0800

till the early hours. In a striking double-storey timber building, **K1** has pool tables upstairs, and dance floors and bars downstairs. Wed night is salsa night with free salsa lessons. Cover charge US$3-7.

**Library Bar**, Windsor Golf Hotel & Country Club, 9 km north of the city centre on Garden Estate Rd, T020-856 2300, www.windsorgolf resort.com. Daily 0700-late. Elegant upmarket wood-panelled hotel bar that's open until the last person leaves, with barmen in black ties, occasional live music and a dance floor, and an excellent selection of cocktails, aged malt whiskies and cigars.

**Lord Delamere's Terrace**, The Norfolk, T020-221 6940, www.fairmont.com/ norfolkhotel. Daily 0900-2300. A popular spot for Kenya's white settlers from 1904 who used to come to the terrace bar for gin and tonics. Named after Lord Delamere, one of the earliest and unofficial leader of the white settlers, whose reputed party trick was riding into the Norfolk on horseback and shooting down bottles off the bar. A man of honour, he would have any damages added to his bill. Very atmospheric. Continental food served.

**Mercury Lounge**, ABC Place, Waiyaki Way, Westlands, T020-445 0378. Mon-Thu 1230-0200, Fri-Sun 1700-0200. Tasteful, modern and spacious cocktail bar, with fabric covered walls and moody lighting, tapas-style snacks, martinis and cocktails, and a DJ plays later in the evening.

**The New Florida**, Koinange St, T020-219 150, and **Florida 2000**, Commerce House, Moi Av, T020-229 036, www.floridaclubskenya.com. Both of these city-centre clubs have been going strong now for 20 years and literally heave at the weekends. They have excellent sound systems and lights and stay open until 0600. These are fun places to visit and are certainly real eye-openers, but it is best to visit in a group and don't take anything valuable with you. Prostitutes abound and think nothing of putting hands in trousers, and have been known to rob tourists.

**The Florida** is probably where the term 'the Nairobi handshake' comes from (use your imagination)! Rather amusingly, security is run by the FBI (Florida Bouncers International), and new additions to the clubs are all-night restaurants serving Kenyan and Chinese food. Cover charge US$3-7.

**Pavement Club & Café**, Westview Centre, Ring Rd, Westlands, T020-444 1711. Wed-Sun 1900-late. A trendy club venue in the basement of this popular restaurant, which serves excellent and expensive international and Thai food until 2300 (see page 91). Very colourful decor, popular with a wide range of ages and groups, predominantly Nairobi residents. Fri and Sat nights are the liveliest. Cover charge US$3-7.

**Safari Bar, Intercontinental Hotel**, City Hall Way, city centre, T020-320 0321, www.ichotelsgroup.com. Daily 1700-late. Comfortable pub atmosphere with good service and a dance floor, different music each night, very popular Salsa nights on Wed and Fri with a Latino band and a DJ on Sun.

**Simba Saloon, Carnivore**, Langata Rd, T020-501 709, www.tamarind.co.ke/simba. Wed-Sun 2100-0400. A huge club with numerous bars and a large dance floor where the likes of Sean Paul and Shaggy have performed. Live bands every Thu, popular with expats, and Sun draws in the Asian community. A fun night out after eating at the restaurant (see page 88), check the website to see what's on. Cover charge US$3-7.

**Soho's**, Maua Close, Westlands, T020-374 5710. Daily 1800-late. Stylish bar/club with bright, yellow, orange and purple decor, popular with an expat crowd, good selection of wines and cocktails, shisha pipes, Mexican snacks, dance floor downstairs and a VIP lounge upstairs, good music, live jazz on Thu, patrons here are series about dancing. Cover charge US$3-7.

**Tacos Club**, Kimathi St. Daily 1000-late. Simple downtown bar that is popular with business people for quick cheap lunches and the informal upstairs bar. With a balcony that overlooks the traffic, a TV showing sport, shakes and juices, and booze. In the evening the tables are pushed aside for dancing.

## ⏺ Entertainment

**Nairobi** p64, maps p64, p70, p79 and p83
Nairobi has a good range of entertainment and the arts scene has particularly come into its own in recent years. To find out what's on, check the local papers, especially the *Daily Nation*, or visit the excellent website of *Nairobi Now*, www.nairobinow. wordpress.com, which, as they say themselves, "is a space where various activities and events taking place in and around Nairobi are posted to create awareness about the local arts and culture scene". *Kenya Buzz*, www.kenyabuzz.com, is another good source of information.

### Arts centres
**The Go Down Arts Centre**, Dunga Rd, industrial area next to **CMC Motors**, T020-555 770, www.thegodownartscentre.com. Home of the **Kuona Trust** (www.kuonatrust.org), a non-profit organisation that supports and promotes the arts in marginalized communities in Kenya. This centre brings together visual and the performing arts under 1 roof and has a theatre, a puppet workshop, rehearsal space for dancers, an acrobat school, a recording studio, a web-design school, a number of studios for artists, and exhibition space. Check the website or local press for what's on, which can be anything from poetry recitals, hip hop competitions, art, sculpture or photography exhibitions, dance, a battle of local bands or lectures. This is an excellent venue and gives the opportunity to see Kenya's contemporary side of art and culture; a far cry from the usual trinkets seen in the touristy souvenir shops or 'traditional' dancing shows in the coastal hotels.

**Rahimtulla Museum of Modern Art (RaMoMa)**, 2nd Parklands Av, Parklands, T020-486 1278, ramoma@africaonline.co.ke. Mon-Fri 0930-1630, Sat 0930-1300, free. This modern art gallery has recently moved from downtown to bigger premises in Parklands. It encourages artistic creativity through exhibitions of Kenya's established artists, the **Safaricom**-sponsored Children's Gallery, temporary exhibitions of young artists and photographers, and hosts numerous art education activities. Occasionally they hold art markets when pieces are for sale. Other spaces in the new premises include a sculpture garden and an outside area for open-air performances.

## Casinos

There are several places advertising themselves as casinos dotted around the city centre, but many of these are just seedy slot-machine joints. The nicest proper casinos with gaming tables, waiter service and bars, are the **RKL Casino**, in the Intercontinental, on Uhuru Highway, **Casino de Paradise**, in the Safari Park on Thika Rd, and the **Mayfair Casino**, in the Holiday Inn on Parklands Rd. They generally stay open until 0300 or 0400.

## Cinemas

Movie listings can be found in the *Daily Nation*. **Fox**, Thika Rd, T020-802 293, a drive-in; **Nairobi**, Uchumi House, Moi Av, T020-241 614; **Kenya**, on Moi Av, T020-227 822; **20th Century**, Mama Ngina St, T020-338 070; **Casino Cinema**, Ndumberi Rd, T020-229 492. South African chain **NuMetro**, www.numetro.com, cinemas can be found at The Junction, Prestige Plaza, both on Ngong Rd, Westgate Mall, Westlands, and Village Market, Gigiri, shopping malls.

## Music

Many of the hotels, bars and clubs already mentioned offer occasional live music. Check the Thu and Fri editions of the *Daily Nation* and the websites above for gigs. Principal venues include the **Carnivore**, which has a live band every Thu night and increasingly it's the venue for large concerts for well-known African music stars and US rap stars in the outside gardens, which can hold over 15,000 people, **The Pavement Club & Café**, and **Klubhouse 1**. The **Alliance Française**, **British Council**, **Goethe Institute**, and the **Italian**

Cultural Institute also host occasional concerts (see page 107). The **Nairobi Music Society** (choral concerts), with or without the Nairobi Orchestra give occasional shows at **All Saints' Cathedral** and various venues around the city. Out of town a popular local venue is the **Wida Highway Motel**, 16 km from the city centre on the Nakuru Rd, T020-476 968, www.hotelwida.com, which regularly hosts live bands, traditional dancing, acrobats and the odd beauty show or boxing tournament. A good venue for *nyama choma* and entertainment on a Sat or Sun afternoon.

## Theatre

The **Kenya National Theatre**, opposite the **Norfolk Hotel**, Harry Thuku Rd, T020-313 171, has productions, but the best option is the **Phoenix Players**, Phoenix Theatre, Professional Centre, Parliament Rd, T020-222 5506, www.phoenixplayers.net, who are the most active theatrical company in the city. They produce a range of drama of a very high standard and perform something new about every 3 weeks at their 120-seat theatre. The **Alliance Française** also hosts performances.

## ○ Shopping

**Nairobi** *p64, maps p64, p70, p79 and p83*
### Bookshops
As well as the bookshops listed below, the museum shops in both the **Nairobi National Museum** (page 73) and the **Karen Blixen Museum** (page 75) have an excellent range of books on East Africa including the classic stories like *Out of Africa* and *Man-eaters of Tsavo*. There are also a couple of decent bookshops at the airport selling books that will appeal to tourists.
**Books First**, Ukay Centre in Westlands, and in most branches of the larger **Nakumatt** stores across the city, www.books first.co.ke. An excellent bookshop chain with a good selection of imported books and cafés with decent coffee, alcoholic drinks, and internet access.

**Legacy Books**, Yaya Centre, Hurlingham, The Mall, Westlands, and on the ground floor of the Kenya International Conference Centre, city centre, www.legacybookshop.com. Sells a wide range of books including a good selection of East African fiction and books covering development issues. The flagship store at the Yaya Centre also has a restaurant, winebar and internet café.

**Nu Metro Media Stores**, The Junction Mall, Dagoretti Corner, Ngong Rd, and Westgate Mall, Westlands, www.numetro.com. Adjoining the cinemas of the same name, this South African company imports a wide range of books, DVDs, CDs, computer games, and holds occasional events such as book readings or live jazz.

**The Stanley Bookshop**, entrance not from the hotel but on Kenyatta Av, T020-212 776. A good selection of fiction and non-fiction, as well as maps, guidebooks and coffee-table books. Staff are helpful.

**Text Book Centre**, Sarit Centre, Westlands, T020-444 9680, www.textbookcentre.com. As the name suggests, sells text books but also has a good range of other books, cards and stationary. It sponsors the bi-annual Jomo **Kenyatta Award for Literature**, which is open to Kenyan writers.

## Clothing

Visitors might want to take home the all-purpose lengths of cotton cloth called *kikoys* and *kangas*. The *kikoy* is striped and comes from the coast, while the *kanga* has patterns and mottos in Kiswahili printed on the hems. They are sold all over Kenya, but there is a good selection in the cluster of shops selling material on Biashara St quite close to the City Market. Here you can also watch tailors on their foot-propelled machines sewing clothes, cushions, etc and stitching some of the most elaborate embroidery at amazing speed. *Kikoys* are now marketed by the **Kikoy Company**, www.kikoy.com. As well as being used as sarongs, they have fashioned the material into other items of clothing, including bikinis,

bags, cushions and other accessories, which can be bought at Kenya's upmarket curio shops, online and **Kenya Airways** carries some products in their duty free selection. There are lots of places that will kit you out in traditional safari gear. **Colpro** on Kimathi St is recommended as good quality and reliable.

## Handicrafts and souvenirs

There are a huge number of souvenir shops in Nairobi and they vary enormously in terms of price and quality. Be sure to have a good look – wood that may look like ebony may in fact just have been polished with black shoe polish. Also cracks may appear in the wood (particularly when placed in a central-heated room) if it has not been properly seasoned. At stalls you will be able to bargain the prices down to between a third and a half of the original asking price. In the city centre there are a number of very similar curio shops on Muindi Mbingu St and the other streets around the City Market, while more specialist shops are in the outlying suburbs and can be visited on the way to one of the sights such as the **Karen Blixen Museum**.

**African Art Shoppe**, Hilton Hotel Shopping Arcade, Mama Ngina St, city centre, T020-222 074, www.allthingsafrican.com. Daily 0900-1900. An upmarket shop with a fine selection of antiques, oil and watercolour paintings, carvings, batiks and sculptures. Expensive but of the highest quality.

**African Heritage**, Libra House, Mombasa Rd, and a gallery at the **Carnivore** restaurant (see page 88), T020-530 054, www.african heritage.net. Mon-Sat 0900-1700, Sun 1000-1600. A vast collection of original works of art and tribal sculptures from all parts of Africa, and authentic artefacts from Kenya. There are 6 lines of jewellery and hand-painted beads and it also has shops in Zanzibar and Paris.

**Collectors Den**, Hilton Hotel Shopping Arcade, Mama Ngina St, city centre, T020-226 990, www.collectorsdenkenya.com. Daily 0800-1800. A good selection of wooden and soapstone carvings, batiks, engraved glass – wine glass sets with the Big Five on them for example – and just about every other kind of Kenyan souvenir.

**Gallery Watatu**, 1st floor, Lonhro House, Standard St, city centre, T020-218 737, www.gallerywatatu.com. Mon-Fri 1000-1700. Showcases contemporary African paintings and has changing exhibitions in the spacious and well-lit formal art gallery and plenty of pieces for sale at the back.

**House of Treasures**, 70 Dagoretti Rd, Karen, T020-883 224, www.treasureskenya.com. Daily 0930-1730. Despite its distance from the city centre, African art lovers should head here for the carefully chosen pieces from all over Africa including antique tribal items, such as bridal corsets and Ashanti stools from Ghana, cowrie shell baskets from Ivory Coast, and ceremonial masks from the Congo. There's also a wide selection of Africana books.

**Kazuri Beads**, branches at the Capital Centre, Mombasa Rd, Village Walk, Gigiri, The Junction, Dagoretti Corner, Ngong Rd, Westgate Mall, Westlands, and on the coast in the Diani Shopping Centre, head office T020-884 058, www.kazuri.com. This company has been going since 1975 and from the outset has provided jobs for women in need, especially single mothers with no other source of income. Clay is purchased from small farmers in the highland region of Muranga, north western Kenya, and the women not only make it into colourful beads, but a stunning range of hand-thrown pottery and ceramics.

**Kitengela Glass**, on the edge of Nairobi National Park, beyond the David Sheldrick Wildlife Trust, 9 km off Mgadi Rd, T020-675 0602, www.kitengela-glass.com. Mon-Sat 0800-1700, Sun 1100-1600. Well worth coming out here is this beautiful sculpture garden, riddled with mosaic pathways leading to the artists' studios, who turn recycled glass and other materials into statues, vases, jewellery and home ware. There are some wonderful items for sale in the shop. Also branches at Village Walk, Gigiri, and The Junction, Dagoretti Corner, Ngong Rd.

**Matbronze**, Langata South Rd, Langata, T020-891 251, www.matbronze.com, phone for an appointment. A fine-art foundry and gallery selling unique bronze wildlife statues by acclaimed sculpture artist Denis Mathews.

**Rupas**, Uganda House, Standard St, city centre, T020-224 417. Mon-Sat 0900-1730. An outstanding selection of gift purchases, good quality, courteous staff and competitive prices.

**Spinners Web**, Viking House, Waiyaki Way, Westlands, T020-444 0882. Mon-Sat 0900-1700. This is a good craft shop, in particular for fabrics and baskets, and its merchandise comes from various self-help groups around the country. The staff are very helpful.

**Zanzibar Curio Shop**, York House, Moi Av, city centre, T020-222 704. Daily 0800-1800. Crammed from floor to ceiling with curios and prices are reasonable, but as they are marked there's no haggling. Established in 1936, it sells batiks, jewellery, safari wear, Arabian chests, sisal baskets, ebony carvings and African semi-precious stones.

### Markets

**City Market**, Muindi Mbingu St, Mon-Sat 0700-1800. Located in a greying, and in some parts crumbling art-deco building, this sells fruit and vegetables, fish, meat and flowers, and the many curio stalls stock armies of wooden giraffes amongst other crafts. Around the market and the Jamia Mosque, other stalls sell baskets, wooden and soapstone carvings, bracelets and lots of other souvenirs. Be prepared to bargain and go in late afternoon, as prices are lowest just before they close.

**Kariakor Market**, Racecourse Rd, Ngara. A huge sprawling congested market selling everything imaginable from fresh produce to household goods and is perhaps the best place to buy sisal baskets. Watch out for pick-pockets here.

**Masai Market**, Fri, on the roof of the Village Market shopping mall, Gigiri. Over 350 traders and artists sell their work and there are contemporary as well as traditional crafts here such as trendy beaded sandals, handbags, cushions, etc. It used to also be at a downtown location on other days of the week, but was recently evicted from the site, so time will tell if it reopens at another venue.

## Shopping malls

**ABC Place**, Waiyaki Way, Westlands. Large and somewhat run-down shopping and business centre in the Westlands/Lavington area. Facilities include a supermarket, a travel agency, a branch of **Nairobi Java House** coffee shop, a small bookshop, gift shops, and a community notice board.

**Capital Centre**, Mombasa Rd, T020-556 176. Good range of shops and restaurants including a large branch of **Uchumi** and furniture and gift shops. There's a large car park here enclosed by a brick wall.

**The Junction**, Dagoretti Corner, Ngong Rd. Pleasant shopping centre that has become a social hub in Nairobi with some good restaurants and coffee shops, a cinema, a **Nakumatt** supermarket, and a number of small gift shops and boutiques.

**Karen Crossroads**, junction of Langata and Ngong rds, Karen. Newly opened shopping mall serving the up-market Karen and Langata communities, with a **Nakumatt** supermarket, restaurants and coffee shops, curio and clothes shops and a travel agency.

**Prestige Plaza**, Ngong Rd, Kilimani. Facilities include a multi-screen cinema and a **Nakumatt** supermarket, which is open 24 hours a day.

**Sarit Centre**, Parklands Rd, Westlands, T020-374 7408/9, www.saritcentre.com. Vast shopping complex on 3 floors with an exhibition hall hosting regular trade fairs, shows and other events, a large food court on the 1st floor, internet cafés, a large bookshop, a branch of **Uchumi** supermarket, a cinema, and the biggest community notice board in the city.

**Village Market**, Limuru Rd, Gigiri, T020-712 2488, www.villagemarket-kenya.com. Large, upmarket shopping complex that has been laid out to resemble (as the name suggests) a village, with a big selection of over 125 boutique-style shops selling shoes, clothes and gift items, an **Uchumi** supermarket, an art gallery hosting regular exhibitions of work by local artists, and a central food court with outside seating, which is phenomenally popular at the weekends. Recreational facilities include a 12-lane 10-pin bowling alley, a cinema, a pool hall, and outside a playground and curly waterslide for kids. There's also a supermarket where diplomats can buy duty-free goods. The Masai Market (see page 97) is also held here. If you're going to visit a mall in Nairobi, make it this one.

**Westgate Mall**, off Waiyaki Way, and within walking distance of the Sarit Centre, Westlands. Nairobi's newest mall, which opened in 2007, is ultra-modern and boasts a waterfall at the entrance. It's the 1st mall to attract international brand shops like Nike, Adidas, United Colors of Benetton, and many South African chain stores, as well as a 24-hr **Nakumatt** supermarket.

**Yaya Centre**, Argwings Kodhek Rd, Hurlingham, T020-271 3360/1, www.yaya-centre.co.ke. Smart shopping centre on 4 floors with a supermarket, a **Nairobi Java House** coffee shop, an internet café, bookshops, and several clothes and gift shops.

## Supermarkets

**Nakumatt**, www.nakumatt.net. Kenya's largest supermarket chain. The hypermarket branches sell just about everything from household goods, furniture and books, to electronics, camping equipment, and clothes. As well as the ones already mentioned in the shopping malls above, there is also a 24-hr Downtown Nakumatt on the corner of Kimathi St and Kenyatta Av in the city centre and 1 on Uhuru Highway opposite the Nyayo Stadium. They've also recently opened a branch in Kigali, Rwanda.

**Uchumi**, is the other supermarket chain with branches in the Sarit Centre and the Village Market among other locations.

## ▲▲ Activities and tours

**Nairobi** *p64, maps p64, p70, p79 and p83*
### Athletics
The **Nairobi Marathon**, T020-329 3811, www.nairobimarathon.com, is in Oct. Established in 2003, every year it gets more popular and now attracts some 20,000 participants from Kenya and all over the world. There's a full and half marathon for runners and wheelchair users, plus shorter family runs, and for spectators it's a marvellous opportunity to see Kenya's famed runners. The marathon starts at **Nyayo National Stadium**, and goes along Uhuru Highway, turns at the University Way roundabout into Kenyatta Av, follows Harambee Av and Haile Selassie Av, back to Mombasa Rd and finishes inside the stadium.

### Cricket
**Aga Khan**, Matam Ln, off Parklands Av, off Limuru Rd, Parklands, T020-374 2930. Exciting league games played on Sat and Sun, with good crowds. Cricket is especially popular with the Asian community.
**Nairobi Gymkhana and Simba Union Club**, next to each other off Forest Rd, in Parklands, T020-374 1310. The Gymkhana pitch is Kenya's main cricket venue, seating 7000, and hosted 2 matches in the 2003 Cricket World Cup.

### Go-karting
**GP Karting**, near the **Carnivore** restaurant, T020-608 444, www.gpkarting.co.ke. Tue-Sun 1000-1900, US$15 for 10 mins. Helmets and suits are provided and there's a computerized timing system plus a sports bar on site.

### Golf
There are a number of very well-kept golf courses in the suburbs of Nairobi, although you will need to take out temporary membership. Information about all of Kenya's 35 golf courses can be found on the **Kenya Golf Union**'s website; www.kgu.or.ke. An advantage of playing golf in Nairobi is because of the high altitude, the ball travels some 10 m further than it would do at sea level.

**Karen Country Club**, Karen Rd, Karen, T020-882 801, www.karencountry club.org.This is famous for its beautiful 18-hole, 72-par championship course and lawn terrace. Many of the trees on the fairways are indigenous to Kenya. The sophisticated irrigation system, the maintenance of the fairways and the flowering bushes and trees give the course the look of a lovingly cared-for garden. It was founded in 1933 by the Karen Estates Company Ltd.
**Kenya Railways Golf Club**, Lower Hill Rd, Nairobi Hill, T020-721 859. This 9-hole course was established in 1922 for the staff of the Uganda Railway and is a fun course to play, especially if you are lucky enough to have your game coincide with a train passing through the course.
**Muthaiga Golf Club**, Kiambu Rd, Karura Forest to the northeast of the city centre, T020-276 2414. This 71-par, 18-hole golf course was first laid out in 1912, and is today home to the Kenya Golf Union and plays host to the most prestigious golfing event in the country, the Kenya Open.
**Windsor Golf & Country Club**, 9 km north of Nairobi on Garden Estate Rd, T020-856 2300 www.windsorgolfresort.com. Another stunning well-tended course, the upmarket resort is best suited for people on specific golfing holidays. For accommodation here, see Sleeping, page 84.

### Horse racing
**Ngong Racecourse**, Ngong Rd, Racecourse, T020-387 3871, info@jockeyclub.co.ke. The Jockey Club of Kenya holds meetings most Sun except in Aug. This is a wonderful setting as well as being a great place to observe all sections of Nairobi society. It's also good for children with extra activities including face painting, camel rides and bouncy castles and there's a good choice of food from *nyama choma* to a buffet restaurant.

## Polo

**Jamhuri Park**, Jamhuri Rd, off Ngong Rd, Jamhuri, T020-564 736. Weather permitting, polo is played on Sat and Sun. In Kenya, polo is a relatively popular sport, although it is considered a sport of the elite. A number of tournaments are held in Nairobi, and have attracted top polo players and international teams. In Jul 2008 a very successful 3-day Rock the Races event was held here and at the Ngong Racecourse, which included polo matches, a ball, and a rock concert. They may run it again so keep an eye on the press.

## Rugby

**Kenya Rugby Union Football Club**, Ngong Rd, Jamhuri, T020-237 0360, www.kenya rfu.com. The Safari Sevens is held each year here in Jun; a major international competition with a wide range of teams coming to play in one of the most popular Rugby Sevens in the world. It's also a major event on the Nairobi social calendar.

## Sporting clubs

British settlers introduced sporting clubs to their colonies and Kenya still maintains a strong legacy of clubs suitable for individuals and families. Most clubs offer standard facilities such as swimming pools, squash and badminton courts and field sports. In addition, there are recreational bars and restaurants. Other clubs offer golf, cricket, rugby, hockey, tennis or sailing. Indoor games and sports include snooker, pool, billiards and darts. Club membership costs vary but most offer temporary membership to visitors.
**Nairobi Railways Club**, Haile Selassie Av, Nairobi Hill, T020-725 125; **Ruaraka Sports Club**, Thika Rd, Mathare North, T020-860 280; **Parklands Sports Club**, Ojijo Rd, Parklands, T020-374 5164, www.parklandssportsclub.org.

## Swimming

Most of the big hotels have swimming pools that can also be used by non-residents for a daily fee of about US$3, or for free if eating at one of the poolside restaurants. The pool at the **YMCA** is particularly good.

## Ten-pin bowling

**The Village Market**, T020-712 3141, www.villagemarket-kenya.com.

## Tours and tour operators

There are a number of minibus tours for either a morning or an afternoon, arranged by any of the tour companies in Nairobi. The cost can vary, but average around US$40, and US$60 for Nairobi National Park.

There are numerous tour operators based in Nairobi where you should be able to get fairly reliable information, book safaris, etc. It is important to find an operator that you like, offers good service, and does not pressurize you into booking something that is not what you are looking for. You can find more at **Kenya Association of Tour Operators**, www.katokenya.org. See below for recommended companies.
**Acacia Safaris**, 4th floor, College House, corner of University Way and Koinange St, city centre, T020-341 997, www.acacia safaris.co.ke. Offers a full range of lodge and camping safaris with regular departures, including an 8-day Lake Turkana tour, plus day trips around Nairobi.
**Adventure Naturetrek Safaris**, Vedic House, Mama Ngina St, opposite International Life House, city centre, T020-341 188, www.naturetreksafaris.com. Small company offering affordable lodge and camping trips from 3 days to the parks.
**Adventure Penfam Tours & Travel**, Summit House, Moi Av, city centre, T020-251 936, www.penfamtours.com. Broad selection of lodge and camping safaris including birdwatching tours.
**AustralKen Tours & Travel**, 8th floor, Sonalux House, Moi Av, city centre, T020-352 5182, www.australken.com. Nairobi day trips and lodge and camping safaris from 2-14 days.
**Best Camping Tours and Safaris**, 1st floor, I & M, Towers, corner of Kenyatta Av and Muindu Mbingu St, T020-229 667, www.best

campingkenya.com. Well-established company offering a half-day trip to Nairobi National Park, plus camping and lodge safaris in minibuses, and tailor-made packages.

**Bike Treks**, T020-444 6371, www.bike treks.co.ke. Organizes reasonably priced walking/cycling tours, supported by a back-up vehicle, including a 3-day Masai Mara safari. Excellent value.

**Breakaway Expeditions Africa**, Thika Rd, T020-811 004, www.breakaway expedition.com. Nairobi excursions, day trips to Amboseli and Nakuru, and longer safaris to the parks.

**Bunson Travel Service**, Pan Africa House, Standard St, city centre, T020-248 371, www.bunsonkenya.com. Good, reliable, well-established travel and tour agent. Offers flight and rail bookings, car hire, safaris and hotel bookings, as well as a number of day trips in and around Nairobi for small groups.

**Bush and Beyond/Bush Homes of East Africa Ltd**, T020-600 457, www.bush-and-beyond.com and www.bush-homes.co.ke. Reservations for some of the more exclusive camps, all in excess of US$600 per person per night in the Masai Mara, Lewa Conservancy and Amboseli.

**Call of Africa Safaris**, 3rd floor, Uganda House, Kenyatta Av, city centre, T020-229 729 www.call-of-africa-safaris.com. Tailor-made safaris using top-end lodges including the Serena chain, can finish in Mombasa.

**Cheli and Peacock Safaris**, Parklands, T020-604 053, www.chelipeacock.com. Represents some of the most upmarket small lodges and tented camps and can arrange 8-10 tailor-made flying safaris between them.

**Dallago Tours and Safaris**, Othaya Rd, Kileleshwa, T020-387 2845, www.dallago tours.com. Park safaris using mid-range lodges and Mt Kenya climbs, can also book flights and hotels.

**East African Wildlife Safaris**, T020-890 711, www.eaws.kenyaweb.com. Very upmarket safaris on offer, all tailor-made to the best lodges and camps, or using their own mobile camps, starting from around US$600 per

person per day. The company was started by Richard Leakey in 1966.

**Express Travel Group**, 2nd floor, Middle East Bank Tower, Milimani Rd, Nairobi Hill, T020-273 4971, www.etg-safaris.com. General agent and tailor-made road and flying safaris for a minimum of 2 people.

**Gametrackers**, 5th floor, Nginyo Towers, Moktar Daddah St, city centre, T020-222 2703, www.gametrackers.com. Well-established company organizing camping safaris with both vehicles and camels to Lake Turkana and the Ndoto mountains, as well as biking and walking safaris. The 8- and 10-day trips to Northern Kenya are probably the best and most affordable on offer. They go to the Kalacha Desert, Lake Turkana and Maralal, including a camel safari. They also offer a number of Nairobi day trips. Recommended.

**Gamewatchers**, Village Market, Gigiri, T020-712 3129, www.porini.com. A good selection of short road or flying safaris to the parks using tented camps.

**Going Places**, Westlands Centre, Mapaka Rd, Westlands, T020-444 2312, www.goingplaces kenya.com. General agent for booking tailor-made safaris and beach holidays.

**Hoopoe Safaris**, inside Wilson Airport, T020-604 303-4, www.hoopoe.com. Consistently recommended by a number of travellers, and *Condé Nast Traveler* (USA) magazine voted them the best eco tourism operator in the world in 2004. This is the first time any African company has won this prestigious award. It has an excellent commitment to the local communities and conservation. A range of safaris and climbs and unusual trekking itineraries. Also has agents in the UK, US and Canada.

**Kenya One Tours**, 84, Riverside Dr, Westlands, T020-445 3318, www.kenyaone tours.com. Good all round tailor-made tour operator that can arrange all accommodation, safaris and flights. Kenyan and German run.

**Malaika Tours**, Ukulima Cooperative House, Haile Selassie Av, city centre, T020-215 7732, www.malaikaecotourism.com. Day tours around Nairobi and longer tours to the parks with cultural experiences included like visiting a Masai *manyatta*.

**Menengai Holidays**, 1st floor, Duplex Apt 40, Bunyala/Lower Hill Rd, Upper Hill, PO Box 2260-00202, KNH, Nairobi, T020-273 3702, www.menengaiholidays.com. Offer a range of tours from 1-day city tours of Nairobi to longer safaris and mountain-climbing trips.

**Mountain Rock Kenya**, Jubilee Insurance House, junction of Wabera St and Kaunda St, city centre, T020-224 2133, www.mountain rockkenya.com. As the name suggests, organizes mountain climbs and hikes including Mt Kenya and the Abedares.

**Origins Safaris**, www.originsafaris.info. A special-interest safari operator with 40 years' experience based in Kenya but covering much of east and central Africa. Main areas of expertise are safaris using a combination of private lodges, tented camps and its own mobile tented camps, cultural expeditions and tours to emerging destinations especially in central Africa. One of Africa's best tour operators, but not cheap, arrangements are US$5000-8000 per person. It does not take direct bookings; you need to go through an agent, if you email, they will send a list of their agents.

**Savage Wilderness Safaris Ltd**, Sarit Centre, Westlands, T020-521 590, www.whitewater kenya.com. Whitewater rafting and kayaking on several Kenyan rivers including a day trip from Nairobi to the Tana River for around US$100.

**Savuka Tours and Safaris**, Pan Africa House, 4th floor, Kenyatta Av, city centre, T020-225 108, www.savuka-travels.com. Good-value budget camping safaris and mid-range lodge safaris to all the parks plus Nairobi ½-day tours and a Lake Nakuru day trip with lunch for US$160.

**Shoor Safaris**, T723-202 188, www.shoor travel.com. Excellent well-established tour operator, offering a variety of safaris, all of which can be customized. Also offer a full hotel-booking service in Kenya, Tanzania and Zanzibar.

**Somak Safaris**, Mombasa Rd, T020-535 508, www.somak-nairobi.com. Safaris using Serena lodges, Nairobi ½-day trips and a full-day Nakuru/Naivasha tour.

**SunTrek Tours and Travel**, Safari Centre, Waiyaki Way, Westlands, T020-444 2982,

www.suntreksafaris.com. Excellent tour operator that organizes tailor-made lodge safaris, plus adventure activities such as trekking, including Mt Kenya climb and scuba diving on the coast, also can combine with safaris to Tanzania, has an impressive fleet of 25 smart safari landcruisers, 4WD vehicle hire, the sample itineraries on the website can be adapted to suit what you want to do and your budget. Very professional.

**Tobs Golf Safaris**, T020-271 0825, www.kenya-golf-safaris.com.Golf specialist that combines hotel accommodation with bookings and transfers to golf courses.

**UNIGLOBE Let's Go Travel**, 1st floor, ABC Place, Waiyaki Way, Westlands, T020-444 7151, Caxton House, Standard St, city centre, T020-340 331, Karen Crossroads, Karen, T020-882 505 (as well as offices in Uganda), www.letsgosafari.com. Very professional tour operator offering reasonably priced balloon safaris, camel safaris, horseback safaris, fishing, golf, walking, trekking and climbing, diving, water sports and whitewater rafting. A well-organized company, it acts as agents for several other companies, and publishes price and information lists of hotels, camps and lodges. Well recommended. Organizes travel allover East Africa.

## ⊕ Transport

**Nairobi** *p64, maps p64, p70, p79 and p83*
Nairobi is fairly central to Kenya and unless you are flying directly to the coast for a beach holiday, most people pass through the city. It's also a popular for getting to the parks of the Northern Circuit in Tanzania as Nairobi is closer than the airport at Dar es Salaam and there are regular transport links between Nairobi and Arusha in northern Tanzania. For getting around the city there are plenty of cheap buses, *matatus* and taxis. Buses and *matatus* are almost always full and you should beware of pickpockets.

### Air
The main airport is **Jomo Kenyatta International Airport**, T020-661 1000, www.kenyaairports.co.ke, 15 km southeast of the city, connected by a good dual carriageway. It costs US$0.75 per car to get into the airport (included in the price of a taxi). There is also **Wilson Airport**, 6 km south of the city, on Langata Rd, T020-501 943, from which smaller planes, including many internal charter flights, leave. See page 64 for further details including transport to and from the airports.

The following airlines offer daily scheduled flights. Specific schedules are detailed under each relevant chapter.

All tickets can also be bought directly from desks at the airports. **Kenya Airways** has daily flights from Jomo Kenyatta International Airport to **Kisumu**, **Malindi**, **Lamu** and **Mombasa**, as well as a number of regional destinations. **Fly 540** has flights from Jomo Kenyatta International Airport to **Eldoret**, **Kisumu**, **Lamu**, **Malindi**, **Masai Mara**, **Mombasa**, and **Entebbe** in Uganda. **Air Kenya** has flights to **Amboseli**, **Kilimanjaro** in Tanzania, **Lamu**, **Lewa Downs**, **Malindi**, **Masai Mara**, **Meru**, **Mombasa**, **Nanyuki** and **Samburu**. They also code share with **Regional Air** in Tanzania and offer flights from Nairobi to **Kilimanjaro**, **Dar es Salaam** and **Zanzibar** in Tanzania. **Safairlink** has flights to **Amboseli**, **Kiwayu**, **Lamu**, **Lewa Downs**, **Masai Mara**, **Nanyuki**, **Samburu** and **Tsavo**. They code share with **Air Excel** in Tanzania so have flights from Nairobi to **Kilimanjaro**.

### Airline offices
**Air India**, Jeevan Bharati Building, Harambee Av, T020-313 300, www.airindia.com. **Air Kenya**, based at Wilson Airport, T020-605 745, www.airkenya.com. **Air Malawi**, International House, Mama Ngina St, T020-333 683, www.airmalawi.com. **Air Uganda**, 5th floor, Jubilee Insurance House, Wabera St, T020-216 5555, www.air-uganda.com. **Air Zimbabwe**, Chester House,

Koinanage St, T020-339 522, www.airzim
babwe.com. **British Airways**, International
House, Mama Ngina St, T020-327 7000,
www.britishairways.com. **Delta**, Ambank
House, University Way, city centre, T020-213
4600, www.delta.com. **Egypt Air**, Hilton
Hotel Arcade, City Hall Way, T020-226 821,
www.egyptair.com.eg. **Emirates**, 20th floor,
Viewpark Towers, Monrovia St, T020-329
0000, www.emirates.com. **Ethiopian Airlines**,
Bruce House, Muindi Mbingu St, T020-311
649, www.ethiopianairlines.com. **Fly 540**,
ABC Place, Westlands, T020-445 3252, airport
T020-827 521, www.fly540.com. **Gulf Air**,
International House, Mama Ngina St,
T020-241 123, www.gulfair.com. **Kenya
Airways**, 5th floor, Barclays Plaza, Loita St,
city centre, T020-327 4747, airport T020-642
2000, www.kenya-airways.com. **KLM/
Northwest Airlines**, Barclays Bank Plaza, Loita
St, T020-327 4210, www.klm.com. **Rwandair**,
4th floor, Arnold Plaza, Westlands, T020-426
6182, www.rwandair.com. **Safairlink**, based
at Wilson Airport, T020-600 777, www.safari
link-kenya.com. **Saudi Arabian Airlines**,
15th floor, Ambank House, University Way,
T020-230 337, www.saudiairlines.com. **South
African Airways**, International House, Mama
Ngina St, T020-224 7342, www.flysaa.com.
**Sudan Airways**, 3rd floor, Sasini House, Loita
St. T020-340 357, www.sudanair.com. **Swiss
International**, 1st floor, Caltex Plaza, Limuru
Rd, T020-374 4045, www.swiss.com.

## Bus
### Local
The main city bus terminal is located at the
end of River Rd and there are main bus stops
outside the Hilton Hotel on Moi Av, outside
Nation House on Tom Mboya St, outside the
Railway Station at the end of Moi Av, and
outside the General Post Office on Kenyatta
Av. The buses cover all the routes and operate
as early as 0600 and as late as 2400, and each
bus has an assigned route number. Useful
numbers are **34** to the airport from the Hilton
stop, **15** to Langata, **24** to Karen, which also
goes past the Bomas of Kenya, and **111** to

Ngong from in front of the Railway Station.
Most buses are pale blue city buses, but
increasingly newer green City Hoppers are
appearing on the streets. Some route numbers
are listed at www.kenyabus.net.

### Long distance
The long-distance bus station is on Landhies
Rd from where buses go from Nairobi to all the
upcountry towns and Western Kenya. There
are at least daily departures to almost every
destination, but generally buses from here
can't be pre-booked and go when full so you
will have to arrive at 0700 or earlier, and wait
until the bus fills up and departs. There are also
a number of coach companies with scheduled
timetables and there is a clutch of offices
along and around Accra Rd to the east of the
National Archives. These include **Coastline**,
**Goldline**, **Kensilver Express**, **Easy Coach** and
**Cross Road Travellers**, but recommended for
long-distance journeys is **Akamba Bus**, Lagos
Rd, T020-556 062, www.akambabus.com, a
private company offering a very good level of
service and you can pre-book tickets. It is not
the cheapest option but the buses are fairly
well maintained and they have a good safety
record. Buses to Mombasa take 9-11 hrs and
cost around US$15. The area around River Rd
where the bus station and offices are located is
unsafe. Beware of robbery and look after your
luggage at all times.

There are also daily services to
neighbouring countries. **Akamba Bus** has
3 departures to **Kampala** (Uganda) US$20,
at 0700, 1900 and 2230, taking 13 hrs.
**Akamba** also operate a Royal Service on this
route where the buses carry less passengers,
have slightly bigger seats and are generally
more comfortable, which departs at 0700 and
costs US$30. **Scandinavian Express** River Rd,
T020-242 523, www.scandinavia group.com
(an equally good Tanzanian company),
also operates on the Nairobi– Kampala route,
with daily departures at 2130, crossing the
border at Busia or Malaba where immigration
procedures are completed, see page 176 for
further details. Also stops at **Jinja**.

**Akamba** and **Scandinavian Express** depart Nairobi daily at 0700 for **Dar es Salaam** (Tanzania) via **Arusha** and arrive in Dar at around 2030, US$45-50. The border at Namanga is efficient and visas can be purchased, see page 244 for further details. **Scandinavian Express** runs a service to **Musoma** and **Mwanza** on Lake Victoria in northwestern Tanzania via **Nakuru** (3 hrs), US$28, departs Nairobi daily at 2130 and takes 13½ hrs. Procedures are straightforward at the Isabania border and visas are available, see page 165 for further details. **Scandinavian** also operates a service between Dar es Salaam and **Lusaka** in Zambia, so die-hard fans of African bus travel can travel all the way from Kampala in Uganda to Lusaka in Zambia with Scandinavian Express.

**Shuttle** There are daily shuttle services to **Arusha** (for Tanzania's Northern Circuit parks) and **Moshi** (to climb Kilimanjaro), from where you can get onward buses to **Dar es Salaam**. The operators utilize 20- to 30-seat buses with comfortable, individual seating and drivers assist passengers during the border crossings. They pick up at the major hotels or the airport by prior arrangement or meet the bus outside the Parkside Hotel, on Monrovia St at least 15 mins before departure especially if you have bulky luggage. They depart Nairobi each day at 0800 and 1400, and take about 5½ hrs to Arusha (US$35), and 6½ hrs to Moshi (US$40). These services can be arranged through the hotel receptions, through a tour operator or directly through **Riverside Shuttle**, Pan Africa Insurance House, Kenyatta Av, T020-229 618, www.riverside-shuttle.com.

## Car

Cars can be rented easily in Kenya, with or without a driver. You will usually need to be over 25 years of age and have a drivers' licence. Driving in Nairobi is a bit of an art and you will have to get used to lots of roundabouts with rather bizarre lane systems. The right of way is usually (but not always)

given to traffic already on the roundabout. Be prepared for a lot of hooting, traffic-light jumping and the odd pothole and watch for *matatus* as they can break very suddenly to pick up passengers. Away from the city centre, driving in the suburbs where there is a lot less traffic is very straightforward. Parking is a problem in the centre and you will be pestered by parking boys. There is no need to pay them to ensure the safety of your vehicle. There is a multi-storey car park at the **Intercontinental Hotel** (around US$3 per hr).

**Car hire** Rates vary, but try **Central Hire a Car** for the best deals. For more information see Getting around, page 32.
**Active Car Hire**, 4th floor, Standard Building, Wabera St, city centre, T020-221 0531, www.activecarhire.com.
**Avis**, College House, University Way, city centre, T020-336 704, airport, T020-213 330 (24 hrs), www.avis.com.
**Budget**, Travel House, opposite Six Eighty Hotel, Muindi Mbingu St, T020-223 581, airport, T020-822 370, www.budget-kenya.com.
**Budget Car Hire Kenya**, Kingsway Nairobi Centre, University Way, city centre, T020-358 1027, www.budgetcarhirekenya.com.
**Central Hire a Car**, Six Eighty Hotel, Muindi Mbingu St, city centre, T020-222 8888, www.carhirekenya.com.
**EuropCar**, airport, T020-822 625, www.europcar.com.
**Glory Car Hire Ltd**, Hilton Hotel Arcade, Mama Ngina St, city centre, T020-214 369, www.glorysafaris.com.
**Hertz**, at the Stanley Hotel on Standard St, T020-311 143, www.hertz.co.ke.
**Kenya Car Hire**, Portal Place House, Muindi Mbingu St, T020-248 453, www.kenya-carhire.com.
**Rent A Fine Car**, Argwing Kodhek Rd, Kilimani, T020-272 8448, www.rentafinecar.com.
**Shoor Safaris**, Corner Plaza, Parklands Rd, Parklands, T020-374 5690, www.shoortravel.com.

## Matatu
### Local

*Matatus* are assigned to set routes within the city and are usually 14-seater minibuses. They collect as many passengers as possible from the outset and along the way, and passengers board and alight wherever they choose. *Matatus* normally have a crew of 2; a driver and a 'tout' who tries to encourage as many passengers as possible to board, and collects their fares. The vehicles are mostly white with a yellow stripe and their destination painted along the side. Also, although it is often flaunted, they are legally only permitted to carry a maximum of 14 passengers on seats with seat belts. They are however, still driven recklessly and drivers will think nothing about driving over central reservations and along pavements to get somewhere quicker. Most *matatu* rides within Nairobi cost around US$0.70.

### Long distance

*Matatus* run to destinations such as **Nakuru**, **Naivasha**, and the **Namanga** border with Tanzania and the main long-distance *matatu* stage is between Tom Mboya St and River Rd. There are regular departures and they go when full. For longer distances you need to swap *matatus* in the regional centres to get any further. They are driven recklessly, road accidents are common, and there's the added problem of petty theft, so only use these as a last resort.

There are regular shuttle buses to Arusha, see page 105, but a cheaper alternative is to do the journey in stages by taking a *matatu* from Ronald Ngala Rd in Nairobi to **Namanga**, crossing the border on foot, then catching another *matatu* to **Arusha**. This takes a little longer than the shuttle, but costs half the price.

## Taxi

Taxis park up outside shopping malls, restaurants, hotels, official taxi stands, are easy enough to find on street corners and any hotel can get one for you. It is recommended that you should always take a taxi to get around at night. A taxi to the airport costs approximately US$20. Although some taxis are metered, they may not always work, so it's best to agree a price with the driver before setting off. Although they start with higher price, they don't intentionally try to rip you off, and if you offer a price that's too low they simply won't accept the fare. A short journey within the city centre should cost US$5-7. Like *matatus*, Nairobi taxis are marked with a yellow line along each side. There is also a fleet of large black London taxis.

## Train

**Nairobi Railway Station**, T020-221 211, is to the south of Haile Selassie Av, at the very end of Moi Av. Despite Kenya's long association with what was the Uganda Railway, which effectively founded the colony, in recent years due to chronic under investment the railway is close to collapse with dilapidated rolling stock, and frequent derailments and breakdowns. A new consortium known as Rift Valley Railways took over the running of the railway in 2006, but little has improved and added to this, part of the railway in the north of the country was ripped up during the post-2007 election violence so the service from Nairobi to Kisumu is no longer operational. For now, only the overnight train between Nairobi and **Mombasa** has a sporadic service. This used to be an historic and authentic rail experience and an excellent way of getting to the coast. However, these days and thanks to frequent breakdowns – not necessarily by the passenger train, but by other freight trains using the same track, which subsequently block the line – the journey can be painfully slow to such an extent that local people have been known to get off the train and take a bus for the rest of their journey. In theory it departs Nairobi at 1900 on Mon, Wed and Fri and arrives in Mombasa at 0830. In the other direction it departs Mombasa on Sat, Tue and Thu at 1900 and arrives in Nairobi at 0900. But the train is often many hours late, so do not arrange onward travel arrangements too close to the scheduled arrival times. 1st class is in cabins that sleep 2 people in bunks and includes bedding and a sink, 2nd class is 4 people in bunks with bedding and a sink, and 3rd class is seating in carriages that take up to 80 people. First class is the best bet as some of the other rickety carriages are almost 90 years old and lights and washbasins may not always function. There is a restaurant car where 1st- and 2nd-class passengers can have a basic dinner and drinks, though you may want to bring additional drinks and snacks with you to last for a journey that could take up to 24 hrs. Tickets: 1st class, adults US$65, children (3-11) US$45, including dinner and breakfast; 2nd class, US$54, children (3-11) US$34 including dinner and breakfast; and 3rd class, US$21. It is essential to make reservations in advance and this can be done at the stations, or through a tour operator or travel agent.

## Tuk-tuk

The 3-wheeled auto-rickshaw or *tuk-tuk* of southeast Asia are becoming increasingly popular as taxis in Nairobi. Like taxis, fares need to be negotiated in advance. They cost around US$3 for a short journey, but as they are open there is the added disadvantage of getting a lung full of traffic fumes and they don't go very fast so are not suitable for all but the shortest journeys.

## ⊕ Directory

**Nairobi** *p64, maps p64, p70, p79 and p83*
**Banks**
There are banks all over central Nairobi that offer foreign exchange services and can give KSh and US$ cash off a credit card. All have ATMs, which can also be found in the shopping malls and at some petrol stations. Try to avoid banks on the last Fri of the month (payday), when there are long queues.

There are also numerous bureaux de change, also known as forex bureaux.

Exchange rates are about the same in most, though commission is charged on changing TCs so shop around for the best deal. Hotels will also change money but at excessive exchange rates. Some shop keepers and curio stall holders will take US$ cash so ensure you know what the current exchange rate is.

### Courier companies
**DHL**, International House, Mama Ngina St, city centre, T020-692 5120, www.dhl.co.ke. **Federal Express**, 12th floor, Bruce House, Standard St, city centre, T020-211 307, www.fedex.com. **TNT**, Kiambere Rd, Nairobi Hill, T020-723 554, www.tnt.com.

### Cultural centres
Regular films, concerts and talks are on offer, and in some, libraries and language courses. The Alliance Française and the Italian Cultural Centre are particularly good venues for the arts. **Alliance Française**, Loita St, city centre, T020-340 054; **British Council**, Upper Hill Rd, Nairobi Hill, T020-283 6000, www.british council.org/kenya; **Goethe Institute**, Maendeleo House, Monrovia St, city centre, T020-222 4640, www.goethe.de/ins/ke/nai; **Italian Cultural Institute**, Woodvale Grove, off Waiyaki Way, Westlands, T020-445 1226, www.iicnairobi.esteri.it.

### Embassies and consulates
**Australia**, ICIPE House, Riverside Drive, Westlands, T020-444 5034, www.kenya. embassy.gov.au. **British High Commission**, Upper Hill Rd, Nairobi Hill, T020-284 4000, www.ukinkenya.fco.gov.uk. **Canada**, Limuru Rd, Gigiri, T020-226 987, www.dfait-maeci. gc.ca/nairobi. **Ethiopia**, State House Av, city centre, T020-273 2050, ethioemb@ kenyaweb.com. **France**, Barclays Plaza, Loita St, city centre, T020-277 8000, www.amba france-ke.org. Issues visas for Togo, Senegal, Burkina Faso, Mauritania and the Central African Republic. **Germany**, 113 Riverside Dr, Westlands, T020-426 2100, www.nairobi. diplo.de. **Netherlands**, Riverside Lane,

Westlands, T020-428 2000, www.nether lands-embassy.or.ke. **South African High Commission**, Roshanmaer Place, Lenana Rd, Kilimani, T020-282 7100, nairobi@foreign. gov.za. **Sudan**, Kabarnet Rd, off Ngong Rd, Kilimani, T020-575 159, www.sudanembassy nrb.org. **Tanzania**, Continental House, Uhuru Highway, city centre, T020-331 056, tanzania@users.africaonline.co.ke. **Uganda**, Uganda House, Kenyatta Av, city centre, T020-311 814, www.ugandahigh commission.co.ke. **United States**, United Nations Av, off Limuru Rd, Gigiri, T020-363 6000, http://nairobi.usembassy.gov.

### Immigration

Nyayo House, Kenyatta Highway, T020-222 022.

### Internet

A vast number of places now offer inexpensive internet access all over the city, including most of the hotels and shopping malls and Wi-Fi is available at the airport and the more expensive hotels. Options range from smart internet cafés with fast reliable connections, to tiny corner shops that have just one computer and sometimes erratic connections.

### Medical services

**Hospitals** The 2 main private hospitals both have world-class facilities: **Nairobi Hospital**, Argwings Kodhek Rd, Nairobi Hill, T020-284 5000, www.nairobihospital.org; **Aga Khan Hospital**, Parklands Av, Parklands, T020-374 2531, www.agakhanhospitals.org. The **Kenyatta Hospital**, on Hospital Rd, Nairobi Hill, T020-726 300, is well equipped, but as a public hospital, has long queues. If you are planning to travel in more isolated areas, consider the **Flying Doctors' Society of Africa**, based at Wilson Airport. For an annual tourist fee of US$50, it offers free evacuation by air to a medical centre or hospital. This may be worth considering if you are visiting remote regions, but not if visiting the more popular parks in the north as adequate provision is made in the

case of an emergency. The income goes back into the service and the **African Medical Research Foundation (AMREF)** behind it. You can contact them in advance on T020-602 495, www.amref.org.

**Pharmacies** These are found all over downtown Nairobi and in all shopping malls but are generally expensive. The major hospitals have 24-hr pharmacies.

### Police

**Police** emergency T999, **Central Police Station**, University Way, city centre, T020-225 685, other police stations can be found on the website; www.kenyapolice.go.ke. Always inform the police of any incidents – you will need a police form for any insurance claims.

### Post office

**Moi Av**, half-way between Kenyatta Av and Tubman Rd on the east side, T020-227 401. There is also a post office on Haile Selassie Av, T020-228 441, where you will find the fairly reliable, and free, poste restante. There are also post offices in the shopping malls and there's a useful branch locator on the post office's website; www.posta.co.ke. Opening hours are generally Mon-Fri 0800-1700 and Sat 0800-1200.

### Telephone

Local and international calls can be made from **Telkom Kenya** public coin and card phones in red or yellow booths on the street or in post offices. Phone cards are available from post offices. Some internet cafés also double up as public phone and fax places. If you are using a Kenya service provider for your cell phone, top up cards for Kenya's 2 cell networks, **Cellnet** and **Safaricom**, are available from their specific shops all around the city and from just about every street vendor.

### Tourist helpline

Based at **Nairobi National Park** main gate, Langata Rd, T020-604 767.

# Contents

## At a glance

**Getting around** Safaris from Nairobi to the parks and lakes; self-drive; buses and *matatus* link the towns; fly-in or drive-in safaris to the Masai Mara.

**Time required** From Nairobi 1 week for the lakes and parks at Naivasha, Nakuru, Bogoria and Baringo; at least 2 nights in the Masai Mara.

**Weather** Overall, the climate is gentle with temperatures rarely above 25°C. Cool season is May-Sep.

**When not to go** All year round, but roads in the Masai Mara deteriorate rapidly in the wet seasons (Nov-Dec, Mar-May).

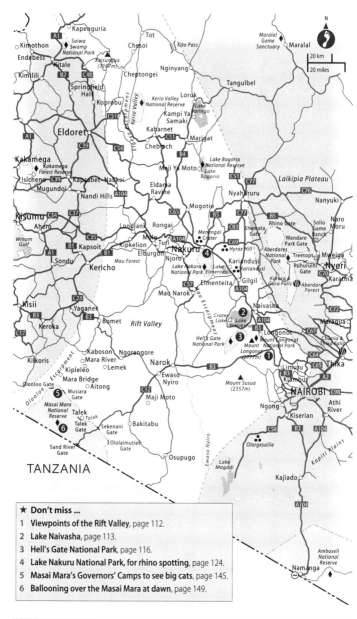

★ Don't miss ...
1 Viewpoints of the Rift Valley, page 112.
2 Lake Naivasha, page 113.
3 Hell's Gate National Park, page 116.
4 Lake Nakuru National Park, for rhino spotting, page 124.
5 Masai Mara's Governors' Camps to see big cats, page 145.
6 Ballooning over the Masai Mara at dawn, page 149.

The Great Rift Valley is one of the most dramatic features on earth, stretching some 6000 km from the Dead Sea in Jordan down to Mozambique in the south. In Kenya, the Rift Valley starts at Lake Turkana in the north, and runs right through the centre of the country. Up to 100 km wide in places, the floor is littered with the famous Rift Valley lakes, such as Nakuru, Naivasha, Baringo and Bogoria, which are surrounded by fascinating cliffs, escarpments, rivers and arid plains. These support an enormous diversity of wildlife, birds, trees and plants. The valley floor rises from around 200 m at Lake Turkana to about 1900 m above sea level at Lake Naivasha to the south.

In the south of the region the Masai Mara, bordering the Serengeti in Tanzania, is one of the most exciting game parks in the world, teeming with wildlife and the site of the quite spectacular wildebeest migration. It is also the most likely place in Kenya to see lions.

No visit to Kenya is complete without spending some time in the Rift Valley. The scenery here is wonderful, with Mount Kilimanjaro acting as the perfect backdrop to miles of arid savannah plains covered with fragile grasslands and scrub bush. Evaporation has left a high concentration of alkaline volcanic deposits in the remaining water. The algae and crustaceans that thrive in the soda lakes are ideal food for flamingos and many of these beautiful birds are attracted here, forming a truly spectacular display.

# Naivasha and around

*Lake Naivasha is a popular weekend destination from Nairobi and there are some excellent accommodation options around its shores. The drive there too is very pleasant with good views of the Rift Valley and Moi South Lake Road runs through pretty countryside and flower farms. In recent years, wildlife numbers in the region have increased thanks to better protection and some re-stocking projects on the private sanctuaries and reserves. It's also a region where there are no large predators, so walking is an option in Hell's Gate National Park and Crescent Island Game Sanctuary. To stroll among zebra and giraffe is a delightful experience.* ▸▸ *For listings, see pages 118-121.*

## Nairobi to Naivasha ☺ ▸▸ *pp118-121.*

### Ins and outs

There are two roads connecting Nairobi and Navaisha; the A104 and the B3. Both roads are tarred, although potholed, and are very busy routes, since they are the main artery between the country's capital, the Rift Valley and ultimately Uganda. The A104 Nairobi–Nakuru road is the starting route for many safaris, so many of visitors get their first sight of the Kenyan landscape from here. Your first glimpse of the huge Rift Valley emptiness is likely to be from the viewpoints just past Limuru, at the top of the escarpments of the valley. Below, the acacia-scattered Kedong Valley bed conveys a neat and archetypal snapshot of the African landscape. Further away, you get a glimpse of Mount Longonot, Hell's Gate National Park and Lake Naivasha, while the plains seem to sweep on forever to the south.

Vehicles of 10 tonnes and over are not permitted on the A104 and instead are routed along the lower B3 road before joining the B4 to the north of Naivasha. This heavy traffic makes it a dangerous route with a high accident rate, so take care if driving. From the old Nairobi–Naivasha road (B3 – the more westerly road), which forks to the left at Rironi, the road continues in a northwesterly direction for approximately 6 km then turns left on a sealed tarmac road in a southwesterly direction around Mount Longonot. The road leads to the small town of Narok, see page 140, the main access point to the Mara. Some interesting diversions along this route are listed below.

### Mount Suswa

From Nairobi, after a drive of about 17 km, a small dirt road leads to the south towards Mount Suswa, 2356 m, an easily accessed volcano in the heart of Masai country only 50 km outside Nairobi. It is not as well known as Mount Longonot to the north. The outer crater has been breached on the southern and eastern sides by volcanoes, and numerous lava flows are visible. This whole area is honeycombed with lava caves and there are many examples of obsidian pebbles and rocks. One of the caves, over 20 km long, is believed to be the longest in Kenya. The caves are home to several small mammals including bats, snake owls, rock hyrax and squirrels, and birds. If you visit the caves, take care as there are some concealed drops in the cave floor.

With a 4WD, it is possible to drive up to the floor of the outer of the two craters, approximately 10 km in diameter. The caldera floor is richly covered with grasses, from which the volcano takes its name. The Masai graze their cattle in this peaceful enclosure, also home to a variety of game. The ring-shaped inner crater has a diameter of approximately 5 km and is covered with dense vegetation. There is a large central lava plug. The inner crater edge offers a good ridge walk of about 1½ hours to the main summit, **Ol Donyo Onyoke**. Circumnavigation of the crater rim is possible, but can take up to eight hours because of the difficulty going over the sharp lava blocks and fields in the southeast section of the crater. It is possible to camp in the caves, but you must bring all supplies, including water, with you.

## Kiambu → Colour map 1, A4.

An indirect route to Naivasha, which need not add more than an hour to your overall journey time (if in your own car), is via Kiambu, a one-way commuter town, and **Limuru**, a lively market town. The drive to Kiambu is hilly but smooth, through corridors of high trees and past the **Windsor Golf and Country Club**. Although neither town is particularly attractive, the Kiambu–Limuru road provides a quite beautiful 30-minute drive through lush, fertile land full of rich tea and coffee plantations, and dotted with the elegant, umbrella-like thorn trees.

This area is on the lower slopes of the Aberdares, and the soil and climate are ideal for growing coffee, which was introduced in 1902. The action of water from many streams flowing southeast from the Kinangop Mountain (3900 m) to join the Athi River has divided the area into sheer ridges and deep valleys. There are several waterfalls in the higher areas.

It is also the centre of one of the main Kikuyu clans (the other is based on Nyeri). The Kiambu Kikuyu were particularly powerful during the presidency of Jomo Kenyatta, who came from this clan. Many displaced Masai refugees settled in this area after the Masai civil wars at the end of the 19th century, and in time intermarried with the Kikuyu people.

## Naivasha ⬤❶ ▸▸ pp118-121. Colour map 1, A4.

→ Phone code: 050.

Naivasha is a small trading centre just off the main road from Nairobi to Nakuru. It was traditionally used as grazing land by Masai, until they were displaced by European settlers at the turn of the 20th century. The most likely reason for stopping in Naivasha town is en route to either Lake Naivasha or Hell's Gate. There are few accommodation options in town and it is far nicer to stay near the lake, where there are resorts, campsites and hotels catering to all budgets. The best reason to stop is for the excellent **Belle Inn**, for fruit juices and pastries.

## Lake Naivasha ⬤❷❸ ▸▸ pp118-121. Colour map 1, A4.

→ Phone code: 050.

Lake Naivasha is one of the few fresh-water lakes in the Rift Valley. It is 170 sq km in size, at about 1890 m above sea level and is a lovely place to come for a weekend if you are staying in Nairobi as it is only a 1½-hour drive away. Strong afternoon winds cause the lake to get suddenly very rough and the local Masai called the lake *Nai'posha* meaning 'rough water', which the British later miss-spelled as Naivasha. Much of the lake is surrounded by forests of the yellow-barked acacia tree, full of birds and black and white colobus monkeys. Acacia were once called 'yellow fever trees' after explorers who camped under them caught malaria. The lake has no apparent outlet, but it is believed to drain underground, and is quite picturesque with floating islands of papyrus. There are hippos that come out onto the shore at night to graze, and there are many different types of waterbirds. The lake is dominated by the overshadowing Mount Longonot (2880 m), a partially extinct volcano in the adjacent national park (52 sq km). On the southern lakeshore, the road goes through a major flower-growing area. Owned by Brooke Bond among other flower growers, it is an important exporter and employs thousands of local people. The flowers are cut, chilled and then air freighted to Europe from the international airport at Eldoret.

## Ins and outs

The Moi South Lake Road is in good condition and has recently been re-tarred. Beyond the village of Kongoni it meets the back road to Nakuru or Moi North Lake Road where it turns into a dirt track that is only suitable for 4WD vehicles. If you are in a saloon car you will have to turn back from here and backtrack to the main Nairobi–Nakuru road. It is possible to come to spend a day at one of the lakeside hotels without staying the night (there may be a small charge or it may be free if you eat there). The lake itself is best explored by boat and a number of the hotels listed rent vessels out for hire. A motorboat can be hired for around US$15 per person per hour to go and see the pods of hippo and there are fish eagle nests near the yacht club. The twin-hulled launch from the Country Club on its 'ornithological cruise' often tries to entice the birds with fish. The evening cruise at about 1800 is a good time to see them. Alternatively you could work your way around the shore by bicycle, and there are a few places that rent out bikes.

## Background

The region was first settled in the 1930s by the notorious British 'Happy Valley' set who bought all the neighbouring farmland – much of which is still owned by white Kenyans. Around this time Lake Naivasha was also Kenya's international airport. Flying boats from Europe used to land on the water and even today, when the water is low, you can see the wooden posts that mapped out the runway. The lake is about 13 km across, but its waters are shallow with an average depth of 5 m. At the beginning of the 20th century, Naivasha inexplicably completely dried up and the land was farmed, until heavy rains a few years later caused the lake to return.

## Sights

**Crescent Island Game Sanctuary** ① *US$20 per person plus boat across the lake*. Morning and evening walks can be made here, a protected reserve where you can walk amongst zebra, antelope and giraffe that come to the water's edge to drink. It is located at the eastern shore of the lake near the Lake Naivasha Country Club, and it is not actually an island, as it is connected to the mainland by a sliver of land. There are no predators so this is one of the few places in Kenya offering the opportunity to walk amongst the animals. Trips can be arranged at the **Lake Naivasha Country Club**, **Fisherman's Camp** or **Fish Eagle Inn**.

**Elsamere** ① *Moi South Lake Rd, 22 km from Naivasha, T050-202 1055, www.elsatrust.org, daily 1500-1800, US$8 includes copious amounts of tea*. A few metres past **Fisherman's Camp** and **Fish Eagle Inn** is Elsamere, the former home of George and Joy Adamson (see box, page 220). It is easy to miss, so look out for the sign to the Olkaria Gate of Hell's Gate; it is a few hundred metres further on the right-hand side. There is a small **museum** with first editions of her books, her typewriter, her dress that she wore for the premier of *Born Free* in London and a selection of her paintings (although the best of her paintings of the various tribes of Kenya hang in the State House in Nairobi). The gardens are very pleasant with lots of birds and black and white colobus monkeys flying among the trees, though in recent years some of the giant acacia trees have had to be felled because of disease. It is open daily in the afternoon for afternoon tea and a video. The aged film shows the life (and death) of Joy. Beware though it lasts well over an hour! Worth sitting through though for the tea – tables in the house are laden with scones, jam and cream, dainty sandwiches, home-made cookies, slices of cake and pots of tea and coffee. See also Sleeping, page 120.

# Lake Naivasha & Hell's Gate

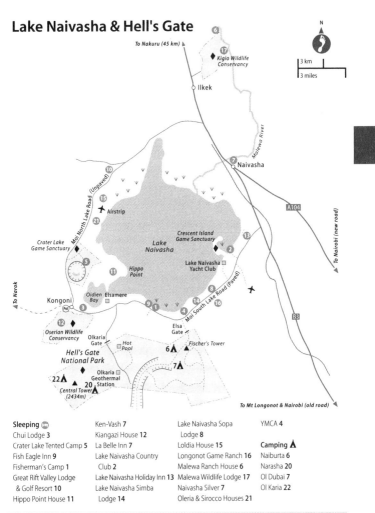

**Sleeping**
Chui Lodge **3**
Crater Lake Tented Camp **5**
Fish Eagle Inn **9**
Fisherman's Camp **1**
Great Rift Valley Lodge & Golf Resort **10**
Hippo Point House **11**

Ken-Vash **7**
Kiangazi House **12**
La Belle Inn **7**
Lake Naivasha Country Club **2**
Lake Naivasha Holiday Inn **13**
Lake Naivasha Simba Lodge **14**

Lake Naivasha Sopa Lodge **8**
Loldia House **15**
Longonot Game Ranch **16**
Malewa Ranch House **6**
Malewa Wildlife Lodge **17**
Naivasha Silver **7**
Oleria & Sirocco Houses **21**

YMCA **4**

**Camping** ▲
Naiburta **6**
Narasha **20**
Ol Dubai **7**
Ol Karia **22**

**Oserian Wildlife Conservancy** ① *T050-202 0792, www.oserianwildlife.com, access is only for guests of the lodges.* Further south of Elsamere the road passes around Oidien Bay, a bottleneck in the extreme southwest corner of the lake, and reaches the village of Kongoni and the turn-off to **Chui Lodge** and **Kiangazi House** (see under Sleeping, page 118). For a few kilometres before Kongoni, the road passes through the Oserian Game Corridor, which allows game to move from Hell's Gate to the lakeshore and is part of the private Oserian Wildlife Conservancy, where the fences on the private land have been removed allowing the game in the area to move freely. If you are not staying, you are likely to see zebra and antelope from the road. The Oserian Wildlife Conservancy is a private reserve that was formed in 1996 on what was formerly a dairy and beef ranch of 1420 ha. The revised management plan was to create a wildlife sanctuary with emphasis on protection of all biodiversity and to create a sustainable ecotourism destination. Wildlife was present on the land but numbers were declining. There are two upmarket accommodation options within the conservancy, and the profits generated by these go towards conservation of the area. In recent years several species have been introduced including Grevy zebra, Beisa oryx and greater kudu, which all came from their native Northern Kenya, and wildebeest and topi were translocated from the Masai Mara. In 1996, six white rhino were introduced and have bred successfully and numbers now on the conservancy are presently 13. The owners of the sanctuary also own the nearby Oserian Flower farm, which among other blooms grows roses and carnations and is the biggest flower-growing operation on the lakeshore.

**Crater Lake Game Sanctuary** ① *US$3.50.* West of Lake Naivasha, one hour's walk from Kongoni and approximately 17 km past **Fisherman's Camp** is Crater Lake. Its often jade-coloured waters are quite breathtaking and it is held in high regard by the local Masai who believe its water helps soothe ailing cattle. There is an animal sanctuary, but some of the tracks in this area are only manageable by foot or with a 4WD. There is a pleasant two-hour nature trail to the lake, you are allowed to walk around by yourself and it's easy to see the rare black and white colobus monkey. Besides the impressive 150 bird species recorded here, giraffe, zebra and other plains wildlife are also regular residents, but if walking, remember that buffaloes lurk in the woods. It is possible to cycle to the game park, although the soft, dusty track after Kongoni is hard going.

---

## Hell's Gate National Park 🌐 ›› *pp118-121. Colour map 1, A4.*

① *Access is south of the YMCA at Lake Naivasha, through Elsa Gate or Olkaria Gate, south of Elsamere, T050-202 0284, www.kws.org. Park entry fee is US$25, children US$10 per day.*
About 90 km from Nairobi and 14 km southeast of Lake Naivasha is this national park, a major attraction in the Rift Valley. It is one of the few parks you are allowed to explore on foot, with bicycles and motorcycles allowed too, all offering excellent ways of exploring its 68 sq km. The flora is mainly grasslands and shrubland with several species of acacias. It is famous for its water geysers, as well as being a breeding area for Verreaux's eagles and Ruppell's vultures. Lammergeyers have also been spotted hovering over the dramatic cliffs of Hell's Gate Gorge. A feature of this landscape is the lustrous acid-resistant volcanic glass, called obsidian, formed from cooled molten lava.

The route through the park is spectacular, leading through a gorge lined with sheer red cliffs and containing two volcanic plugs – **Fischer's Tower** and **Central Tower**. The park is small and, although there is a wide variety of wildlife – including eland, giraffe, zebra, impala and gazelle – you may not see many of them as they are few in number. What you will see though is the incredibly tame hyrax that looks like a type of guinea-pig but is actually more closely related to the elephant, and a host of different birds of prey.

Within the park is the substantial **Olkaria Geothermal Station** generating power from underground – lots of large pipes and impressive steam vents in the hills. Near Central Tower is a smaller lower gorge that extends out of the park to the south. Here is a ranger post where drinks and sodas can be purchased, and a path that descends steeply into the gorge. The path skirts along the river in the bottom, into which hot springs in the cliffs flow, and then climbs back to the ranger post. While in the gorge you can branch off into an even smaller gorge that has high, water-eroded walls that are so narrow in places that the sky is almost blocked out. After about 700 m there is a high wall that will force you to turn back, but on your return you will get a great view of Central Tower rising up.

## Kigio Wildlife Conservancy ● ▸▸ pp118-121.

ⓘ *www.kigio.com, access only to guests at the lodges.*
This is another former cattle and dairy farm that now operates as a private wildlife conservancy. Located in the hills to the northeast of Naivasha off the road to Nakuru, it covers 1420 ha and has breathtaking views of the Rift Valley, Mount Longonot and Lake Naivasha. Guests can walk or cycle amongst the wildlife and birds, or enjoy a splash in the Malewa River that runs through the conservancy.

The last remaining giraffe in the Naivasha region died as a result of poaching in 1996. Following an application by the management to the Kenya Wildlife Service, the request to relocate Rothschild's giraffe to the conservancy was granted, provided the property was fenced. Funding for this was sourced amongst others, from the European Union, and the Born Free Foundation. With these facilities in place, eight Rothschild's giraffe were relocated from Lake Nakuru in 2002. The entire event was filmed by the BBC for the *Born to be Wild* series. The giraffe have settled well and the population now numbers 29. The conservancy also has around 300 identified bird species, including the reputedly largest population of grey crested helmet shrikes in the world, and is home to 45 different mammals, including leopard, topi, hippo, spotted hyena, most of the plains game and a 200-strong herd of buffalo. In 1996, the large mammal count was only about 100, but today it is up to 3500, so the conservancy has been an exceptional success.

## Mount Longonot National Park ▸▸ *Colour map 1, A4.*

ⓘ *www.kws.org, daily 0600-1800, park entry fee US$20, children US$10 per day.*
This 52-sq-km park encompasses Mount Longonot, which is a dormant volcano standing at 2886 m. The name is derived from the Masai word 'Oloonong'ot' meaning mountains of many spurs or steep ridges. The mountain cone is made up of soft volcanic rock that has eroded into deep clefts, v-shaped valleys and ridges. There is little vegetation on the stony soil. However, the crater is very lush and green, with fairly impenetrable trees. There are fine views over the Rift Valley on one side and into the enormous crater on the other. To climb Mount Longonot you need to get to Longonot village, about 12 km south of Naivasha town along the old road; from there it is about 6 km to the base of the mountain. There is a marked gate, where there is a secure parking area and Kenya Wildlife Services office. You can be escorted up by Kenya Wildlife Service rangers and the fairly straightforward climb takes about an hour, but be prepared for the last section which is quite steep. A wander round the rim of the mountain takes a further two to three hours.

## ◉ Naivasha and around listings

*For Sleeping and Eating price codes and other relevant information, see Essentials pages 34-38.*

## ◉ Sleeping

There is plenty of excellent accommodation in this popular and expanding weekend retreat for Nairobians, although there is little of attraction in Naivasha itself except for **La Belle Inn**; its far nicer to stay near the lakeshore. Some of the accommodation is exceptional and thanks to the conservation projects in the region, increased game numbers has caused a mushrooming of game lodges.

Lake Naivasha is home to several hundred hippos. At the lakeshore hotels, lodges and campsites, be very wary of the hippos that feed in the grounds at night. There have been accidents, including a fatality in 2005, from people getting too close.

### Naivasha *p113*

**D La Belle Inn**, Moi Av, T050-202 1007, labelleinn@kenyaweb.com. Popular place with very attentive staff and a selection of comfortable rooms at different prices, all including huge and very good breakfast (fresh fruit juice, croissants, home-made jam, butter, bacon, eggs and lots of coffee). This is an institution in Kenya and the large terrace restaurant is an excellent place to stop for a break from driving for the selection of pastries, sandwiches, pies, cakes and full meals (many vegetarian, which is unusual for Kenya). The hotel also has 3 lively bars, and contains the Naivasha Business Centre, with internet access.
**F Ken-Vash Hotel**, Posta Lane, just up from Moi Av, T050-203 1503. The best of the basic hotels in an enormous white building, the tallest in town, with spacious and comfortable rooms with balconies, and friendly staff. It has a good, cheap restaurant and a lively bar.
**F Naivasha Silver Hotel**, Kenyatta Av, T050-202 0580. Above the **Jolly Café**, basic but clean and comfortable rooms with hot water, serving African staples and beer.

### Lake Naivasha *p113, map p115*

**L Chui Lodge**, Oserian Wildlife Conservancy, T050-202 0792, www.oserianwildlife.com. Exclusive lodge overlooking a waterhole with the dramatic Mau Escarpment as a backdrop, crafted from simple bush stone, local acacia and olive woods. The 8 individual and well-spaced cottages each has a veranda with its own view, log fire, marble bathroom and 4-poster beds. Features a heated swimming pool, Japanese Teppanyaki hot plate and African antiques.
**L Hippo Point House**, at Hippo Point to the southwest of the lake, T050-202 1295, www.hippo-pointkenya.com. From around US$600 per person, this is 1 of the most expensive places to stay on the lake, which has 2 private homes, the unusual 35-m-high Hippo Point Tower, which has room for 9 guests on 8 floors, and Hippo Point House, an old colonial house with 8 rooms for up to 14 guests. Built in 1933 and lovingly restored in 1998 to the highest standards. The cuisine is superb, game drives are included, horse riding, sailing, water-skiing and day trips are also available and there's a swimming pool. Closed May.
**L Kiangazi House**, also in Oserian Wildlife Conservancy, T050-202 0792, www.oserian wildlife.com. Delightful gardens, rolling lawns, swimming pool, private country house with 3 double rooms in the house and 2 doubles and 1 single room in garden cottages, satellite TV lounge and library, tennis court and gourmet food in the dining room. A salt lick and waterhole is excellently located at the bottom of the garden and attracts the local game and game drives are included in the rates.
**L Loldia House**, a prestigious Governors' Camp, book through an agent or at www.governorscamp.com. Among Kenya's oldest farms on the western shore, with lush lawns that run down to the lakeshore, with 8 en suite rooms in the main house or in garden cottages, colonial style with original furniture. Very atmospheric; you'll experience the life of Kenya's early settlers – the ranch was

established by a family who trekked by ox-wagon from South Africa a century ago, and the property is still owned by their descendants. Rates from US$560 for a double.

**L Longonot Game Ranch**, www.sama wati.co.ke. A local homestay situated on the 324-sq-km Kedong Game Ranch, overlooking Lake Naivasha off the South Lake Rd. Beautiful and rustic, small groups of up to 6 people are catered for. Rooms are very comfortable with en suite bathrooms. If you want to see some wildlife on horseback, this would be a good option.

**L Oleria and Sirocco Houses**, Moi North Lake Rd near the airstrip and Loldia House, reservations Nairobi T020-334 868, www.olerai.com. Oleria and Sirocco are the homes of Iain Douglas-Hamilton and his wife Oria. Iain is a leading conservation specialist who has been instrumental in protecting elephants in Kenya for decades (see also Elephant Watch Safari Camp at Samburu on page 359). The houses have been the family's home for many years. Accommodation is in very tranquil garden cottages decked with crawling vines and flowers, or in superbly luxurious rooms in the main houses. Rates are around US$300 per person per day, and are all inclusive of drinks and food. Activities include *pirogue* trips on Lake Naivasha with the Masai.

**A Great Rift Valley Lodge and Golf Resort**, about 11 km from Naivasha on the northern lakeshore road, best accessed from the main Nairobi–Nakuru road, reservations through **Heritage Hotels**, Nairobi, T020-444 6651, www.heritage-eastafrica.com. Perched on the panoramic shoulder of the Eburu Escarpment overlooking Lake Naivasha and home to Kenya's newest championship 18-hole golf course. Private airstrip, 2 clay tennis courts, swimming pool, activities include walking and horse-riding safaris and fishing. Accommodation is in 30 twin and double rooms with private balconies, 4-poster beds, luxurious furnishings, 2 bars, very good food.

**B Crater Lake Tented Camp**, Crater Lake Game Sanctuary, reservations though **Merica Hotels**, Nairobi, T020-316 696,

www.mericagrouphotels.com. This small camp has a great position on the shores of the lake and is near the grave of Lady Diana Delamere, the 11 tents sit in secluded clearings in the lakeside forest with sweeping views, good food, a fully stocked bar and overall a relaxing spot, although it may lose its exclusivity as the owner recently died and its now marketed as a local conference venue through **Merica Hotels**. The honeymoon suite has a sunken bath and 4-poster bed.

**B Lake Naivasha Country Club**, reservations Nairobi T020-445 0693, www.kenyahotels ltd.com/lake. This 22-ha property boasts green lawns shaded by mature acacias and spreading fever trees that stretch down to the lakeshore. Although the rooms are overdue for refurbishment the amenities are good and include a swimming pool, and it's one of the cheaper options on the lakeshore at around US$210 for a double. The reception area has been recently renovated. Children are welcome and there is a small adventure playground. Good food with an excellent buffet lunch on Sun (on lawns if the weather is good) – eat as much as you like for around US$14 – only drawback is it often gets crowded with tour groups from Nairobi. Boat trips are on offer and you can hire bicycles.

**B Lake Naivasha Simba Lodge**, reservations Nairobi, T020-434 3960, www.mara simba.com. Opened in 2003, this is a large modern lodge built in expansive grounds full of giant acacia trees. 70 rooms in several blocks of stone buildings with slate roofs, disabled rooms, heated swimming pool, restaurant and pub, bike hire, tennis courts, and a health club with gym, massage and sauna. A good set-up but primarily a conference venue so give it a miss if there is a large conference on.

**B Lake Naivasha Sopa Lodge**, reservations Nairobi T020-375 0235, www.sopa lodges.com. Part of the popular Sopa safari lodge group, this is a large lakeside resort with 84 very attractive rooms built in a crescent of cottages, some interconnecting and 1 with disabled facilities. The stunning lobby and bar has high ceilings, wrought-iron chandeliers and 3 fireplaces, the restaurant opens up to the manicured gardens and there's a lovely swimming pool.

**C Elsamere**, Moi South Lake Rd, 22 km from Naivasha, T050-202 1055, www.elsatrust.org. Joy and George Adamson's house (see page 114). The conservation centre provides accommodation for 16 people in cottages set in the gardens around the main house. The rooms are bright and attractive and all have en suite bathrooms. Guests may also choose to stay in the main house in the Joy Adamson bedroom (has easy wheelchair access). Dinner is hosted each night and it is the perfect opportunity to get to know other guests, many of whom may be visiting researchers and conservationists, no bar but guests are invited to bring their own alcohol.

**D Lake Naivasha Holiday Inn**, roughly 3 km down the lakeshore road from the turn-off, reservations Nairobi, T020-359 2627, www.lakenaivashaholidayinn.com. There are 25 comfortable rustic en suite rooms here in cottages or in a delightful thatched old farmhouse, each is individually decorated and have mosquito nets. Facilities include a bar and restaurant and a fire is lit in the outdoor pit in the evening. Pretty gardens. You can organize boat trips from here.

**D-F Fish Eagle Inn**, 20 km from Naivasha on Moi South Lake Rd, T050-2030306, www.fish eagleinn.co.ke. Decent *bandas* available, as well as small but clean dorms made with local materials, and camping facilities. There is an excellent swimming pool, steam room, sauna and gym available at extra cost. Hippos come out of the water at night and graze a stone's throw away and staff can organize boat rides and bicycle hire. There's a good and affordable terrace restaurant and bar.

**E-F Fisherman's Camp**, next door to **Fish Eagle Inn**, T050-2030 088, www.fisher manscamp.com. This is set in beautiful surroundings, shaded by huge acacia trees. There are comfortable *bandas* with reasonable facilities including showers, bed linen and electricity. There are also cheaper spartan dorm-type bunks. Camping is on

springy grass beneath the huge arms of the trees, with showers and toilets in tin sheds, and a communal washing-up area and tents can be hired. Hot water is available in the evenings. There is also a bar and restaurant in a rustic thatched shed. Motor boat trips to Crescent Island can be arranged with plenty of time for walking before the ride back. Recommended budget option.

**F YMCA**, 14 km from Naivasha on Moi South Lake Rd, T020-205 0109, www.kenya ymca.org. This is the closest accommodation to the main gate of Hell's Gate National Park but is a good 15 mins from the lakeside, set in beautiful gardens. It's sometimes possible to buy provisions here such as fish, eggs and firewood and plates of local food can be arranged. Accommodation is in dorms (you'll need bedding), simple *bandas* with bedding and you can also camp in the grounds. There are decent shared bathrooms with hot water.

**Hell's Gate National Park** *p116, map p115*
There are a few campsites within the park; **Narasha**, **Naiburta**, **Ol Dubai**, and **Ol Karia**, see map. Each has water and pit latrines. Contact the warden, T050-202 0284, or **Kenya Wildlife Services**, Nairobi, T020-600 800, www.kws.org.

**Kigio Wildlife Conservancy** *p117*
**L Malewa Ranch House**, reservations Nairobi T020-353 5878, www.malewaranch.com. To the northeast of the lake off the road to Nakuru, this is small exclusive 10-bed ranch house with a tin roof that can be rented as a whole with country-style floral decor and Persian rugs on wooden floors. There's a large sitting room, open fire, spacious veranda, bar and dining area with views over the Malewa River. Rates from US$485 for a double and include all meals and game activities.

**L Malewa Wildlife Lodge**, reservations Nairobi T020-374 8369, www.kigio.com. A small exclusive 'eco-friendly' lodge, with cottages nestled in the shade of huge acacia trees, and 4 river suites built on stilts over the Malewa River. Rates are full board with very good cuisine, and walking or cycling are on offer. The beds, tables and chairs are constructed using the timbers from old fencing posts taken from the former cattle ranch that was on the conservancy.

## ❼ Eating

All the hotels have their own restaurants; many are extremely good. In Naivasha itself **La Belle Inn** is easily the best place to eat whatever your budget. There is a stall opposite that sells fresh fish and crayfish. See Sleeping, above, for more information.

## ❽ Transport

### Mount Suswa *p112*
*Matatus* serve the B3 Narok Rd, but there is little traffic or hitching opportunities along the last 12 km south on rough unmade roads. The road skirts the northeast flank of the mountain until it reaches a crossroad. Turn right here along a rough track until you reach a group of *manyattas* (Masai villages) that extend over a distance of 1.5 km. From here a rough track leads up to the caldera. The only identifying marks are the deeply grooved water channels lying to the sides of the track. The distance to the caldera is approximately 7 km. Turn left for the caves or right to reach the inner crater, a distance of another 8 km.

### Lake Naivasha *p113, map p115*
If you are coming by road from Nairobi there are 2 routes. The 1st is along the old road that nowadays is the preserve of hundreds of lorries driving between Mombasa and Uganda. The road is poor, although the views are great and you are likely to see herds of zebra and other wildlife roaming the vast valley. The other route is along the new A104 road that does not come into Naivasha town. It is in good condition and has the advantage of having the most wonderful views of the Rift Valley.

There is regular public transport between Naivasha, **Nairobi** and **Nakuru**(1½ hrs). Buses and *matatus* arrive and depart at the bus stand on Kariuki Chotara Rd in Naivasha. There are also regular *matatus* from the centre of town along the southern lakeshore road as far as **Kongoni**.

There is bike hire available from various places from around US$10 a day, greatly increasing your options for exploration, particularly to Hell's Gate National Park. Try **Fisherman's Camp** and **Fish Eagle Inn**, or the stall at the turn-off to the Elsa Gate of Hell's Gate National Park.

## ❶ Directory

**Lake Naivasha** *p113, map p115*
**Banks** Barclays Bank and **Kenya Commercial Bank**, are both on Moi Av, and will change money and have ATMs. **Internet** From **Naivasha Business Centre** at La Belle Inn. **Post office** On Moi Av. **Securicor**, along Moi Av, offers **DHL** parcel services.

# Nakuru and around

*Nakuru is the largest town in the Rift Valley lakes region and is a good place to stock up on provisions and browse in the good curio market. It's also on the edge of the Lake Nakuru National Park, which is one of Kenya's most popular parks to visit thanks to its accessibility and proximity to Nairobi. The chances of seeing animals like rhino and leopard here are much better than in other parks and reserves and the flamingos on the lake itself, and other lakes in the region, are a spectacular sight.* ▶▶ *For listings, see pages 129-133.*

## Lake Elementeita ● ▶▶ *pp129-133. Colour map 1, A3/4.*

From Naivasha the road continues towards Nakuru, a 1½-hour drive, via the uninspiring town of **Gilgil**. The small 18-sq-km lake is the notable attraction on this route. Elementeita

## Nakuru

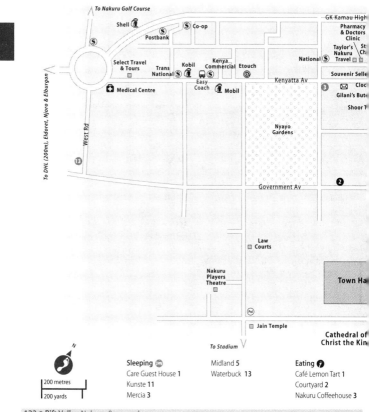

| Sleeping ⬤ | Midland 5 | Eating ⬤ |
| --- | --- | --- |
| Care Guest House 1 | Waterbuck 13 | Café Lemon Tart 1 |
| Kunste 11 | | Courtyard 2 |
| Mercia 3 | | Nakuru Coffeehouse 3 |

200 metres
200 yards

lies in the shadow of an impressively peaked hill known locally by the Masai as the 'Sleeping Warrior' and is roughly halfway between Naivasha and Nakuru, just off the main road. It is a shallow soda lake, similar to Lake Nakuru, although it does not attract such enormous numbers of flamingos, which apparently fled due to encroachment by pelicans; Elmenteita is now one of Kenya's main breeding grounds for the great white pelican. Other birds include the great egret, great crested grebe, maccoa duck, and in total about 450 species of bird live in and around the lake. It was designated as a **RAMSAR** wetland of international importance in 2005. (The **RAMSAR** treaty, signed in 1971, ensures the conservation of wetlands.) As it is not a national park, you can walk around it and you don't have to pay. Most of the safaris covering the trip from Naivasha to Nakuru only stop at the viewpoint overlooking the lake on the main road.

Near the lake are several prehistoric sites, indicating that this area was once densely populated. The best-known archaeological site is **Gambles Cave**, 10 km southwest of Elmenteita. There are few facilities at the lake or in Elmenteita town, but it is an easy day

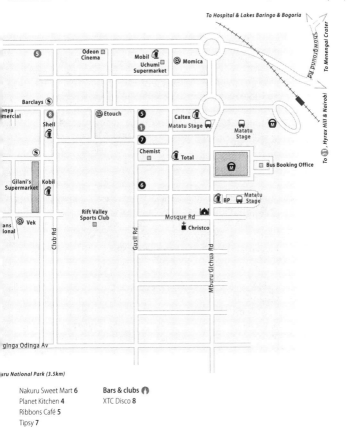

Nakuru Sweet Mart **6**
Planet Kitchen **4**
Ribbons Café **5**
Tipsy **7**

**Bars & clubs** 🏠
XTC Disco **8**

trip from Nakuru with direct *matatus* (one hour) or 30 minutes from Gilgil. It is an easy walk from the main road down to the edge of the lake, but fairly steep coming back up. Be very wary of driving too close to the lake down this track as it's easy to get a vehicle stuck in the ground. **Kariandusi** ① *www.museums.or.ke, daily 0930-1800, US$7.50, children (under 18) US$3.50*, is a prehistoric site of the Acheulean period to the right of the Naivasha–Nakuru road (A104) discovered by Dr L Leakey in 1928 and excavated from 1929 to 1947. Studies suggest that it was not an area of permanent habitation and the findings indicate that the people who lived here were of the genus *Homo erectus*. There is a small museum housing obsidian knives, Stone Age hand axes and a molar of the straight-tusked elephant, a variety that roamed in Northern Europe before extinction. The nearby diatomite (a type of algae) mine produces a white stuff used for paints, insulation and as a face paint by the Masai.

## Nakuru ●❷🐾⛰️●●❸ ›› *pp129-133. Colour map 1, A3.*

→ *Phone code: 051.*

The next major town along from Naivaisha, Nakuru is Kenya's fourth-largest town and is in the centre of some of the country's best farming land. It is a pleasant, slightly dusty agricultural town with many supermarkets, and shops mostly selling farming equipment and supplies and the main crops grown around town include coffee, barley, maize and wheat. Indeed, the name derives from a Masai word meaning 'place of dust'. Although its history can be dated back to the prehistoric period thanks to archaeological findings at Hyrax Hill, modern Nakuru came into existence in 1900 when the building of the railway opened up access to the surrounding lush countryside attracting hundreds of white settlers to the area. Lord Delamere, one of the most famous figures in colonial times, collected around 600 sq km of land here and developed wheat and dairy farming. The 2007 post-election violence took its toll on this town and many buildings were burnt down.

### Ins and outs

There are frequent buses and *matatus* from just about everywhere in the highlands region of Kenya to and from Nakuru. The main road from Nairobi passes by Naivasha and Gilgil and Lake Elmenteita on the way. Nakuru town itself is compact enough to walk around, though *boda bodas*, regular taxis and the odd *tuk-tuk* are available to get around. Many of the more upmarket hotels and lodges in the region can arrange transfers to and from Nairobi.

### Sights

The only notable building in town is the **Rift Valley Sports Club** ① *T051-221 2085*. This was formerly the Nakuru Club, first built in 1907, burnt down in 1924 and then restored. A patio restaurant looks out over the cricket pitch. The cricket pavilion has photos of past teams and the ground is prettily surrounded by jacarandas and mango trees. In the Men's Bar (women still not allowed) there are sporting prints and etchings. Tennis, squash and a small swimming pool are available as well as cricket nets for a small fee for non-members.

## Lake Nakuru National Park ● ›› *pp129-133. Colour map 1, A3.*

① *T051-224 4069, www.kws.org, 0600-1900, park entry fees per day US$60, children US$30.*
This national park is just 4 km south of Nakuru town in central Kenya and 140 km northwest of Nairobi. It was established in 1960 as the first bird sanctuary in Africa to

protect the flamingos and the other birds in the hills and plains around the lake. It covers 188 sq km and the lake is fringed by swamp, and surrounded by dry savannah. The upper areas within the national park are forested. The lake itself is in the centre of the park surrounded by huge white salt crusts, whose surface area varies from five to 40 sq km.

## Ins and outs

Game viewing is very easy and rewarding here, and the whole park can be driven around in half a day. You will need to be in a vehicle, although you are allowed to get out at the picnic and camp sites. If you don't have your own car the most logical way of exploring is by picking up a taxi in Nakuru and negotiating a price for half a day, which obviously can be shared among a group. Alternatively arrange an excursion through **Shoor Travel** on Moi Road. The most frequent way of accessing the park is through the Main Gate, 4 km south of Nakuru centre, next to the park's headquarters, where you can also obtain and reload your Smartcard. From Kenyatta Avenue, take Moi Road and turn left to Stadium Road, which will lead you right to the gate. Here there is also a map on a board showing the spots of the latest animal sightings. If you come from Nairobi and you want to avoid Nakuru altogether, you can enter the park through Lanet Gate, although this is not very well signposted off the main road. The turn-off is about 3 km before you reach town. Finally, Nderit Gate lies at the east side of the park, close to **Lake Nakuru Lodge**. This is a suitable way for visitors arriving from Mau Narok or Lake Elmenteita on the back road. The park's tracks are usually well kept, although you may find some mud during the rains. The main road circles the lake completely. The north drive is very busy and is hence less interesting for wildlife viewing. The biggest stretch of land in the park is located south of the lake. There is a track network here which is much less visited and where you will have the chance to see some of the park's herbivores, such as Rothschild's giraffe, black and white rhino and eland.

## Sights

The blue-green algae *Spirulina platensis* flourishes in the alkaline waters and is a primary food source for the flamingo

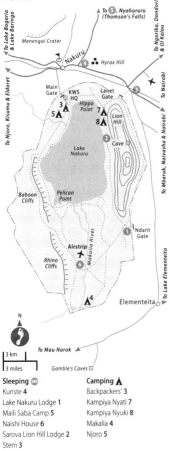

# Lake Nakuru National Park

To Lake Bogoria & Lake Baringo

To ⑤, Nyahururu (Thomson's Falls)

Menengai Crater

Nakuru

To Njoro, Kisumu & Eldoret

To Ngorika, Dondori & Ol Kalou

④ Hyrax Hill

To Nairobi

Main Gate

KWS HQ

Lanet Gate

3▲ 5▲

Hippo Point

7▲ 8▲

Lion Hill

② Cave

Lake Nakuru

To Mbaruk, Naivasha & Nairobi

Baboon Cliffs

Pelican Point

Ndarit Gate

Rhino Cliffs

Airstrip

Makalia River

⑥

▲4

To Lake Elementeita

Elementeita

N

3 km
3 miles

To Mau Narok

Gamble's Caves

**Sleeping** 🛏
Kunste **4**
Lake Nakuru Lodge **1**
Maili Saba Camp **5**
Naishi House **6**
Sarova Lion Hill Lodge **2**
Stem **3**

**Camping** ▲
Backpackers' **3**
Kampiya Nyati **7**
Kampiya Nyuki **8**
Makalia **4**
Njoro **5**

population. Both the lesser and greater flamingo is present. In 1958 alkaline-tolerant *Tilapia grahami* were introduced to the lake to try to curb the problem of malaria in the nearby town. **Fish eagles** appeared in this area shortly afterwards thanks to the abundant supply of these fish. There is a wide variety of wildlife: bat, colobus monkey, spring hare, otter, rock hyrax, hippo, buffalo, waterbuck, lion, hyena, and giraffe, but the most popular reason for visiting is the wonderful sight of hundreds of thousands of flamingos. At one time there were thought to be around two million flamingos here, about one third of the world's entire population, but the numbers have considerably diminished in recent years. Now, the number of flamingos varies from several thousand to a few hundred, depending on the water level and their frequent migration to the other lakes in the Rift Valley. Usually, the lake recedes during the dry season and floods during the wet season, and in recent years, there have been wide variations between the dry and wet seasons' water levels. It's suspected that this is caused by increasing watershed conversion to intensive crop production and urbanization, both which reduce the capacity of soil to absorb water, recharge groundwaters and increase seasonal flooding. This has caused the flamingos to migrate to other lakes; namely Elmenteita, Simbi Nyaima and Bogoria.

The best viewing point is from the **Baboon Cliffs** on the western shores of the lake. There are also more than 450 other species of bird here. Thousands of both little grebes and white winged black terns are seen as are stilts, avocets, ducks, and in the European winter the migrant waders. Another highlight is the very healthy population of black and white rhino; Nakuru was declared a sanctuary for the protection of these endangered animals in 1987. Both black and white rhino have been reintroduced, and the park has become the most successful refuge for rhino in East Africa – you'll literally trip over them here. There are quite a few leopard too, which are often, and unusually, spotted during the day in the acacia forest at the entrance to the park. Lion favour the savannah area to the south of the lake. In 1974 the endangered Rothchild's giraffe was introduced from the Soy plains of Eldoret where they have bred successfully. There are also a fair number of pythons, which may be seen crossing roads or dangling from trees. Because of its proximity to Nakuru town, the park is fenced, to stop the animals wandering into town and, previously, to stop poachers wandering into the park. It's so close to the city that it's not out of the ordinary to be watching a lion within the park, and at the same time watching a woman doing her washing outside her house beyond the fence! The advantage of being so close is that local people get to know the wildlife – the park buses in local school children for game drives.

## Hyrax Hill prehistoric site ›› *Colour map 1, A4.*

① *Just off the Nairobi Rd. www.museums. or.ke, 0930-1800, US$7.50, children (under 18) US$3.50. Take a matatu heading for Gilgil and ask to be dropped off at the turning for Hyrax Hill. It is about 1 km from here to the museum. You can camp here.*

About 4 km from Nakuru, Hyrax Hill contains Neolithic and Iron-Age burial pits and settlements, first investigated by the Leakeys in the 1920s and work has been going on there, periodically, ever since. The excavations have found evidence of seasonal settlements from 3000 years ago, and there are signs of habitation here up until about 300 years ago. The presence of beach sands is an indicator that Lake Nakuru may have extended right to the base of the hill in former times, turning Hyrax Hill into a peninsula or even an island. It is possible that 9000 years ago this vast prehistoric lake extended as far as Lake Elementeita. The hill was given its name during the early part of the 20th century, reflecting the abundance of hyraxes in the rocky fissures of the hill.

The northeast village has some enclosures where the digging was carried out although only one is not overgrown. It dates back about 400 years and the finds have been pieced together and are exhibited in the museum. There is no evidence of human dwelling suggesting this may have been used for livestock.

Up at the top of Hyrax Hill are the remains of a stone-walled fort and on the other side of the hill you can see the position of two huts in a settlement that has been dated back to the Iron Age. A series of burial pits with 19 skeletons were found, most of them decapitated, dating back to the same time. The remains are all in a heap and all appear to be young men suggesting they were buried in a hurry – possibly the remains of the enemy after a battle. On the path back to the museum, a *bau* board has been carved into the rock. One very curious find was six Indian coins dating back 500 years – no one knows how they got here.

Underneath the Iron Age site, a neolithic site was found and the neolithic burial mound has been fenced off as a display, the stone slab which sealed the mound having been removed. Nine female skeletons were found at the site. Unlike the male remains, the female remains have been buried with grave goods including dishes, pestles and mortars. No one can be sure why the women were buried with grave goods and not the men, but it could indicate that women were more politically powerful. Oral history in the region suggests this may have been the case. Why the Iron Age burial site is directly on top of the neolithic one also remains a mystery. Hyrax Hill was gazetted a National Monument in 1943. The **museum**, which contains artefacts from the site, was previously a farmhouse. Guides are on hand to take you around.

## Rongai ➤ *Colour map 1, A3.*

Rongai is a small, pretty village about 25 km west of the Nakuru in the valley of the Rongai River, which rises in the Elburgon Hills. Originally the area was inhabited by the Tugen and Njembs tribes, before they were driven out by the Masai. But the Masai never settled and there is no record of their ever constructing *manyatta* (Masai villages) in the valley.

### Ins and outs
Rongai is a short diversion off of the A104 Nakuru–Eldoret road. Numerous *matatus* go from Nakuru along the A104 past the turning to Rongai. Here you can swap for another going from the turn off to Rongai. From Nakuru there are also four or five direct *matatus* each day in both directions.

### Background
The land was part of the great tract leased to Lord Delamere, who then rented it out to settlers. In the colonial period Rongai grew to prominence as a maize-growing area. This crop was first introduced to Kenya by the Portuguese, but it did not do well. Then an American variety was used to develop a hybrid known as Kenya White, which flourished. The land was tilled by teams of oxen, maize was being exported by 1910, and by 1917 there were 3000 ha under maize around Rongai. The railway arrived in 1926 as part of the line onward from Nairobi to Uganda. A branch line was built from Rongai northeast to Solai, now disused, although you can still see the tracks. The branch went entirely through settler country and, as there was no 'native land' along the route, it was criticized as an example of the colonial administration favouring the interests of the settlers over those of the Africans.

## Sights

One notable feature of Rongai is the number of churches. **Africa Inland Church** has arched windows in pairs, glazed in yellow, green and orange, with sunrise airbricks above each pair. The walls are of grey volcanic stone, and it has a tin roof. The **Catholic Church of St Mary** is a modern, neat, functional structure of grey stone with timber panelling. **Heart of Christ Catholic Seminary**, dates from 1986, but is cloistered and quiet, with well-tended flower beds, run by Italian Fathers.

The prettiest of the churches, and a testament to the determination of the settlers to reproduce rural England on the equator, is **St Walstan's**, built in 1960. It is an exact replica of an early English (1016) country church at Bawburgh, 6 km east of Norwich in the UK. St Walstan is known as the 'Layman's Saint'. He came from a wealthy land-owning family, was fond of farm animals, and he insisted on working in the fields with the farm labourers. He collapsed and died while working one day, and a spring bubbled up on the very same spot. The church building has a square tower with battlements, pointed windows, and a shingle (wooden tile) roof. In the vestibule is a piece of flint from the church in Bawburgh. Inside there is a tiny gallery with steps up to it cut into the wall. The saints are depicted in orange, yellow and blue stained-glass windows. The roof is supported by timber beams and there is a small bell. The approach to the church is bordered by jacarandas that carpet the path with fallen blue blossoms when the trees are in flower.

## Menengai Crater ◉ ▸▸ pp129-133. Colour map 1, A3.

This extinct volcano on the northern side of Nakuru is 2490 m high and is the second-largest surviving volcanic crater in the world, with a surface area of 90 sq km. However, it is not easy to see it from the town. A sign erected at the highest point by the Rotary Club shows the distances and general directions of several places worldwide. The crater is 8 km from the main road. As you ascend, the views over Lake Nakuru are excellent, although it is not visible from the top. If walking, leave from the Crater Climb Road, then Forest Road (it takes a couple of hours but is pleasant enough). However, recent reports of robberies makes this a less safe option, and an alternative is to drive along Menengai Drive out through the suburbs. It is fairly well signposted. There is no public transport from the town to the Menengai Crater, and as few people visit it there is scant hope of hitching a lift.

In the 19th century the Menengai Crater was the site of a bloody battle between different Masai clans, vying for the pastures of the Rift Valley slopes and Naivasha. The Ilaikipiak Moran (warriors) were defeated by their southern neighbours the Ilpurko Masai, who reputedly threw the former over the crater edge. According to legend the fumaroles rising from the crater bed are the souls of the vanquished seeking to find the way to heaven. The Maa word *Menenga* means 'the dead'.

The views over Lake Nakuru are excellent as are the views towards Lake Bogoria over the other side. The crater itself is enormous, about 12 km across and 500 m deep. The mountain is surrounded by a nature reserve.

## Nyahururu and Thomson's Falls ◉ ▸▸ pp129-133. Colour map 1, A4.

→ Phone code: 065.

The small town of Nyahururu lies at high altitude (2360 m) with a splendid climate and is Kenya's highest town, surrounded by pretty tracts of forest and agricultural land, and the region benefits from high rainfall. The surrounding plateau is highly cultivated with maize, beans and sweet potatoes, which are well represented in Nyahururu's lively market. It originally served the colonial settler farmers in the area and was boosted when a branch line of the railway reached the town in 1929. This still runs, but only carries freight. In the post-war period the town was prosperous enough to boast a racecourse. Lately, flower farming has brought new life to Nyahururu. Although only a few kilometres north of the equator, nights can be cold, with occasional frosts in the early months of the year. Samuel Wanjiru, the long-distance runner and now Olympic marathon record holder and the first Kenyan to win the marathon at the Olympics in Beijing in 2008, calls Nyahururu home.

An explorer, Joseph Thomson, came across the waterfall to the north of the town in 1883 which he named Thomson's Falls after his father. He was the first European to walk from Mombasa to Lake Victoria. The cascade plunges 75 m, and is a pretty area to walk around. A stony path of sorts leads down to the bottom of the ravine. Do not attempt to go down any other way as the rocks on the side of the ravine are very loose. It's more commonly known as 'T-falls'. Upstream on the **Ewaso Narok River** is found one of Kenya's highest altitude hippo pools in an area of marshy bogland, about 2 km from the falls.

---

## ◉ Nakuru and around listings

*For Sleeping and Eating price codes and other relevant information, see Essentials pages 34-38.*

## ⊜ Sleeping

### Lake Elementeita *p122*
**B Sunbird Lodge**, 30 km south of Nakuru off the main road to Nairobi, T0723-702 181, www.sunbirdkenya.com. This is a new eco-lodge with 10 thatched chalets overlooking the lake with nice bathrooms with double sinks, wide wooden verandas, and 1 king size and 1 single bed in each room. The restaurant has sliding glass doors and fireplaces, buffet meals are included in the rates, swimming pool and local guided walks can be arranged.
**D Pink Lake Man's Ecolodge**, 30 km south of Nakuru off the main road to Nairobi, 1.5 km off the main road, T0721-842 811, www.pink lakeman.com. This is another new eco-lodge with 3 lovely wooden cottages set in a lush tract of woodland and each is surrounded with earthenware pots of flowering shrubs and there's a pleasant campsite (**F**) with hot showers. Bar and restaurant decorated with African touches, solar power, and locally managed by the affable Francis.

### Nakuru *p124, map p122*
Nakuru has a crop of basic board and lodgings, which are fairly dirty and dingy and best avoided as they are in the rough part of town on the of streets around Mosque Rd. Consider staying in Lake Nakuru National Park or one of the better larger hotels listed here instead.
**L Deloraine**, 33 km from Nakuru on the A104 (6 km northwest of the turning to Rongai), T062-31081, www.offbeatsafaris.com. On the Deloraine Estate, this is an exclusive homestay in a classic colonial house on the lower slopes of Londianin Mountain, set on a 2000-ha farm. 6 double bedrooms with bathrooms. All meals are taken in the dining room and guests are expected to be part of the family in a house party atmosphere. There are small children and dogs in the family too. Croquet, lawn tennis, horse-riding safaris. There is no electricity and lighting is by gas and hurricane lamps. The house was built in 1920 and there are some fine antiques.
**D Kembu Cottages and Campsite**, take the main A104 road from Nakuru towards Eldoret and after a few km turn off to the C56 to Njoro. From Njoro take the Molo road; the farm is 8 km beyond Njoro. *Matatus* from Nakuru to Molo will drop you off to the turning to the farm. T0722-361 102, www.kembu.com. The cottages and campsite are located on a large

364-ha working farm, children can help feed horses, calves and chickens, mountain biking and horse riding is on offer. Accommodation is in en suite cottages (one of which was built in 1915 and was a former home of Beryl Markham), rooms in the family house, and 1 unique treehouse with double bedroom only, for which guests use toilets and showers in the campsite. The campsite (**F**) itself is a fantastic swathe of springy green grass surrounded by bushes full of chameleons. There's a lovely rustic bar and restaurant with wood fire and superb farm cuisine. Activities include playing football with the farm team and visiting the local school. Well recommended and the Nightingale family that run the farm are very hospitable.
**D Kunste**, about 2 km out on the Nairobi road, T051-221 2140, www.kunstehotel.com. Large spacious hotel with secure parking, outside bar with kids' playground, restaurant, 105 comfortable rooms, singles, doubles and triples, the bigger suites also have TV, old-fashioned decor but well run with friendly staff.
**D Mercia Hotel**, Kenyatta Av, T051-221 6013, www.mericagrouphotels.com. A surprise for dusty little Nakuru, this is a modern block that opened in 2003 with a fabulous atrium-style lobby where all the doors to the rooms look inward on several storeys and are reached by glass elevators, with 89 rooms and 4 suites, doubles cost about US$75, and breakfast is US$10, if you are not staying buffet dinner is US$15. There's a bar, gym, a good swimming pool at the rear where non-residents can swim for a small fee and secure parking.
**D Midland**, Geoffery K Kamau Rd, T051-221 2125, enquiries@midland.co.ke. Comfortable, well-appointed rooms with en suite bathrooms and satellite TV, breakfast is included, car washing for a small tip, newspapers in the morning, 2 bars with giant TVs, and an excellent restaurant serving reasonably priced steaks and pork chops, fresh tilapia fish, pasta and delicious filled pancakes. Recommended.
**D Stem Hotel**, 8 km from Nakuru on the A104 towards Naivasha, www.thestem hotel.com. Old-fashioned rooms with heavy

dark furniture in a 1970s-built block, but comfortable and the 'executive' rooms have TVs. The restaurant serves a good range of tasty Indian dishes and there's a swimming pool, sauna, steam room and gym.
**D Waterbuck**, West Rd, T051-221 5672. Modern hotel with good facilities. Brightly coloured rooms with touches of African decor, very clean and spacious, the double rooms have balconies. The restaurant is affordable and good and the swimming pool here is popular with Kenyan families at the weekend. Can organize game drives into the park.
**E Care Guest House**, Gusii Rd, very central, T0721-636 447 (mob). The best at the cheapest end of the scale in an unmissable bright pink building on several storeys with 70 rooms. A double is just over US$5, clean rooms with simple concrete shower and loo, hot water, mosquito nets, very secure and there are additional locked gates at the end of each corridor. Restaurant serves good simple snacks and breakfasts but no booze.

## Lake Nakuru National Park p124, map p125

The rates of the accommodation options within the park do not include park entrance fees or vehicle costs.
**A-B Lake Nakuru Lodge**, T051-850 518, www.lakenakurulodge.com. Medium-sized lodge situated to the southeast of the park near the Ndarit Gate, with pleasant gardens and pool overlooking the park, space for 176 people in cottages, *bandas* and suites, friendly service, bar and dining room, and 24-hr room service. The original house was part of Kenya pioneer Lord Delamere's estate.
**B Sarova Lion Hill Lodge**, close to eastern shore of lake, access from Lanet Gate, T051-208 5455, www.sarova.co.ke/lionhill. Each of the 67 chalet-style rooms and suites have a private bathroom and veranda where meals can be served. Swimming pool, sauna, massages and boutique available on site. There are good views and it is popular with tour group. Full board from US$230 for a double but rates vary depending on season.

**B Naishi House**, Kenya Wildlife Service, Nakuru Warden, T051-204 4069, Nairobi, T020-600 800, www.kws.org. National park self-catering accommodation in the south of the park, near **Makalia Campsite**. The house is furnished with rugs and paintings by local artists and has a fully equipped kitchen (including fridge), lounge, dining room and 2 bedrooms, each with a double and a single bed. There are also 2 single rooms in an adjacent cottage. Bring all food, firewood and drinking water and electricity is provided by generator from 1900-2200. Escorted game drives can be organized from here. The whole house rents for US$250, including the cottage, but other arrangements may be possible.

## Camping

There are 2 public campsites within the park, **Backpacker's** and **Makalia**, which cost US$10 per person and 3 'special' campsites, which cost US$25 per person, reservations through the warden, T051-204 4069, www.kws.org, or simply book and pay for camping when you arrive at the main gate.

**E-F Backpackers' Campsite**, just inside the Main Gate with basic facilities including a communal tap and cold showers, in a good location under shady yellow acacias, but the monkeys and baboons can be bothersome so look after your stuff. You can camp here even if you do not have a vehicle, and there is no entry fee to the park. However, the park cannot be explored on foot, so to go on a game drive you would have to hitch from the main gate, and if you were lucky enough to get a lift (remember safari companies are unlikely to pick up non-paying passengers), then you would have to pay park entry fees. **Kampi ya Nyati** (Buffalo) and **Kampi ya Nyuki** (Bee), both lead down to quiet viewpoints on the lakeshore and are near the northeast entrance. **Makalia Campsite** is by the southern boundary of the park and close to the waterfall – exercise caution: lions are often spotted here, and **Njoro Campsite**, is about 1 km into the park on the northwest side of the lake.

**Menengai Crater** *p128*
**B Maili Saba Camp**, at Hotel Kunste 2 km outside of Nakuru turn left and the camp is 11 km, T050-50845, www.mailisabacamp.com. Just 10 comfortable permanent en suite tents set under thatched roofs with wooden decks, on the lower slopes of the Menengai Crater with excellent views. Well-stocked bar, restaurant serving Western and Swahili dishes which is atmospherically lit at night with oil lamps, swimming pool, and can organize local excursions to Lake Nakuru National Park and Thomson's Falls.

**Nyahururu and Thomson's Falls** *p128*
At the time of writing a sports camp was being developed on the outskirts of Nyahururu, **Thomson's Falls Sport Camp**, which will offer accommodation and a camp site and will be affiliated with the **Kenya Youth Hostel Association** and offer facilities for athletes wanting to train at high altitude. Visit www.sportscamp-hostel.com for progress.
**D Thomson's Falls Lodge**, T065-22006, www.tfalls.co.ke, is the most popular choice, just off the road out of town toward Nyeri and Nanyuki. Built in 1931, it is set in pleasant gardens next to the waterfall. Charming colonial atmosphere, there is a choice of rooms in the main building or cottages. More people visit to see the falls and have a drink at the bar than stay but the rooms are well furnished, if a little cheerless and all have fireplaces. The restaurant is good and the staff are friendly. There's also a campsite (**F**), with hot showers.
**F Ranika Baron Hotel**, Ol Kalou Rd, T065-320 56. Some rooms have baths others have showers, it is clean and comfortable although less than lavish. There is a bar-restaurant, disco at weekends. One disadvantage is that it is very noisy from 0600 when the *matatus* get going.

## 🍴 Eating

**Nakuru** *p124, map p122*
The best restaurants are attached to hotels, and represent the limited choices after dark;

the **Midland** and **Mercia** hotels are especially good. There are a number of places for cheap snacks around town. The many supermarkets also sell pies, samosas and pieces of fried chicken. About 2 km outside Nakuru on the road to Nairobi on the left-hand side there is a shopping centre with good snacks for a short stop if you are only driving through.

**Courtyard**, Government Av, T051-221 1585. Daily 1200-2200. Formal and very comfortable restaurant that offers an excellent choice of hot and cold starters, salads, Indian food, seafood, pizza or grills, huge varied menu and not unreasonably priced. The pan-fried chicken flavoured with coconut cream, green chillies and turmeric is rather good. You can choose to eat inside, on the terrace at the front, or in the lovely courtyard decked with plants to the rear. Full bar including some wines.

**Café Lemon Tart**, corner of Moi Rd and Kenyatta Av, T051-221 3208. Daily 0800-1700. Excellent breakfasts and light snacks, simple café environment, good freshly ground filter and espresso coffee.

**Gilani's Restaurant**, in the Gilani's Supermarket on Club Rd. Daily 0800-1730. Run by one of Nakuru's biggest Muslim business families in this large supermarket, the cafeteria serves affordable and generous portions of fresh juices, pastries, and some Indian curries and continental dishes.

**Nakuru Coffeehouse**, Moi Rd, T051-221 4596. Serves very good coffee, snacks and ice cream, although the café is a little dim inside and seating is on plastic bucket chairs. This is a recommended stop to buy fresh coffee beans and if you wish they will grind them for you in a wonderful old-fashioned grinder.

**Nakuru Sweet Mart**, there are 2 branches in town. Daily 0830-1700. The bakery on Gusii Rd sells vegetarian Indian snacks like samosas and bhajis, puff pastries, proper French bread, and unusual sweets like gingerbread men, and cold drinks including good passion juice. The second outlet on Moi Rd is more of a sit-down option and serves sandwiches, burgers, and greasy fried chicken and chips.

**Planet Kitchen**, Government Av. Mon-Sat 1000-late. Very nice terrace with lots of pot plants, snacks and full meals like grilled chicken or fish, friendly atmosphere, good place for a cold beer, popular after work venue for business people. Notice the bike park across the street, where hundreds of tightly packed bicycles are chained up.

**Ribbons Cafe**, Gusii Rd. Daily 0800-1730. Nice 1st-floor terrace, popular with bank workers at lunchtime, cold drinks and snacks, and typical Kenyan dishes like chapattis, ugali and *nyama choma*, and *githeri* – a combination of beans and corn, which traditionally was a Kikuyu dish and now features in many poorer Kenyan's diet as a good source of protein.

**Tipsy Restaurant**, Gusii Rd. Daily 0730-1700. Popular with local people and good value, they have Western dishes as well as good curries and tilapia fish in a fast-food atmosphere complete with 1970s swivelling chairs.

## 🜚 Bars and clubs

**Nakuru** p124, map p122
Many of the hotels have discos or live music at the weekends.
**XTC Disco**, Club Rd. Popular local disco, open Wed-Sat, sometimes has live bands. With strobe lights and a dark dance floor, the nearest thing to a proper nightclub in Nakuru.

## ▲ Activities and tours

**Nakuru** p124, map p122
**Select Travel and Tours**, Kenyatta Av, T051-221 4030/1, select@multitech web.com. Arranges hotel bookings, car hire and flight ticketing.
**Shoor Safaris**, Moi Rd, T051-221 1408, www.shoortravel.com. Quality safari operator and travel agent that also has an office in Nairobi. Best in Nakuru with very helpful staff, members of the Kenya Association of Travel Agents, organize local tours as well as packages throughout East Africa. If you

haven't arranged tours to lakes Baringo and Bogoria or Nakuru National Park by the time you get to Nakuru head here. **Taylers Nakuru Travel**, Kenyatta Av, near **Standard Chartered Bank**, T051-221 1173, taylers@multitechweb.com. All airline ticketing, useful and efficient general travel agent.

**Nakuru Golf Club**, 2 km northwest of town on the lower slopes of the Menengai Crater, T057-224 0391. This is the only uphill course in Kenya, and was opened in 1929 and extended to 18 holes in 1935. Lake Nakuru can be seen from the 8th and 18th tees. Visitors are welcome and there's an attractive clubhouse with restaurant and bar.

## ⦿ Shopping

**Nakuru** *p124, map p122*
There are several well-stocked supermarkets around town including Gelani's on Club Rd, which also has a good butchery 1 block back on Moi Rd that also sells some dairy produce such as yoghurt and cheese. Surprisingly for such a large town there isn't a branch of **Nakumatt**. The market has an excellent selection of fresh fruit and vegetables but be wary of petty thieves here. For souvenirs, an obligatory stop for anyone passing through Nakuru is at the large craft market in the car park near the clock tower where there is fine selection of items from all over Kenya. The traders are well used to tour groups and don't hassle you too much.

## ⊖ Transport

**Nakuru** *p124, map p122*
The main bus station is on the eastern edge of town. **Easy Coach**, which has a terminal in town at the Kobil petrol station on Kenyatta Av,

is recommended as all its vehicles are very new. It has services to **Nairobi**, **Eldoret** and **Kakamega**.

### Nyahururu and Thompson's Falls
*p128*
There are regular buses and minibuses linking to **Nakuru** (1¼ hrs) to the west and **Nyeri** (2 hrs) to the east. Less plentiful are services to **Naivasha** (1½ hrs) and **Nanyuki** (2 hrs). Several early-morning buses also serve **Nairobi** (3 hrs). If you are driving north from here fill up on petrol, as it is much pricier in Mararal.

## ⦿ Directory

**Nakuru** *p124, map p122*
**Banks** Most of the big banks have a bureau de change and ATMs including **Barclays** and **Standard Chartered** on Kenyatta Av. The **Postbank** on GK Kamau Highway can arrange Western Union money transfers. **Internet** There are a number of internet cafés around town but the best is the **Cyber Café**, Kenyatta Av, which has lots of terminals, is cheap at about US$1 per hr and has surprisingly fast access by Kenya's standards. **Medical services** Pharmacy: there is a well-stocked pharmacy next to a doctor's clinic near the Standard Chartered Bank. **Post office** The post office is close to the clock tower on Kenyatta Av.

### Nyahururu and Thompson's Falls
*p128*
**Banks** Barclays, Kenya Commercial Bank and Kenya Co-op Bank are all in the vicinity of the post office, which is on the town's main square near the (unused) railway station. **Medical services** Mbaria Centre, opposite the town hall, has a medical centre.

# Further north

*The Rift Valley lakes of Baringo and Bogoria are not far from Nakuru and make an interesting diversion away from the game parks. The lakes are in attractive settings with Bogoria being best known for its hot springs and flamingos and Baringo for its large pods of hippos and excellent birdlife. Serious twitchers should head to this region as it offers some of the best birding in East Africa. Mosquitoes are a problem in this region so sleep under nets and use plenty of repellent.* ➥ *For listings, see pages 138-139.*

## Lake Bogoria National Reserve ●●● ➥ *pp138-139. Colour map 3, C6.*

➔ *Phone code: 037.*
ⓘ *US$20 entrance fee plus US$1.50 per vehicle and US$3 per person for camping.*

This reserve, which covers an area of 107 sq km in the Rift Valley, is 40 km south of Lake Baringo and 80 km north of Nakuru, and is mainly bushland with small patches of riverine forest. The main reason people visit Lake Bogoria is to see the thermal areas with steam jets and geysers and the large number of flamingos that live here.

### Ins and outs

It is an easy drive from Nakuru taking less than one hour along the Baringo road. Motorbikes are allowed into the park and the road is paved up to the hot springs, after which it becomes very rough. It is not possible to drive all around the lake as the road is closed on the east side between just north of **Fig Tree Camp** to just east of Loboi Gate. There are three gates, all accessible from by-roads off the B4 main road leading to Baringo. The main gate is Loboi Gate, at the lake's north end. The detour eastward from the B4 is 4 km south of Marigat. A paved road, the E461, heads for Loboi and the gate after a 21 km stretch. The other two gates are to the south of the reserve. Take the east turn-off the B4 at Mogotio, 59 km south of Marigat. This road covers some 20 km up to Mugurin. One kilometre ahead, the road splits into two. The left track heads on for some 20 km until a right turn-off which leads you to Maji Moto Gate, close to the hot springs. The other track at the right is badly damaged and quite steep at some stretches, and covers 14 km before reaching Emsos Gate, the southernmost gate, at the reserve's forest area. ➥ *See Transport, page 139.*

### Sights

There are now thought to be over two million flamingos, predominantly the lesser flamingo, that feed on *Spirulina platensis*, the blue-green algae. Many of the flamingos have moved here from Lake Nakuru, possibly because the water level there fell so dramatically. Lake Bogoria's geysers are located mostly on the western side of the lake. There are pools with foul-smelling sulphurous steam bubbles, some of which send up boiling hot water spumes several metres high. Take care, the water is very hot and you can get badly burnt.

This is the least-visited of all Kenya's Rift lakes, but it can conveniently be included in a visit to Lake Baringo and the Kerio Valley, all of which are in this extremely hot area of the Rift Valley. The lake itself lies at the foot of the Laikipia Escarpment and its bottle-green waters reflect woodlands to the east. It is a shallow soda lake, between 1 m and 9 m in depth, and the shoreline is littered with huge lava boulders, surrounded by grassland. On the eastern side of the lake are found a number of greater kudu; they can best be seen in the evening when they come down to the lake to drink. The northern and eastern

# Lakes Bogoria & Baringo

To Kapedo Springs, Silali
Volcano & Lake Turkana

Karosi
Volcano
(1449m)

Lake
Baringo

Tugen Hills

6 Kampi Ya
5 ○ Samaki 7

2 1 Ol Kokwe
Island

To Maralal (170 km)

B4

To Kabarnet & Eldoret

Marigat

To Nakuru

E461

8 Loboi Gate
KWS HQ

Road closed

Lake Bogoria
National Reserve

Maji Moto Gate

Lake
Bogoria

Geysers

Bogoria River

3▲ ▲4

Road closed

Laikipia Escarpment

Road closed

Waseges River

Emsos Gate

Moto River

To Mugurin (19 km)

N

3 km
3 miles

Lake Bogoria **8**
Roberts Camp **5**
Samatian Island **7**
Soi Safari Lodge **6**

**Sleeping** 🛏
Island Camp **1**
Lake Baringo Club **2**

**Camping** ▲
Acacia Tree **3**
Fig Tree **4**

shoreline is swampy and attracts many waders. Along the eastern end of the lake you can see the northernmost part of the Aberdares. Trees including wild fig and acacia grow densely alongside the dry river beds and this is the best place for birdwatching. A total of about 375 bird species have been recorded here.

## Lake Baringo 🛏🍴 ▸▸ pp138-139.
Colour map 3, C6.

Lake Baringo, 20 km north of Marigat, is a peaceful and beautiful freshwater lake covering about 168 sq km, at an altitude of about 1000 m. It is a shallow lake (maximum depth is 12 m) and like Lake Naivaisha, Lake Baringo appears to have no outlet. It's thought it drains to the north through an underground series of fissures, possibly re-appearing at Kapedo, 80 km away, where steaming water tumbles over a 10-m cliff. This part of Kenya used to be heavily populated with game, but rinderpest greatly reduced the wildlife numbers in the early part of the 20th century. Nevertheless in 2002, and on their way from the Kerio Valley to the Laikipia Plateau, a herd of elephant swam across Lake Baringo, an event never seen at the lake before.

### Ins and outs
Some 30 km past Nakuru on the B3 is the right turn-off to the B4, toward **Kampi Ya Moto**, **Bogoria**, **Marigat** and **Kampi Ya Samaki**, the latter town being at the lakeshore 2 km away from the main road. The road is tarmac up to the north tip of the lake. From Eldoret, take the C51 heading northward to Cherangani Hills. Some 33 km ahead, at the town of Iten, the road turns southeast. From there you will pass the towns of **Kamarin**, **Tambach**, **Chebloch** and **Kabarnet** and finally reach the junction with the B4 in Marigat, where you turn left for Kampi Ya Samaki and Lake Baringo. ▸▸ See Transport, page 139.

## Born to run

The Kalenjin people have attracted world-wide attention for excelling in world-class middle- and long-distance running championships. They are also sometimes referred to as the 'running tribe' and the Kalenjins have won some 75% of Kenya's distance running races from the 800 m to 10,000 m, as well as the marathon, and 40% of international honours in the same races in the past 40 years. The first of these amazing athletes was Kip Keino, who rose to world prominence in the Mexico Olympics in 1968. Despite suffering severe pain from gallstones he competed in the 10,000-m race. With two laps to go, whilst in the lead pack, he collapsed in pain, but before the stretcher arrived he returned to the track and completed the race, despite having been disqualified. Four days later he won the silver medal in the 5000 m, and beat the American Jim Ryun for the gold in the 1500 m. In the 1972 Games, Kip Keino won the gold in the steeplechase and silver in the 1500 m. Nowadays he helps to run a children's home with his wife in Western Kenya and presently serves on the Kenya Olympic Committee. His success in Mexico spawned a dynasty of Kenya runners and the reason for their success has been ascribed in part to their 'altitude' training as their homesteads and farms, mostly located above 2000 m, which have known aerobic benefit, plus their normal diet that contains a high percentage of complex carbohydrates. Most recent successes include the Kenya team picking up 13 medals at the 2007 International Association of Athletics Federations World Championship in Japan, including gold for the men's and women's marathon, and gold, silver and bronze for the men's steeplechase, and of course Kenya's phenomenal success in the 2008 Beijing Olympics. At this, Kenya had their best-ever performance at the Olympics by winning 15 medals in track and field events of which five were gold: Women's 800 m for Pamela Jelimo; Men's Steeplechase for Brimin Kipruto; Men's 800 m for Wilfred Bungei; Women's 1500 m for Nancy Lagat; and the final event of the Olympics, the Men's Marathon, won by the tiny figure of Samuel Wanjiru.

### Sights

It is an extremely attractive lake with small, wooded creeks, little islands and white pebble beaches, framed by the mountains to the east and west. The Njemps fishermen can be seen on the lake, and the imposing Laikipia Escarpment creates a magnificent backdrop. The lake contains large schools of hippo and crocodile, and the delicious fish, tilapia, is caught here. There are several islands, **Ol Kokwe** being the biggest of them at approximately 1200 ha while the other islands include **Parmolok**, **Willys Island**, **Devils Island** and many others. The lake's greatest attraction is the huge number and variety of birds. There are said to be 450 species of bird here, including the Hemprich's hornbill and Verreaux' eagle. On **Gibraltar Island** there is a very large colony of the Goliath heron, the largest concentration of these magnificent birds in East Africa. Mammals found locally include Grant's gazelle, waterbuck, mongoose and dikdik. The extended area around the lake is very hot and dry.

If you continue driving north past Lake Bogoria you will start noticing large sawn-off tree trunks lying horizontally in the higher branches of many of the trees. This odd sight is in fact a method of honey cultivation (the trunks are hollowed out to the bee's taste); the effort to get the branches up there is quite amazing. The result is the delicious Asilah honey on sale at the roadside.

Much of the northern part of the Rift Valley remains relatively unexplored by travellers and facilities are few and far between. The landscape is quite different from the central and western parts of the Rift and this region is the location of the **Elgeyo Escarpment**, **Tambach Escarpment** and the **Tugen Hills**, which rise to heights of over 2000 m and are intercepted by deep valleys. Climatic conditions at the bottom of the valleys are arid and hot, while at the top, cool and sometimes misty, which contribute to a diverse range of landscapes. It is only sparsely inhabited, but the stark beauty provides an adventurous route to Eldoret in Western Kenya (see page 175) and further north the Cherangani Hills (see page 350).

### Kabarnet → *Colour map 3, C6.*

Once past the lakes of Bogoria and Baringo you are heading up into the less-frequented regions of Kabarnet in the Tugen Hills. Marigat to Kabarnet is a torturously slow drive. The extremely steep climb and slow *matatus* make for a trotting pace in first gear. The advantage though is of lingering views back over the Rift Valley and the lakes below. Kabarnet itself is a quiet, unimposing town despite the fact that it is the capital of Baringo district. It was established around 1907 as a colonial administrative post and named after a local missionary with the surname of Barnet. 'Ka' is homestead in the Kalenjin language. Its high altitude means it is cool (especially noticeable if you've come from the heat of Marigat), with an Alpine summer feel and there are great views northwest 1500 m down into the Kerio Valley. It is the hometown of Daniel Arap Moi, ex-president of the Republic of Kenya. In town there are two banks, a post office, petrol station and a good supermarket and covered market. **Kabarnet Museum** ① *Hospital Rd, T053-21221, www. museums.or.ke, 0900-1800, US$7.50, children (under 18) US$3.50.* This is housed in the former residence of the District Commissioner and exhibits elements from the local culture and traditions, as well as information on Lake Baringo and its environment. Lush vegetation growing in its broad gardens makes it almost a small botanic park and there are some mock-up homesteads of the Pokot and Nandi peoples.

### Kerio Valley

From Kabarnet, the road zigzags down into the Kerio Valley, part of which was designated a national reserve in 1983. The deep valley covers an area of 66 sq km and is carpeted with lush, semi-tropical vegetation on the slopes, and thorn bush on the dry valley floor. It offers stunning scenery and magnificent views and is surrounded by the Elgeyo Escarpment, Tambach Escarpment and the Tugen Hills. Waterfalls splash down, and isolated *shambas* (small farms) of the **Kalenjin** are dotted around the mountainous countryside. The Kalenjin people are very successful in world-class middle- and long-distance running championships, see box, page 136. Apart from the Kalenjin herders and their livestock, there is little else but the unspoilt beauty and quiet. If you are driving and heading from Nakuru to western or north western Kenya and have the time, this route makes for a much better alternative to the busy main Nairobi–Uganda road. The good tarred C51 twists and turns up from Mariget and then down from Kabernet, a descent of around 1000 m in about the same distance, and then rolls through Chebloch Gorge, a deep and narrow gorge with sheer rock walls and over the Kerio River before climbing up the other side again towards Eldoret via the settlements of Tambach and **Iten**. On this western side of the valley, the best place to appreciate the magnificent views is from the **Kerio View** lodge and restaurant (see page 139) near Iten. After Iten, the road flattens at at the top of the Elgeyo Escarpment and continues through pine plantations to Eldoret, about 30 km. From Marigat to Eldoret it's about 120 km, but allow plenty of time to navigate the bends and stop at the view points, and if possible lunch at Kerio View.

## ⊕ Further north listings

*For Sleeping and Eating price codes and other relevant information, see Essentials pages 34-38.*

## ⊜ Sleeping

### Lake Bogoria National Reserve
*p134, map p135*
**C Lake Bogoria Hotel**, outside of the reserve, 2 km from Loboi Gate, T037-40225, www.bogoriasparesort.com. 23 slightly faded, old-fashioned private cosy cottages with en suite bathrooms and a/c, and the only natural heated health spa in Kenya. The spa pool feeds from the hot springs of Bogoria, and the gates to the park are only a 5-min drive away. The restaurant is a reasonable stop over for lunch.

### Camping
**F Acacia Tree**, on the western shore, has pit latrines but no other facilities, bring all equipment, food and drinking water.
**F Fig Tree Campsite**, on the southern shore, is pleasant and quiet. There is a freshwater stream running through the campsite that is just big enough to get into. Beware of the baboons: secure your property and avoid camping directly under the fig trees as they enjoy the fruit enormously with predictable results. Access to the site is a winding rocky narrow track for 4WDs only.

### Lake Baringo *p135, map p135*
**L Samatian Island**, reservations Nairobi, T020-211 5453, www.samatianislandlodge.com. A small private island with breathtaking views, luxury accommodation for up to 12 guests in 5 comfortable, open-plan cottages, each with bathroom and sitting area.
1 is a family cottage 2 bedrooms, sharing a bathroom, sitting room and veranda, all very well decorated. Stunning infinity pool and very good food, all-inclusive rates. Closed Apr-May.

**B Island Camp**, on Ol Kokwe Island at the centre of Lake Baringo, T051-850 858, admin@islandcamp.co.ke This is quite an experience, even if only for a day trip. There is a swimming pool at the highest point of the camp, with very good views. Paths lead down from the pool to the informal dining and bar areas. All 23 tents have own bathroom with flush toilet and shower, and a shaded veranda. Activities on offer include waterskiing and windsurfing, guided birdwatching walks and champagne bush breakfasts. All meals and boat transfers are included in the room rates.
**B Lake Baringo Club**, reservations Nairobi T020-4450 693, www.kenyahotelsltd.com/lakebaringo. With 10 ha of colourful gardens, a swimming pool and good buffet-style food. 48 rooms are spread out in the gardens. Non-residents can use facilities for a small fee. An ornithologist can accompany you on bird walks before breakfast and in the evening. Don't miss the bird boat trip; highly recommended for birdwatchers. A nice touch is a newsletter in the rooms telling guests what birds are nesting in the hotel grounds. Boats take 8 people, and the tour is 2 hrs to see the lake, islands, crocodiles, hippos and birds.
**C Soi Safari Lodge**, just north of Kampi ya Samaki, reservations Nairobi, T020-318 774, soisafarilodge2003@yahoo.com. Relatively new camp with a/c cottages. Bar and restaurant overlook the lake and its imposing islands from a double-storey building with a pagoda-style tiled roof. Buffet lunches and BBQ dinners are served, and there is a swimming pool.
**C-F Roberts Camp**, T053-51431, www.robertscamp.com. A lovely spacious set-up near the lake and well shaded by giant acacia trees. Camping is US$5 per person, *bandas* with kitchens are US$55 for 2 people with shared hot showers, and larger ones sleeping 4-6 are US$108 and have additional bathrooms.

Activities include boat rides and bird walks. The **Thirsty Goat Pub and Restaurant** prides itself on an astonishing range of ice cold beers, wines, spirits and exotic cocktails, as well as a very good menu that includes vegetarian dishes and they can organize packed lunches and bush barbeques. Watch out for hippos in this area and don't approach them; although they seem docile they can be dangerous. For a small fee you can swim in the pool at the Lake Baringo Club next door.

## Kabarnet p137
**E Kabarnet**, a 5-min walk from the post office, T053-22150. A faded small town hotel with tatty furnishings, but nevertheless set in well-tended gardens, with fine views of the Kerio Valley and it has a lovely cool swimming pool (non-residents US$2), restaurant and bar with set meals. Its run by the **Kenya Tourist Development Corporation** so may refurbished in the future.

## Kerio Valley p137
**C Kerio View**, T053-44206, 1 km north of Iten and 35 km from Eldoret on the C51, Elgeyo Escarpment, T053-44206, www.kerioview.com. Set in an unbeatable location with glorious endless views over the Kerio Valley, this is worth stopping for the fantastic food in the double storey glass-walled restaurant even if not staying. Accommodation is in 12 simple *bandas*, though they are hoping to extend soon. Bring a sweater as it can be cold up here at night, although there is a roaring fire in the main building. There are good-value set lunches and dinners for US$13, plus light meals, and a very long à la carte menu. There's a children's playground and unlimited hiking including the 1000 m descent into the valley over 10 km. A stunning spot.
**D High Altitude Training Centre**, www.lorn ah.com. Interested athletes may want to contact this high-altitude running centre in Iten, which lies at 2400 m above sea level and offers simple full-board accommodation, a gym, a 400-m dirt track, coaching, and there are dozens of long-distance running routes

across the top of the Elgeyo Escarpment. It was founded by acclaimed Kenyan female long-distance runner Lornah Kiplagat.
**D Sego Safari Lodge**, near Chebloch, 31 km after Kabarnet, turn left for 1 km at the signpost, T053-21399, www.segosafari lodge.co.ke. This is a rural budget option on the lower slopes of the valley, still with tremendous views, a small swimming pool, bar with pool table and satellite TV, restaurant for basic meals and 10 simple en suite rooms with hot showers and Masai blankets. It has orange and pawpaw orchards and gets all its milk, meat and eggs from nearby farms. Activities include walks to local homesteads.
**E-F Lenlin Campsite**, 6 km from Iten towards Kabarnet on the C51, Elgeyo Escarpment, T0722-900 848, www.lelin campsite.com. Popular with overlanders, this campsite has flush toilets, hot showers and grassy sites with spectacular views down the valley, though it can get cold here at night, plus some simple double rooms. A bonfire is lit at night, and there is a restaurant and bar though meals need to arranged with a little notice. The camp has provided the nearby primary school with piped water.

## ⊖ Transport

**Lake Bogoria National Reserve**
*p134, map p135*
Several *matatus* a day run between Nakuru and **Loboi**.

**Lake Baringo** *p135, map p135*
From Nakuru, there are 2 buses daily to **Kampi Ya Samaki**, but *matatus* only reach **Marigat**. The boats for **Ol Kokwa** island, where **Island Camp** is located, may be hired at the jetty north of Kampi Ya Samaki.

**Kabarnet** *p137*
Buses to **Eldoret** (3 hrs) and **Nakuru** (2 hrs) leave early in the morning. There are regular and quicker *matatus* to Eldoret, Nakuru and **Marigat**.

# Masai Mara National Reserve

→ *Colour map 1, B2/3.*

*This is the most popular of Kenya's parks, with very good reason. Almost every species of animal you can think of in relation to East Africa lives on the well-watered plains in this remote part of the country. One of the unique, spectacular and most memorable sights is the annual migration of hundreds of thousands of wildebeest, gazelle and zebra. The landscape is mainly gently rolling grassland with the rainfall in the north being double that of the south. The Mara River runs from north to south through the park and then turns westwards to Lake Victoria. Most of the plains are covered in a type of red-oat grass with acacias and thorn trees.*
⇥ *For listings, see pages 145-150.*

## Ins and outs

### Getting there

**Road** The Mara is 275 km southwest of Nairobi (five hours by road) in the remote southwestern corner of the country right on the Tanzanian border. The main access to the reserve is through the town of **Narok**, 141 km to the west of Nairobi. It is the main trading centre for the Masai people in southwestern Kenya and the last place you can get a cold drink or refuel if travelling there. Narok has two banks (one with an ATM), a post office and a museum plus countless souvenir stalls. Public buses from Nairobi only go as far as Narok and the chances of hitching a lift to and through the reserve are slim. From Narok, there is no singular major road into the reserve, which makes it advisable to study your route into the Mara depending on what your destination is once there. None of the access roads to the Masai Mara are in good condition and during the wet season they become quagmires, and a 4WD is essential.

To get to Narok from the capital take the old Nairobi–Naivasha road (B3 – the more westerly road) that forks to the left at Rironi, the road continues in a northwesterly direction for 6 km then turns left on a sealed tarmac road in a southwesterly direction south of Mountt Longonot. From here it is 82 km to Narok. The route is well served by *matatus* and share-taxis. From Narok to the reserve, if you are driving yourself there are a number of possibilities of accessing the reserve. Some 15-20 km past Narok, the B3 road reaches Ewaso Ng'iro, where there is a crossroads, and from here there are two options. The first is the most frequent route, leading to the eastern sector of the park, where **Keekorok Lodge** is located. At Ewaso Ng'iro, there is a left turn on to the C12. Some 40 km ahead the road divides. Both tracks lead to the Masai Mara, but to different gates, and converge within the reserve at **Keekorok Lodge**. The one at the right is the main access, leading to Sekenani Main Gate, the left route reaches Ololamutiek Gate crossing a collapsed bridge, but it is passable for a 4WD vehicle. The second option from Ewaso Nyiro is less used because of its worse condition and abundance of mud after the rains. At Ewaso Ng'iro, go straight ahead along the B3 some 40 km more up to Ngorengore. At this village turn left on to the C13. From here there are two further choices. The first one is driving straight to Oloololo Gate and Kichwa Tembo Camp, at the western side of the reserve. The second option is turning left at Aitong to the E177. This track leads to the eastern sector through Talek Gate. If arriving from Kisii from Western Kenya, take the main A1 highway heading south for Tanzania. Past Migori, at Suna, just before reaching the border, there is a left turn off toward Lolgorien and the Masai Mara. This track crosses the

Soit Ololol Escarpment and is very steep in places. You'll enter the reserve through Oloololo Gate, at the western sector of the reserve. There are two bridges that cross the Mara River, the New Mara Bridge is along the reserve's main road, the E176, which connects Keekorok Lodge with Oloololo Gate. The second bridge over the Mara, lies outside the reserve, northwest of the limits shortly after Oloololo Gate. Apart from this main network, there is a web of minor roads in different conditions, some of them passable all the year round and others flooded during the rainy season. Off-track driving over the years has caused wheel-track tangles that are hard to discern from the authorized roads, and the maps available are generally far from perfect.

Air A large number of visitors choose to travel to the Mara by plane although it is of course more expensive. **Air Kenya** operates daily flights from Nairobi to seven airstrips in the Masai Mara, and a daily flight from Nanyuki to the Mara, **Fly 540** operates a daily flight from Nairobi, **Tropic Air**, **Safarilink** and **Mombasa Air Safaris** all offer daily scheduled flights to the park lodge airstrips. From Nairobi, the flight lasts little more than an hour compared to the five or more hours by road. ▸▸ *See Transport, page 150.*

## Tourist information

Daily 0630-1900, adults US$60 per day, children (under 11) US$30, vehicle 300KSh, which covers entry to the national reserve and the Greater Mara region, which also includes a number of group ranches and conservancy regions. The fees can also be paid at many of the lodges and camps, or will be part of your safari package if you are on an organized tour.

## Safety

If you are exploring the Masai Mara independently in your own vehicle let someone know where you are going, travel in groups of two or more vehicles if possible, seek advice about the state of the roads especially in the wet seasons, and remember, in the event of an emergency mobile phones to do not yet get full coverage in the reserve.

## Sights

The Mara covers some 1510 sq km ranging between 1500 m and 2100 m above sea level. The reserve receives a high rainfall as a result of the altitude and humidity of nearby Lake Victoria, 160 km west. It is an extension of Tanzania's Serengeti National Park, a small part of the Serengeti ecosystem covering some 40,000 sq km between the Rift Valley and Lake Victoria.

If you can, time a visit with the annual migration, which although is determined by the times of the rains generally runs as follows: hundreds of thousands of wildebeest (estimated at 500,000 animals), gazelle and zebra move northwards from the Serengeti Plains in January, having exhausted the grazing there, and arrive in the Masai Mara by about July-August. In the Mara, the herbivores are joined by yet another 100,000 wildebeest coming from the Loita Hills, east of the Mara. Once the Mara's new grass has been eaten, the wildebeests, zebra and gazelles retrace their long journey south to Tanzania in October, where their young are born, and where the grasslands have been replenished in their absence. It is estimated that in four or five months, the wildebeest alone deposit 60,000 tonnes of dung, which fertilizes the grasslands for the next year's migration. One of the highlights of the migration is seeing the animals crossing the Mara River. Sometimes thousands of animals will amass on the banks, waiting for an opportunity to cross. Eventually they will choose a crossing point, which can vary from year to year and cannot be predicted with any accuracy. Usually it will be a fairly placid stretch of water without too much predator-concealing vegetation on the far side, although occasionally they will choose seemingly suicidal places and drown in their hundreds. Below, waiting knowingly in the river, are the enormous Mara crocodiles. First one, then another and then the whole frenetic herd leap into the water. In places, the river

# Masai Mara National Reserve

**Sleeping**
Acacia Camp **11**
Basecamp Masai Mara **15**
Bateleur Camp **16**
Cottars' 1920s Safari
   Camp **17**
Fig Tree Camp **1**

Governors' Il Moran
   Camp **18**
Governors' Camp **2**
Governors' Private Camp **19**
Keekorok Lodge **3**
Kicheche Mara Camp **20**
Kichwa Tembo Camp **4**
Kilima Camp **38**

Little Governors' Camp **5**
Mara Explorer **21**
Mara Intrepids **6**
Mara Safari Club **22**
Mara Serena Lodge **8**
Mara Simba Lodge **23**
Mara Sopa Lodge **9**

banks have been worn down considerably after centuries of crossings. Most make it to the other side but many hundreds are either taken by crocodiles or drown. This lengthy trek costs the lives of many old, young, lame and unlucky animals, picked off by predators like lions, leopards and hyenas.

The reserve is teeming with herbivores – numbering around 2.5 million including wildebeest, Thompson's and Grant's gazelle, zebra, buffalo, impala, topi, hartebeest, giraffe, eland, elephant, dik-dik, klipspringer, steinbok, hippo, rhino, warthog and bushpig. There are also large numbers of lion, leopard, cheetah, hyena, wild dog and jackal, as well as smaller mammals and reptiles. In the Mara River hippo and usually sleepy crocodiles can be seen. The number of animals suited to grasslands living in this area has increased enormously over the last 30 years due to woodland being cleared. In addition to the numerous mammals, over 450 species of bird have been recorded, including 57 species of bird of prey. The Masai Mara has a very high density of lion with about 500 in just over 1500 sq km. Among the rarer mammals found here are the Roan antelope in the southwest sector, and the thousands of topi only found here and in the Tsavo National Park. Another shy mammal is the bat-eared fox sometimes seen peering out of their burrows.

The **Oloololo Escarpment** on the western edge of the park is the best place to see the animals, although it is also the hardest part to get around, particularly after heavy rain, when the swampy ground becomes impassable.

The Masai Mara is not a national park but a game reserve, divided into an inner and outer section. The inner section covers an area of 520 sq km, and the greater conservation area is 1810 sq km. The inner section has no human habitation apart from the lodges. In the outer reserve area the Masai coexist with the game and evidence of their communities can be seen in the many *manyattas* (villages). The essential difference between a game reserve and a national park is that the indigenous people (the pastoral Masai) have the right to graze their animals on the outer part of the reserve and to kill animals

Mara Springs Safari
  Camp **24**
Mpata Safari Club **33**
Olonana Camp **25**
Rekero Tented Camp **28**
Richard's Camp **29**
Saruni Camp **30**

Sekenani Camp **12**
Siana Springs Intrepids **13**

**Camping** ⚠
Musiara Gate **34**
Ololaimutiek **35**
Sand River **36**
Talek River **37**

## Big Cat Diary

The BBC Natural History Department's phenomenally successful *Big Cat Diary* series has been filmed in the Masai Mara since 1996, and has given viewers an extraordinary insight into the lives of Africa's greatest cats. It's been described as an animal soap opera, with each episode following the same characters around as they go about their daily lives, and it certainly reflects all the drama, tears and joy of a regular human soap opera. The first series concentrated on a family of lions, while subsequent ones have covered cheetahs and leopards. To date eight series have been filmed and broadcast all over the world, and in the UK the show attracts some seven million viewers per episode. The crew follows the cats around the Mara, tracking, spotting and filming them, while the presenters also travel in the vehicles addressing the camera as the action unfolds. *Big Cat Diary* has spawned a number of similar shows using the same format, including *Elephant Diaries* (2005 and 2008), *Chimp Week* (2005), *Big Bear Week* (2006) and *Orangutan Diary* (2007). So, if you are familiar with the dominant male lion Simba of the Marsh pride, Shakira the cheetah and her three cubs or Olive the leopard, one of the 'Jackson Five', and her three cubs, than you might just see the stars of the show for yourself in the Masai Mara. Interestingly, allegedly the original first show back in 1996 was planned to be filmed in Tanzania's Serengeti National Park, but the BBC considered the costs to be too prohibitive. Bet the Tanzania park authorities are kicking themselves now ...

if they are attacked. However, the game does not recognize these designated boundaries and an even larger area, known as the 'dispersal area' extends north and east contiguous with the reserve, where the Masai people live with their stock. However, the Masai have never hunted wild animals for food but depend on their cows, and effectively live in peace with the wildlife. The reserve is controlled by the Narok and Trans-Mara County Councils and not by Kenya Wildlife Services. At many of the lodges guests are also introduced to the cultural side of the Mara as well as seeing the wildlife and visits to Masai *manyattas* are on offer, which you can wander round taking as many photographs as you wish. The money generated by these ecotourism initiatives goes directly to the local communities.

There is increasing concern about the impact that the servicing of the requirements of the tourists is having on the finely tuned ecological balance of the reserve. A couple of the identified concerns are the impact that the off-road driving is having on the flora. Many vehicles criss-cross the area causing soil erosion by churning up the grasslands. However, the animals do not appear to be adversely affected by the huge number of visitors to the reserve. Another concern regards the disposal of waste generated by the tourist industry, as some of the predators like hyenas are discovering an easier food source by rummaging through garbage.

East African wildlife

# Introduction

A large proportion of people who visit East Africa do so to see its spectacular wildlife. This colour section is a quick photographic guide to some of the more fascinating mammals you may encounter. We give you pictures and information about habitat, habits and characteristic appearance to help you when you are on safari. It is by no means a comprehensive survey and some of the animals listed may not be found throughout the whole region. For further information about East Africa's mammals, birds, reptiles and other wildlife, see the Land and environment section of the Background chapter, page 391.

## The Big Nine

It is fortunate that many of the large and spectacular animals of Africa are also, on the whole, fairly common. They are often known as the 'Big Five'. This term was originally coined by hunters who wanted to take home trophies of their safari. Thus it was, that, in hunting parlance, the Big Five were elephant, black rhino, buffalo, lion and leopard. Nowadays the hippopotamus is usually considered one of the Big Five for those who shoot with their cameras, whereas the buffalo is far less of a 'trophy'. Equally photogenic and worthy of being included are the zebra, giraffe and cheetah. But whether they are the Big Five or the Big Nine, these are the animals that most people come to Africa to see and, with the possible exception of the leopard and the black rhino, you have an excellent chance of seeing them all.

■ **Hippopotamus** *Hippopotamus amphibius*. Prefers shallow water, grazes on land over a wide area at night, so can be found quite a distance from water, and has a strong sense of territory, which it protects aggressively. Lives in large family groups known as 'schools'.

■ **Black rhinoceros** *Diceros bicornis*. Long, hooked upper lip distinguishes it from white rhino rather than colour. Prefers dry bush and thorn scrub habitat and in the past was found in mountain uplands. Males usually solitary. Females seen in small groups with their calves (very rarely more than four), sometimes with two generations. Mother always walks in front of offspring, unlike the white rhino, where the mother walks behind, guiding calf with her horn. Their distribution was massively reduced by poaching in the late 20th century, and now there are conservation efforts in place to protect black and white rhino and numbers are increasing. You might be lucky and see the black rhino in Nakuru, Tsavo and Aberdares national parks.

■ **White rhinoceros** *Diceros simus*. Square muzzle and bulkier than the black rhino, it is a grazer rather than a browser, hence the different lip. Found in open grassland, it is more sociable and can be seen in groups of five or more. Probably extinct in much of its former range in East Africa, it still flourishes in some places.

**Opposite page:**
Leopard with a kill.
**Above left:**
Black rhinoceros.
**Above right:**
White rhinoceros.
**Right:**
Hippopotamus.

■ **Common/Masai giraffe** *Giraffa camelopardis*. Yellowish-buff with patchwork of brownish marks and jagged edges, usually two different horns, sometimes three. Found throughout Africa in several differing subspecies.

■ **Reticulated giraffe** *Giraffa camelopardalis reticulata*. Reddish-brown coat divided up into polygonal shapes by a network of distinct, pale, narrow lines. Also known as the Somali giraffe, it is native to Somalia, Ethiopia and Northern Kenya, but has been relocated to reserves further south.

■ **Common/Burchell's zebra** *Equus burchelli*. Generally has broad stripes (some with lighter shadow stripes next to the dark ones) that cross the top of the hind leg in unbroken lines. The true species is probably extinct but there are many varying subspecies found in different locations across Africa.

■ **Grevy's zebra** *Equus grevyi*. Grevy's is larger than Burchell's and has much narrower white stripes, which are arranged in such a way as to meet in a sort of star-shaped arrangement at the top of the hind leg. Prefers more arid areas.

■ **Leopard** *Panthera pardus*. Found in varied habitats ranging from forest to open savannah. It is generally nocturnal, hunting at night or before the sun comes up to avoid the heat. Sometimes seen resting during the day in the lower branches of trees.

■ **Cheetah** *Acinonyx jubatus*. Often seen in family groups walking across plains or resting in the shade. The black 'tear' mark is usually obvious through binoculars. Can reach speeds of 90 kph over short distances. Found in open, semi-arid savannah, never in forested country. Endangered in some parts of Africa. More commonly seen than the leopard, but not as widespread as the lion.

**Opposite page left:**
Common giraffe.
**Opposite page right:**
Reticulated giraffe.
**Top left:** Common zebra.
**Top right:** Grevy's zebra.
**Above:** Cheetah.
**Right:** Leopard.

v

Top: Buffalo. **Bottom:** Elephant.

■ **Lion** *Panthera leo* (see page i). The largest (adult males can weigh up to 200 kg) of the big cats in Africa and also the most common, they are found on open savannah all over the continent. They are often not at all disturbed by the presence of humans and so it is possible to get quite close to them. They are sociable animals living in prides or permanent family groups of up to around 30 animals and are the only felid to do so. The females do most of the hunting (usually ungulates like zebra and antelopes).

■ **Buffalo** *Syncerus caffer*. Were considered by hunters to be the most dangerous of the big game and the most difficult to track and, therefore, the biggest trophy. Generally found on open plains but also at home in dense forest, they are fairly common in most African national parks but, like the elephant, they need a large area to roam in, so are not usually found in the smaller parks.

■ **Elephant** *Loxodonta africana*. Commonly seen, even on short safaris, elephants have suffered from the activities of ivory poachers in East Africa and by 1990 numbers in Kenya were critically just 16,000, down from 170,000 at Independence in 1963. Today, numbers are around 28,000 thanks to better protection by the Kenya Wildlife Services.

## Larger antelopes

■ **Beisa oryx** *Oryx beisa*, 122 cm. Also known as the East African oryx, there are two sub-species; the **common Beisa oryx** is found in semi-desert areas north of the Tana River, while the **fringe-eared oryx** is found south of the Tana River and in Tanzania. Both look similar with grey coats, white underbellies, short chestnut-coloured mane, and both sexes have long straight ringed horns. They gather in herds of up to 40.

■ **Common waterbuck** *Kobus ellipsiprymnus* and **Defassa waterbuck** *Kobus defassa*, 122-137 cm. Very similar with shaggy coats and white markings on buttocks: on the common variety, this is a clear half ring on the rump and around the tail; on the Defassa, the ring is a filled-in solid area. Both species occur in small herds in grassy areas, often near water.

**Top:** Beisa oryx. **Bottom left:** Defassa waterbuck. **Bottom right:** Common waterbuck.

■ **Sable antelope** *Hippotragus niger*,
140-145 cm, and **Roan antelope**
*Hippotragus equinus* 127-137 cm. Both are
similar in shape, with ringed horns curving
backwards (both sexes), longer in the sable.
Female sables are reddish brown and can
be mistaken for the roan. Males are very
dark with a white underbelly. The roan
has distinct tufts of hair at the tips of its
long ears. The sable prefers wooded areas
and the roan is generally only seen near
water. Both species live in herds.

■ **Greater kudu** *Tragelaphus strepsiceros*,
140-153 cm. Colour varies from greyish to
fawn with several vertical white stripes
down the sides of the body. Horns long and
spreading, with two or three twists (male only).
Distinctive thick fringe of hair running from the
chin down the neck. Found in fairly thick bush,
sometimes in quite dry areas. Usually lives in
family groups of up to six, but occasionally in
larger herds of up to about 30.

■ **Topi** *Damaliscus korrigum*, 122-127 cm.
Very rich dark rufous, with dark patches on
the tops of the legs and more ordinary looking,
lyre-shaped horns.

**Top**: Greater kudu. **Middle**: Sable antelope. **Bottom**: Topi.

■ **Hartebeest** The horns arise from a bony protuberance on the top of the head and curve outwards and backwards. There are three sub-species: **Coke's hartebeest** *Alcephalus buselaphus*, 122 cm, is a drab pale brown with a paler rump; **Lichtenstein's hartebeest** *Alcephalus lichtensteinii*, 127-132 cm, is also fawn in colour, with a rufous wash over the back and dark marks on the front of the legs and often a dark patch near the shoulder. All are found in herds, sometimes they mix with other plains dwellers such as zebra.

Top: White-bearded wildebeest. Middle: Coke's hartebeest. Bottom: Eland.

■ **White-bearded wildebeest** *Connochaetes taurinus*, 132 cm. Distinguished by its white beard and smooth cow-like horns, often seen grazing with zebra. Gathers in large herds, following the rains.

■ **Eland** *Taurotragus oryx*, 175-183 cm. The largest of the antelope, it has a noticeable dewlap and shortish spiral horns (both sexes). Greyish to fawn, sometimes with rufous tinge and narrow white stripes down side of body. Occurs in groups of up to 30 in grassy habitats.

## Smaller antelope

■ **Bushbuck** *Tragelaphus scriptus*, 76-92 cm. Shaggy coat with white spots and stripes on the side and back and two white, crescent-shaped marks on neck. Short horns (male only), slightly spiral. High rump gives characteristic crouch. White underside of tail is noticeable when running. Occurs in thick bush, often near water, in pairs or singly.

■ **Kirk's dikdik** *Rhynchotragus kirkii*, 36-41 cm. So small it cannot be mistaken, it is greyish brown, often washed with rufous. Legs are thin and stick-like. Slightly elongated snout and a conspicuous tuft of hair on the top of the head. Straight, small horns (male only). Found in bush country, singly or in pairs.

■ **Gerenuk** *Litocranius walleri*, 80-105 cm. A curious antelope found in dry bushy scrub in Northern Kenya, also called the giraffe-necked antelope for its long, slender neck and tiny head with large ears and eyes. Is able to stand on its hind legs to reach for food in trees. Seldom needs to drink; gets moisture from fruit and shoots.

■ **Steenbok** *Raphicerus campestris*, 58 cm. An even, rufous brown with clean white underside and white ring around eye. Small dark patch at the tip of the nose and long broad ears. The horns (male only) are slightly longer than the ears: they are sharp, smooth and curve slightly forward. Generally seen alone, prefers open plains and more arid regions. A slight creature that usually runs off very quickly on being spotted.

■ **Bohor reedbuck** *Redunca redunca*, 71-76 cm. Horns (males only) sharply hooked forwards at the tip, distinguishing them from the oribi (see page xiii). It is reddish fawn with white underparts and has a short bushy tail. It usually lives in pairs or in small family groups. Often seen with oribi, in bushed grassland and always near water.

■ **Grant's gazelle** *Gazella granti*, 81-99 cm, and **Thomson's gazelle** *Gazella thomsonii*, 64-69 cm (see page xii). Colour varies from a bright rufous to a sandy rufous. Grant's is the larger of the two and has longer horns. In both species the curved horns are carried by both sexes.

■ **Common (Grimm's) duiker** *Sylvicapra grimmia*, 58 cm (see page xii). Grey-fawn colour with darker rump and pale colour on the underside. Its dark muzzle and prominent ears are divided by straight, upright, narrow pointed horns. This particular species is the only duiker found in open grasslands. Usually the duiker is associated with a forested environment. It is difficult to see because it is shy and will quickly disappear into the bush.

Bushbuck.

**Oribi** *Ourebia ourebi*, 61 cm (see page xiii). Slender and delicate looking with a longish neck and a sandy to brownish-fawn coat. It has oval-shaped ears and short, straight horns with a few rings at their base (male only). Like the reedbuck, it has a patch of bare skin just below each ear. Lives in small groups or as a pair and is never far from water.

**Suni** *Nesotragus moschatus*, 37 cm (see page xiii). Dark chestnut to grey-fawn in colour with slight speckles along the back, its head and neck are slightly paler and the throat is white. It has a distinctive bushy tail with a white tip. Its longish horns (male only) are thick, ribbed and slope backwards. They live alone and prefer dense bush cover and reed beds.

**Clockwise from top left**: Kirk's dikdik; gerenuk feeding; steenbok; bohor reedbuck.

■ **Impala** *Aepyceros melampus*, 92-107 cm. One of the largest of the smaller antelope, the impala is a bright rufous colour on its back and has a white abdomen, a white 'eyebrow' and chin and white hair inside its ears. From behind, the white rump with black stripes on each side is characteristic and makes it easy to identify. It has long lyre-shaped horns (male only). Above the heels of the hind legs is a tuft of thick black bristles (unique to impala), which are easy to see when the animal runs. There is also a black mark on the side of abdomen, just in front of the back leg. Found in herds of 15 to 20, it likes open grassland or sometimes the cover of partially wooded areas and is usually close to water.

**Top**: Thomson's gazelle. **Bottom**: Common duiker.

**Top left:** Oribi. **Top right:** Suni. **Bottom:** Impala.

## Other mammals

There are many other fascinating mammals worth keeping an eye out for. This is a selection of some of the more interesting or particularly common ones.

■ **African wild dog** or **hunting dog** *Lycacon pictus*. Easy to identify since they have all the features of a large mongrel dog: a large head and slender body. Their coat is a mixed pattern of dark shapes and white and yellow patches and no two dogs are quite alike. They are very rarely seen and are seriously threatened with extinction (there may be as few as 6000 left). Found on the open plains around dead animals, they are not in fact scavengers but effective pack hunters.

■ **Spotted hyena** *Crocuta crocuta*. High shoulders and low back give the hyena its characteristic appearance and reputedly it has the strongest jaws in the animal kingdom. The spotted variety, larger and brownish with dark spots, has a large head and rounded ears. The **striped hyena**, slightly smaller, has pointed ears and several distinctive black vertical stripes around its torso and is more solitary. Although sometimes shy animals, they have been known to wander around campsites stealing food from humans.

**Top:** African wild dog. **Middle:** Spotted hyena. **Bottom:** Chacma baboon.

■ **Warthog** *Phacochoerus aethiopicus*.
The warthog is almost hairless and grey with a very large head, tusks and wart-like growths on its face. It frequently occurs in family parties and when startled will run away at speed with its tail held straight up in the air. They are often seen near water caking themselves in thick mud, which helps to keep them both cool and free of ticks and flies.

■ **Chacma baboon** *Papio ursinus*.
An adult male baboon is slender and weighs about 40 kg. Their general colour is a brownish grey, with lighter undersides. Usually seen in trees, but rocks can also provide sufficient protection, they occur in large family troops and have a reputation for being aggressive where they have become used to the presence of humans.

■ **Rock hyrax** *Procavia capensis*. The nocturnal rock hyrax lives in colonies amongst boulders and on rocky hillsides, protecting themselves from predators like eagles, caracals and leopards by darting into rock crevices.

■ **Caracal** *Felis caracal*. Also known as the African lynx, it is twice the weight of a domestic cat, with reddish sandy-coloured fur and paler underparts. Distinctive black stripe from eye to nose and tufts on ears. Generally nocturnal and with similar habits to the leopard. They are not commonly seen, but are found in hilly country.

**Top**: Warthog. **Middle**: Rock hyrax.
**Bottom**: Caracal.

# Masai Mara National Reserve listings

*For Sleeping and Eating price codes and other relevant information, see Essentials pages 34-38.*

## Sleeping

### Masai Mara National Reserve
*p140, map p142*

There is an abundance of luxury lodges and tented camps and some careful thought needs to go into choosing one. However thanks to the competition most offer excellent standards and service. All must be booked in advance. At the more expensive, game drives are included in the price, but are for an additional expense in some of the less expensive; budget about US$50-70 per person per 2-hr game drive. Night game drives with spotlights are only on offer from the lodges in the Greater Mara area as vehicles are not allowed out after dark in the reserve itself. Low season is after the long rains, usually April to June, when room rates drop significantly but the state of the roads may be at their worst. It's not necessarily a bad time to visit in terms of game viewing, though you may want to consider opting for a flight into the reserve using the money you have saved on accommodation. Always enquire about children policies; some places are very family friendly, while others do not accept children at all. The Masai Mara also offers a number of campsites, really the only option for budget travellers, where they may find themselves if booked on to a budget camping safari, although almost all are accessed on poor roads.

### Lodges in the reserve
**A Keekorok Lodge**, in the southeast of the reserve, reservations **Wilderness Lodges**, Nairobi T020-532 329, www.discover wilderness.com. Oldest lodge in the Mara, set in a grassy plain in a good position for the migration, swimming pool, wildlife and local culture lectures, game drives arranged. 101 high-standard rooms that were refurbished in 2006, cosy lounge, outside dining room, and an elevated walkway to a bar overlooking a hippo pool.

**A Mara Serena Lodge**, T050-22253, www.serenahotels.com. Well designed, 74 boma-style rooms with balconies with a superb view over the Mara River and plains beyond, restaurant overlooking a waterhole, swimming pool, wildlife films, Masai dancing. 2-day packages include return flights from Nairobi or Mombasa, full board and 3 or 4 game drives.

### Tented camps in the reserve
A stay in a tented camp, with perhaps a dawn hot-air balloon safari (around US$425), is an unforgettable experience (book well in advance for both).

There are 4 **Governors' Camps** grouped around the Musiara Swamp near the Musiara Gate, all different and all expensive although all meals and game drives are included. They are unfenced, but patrolled by Masai guards just in case the animals get too curious. All the Governors' Camps are consistently rated in the Gold List of *Condé Nast Traveller*'s 'Best Place to Stay in the World'. Rates in the camps vary between US$260 and US$640 per person per night, depending on season, with Governors' Camp being the least expensive. Reservations, Nairobi, T020-273 4000, www.governorscamp.com.
**L Governors' Camp**, solid floors for the 37 tents, very spacious and nicely decorated, verandas, bar lounge, candlelit dinners, small museum, balloon safaris, no swimming pool, beautiful site by the Mara River and excellent game viewing. The guides on the game drives and walks are very knowledgeable.
**L Governors' Il Moran Camp**, in bush along the Mara River. Small and intimate camp

hidden under ancient trees. The 10 tents are very private and furnished to a superior standard, with antiques, stunning beds hand-made from olive trees, large bathrooms with showers and Victorian baths, you can take dinner at your tent if you wish. Game drives and game walks are included in the rate and complimentary wine is served with dinner.

**L Governors' Private Camp**, on a bend of the Mara River. A private camp that can only be booked by 1 family/group at a time, up to 16 people (minimum of 4), and usually for a minimum of 3 nights. The food is delicious, and served on fine china and crystal, and guests can design their own menus.

**L Little Governors' Camp**, access by ferry across the Mara River followed by a short walk with guards. Very special, a splendid site with very high standards. 17 comfortable and tasteful tents with solid floors are tucked around a large watering-hole that teems with animal and bird life. In keeping with safari tradition lighting is by gas and kerosene lantern or candlelight. Flickering lights at dusk make this an atmospheric place.

**L Mara Explorer**, reservations **Heritage Hotels**, Nairobi T020-444 6600, www.heritage-eastafrica.com. On a bend of the Talek River, this is intended to provide ultra-exclusive sophistication and style for couples. 10 tents where a personal butler is on hand at all times, elephants can be watched from the outside claw-foot bath tubs, lovely riverside dining area, lounge and camp library and guests can swim at the pool at the nearby Mara Intrepids. Rates upwards of US$800 for a double. Closed Apr-Jun.

**L Rekero Tented Camp**, very close to the confluence of the Mara and Talek rivers, send them an email and they'll recommend the nearest of their agents to you, www.rekero.com. Mobile camp situated for the annual migration, set up seasonally (Jun-Oct, and Dec-Mar), takes up to 14 guests in 5 spacious tents, farmhouse meals, picnics in the bush and sundowners, very good guides for game activities.

**A Mara Intrepids**, reservations **Heritage Hotels**, Nairobi, T020-444 6600, www.heritage-eastafrica.com. By the Talek River, 30 tents with large 4-poster beds, en suite bathrooms, divided up into 4 different sections each with their own dining areas and mess tents. Swimming pool, elevated viewing platform with bar service, and family orientated with kids' educational activities.

## Greater Mara lodges

**L Mpata Safari Club**, Oloololo Escarpment, reservations Nairobi, T020-221 7015, www.mpata.com. A lodge popular with Japanese cliental with restaurant, library, bar, pool, jacuzzi, very stylish modern decor, very good views, designed by one of Japan's leading architects, 23 cottages with verandas, some with private plunge pool, game drives, walks, and visits to Masai villages.

**L Saruni Camp**, on the Lemek Koyiaki Group Ranch, to the north of the Mara, near Aitong, www.sarunicamp.com, reservations through **Cheli & Peacock**, Nairobi, T020-604 053, www.chelipeacock.com. Intimate lodge with 6 large and very elegant cottages furnished with colonial antiques, Persian carpets and African art, Italian bathroom fittings, polished wooden floors and large bathrooms with a view, plus 3 luxury tents. Very good mostly Italian cuisine in the dining room, a well-stocked library, and massages on offer.

**B Mara Simba Lodge**, overlooking the Talek River just north of the Talek Gate, reservations Nairobi, T020-434 3960, www.mara simba.com. 84 guest rooms arranged in clusters of 6 natural wood and stone thatched *bandas*, each has 4 rooms on the ground floor and 2 interconnecting rooms on the 1st floor, all have en suite bathrooms and verandas overlooking the river. Restaurant and bar,

wildlife and ecology talks, swimming pool, room service and evening entertainment.
**B Mara Sopa Lodge**, near to Ololaimutiek Gate, reservations, Nairobi, T020-375 0235, www.sopalodges.com. Well located this recently refurbished 200-bed lodge: 77 rooms, 12 suites and 1 presidential suite, is one of the most popular in the reserve. Rondavel rooms with balconies/verandas, grand African-style public areas, fine food, friendly staff, excellent swimming pool, balloon safaris and night game drives.

### Greater Mara tented camps
**L Bateleur Camp**, reservations, **And Beyond**, until recently known as **CC Africa**, Johannesburg, T+27-118 094 300, www.andbeyondafrica.com. On the Mara River, below the location where *Out of Africa*'s final scene was filmed. Romantic and totally private exuding the ambience of Kenyan safaris of the 1920s and 1930s, with 9 exclusive tented suites, with expansive en suite bathrooms, ceiling fans, private butler service, decorated with beautiful antiques and framed maps, and there's crystal, bone china and silverware in the restaurant. Walking safaris and day/night game drives are included. Rates from US$490 per person.
**L Cottars' 1920s Safari Camp**, www.cottars.com. An award-winning camp on an unspoilt and remote site near the Tanzania border, specialist walks and lectures with renowned guide Calvin Cottar, swimming pool, the 12 authentic white canvas tents are luxuriously furnished with original safari antiques from the 1920s, and have private en suite dressing rooms and bathrooms with old-fashioned tubs. Butlers and beauty therapist for massages and treatments and game drives in a vintage car. Rates from US$490 per person.

**L Kicheche Mara Camp**, on the Aitong Plains in the northern Koiyaki Lemek region, reservations Nairobi T020-890 358, www.kicheche.com. 11 comfortably furnished tents with en suite bathrooms, most are secluded and overlook the plains and hills, others are closer together for families/groups and family tents with 4 beds available. Lounge with comfortable seating, library and games, dining is either alone or with the hosts, good fresh food. From US$270 per person. Closed Apr-May.
**L Kilima Camp**, in a great position on top of the Siria Escarpment, overlooking the Mara River in the distance, reservations Nairobi T020-208 1747, www.kilimacamp.com. Opened in 2006, this has 12 very comfortable tents decorated in earthy tones, bush bar, lounge areas and dining area with great views over the savannah. Game walks and visits to a Masai *manyatta* within a 30-min walk can be arranged. From US$290 per person.
**L Mara Safari Club**, at the foot of the Aitong Hills, positioned on an ox-bow of the Mara River, reservations **Fairmont Hotels**, Nairobi T020-221 6940, www.fairmont.com/Mara SafariClub. This has just reopened after a refit and now features 50 tents with 4-poster beds, 10 of which have sunken baths, outdoor showers and platforms for private dining, surrounded by well-cultivated gardens, with a heated swimming pool. Wildlife slide shows, dancing and talks on Masai culture on offer.
**L Olonana Camp**, www.olonana.com. A lavish camp on the Mara River, 14 spacious tents, each tastefully appointed with large, river view verandas overlooking a pod of hippos, superb food in the dining room, comfortable sitting area and library, swimming pool. Rates from US$360 per person include game activities and a visit to a Masai *manyatta*.

**L Richard's Camp**, on the Aitong Plains, safaris@richardscamp.com, www.richardscamp.com. Originally built as the Roberts' family home whilst carrying out conservation work, this small and exclusive tented camp has 6 individually decorated tents, all meals are taken outside, and there is a cosy sitting room with roaring fire. A Victorian bath has been tucked away in the bush where you can bathe by candlelight. Activities include game drives and walks and visits to the Masai.

**L Sekenani Camp**, near the gate of the same name, reservations Nairobi, T020-571 597, www.sekenani-camp.com. Intimate, luxurious and very charming, the 15 tents are raised on wooden platforms and set well apart amid lush vegetation, and have polished wooden floors, grand baths and hurricane lamps. A suspension bridge leads to the dining room serving fresh gourmet meals.

**A-L Kichwa Tembo Camp**, at the base of the Oloololo Escarpment, reservations, **And Beyond**, until recently known as **CC Africa**, Johannesburg, T+27-118 094 300, www.andbeyondafrica.com. 40 Hemingway-style safari tents, with en suite bathrooms and private verandas, the main thatched guest areas include a bar/sitting area, indoor/outdoor dining areas and a rather stunning infinity swimming pool. Bush breakfasts or dinners, bush walks and night game-drives can be organized and 2 game drives per day are included. Rates vary enormously from US$200 per person in Apr and May (off season) to US$895 per person during the height of the migration.

**A Basecamp Masai Mara**, on a peninsula by the Talek River, reservations Nairobi, T020-577 490, www.basecampexplorer.com. 15 spacious, comfortable tents shaded by grass roofs, each has own terrace and a hot shower open to the sky. Restaurant, bar, game viewing tower, Masai entertainment.

Popular with Scandinavians. Makes use of dry toilets, waste recycling, solar energy, etc. Can organize walking safaris.

**A Fig Tree Camp**, in a good location on the Talek River, reservations **Mada Hotels**, Nairobi, T020-605 328, www.mada hotels.com. One of the original camps, lately refurbished, with 70 units, some tented camp and some timber cabins with electricity, pool, 2 bars and restaurants, a treehouse coffee deck, Masai dancing and wildlife lectures. Rates from US$360 for a double and there are some affordable packages from Nairobi including flights.

**A Siana Springs Intrepids**, at the base of the Ngama Hills, reservations **Heritage Hotels**, Nairobi, T020-444 6651, www.heritage-eastafrica.com. Set in a lush indigenous forest watered by the largest natural springs in the Mara ecosystem known as *Siana* meaning 'the plentiful' in the local language. 38 luxury tents, bar and large dining area, swimming pool, adventure club for kids. Walking safaris, night drives and fly camping along the seasonal streams beneath the Ngama Hills.

**B Sarova Mara Game Camp**, reservations, Nairobi T020-716 688, www.sarova.co.ke. Good tents and food, beautiful views, swimming pool, bar with large fireplace, meals can be taken in the restaurant or out bush, large with 75 tents, so rather impersonal but cheaper than many camps and low-season rates start from US$140 per person.

**C-D Mara Springs Safari Camp**, at the foot of Naunare Hills alongside the forested banks of Sekenani River, 3 km from the Sekenani Gate, reservations Nairobi, T020-224 2133, www.mountainrockkenya.com. Very basic with tents with beds and bedding or pitch your own tent on the well-shaded campsite (**F**). Self catering in the fully equipped kitchen or meals from the restaurant, shared bathrooms with hot showers and flush toilet, and small shop/bar. US$55 per person for pre-erected tent.

**E-F Acacia Camp**, not far from the Olelemutia Gate, reservations, Nairobi, T020-210 024, www.acaciacamp.com. Simple and cheap, 34 walk-in tents, built up on wooden platforms under a thatch cover, each tent has 2 single beds and a small table, shared hot showers and toilets. Without bedding, US$40, with, US$47. Camping with own tent US$8. Fully operational kitchen with gas stoves, but you will need to bring all food, and Masai dancing can be arranged in the evening around a bonfire. You'll need to be in your own vehicle to get here, though some of the budget safari operators use it.

### Greater Mara camping

The Masai Mara hardly caters for budget travellers apart from a few campsites. In theory, they should be booked in advance, but for public camp-sites it is possible to do this once at the reserve. Camping fees of about US$6 per person are paid at the gates, but if you want to hire a Masai *askari*, you will pay for his services directly to him. There are campsites close to every gate and 1 public campsite within the reserve near the **Serena Lodge**. Few have any facilities, although firewood is usually available.

**F Musiara Gate**, there are no facilities but you should be able to get water from the wardens. This is very popular for being a safe area, shaded and with plentiful wildlife.

**F Ololaimutiek Campsite**, at the eastern side of the park, is the most lively place to stay. It is Masai-run and is where most budget safari outfits stay. Water is limited and you have to buy it if you need it. You can visit the nearby **Mara Sopa Lodge** to eat in the restaurant.

**F Sand River Gate**, has lavatories, water from a stream, and is located by a waterhole usually visited by animals at night. However

the Sand River Gate into Tanzania is seldom used so this is now a very isolated spot and you'll definitely need an *askari*.

**F Talek River Campsites**, close to the Talek Gate, at 10 locations. These are located east of the gate, bordering the river at the north bank, which is also the reserve's limit. Several of them are nearly always booked up by safari companies.

---

## ▲ Activities and tours

### Masai Mara National Reserve *p140, map p142*

For details of tour operators that arrange multi-day safaris to the Masai Mara see Nairobi tour operators, page 100.

A very popular activity in the Masai Mara is a hot-air balloon flight above the plains to watch the big herds from the above. Most of the lodges and camps offer this activity, which always works in a similar way. Tourists are picked up around 0530 and driven to the site where the lift-off will take place. The balloon blow-up is part of the experience. Once the balloon rises, passengers have the chance to watch the sunrise high above the plains when the sun comes up and turns the grasslands from blue to gold. Especially during the months of the migration, this is often the highlight of visitors' trips to Kenya. The flight lasts 60-90 mins. Finally, the price usually includes a bush breakfast, made on firewood stoves beneath a tree, frequently served with champagne. If your lodge does not offer this service, they can arrange it and book the day before with one of the lodges that does. Even better, if you know you want to do this before arrival, book it along with your accommodation or safari. The following lodges have balloons; **Little Governors' Camp, Keekorok Lodge**,

**Fig Tree Camp** and the **Mara Serena**. Flights cost in the region of US$425.

## ⊕ Transport

**Masai Mara National Reserve** *p140, map p142*

### Air
Small planes are used on the Nairobi–Masai Mara route, so baggage allowance is only 15 kg on these flights. You may have to arrange to leave excess luggage in hotels in Nairobi, and most offer this service for a small fee.

**Air Kenya**, based at Wilson Airport, Nairobi, T020-605 745, www.airkenya.com. Operates 5 daily flights between **Nairobi** and 7 airstrips in the Masai Mara taking about 1 hr 15 mins (remember they touch down a few times), which cost US$105 1 way and US$190 return, slightly more in high season. **Air Kenya** also has a daily 1-way flight from **Nanyuki**, which leaves at 1000 and arrives about 1130, US$181.

**Fly 540**, ABC Place, Westlands, Nairobi, T020-445 3252, Jomo Kenyatta International Airport, T020-827521, www.fly540.com. They operate the same service as Air Kenya but have only 1 flight a day that leaves Nairobi at 1000 and departs the Mara lodges again at 1400, US$99 each way.

**Safairlink**, based at Wilson Airport, Nairobi, T020-600 777, www.safairlink-kenya.com. Again 1 daily service departing Nairobi at 1000 and returning from the Mara lodges at 1500, US$139 1 way, US$222 return.

**Mombasa Air Safaris**, Moi International Airport, Mombasa, T041-343 3061, www.mombasaairsafari.com. Operates a daily scheduled 'Beach to Bush' service between **Mombasa**, and the airstrip at **Diani Beach**, to **Amboseli**, **Tsavo**, and the Masai Mara airstrips. It leaves Mombasa at 0800 and Diani at 0830 and leaves the Mara again at 1400.

## Footprint features

## Border crossings

# Western Kenya

## At a glance

**Getting around** Buses and *matatus* link the regional towns, or you can self-drive.

**Time required** 3- to 4-day drive around the Western Kenya circuit; 1 day for walking in Kakamega Forest.

**Weather** Variable; mostly hot and dry near Lake Victoria, cooler and wetter in the higher hills and forests.

**When not to go** Can be visited year round except for Mount Elgon National Park, which is very wet in the rainy seasons (Nov-Dec and Mar-May).

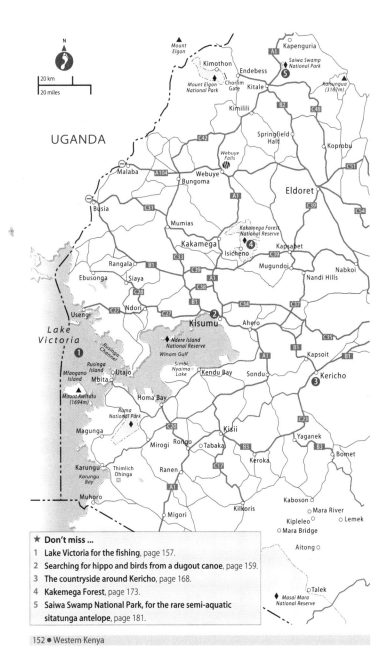

Western Kenya is the most fertile and populous part of the country, teeming with market towns and busy fishing villages. There are also a number of national parks and reserves in this region. Kakamega Forest National Reserve is the only tract of equatorial rainforest in Kenya that was once linked to the mighty forests of Central Africa. It contains many species of bird, tree and butterfly that are found nowhere else in the country and is a delightful and tranquil place for walking. Saiwa Swamp National Park, near Kitale, is worth a visit to see the rare sitatunga antelope. Mount Elgon National Park has good climbing and is accessed from Kitale and is home to the famous elephants that enter its caves in search of salt. To the south of this region is Kenya's share of Lake Victoria, Africa's largest lake, which provides a living for many of the Lou people on its shore who fish for tilapia and Nile perch from small picturesque dugout canoes, equipped with lateen sails. On Lake Kisumu is Kenya's third largest town. Unfortunately it is now pretty ravaged as it witnessed the worst of the ethnic violence over the 2007 disputed elections, and it will take many years to overcome this slice of tragic recent history.

For some reason the region is not that popular with the big tour operators and has few upmarket establishments, which is all to the benefit of the independent traveller. In fact, conditions for budget travellers are perfect; over half the population of the whole country lives here so public transport is excellent and the main road surfaces tend to be above average. There are numerous cheap hotels and restaurants, and there is plenty to see and do.

## Ins and outs

Getting around Western Kenya is pretty straightforward. All the regional towns are linked by a steady stream of buses and *matatus* and most (not all) of the roads are in a reasonable tarred condition with only the occasional pothole. The main A1 south of Kisumu that goes to Tanzania is good all the way through to Mwanza, and there are frequent buses to the border and beyond. Indeed some Tanzanian long-distance buses between Mwanza to Arusha and Dar es Salaam take the route via Kenya as the roads are better than in the interior of Tanzania. From the border, the Western Corridor of Tanzania's Serengeti National Park is less than 200 km from Kenya, so there is the option of exploring some of Tanzania along with Western Kenya. Self driving is also a good option in this region; distances between the towns and sights are relatively short and there are plenty of places to stop for petrol and take a break. The towns themselves hold little interest, but driving around the region gives a good opportunity to enjoy the countryside, especially the impossibly scenic hills covered in the brilliant green tea plantations around Kericho and Kisii. There are a few tour operators that are doing much to promote this region and a number of safaris are on offer that are way off the normal tourist trail.

# Kisumu and around

→ *Phone code: 057. Population 330,000.*

*Kisumu, on the shore of Lake Victoria, is the principal town in Western Kenya and the third-largest city in the country. It has a slow, gentle pace of life, a relaxed ambience, and the whole town comes to a standstill on Sunday. The sleepy atmosphere is as much due to lack of economic opportunities as to the extremely hot dry weather, which makes doing almost anything in the middle of the day hard work. However, the town is not economically prosperous; it has been bypassed by post-Independence development and has had little investment in infrastructure and basic services – the signs are all too visible. Warehouses by the docks remain empty and the port does not have the bustling atmosphere you would expect in such an important town. There is little formal employment and the poverty rate is among the highest in the country. The city is also not looking at its best physically at the moment because of damage caused by the 2007 post-election violence and many buildings have been wrecked or burnt out.* ▸▸ *For listings, see pages 159-163.*

## Kisumu ⊖⊕⊕▲⊖⊕ ▸▸ *pp159-163, Colour map 1, A2.*

### Ins and outs

Kisumu is an excellent base for exploring the region with good bus and *matatu* links to nearby towns, as well as to Western Kenya and Uganda. It is a six- to seven-hour drive from Nairobi. **Kisumu Airport** ① *T057-202 0811, www.kenyaairports.co.ke*, is 3.5 km to the northwest of the city off the Busia road, and **Kenya Airways** and **Fly 540** have daily flights to and from Nairobi. A taxi from the airport shouldn't cost more than US$8 and taxis are waiting in the car park to meet the planes. The airport is tiny and you walk from the plane, pick up your luggage off the tarmac and walk out of the gate. There's a small garden café for passengers waiting for flights. Most local people come to and go from here by bus or *matatu*, of which there are frequent departures to all the upcountry towns in Western Kenya and the Rift Valley as well as Nairobi. The city is the historic western terminus of the

## Rat tales

Around 1916 or 1917 the plague spread across parts of Kenya and Uganda. It was spread by rats, or rather the fleas that live on rats, and in an effort to curb the problem the medical authorities in Kisumu had a plan. They offered 10 cents for every dozen rats' tails that were brought in to them. About 29 km from Kisumu, at Maseno, many dozens were collected – but it was a long walk to take them into

Kisumu. So the collectors approached the missionary authorities and asked whether they could give the rats' tails as collection in church. This was agreed, and provided they were sun-dried, and correctly bundled, there was no objection. Every Sunday the collection tray was passed around, many bundles were collected and on Monday the mission sent someone to Kisumu with them, for payment.

Uganda Railway from the Indian Ocean to Lake Victoria, and until recently there used to be an overnight passenger rail service between Nairobi and Kisumu. However, for many years this suffered from neglect of the rolling stock and frequent derailments, there were two serious rail accidents in 2000 and again 2005 when many people were killed, and parts of the railway line between Nakuru and Kisumu were ripped up or vandalised during the 2007 post-election violence. However, the service may resume soon once the damage has been fixed as this line is not only used by passenger trains but is also an important link to Nairobi and Mombasa for the transportation of the tea, coffee, maize and sugar grown in Western Kenya. Despite the hilly terrain, you will have no problem getting around Kisumu itself as there are plenty of taxis and literally thousands of *boda bodas* (bicycle taxis) – so much so it is quite difficult to drive through central Kisumu because of the barrage of bikes. Some *boda boda* drivers have upgraded to motorbikes and new on the scene are motorized three-seater *tuk-tuks*. ▶▶ *See Transport, page 163.*

### Background

Kisumu developed during the colonial era into the principal port in the region. The railway line reached Lake Victoria in 1902, five years after plate laying began 1000 km away in Mombasa, opening up trade opportunities. It was briefly called Port Florence. By the 1930s it had become the hub of administrative and military activities on the lake. Kisumu was a difficult place at this time, bilharzia was endemic, malaria and sleeping sickness were common and the climate was sweltering. However, the area attracted investment from many different quarters, including Asians ending their contracts to work on the railway.

Kisumu and the region of Western Kenya near Lake Victoria are dominated by the Luo people, whose traditional livelihood is fishing. The Luo and the Kikuyu inherited the bulk of political power following Kenya's Independence in 1963, and a prominent Luo Oginga Odinga became vice-President under Jomo Kenyatta (a Kikuyu). However a difference of opinion between them caused Odinga to resign, which resulted in the Luo becoming politically marginalized under the Kenyatta and then the Moi governments. The breakdown of trade between Kenya, Uganda and Tanzania and the collapse of the East African Community in 1977 badly affected Kisumu and there was no compensating expansion of manufacturing in the area. In addition to this, in recent years the water-hyacinth problem in Lake Victoria has proved to be an impediment to the local fishing industry and put a stop to ferry services on the lake. The choking prolific weed formed great mats, inhibiting even large boats from using the port and it got so bad around a decade ago, people could actually walk across it to reach their marooned boats. Today it is still a problem and the main bay in front of Kisumu's port is still covered with it, but 'swamp devils', which regularly chop, shred and remove the weed, have contributed to reducing it. Nevertheless, while the fishing industry may have recovered a little, ferry services are still suspended because of falling water levels (see box, page 157).

Overall, Kisumu is not in economic good health. It has one of the highest population densities in Kenya and with little formal employment the poverty rate here of 48% is much higher than the national average of under 30%. In turn this has caused the rapid expansion of informal settlements, informal trading and a marked increase of disease infection, especially HIV/Aids, associated to areas without enough healthcare facilities.

Over the years it has also unfortunately been a hotbed of ethnic violence, predominantly between the Luo and Kikuyu. The unexplained murder of Robert Ouko in 1990, a Luo

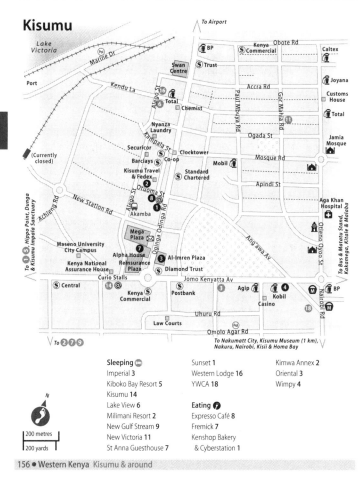

# Kisumu

**Sleeping**
Imperial **3**
Kiboko Bay Resort **5**
Kisumu **14**
Lake View **6**
Milimani Resort **2**
New Gulf Stream **9**
New Victoria **11**
St Anna Guesthouse **7**

Sunset **1**
Western Lodge **16**
YWCA **18**

**Eating**
Expresso Café **8**
Fremick **7**
Kenshop Bakery
  & Cyberstation **1**

Kimwa Annex **2**
Oriental **3**
Wimpy **4**

200 metres
200 yards

# Lake Victoria

Lake Victoria is one of the most important natural water resources in the sub-Saharan region of Africa. It is the second biggest freshwater lake in the world, with a surface area of approximately 69,500 sq km. The Tanzanian share of the lake is 49%, whilst the Kenyan share of the lake is 6% and Uganda has 45%. The surrounding lake communities in all three countries equal around 30 million people, with a large proportion being totally dependent on the lake for water, food and economic empowerment.

Despite its vast size, Lake Victoria remained one of the last physical features in Africa to be discovered by the 19th-century explorers from Europe. Early charts depict a vague patch of water lying to the north and east of the 'Mountains of the Moon' (today's Rwenzori Mountains in Uganda), but it was not until 1858 that explorers Speke and Burton stumbled on its southern shore near Mwanza in Tanzania, saying "the lake at my feet is the most elusive of all explorers' dreams, the source of the legendary Nile".

Lake Victoria is relatively shallow and has a gentle slope on the shores, hence any slight change in lake level affects a considerably large land area. The lake has a mean depth of about 40 m, with the deepest part at 82 m.

Scientifically, it is puzzling that so many diverse species unique to these waters could evolve in so uniform an environment. Biologists speculate that hundreds of thousands of years ago, the lake may have dried into a series of smaller lakes causing brilliantly coloured cichlids to evolve differently. These fish are greatly sought after for aquariums. One unique characteristic for which cichlids (tilapia being the best known) are noted for is the female's habit of nursing its fertilized eggs and young in its mouth. To the people of Lake Victoria, the cichlids have been their livelihood. Lake Victoria is also a home to a predator fish, the Nile perch, introduced into the lake 20 years ago as a sport fish. The lake once had abundant hippo and crocodile but these are reduced.

politician who at one time served as Kenya's Foreign Minister and administered a report on corruption of the Kenyan government, led to riots where many people died and much property was destroyed. Later, in the build-up to multi-party elections in Kenya in 2002, the nearby area was the scene of outbreaks of ethnic violence and thousands of people fled their *shambas*, coming into Kisumu or heading up to Eldoret. Then Kisumu and much of Western Kenya witnessed the worst of Kenya's 2007 post-election violence, when hundreds of people were killed or injured and many Kikuyu people fled Western Kenya in fear of the lives. Although not Prime Minister Raila Odinga's constituency, the province of Nyanza is where he was born and is a predominate stronghold of his support. Kisumu's main street is named after his father, Oginga Odinga, who was a prominent figure during Kenya's struggle for Independence. On the 30th December 2007, when the disputed election results turned to favour Mwai Kibaki (a Kikuyu) and not Odinga (a Luo), the town exploded and what followed was 10 days of rioting, looting and killing, and afterwards 120 bodies were counted in the city morgue. Most of the violence occurred in Kisumu's slums, but furious mobs stormed Oginga Odinga Street, and looted or burnt out shops, supermarkets and even internet cafés. Many of these were Kikuyu owned and about 90% of the businesses in town were affected. Today, a large supermarket in the Alpha Centre near the main roundabout remains a burnt out shell, the Swan Centre further north on

Oginga Odinga Street stands empty and shattered and many other buildings are boarded up or are in tatters. You can also see on the streets themselves, black spots on the tarmac caused by burning tyres. Physically it will take many years for Kisumu to recover, but nevertheless it's more or less business as usual and it has now reverted to its former sleepy self. Again, women sit on the side of the road braiding each other's hair while tempting shoppers with their beautifully arranged pyramids of tomatoes or split sun-dried tilapia fish, and *boda boda* drivers park their vehicles in the shade and somehow catnap straddled across them while batting away mosquitoes in their sleep.

## Sights

**Kisumu Museum** ① *east of the town's main market off the Nairobi Rd, www.museums.or.ke, daily 0930-1800, US$7.50, children under 18 US$3.50*, is set in a lovely garden where paths have been laid out and the trees labelled, and offers a pleasant distraction for an hour or two. Its small yet comprehensive exhibit gallery focuses on displays of material culture of the peoples of the Western Rift Valley and Nyanza Province. This includes traditional clothing and adornment, basketry, fishing gear, agricultural tools and hunting weaponry. There are also a number of stuffed birds, mammals, reptiles and fish. Most impressive is a lion bringing down a terrified wildebeest and a 190-kg Nile perch, thought to be the largest ever caught in Kenya. The ethnographic exhibits centre on the customs and traditions of the tribal groups who lived in this area, and there is a life-size replica of a traditional Luo homestead, which has livestock pens and a granary and local vegetables are grown in the garden. There's also a tiny aquarium, which displays small fish found in Lake Victoria such as tilapia, a snake pit with some rare species found in Kakamega Forest, and a couple of dead-looking crocodiles in a small pool. Look up from here and you'll see a magnificent collection of weaver bird nests balancing precariously from the branches of a tree that hangs over the crocodile pen. If the branches of the tree get any lower and the crocodiles decide to wake up, the nests will easily be within snappable distance.

The majority of people in Kisumu are Christian (mainly Roman Catholics), but there are a significant number of Muslims. **Jamia Mosque**, on Otieno Oyoo Street, is testament to the long tradition of Islam here and is one of the most striking buildings in the city. Built in 1919, this green and white building has two imams and calls to prayer can be heard in much of the town. Non-Muslim males may be permitted to enter the enclosure, ask the gateman, and everyone else can admire the gleaming silver domes from the street.

## Around Kisumu

**Dunga** is a small Luo fishing village just 4 km outside Kisumu and is located by following the shoreline road south past the **Sunset Hotel**. It takes about an hour to walk, or get a motorbike *boda boda*. To get back to town, ask around in the village and someone will find a driver and bike. It is a lovely, peaceful place to visit on the shores of Lake Victoria, and given that the views of the lake from the city centre of Kisumu are curiously very limited (only from the tops of tall buildings), this is the best place to come to see the lake itself. Here the fairly new **Kiboko Bay Resort** (see Sleeping, page 160) has great views and a lovely restaurant with tables in the garden to have cold soda or beer and admire the little fishing boats on the lake. The delightful swimming pool, which non-residents can use if they are utilizing the restaurant or bar, sits on a little hill right above the lake. Do not be tempted to swim or even paddle in the lake itself as bilharzia is present. Watching the sun set over the lake is a very pleasant way to end the day and remember being so close to the equator sunset is between

1800 and 1900 throughout the year. There are hippos here, and once night has fallen they come out of the water to graze on land. You can negotiate with a fisherman in Dunga, or organize it at the resort, to take a rowing boat out to nearby Hippo Point where you can see the hippos in the water during the day for about US$15 per boat.

**Dunga Swamp** is a belt of papyrus on the lake's edge popular with birdwatchers and is home to the rare *Papyrus gonolek*, which faces extinction due to the cutting of papyrus reeds along the shores of Lake Victoria. The papyrus yellow warbler is relatively common.

Tiny **Kisumu Impala Sanctuary** ① *on the way up the dirt track to Dunga, 3 km from Kisumu, www.kws.org, daily 0600-1800, US$10, children US$5*, only 40 ha of marsh, forest and grassland, was created to protect the few remaining impala in the region, decimated over the last century by hunting. The sanctuary was expanded to act as a holding point for captured animals. Nowadays it is home to a lonely old male lion, two leopards, a spotted hyena and several vervet monkeys in addition to several reptiles and birds, but they are all in cages and it is nothing more than a sad-looking zoo. Hippos come up to the sanctuary to graze, and in the past there have been sightings of the rare Sitatunga antelope. You can get a boda boda to the gate and ticket office. A guide takes you around to give you a rather school-child account of the animals and again you can hire a boat to take you out to Hippo Point. The boatmen here are particularly knowledgeable about the birdlife.

**Ndere Island National Reserve** ① *www.kws.org, daily 0600-1800, US$20, children US$10*, gazetted in 1986, covers a small island of just over 4 sq km off the northern shore of Lake Victoria, 30 km from Kisumu. In the local Luo language Ndere means 'meeting place' and, according to legend, Kit Mikayi, mother of the tribe, rested up near here following her long journey south down the Nile Valley. Bird life teems in the park, from pied kingfishers and swifts to the African fish eagle and the dazzling malachite kingfisher. Hippos and crocodiles are plentiful on the shoreline, and there is also a small herd of impalas. Other animals present include pythons and monitor lizards. Very few visitors make it to Ndere Island, due to its small size and lack of terrestrial wildlife. Bird enthusiasts, however, would find a visit to Ndere Island very rewarding. The island vegetation is primarily glades in the upland areas, with a shoreline fringe of woodland. However, as with other parts of this area of Kenya, tsetse flies are common, along with the ubiquitous malaria-vector mosquitoes. There is no regular boat service to the park, so transport has to be negotiated with the local fishermen. Small boats can be hired at the fishing villages of Kamuga or Asembo on the nearby mainland for the short distance to Ndere Island. Alternatively you can organize a motorized canoe to take you the 30 km from Kisumu, which is quite a good way to explore Lake Victoria. The best bet is from the Kiboko Bay Resort (see page 160), which has two modern speed boats and can also organize a packed lunch. It is possible to camp on the island but you have to be completely self sufficient.

---

### ⊙ Kisumu and around listings

*For Sleeping and Eating price codes and other relevant information, see Essentials pages 34-38.*

### ⊙ Sleeping

**Kisumu** *p154, map p156*
Hotel accommodation is now fairly limited in Kisumu and some establishments were either damaged or destroyed in the 2007 post-election violence. However, the few larger hotels in Kisumu more or less survived unscathed thanks to good hotel security. There is no choice of up-market accommodation, consider the Imperial the best, but if you want lake views, also consider the Sunset or Kiboko Bay Resort. Kisumu is

swarming with mosquitoes. If you don't have a net, get a room with one. Use cover up and repellents. A fan is a boon, too.

**C Kiboko Bay Resort**, Dunga, 4 km south of Kisumu, T057-202 5510, www.kiboko bay.com. This is the nicest accommodation in Kisumu, in a lovely lakeside setting, and is exceptionally friendly and worth coming here (even if not staying) for the charming restaurant, swimming pool and boat excursions. The 12 en suite rooms are set in spacious and comfortable permanent tents on elevated wooden decks under thatched roofs, with chunky home-made furniture and are dotted around manicured gardens. A lovely spot and well recommended.

**C-D Imperial**, Jomo Kenyatta Av, T057-202 0002, www.imperialkisumu.com. This has made-for-hotel furniture, plush carpets and fittings, a/c, a very good swimming pool and friendly staff. The rooms on the 3rd and 4th floors have views of the lake. Facilities include 2 bars (1 rooftop), restaurant, coffee shop and internet access. A standard double room is US$95 a night (with rates significantly lower Fri-Sun). It's very popular so book ahead.

**D Kisumu**, Jomo Kenyatta Av, T057-202 2833, www.maseno.ac.ke/hotelkisumu. Very large and grand colonial building that was bought by Kisumu University, who completely refurbished and reopened it in 2004. Despite being very run-down before this, it did have a certain dilapidated colonial charm. Now, with a modern tiled lobby, made-for-hotel furnishings and wall-to-wall carpeting, the atmosphere has been somewhat lost and it's a shame they didn't refurbish it in the style of its era. However, the 80 rooms are neat with good bathrooms, phone and TV, and there's a decent bar and restaurant, lovely pool, and car park.

**D Milimani Resort Hotel**, T057-202 3245, www.milimaniresort.com. Modern hotel with car parking in a quiet location, a fair distance south of the town centre, but signposted from Jomo Kenyatta Av from the **Kisumu Hotel**. The recently renovated rooms have different prices, are well equipped with fans,

nets and TVs but a little on the small side. Breakfast included. Restaurant, bar, pool and conference centre.

**D Sunset**, Aput Lane, south of town, T057-202 217. A faded 3-star hotel but with adequate rooms with satellite TV and a/c. The veranda looks over beautiful lawns, restaurant and bar, secure parking and a good swimming pool. All 50 rooms have balconies and views of the lake and sunset, and you can take a good photograph of the lake from the hotel roof.

**E New Gulf Stream**, around the corner from the **Millimani Resort Hotel** and clearly signposted in town from Jomo Kenyatta Av, T057-202 5460. Big down-at-heel concrete block, adequate rooms, if a little plain, with satellite TV and fan, tiled floors, pleasant outside restaurant and bar terrace with plants, rates include breakfast. It's predominantly used as a local conference venue.

**E New Victoria**, Gor Mahia Rd, T057-202 1067. Excellent value, clean and large rooms with fans but check mosquito nets for holes, in an unmissable building brightly painted green and yellow. Triple rooms available, 2nd-floor rooms have pleasant balconies (rooms 205-209 have views of the lake). Good basic food like stews and curries, but Muslim-owned, so no alcohol and the rules stress that there should be no 'private meetings' in rooms.

**E St Anna Guesthouse**, 3 km south of town in the Milimani Estate, follow signboards from the Central Bank of Kenya in town, T057-202 4792, www.stannaguesthouse.com. This is a Christian-run establishment and a popular local conference venue, in a very pleasant double storey stone house set in nice gardens, with 35 en suite 2-3 bed rooms with hot showers, very bare but spotlessly clean. Breakfast is included, and basic African meals and some oriental dishes can be arranged in advance for supper. There's a common room with TV and a computer for internet access.

**F Lake View**, Alego St, T057-204 5055. Friendly hotel from where the lake can only just be seen, mirrored exterior, basic rooms with nets are on the 1st floor but the very heavy dark brown curtains make them a little gloomy. There's a bar next door.

**F Western Lodge**, Kendu Lane, T057-202 3707. Good cheap rooms and good security with an *askari* at the door, and a safe in each room. Nice little upstairs terrace with pot plants and tables for breakfast from where you can get a slight view of the lake, but it does suffer from noise as it's so central.

**F YWCA**, off Ang'awa Av, T057-204 4788. This used to offer 3-4 bed very simple and cheap rooms, mostly used by church groups, but at the time of writing it was still being used to house displaced women from the 2007 post-election violence. Check locally.

# ⊘ Eating

## Kisumu *p154, map p156*
Some of Kisumu's restaurants were damaged in the 2007 post-election violence. Those that are open usually close on a Sun. The fish dishes using fresh tilapia from the lake, which is quite delicious, are good value. The large Asian community that has settled here means it is possible to get excellent Indian meals. Cheap kiosks near the bus station and more in the car park of the Maseno University City Campus, sell grilled meat on skewers or tilapia fish with *ugali* (maize dough).

**†† Kiboko Bay Resort**, Dunga, 4 km south of Kisumu, T057-202 5510, www.kiboko bay.com. Daily 0700-2300. Very pleasant bar/restaurant with chunky wooden tables inside and plastic tables scattered on the terrace overlooking the lake and in the gardens. You can get a simple toasted sandwich here and main meals include creamy masala curries and whole baked tilapia fish straight from the lake. Look out for the modern paintings on the wall from local artists, which are for sale, and diners can use the swimming pool and pool bar.

**†† Sunset Hotel**, Aput Lane, out of town to the south, T057-202 217. Downstairs is

a bar and terrace overlooking the lake and although the view is mostly obscured by trees you can walk down through the gardens to the lake's edge. You can get snacks here throughout the day such as chicken or sausage and chips, while upstairs is the more formal restaurant that is open from 1900 for à la carte dinners of stews and curries and the like. Excellent friendly service.

**†† Victoria Terrace**, in the Imperial Hotel, Jomo Kenyatta Av, T057-202 0002, www.imperialkisumu.com. Daily 1230-1500, 1900-2200. Kisumu's best restaurant, which has a good value daily lunch buffet of mixed African and European food for around US$9 and an evening à la carte menu of curries, steaks, chicken and pasta dishes, occasionally Nile perch, and there's always something for vegetarians. The hotel's poolside bar is open daily from 1030-2300 and serves *nyama choma*.

**† Expresso Café**, Otuoma St. Mon-Fri 0700-1800, Sat 0800-1300. Popular with office workers during the day, this is a simple canteen serving good and cheap grills, curries, burgers and sandwiches, hot and cold drinks, and nice fresh fruit juice.

**† Fremick**, Alpha House, Oginga Odinga Rd. Mon-Sat 0800-1700. Bar and restaurant with simple but good food, nice terrace area with wrought-iron furniture but it overlooks a car park. Local food such as rice and beans or *ugali* and stew, plus omelettes, burgers, sandwiches.

**† Kenshop Bakery & Cyberstation**, Oginga Odinga Rd. Mon-Sat 0900-1500. Branch of a popular bakery chain with a few tables selling very good pies, pastries, bread, pizza slices and ice cream as well as hot drinks and juice, including freshly squeezed sugarcane juice. Also has internet access.

**† Kimwa Annex**, Otuona Rd. A clean, tiled local canteen with plastic tables that's very popular for huge plates of cheap local fare, served up self-service style from big catering tins, there's also a bar with pool table, open 24 hrs.

**† Kisumu Hotel**, Jomo Kenyatta Av. Daily 0800-2100. Large brilliantly white canteen with CNN on TVs and very popular for the school-dinner type of fare of pork chops and vegetables or chicken and chips followed by sponge and custard or fruit salad and ice cream.

† **New Victoria Hotel**, Gor Mahia Rd. Does a substantial breakfast from 0700-0900, good Indian menu with lots of vegetarian options, owned by a family from Yemen, very quick service and large portions. Can get quite busy, the menu states all food will be served within 15 mins.

† **Oriental Restaurant**, in the Al-Imren Plaza, Oginga Odinga Rd, T057-202 0579. Mon-Sat 1200-1400, 1800-2200. Actually run by Chinese people, this is excellent value, and offers tasty authentic, if not imaginative, Chinese dishes in generous portions and good service in typical red-lantern type decor.

† **Wimpy**, Jomo Kenyatta Av, towards the market. Burgers, chicken, fries, good fry-up, and coffee, best pineapple milkshake ever.

## ○ Shopping

**Kisumu** *p154, map p156*
### Handicrafts
There are many artefacts from other parts of the country available here. *Kisii* stone is a particularly good buy as are *kikois* (woven cloth). Street vendors are outside the post office and at a line of stalls opposite the **Kisumu Hotel** on Jomo Kenyatta Av. In *Kisii* stone there are chess boards, bowls, pots, candleholders and sculptures. There are also wooden animals, Masai warriors, drums, spoons/forks, masks and trinkets. These are excellent quality and good value, but you will need to barter hard to get a good price.

### Markets
Kisumu's main fruit and vegetable market on Nairobi Rd is one of the largest in Western Kenya, and worth a wander to soak up some of the atmosphere. The market bustles every day, although Sun tends to be quieter. You'll find that most things on offer tend to be

quite similar. Look out for *kikois*, some real gems are available if you look hard enough. Otherwise it's run-of-the-mill stuff: fruit and vegetables, children's clothes, tools, flip-flops, radios, batteries, bags, sheets, etc, but also a surprisingly large number of trainers/sneakers along Jomo Kenyatta Av. There are 2nd-hand clothes and shoes stalls all over town.

### Supermarkets
**Nakumatt Nyanza**, Mega Plaza, Oginga Odinga St, has a good selection of goods and rather remarkably this is now one of Kenya's Nakumatt branches that is open 24 hrs. The larger **Nakumatt City,** out of town on Nairobi Rd on the left just beyond the museum has just about anything for sale and is in a modern complex with a number of other shops and coffee shops.

## ▲▲ Activities and tours

**Kisumu** *p154, map p156*
### Boat trips
**Kiboko Bay Resort**, Dunga, 4 km south of Kisumu, T057-202 5510, www.kiboko bay.com, has 2 motorized boats and 30-min sightseeing trips can be arranged for up to 5 people for US$35 to see the birdlife and hippos around Dunga, or they can arrange 1 hr's fishing for 2 people for about US$50. You can also arrange canoe trips with the local fisherman in Dunga or from the Kisumu Impala Sanctuary for about US$15 per boat.

### Swimming
Do not swim in the lake as bilharzia is rife, so use the hotel pools at the **Sunset, Kisumu, Milimani Resort, Imperial** or **Kiboko Bay Resort**. Each charge around US$2 for non-guests to use the pool or you may be able to use them for free if you are utilizing the restaurants.

### Tour operators
**Kisumu Travels Ltd**, Oginga Odinga Rd, T057-202 4582 www.kisumutravels.com.

General travel and flight agent and can also arrange car hire but only with a driver.

## ⊖ Transport

**Kisumu** *p154, map p156*
### Air
**Fly 540**, Nairobi T020-4453252, www.fly 540.com. Has 5 daily flights in each direction between Kisumu and **Nairobi** taking 45 mins, 1 way from US$69. The early-morning flight at 0750 also touches down in **Eldoret**, which takes 20 mins and costs US$30 1 way – the plane hardly gets up into the air. It doesn't stop in Eldoret on the way to Kisumu however. **Kenya Airways**, Alpha House, Oginga Odinga Rd, T057-205 6000, www.kenya-airways.com. There are 4-5 daily flights between Kisumu and **Nairobi** taking 50 mins and costing US$105, 1 way.

### Bus and matatus
The main *matatu* and bus stopping point is behind the covered section of the main market. There are regular *matatus* and buses travelling between Kisumu and most major towns in Western Kenya. There are also many leaving for **Nairobi** passing through **Nakuru** and **Kericho** on the B1. Approximate times: **Nairobi**, express 6 hrs or normal 8 hrs, 2 hrs to **Kericho**, 5 hrs to **Nakuru**, 2 hrs to **Eldoret**, 1 hr to **Kakamega**. The offices of **Akamba Buses** are in the town centre, on Alego St just off New Station Rd.

### Ferry
Small motor ferries running between Kisumu and a number of lakeshore towns were a very cheap and nice way of seeing around Lake Victoria. However, all operations are currently suspended because of low water levels.

## ⊕ Directory

**Kisumu** *p154, map p156*
**Banks** Barclays, **Co-op Bank**, and **Standard Chartered**, all on Oginga Odinga Rd, and **Kenya Commercial Bank** at the roundabout on Jomo Kenyatta Av, are all efficient for changing money and have ATMs. **Western Union** money transfer can be organized at the **Post Bank** on Jomo Kenyatta Av. Banking hours are Mon-Fri 0900-1500 and Sat 0830-1100. **Immigration** 2nd floor Reinsurance Plaza, T057-202 4935. **Internet** Given that Kisumu is a university town, access is available at a number of places around town including the **Imperial Hotel**, and **Kisimu Hotel**. There are also 2 cyber cafés in the Al-Imren Plaza, Oginga Odinga Rd. The best of the lot is **Cyberstation**, Oginga Odinga Rd, at the Kenshop Bakery, which is also a coffee shop. **Medical Services** Aga Khan Hospital, Otiena Oyoo St, T057-202 0005, www.agakhanhospitals.org. Kisumu's private hospital and the best bet if you fall sick. **Police** Omolo Agar Rd, T057-202 4719. **Post office** Oginga Odinga Rd, Mon-Fri 0800-1700 and Sat 0900-1200, has a reliable poste restante service. **DHL**, delivery services from **Securicor**, **Fedex** from Kisumu Travel, Oginga Odinga Rd. **Telephone** Direct calls from the card phone outside the post office.

# South of Kisumu

*The main A1 road heads south to Tanzania via the rambling market town of Kisii. This area receives abundant sunshine and rainfall and the hillsides feature terraced fields of subsistence farmers. Another road to the west of here joins the simple fishing settlements located on the shores of Lake Victoria, while on the lake itself are a couple of upmarket island fishing lodges. To the southeast of Kisumu, tea is the mainstay of the local economy around Kericho and the countryside is blanketed with glistening green tea plantations.* ▶▶ *For listings, see pages 170-172.*

## Kisumu to the Tanzanian border ● ▶▶ *pp170-172.*

The main route from Western Kenya to Tanzania, the A1, runs from Kisumu via Oyugis and Kisii, and is in reasonable condition, except for a few patches of potholes. Mgori is the last town along this stretch, on the Tanzanian border. See page 165 for border crossing information. This small town is a transit stop for people travelling to Musoma and Mwanza in Tanzania. The lakeshore region to the south of Kisumu is known as South Nyanza is an easy enough area to explore by *matatu*. However, there is limited accommodation in this region. Self-drive (in a 4WD vehicle) is probably recommended to get to some of the more remote spots, such as the prehistoric site of Thimlich Ohinga, and Ruma National Park.

Fishing (a male activity) and the smoking of fish (a female activity) are important occupations around this region. Homa Bay is the biggest town in the area and here there is a branch of **Kenya Commercial Bank**, a post office and a petrol station. Out on the lake are two islands, Rusinga and Mfangano. Rusinga is the burial place of Tom Mboya, a great son of Kenya who was assassinated in Nairobi in 1969. On each of the islands there are fishing camps providing boats for hire and some accommodation in sublime settings. Much of the business comes from the Masai Mara lodges where, every morning, small planes pick up upmarket safari goers that also want to go fishing.

### Kendu Bay → *Colour map 1, A2.*

Kendu Bay is a small town in South Nyanza, now Homa Bay District. It is an hour's drive from Kisumu, on the Homa Bay–Katito road, off the Ahero–Sondu-Kisii road. The main reason for coming here is to visit the curious **Simbi Nyaima Lake** – a deep volcanic lake, steeped in myths and legends. It has bright green opaque water, is located only a few kilometres from Lake Victoria and as it is rich in algae, attracts a few hundred flamingos. To get there take the road towards Homa Bay and it is a 4-km walk from Kendu Bay. It takes about two hours to walk around the lake. There are no facilities so take food and drink. No one knows what the source of the lake is and its size is constantly changing. Local people believe it to be unlucky and the surrounding area is certainly devoid of vegetation. It is not fished and the area is uninhabited. According to one legend, a hungry and tired old woman called Ateku arrived in this area, where she found the villagers celebrating by eating, drinking and dancing. Only one caring female villager gave her food and drink and a bed in which to rest her weary bones. To give thanks, Ateku ordered water to spring from the ground, which later went on to flood the area. Another version of the legend was that the old lady was denied food and lodgings and in wrathful vengeance induced a massive flood that swamped the village.

# Border essentials: Kenya–Tanzania

### Isebania

Isebania is a small settlement that straddles the A1 road. Crossing is efficient and quick and visas for both Tanzania and Kenya are available, but remember that if you've only gone into Tanzania and go back to Kenya you don't need to buy another visa to re-enter as long as your original one is still valid. If you are in your own vehicle travelling on a carnet de passage, its needs to be stamped here and third-party insurance for both countries is available at kiosks on either side of the border. Once in Tanzania the road continues south past the Western Corridor of the Serengeti National Park and on to Mwanza, which is Tanzania's principal town on Lake Victoria.

**Note** If you have arrived from Tanzania, you will need to have a valid certificate to prove vaccination against yellow fever.

## Homa Bay

About 35 km southwest of Kendu Bay, Homa Bay is an unremarkable ramshackle market town running along two main streets, with a covered market and one reasonable place to stay on the lake – the **Homa Bay Tourist Hotel**, see page 170. Most people rely on fishing here though over recent years, water hyacinth has periodically plagued the lakeshore. Above town rises the 1751 m Mount Homa, known by the Luo as Got Asego ('famous mountain'), which is the highest of many extinct volcanic plugs that scatter the region. It is possible to climb to the top but it's a scramble through thick thorny bushes and the only paths are those made by goats. Beyond Homa Bay, the road goes to Mbita Point, a small rural community and a collection point for boats to Lake Victoria's islands (below).

## Ruma National Park → *Colour map 1, A2.*

ⓘ *www.kws.org, daily 0600-1800, US$20, children US$10.*

Ruma National Park is 10 km east of Lake Victoria in the Lambwe Valley in the Suba District, 140 km from Kisumu. The park was established in 1966 to protect the rare roan antelope, found only in this part of Kenya. The land is a mixture of tall grassland and woodlands of acacia, open savannah and riverine forests interspersed with scenic hills. There are abundant wild flowers. In addition to the roan antelope, other mammals found here include the Bohor reedbuck, Jackson's hartebeest, hyena, leopard, buffalo and topi. Rothchild's giraffe, zebra and ostrich have been introduced in recent years. Oribi, one of the smallest of the antelope family, are also present. Birdlife is plentiful and diverse, and Ruma is the only protected area in Kenya where the globally threatened blue swallow, a scarce intra-African migrant, is regularly recorded. Blue swallows arrive from their breeding grounds in southern Tanzania around April and depart in September. They depend on moist grassland for feeding and roosting. The diurnal yellow-eared bat is also found.

This is a delightful park for anyone wishing to achieve isolation on their safari, although there is no accommodation and the roads are pretty rough. From Kisumu, follow the A1 south onto the C18 Homa Bay turn-off. Continue along the C18 past the Homa Bay turn-off to the north (the C20) and access to the park is on a turn-off to the right soon after the town of Mirogi. From the Migori Shopping Centre it is 10 km to the park headquarters along a *murram* road. Within the park are also unsealed *murram* roads, which become impassable with black sticky mud, known locally as black cotton, when it rains. A 4WD is needed and is essential during the rainy season.

There are two camping sites here, **Sigama Hill** and **Fig Tree**. However, there are no facilities and, given the tsetse fly situation, you may want to give camping a miss.

## Rusinga Island → *Colour map 1, A2.*

Rusinga Island lies in the northeastern corner of Lake Victoria in Kenyan waters. Ferry access from Homa Bay is restricted due to the water-hyacinth problem in Lake Victoria, but the island is now linked to the mainland by a causeway. Rusinga is an austerely scenic island with high crags dominating the desolate goat-grazed landscape. A single dirt road runs around its circumference. The main town on Rusinga Island, Mbita, is unexceptional, though the excellent **Lake Victoria Safari Village** (see page 170) is nearby, but inland foreigners are rare and you are sure of a welcome. Life here is difficult, drought commonplace, and high winds a frequent torment. The occasional heavy rain either washes away the soil or sinks into the porous rock, emerging lower down where it creates swamps. Almost all the trees on the island have been cut down for cooking fuel or been converted into lucrative charcoal although there has recently been an initiative to plant new trees. These conditions make farming highly unpredictable and most people rely on fishing to make ends meet.

The island is rich in fossils, and famed for the 1948 discovery by Mary Leakey, the anthropologist, of one of the earliest austrapithecines remains, the skull of *Proconsul africanus* (*P. heseloni*), a sub-group of *Dryopithecus*, said to be 17.5 million years old. This anthropoid ape lived on the island three million years ago, and is believed to be a probable ancestor of the chimpanzee. Aside from the public interest it spurred, the discovery of the skull also ensured the Leakeys' funding for their next expeditions. Louis and Mary, thrilled at the discovery, decided the best way to celebrate would be by having another child. Their third son, Philip, was born in 1949 almost nine months later to the day that the skull was discovered. The skull can be seen in the Nairobi National Museum.

Rusinga Island was also the birthplace of Tom Mboya, an important Kenyan political figure during the fight for Independence. A civil-rights champion, trade unionist and charismatic young Luo politician, he was gunned down in Nairobi by a Kikuyu policeman in 1969, sparking off a crisis that led to over 40 deaths in widespread rioting and demonstrations. There is a school and a health centre named after him, and Tom Mboya's mausoleum lies on family land at Kasawanga on the north side of the island, about 7 km by the dirt road from Mbita, or roughly 5 km directly across the island. The mausoleum (open most days to visitors) contains various mementoes and gifts Mboya received during his life. The inscription on the grave reads: *Go and fight like this man, Who fought for mankind's cause, Who died because he fought, Whose battles are still unwon*. You don't have to know anything about the man to be impressed. In any other surroundings his memorial might seem relatively modest, but on this barren, windswept shore, it stands out like a beacon. Mboya's family live right next door and are happy to meet foreign visitors, who rarely come here. A small donation towards the upkeep of the mausoleum would also be gratefully appreciated.

The island is popular with game fishermen and holds the IGFA all-tackle record for the heaviest Nile perch ever caught. Over 80 species of bird are found here, including fish eagles and bee-eaters. On the shores of the island you may see the rare spotted-necked otter, giant monitor lizards or hippos. Lake Victoria is renowned for its glorious sunsets, and after dark the Luo fishermen from the villages scattered along the lakeside can be seen out on the lake in their beautifully painted boats, lit by paraffin lamps. Boat trips to visit other nearby islands can be arranged locally with these fishermen.

## Mfangano Island → *Colour map 1, A1/2.*

Further along Lake Victoria, slightly bigger than Rusinga Island, Mfangano has shade from giant fig trees, and is much more remote and primitive, with few tourist facilities except for the luxury **Mfangano Island Camp**, see page 170. Until recently there were no roads, but now a road has been cut that circles the island and the first car was driven on the island in 2007. Mfangano's greatest economic resource is still the lake itself and the islanders fish with floating kerosene lamps to draw in the fish to be netted. Hippos are very much in evidence, as are monitor lizards basking in the sun. There are interesting prehistoric rock paintings here showing signs of aeons of habitation. The rock paintings are in a gently scooped cave on the north coast of the island and are reddish coloured shapes. It is not known who drew them, when or why, although one theory is that they were the work of Twa Pygmy hunters from Congo, and could be 8000 years old. Local people associate the site with supernatural powers and miraculous events, and in some measure fear them too, which has so far helped prevent the vandalism which has afflicted other rock art sites in Kenya.

A large wooden boat shuttles people between Mbita and surrounding places. It leaves Mbita at 0830 and takes about 90 minutes to Sena on the east of Mfangano and leaves there again for Mbita at about 1400. The island is has neither electricity nor piped water, so bear this in mind if you intend to visit. Mfangano's people rely on a network of temporary footpaths that are constantly changing course, so you can walk all over the island.

## Thimlich Ohinga → *Colour map 1, A2.*

Some 60 km southwest of Homa Bay or 55 km northwest of the town of Migori on the main A1 to the border with Tanzania, the Thimlich Ohinga Prehistoric Site is one of the most significant archaeological sites in East Africa. The name means 'thick bush' or 'frightening dense forest' in the local DhoLuo language. It was declared a national monument in 1983, and consists of dry stone enclosures of what appears to be one of the earliest settlements in the Lake Victoria area. It is an impressive example of a style of architecture whose remnants are found all over the district. The main structure consists of a compound about 140 m in diameter with five smaller enclosures in each and at least six house pits. The drystone walls range from 1-4 m high and from 1-3 m wide. The materials used were collected locally from the nearby hills. Several parts of the enclosing wall have caved in, and conservation work is urgently required. A giant *Euphorbia candelabrum* towers over the site.

The design of these structures would appear to indicate that the dry stone enclosures were built by a cohesive community, thought to date from about the 14th century, believed to be mostly of Bantu origin. It is believed that the Bantu lived here prior to the arrival of the Luo people. Between them, the early Bantu settlers and later Nilotic settlers built about 521 enclosures in over 130 locations in the Lake Victoria region. They are similar to the 17th-century stone ruins in Zimbabwe. Later settlers appear to have carried out repairs to the stonework between the 15th and 19th centuries. It is unclear as to why the area was abandoned by the Ohingnis in the early 20th century. A similar style of dwelling is used in some places by Luos today.

There is no public transport to get here. If driving you need to follow the A1 road through Migori and after 4 km turn right onto a rough *murram* road at the junction of Muhoro Bay where there is National Cereals and Produce Board depot. Take the first right after the depot for 55 km. This road is accessible by a normal car if it's dry but only in a 4WD if it's wet. If there is anyone here to collect it, there is a small entry fee and the ruins are generally accessible during daylight hours but remember there are no facilities.

## Kisii and the Western Highlands ⬤➊➋➌➍ » *pp170-172.*

The Western Highlands are the agricultural heartland of Kenya, separating Kisumu and its environs from the rest of the country. The Highlands stretch from Kisii in the south up to the tea plantations around Kericho, through to Kitale, Mount Elgon and Eldoret. Away from the towns other highlights in this region include the Saiwa Swamp National Park. This is one of the few parks that permits walking, and is an ideal place for a day's hike. This wild country is home to many and varied species, the best known being the very rare sitatunga, a semi-amphibious antelope that lives in the depths of these swamps. The Western Highlands have become a major draw for sporting tourists. This is the home of many of Kenya's world-famous runners. This is probably the finest place on earth for high-altitude athletic training, and many international athletes visit training camps around Iten and Kaptagat. There are good bus and *matatu* connections among most towns and villages and it is an easy region to get around, although the roads around Kisii are in a poor shape.

### Kisii → *Colour map 1, A2. Phone code: 058.*
Set in picturesque undulating hills in some of the most fertile land of the country and with abundant sunshine and rainfall, Kisii is a very lively and fast-growing town, although unfortunately it was another Western Kenyan town hit hard by the 2007 post-election violence. As with so many other towns in agricultural areas, the market here is buzzing and has an excellent array of fresh fruit and vegetables. The town lies on a fault line, so earth tremors are not uncommon. This is the home of the Gusii people, and is famous for its **soapstone**, although you may try to buy some in vain as most of what is locally produced is bought up by traders to stock the tourist shops in Nairobi and on the coast.

### Tabaka → *Colour map 1, A2.*
This village is the most important producer of soapstone and the centre of carvings in the country. The left turn-off to Tabaka is 18 km west of Kisii off the A1, and the village is 6 km from the turnoff. This road can be fairly dire in the wet. Direct *matatus* come from Kisii. You can visit the quarries and watch the carvers at work, who are members of the **Kisii Soapstone Carvers Co-operative**. The soft pliable stone is fashioned into all sorts of items for practical use such as bowls and plates, as well as tourist items such as animal statues, chess sets, and abstract figures, and there are lots of local stalls where you can buy soapstone artefacts. The stone comes in a variety of colours from orange (the softest) to deep red (the heaviest).

### Kericho → *Colour map 1, A3. Phone code: 052.*
Perched on the top of a hill, the tea plantations stretch for miles on either side of the road, their bright green bushes neatly clipped to the same height with paths running in straight lines in between. At 1800 m above sea level, the tea plantations stretch along the western edge of the Great Rift Valley. The tea bush is an evergreen in tropical climates, so the bushes are harvested throughout the year. An evocative image of this region is of the many hundreds of men and women plucking the tea leaves in the plantations with their distinctive white polythene sacks on their backs. The predictable weather (it rains every afternoon here) and the temperate climate giving a high ground temperature, make this the most important tea-growing region in Africa. Tea was introduced in Kenya in 1903 and it is now the world's third largest tea-producing nation, after India and Sri Lanka. This is an orderly part of Kenya, very different from the *shambas* further down the slopes, and

very English, exemplified by the **Tea Hotel** with its lovely gardens that used to be owned by Brooke Bond. Kericho is named after Ole Kericho, a Masai chief who perished in battle at the hands of the Gusii in the 18th century. The town's main purpose is to service the enormous tea plantations, so it has most of the basic amenities on the main road, Moi Highway: branches of the main banks, post office, market, library, village green, the English-style Holy Trinity Church, War Memorial and cemetery. There's also an impressive **Sikh Temple**, which is Africa's largest Gurudwara temple, and is dedicated to Baba Puran Singh Ji of Kericho, who was an eminent spiritual Sikh figure. He was born in 1898 in Panjab and emigrated to Kenya in 1916, set up Kericho Wagon Works and was a major benefactor to the town. In the 1970s he went to the UK and became a leading campaigner for getting Sikhs protected under the Race Relations Act there.

For tea tours, where the growing and picking procedures are explained, enquire at the **Tea Hotel** who have a resident guide who will take you for a walk to the hotel's own estate and explain all about how tea was introduced into the region and the tea-growing process. Tea tasting is included in the excursion and it costs about US$3.50 per person. If you would like to visit a tea-processing factory around Kericho, get in touch with the hotel two weeks in advance and they will be able to arrange this.

### Chagaik Dam and Arboretum

About 8 km to the northeast of Kericho off the road to Nakuru is this exceptionally attractive arboretum. It was established after the Second World War by a Kericho tea planter, Tom Grumbley, and is home to many tropical and sub-tropical trees surrounded by well-tended lawns running down to the lake's edge. The lake is covered in water lilies and fringed with stands of bamboo. It's a good spot for birdwatching and at least one troop of black and white colobus monkeys live in the trees. Trout fishing is available in the Kiptariet River. The **Tea Hotel** will arrange for permissions and equipment hire. The river runs close by the hotel.

# Kericho

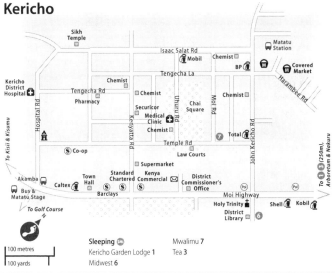

Sleeping
Kericho Garden Lodge 1
Midwest 6

Mwalimu 7
Tea 3

*For Sleeping and Eating price codes and other relevant information, see Essentials pages 34-38.*

## ☁ Sleeping

### Homa Bay *p165*
**D Homa Bay Tourist Hotel**, T059-22788, www.homabaytouristhotel.com. Although this was built in the 1970s, it's recently been refurbished and occupies a pleasant site on the lakeshore. The 23 rooms have fans, mosquito nets, fridges and rather shiny bedspreads, and facilities include a good restaurant serving both local and international food, bar, a spacious lawn with garden furniture, internet access, and the hotel has its own motorized boat for lake excursions and rents out bikes.

### Rusinga Island *p166*
**L Rusinga Island Lodge**, reservations **Private Wilderness**, Nairobi, T020-882 028, www.rusinga.com. 6 cottages with their own veranda, and 1 family cottage made up of 2 rooms with shared veranda, all overlooking the lake, made from stone, wood and grass thatching, and decorated with traditional fabrics and baskets. Game drives at Ruma National Park are on offer, as is waterskiing and fishing for Nile perch on the lake. It's usually accessed by private air charter and is a 20-min flight from Kisumu and 35 mins from the Masai Mara. Rates are from US$400 per person sharing and including meals and drinks and all activities except air transfers.
**C-D Lake Victoria Safari Village**, 3 km to the southwest of Mbita, clearly signposted, T0721-912 120, www.safarikenya.net. Owned by a local lady and her Norwegian husband, who also own the 2 local board and lodgings in Mbita below, this is a great, remote place to stay. The clump of thatched rondavels are set in a lush tract of indigenous woodland on the lakeshore where there is a little beach. En suite rooms are neat with mosquito nets and bunches of flowers, there's a rather

remarkable 'honeymoon suite' in a 2-storey bright white mock lighthouse, which has an additional stone bath, and a shady restaurant and bar. Boat trips to the islands and fishing for Nile perch can be arranged (much cheaper than the island lodges), they can take you to Ruma National Park if you don't have a 4WD, and have compiled a local bird list for birdwatching.
**F Elk Guesthouse**, next to the bus stand in Mbita. A very basic local guest house but clean and all beds are fitted with mosquito nets. Does not have a restaurant or bar but there are several cheap eating places nearby.
**F The Viking Guest House**, to the right of the bus stand is very similar, although with shared bathrooms, and it also has a bar in a bougainvillea shaded courtyard.

### Mfangano Island *p167*
**L Mfangano Island Camp**, reservations **Governors' Camp**, Nairobi, T020-273 4000, www.governorscamp.com. This is set in beautiful gardens that mostly attracts serious (and wealthy, at US$445 per person) fishermen. There are just 6 rooms made from natural clay and banana thatch, with private verandas and lovely stone bathrooms, beautifully decorated with 4-poster beds with mosquito nets, very good food, bar, and swimming pool. All fishing activities are organized, especially for Nile perch, and are included in the price. Set in a secluded bay surrounded by fig trees. Very high standards here to match the Governors' Camps in the Masai Mara, and most guests arrive here by plane from the Mara. Closed Apr-May.

### Kisii *p168*
**E Zonic Hotel**, at the corner of Hospital Rd and Ogemba Rd, T058-30298. Although this very large hotel on 5 storeys was only built in 2002, it's starting to look worn already (some missing door handles and toilet seats) and there's no parking. Nevertheless it's the best option in town and all rooms have

bathrooms and some have balconies. On the roof is a nice terrace, the restaurant does decent food, at the weekends there is sometimes a disco, rates include breakfast.

**F Kisii**, north of town centre on the Kisumu Rd, T058-30134. Probably the best of the budget places, the rooms are spacious with bathrooms but very basic. It is an old slated wooden building in a compound with secure parking, there is a comfortable colonial atmosphere, with attractive gardens and OK food in the restaurant and there's a bar.

**F Kisii Sports Club**, behind **Barclays Bank** on the main road, has quite spacious rooms within the clubhouse, with nets and bathroom but a little gloomy. Has a bar and restaurant. Price includes breakfast, but the use of the facilities (swimming pool, squash, snooker and pool tables) requires an extra small payment. Club membership fee is necessary to play golf.

### Kericho p168, map p169

**D Tea Hotel**, east of town centre, on Moi Highway on road to Nakuru, T052-30004/5, teahotel@africaonline.co.ke. Set in lush gardens and backing directly on to the tea plantations this is the best hotel in Kericho. It was built in 1958 by Brooke Bond. Although now looking slightly drab the 45 rooms in the old colonial building and garden cottages are spacious and some have TVs. It has a swimming pool, and a reasonable restaurant with a solid and dependable English-style menu and some Indian dishes. Visa and Mastercard accepted. There's also a very pleasant campsite here (**F**) in the grounds with toilets and hot showers, a tap for filling water tanks for overland vehicles and an electric point for charging batteries.

**E Midwest**, John Kericho Rd, turn off Moi Highway opposite the police station, T052-20611. A large ugly 1970s block with 70 soulless rooms with old-fashioned furnishings and TVs, set in nice gardens though, plus there's a gym with steam

room and sauna, and a passable restaurant with a reasonable daily set menu of Western dishes. It's a popular local conference venue.

**F Kericho Garden Lodge Hotel**, Moi Highway, close to **Tea Hotel**, T052-20878. Very basic board and lodgings with singles with shared bathrooms and some doubles with en suite, but reasonably friendly, sporadic hot water in the showers, breakfast included, garden bar with *nyama choma*, and satellite TV, but note women may feel exposed here as the bar is popular with male drinkers. There's parking in the sweeping drive and you may be able to negotiate to camp.

**F Mwalimu**, Temple Rd, just to north of Chai Sq in town centre, T052-20601. Basic board and lodgings, corridors are quite dark but the rooms are OK, and clean, with own bathroom, restaurant and bar though this gets noisy on weekend nights, price includes breakfast.

## 🍴 Eating

### South of Kisumu p164

Most of the small towns have small *hotelis* (kiosks) selling the likes of *nyama choma*, *ugali*, chips and omelettes and sodas. For more substantial meals, go to the larger hotels. See under Sleeping, above.

## 🛍 Shopping

### Kisii p168

There's a branch of **Nakumatt** supermarket on Moi Highway.

## 🚌 Transport

### Kisii p168

Kisii is about 115 km from Kisumu on the A1. At the time of writing the road was in a terrible state and was severely damaged during the 2007 post-election violence as barricades were put up outside of Kisii, but it has been ear-marked to be re-tarred. *Matatus* to **Kisumu** take 2 hrs and the *matatu* stand is on the main road that runs through town, Moi Highway. There is another *matatu* stand 2 blocks east of the market. Buses to **Nairobi** go via **Kericho** and **Nakuru** and the **Akamba Bus** office is also on Moi Highway near the post office.

### Kericho *p168, map p169*

The *matatu* and bus station is at the northern end of Isaac Salat Rd and is well organized. There is plenty of transport, both buses and *matatus* run regularly throughout the day for **Nakuru** and **Kisumu** where you can pick up onward transport. **Akamba Bus** has a stand on the corner of Moi Highway and Hospital Rd, and runs daily services to **Nairobi**.

### ⊙ Directory

**Kisii** *p168*

**Banks** Barclays Bank, Moi Highway, open Mon-Fri 0830-1300 and Sat 0830-1100.

**Kericho** *p168, map p169*

**Banks** Barclays and Standard Chartered banks are both on Moi Highway and both have ATMs. **Western Union** money transfer is available at the post office and post bank. **Internet** Email from **Tea Hotel** or post office. **Medical services** Kericho District Hospital is on (naturally) Hospital Rd, T052-31192. **Police** The main police station is just to the southwest of the Tea Hotel on Moi Highway. **Post office** A few metres to the east of the **Kenya Commercial Bank** on Moi Highway.

# Kakamega and around

*To the north of Kisumu is the beautiful Kakamega Forest National Reserve, which will appeal to the nature lover for its walks through the dense canopy of trees and rich ground foliage. It's also home to a number of interesting and unusual primates and small mammals, snakes and reptiles, and butterflies and birds. Further north, the industrial town of Eldoret won't hold the attention of visitors for long, but it is the gateway town to the more remote regions of Northern Kenya.* ▸▸ *For listings, see pages 176-179.*

## Kakamega ●●●● ▸▸ *pp176-179. Colour map 3, C5.*

→ *Phone code: 056.*

This pleasant lively place is the main town of the Luhya people. A major attraction is the Kakamega Forest (below), and the town is the place to buy provisions for an excursion there. At the end of November is the **Kakamega Show**, an agricultural festival at the showground just to the north of the town, on the Webuye Road. Most travellers tend to head straight out to the forest reserve and stay there, which is a much more pleasant alternative than staying in town. Kakamega is famous for being the centre of a gold rush in the late 1920s, which attracted huge numbers of hopeful prospectors. The largest nugget found was named the **Elbon Nugget**, so named by reversing the surname of Dan Noble, a postman, who later bought Nairobi's first hotel, the old **Hotel Stanley**.

Kakamega

Sleeping ●
Franka 1
Golf 2
Savona Isle Resort 3

## Kakamega Forest National Reserve
● ▸▸ *pp176-179. Colour map 3, C5.*

ⓘ *Open 0600-1800. Entry fee US$25, children US$10, vehicle US$4.50. Guide fee is US$4 per hr and represents excellent value as the guides are extremely knowledgeable.*

Western Kenya's Kakamega Forest would not look out of place on the set of a Tarzan movie – tangled vines, intermingled branches, and a chorus of screeches and mutterings from a whole host of African creatures. Declared a forest reserve in 1966, Kakamega Forest's headquarters lie 12 km from the town of Kakamega on the Kisumu–Eldoret road, the A1. One of the last remaining (and fast diminishing) tropical rainforests of East Africa, Kakamega is a remnant of the Guineo–Conglian equatorial belt that once covered all land from the Atlantic to the Rift Valley as little as

400 years ago. Its closest relation, to whom it once joined, is Bwindi Impenetrable Forest on Uganda's western border with the DRC. Kakamega Forest is only 45 sq km and is the sole remnant of tropical rainforest in Kenya and has been a protected area since the 1930s. It is an extraordinarily beautiful forest, with at least 150 species of tree, shrub and vine, including the Elgon teak, 90 dicotyledenous herbs, 80 monocotyledonous herbs of which 60 are orchids (nine unique to Kakamega), and a further 62 species of fern, making a total of 380 different plants in one small area. The indigenous trees along the trails are identified with small plaques giving their Latin as well as their local names. Many of these provide a valuable source of fruits and green vegetables for the local people and about 50 herbs are used for medicines and ritual events. Approximately 20% of the flora and fauna in the Kakamega Forest is not found anywhere else in Kenya.

### Ins and outs

For **Isecheno** take the Kisumu road south of Kakamega for about 10 km and turn left at Khayega. Carry on down this road for about 7 km when you will reach the village of **Shinyalu** where the forest is signposted. Take a right and after about another 5 km you will reach the forest reserve. **Buyangu** is much easier to get to than Isecheno if you do not have your own transport as it is a walk of less than 1 km from the main road, about 20 km north of Kakamega, on the way to Webuye. This route is served by countless *matatus*, but watch out, very few of the drivers or conductors seem to recognize the name Buyangu.

### Wildlife and vegetation

There are a number of animals here including the grey duiker, bushpig, bush-tailed porcupine, giant water shrew, clawless otter and a few leopards. There are also several primates including the olive baboon, the red-tailed monkey, the black and white colobus and blue monkey. The forest is also home to the hairy-tailed flying squirrel that can 'fly' as far as 90 m, bush babies and the lemur-like potto can be spotted amongst the branches at night, along with the hammer-headed fruit bat – the largest in Africa with a wing span of over 1 m and an exceptionally big head.

The forest is also of great ornithological interest as many birds found here are not seen elsewhere in Kenya. Hornbills, woodpeckers, honeyguides, both Ross's and the great blue turaco, grey parrot and the rare snake-eating bird are among the avian residents. In addition, several varieties of barbet including the double-toothed, speckled and grey-throated are found here. Butterflies are abundant, and snakes normally only found in West Africa, can be seen too. Look out for the Gabon viper, a particularly nasty, deadly but fortunately very shy snake that lives in the forest. Near to

# Kakamega Forest National Reserve

*To Webuye & Eldoret*

Kenya Wildlife Service HQ

*Isiukhu Falls*

Buyangu

Kakamega

*Weeping Stone*

Isecheno

Shinyalu

*To Kapsabet*

Khayega

Chepsonoi

*To Kisumu*

Kaimosi

Chavakali

N

5 km
5 miles

**Sleeping**
Forest Rest House 3
Isecheno Bandas 2
Rondo Retreat Centre 1
Udo's Bandas & Campsite 4

the reserve on the Kakamega–Kisumu road is a curiosity called the **Weeping Stone**. This is an 8-m-high rock upon which a smaller rock is balanced, and between the rocks a small trickle of water emanates, and continues to flow even during the dry season.

The most rewarding way to appreciate Kakamega is to walk through the narrow winding paths accompanied by a knowledgeable guide from the forestry station. These dedicated local people, who are often self-taught, make excellent and informative guides and know the flora and the fauna intimately. The enthusiastic welcome by the proud employees of the Forestry Service is almost overwhelming, and if given the chance, they will reel off every species name in Latin. Birdsong and the occasional whoop of a black and white colobus monkey accompany walks ranging from 1 to 6 km through the peaceful interior. If you wish to see the flowers at their best, plan your visit during the rainy season from April to July. Exotic orchids grow in the junctions of the tree branches. There are two areas in the forest that cater for tourists: **Isecheno** towards the south/centre of the forest and **Buyangu** in the north. At Buyangu. several walks are possible, the longer of which offers the chance to reach **Buyangu Hill**, from where there is a good view over the tree canopy or to a small waterfall (**Isiukhu Falls**). Here the canopy spreads out like a thick green blanket and on a clear day a brooding Mount Elgon can be sighted in the distance. On the banks of the Yala River you can see deep pits, which were dug to extract gold, and occasionally you may see local people panning for the precious metal. It is advisable to wear waterproofs, as the rain is heavy, regular and predictable, but it is beautiful walking country.

## Eldoret ⬤🕓▲⬤🅱🅖 ➠ pp176-179. Colour map 3, C5.

➔ Phone code: 053.

The journey from Kericho due north to Eldoret passes through the **Nandi Hills**, some of the most spectacular scenery in this part of the country, and the **Kano Plain**s, bleak mountainous scrubland and ravines. Eldoret was originally settled by South African Boers who sailed from the Cape to Mombasa after the Boer War. They then travelled from the coast inland by ox wagon to what was 'plot 64', the number of the farm plot that had a post office on it, which was renamed Eldoret in 1912. This pleasant, busy and fairly prosperous highland town is surrounded by fertile countryside growing a mixture of food and cash crops. There is large-scale maize and wheat farming, and cattle keeping of the Ayrshire breed. The market is good and there are some useful shops if you are stocking up on provisions. Eldoret is dubbed 'home to running' thanks to a number of Olympic medal-winning athletes that have come from the region. An international airport opened at the end of the 1990s used to transport fresh flowers from the Naivasha region directly to the flower markets of Amsterdam and elsewhere in Europe. It is home to **Moi University** and this appears to be benefiting the town and expanding its economic potential. It is also home to a large teaching hospital, which attracts many European medical professionals on placements. It is a very busy town, with banks, supermarkets, trading stores and dozens of internet cafés, but there's no special reason you should stay here, unless en route to the Cherangani Hills. Again, Eldoret is another Western Kenyan town that suffered during the 2007 post-election violence and the worst incident was on New Year's Day 2008, when a mob attacked and set fire to a church in the town where hundreds of people had taken refuge. As a result, up to 40 people, mostly Kikuyus, were burned to death.

# Border essentials: Kenya–Uganda

Visas for Uganda and Kenya can be bought at the border posts below and the crossings are quick and efficient. Remember that if you go into Uganda and return to Kenya, the Kenyan visa is still valid as long as the date is still valid and you do not need to get another one. However, if you go into Uganda and then into Rwanda or the Democratic Republic of Congo to see the mountain gorillas, for example, and then return to Kenya via Uganda, the Kenyan visa will not be valid and you will have to get another one. This visa agreement is only between Kenya, Uganda and Tanzania.

There are money changers on both sides of the border at both Malaba and Busia and you can change up a small amount of currency until you get to the next bank. If coming from Uganda, the first bank you'll reach in Kenya is in **Bungoma**, 32 km from the Malaba border, and there's a branch of **Kenya Commercial Bank** in Busia. Going in the other direction the first Ugandan banks are in **Tororo**, 18 km beyond the Malaba border, or **Jinja**, about 90 km from the Busia border. If you are on a through bus, then wait until you get to a bank at your final destination.

### Malaba

From Eldoret the A104 passes through **Webuye** and **Bungoma** to reach Malaba, the most common border crossing into Uganda. These towns are all geared toward the transit traffic heading for Uganda. The Malaba border itself is very busy especially with trucks and if you are in your own vehicle it may be better to cross at Busia (see below).

### Busia

Busia is some 30 km to the south of Malaba and more easily accessed from Kisumu; most of the buses between Nairobi and Kampala use this border. It is a small town that primarily consists of one road lined with shops, kiosks and cafés that serve the busy border post, which is actually two sets of worn metal gates with a few metres of no-man's land between them.

The settlement teams with *boda bodas*, the bicycle taxis that now feature in many Kenyan towns and the name was thought to have originated from Busia as drivers call out 'border border'.

---

## ⦿ Kakamega and around listings

*For Sleeping and Eating price codes and other relevant information, see Essentials pages 34-38.*

### ⬤ Sleeping

**Kakamega** *p173, map p173*
**C-D Golf**, just off main road, T056-30150/1/2, www.golfhotelkakamega.com. Modern, very pleasant, excellent service and food, the 60 en suite rooms have mosquito nets and TV, there is a swimming pool and facilities for

golf, tennis and squash at the **Sports Club** next door. The bar and restaurant is open to non-residents, and offers English-style cooking with some Indian dishes. Can arrange tours into the Kakamega Forest. Room rates include a buffet breakfast.
**E Franka**, southwest of the clocktower, T056-20086. Basic and quite small but clean rooms with hot water, bar and restaurant. Overall this hotel is quite reasonable and is the best of the basic board and lodgings in

town, although the bar can get noisy. Rates include breakfast and there's *nyama choma* in the evening.

**E Savona Isle Resort**, 1.5 km out of town near the Kakamega airstrip, T056-30593, www.savona isleresort.com. This is a simple local predominantly conference venue set in a pretty forested location on the Isiukhu River, and is reached over an attractive white pedestrian bridge complete with 2 thatched entrance gates from the parking area. The 8 thatched *bandas* have 2 rooms each plus a bathroom with hot water and veranda, and there's a bar and restaurant with some international dishes. It's currently a bit of a building site as they are expanding with 10 additional *bandas* and a swimming pool, but should be very nice when it's all up and running properly.

### Kakamega Forest National Reserve
*p173, map p173*

**C Rondo Retreat Centre**, T056-30268, www.rondoretreat.com. This is a religious centre open to the public, in a serene location within the forest. Originally Rondo was owned by a sawmiller who, in 1948, built a house at his wife's request at the base of what was thought to be the biggest tree in the Kakamega Forest, an Elgon olive tree that still stands today. The sawmiller left Kenya in 1961, leaving the property to the Christian Council of Kenya. It was first used as a youth centre and orphanage, but more recently it has been involved with conservation efforts for the forest and it produces its own field guidebook. The homestead consists of the main house of clapboard and colonial-era corrugated iron and 5 cottages in the same style – 18 rooms in total. Very good wholesome food in the dining room, but you need to be on best behaviour here. It's not suitable for children and there is no alcohol or smoking.

**E Isecheno Bandas**, Isecheno Forest Station, 20 km from Kakamega town on Shinyala Rd, T0722-619 150, keeporg@yahoo.com. There are 6 *bandas* that in total can sleep 18 people, a shared kitchen, bathroom and dining area.

You need to bring your own bedding, food and firewood, though meals can be arranged on request with notice. This project is owned and run by the Kakamega Environmental Education Program (KEEP), which can provide guides for walks into the forest; you can also visit its resource centre nearby.

**E Udo's Bandas and Campsite**, just outside the entrance gate in the north of the forest at Buyangu. Reservations **Kenya Wildlife Service Nairobi**, T020-600 800, www.kws.org. 7 2-bed *bandas*, communal cooking area but no utensils, you need to bring firewood and water as well as linen and towels, US$10 per person, bucket showers and long-drop loos. You can also camp next to the stream for US$3. A small shop sells a few basic supplies such as bread and soda, and there are small shops and tiny local restaurants in the village.

**F Forest Rest House**, within the forest reserve not far from the park office at Isecheno. It is a small building on stilts, with 4 bedrooms, all with private bathrooms but it's pretty filthy and unkempt with no electricity and an erratic water supply. Nevertheless it's in a beautiful forest glade where you can also camp. You will need to bring all food supplies from town although nearby there is a very small shop/restaurant where you can arrange a plate of food in advance.

### Eldoret *p175*

**C-D Eldoret White Castle**, Uganda Rd, T053-203 3095, www.eldoretwhitecastle.com. 120 very pleasant, clean rooms with TV and good modern facilities including a restaurant, bar, health club and disco. However, it is bang in the middle of town with no parking but a few spaces on the street, although you can arrange for an *askari* to watch your car overnight.

**D Eldoret Wagon**, Elgeyo Rd, T053-200 2270, wagonhotel@africaonline.co.ke. Comfortable, some triple and family rooms, there are new and old blocks so some rooms are better than others, has restaurant, bar, secure parking and swimming pool. This started life as a members' club for senior railway staff, notice the dining room was built in the shape of a railway carriage with a hooped roof. There's a casino here too with some slot machines.

**D Sirikwa**, Elgeyo Rd, reservations Nairobi, T053-206 2499, sirikwahotel@yahoo.com. Large hotel with over 100 rooms in an imposing white block located in well-tended gardens, with an impressive entrance hall and good swimming pool, which non-guests can use for a small fee. Rooms are a worn but comfortable with bathrooms, there's a Presidential Suite, price includes breakfast. There's a relaxed bar and good food in the restaurant. A double room goes for a not unreasonable US$75.

**D-F Naiberi River Campsite & Resort**, T053-206 3047, www.naiberi.com. 16 km from Eldoret on the road to the Kerio Valley, the C54 to Kaptagat, this turn-off is a few kilometres south of Eldoret at the Shell petrol station on the Nairobi road. *Matatus* from Eldoret to Kaptagat can drop at the entrance to the resort. Unique in its design, with a tunnel leading to a cool bar with running streams, huge central fire place, glass roof with views of the moon and the setting sun over the forest. Lovely stonework, dorms, en suite double rooms in a log cabin, and luxurious doubles in stone cottages, kitchens, spotless ablution blocks and beautiful gardens with a swimming pool and ponds. A very popular spot for overlanders, the parties here can be huge if large groups are staying, good food on offer including Indian snacks, run by the affable Raj who owns a big textile factory in Eldoret. Prehistoric remains have recently been discovered here. A magical spot, well recommended.

**F Eldoret New Lincoln**, Oloo Rd, T0721-466 162. Colonial-style hotel with some character and helpful staff with 46 rooms, but hopelessly dilapidated with leaky toilets and sporadic water.

## 🍴 Eating

### Eldoret *p175*
There are a few canteen-type establishments around town but after dark the best choice for eating is at the hotels.

🍴 **Arcade**, is a fairly new food court type complex on Oloo Rd, which has the **Swiss Restaurant,** which serves pizza, a branch of **Paul's Bakery**, for pies, sandwiches and cakes, the **Spree Club**, which is a bright and modern bar and disco, and an internet café.

🍴 **Paul's Bakery**, to the north of town on Uganda Rd. Good place to stop for fresh bread, pies, cakes, etc.

🍴 **Sizzlers Cafe**, Kenyatta St. American-style diner, good local food, snacks and milkshakes, good service too.

🍴 **Sunjeel Palace**, Kenyatta St. Cheap daytime café serving good-value and tasty Indian dishes with good choices for vegetarians and popular with the local Indian community, a good sign that the food is authentic.

## ⛰ Activities and tours

### Eldoret *p175*
**Eldoret Travel Agency**, Corner House, Kenyatta St, T053-206 3588. General agent and can book flights.
**Elgeyo Travel and Tours**, Uganda Rd, T053-206 2006. Again, a general agent.

## 🛍 Shopping

### Eldoret *p175*
There's a large branch of **Nakumatt** supermarket on Oginga Odinga Rd. The main market around Kimathi Av has a huge selection of fruit and vegetables. There is also a good shop at the cheese factory located to the south of the roundabout at the end of Kenyatta St, which sells a surprising range of very good cheeses and excellent ice cream

plus other dairy products. On the main road coming into Eldoret from the southeast look out for people selling fresh mushrooms on the side of the road around the large Shell petrol station at the turn-off to Kabernet.

## ⊖ Transport

**Kakamega** *p173, map p173*
The town is less than 1 hr from **Kisumu** along the very busy A1 and there are plenty of buses and *matatus* travelling this route. The main bus stand is close to the market. The **Akamba** bus service has its stand opposite the Hindu Temple, off the Mumias Rd, for **Nairobi**.

**Eldoret** *p175*
### Air
Some 16 km south from Eldoret on the Eldoret–Kisumu Rd is Eldoret Airport www.kenyaairports.com, which although predominantly used for freight is served by **Fly 540**, Nairobi T020-445 3252, www.fly540.com. There are 2 daily flights in each direction between Eldoret and **Nairobi** taking 45 mins, 1 way from US$69. The early-morning flight at 0750 from **Kisumu** also touches down in Eldoret, which takes 20 mins and 1 way costs US$30, but it doesn't stop in Eldoret on the way to Kisumu. Taxis meet the flights.

### Bus and matatu
The *matatu* stand is in the centre of town just off Uganda Rd and there are a number of *matatus* and buses throughout the day. The journey direct to **Nairobi** takes 4-6 hrs.

Recommended is **Easy Coach**, which has its office next to Eldoret Valley Board and Lodging on Uganda Rd. It has a daily service between Eldoret and **Nairobi** via **Nakuru** (2 hrs). **Akamba Bus** also offers daily services and the office is on Arap Moi St to the west of the market.

## ⊕ Directory

**Kakamega** *p173, map p173*
**Banks** Barclays is to the south of town towards Kisumu, **Standard Chartered** and **Kenya Commercial** banks are both on Kenyatta Av and all have ATMs. **Internet** There is internet access at the Kakamega post office. **Police** opposite the post office on the Kisumu road, T056-31486. **Post office** In the middle of town.

**Eldoret** *p175*
**Banks** There are several banks in Eldoret with ATMs and foreign exchange facilities. Most are on Uganda Rd or Kenyatta St. **Internet** Thanks to Eldoret being a university town, there are dozens of internet cafés. Try **Cyber Café**, next to Barclays Bank, on Uganda Rd, **Cyberhawk**, Nandi Rd, or **Jambo Internet Café**, Uganda Rd, next to Standard Chartered Bank. **Medical services** Moi Teaching and Referral Hospital, southwest of the centre at the end of Nandi Rd, T053-203 3471, www.mtrh.or.ke, is very good with a large casualty department. **Police** On Uganda Rd near the National Bank of Kenya, T053-203 2900. **Post office** Uganda Rd, opposite is the Post Bank which offers **Western Union** money transfer.

# The far north

*The busy main A104 heads west of Eldoret and into Uganda; a route heavily used by trucks taking goods over the border. To the north the small market town of Kitale has an interesting museum and serves as the access point to both the Mount Elgon and Saiwa Swamp national parks.* ➤➤ *For listings, see page 184.*

## Webuye ➤➤ *Colour map 3, B5.*

Webuye is an industrial town straddling the main A104 Uganda road and is home to the large **Panafric Paper Mills**, which omits a very unpleasant smell of sulphur dioxide, and some sugar refineries. **Webuye Falls** are about 5 km from the road, and provide the water for the mills. You can hire a *boda boda* to take you up there; it's a fairly scenic spot with a short drop of foamy water tumbling over some rocks and behind the main falls, huge stones dominate the countryside creating a series of smaller falls and rapids.

## Kitale ●● ➤➤ *p184. Colour map 3, C5.*

→ *Phone code: 054.*

A pleasant, small town, Kitale is in the middle of lush farmland between Mount Elgon and the Cherangani Hills. Originally this was Masai grazing land, but it was taken over by European settlers after the First World War. The town did not really develop until after 1925 and the arrival of the railway. The region is known for its fruit and vegetables, including apples, which are rare in East Africa. Kitale's main attraction for tourists is as a base from which to explore the Cherangani Hills, see page 350, or Mount Elgon and the Saiwa Swamp National Park, see page 181. It's also a stopping-off point on the route to Lake Turkana in the north.

### Ins and outs

Getting to and from Kitale is relatively easy as it is on the A1 heading for Kakamega and Kisumu in the south, and is the main route to Lake Turkana in the north. There are regular buses and *matatus*. In Kitale there are various bus stands and *matatu* stops at the western end of the road to Mount Elgon. An **Akamba Bus** stand is on the corner of Moi Avenue and Bank Street. The road north is reasonable until Marich Pass and then rapidly deteriorates on the route to Lake Turkana.

### Sights

**Kitale Museum** ① *close to the Eldoret Rd, T054-20670, www.museums.or.ke, 0930-1800, US$7.50, children under 18 US$3.50*, contains ethnographic displays of the life of the people of Western Kenya with lots of tribal artefacts, and has a section on the evolution of man. The museum also boasts a very comprehensive insect collection as well as birds, reptiles and wildlife exhibits. Murals on local life can be viewed in the Museum Hall. The museum buildings are set in spacious gardens, and the indigenous trees are labelled. There is an excellent nature trail through local forest, the remnants of a much larger forest that once clothed this area, that is rich in birdlife and monkeys, terminating at some very pleasant picnic sites. There is also a **Snake Park**, home to both non-venomous and venomous snakes, in addition to an enclosure containing two crocodiles. Another enclosure contains tortoises. Nearby is a display of traditional homesteads of the Luhya, Nandi, Luo and Sabaot peoples. A bio-gas generation unit to demonstrate the use of animal waste to produce methane is an unusual exhibit.

**Olaf Palme (Vi) Agroforestry Centre** ① *next door to the Kitale Museum, T054-31498, run by the Swedish Cooperative Centre, www.sccportal.org, daily 0800-1700, free*, was established by a Swiss NGO to assist and educate local farmers in soil conservation and improvement techniques, with advice and support about methods of tree planting and preventing soil erosion. There is an arboretum, an indigenous tree nursery and an agro-forestry demonstration area, in addition to a conference centre with educational displays.

## Saiwa Swamp National Park 🖰 ⇸ *p184. Colour map 3, C5.*

① *0630-1800, US$20, children US$10. Reached via the sealed well-signposted road, 24 km northeast of Kitale on the Kitale–Kapenguria road. There is a 5-km murram road linking Saiwa to the main road. You can reach here by public transport on matatus from Kitale to Kapenguria and beyond and then walk the last 5 km or there may be boda bodas around.*

Kenya's smallest national park, at 2.9 sq km, was established to protect the rare semi-aquatic sitatunga antelope (*Tragelaphus spekei*). The park is a perfect example of how a small area can survive as a complete ecological entity; it encloses the swamp fed by the Saiwa River together with its fringing belts of rainforest. The star of the show, the sitatunga, has splayed hooves, allowing it to walk on the swamp vegetation. There are a sufficient number here to ensure a sighting. Other animals here include the giant forest squirrel, bushbuck, Bohor reedbuck, bush duiker, the de Brazza monkey and both the spotted-necked and clawless otter. There is prolific birdlife estimated at over 400 species of bird and includes the great blue turaco, several varieties of kingfisher and the bare-faced go-away-bird. There is also a very large variety of reptiles, amphibians, butterflies and other insects. There are about three nature trails, totalling 10 km, on duckboards, and there are rest areas and picnic areas along the way. Several tree hides with viewing platforms have been built along the western boundary from where it is possible to view the mammals and birds. The best time to see the sitatunga is in the early morning or evening, as it rests semi-submerged and very well hidden during the heat of the day. The park has three distinctive vegetation types: wetland vegetation with stands of bullrush, reeds and sedges; wooded grasslands containing shrubs and grasses; indigenous forest as the national park contains remnants of tropical forest including wild fig and banana trees.

## Mount Elgon National Park 🖰 ⇸ *p184. Colour map 3, C5.*

→ *Phone code: 054.*

① *T054-310 456, www.kws.org, park entry fee US$25, children US$10, vehicle S$4.50 per day.*

Mount Elgon National Park is in the Rift Valley on the western border with Uganda, covering 169 sq km on the Kenyan side. The peak of the extinct volcano, which reaches 4322 m, the second-highest mountain in Kenya with a radius of about 100 km, is estimated to be more than 15 million years old. The Kenya/Uganda border cuts through the caldera, giving half the mountain to Uganda, including the highest peak Wagagai (4320 m), with Lower Elgon Peak (also sometimes called Sudek Peak) (4307 m) in Kenya.

The brooding flat-topped Mount Elgon, which straddles the border with Uganda, is a distinctive feature of this region of Western Kenya. Located in the National Park, the mountain is home to a wide diversity of habitats created by the changing altitude at differing heights. From the base of the mountain to the top are a number of ecological zones going from mixed deciduous and evergreen forest, which include wonderful specimens of the Juniperus procera more commonly known as the East African cedar, as well as the Elgon teak and the great podos. With increasing altitude the vegetation changes to bamboo forest, and then to Afro-alpine moorlands. Several rivers rise in these peaks including the Malakis and the Nzoia that feed Lake Victoria, and the Suam and the Turkwell that feed Lake Turkana. The park also contains several beautiful waterfalls, dramatic cliffs and gorges, and hot springs. The name Elgon is said to be derived from the Masai *ol doinyo ilgoon* meaning 'the mountain with the contours of the human breast'. This area is known as Koitoboss meaning 'table rock' by virtue of its flat-topped basalt columns. There are a number of lava-tube caves formed by the action of water on volcanic ash, some are over 60 m wide and attract elephants and other herbivores in search of salt. Some of them can be explored (see below). The El Gonyi people, a Masai tribe, lived in the caves for hundreds of years with their cattle, and the caves were used for many of their ceremonies. The mountain peak is considered to be a sacred place of worship, home to the gods.

The Sabaot Land Defence Force (SLDF) is an armed militia group that has been operating in the Mount Elgon district since 2005. They seem to be some kind of rural mafia, and it appears their motives are about land claim issues. They have been accused of the deaths of over 600 people since 2005, and while the government at first considered them common criminals, more recently and given that members of the group wear army fatigues and carry AK47s, they are now considered an organized militia group. There was a large-scale military assault in May 2008 to try and flush out members of the group from their hideouts in the Mount Elgon region and the leader of the group, who was only 24, was shot dead in a cave on Mount Elgon. This appears to have abated their activities but check locally.

# Mount Elgon National Park

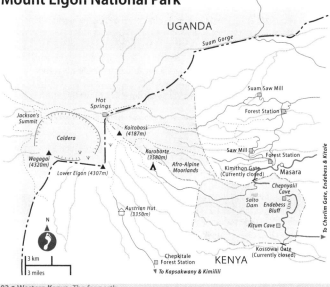

## Ins and outs

The park is about 26 km northwest of Kitale, and the roads are clearly signposted. The most popular entry to the national park is by Chorlim Gate. There are other gates but they are presently closed and Chorlim Gate is the only place you can pay park fees. Two routes to the gate can be used, either via Endebess, about 15 km from Kitale, or take the tarmac road 11 km past Kitale and turn left onto a *murram* road leading to the gate. Most roads in the park are in good condition but a 4WD is recommended and is essential in the wet season.

## Sights

Four of the lava-tube caves can be explored. **Kitum** is the largest cave extending to over 180 m in depth with a width of 60 m, and overhanging crystalline walls. This is the cave most favoured by the elephants. Using their tusks the elephants scrape away at the rock face and pick up the shards with their trunks. At night it is possible to see elephant convoys entering the cave to supplement their diet on the rich salt deposits. Kitum is also home to a large population of fruit bats. **Makingeni Cave** is not far from Kitum, and is favoured by buffalo, and both **Chepnyalil** and **Ngwarisha caves** can also be explored. **Endebess Bluff** offers a panoramic view of the surrounding area. Animals likely to be here include colobus monkey, blue monkey, forest elephant (sometimes called cave elephant), leopard, giant forest hog, bushbuck, eland, buffalo, duiker and golden cat. It is possible to drive up to about 4000 m – the road passes through forest that is later supplanted by montane bamboo – and then hike over the moorlands with tree heathers up to 6 m tall, to Koitoboss peak. In the Afro-alpine zone are found giant lobelia and groundsels, believed to be survivors from the Ice Age. From there it is possible to climb over the crater rim and descend to the floor of the caldera.

## Climbing Mount Elgon

It is possible to climb Mount Elgon at any time of year, but the crater gets very cold and snow and hail are common, so the best times are December to March. A KWS ranger is required to accompany you, which can be arranged at the gate, or in advance at the KWS HQ in Nairobi. You can reach the summit and back in a day in dry weather when you are able to drive to within a few hours' hike of the highest point. Ensure you are suitably equipped with warm and waterproof clothing and appropriate footwear. There is not such a severe problem with altitude sickness as on Mount Kenya, but a night spent en route will lessen any problems. If you do not have a 4WD, the ascent can be hiked in a fairly leisurely manner, three days up and two down. The usual entry to the park is through the main Chorlim Gate and then driving through the park to the end of the road track at Koroborte (3580 m), where there is a campsite and water. From here it is then about three hours to the Koitoboss summit. The following two routes may be closed; enquire with KWS.

**Kimilili route** This runs south of the park route. From the village of Kimilili, there is a track to Kapsakwany (8 km). Another 2 km on is the turning to the forest gate, which is a further 2.5 km. It is then 26 km, which can be driven in dry weather, to the **Austrian Hut** (3350 m), where you can stay or camp (water nearby). There is 3 km more of driveable track. From here it is about a four-hour hike to Koitoboss. Picnic sites at Elephant Platform and Endebess Bluff.

**Kimithon route** This runs north of the park route. Starting from Endebess, it is 16 km to Masara village. About 1 km further on take the right fork (not the left to the Kimithon Gate). The middle of three tracks leads to Kimithon Forest Station, where it is possible to camp. Koitoboss is then about six hours' hike away.

*For Sleeping and Eating price codes and other relevant information, see Essentials pages 34-38.*

### ⬤ Sleeping

**Kitale** *p180*

**C-E Kitale Club**, Eldoret Rd, T054-31330. This old colonial sporting club is said to have been built on the site of the old slave market. Rooms are in cottages with own bath and shower, or there are simple single rooms with shared bathrooms and hot water in the older rundown buildings. The restaurant serves English fare with some Indian dishes, and there's satellite TV in the bar, a swimming pool, tennis, squash, snooker, and an 18-hole golf course, which can be used for an extra fee.

**D Mid Africa Hotel**, Kenyatta St, T054-202 017, www.midafricahotel.com. A good option in the middle of town, set in a neat 5-storey block, with clean double and single rooms with TV, en suite or sharing a bathroom, which are modern and tiled and have hot water. The nicest rooms face the front and have balconies, avoid the ones with only windows facing on to the corridors as they can be noisy. There's an excellent and affordable restaurant serving European and Indian food, a *nyama choma* bar on the roof and internet facilities.

**E-F Karibuni Lodge**, off Hospital Rd, T0735-573 798, www.karibunikitale.com. European-run, this is an excellent and fairly new backpackers' set up with dorm beds, some doubles with or without bathrooms and plenty of camping in the spacious gardens of a homely colonial-style house. All the showers have hot water and meals are taken communally around a large table. Rents out tents and bikes and can organize local excursions to Saiwa Swamp and Mt Elgon.

**F Alakara**, corner of Kenyatta St/Post Office Rd, T054-31554. Secure, friendly staff, and basic rooms are comfortable enough, but an intermittent water supply. Restaurant serves fairly simple food but is good value, and a generous breakfast is included in the rates.

**Saiwa Swamp National Park** *p181*

**F Campsite**. There's a small site near the park entrance at Saiwa Swamp, but with no facilities or water. You need to bring all camping equipment, food and firewood. Better to stay in Kitale and visit on a day trip.

**Mount Elgon National Park** *p181*

**A Lokitela Farm**, 19 km west of Kitale, in the foothills of Mt Elgon, reservations **Bush and Beyond/Bush Homes of East Africa**, Nairobi, T020-600 457, www.bush-and-beyond.com and www.bush-homes.co.ke. This farm mainly produces maize and milk and covers an area of 365 ha, of which 30 ha are riverine forest. 350 different species of birds and mammals have been identified here. 3 comfortable rooms and cosy sitting with a fireplace, good wholesome food using farm fare. This is a homestay hosted by the Mills family who are a wealth of information about the Elgon region, they offer nature walks, trips to Saiwa Swamp National Park, as well as Mt Elgon, also overnight stays in the Cherangani Hide, a shelter built on wooden stilts beside the Suam River.

**E Kapkuro Bandas**, 1 km from Chorlim Gate within the park, reservations **Kenya Wildlife Service**, Nairobi, T020-600 800, www.kws.org. In a forest glade, 4 semi-detached self-catering *bandas* with 1 double and 1 single bed, en suite bathrooms with showers and kitchen with gas cooker. Utensils in the kitchen are provided but no sheets and towels, blankets and lanterns are supplied, guests need to bring firewood and drinking water. You can also camp (**F**).

### ◉ Directory

**Kitale** *p180*

**Bank** The main banks **Barclay's** and **Standard Chartered** are pretty close to Bank St. **Post office** On Post Office Rd.

# Contents

## Footprint features

# Central Highlands

## At a glance

◉ **Getting around** Car hire from Nairobi is best to drive around Mt Kenya; flights to lodges on the Laikipia Plateau.

◉ **Time required** At least 3-4 days to drive around Mt Kenya and visit the Aberdares National Park; 2-3 days at a game lodge in the region.

◌ **Weather** Moderate temperatures year round of 15-25°C but often it's cloudy and gets cool at night.

✘ **When not to go** Avoid the rainy season Mar-May as it's wet and cold.

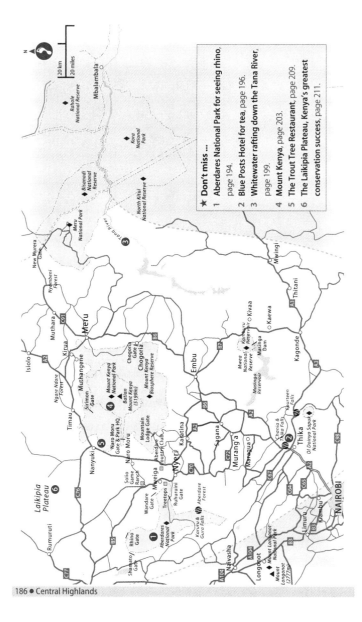

★ **Don't miss ...**

1 Aberdares National Park for seeing rhino, page 194.

2 Blue Posts Hotel for tea, page 196.

3 Whitewater rafting down the Tana River, page 199.

4 Mount Kenya, page 203.

5 The Trout Tree Restaurant, page 209.

6 The Laikipia Plateau, Kenya's greatest conservation success, page 211.

The Central Highlands, to the north of Nairobi and forming the eastern boundary of the Rift Valley, is the heartland of the Kikuyu people who make up the largest ethnic group in Kenya. It used to be known as the 'White Highlands' because – being fertile and well watered – many of the white settlers chose it for their farmland. Thanks to the nutritious volcanic soils of Mount Kenya, this region is now home to much small-scale farming, including coffee, and is very densely populated.

There are a number of towns in the Central Highlands, often referred to as upcountry, and these are useful for shops and communications but have few distractions and will not hold the attention of visitors for very long. The real reason people come to the Central Highlands is to visit the Aberdares National Park – home to the famous hotels, the Ark and Treetops – the more remote Meru National Park, and also to climb Mount Kenya. The newest attraction of the region, and one of East Africa's wildlife conservation success stories, is the Laikipia Plateau. Here the many farms and ranches across a vast area have joined forces to protect the wild animals on their land and start tourism initiatives to support their gallant efforts. After the Masai Mara, it's now the best place to view wildlife, including the Big Five, and is home to over 50% of Kenya's rhino. This area is over 9500 sq km and covers not only much of the Central Highlands but also stretches into the Northern Territory and into Western Kenya. It is, however, best accessed from the town of Nanyuki so it is included in this chapter.

## Ins and outs

### Getting there and around

There are a number of towns located along the Kirinyaga Ring Road at the base of Mount Kenya. The route round the mountain is becoming increasingly popular as a tourist circuit, which is not surprising for it is a really beautiful part of the country, and the mountain and nearby game parks nearby are an added attraction. From Nairobi the main A2 heads north, firstly along a dual carriageway through the outskirts of the city to Thika, a distance of 42 km. It then continues northwards through the lush, verdant countryside. Almost every inch of ground is cultivated and you will see terraces on some of the steeper slopes. You will soon notice that this is pineapple country and many hectares are taken up with plantations; the 'man from Del Monte' is the region's largest producer. There are a number of routes to choose from: you can go north to Nyeri and the Aberdares National Park, then clockwise round the mountain via Naro Moru, or anti-clockwise via Embu. The following section will cover the clockwise route around Mount Kenya, taking in Nyeri and Naro Moru, to Nanyuki. It is possible to continue on all the way around the mountain via Meru to Embu and rejoin the A2 at Thika. The towns are linked with a steady stream of *matatus* and long-distance buses operate services to and from Nairobi. There are also bus and *matatu* links across country to Naivasha and Nakuru in the Rift Valley. Main access points to the lodges in the Laikipia Plateau region is from Nanyuki, Isiolo, Nyahuru or Maralal, depending on where the lodges are located. ▶▶ *See Transport in the relevant sections.*

### Best time to visit

This area is very high, with peaks in the Aberdares of up to 4000 m, and Mount Kenya, which is 5199 m. You should therefore expect it to get fairly chilly, especially at night. The maximum temperature range is 22-26°C and the minimum 10-14°C. It is also very wet here, with annual rainfall of up to 3000 mm not unusual.

# Nyeri and around

*The region directly to the northeast of Nairobi provides access to one of the highlights of the Central Highlands, the Aberdares National Park, and, if the cloud lifts, good views of Mount Kenya to the right of the main A2 road. This is a heavily cultivated area thanks to the rising elevation on the lower mountain slopes, and the market towns have good displays of fresh produce in their markets. Thika can be easily reached from Nairobi for lunch at the Blue Posts Hotel, while the Outspan and Aberdare Country Club make fine country retreats.* ▶▶ *For listings, see pages 196-200.*

## Thika to Nyeri 😊🕖🏕️🚌🚍 ▶▶ *pp196-200.*

**Thika →** *Phone code: 067. Colour map 1, A4.*

Directly from Nairobi, the four-laned A2 continues up towards Thika, which is actually off the main road. This town was made famous by the book (and later the television series) *The Flame Trees of Thika* by Elspeth Huxley. It is about her childhood when her parents came out to Kenya as one of the first families, and their attempts to establish a farm. However, there is little special about Thika – not even many flame trees to brighten it up.

# Baden-Powell

Lord Baden-Powell distinguished himself in the Boer War during the seige of Mafeking. At the time he was 45 years old, the youngest General in the British Army.

He is best known as the founder of the Boy Scout movement. Guides were soon to follow and, for younger children, Cubs and Brownies. The movement was very successful, and is still popular around the world.

Baden-Powell once visited a small boarding school in the Rift Valley that was popular amongst British settlers and missionaries. Some of the children there were as young as six, and considered to be too small to join the Brownies or the Cubs. Baden-Powell therefore decided to establish something for the youngest children and so the 'Chippets' were born. The school remembers Baden-Powell each year. They also have a flag mounted in a corridor, which was presented to the school by Baden-Powell's wife after his death.

Nyeri was Baden-Powell's great love and he once wrote that "The nearer to Nyeri the nearer to bliss". In the grounds of the **Outspan Hotel** is the cottage, Paxtu, built with money collected by guides and scouts from around the world, where Baden-Powell spent his final years. He died in 1941 and his obituary states: "No Chief, no Prince, no King, no Saint was ever mourned by so great a company of boys and girls, or men and women, in every land." He is buried in Nyeri cemetery, and his wife's ashes are buried beside him. Lady Baden-Powell was World Chief Guide until her death (in England) at the age of 88 on 25 June 1977.

It is primarily a market town that was established during the white settler period and is today a base for manufacturing activity and there are a number of factories around town.

The singular attraction is the **Blue Posts Hotel**, a famous colonial landmark. A visit is a must if you're in the area. It is nestled between Chania and Thika Falls with shaded tables in sight of the falls, where all you hear is the crashing water, birdsong and the rustling of leaves. There are also easy trails around the base of the falls, thick with flowers and foliage, and teeming with butterflies and dragonflies.

## Ol Doinyo Sapuk National Park → Colour map 1, A5.

① T067-435 5257, www.kws.org, open daily 0600-1900, adults US$20, children US$10 per day, plus vehicle fee US$4.50, smartcards not accepted, cash only in KSh or US$.

The park, 27 km southeast from Thika on the Garissa road and 85 km northeast of Nairobi, is named after the extinct volcano, Ol Doinyo Sapuk, 2150 m, which means 'the mountain of the buffalo'. To get here, follow the main A3 Thika–Garissa road for 22 km from Thika to the Makutano junction where there is a signpost to the right. Follow this road 3 km to the village of Donyo and turn right again; it is 2 km to the main gate and car park. Buses run regularly from Thika towards Garissa and you can get off at the Makutano junction. However, from there, transport to the park is irregular and walking within the boundaries of the park is prohibited without an armed escort. Ol Doinyo Sapuk is best visited by organized tour from Nairobi. The mountain can be climbed and it's 9 km to the top from the car park, but you must be accompanied by an armed KWS ranger, which must be pre-arranged. Alternatively, you can drive to the summit in a 4WD. From the top are views of Nairobi, Mount Kenya and even Mount Kilimanjaro on clear days. The top of the volcano is covered in dense forest vegetation and afro-alpine

## Wangari Maathai

A Kikuyu born in Nyeri in 1940, Wangari Muta Maathai has achieved some acclaimed 'firsts' in her lifetime. She was the first woman in East Africa to earn a university doctorate degree, (a PHD in veterinary medicine from the University of Nairobi in 1971); the first woman to head up a university department in Kenya (the Veterinary Department, also at the University of Nairobi); and the first African woman to win the Nobel Peace Prize. This was awarded to her in 2004 for her astonishing work in replanting trees in regions where it was estimated about 30 years ago that only 10% of the trees that were being cut down were being replaced. In 1977, she founded the Green Belt Movement, which to date has planted more than 30 million trees in Kenya to prevent soil erosion and provide wood for cooking fires. Most are planted by women in Kenya's rural areas and as they are paid to plant a tree, this income empowers them and their children financially in addition to protecting their own environment. The project has made significant headway against Kenya's deforestation and the Green Belt Movement also raises awareness about other environmental issues and conducts educational campaigns on women's rights and empowerment. In 1986, it established the Pan African Green Belt Network that has exposed many leaders of other African countries to its unique approach. Countries that have

successfully launched similar tree-planting initiatives include Tanzania, Uganda, Malawi, Lesotho, Ethiopia and Zimbabwe among others. In 2002, under the new Kibaki government, Maathai was elected to parliament and became Deputy Minister of Environment, Natural Resources and Wildlife until 2005, after which she turned her attention to the protection of the Congo rainforests of Central Africa and is presently the co-chair of the Congo Basin Fund. She is internationally recognized for her persistent struggle for democracy, human rights and environmental conservation and presently serves on the boards of some very powerful and influential organisations. These include the UN Secretary Generals Advisory Board on Disarmament, the Jane Goodall Institute, the Women and Environment Development Organization, World Learning for International Development, Green Cross International, Environment Liaison Centre International, the Worldwide Network of Women in Environmental Work, the Global Crop Diversity Trust, Prince Albert II of Monaco Environmental Foundation, and the National Council of Women of Kenya. In 2005, Professor Maathai was honoured by Time Magazine as one of the 100 most influential people in the world, and by Forbes Magazine as one of the 100 most powerful women in the world. For more information, visit www.greenbeltmovement.org.

vegetation including the giant lobelia, and the area is home to 45 species of bird. There is some game including monkeys and small antelope but it is difficult to spot them in the heavily wooded terrain.

Sir William Northrup MacMillan, a well-heeled gentleman of St Louis, bought the mountain and much of the surrounding land in the early part of the 20th century. This immensely wealthy, 158-kg American came to the protectorate in 1904 and received a knighthood from the British in recognition of his support during the First World War. He was famous among the early settlers for his generous entertainment of most of the people of note who passed through Kenya, including Roosevelt and Churchill. After his death he bequeathed the mountain to the nation and was buried at the 7-km mark along the road to the summit. It had been intended that his remains would be interred at the summit, but they proved to be too heavy for the hearse, supported on skis and pulled by a tractor, to complete its ascent. Oak trees were planted by the graveside.

## Fourteen Falls → Colour map 1, A5.
ⓘ Daily 0900-1700, US$2, car US$3.
Located about 65 km northeast of Nairobi off the Thika–Garissa road, these falls are particularly splendid during the rainy season. Recently declared a national park, this broad plume of water plummets 30 m over a multi-lipped precipice. There is a path leading from the car park to the base of the falls. The falls derive the name from their 14 successive falls of water along the Athi River.

## Murang'a → Colour map 1, A4.
This small, bustling town is situated 11 km west off the main A2 road north. The town has become known as the Kikuyu Heartland because it is close to **Mugeka**, the *Mukuruwe wa Gathanga* (Garden of Eden of the Kikuyu), which has an important place in Kikuyu mythology. The legend is that it was here that N'Gai (God) led Gikuyu to the mountain and told him to build his home there. He was given his wife Mumbi and in time they had several daughters. N'Gai found nine husbands under a fig tree for the nine daughters of Gikuyu and Mumbi, who in mythology are the ancestors of all Kikuyu. These nine became the forefathers of the nine Kikuyu clans – in alphabetical order: Achera, Agachiku, Airimu, Aithaga, Aitherandu, Ambui, Angare, Angui and Anjiru. There was actually also a tenth daughter. However, the Kikuyu are very superstitious and one of their beliefs is that the number 10 is unlucky, so the term the 'full nine' is often used instead, and is still in use today especially by older Kikuyus.

The **CPK Cathedral** is not particularly old but has some interesting decorations painted in 1955 by a Tanzanian artist named Elimo Njau. It shows various scenes from the Bible with an African Christ and in African surroundings. The church was founded in the 1950s in memory of the Kikuyu who died at the hands of the Mau Mau.

It is possible to take a detour into the **Aberdare Forest**. Follow one of the minor roads from Murang'a, which eventually leads to Othaya and on to Nyeri – the turning for this is to the left just before you get to Murang'a. Back on the A2, the road continues north towards Nyeri, Naro Moru and Nanyuki.

## Sagana and Karatina → Colour map 1, A4. Phone code: 061.
The main road continues north through the small settlement of **Sagana**, where **Savage Wilderness Safaris** has its base for whitewater rafting (see under Activities and tours, page 199), to **Karatina**, which is the next town you will reach. There are baskets for sale from the Kikuyu women who sit by the roadside. It is often the vendors themselves who make the baskets, and they are good value. Worth a visit on market days (Tuesday, Thursday and Saturday), this is one of the biggest fruit and vegetable markets in East Africa, and it attracts buyers from as far away as Mombasa.

→ *Phone code: 061.*

Nyeri, 154 km from Nairobi, is the administrative capital of the Central Province. The town was founded by Richard Meinertzhagen in 1902 (who, despite his name, was British), as he camped at Nyeri Hill during a revolt against the Tetu (a sub-group of the Kikuyu) who had ambushed an Arab caravan. He was a man with an astonishingly accurate foresight and in 1904 wrote in his diary, "I am sorry to leave the Kikuyu, for I like them. They are the most intelligent of the African tribes that I have met; therefore they will be the most progressive under European guidance and will be the most susceptible to subversive activities. They will be one of the first tribes to demand freedom from European influence and in the end cause a lot of trouble. And if white settlement really takes hold in this country it is bound to do so at the expense of the Kikuyu, who own the best land, and I can foresee much trouble".

During the British colonial period the land around Nyeri was taken from the Kikuyu and given to white settlers and the town developed as an army base and important trading centre for farmers. It was here that General Dedan Kimathi, the last Mau Mau leader, was captured in 1956 along with 13 other Mau Mau rebels and subsequently executed by the

**Nyeri**

To 7 8 9 10 11 & Nyahururu

Anglican & Grave of Baden Powell

Caltex

To Baden Powell's Home, Italian Church & Aberdares National Park

Kanisa Rd

Consolidated

Provincial HQ

Clocktower

Standard Chartered

Bishop Gatimu Rd

Kobil

Cenotaph

Pharmacy

Medical Centre

Kenya Commercial

Nyeri Town Medical Centre

Matatu Stand

Mobil

Nibco Stationers

Kimathi Way

Shell

Matatu Stage

Kenyatta Rd

Moi Nyayo Way

Market St

Town Hall

Medical Centre

Co-op

Barclays

Library

BP

Medical Centre

Kimathi Way

Covered Market

Bus Stage

Matatu Stand

Caltex

Cathedral

To Thika & Nairobi

N

200 metres
200 yards

| Sleeping | | Eating |
|---|---|---|
| Aberdare Country Club 7 | Itara Garden Park 5 | Bahati 1 |
| Ark 11 | Outspan 4 | Green Oaks 2 |
| Batian Grand 1 | Sangare Tented Camp 9 | Impala Pub 3 |
| Central 2 | Treetops 10 | |
| Green Hills 3 | White Rhino 8 | |

British in 1957, which effectively ended the Mau Mau campaign. After Independence most of the fertile land was returned to the Kikuyu and as you drive into Nyeri you will see the many *shambas* (farms) growing maize, bananas and coffee, as well as many varieties of vegetables. A few famous people have hailed from Nyeri including President Mwai Kibaki, 2004 Nobel Peace Prize winner Wangari Maathai (see box, page 190), and acclaimed runner Catherine Ndereba (known as Catherine the Great in Kenya), who broke the women's marathon world record in 2001 and picked up the silver medal for the marathon at the 2008 Olympics in Beijing.

## Ins and outs

**Getting there and around** There are regular *matatus* from Nairobi and other main towns in the area. The main street, Kimathi Way, is where you will find banks and the post office, while running parallel Kenyatta Road has more banks and petrol stations. To the southeast of the two is the market and the bus and *matatu* stands.

**Best time to visit** Although it is one of the wettest parts of Kenya with a cool climate, and it can get cold in the evenings, outside of the rainy seasons the sun shines most afternoons and the cloud lifts from the mountain.

## Sights

On the main road you can see a **cenotaph** to those who died during the Mau Mau. It has the inscription: to the Memory of the Members of the Kikuyu Tribe Who Died in the Fight for Freedom 1951-1957.

It is possible to visit **Lord Baden-Powell's home** ① *US$5, free to scouts and guides, pay at the hotel reception*, which contains a small **museum** with a display of memorabilia. The cottage *Paxtu* lies in the grounds of the **Outspan Hotel**. Baden-Powell's home in England was named *Pax*, and the name of his Kenyan home was a pun on the original (*Pax Two*). In the living room are some of the greeting cards Baden-Powell drew for friends. Outside, two big scout movement emblems are surrounded by a tropical garden. See box, page 189.

After Baden-Powell's death, *Paxtu* was the home of Jim Corbett, famous hunter/destroyer of several man-eating tigers in India in the 1920s and 1930s. In 1947 Jim Corbett and his sister Maggie moved to Nyeri where he wrote most of his books. In 1952 (when aged 80 years) he received a request to meet Princess Elizabeth and Prince Philip at **Treetops** (see page 195), where he identified animals for the Royals.

Out of town on the D435 road that leads to the Ruhuruini Gate is an enormous **Italian church** built in remembrance of the Italian soldiers who died in East Africa during the Second World War. In front of the main altar lies the grave of Amadeo di Savoia, Duce d'Aosta, the commander of the main Italian armies in Ethiopia, who formally surrendered to the Allied army at Amba Alagi, 20 May 1941, and died in Nairobi in 1942.

## Solio Game Ranch ›› *Colour map 1, A4.*

① *T061-55271, daily 0700-1800, US$22, under 12s free, closes if it's very wet, 4WD only.*
About an hour's drive north of Nyeri is this private ranch that incorporates one of the most successful rhino-breeding programmes in Africa. It's presently home to around 120 black and white rhino and is located a little north of Mweiga, along the B5 towards Nyaharuru, between Solio and Naro Moru. Its conservation and breeding programme has been so successful that Solio Park has provided stock that has been translocated to other

sanctuaries, such as Nakuru, Tsavo and the Aberdares national parks. In 2004, six white rhino were also relocated to the Lewa Wildlife Conservancy and in 2005, four were sent to a park in Uganda. In February 2007 the Ol Pejeta Conservancy, Kenya Wildlife Service (KWS) and Lewa Wildlife Conservancy undertook the largest ever rhino translocation in East Africa when they moved 34 black rhinos from Solio to Ol Pejeta on the Laikipia Plateau. Trips to visit the ranch can be arranged at the **Aberdare Country Club**, see page 197.

## Aberdares National Park 🖨 ↠ pp196-200.

→ *Phone code: 061.*
ⓘ *Park entry fee US$50, children US$25, vehicle US$4.30 per day, gates open 0600-1900 (no entry after 1815).*

The national park, established in 1950, encompasses an area of around 715 sq km and is one of Kenya's only virgin forest reserves. The Aberdares are the third highest massif in

# Aberdares National Park

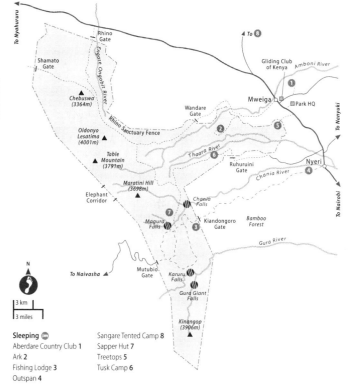

**Sleeping** 🛏
Aberdare Country Club **1**
Ark **2**
Fishing Lodge **3**
Outspan **4**

Sangare Tented Camp **8**
Sapper Hut **7**
Treetops **5**
Tusk Camp **6**

## Treetops

Originally, Treetops was nothing more than a two-room treehouse sitting on top of a fig tree. Intrepid travellers reached it on foot escorted by armed rangers that protected them from wild animals during the walk. Then guests were left on their own with just a picnic supper and some oil lamps. At dawn, the rangers returned to escort them back, after an exciting and chilling night in the midst of the forest watching the wildlife roaming below their feet. In 1952, Treetops was enlarged for a royal visit from Princess Elizabeth and her husband Philip. A third room was added and a small cabin for the ranger on duty was attached. During their overnight stay, the young princess and her husband witnessed a thrilling fight between two male waterbucks that ended with one killing the other. However, that night would become historical because of a different reason as the princess's father, King George VI, died in London. Although the princess was not aware of the bad news until her next stop at Sagana, the morning she descended from Treetops she had become the Queen of England. The hotel was burnt down by the Mau Mau two years later, but it was rebuilt in 1957 at the opposite side of the waterhole. The modern building, several times enlarged since then, is a pillared wooden house embracing the branches of a chestnut tree. A second waterhole was artificially opened at the back side of the building, although for some reason the animals prefer the original pond. The lodge's employees spread salt on the soil, which the animals lick.

the country, with dramatic peaks, deep valleys, enormous spectacular waterfalls cascading down the rock face, volcanic outcrops of bizarre proportions and undulating moorlands. There isn't a huge amount of wildlife (comparatively) although birdlife is rich, and the walks around the park offer tremendous views.

### Ins and outs

The park is 10 km from Nyeri and 165 km from Nairobi. From Nyeri you can enter the park through three gates: Ruhuruini Gate, Wandare Gate and Kiandongoro Gate. **Outspan Hotel** is the base hotel for Treetops and visitors usually come here first. From Nyeri there is a road to Mweiga, the town close to the **Aberdare Country Club**, the base for **The Ark**. Also in Mweiga is the **KWS headquarters**, where you can obtain or reload your Smartcard. The lodges and hotels organize transfers and game drives, and there are hiking trails, although a ranger guide is compulsory.

The park is not often visited primarily because of the weather. It rains heavily and frequently, making driving difficult and seeing the game and mountain peaks almost impossible. Set off early in the day, as it frequently clouds over by late morning, and during the wet season roads turn into mudslides and are often closed.

### Sights

The Aberdares is a range of mountains to the west of Mount Kenya, running in a north-south direction between Nairobi and Nyahururu (Thomson's Falls). The Aberdares come to a peak at about 4000 m and the middle and upper reaches are densely forested with thickets of bamboo, giant heath and tussock grass. The eastern and western slopes in particular are covered with dense forest and tree ferns in places.

The Kikuyu call these mountains *Nyandarua* (drying hide) and they were the home to Mau Mau guerrilla fighters during the struggle for Independence. Nowadays the mountains are home to bongo (elusive forest antelope), buffalo, elephant, giant forest hog, red duiker, and Syke's and colobus monkeys. The rare, handsome bongo is most likely to be spotted near **The Ark**, which is sited close to a swampy glade, waterhole and salt-lick, or up in the bamboo zone. Dawn and the following hour is the optimum time to see these elusive forest antelopes. At about 3500 m, where the landscape opens up, is the terrain of lion, leopard and serval cat, but these are rarely seen and most of the lion from the park have been removed to protect the bongo. Birdlife is prolific here; most obvious are the four species of sunbirds. Among the birds of prey are the crowned hawk eagles, mountain buzzard and the African goshawk. Wildlife is comparatively scarce, but the views in the park are spectacular. Particularly good walks include trekking up the three peaks, **Satima**, 3998 m, **Kinangop**, 3906 m, and **Kipipiri**, 3348 m. You can hire a guide if you wish, but, if walking, an armed guard (costing US$15 daily) is obligatory to protect you from the wildlife. Trout fishing is very popular, especially high up in the moors. A fishing licence is required, obtainable from the park headquarters for US$5.

The park is split into two sections, the beautiful high moorland and peaks with sub-alpine vegetation, and the lower Salient, which is dense rainforest and where much of the wildlife lives. The Aberdare Salient is closed to the public and the animals can only be viewed from **Treetops** or **The Ark** (details below). Access to these lodges is prohibited to private vehicles; visitors are obliged to use the hotels' buses.

There are a number of spectacular waterfalls in the park including the **Chania Falls** and the **Karuru Falls**, which have a total drop of 273 m in three steps. The more remote and inaccessible **Gura Giant Falls**, to the south, have a higher single drop of over 300 m. There are a few roads traversing the centre of the national park from Nyeri to Naivasha, giving access to most of the waterfalls.

A major project in recent years has been the building of the **rhino sanctuary**, funded by the Kenya Wildlife Services, the Overseas Aid Agency and conservation organizations including **Rhino Ark** ① *www.rhinoark.org*. Other wildlife also live within the fence including elephant and various members of the cat family. The electricity for the fence is generated locally using waterwheels to harness water from within the forest, a project that also provides power for local people living in the surrounding villages. The local villages support and raised money for this project, which also protects their livestock and crops from the animals. Various fund-raising activities in support of the project include the 'Rhino Charge' motor rally (see page 40).

---

## ◉ Nyeri and around listings

*For Sleeping and Eating price codes and other relevant information, see Essentials pages 34-38.*

## ● Sleeping

### Thika *p188*
**C Blue Posts Hotel**, just north of Thika, towards Murang'a (take the first slip road off the main A2 after the main junction for Thika), T067-22241. Established in 1908 as a stopover for white settlers who farmed and lived in central Kenya, it is still a popular hotel, with a very good view over the falls. (Thika and Chania rivers surround the hotel, each with a natural waterfall). Easily the nicest place to stay in the area, rustic, sprawling, country-style lodge, with large gardens and ostrich farm, 32 rooms with TV and veranda,

good food and the buffet lunches (US$9) on a day trip from Nairobi are recommended.
**F New Fulia Hotel**, there are 2: Kwame Nkrumah Rd, T067-21840; and 2 blocks east on Uhuru St. Go to the former first and you may be directed to the latter if it's full. Both are good value, reasonably clean and basic board and lodgings.
**F White Line**, in the centre of Thika on Stadium Rd, T067-22857. Simple but acceptable board and lodgings, the double rooms have bathrooms, the singles have shared bathrooms and there is sometimes hot water, usually in the evenings, and a bar. Good value for the price.

**Ol Donyo Sapuk National Park** *p189*
**F Camping**, T067-4355257, www.kws.org, US$15 per person. There's a very basic KWS campsite near the main gate with water and a pit latrine, so you will need to bring everything with you.

**Karatina** *p191*
**E Karatina Tourist Lodge**, T061-533 968. Set back from the main road in the centre of town in a squat dark grey concrete building with secure parking, simple rooms, everything is worn and old fashioned but it is well run and rates include breakfast.
**F Hotel Ibis**, there are 2 Ibis hotels in town, 1 on the main road opposite the Agip petrol station, T061-772 777, and the other is 1 block back from the BP garage on the main road, T061-772 800, in a striking and modern pink and blue tower. Both are smart and good value with modern bathrooms, the first has a restaurant and bar, but there is no parking at either.

**Nyeri** *p192, map p192*
**L Aberdare Country Club**, 12 km to the north of Nyeri, reservations Nairobi, T020-216 940, www.fairmont.com. Formerly a farmhouse, it is another old colonial-type country hotel with 46 rooms arranged in garden cottages, very luxurious with tennis courts, a swimming pool, a 9-hole golf course

and baboons and antelope can be seen in the extensive grounds. You can arrange game drives into the national park and this is the springboard point to excursions to **The Ark** (see page 198). Rates are full board.
**A Sangare Tented Camp**, north of the Aberdare Country Club, but access is by a 27-km 4WD transfer from the Green Hills Hotel in Nyeri where you can leave your car, which must be arranged in advance. Reservations Nairobi, T020-272 2451, www.sangaretentedcamp.com. This is a wilderness camp in the foothills of the Aberdare Mountains set on 2630 ha with a private airstrip, and guest rooms in 12 en suite tented units with 4-poster beds and rustic African decor. An attractive cedar wooden cottage is the bar and dining room. The camp overlooks a small lake and is encircled by yellow acacia trees where elephant and buffalo visit. Rates are all-inclusive – food, drinks, laundry, game drives, mountain biking and horse riding and, for an extra fee, trips to the Solio Game Ranch.
**B Outspan Hotel**, Baden Powell Rd, 1 km from Nyeri, well signposted from town, T061-203 2424, reservations **Aberdare Safari Hotels**, Nairobi, T020-445 2095, www.aberdaresafarihotels.com. Built in the 1920s, it contains within its grounds the cottage that was the last residence of Lord Baden-Powell (see page 189). With 42 spacious rooms, all with TV and many with fireplaces, and 3 cottages, this has a wonderful atmosphere. It is set in the most beautiful gardens, with swimming pool, tennis and squash courts, and golf at the adjacent Nyeri Golf Club, and the restaurant and bar has a wide veranda. Activities include a 2-hr game drive into the Aberdares National Park (US$45 plus park entry fees), a 2-hr guided nature trail along the Chania River (US$15), which is great for birdwatching, and for groups, a guided tour of a nearby coffee farm can be arranged. Also in the hotel grounds, Kikuyu ceremonies and songs take place

in a typical Kikuyu Village of thatched huts and ceremonial trees every day at 1330 (US$10).

**D Green Hills**, Mumbi Rd, on the top of a hill to the southwest of the town, T061-203 0604, www.greenhills.co.ke. Spread over extensive gardens where on a clear day you can see Mt Kenya, this is large and predominantly a popular local conference venue, with 112 rooms in a 1970s block with balconies and TV. Decor is slightly dated – embroidered 'arm covers' over the sofas, etc – but friendly staff and excellent facilities including restaurant, bar, swimming pool, laundry and parking. Price includes breakfast. Every Sun, there are activities on like a children's puppet show and dancing and it's a popular venue for locals to come and eat, drink and swim.

**E Batian Grand Hotel**, Temple Rd, on the east side of town, near the bus and *matatu* stands, T061-203 0783. Best of the basic board and lodgings in a large modern block with central courtyard, the rooms looking inwards are much darker than the larger, carpeted ones looking outwards, some of which on a clear day have views of Mt Kenya, hot water, although leaky boilers, simple restaurant with bar with pool table, and secure parking with a guard.

**E Central**, Kanisa Rd, T061-203 4233. A fairly modern hotel close to the post office in the north of the town, with basic but clean and comfortable rooms and good value. All the rooms have bathrooms with hot water, some have balconies and it has secure parking, a restaurant and a pleasant open-air bar and a disco at weekends.

**E Itara Garden Park Hotel**, Moi Nyayo Way, T061-203 2537. A fairly new hotel with basic but clean rooms in the main modern building or thatched wooden complex, most with en suite bathrooms and hot water. Has a restaurant and good outdoor bar with pool tables.

**E White Rhino**, Kenyatta Rd, T061-203 0934. This colonial hotel is located fairly centrally in Nyeri. One of the oldest buildings in the town and starting to feel its age, the facilities are not that extensive, but the atmosphere, friendly staff and pleasant gardens make it worthwhile. It has a bar with a pool table, restaurant, lounge and laundry service.

**Aberdares National Park** *p194, map p194*
As accommodation is expensive and limited in the park, an alternative option is to stay at Nyeri and visit on an organized game drive from the **Outspan** or **Aberdare Country Club** (see page 197). Remember it gets freezing at night in the park.

**A-B Treetops**, inside the park entrance, T061-203 4914, reservations **Aberdare Safari Hotels**, Nairobi, T020-445 2095, www.aberdaresafarihotels.com. Built on stilts, this has 50 small cabin-type rooms with shared bathroom facilities, and a number of decks from where you can safely view the animals at night at the 2 waterholes. See box, page 195. Access is from the **Outspan Hotel** in Nyeri, you need to arrive for lunch at 1130, the bus leaves for the park at 1430. No children under 5. Rates vary depending on season.

**B The Ark**, reservations well in advance through **Fairmont Hotels**, Nairobi T020-216 940, www.fairmont.com. Wooden lodge with 46 twin, 5 single and 7 triple small cabin-style rooms with en suite bathrooms, located in the centre of the park. This tree lodge is uniquely shaped to resemble the actual Ark, designed with decks from which numerous balconies and lounges provide superb vantage points for viewing the animals visiting the salt-lick and waterhole. A ground-level bunker provides excellent photographic opportunities, and the waterhole is floodlit at night. Rates are full board, and include transfer to the hotel from the **Aberdare Country Club** but exclude park entry fees, children under 7 are not allowed.

**B Fishing Lodge**, T061-55465, or **Kenya Wildlife Service**, Nairobi, T020-600 800, www.kws.org. 2 stone-built cottages each with 2 bedrooms (each with a double and single bed), and a 3rd smaller bedroom (has a single bed), plus 2 bathrooms. Everything is provided except for food, firewood (though there is a gas cooker) and drinking water. Facilities are shared by everyone and include a communal eating area. A 4WD is recommended at all times of year to get here because of the steep hills. It is usual for a whole cottage to be rented out for US$180 per night, but it is possible to share.

**C Tusk Camp**, just inside the park at the Ruhuruini Gate, 20 km from Nyeri, reservations through Kenya Wildlife Service as above. Here is 1 simple *banda* with 2 double beds and 1 *banda* with 4 single beds, and sleeps 8 in total for US$$120. There is an external bathroom with pit latrine and kitchen with gas cooker, some kitchen utensils, caretaker on site, linen and lanterns supplied but guests must provide firewood and drinking water, and a 4WD is essential in the wet.

**D Sapper Hut**, about 10 km west of the Fishing Lodge where you collect the key from, reservations through Kenya Wildlife Service, page 198. Just 1 small *banda* sleeping 2 people with separate living room, veranda, basic outside bathroom and cooking facilities, firewood, linen and lamps are provided but bring everything else including paraffin for the lamps, a 4WD is recommended all year round.

## 🍴 Eating

### Thika *p188*

🍴🍴 **Blue Posts Hotel**, very good food and wide selection of dishes, the buffet lunches are recommended. Lovely place in extensive grounds and very attentive staff. Kids will enjoy the ostrich farm, pony rides and playground.

🍴 **Prismos Hotel**, Kwane Nkrumah Rd. Large popular canteen-style restaurant with covered balcony serving the usual chicken and chips, cold drinks, stews, basic grills and the like.

### Nyeri *p192, map p192*

If you are staying in a top-range hotel you will probably eat there. Otherwise the **Central** and **White Rhino** both have good-value restaurants. Many small restaurants offer cheap meals.

🍴 **Outspan**. A good place to stop for breakfast or lunch – you can admire the gardens and, as long as the clouds are not down, you will get a good view of Mt Kenya and the Aberdare range behind. There is also a pub on site serving good food and for a small fee day visitors can use the swimming pool.

🍴 **Bahati**, opposite **Green Oak**. Local canteen in which if you ask the staff for a menu, you'll get "we do chicken and chips". Enough said.

🍴 **Green Oaks**, Kimathi Way. Local restaurant with a covered balcony where you can look down on to the street, serving mostly African food, including very cheap *nyama choma*, curries and stews and occasionally has good local fresh trout. Very popular with office workers at lunch time and there is a TV in the bar that mostly shows European football.

🍴 **Impala Pub**, on the corner opposite the **Central Hotel**. Daily 1200-1600. A popular, relaxed local bar that offers simple buffet lunches and is a favourite of local business people.

## ⛰ Activities and tours

### Sagana and Karatina *p191*

**Savage Wilderness Safaris**, Nairobi, T020-521 590, www.whitewaterkenya.com. Its base is on the Tana River just south of Sagana, which is clearly signposted and offers whitewater rafting on the river as well as climbs of Mt Kenya. A 1-day rafting trip from Nairobi costs US$100 and includes transport from **The Norfolk Hotel** at 0800, tea and coffee on arrival at the river, and a 4-hr rafting trip. Most of the rapids are classed as Grade III but on the last 7 km there are some Grade IV and V rapids. Afterwards there is time to relax at the Savage Camp, have a hot shower or a swim in the pool, plus a BBQ lunch. Longer 3-day, 65-km rafting trips on the Athi River further south that borders Tsavo National Park can be arranged for US$390, 2 nights are spent camping on sandbanks and rates include transfers to and from Nairobi and food. Most of the route is on fairly calm water, though there are some Grade II and III sections of rapids and 2 Grade IV drops. This is excellent for game viewing and birdwatching. There's a minimum of 3 people for the Tana River and 6 for the Athi River.

**Nyeri** *p192, map p192*
Nyeri is the gateway to the Aberdares National Park and you will come here before you go to the park. If you do not already have a trip arranged you can organize a 2-hr game drive from the **Outspan** for US$45 per person (minimum 3).

## ⊖ Transport

**Thika** *p188*
There are frequent *matatus* from **Nairobi** to Thika from Racecourse Rd and Ronald Ngala Roundabout (45 mins). Note that the Thika Road can get horribly congested and it's a black spot for accidents. In Thika the *matatu* stand is at the end of Commercial St opposite the **White Line Hotel**. From here *matatus* also go to **Nyeri** and beyond to the north along the main highway, and across country to **Naivasha** and **Nakuru**. Getting around town is simple enough as there are plenty

of taxis, *boda bodas* and the odd *tuk-tuk*. If you arrive in town on public transport and want to go to the **Blue Posts Hotel** you will need to take a taxi, but it's not far.

**Nyeri** *p192, map p192*
*Matatus* ply the route to **Nairobi** and there are good connections with the main towns in the area. The bus and *matatu* stands are on or around Kimathi Way in the centre of town.

## ⊙ Directory

**Thika** *p188*
**Banks** Barclays Bank is on Kenyatta Highway to the south of town, **Standard Chartered** is on the corner of Commercial St and Uhuru St, and both have ATMs that accepts most cards. **Internet** Emails can be checked at **Mbambu Cyber Café** on Uhuru St north of the post office.

**Nyeri** *p192, map p192*
**Banks** Money can be changed at the several banks around town including **Barclays** opposite the library on Kenyatta Rd, **Kenya Commercial Bank** further west on Kenyatta Rd, and Standard Chartered on Kanisa Rd, which all have ATMs. **Internet** Available from **Nibco** stationers on Kimathi Way and several other places in the centre of town including the post office also on Kimathi Way, but service can be slow.

# Mount Kenya and around

*The second tallest mountain in Africa, Mount Kenya is about 150 km northeast of Nairobi and is protected in the Mount Kenya National Park, which is a UNESCO World Heritage Site. It's a stand-alone extinct volcano and the fertile soil on its lower slopes supports the market towns on the road that circles the mountain. Although it's not as popular a climb as Kilimanjaro in Tanzania, trekkers will be well rewarded with the climb up through montane forest and giant bamboo and lobelia to the snow line.* ▸▸ *For listings, see pages 207-210.*

## Naro Moru ▸▸ *Colour map 1, A4.*

The A2 road from Nyeri climbs gradually up to Naro Moru, which is little more than a village located at the base of the mountain. It has a few shops, guest houses and a post office and is clustered around the railway station that no longer functions as a passenger terminal. Bear in mind before you arrive here that there are no banks in the village. There are no restaurants apart from the one at the **Naro Moru River Lodge**, see page 208, and if you are cooking your own food, you are advised to stock up before you get here. However, the village does receive quite a few visitors as it serves as the starting point of the **Naro Moru Trail**, one of the most popular routes up Mount Kenya. Before you set off on this route you have to both book and pay for the mountain huts that you will stay in on the way up. This must be done through the **Naro Moru River Lodge**, if you are not already on an organized climb.

## Nanyuki ⬤🅿️⬤▲⬤⬤ ▸▸ *pp207-210. Colour map 1, A4.*

→ *Phone code: 062. Population: 32,000.*

Nanyuki (meaning 'place of red water' in the Masai language) is a small upcountry town, located to the northwest of Mount Kenya, which dates back to about 1907 when it was used by white settlers as a trading centre and for socializing. The first settlers arrived to find a few Masai *manyattas* and a great deal of game. The town was established as a trading centre and still has a country atmosphere; today it is home to the Kenyan Air Force as well as a British army base. Despite this it is a fairly sleepy kind of town and retains some of its colonial character. Nanyuki is usually visited by people planning to use the Sirimon or Buguret trails up Mount Kenya. Its good range of shops provides its only interesting diversion. The town serves as the supply centre for ranchers on the Laikipia Plateau (see page 211), as well as the nearby tourist hotels in the foothills of the mountain. On the main road just 1.5 km to the south of Nanyuki there are signposts marking the equator, and more than a few pushy souvenir sellers.

## Mount Kenya Biosphere Reserve ⬤🅿️ ▸▸ *pp207-210.*

This reserve includes the **Mount Kenya National Park**, 715 sq km, which straddles the equator about 200 km northeast of Nairobi in Central Province. Mount Kenya, or *Kirinyaga* (the shining mountain), also sometimes referred to as the black-and-white-striped mountain, is the sacred mountain of the Kikuya (Gikuya) people, who believe that it is where their God 'Ngai' lives. The Kikuyu who live on the slopes always build their homes facing this sacred peak. It is actually an extinct volcano that last erupted between 2.8 to

3.2 million years ago, and was gazetted as a National Park in 1949 and a Biosphere Reserve in 2000 and is managed by Kenya Wildlife Service. As you drive around the road that circles Mount Kenya you will spend much of the time looking towards the mountain – however, much of the time it is shrouded in cloud. There are some clear days; otherwise very early in the morning or just before nightfall the cloud will often lift suddenly, revealing the two snow-capped peaks for a few minutes. The upper base of the mountain is nearly 100 km across and has two major peaks, **Nelion** at 5199 m and **Batian** at 5189 m. Mount Kenya has a vital role in ecosystems in the area. It is Kenya's most important

## Mount Kenya region

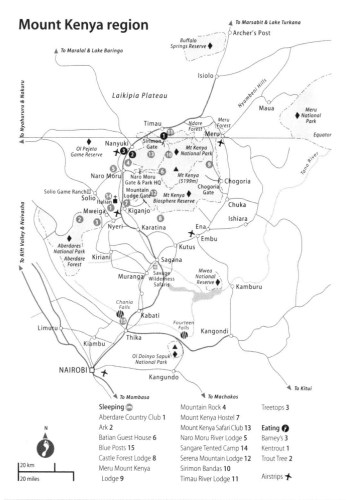

**Sleeping** 🛏
Aberdare Country Club **1**
Ark **2**
Batian Guest House **6**
Blue Posts **15**
Castle Forest Lodge **8**
Meru Mount Kenya
   Lodge **9**

Mountain Rock **4**
Mount Kenya Hostel **7**
Mount Kenya Safari Club **13**
Naro Moru River Lodge **5**
Sangare Tented Camp **14**
Serena Mountain Lodge **12**
Sirimon Bandas **10**
Timau River Lodge **11**

Treetops **3**

**Eating** 🍴
Barney's **3**
Kentrout **1**
Trout Tree **2**

Airstrips ✈

20 km
20 miles

watershed and its largest forest reserve and the lower slopes make up the country's richest farmlands. The dramatic landscape includes glaciers, moraines, waterfalls, precarious-looking rock pinnacles and hanging valleys. At the very top is permanent ice in some 11 glacier lakes, though due to global warming these are shrinking fast and seven glaciers have disappeared in the last 100 years.

Mountain flora includes a variety of different vegetation over altitudes ranging from 1600 m to 5199 m. From bottom to top, it goes from rich alpine and sub-alpine flora to bamboo forests, moorlands with giant heathers and tundra. Over 4000 m some extraordinary vegetation is found including the giant rosette plants.

In the lower forest and bamboo zones, giant forest hog, tree hyrax, white-tailed mongoose, elephant, suni, duiker and leopard roam. Further up in the moorlands there are hyrax, duiker and Mount Kenya mouse shrews. In higher altitudes still there are the fairly common mole rat and the very rare golden cat.

## Mount Kenya → *Colour map 1, A4/5.*

Fewer people go trekking on Mount Kenya than Kilimanjaro in Tanzania, but those that do rate the experience far better than the Kili climb. There are several routes up the mountain. The three most popular routes are described here. They are best taken leisurely in six days, although they can be done in four. It is an interesting variation to ascend by one route and descend by another (but make sure you keep the park fee receipts for the exit). Point Lenana at 4986 m is your destination; it is a strenuous hike, but quite manageable if you are reasonably fit and allow sufficient time to acclimatize to the rarefied atmosphere. It is sometimes called the trekker's or tourist's peak. The trek is an excellent opportunity to enjoy the beautiful scenery on the mountain and the snow on the equator.

**Ins and outs** There are a number of towns located along the Kirinyaga Ring Road at the base of Mount Kenya, which serve as starting points for the various climbs up the mountain. Main road access is via Nanyuki or Naro Moru, from where roads go further into the foothills. Trekkers attempting the Chogoria route access the mountain from the small village of Chogoria on the eastern side, see page 219.

**Getting up** Prior to climbing Mount Kenya it is a good idea to get in touch with the **Mountain Club of Kenya**① *based at Wilson Airport in Nairobi, T020-501 747, www.mck.or.ke*. It has lots of maps and books in its library, non-members can attend the open night on Tuesdays at the club house at Wilson Airport, and the website is an excellent resource for information. Take great care over equipment and altitude sickness precautions, otherwise the climb can be sheer misery. Trekkers should be aware that sudden storms, heavy cloud cover and fog can lead to climbers getting lost on the mountain, and it is prohibited to hike alone without a guide. Many of the tour operators listed under Nairobi can organize climbs, and the lodges in the vicinity of the mountain can organize porters and guides, which cost about US$15 each per day, plus their daily park entry fees (much reduced as they are both licensed guides and Kenya residents) and trekkers need to cover the costs of transporting them to the roadheads on each of the trails. Make sure that the agreement with any guides or porters is clear before you set off and that the guides are carrying a KWS identity card, which also gives them a discount on park fees. Guides and porters can be arranged at **Naro Moru River Lodge**, **Mountain Rock Hotel**, **Serena Mountain Lodge**, **Castle Forest Lodge**, or contact the **Mount Kenya Guides and Porters Association**① *T0722-751 919, www.gotomountkenya.com*, located on the road to the main gate of the park from Naro Moru. Evans Mwangi has been voted as one of the top 10 guides for Mount Kenya by the club and has been climbing the mountain since 1989.

**Costs and climate**  Park entry fee is US$55 adults, US$20 children per day, or for the climb, a fixed minimum for the first three days of US$150 adults, US$70 children and then US$55/US$20 per day after that, which includes camping but not huts, which cost an additional US$10-12 per person per night. Costs for climbing vary depending on which route you choose and over how many days, but expect to pay in the region of US$550-80 for a five-day climb, although the price goes down for larger groups. Only experienced climbers can climb the highest peaks of Nelion (5199 m) or Batian (5189 m) and the summit of Mount Kenya, as this involves the use of ropes, ice-axes, crampons and other specialized climbing gear. Kenya Mountain Club owns some of the mountain huts for these ascents, which are reserved for members only, although there may be reciprocal arrangements with other clubs. The best months to climb Mount Kenya are January to March or July to August. Avoid the rainy seasons April to May and November to December. In case of an emergency (a severe injury or illness where outside help is needed) contact a KWS official immediately. The ranger station at the head of the Teleki Valley, the Austrian Hut, the Met Station, and the Naro Moru, Sirimon and Chogoria gates are all permanently manned and have radios. Be familiar with the nearest source of help while on the mountain.

**Equipment**  Very little camping gear and appropriate warm and waterproof clothing is available locally so you need to bring everything with you. Alternatively, hire at **Naro Moru River Lodge** (see page 208) although items available cannot be relied on. It is essential to take effective waterproofs, gloves, headgear, spare boots/shoes, as well as warm/windproof clothing (several layers are preferable) as many of the huts have no drying facilities. Also ensure that you have at least a three-season sleeping bag and a sleeping mat because above 3000 m the night temperatures can fall to as low as -10°C, and if camping the ground can be very, very cold. Sunglasses are also useful as the glare off the snow and ice can be very uncomfortable. There are mountain streams to collect water, but ensure you set off with an adequate supply and you must carry out all litter. If possible try and get a map of the mountain showing the trails in some detail, though the guides know the routes well enough. If your gear is being carried by porters (who often hike separately from the group and guide) or you are on a summit bid, then ideally it's a good idea to have a day-pack containing at least the following essentials: instant body shelter (warm and waterproof), signalling capability (small mirror), food and drink, first aid kit, compass, torch, and matches/lighter to light a fire in the case of an emergency.

**Maps and guides**  *Mount Kenya Map and Guide*, by M Savage and A Wielochowski, is available at **The Stanley** bookshop in Nairobi, see page 96, **Stanfords Bookshops** in the UK, and from **Amazon**. The Mountain Club of Kenya has published the excellent detailed *Guide to Mt Kenya and Kilimanjaro*, listing all the routes, edited by Iain Allan. It is available in the Nairobi bookshops or directly from the club and you may find it on Amazon.

**Naro Moru approach**  Naro Moru approaches from the west and is the most direct, popular but least scenic route, and includes trekking through a long vertical bog. Opposite the Naro Moru police station is a signposted road that leads to the park entrance. It is possible to drive as far as the Meteorological Station, although inexperienced climbers are less likely to suffer from altitude sickness if they walk the 26 km.

**Day 1** Is best spent travelling from Naro Moru to the Meteorological Station at 3050 m. A ride can be hired from the Naro Moru River Lodge part or all of the way. There are some *bandas* here or some permanent tents.

**Day 2** Is to Mackinder's Camp (sometimes referred to as Teleki Valley Lodge), located at an altitude of 4200 m, through terrain that is often very wet underfoot. An early departure is recommended as fog and rain are more commonplace during the afternoon. This section includes a very tiring climb through a steep vertical bog, and when you've cleared the bog the route then continues along a ridge on the southern side of the Teleki Valley, gradually descending to the valley floor. This section is much more attractive with *Senecio* (giant groundsel), heathers, the broad-leafed *Lobelia keniensis* and the feathery *Lobelia telekii*. The camp, a stone building, has about 40 bunks and some tents. It is possible to visit the Teleki tarn from here, taking about 1-1½ hours, if the weather holds out.

**Day 3** It is possible to make the final leg to Point Lenana, 4895 m, although it is more comfortable to spend Day 3 in and around the surrounding area known as Mackinder's, getting acclimatized to the altitude. From here there are some of the best views of the central peaks. Alternatively, climb another 500 m to the Austrian Hut, 4790 m.

**Day 4** Climb to Point Lenana. Most trekkers leave Mackinder's at between 0200-0400 to ensure that they reach the summit at sunrise (so a powerful torch is an essential piece of equipment), climbing past the Austrian Hut, 4790 m. From here it is about 30 minutes to an hour scramble, depending on fitness, to reach Point Lenana.

**Day 5** It is possible to descend all the way to Naro Moru (with a lift from the Meteorological Station), but it is more leisurely to return to Mackinder's Camp for a night, and then on to Naro Moru on Day 6.

**Chogoria approach** The Chogoria approach is from the east between Embu (96 km) and Meru (64 km), and is the most scenically attractive of the routes, although it can be wet. It is a tent route, and you are required to show your tent at the park gates before you will be let in. The Minto's Hut is for porters' use only. Chogoria village, see page 219, is the starting base for the deeply rutted road (4WD essential), which takes you past small, intensively cultivated *shambas* within the lowland forest rising to become bamboo forest. Colobus monkeys can occasionally be seen here. Most trekkers organize the 32-km ride from Chogoria to approximately 6 km beyond the park gate to the roadhead, 3110 m. However, if you walk this stretch you will greatly reduce the possibility of developing altitude sickness.

**Day 1** From village to the roadhead by vehicle or on foot and camp there.

**Day 2** From the roadhead cross the stream and follow the path going in a southwesterly direction. The route continues along the west side of the Nithi Gorge and it is about a six-hour hike to Minto's Hut, 4300 m. En route there are spectacular views of the Gorges Valley. The path leads through dramatic rock fields and later through the heather moors to Vivienne Falls, 3650 m, where you can swim in the bracing waters. As you progress upwards, Lake Michaelson can be seen on the valley floor 300 m below Hall Tarns.

**Day 3** It is possible to reach Point Lenana, but it may be more comfortable to spend the day getting acclimatized in and around Minto's Hut, located close to Minto's Tarn, 4540 m, which is framed by lofty pinnacles, the scree slopes flecked with giant lobelia and senecio.

**Day 4** From Minto's Hut it is about a four- to five-hour climb to Point Lenana, via the Austrian Hut, close to the Lewis Glacier. In recent years, the Lewis Glacier has receded significantly, and has left behind steep ice, covered with small stones on the western flank of Point Lenana, which is slippery and loose. Anyone attempting this route during the warmth of the day should take great care.

**Day 5** It is possible to descend all the way back to Chogoria (with a lift from the park gate), but it is more leisurely to return to Minto's Hut for a night, and then on to Chogoria on Day 6.

**Sirimon Approach** The Sirimon Gate is 15 km northeast of Nanyuki. This is probably the driest route and goes over much open moorland covered with heather so there is a good chance of spotting wildlife. It's popular alternative to Naro Moru, and has a gentler rate of ascent; although it is still easy to climb too fast so allow five days for the trek. Huts on this route can be booked through the Mountain Rock Hotel (page 208).

**Day 1** From the gate, it's about 9 km or around a two- to five-hour hike through the forest to Old Moses Hut, 3300 m, where you can spend the first night.

**Day 2** On the second day, you could head straight through the moorland for Shipton's Camp, 4050 m, but it is worth taking an extra day to go via Liki North Hut, 3993 m, which is actually a complete wreck and is only meant for porters, but has a good campsite with a toilet and stream nearby. You can also walk further up the hill to help acclimatize.

**Day 3** From Liki North Hut, head straight up the western side of the Liki North Valley and over the ridge into Mackinder's Valley. After crossing the Liki River, follow the path for another 30 minutes until you reach the bunkhouse at Shipton's Camp, 4200 m, which is set in a fantastic location right below Batian and Nelion. The camp is also within sight of two glaciers, which can also be heard cracking.

**Day 4** From Shipton's you can push straight for Point Lenana, a tough three- to four-hour slog via Harris Tarn and the tricky north face approach, or take the Summit Circuit in either direction, which encircles the main peaks of the mountain between the 4300 m and 4800 m contour lines, to reach Austrian Hut, 4790m, about half an hour below the summit where you can also spend the night. The left-hand (east) route past Simba Col is shorter but steeper while the right-hand (west) option, takes you on the Harris Tarn trail nearer the main peaks.

**Day 5** It is possible to descend all the way back to Chogoria or Naro Moru (see above).

*For Sleeping and Eating price codes and other relevant information, see Essentials pages 34-38.*

## ⊜ Sleeping

### Nanyuki *p201*

**C-D Sportsman's Arms**, located across the river, 500 m east of town, T062-314 448. The best-value hotel in Nanyuki, surrounded by gardens and in a lovely setting. Built in the 1930s, but extended more recently so there are smart rooms in modern blocks with satellite TV and older cottages with fireplaces. Price includes breakfast, and full board is also available. Excellent facilities include fitness centre, Olympic-sized swimming pool, sauna, tennis, good restaurant and bar with pool tables and a disco at the weekends. You can also camp here, US$4 with your own tent, US$6 with tent hire.

**E Simba Lodge**, opposite the **Sportsman's Arms**, 500 m from the main road on a very rough road, T062-31723. Clean, comfortable and secure in a neat compound. 32 rooms with hot water in either a block or individual chalets, TV room, bar with pool tables and *nyama choma*, good set menus in the restaurant, breakfast included, secure parking.

**F Equator Chalet**, Kenyatta Av, T062-318 011. Newly painted block on the main road with an enormous sign and above a supermarket, rooms surround an internal courtyard that open on to 2 balcony areas and a roof terrace, and have 4-poster beds with nets and modern bathrooms with hot water. Very nice terrace restaurant. A recommended budget option.

**F Ibis**, Lumumba Rd, close to the *matatu* stand, T062-31536. Comfortable rooms with hot water and mosquito nets, fresh tiles and woodwork, ask for a room with Mt Kenya view, above its own bar/restaurant and bright covered courtyard. Secure parking, laundry service available.

**F Jambo House Hotel**, Bazaar St, T062-31894. Located at west corner of the park, 1 of several cheap board and lodgings along Bazaar St, and not the worst despite the rather dark, dingy rooms. Reasonably quiet, has hot water, plus a bar with a pool table.

### Mount Kenya Biosphere Reserve *p201, map p202*

There are a couple of cheap basic places for board and lodgings in Naro Moru, but for budget travellers it is best to camp at the **Naro Moru River Lodge** or the **Mountain Rock Hotel**, see below, which both hire out tents, and make use of the excellent facilities. There are other accommodation options that provide access to the mountain in Nanyuki itself.

**A Mount Kenya Safari Club**, 15 km east of Nanyuki in the foothills of the mountain, reservations **Fairmont Hotels**, T020-221 6940, www.fairmont.com. The region's most exclusive and luxurious hotel with 115 guest rooms in cottages with wooden floors, colourful rugs and fireplaces set in over 40 ha of landscaped gardens. The club was originally founded by movie star William Holden (of *Bridge over the River Kwai* fame) and the club's illustrious former members have included Winston Churchill and Bing Crosby. Facilities include horse riding, golf, croquet, a putting green, a bowling green, table tennis, swimming, a beauty salon, an animal orphanage, several restaurants, lounges and bars and excursions include day trips to the Aberdares National Park.

**A Serena Mountain Lodge**, 5 km inside the park from the Mountain Lodge Gate, T061-203 0785, reservations **Serena Hotels**, Nairobi, T020-284 2333, www.serena hotels.com. Quality lodge of the Serena group situated at 2194 m on Mt Kenya's slopes overlooking a waterhole, with similar architecture to the **Ark** and **Treetops** in the Aberdares, and built on stilts. 42 wooden cabin-style double bedrooms with en suite bathrooms, fireplaces and hot-water bottles. A close-up viewing bunker is connected to the hotel by a tunnel, post-climb massages and trout fishing on offer, very good guides for walking and climbing excursions, restaurant and bar.

**B Batian Guest House**, inside the park from the main Naro Moru Gate, reservations **Kenya Wildlife Service**, Nairobi, T020-600 800, www.kws.org. A KWS cottage, with 2 bedrooms sleeping up to 6 people for US$180 per night. Linen, towels and cooking equipment are provided and there's a gas cooker and a generator is switched on the evenings (1900-2230) for electricity, but guests need to bring own food, firewood and drinking water.

**B Naro Moru River Lodge**, 2 km from Naro Moru off the main road, reservations **Alliance Hotels**, Nairobi, T020-444 3357, www.alliancehotels.com. At an elevation of 1982 m and overlooking the Naro Moru River, this is a popular place to stay for all budgets and it organizes climbs up the mountain. 19 de luxe cottages with 2 double beds, bathrooms, sitting room area with fireplaces, all elegantly furnished in pine, 12 standard cottages, which are a bit cheaper, and 12 self-catering cottages aimed at families. Facilities include a swimming pool, tennis and squash courts, 2 restaurants, bar with roaring log fire. Also a campsite (**F**) where you can hire the necessary equipment and use all the hotel facilities.

**C Castle Forest Lodge**, 22 km north of Kutus, on the slopes to the south of Mt Kenya, accessed from Sagana and the C73, T0721-422 908 (mob), www.castleforest lodge.com. Set in a natural surrounding of rainforest and rivers with falls on either side of the lodge, the main house was built in 1910 of river stones and wood, and both Queen Elizabeth and former President Jomo Kenyatta have stayed here in the past. A charming old building with a cosy dining and bar and a veranda overlooking a waterhole and the valley below. Recently renovated, the main house contains

3 double rooms, in the gardens is a bungalow that sleeps 4, and 8 double cottages, each en suite with a fireplace. Rates are full board. Can organize climbs from US$85 per day.

**D Mountain Rock Hotel**, 7 km north of Naro Moru on the road to Nanyuki, 1 km off the main road, T062-62625, www.mountainrockkenya.com. Lovely surroundings and 28 simply decorated cottages with fireplaces, welcome on cold evenings, and restaurant and bar. The hotel, which arranges a wide range of activities including horse riding, fishing and birdwatching, is known for its very well-run treks up the mountain (taking the Naro Moru, Sirimon or Burguret routes). There is also a quiet, secure campsite (**F**) with toilets, hot showers, kitchen area with firewood available, and if you don't have a tent or equipment you can hire everything here.

**D Sirimon Bandas**, near Sirimon Gate, 9 km along a turning off the main road, 15 km north of Nanyuki, reservations **Kenya Wildlife Service**, Nairobi, T020-600 800, www.kws.org. Managed 2 self-catering furnished cottages, each has 1 room with a double bed, 1 room with 2 single beds, fitted kitchen with gas cooker and lounge, linen, towels, and kitchen utensils are provided but you will need to bring your own food, firewood and drinking water. Each cottage is rented out as a whole for US$78.

**E-F Timau River Lodge**, 20 km north of Nanyuki towards Isiolo 1 km after Timau, 1 km off the main road, T0177-41230, www.timauriverlodge.8m.com. On the forested slopes of Mt Kenya, several simple *bandas* built of cedar logs sleeping 2-4 people and campsites located amongst trees at the top of a very pretty waterfall, where geese and ducks wander around. There is a restaurant and bar with fireplace and pool table, electricity is provided by a generator from 1800-2100, kerosene lamps are available at other times. Local guides can take guests on walks through the forest and to local villages.

**F Mount Kenya Hostel**, T062-62414, about 12 km from Naro Moru off the main highway along the dirt road towards the Naro Moru Gate, about 4 km from the park entrance gate. Popular with budget travellers, simple bunk beds, hot showers and cooking facilities, and you can also camp here. There's a rustic thatched bar called Summit View Pub and meals are available but you will have to give some notice. The hostel has some equipment for climbing to hire, and it can organize guides and porters.

## 🍴 Eating

### Nanyuki *p201*

Apart from the restaurants attached to the hotels of which in town, the one at the **Sportsman's Arms** is the best, there are few other places to eat in Nanyuki.
🍴 **Marina Grill**, opposite the post office, Kenyatta Av. Daily 0900-2100. Popular with locals and visiting British soldiers and offers friendly service, an attractive rooftop bar with BBQ and pool table. Convenient for a cold beer and a snack like burgers and pizzas, and has a good selection of desserts. There is also an internet café here.

### Mount Kenya Biosphere Reserve
*p201, map p202*

There are 3 very good options on the road running around the mountain.
🍴 **Kentrout**, clearly signposted, located about 2.5 km down a track from the village of Timau, 35 km north of Nanyuki, T062-41016. Daily 1200-1700. This is primarily a trout farm that serves delicious buffet lunches to passing visitors, eaten in the very pretty gardens next to the Teleswan River where you may spot monkeys. There are also 3 comfortable cottages with bathrooms (**D**), and you may be able to negotiate camping in the grounds.
🍴 **Trout Tree Restaurant**, about 12 km south of Nanyuki, T062-62059. A similar set-up to **Kentrout** above, fantastic 3-course lunches

served daily 1100-1600, the very attractive restaurant is constructed around a giant fig tree and overlooks the fish ponds, and a patch of lovely forest which is home to 2 troops of curious black and white colobus monkeys. The menu is superb and there's tandoori trout, masala trout, grilled trout, char-grilled trout, farm-smoked trout and trout chowder soup, as well as steaks, fresh salads and vegetables, and strawberries grown on the farm and fresh cream for dessert.
🍴 **Barney's**, at the Nanyuki airfield, 5 km to the south of town. Daily 0800-1800. This primarily serves Tropic Air's passengers but since it opened in 2005, has become very popular with locals and road travellers can pull in. An excellent and friendly cafe overlooking the planes parked up on the apron with outside tables, colourful decor, a full bar, and offering homemade soups, sandwiches, burgers, salads, coffees, milkshakes, and they can make up a picnic hamper for you to take away.

## 🛍 Shopping

### Nanyuki *p201*
**Nanyuki Spinners and Weavers Workshop**, 1 km from town on the Nyahururu road, T062-32062, www.spinnersandweavers.org. The shop here sells hand-woven items and is run by a women's cooperative group that was established in 1977. It's an interesting place to visit, and the group are pleased to give you a full guided tour. The Kenyan Highlands wool is very good for hand spinning, and there is a good selection of rugs, tablemats, sweaters and shawls.
**Settlers Stores**, on the main street, is 1 of the oldest shops in town (founded in 1938) and sells hardware and groceries.

## ⛰ Activities and tours

### Nanyuki *p201*
**Nanyuki Sports Club**, east of **Sportsman's Arms**, T062-22623. Opened in 1937, this is

another sports club established in the colonial years and offers tennis, squash, a 9-hole golf course, swimming and snooker, but you will need to take out temporary membership.

**Sportman's Arms Hotel** has facilities that can be used, including the very large swimming pool, for a small fee to day visitors and this is a pleasant place to come for lunch.

---

## ⊕ Transport

**Nanyuki** *p201*
### Air
The airstrip at Nanyuki is 5 km to the south of town on the Nairobi (A2) road. Even if you're not flying, it's well worth stopping here for Barney's restaurant (see eating above). **Air Kenya**, Wilson Airport, Nairobi, T020-606 539, www.airkenya.com, has a daily flight from Wilson Airport, **Nairobi**, leaving at 0915 and arriving 35 mins later, US$80 1 way. The return flight leaves Nanyuki at about 1140, depending on passenger loads. **Tropic Air**, T062-32890, www.tropicairkenya.com, is an air-charter company operating out of Nanyuki. Destinations include the airstrips on the **Laikipia Plateau**, **Samburu**, **Masai Mara** and **Meru**, and they have a daily service to and from Nanyuki linking the more popular lodges in these areas. Prices for flights start at around US$175 per person. Tropic Air also has 3 helicopters and 2 bi-planes in their fleet and can organize unique sightseeing and game-viewing flights to various destinations.

### Bus and matatus
The bus and *matatu* stage is located next to the park off Bazaar Rd. There are frequent buses and *matatus* running between Nanyuki and **Nairobi**. If you are heading north to Marsabit and Northern Kenya you can get buses and *matatus* from Nanyuki to **Isiolo**, which is the last town on the good tarred road before the A2 heads north on a rough track.

### Car
Nanyuki is located about 60 km from **Nyeri** and 190 km from **Nairobi** – a drive that will take you about 3 hrs.

---

## ⊖ Directory

**Nanyuki** *p201*
**Banks** On the main street, Kenyatta Av, there are branches of **Barclays Bank**, **Kenya Commercial Bank** and **Standard Chartered Bank**, which all have ATMs. **Internet** Services are available at **Global Information Centre** next to Barclays Bank and at the **Marina Grill Restaurant**, a few doors along on Kenyatta Av. **Medical services** Nanyuki Cottage Hospital is located about 1 km out of town to the east, T062-32666, which is privately run and has a good reputation. **Post office** On the main street.

# Laikipia Plateau

*Laikipia Plateau has only recently been recognized as a wildlife area in its own right, and this spectacular region is considered the gateway to Kenya's wild northern frontier country. The plateau covers an area of 9723 sq km – roughly half the size of Wales in the UK. Altitudes range from 1700 to 2600 m above sea level. Wild and sparsely populated, much of Laikipia is covered by large privately owned ranches. These ranches cover a wide range of landscapes, and the plateau is dominated by acacia bushland with large areas of open grasslands to the north and south of the district, and dense olive and cedar forests to the east. It is, without doubt, Kenya's greatest conservation success story over the last 15 years or so; an area of beautiful wilderness, where protected game roams freely and safely, while preserving traditional farming methods and ways of life.* ►► *For listings, see pages 214-216.*

## Ins and outs

This area of wilderness is a sprawling, rather loosely defined area, accessible by road from Nanyuki, Baringo, Eldoret or Isiolo. The main roads that cross this region are the C76, which connects Nanyuki with Nyaharuru, the C77, which runs between Nyaharuru and Maralal, and the C78, which joins Maralal with Isiolo. It is important to remember that many of the ranches, and the roads therein, are privately owned. Some ranches allow day visitors with their own transport, others do not. Visitors should always make enquiries in advance. If you are visiting a ranch with your own private transport, and it is essential to have a 4WD, ask for directions and preferably a map, in advance. Many ranches and sanctuaries have their own airstrips, which can be used by charter aircraft. Between them, **Air Kenya** and **Safarilink** run scheduled services from Nairobi to Samburu, Nanyuki, and Lewa Downs. **Tropic Air** based at Nanyuki offers a charter service directly to the lodges, see page 205. Most ranches will arrange to transfer guests directly by air or road from Nairobi or any other destination, as part of their service. Nanyuki serves as the supply centre for ranchers on the Laikipia Plateau. Many of the ranches and game reserves work closely with the Kenya Wildlife Service in conservation and poaching control. Consequently there is often an additional conservation fee of US$20-30 per person on top of the accommodation rates.

## Sights

The district is located on the leeward side of Mount Kenya, forming the arid and semi-arid highlands west and northwest of the mountain. The region spreads north from Nanyuki from the northern foothills of Mount Kenya to Maralal, northeast to Isiolo, and west to Nyahuraru. The region is dominated by the Ewaso Ng'iro and Ewaso Narok rivers, and it incorporates the entire Ewaso rivers ecosystems, the Laikipia National Reserve and the Lewa Wildlife Conservancy. On most ranches cattle share the land with free-ranging wildlife. In recent years this wildlife has become a valuable asset, with many ranches now establishing guest houses, homestays and private camps within their boundaries. Some of these are now the most luxurious places to stay in Kenya, and most people visit on specialist tailor-made safaris and they offer a growing wealth of activities and game-watching experiences. Lewa Safari Camp for example is a firm favourite with Britain's Prince William, and Princess Anne has stayed at Borana Lodge. Increasingly, some of these lodges have become popular as wedding destinations.

The **Laikipia Wildlife Forum (LWF)** ⓘ *www.laikipia.org*, was formed in 1992 by private and communal landowners with a common interest in preserving the wildlife. This has proven a great success, and many ranches now rely on a thriving tourist trade. There are currently over 40 tourism operations active in the region, and collectively they promote their region through the LWF. Importantly, community ranches have also been formed. These are sanctuaries created by local communities, who have combined small-scale farms and grazing land into large group ranches. Once again, the tourist trade has proved infinitely more profitable than agriculture or herding, and this allows them to use their traditional lands in a way that is sustainable and productive. Significantly, they are conserving more than just wildlife, but also a way of life. These ranches have bolstered a sense of local identity and strengthened community ties.

## Wildlife

Centred around the original Laikipia National Reserve, this area has become a sanctuary for elephant, lion, leopard, buffalo and a wealth of plains game, including many endemic northern species such as the Grevy's zebra, gerenuk and reticulated giraffe. It has one of the highest diversity of large mammals in all of Kenya, including significant populations of all the major predators and the Big Five. Almost 6000 elephants migrate through the region each year. Laikipia has also become a focus for many conservation efforts; some ranches have become breeding sanctuaries for rhino, and now the region protects over 50% of Kenya's population of black and white rhino. Wild dog and the sitatunga antelope are also present, and these days the region is widely believed to have an animal diversity

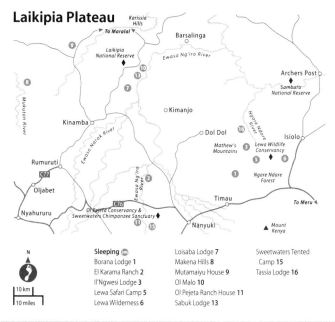

**Laikipia Plateau**

**Sleeping**
Borana Lodge **1**
El Karama Ranch **2**
Il'Ngwesi Lodge **3**
Lewa Safari Camp **5**
Lewa Wilderness **6**

Loisaba Lodge **7**
Makena Hills **8**
Mutamaiyu House **9**
Ol Malo **10**
Ol Pejeta Ranch House **11**
Sabuk Lodge **13**

Sweetwaters Tented
Camp **15**
Tassia Lodge **16**

second only to the Masai Mara. On Ol Pejeta Ranch, a refuge for chimpanzees rescued from the pet and bush-meat trade has also been established. Visiting a private ranch in this region is an ideal way of exploring the Kenyan wilderness while getting off the well-beaten paths of the national parks. The real attraction of Laikipia is a wonderful sense of freedom. Staying on a private ranch gives a wide range of options for both activities and relaxation, and game viewing tends to be more intimate and adventurous.

## Lewa Wildlife Conservancy

ⓘ *T064-31405, www.lewa.org, entry by prior arrangement only. To visit here you will need to be staying at Lewa Safari Camp, Il'Ngwesi Lodge, Tassia Lodge or Lewa Wilderness Trails (see Sleeping, page 214).*

The 251-sq-km Lewa Wildlife Conservancy is situated about 15 km southwest of Isiolo on the northern foothills of Mount Kenya on the Laikipia Plateau, approximately 65 km northeast of Nanyuki. It was originally a 180-sq-km cattle ranch. The land comprises savannah, wetland, grassland and indigenous forest. It was officially registered as a Non-Profit Organization in 1995. The conservancy project aims to minimize the conflict between conservation and human settlement and protect and encourage the rhino and other endangered species. The Lewa Downs and later the adjoining state-owned **Ngare Ndare Forest** were fenced to reduce the human/wildlife conflict and loss of smallholders' crops to elephants. Numbers of both black and white rhino have increased, with none lost to poachers, and in 2008 it celebrated the birth of its 100th rhino. It is possible to see the Big Five. Lewa Downs also contains an archaeological site where Mary Leakey found prehistoric tools and artefacts, some of which are on display in the Meru Museum. Tourism has been expanded to help cover the cost on the conservancy, but has been kept within clear limits: low-impact/high-income tourism with a maximum of 60 tourist beds. The original homestead has been converted into a Conservation Centre. As it is a non-profit organization all tourist-generated income goes to pay for security and management of the wildlife. The unique and hugely popular Safaricom Marathon (see page 40) is run in Lewa every June.

## Ol Pejeta Conservancy and Sweetwaters Chimpanzee Sanctuary

ⓘ *The main gate is 14 km from Nanyuki off the road to Nayahururu, T062-32408, www.olpejetaconservancy.org, daily 0700-1900, US$40, children (2-12) US$20. Accommodation in the conservancy is offered by Sweetwaters Tented Camp and Ol Pejeta House, and a number of seasonal bush camps. Day visitors are permitted by prior arrangement.*

Ol Pejeta Conservancy covers 364 sq km and was established in 1988 on what was a cattle ranch originally owned by Lord Delamere, whose later owners included Christina Onassi's father-in-law, Roussel, and arms dealer Adnan Khashoggi. It is home to all the Big Five, and has the highest ratio of game-to-area of any park or reserve in Kenya. It has the fastest-growing population of rhino in the country and now with 78, is home to East Africa's largest population of black rhino and rather staggeringly some 10,000 other large mammals. The Laikipia Environmental Conservation Centre is visited by over 100 Kenyan schools each year and teaches the students about ecology, wildlife management and culture. Apart from safaris in vehicles, game walks and horse rides are available, plus camel riding and night game drives. A new addition is the cultural *manyatta* where visitors can meet Masai, Pokot, Samburu and Turkana people and learn a little about traditional ways of life.

**Sweetwaters Chimpanzee Sanctuary** ① *daily 0900-1030, 1500-1630*. This is the only place in Kenya to see (non-indigenous) chimpanzees and was established in 1993 in collaboration with KWS and the Jane Goodall institute. An initial group of chimpanzee orphans were brought to the sanctuary from a facility in Bujumbura, Burundi as they needed to be evacuated due to the outbreak of civil war in Burundi. It is now home to 42 rescued chimps, which live in two groups on an island in the Ewaso Ng'iro River and visitors can view them from a boat. Sweetwaters is a member of the **Pan African Sanctuary Alliance (PASA)**, an alliance of 18 sanctuaries in 12 African countries, which between them currently care for over 800 orphaned and/or confiscated chimpanzees.

---

## ◉ Laikipia Plateau listings

*For Sleeping and Eating price codes and other relevant information, see Essentials pages 34-38.*

### ● Sleeping

**Laikipia Plateau** *p211, map212*
All the places to stay here are very expensive. However, most rates are full board and include game activities. Expect to pay in the region of US$300-500 per person sharing. For this, however, you will get an impeccable and private safari experience a long way from the hoards in the national parks and game reserves. This is just a selection of accommodation on the plateau, for a full list visit, www.www.laikipia.org. Horseback expeditions and camel safaris are available from most of the lodges and all use local guides.
**L Borana Lodge**, www.borana.co.ke, reservations **Bush and Beyond**, Nairobi, T020-600 457, www.bush-and-beyond.com. This lodge is situated on a 14,200-ha, wildlife-rich, private, working cattle ranch, adjacent to the Lewa Wildlife Conservancy on the edge of the Samangua Valley with panoramic views of Mt Kenya and the plains below. The 8 en suite cottages have been built from local materials, 1 has an extra bedroom for children, the central lounge and dining room is decorated with local art, swimming pool, and a hide overlooking a dam which is a popular spot for swimming elephants. From US$480 per person per night.
**L El Karama Ranch**, 40 km to the north of Nanyuki, www.horsebackinkenya.com, or reservations **Let's Go Travel**, Nairobi,

T020-444 7151, www.lets-go-travel.net. Attractive stone and canvas, thatched *bandas* with en suite bathrooms, beautifully situated along the banks of the Ewaso Nyiro River on a working cattle farm. There is a large open-fronted dining and sitting area with a big fireplace and view over the river to a salt lick on the opposite bank, which is visited by a variety of animals. Game walks and drives can be arranged. It also offers horse-riding safaris combined with mobile camping in lovely wilderness places, accompanied by a pack string of camels. From US$250 per person per night.
**L Il'Ngwesi Lodge**, Mathew's Mountains north of the Lewa Wildlife Conservancy, reservations **Lets Go Travel**, Nairobi, T020-444 7151, www.lets-go-travel.net. Constructed with materials from the local area, this community-owned lodge comprises 6 individual thatched *bandas* with open-air showers and good views. There's a large sitting area, a strikingly designed swimming pool and a covered hide overlooking a waterhole. All profits go to the local Masai community and are spent on schools, health, water supplies, and cattle dips. From US$250 per person.
**L Lewa Safari Camp**, Lewa Wildlife Conservancy, www.lewasafaricamp.com, reservations **Bush and Beyond**, Nairobi, T020-600 457, www.bush-and-beyond.com. Lush green lawns, swimming pool and tented accommodation; guests get a real insight to conservation and wildlife management. The camp has 10 doubles

and 2 family/triple tents and a main building with a lounge and dining area and veranda with good views over a waterhole frequented by rhino and elephant. Closed Apr–May and Nov. From US$290 per person.

**L Lewa Wilderness**, Lewa Wildlife Conservancy, reservations **Bush and Beyond**, T020-600 457, www.bush-and-beyond.com. This has been the Craig family home since 1924 when the family came from England and began raising cattle here, and accommodates 16 guests in 8 comfortable thatched cottages with en suite bathrooms, fireplaces and verandas. The food is wholesome and organically grown. There is a cosy sitting room and meals are eaten on a long banquet table in the open-air dining room. Rhino, Grevy's zebra and the sitatunga are among many other species of game found here. Closed Apr–May and Nov. From US$450 per person.

**L Loisaba Lodge**, T062-31072, www.loisaba.com, or **Bush and Beyond**, Nairobi, T020-600 457, www.bush-and-beyond.com. A 150-sq-km private wildlife conservancy in the centre of Laikipia Plateau with 4 double and 3 twin bedrooms with en suite bathrooms and verandas perched over an escarpment, with commanding views of Mt Kenya. This area is especially known for sightings of big cats. Facilities include swimming pool, tennis court, bocce court and croquet lawn and the spa offers massages and beauty treatments and a romantic open-air bubble bath. There are also 'skybeds': 4 wooden platforms set against rocky outcrops and partially covered by a thatched roof, with shower and flushing toilet, which form part of optional walking, horse or camel safaris. The 1st and original set are located amongst a kopje of rocks in one of the eastern valleys overlooking a waterhole. The second and newer set is located about 8 km further south on the banks of the Ewaso Ng'iro River. Finally, Loisaba is the only location of a hot-air balloon on the Laikipia Plateau: 1-hr sunrise balloon trips cost US$425 per person. Closed Apr–May. From US$470 per person per night.

**L Makena Hills**, gmf@gallmankenya.co.ke, www.gallmankenya.org. Situated on the extreme west of Laikipia on the edge of the Great Rift Valley, and home to Kuki Gallman – conservationist and author of *I Dreamed of Africa* – who guests can meet if she's home, and it's where the subsequent movie was filmed starring Kim Basinger. 6 enormous Arabic desert-style tents with attached dressing room and bathrooms, and facilities include a central reception area with 2 giant fireplaces, front terrace with a camp fire, dining room, bar, shop and swimming pool. Quality organic food is served. From U$$325 per person per night.

**L Mutamaiyu House**, www.mutamaiyu.com, is on Mugie Ranch at the northern end of the plateau, reservations, **Exclusive African Treasures**, Nairobi T020-712 330, www.eatreasures.co.ke. A magnificent family-owned house built in a grove of ancient, twisting olive trees. It is a 19,800-ha working ranch, home to all the Big Five and 20 black rhino were relocated here in 2004; these were previously not seen in the area for 25 years. Mutamaiyu comfortably accommodates up to 8 people in 4 African-style thatched cottages built of local stone, and there's a comfortable lounge with fireplace and a swimming pool. One of the more unusual activities here is painting safaris with a local artist. From US$380 per person per night.

**L Ol Malo**, halfway between Archer's Post and Loruk, to the west of Samburu National Reserve, reservations Nairobi, T062-32715, www.olmalo.com. A ranch and game sanctuary near the Ewaso Ng'iro River with 4 expensive and exclusive guest cottages spread out along the cliff edge and built out of natural rock and ancient olive wood, with thatched roofs and huge glass windows. You can soak in the bath whilst looking at the animals at the waterhole. There is a dining room, sitting room and swimming pool, and most of the food is home grown. From US$490 per person per night.

**L Ol Pejeta Ranch House**, 40 km west from Nanyuki in the Ol Pejeta Consevancy, reservations, **Serena Hotels**, T020-284 2333, www.serenahotels.com. 6 elegantly appointed suites overlooking extensive tropical gardens and 2 swimming pools. **Ol Pejeta** was formerly owned by Lord Delamere and was also one of the holiday homes of the international arms dealer Adnan Kashoggi. An 8-ft basket, which can be winched down by a pulley system, hangs above the main dining room table – it is said that a naked young lady covered in fruit, hidden in the basket, was a treat for guests when Khashoggi owned the ranch! From US$495 per person per night.

**L Sabuk Lodge**, at the northern edge of the plateau on the banks of the Ewaso Ng'iro River, reservations **Cheli and Peacock**, Nairobi, T020-603 054, www.cheli peacock.com. Perched on the edge of the gorge overlooking the river, the 5 thatched cottages have stunning views and each has its own unique design, crafted from local stone and ancient cedar and olive wood. The lodge is the starting/finishing point for camel-assisted walking safaris, when guests are guided through completely deserted tracts of wilderness. Most of the walking is done in the morning, leaving the afternoon free to enjoy the river, swim, fish, or learning bush crafts with the guide. From US$360 per person per night.

**L Tassia Lodge**, T0725-972923, www.tassiasafaris.com. A community lodge north of **Borana Lodge** where elephants can be observed. The ranch is covered with original cedar forest to the west, it then stretches down the Mokogodo Escarpment onto the plains. 5 double bedrooms and 1 twin room, all with en suite bathrooms, extra beds can be provided for children. A comfortable sitting and dining area overlooks a stunning swimming pool, which is built into rocks and surrounded by fig trees. From US$400 per person.

**L-B Sweetwaters Tented Camp**, Ol Pejeta Conservancy, reservations **Serena Hotels**, Nairobi, T020-284 2333, www.serena hotels.com. One of the larger camps with 39 luxury tents under thatch overlooking a waterhole, floodlit by night, swimming pool, restaurant and 2 bars in what was the original homestead. Safaris in vehicles, game walks and horse rides are available, plus camel riding, night game drives and bush lunches or dinners. High season rates are US$575 for a double or twin but drop to US$295 in low season.

# East from Nanyuki

*From Nanyuki, the road turns southeast through Meru and Embu and joins the A2 again in Sagana, completing its loop around Mount Kenya. The eastern side of the mountain is heavily cultivated and coffee is grown on the higher volcanic slopes. Meru National Park lies to the east, and although little visited does offer a couple of upmarket lodges, and a number of black and white rhino have recently been reintroduced.* ▶▶ *For listings, see pages 222-224.*

## Nanyuki to Embu

Northeast from Nanyuki the road continues around Mount Kenya. The next village that you will reach after Nanyuki is **Timau** – there is very little here except for the excellent Kentrout, see Eating, page 209. Another 35 km or so down the road is the turning off to the left that goes up on to **Marsabit** and Northern Kenya. The first town on this road is Isiolo, which is located about 30 km off the Nanyuki–Meru road and is where the good road ends, see page 356.

Continuing around the mountain about 30 km on after the turning off to Isiolo, you will reach the town of Meru. The journey from Nanyuki to Meru is very beautiful, and shows the diversity of Kenya's landscape. To the south is Mount Kenya, to the north (on a clear, haze-free day) you can see miles and miles of the northern wilderness of Kenya.

## Meru ●●● ▶▶ *pp222-224. Colour map 1, A5.*

→ *Phone code: 064.*

Meru, a thriving and bustling trading centre, is located to the northeast of Mount Kenya, about 70 km from Nanyuki. It stands in a heavily cultivated and forested area at an altitude of about 3000 m and it can be cold and damp. It's quite a climb up to Meru from either Isiolo or Embu, and in the rainy season you will find yourself lost in the clouds. However, if you are here on a clear day you may get good views of the mountain peaks. It is an important coffee-producing region, which is grown in small holdings on the higher slopes above town in Mount Kenya's rich volcanic soil. From Meru the road to Embu is good, and about 5 km to the south of town, the road crosses the equator again where there is a sign and a few curio stalls. Although it serves as an important trading centre it does not receive many visits from travellers. As it is not close to any of the trails up the mountain, it has not been developed for this. It is, however, the base for visits to the Meru National Park, the entrance of which is just over 80 km from the town. There is a noticeable military presence here and a good range of shops, banks and internet facilities.

**Meru National Museum** ① *down the road roughly opposite the Meru County Hotel, T064-20482, www.museums.or.ke, Mon-Fri 0930-1800, Sat 0930-1400, US$7, children (under 18) US$3.50,* is housed in the oldest building in town, built in 1916, and was formerly a District Commissioner's Office. It has several small galleries, with displays ranging from local geology, stuffed birds and animals, to innovative toys made from scrap materials. The most interesting section of the museum is that related to the customs and culture of the local Meru people: various ethnographic artefacts are exhibited, as well as examples of local timber and stone and tools from the prehistoric site at Lewa Downs. There is a Meru homestead that gives a good idea of how the Meru people live. In the museum shop is a relic of colonial days – a wind-up gramophone made by His Majesty's

Voice. This particular model came via Pakistan where the then owner was stationed with the King's African Rifles. There is a small selection of bakelite 78 records, which can be played for KSh10. Outside there is a display of various herbs and other medicinal plants, including an example of a *miraa* plant. A craft shop sells locally produced items.

There are two **markets** at Meru: one on the main road towards Nanyuki and the other on the opposite side of town. The merchandise on sale is very cheap and includes not just agricultural produce from the farms around Meru, but also baskets and household goods.

---

## Meru National Park ⊜ ➤ *pp222-224. Colour map 1, A5.*

① *T064-20613, www.kws.org, entry fee US$50, children US$25, car US$4.20 per day. To get here take the C19 from Meru to the settlement of Maua, and the park's New Murera Gate is 30 km to the west on a rough road. The park has a road system of over 600 km, much of which has recently been upgraded, but many roads become impassable in the wet.*

With just a few tourist package tours visiting Meru National Park, it makes it one of the least trampled and unspoiled of Kenya's parks. Some 85 km away from Meru town and 370 km northeast of Nairobi, straddling the equator, the 1810 sq km is mainly covered with thorny bushland and wooded grasslands to the west. There are 13 rivers and numerous mountain-fed streams that flow into the Tana River from the south. Dense riverine forests grow along the watercourses surrounded by the prehistoric-looking doum palms. There are hundreds of species of birds including the Somali ostrich, the red-necked falcon and Pel's fishing owl, which can be heard at night by the Tana River. Animals include lion, leopard, cheetah, elephant, Grevy's and plains zebra, gerenuk, reticulated giraffe, hippo, lesser kudu, oryx, hartebeest and Grant's gazelle and some fairly large herds of buffalo.

The national park suffered greatly from poachers during the late 1980s, which resulted in the deaths of several rangers and two French tourists, along with the annihilation of the introduced white rhino population. Following these incidents the option of visiting Meru National Park was effectively withdrawn by all the safari operators. The Kenyan government have now driven out the poachers and restored security. However, much of the wildlife in the park was decimated and it will be some time before numbers are fully recovered. Nevertheless there have been some success stories and in 2001 Kenya Wildlife Services embarked on an elephant translocation initiative and moved 56 elephants (nine different families) from the Laikipia Plateau to Meru National Park. Since then a variety of other game has also been relocated into Meru, including 20 Grevy's zebra in 2002, 39 giraffe in 2003, and 20 black rhino and 10 white rhino in 2006, as well as very large herds of plains zebra and reedbuck.

The park was opened in 1968 and became famous for its role in the *Born Free* story. The late Joy Adamson hand-reared the orphaned lioness Elsa here, later releasing her into the wild. Elsa died of tick-borne fever and was buried in a forest clearing by Joy. After her death, Joy was also buried at the same site near the Adamson's Falls next to the Tana River, where the grave is marked by a small plaque. For the full *Born Free* story see box, page 220. In recent years, Kenya Wildlife Services has built a three-span galvanized Bailey bridge across the Tana River. Funded by the World Bank, the 138-m galvanized steel bridge links Meru National Park to Kora National Park and allows for the free movement of animals between the parks. The bridge has been named the Adamson Bridge in honour of George Adamson, who lived in Kora with his beloved lions at Kampi ya Simba.

## Leafy streets

*Miraa*, also known as *qat* and *gatty*, is produced in large quantities around Meru. It is a leaf that is chewed and is a mild stimulant as well as acting as an appetite suppressant. You will see people all over Kenya (but particularly in the north) holding bunches of these leaves and twigs and chewing them. In Meru there is a street corner devoted to the selling of *miraa*. It is a small tree that grows wild here and is also grown commercially. It is produced legally and it is also sold to the northeast of Kenya and exported to Somalia, Yemen and Djibouti.

Meru National Park is close to several national reserves including Bisanadi, North Kitui and Rahole. They have no tourist facilities at present. Kora was upgraded from reserve to national park following the death of George Adamson and there are plans to open it up in the near future.

## Chogoria village ⬤⬤⬤ ▸ *pp222-224. Colour map 1, A5.*

Between Meru and Embu is the village of Chogoria, which is the starting point for the **Chogoria trail**. This is the only eastern approach up the mountain and it is generally considered to be the most beautiful of the routes. It is also supposed to be the easiest as far as gradients are concerned. For the Chogoria trail, see page 205.

**Embu** is the final town in the clockwise circuit around Mount Kenya, before rejoining the road south to Nairobi. Named after the Embu people who live in this area, it is the provincial headquarters of the Eastern Province. The town is strung out along the main road and it's a busy place, with the bars staying open late. There's not a great deal to see here although the old Isaac Walton Inn is a reasonable place to stay. The surrounding area is densely populated and intensively cultivated.

## Mwea National Reserve ▸ *Colour map 1, A5.*

ⓘ *Adults US$20, children US$10. Check with the Kenya Wildlife Service, Nairobi, T020-600 800, www.kws.org, for current camping regulations. Basic road network: a 4WD is required.*

Mwea National Reserve is a small reserve of 6800 ha, gazetted in 1976, located southeast of Embu. It lies immediately north of the Kamburu Reservoir, constructed at the confluence of the Tana and Thiba rivers, and the Kaburu and Masinga hydroelectric dams are sited in the reserve. The vegetation is mainly thorny bushland with patches of woodland and scattered baobab trees. Part of the park has been enclosed with an electrified fence to stop the animals wandering into settlements, and it provides a home for elephant, buffalo, impala, lesser kudu, baboon, vervet and Sykes' monkeys, hippos and crocodiles in the rivers and the dam, There is also a profusion of birdlife and the adjacent rice-growing paddies and fields have attracted large number of waders and waterbirds and this area is also rich in birds of prey.

The most direct route from Embu is to follow the infrequently used B7 road towards Kangonde, south of Mount Kaniro, 1549 m, and branch off to the right on a small road approximately 10 km before Iriamurai. Or, travellers coming from Nairobi, 180 km away, can take the A3 towards Garissa, branching north on the B7 as far as the town of Kaewa where you can branch left onto the same road to Mwea but approaching from the south.

## A real tear jerker

Joy and George Adamson were one of the 20th century's most famous champions of wildlife. Their relationship with Elsa the lioness in the 1950s and 1960s is one of the best-known animal stories ever told – immortalized in the book and film *Born Free*. The public image of their lives in the inhospitable bush lands of Kenya was of romantic safaris and tireless commitment. Joy with her tight knit of blond curls and easy laugh was a colonial queen and George with his suntanned chest, khaki shorts and white beard, a legend of the bush. George grew up in India but moved to Kenya as a child, and after working on farms in the Rift Valley, he turned his hand to hunting but had a change of heart about killing lions when he came across one sitting on a rock: "She was sculptured by the setting sun, as though she were part of the granite on which she lay. I wondered how many lions had lain on the self-same rock during countless centuries while the human race was still in its cradle". This passage from his diary was read by Bill Travers, the actor who played George in *Born Free*, at his 1989 memorial service in London. George decided on a career as a game warden and got a job in the remote and unexplored Northern Frontier of Kenya on the border with Somalia and arrested 25 poachers in the first few months.

Joy was born Friederike Gessner in 1910 in what was then the Austro-Hungarian Empire (later to become part of Austria). She set sail for Africa in 1937 and met Peter Bally, a botanist, on the boat between Cairo and Mombasa. They married in Nairobi in 1938 and he renamed her Joy, after the joy that she had bought into his life. Ironically, the marriage was unhappy and didn't last long. Joy met George on safari and seduced him in the Norfolk, the famous hotel in Nairobi, a month later. She shared his passion, respect for the Northern Frontier, an adventurous spirit and a love of wildlife. She was also a fine artist and was commissioned to paint a collection of the tribes of Kenya (which today hang in the Kenya State House and the National Museum). Successful in her own right, her frequent affairs were legendary amongst the tight-knit community of colonial Kenya.

Their safari in 1955 was the one that changed their lives forever. After shooting a dangerous man-eating lioness, George found her three newborn cubs in a cleft of rock and took them home to Joy. When they opened their eyes a few days later, they immediately imprinted on her as their mother. For the first few months, she raised all three, but they grew big and boisterous and two were sent to a zoo in Rotterdam. Elsa stayed and was doted on by Joy, who showered her with affection and attention. The lioness went everywhere with the Adamsons and Joy adored her. Despite their affection for the lioness, they both agreed she must be set free. George taught her to hunt and kill, which involved dragging a carcass behind his Land Rover for Elsa to chase. When she could fend for herself, she was released in the bush but visited the Adamsons almost daily and retained her old friendship with Joy. Elsa's unique rehabilitation became the success it was, when she mated with a wild male and bore three cubs, which she introduced to Joy. Only once before had captive lions successfully been released in the wild but with no contact, it was never known if they reproduced. Joy took her story to London and the publishing house of Collins. *Born Free* became an instant success and sold over 5 million copies in 12 languages. Her publisher Billy Collins came to Kenya to meet Elsa, where he was seduced by Joy. In January 1961, whilst Joy was away on business with Billy, Elsa became ill from tick-bite fever and died with her feverish head resting in George's lap. Joy returned grief-stricken and buried Elsa next to the Tana River at Meru, causing a worldwide reaction of condolence never before seen for an animal. In 1964 Columbia Pictures started filming *Born Free*, and George was hired as the technical adviser on lion handling. George selected the lions (over 20 were needed) from zoos and circuses, and trained them. Virginia McKenna and Bill Travers who played the parts of Joy and George (married in real life), refused to use doubles in their scenes with the lions but the crew worked from within cages. After the film was finished, George was able to keep three of the lions and Joy agreed to finance their rehabilitation at Meru Reserve. She had a cheetah cub to set free, so they both set up camps 15 miles apart where they lived for over four years, as cheetah and lion cannot share the same territory. Bill Travers returned to Kenya to make a documentary on the Adamsons, but Joy withdrew because she was jealous of the amount of coverage of George. Travers apologized, but she never spoke to him or Virginia McKenna again. An audience of 35 million saw the finished film, *The Lions are Free*. George earned royalties, and made money from his autobiography, aptly entitled *My Pride and Joy*. In 1969, Joy moved to Elsamere, her new house on Lake Naivasha, which is today a museum. George's pride of 15 lions was faring well for themselves in the bush and in 1970, George moved to the isolated wilderness of Kora on the Tana River where he spent the rest of his life. He re-released Boy, his favourite lion who played Elsa's mate in the movie and another young cub that had been found by Bill Travers in a furniture shop at the bottom of the Kings Road in Chelsea. Over the next seven years George released a further 17 lions, and became known as *baba ya simba* (father of the lions). Despite being awarded the Austrian Cross of Honour for Science and the Arts from her country of birth and contributing to wildlife projects throughout the world (and her celebrity status increasing), Joy resented George's obvious contentment at Kora, his activeness, deep concern for his lions, and popularity. Her mood was revived when she was given another leopard cub, Penny, in 1977, which she raised and released at her camp at Shaba, and in 1979 she invited George to come to her camp and celebrate Christmas. At the last minute, he couldn't make it due to problems with his plane. On the 3 January 1980, Joy Adamson was found in a pool of blood after being stabbed. One of her ex-workers later confessed to her murder in retaliation for being sacked. George buried his wife's ashes beneath the graves of Elsa and Pippa, a cheetah she had released, at Meru. Nine years later George was killed by Somalia Shifta poachers carrying automatic weapons at his beloved camp in Kora. On the Sunday morning of 20 August 1989 after his usual 11 o'clock gin, a 50-year ritual, he rushed in his battered Land Rover to investigate a commotion in the bush. Poachers were ambushing a female German guest and threatening her with rape, and he charged forward in the vehicle firing his pistol. George and two of his employees were shot dead in a hail of bullets. He was 81. Hundreds of people came to his funeral at Kora and he was buried alongside Boy. A bottle of gin was placed beneath his coffin, and after the funeral, a wreath was dragged away by a lion – evidence that his pride had visited the grave of the father of the lions.

## ✪ East from Nanyuki listings

*For Sleeping and Eating price codes and other relevant information, see Essentials pages 34-38.*

## ● Sleeping

**Meru** *p217*
There's no really decent accommodation in Meru, just a string of basic board and lodgings, so it's better to move on if you can.
**D-E Meru Country**, on the main road next to the post office, T064-20432. Probably the best hotel in the town centre, with simple but clean, reasonably modern and comfortable rooms and friendly staff. All rooms have hot water but make sure the showers work and it's worth paying a little more for the ones with TVs and balconies. It has a decent restaurant that serves *nyama choma* and Indian curries, a bar with a patio, and plenty of secure parking.
**E Meru Safari Hotel**, Tom Mboya St, T064-31500. A big block with a range of rooms, but look at them first as some are rather small, all with hot water, although this is often provided in a bucket from the kitchen, and some have TVs. There is secure parking, laundry services, and a simple restaurant with an outside terrace.
**E Pig and Whistle**, off Kenyatta Highway, T064-31411. A ramshackle run-down hotel on a hill off the road to Embu and it was here that the then Joy Bally committed adultery with George Adamson which led to her divorce her husband, Peter Bally, see box, page 220. There are cottages in the grounds, hot water, and some of those built in the 1930s have original furnishings and fittings. The hotel has a handsome central building from the colonial period with a good restaurant (mid-range), with outside tables separated by flowering hedges, friendly staff and excellent security.
**F New Milimani**, roughly 2 km from town on Moi Stadium Rd, off the Nanyuki road, T062-20224. Rooms are bare but clean, but often have water supply problems and avoid

it at weekends when the hotel hosts a very noisy disco. The basic and cheap restaurant serves a wide-ranging menu including curries and stews and there's plenty of safe parking.
**F White Star**, some distance from the town centre on the road to the Meru National Park, just before the Teacher's College, T063-20989. Simple en suite rooms in a squat block in a compound with parking, you can get basic food here on the attractive leafy terrace but no beer as it is Muslim owned.

**Meru National Park** *p218*
For now there is only the choice of 2 exceptionally good but pricey top-end camps or very basic KWS *bandas*. However, a 60-bed tourist facility to be called **Meru Mulika Lodge** is presently being constructed a few metres from the New Murera Gate.
**L Elsa's Kopje**, www.elsaskopje.com, reservations **Cheli and Peacock**, Nairobi, T020-603 054, www.chelipeacock.com. A luxury camp perched on top of a kopje with 9 thatched stone cottages, all with en suite stone bathrooms and locally made furniture, 2 of the cottages have an outside bath with views over the park, and all have their own butler. There's a central dining and lounge area, a stunning infinity swimming pool built into the rocks with sweeping views. Set slightly apart from the camp on a hill where George Adamson set up a camp after filming *Born Free* is Elsa's House, with 1 twin and 1 double en suite bathroom and its own swimming pool, ideal for families. The camp has its own airstrip and helicopter pad, or road transfers can be arranged from Meru airstrip. Rates from US$330 per person and include food, day and night game drives, nature walks and fishing.
**L Leopard Rock Lodge**, reservations T020-600 031, www.leopardmico.com. This is a beautiful lodge decorated with exquisite antique furniture and Persian rugs

on hardwood floors, built on a 3.5-km frontage on the Murera River offering luxury full-board accommodation in 15 *bandas*, each one with 2 bathrooms. Very fine cuisine, in a high-class restaurant with special service and a broad selection of wine and champagne. It has a small museum with library and video room, African-style open-air kitchen, pottery workshop, jacuzzi and pool bar. A simply stunning swimming pool, which has a perspex wall at one end so it's actually possible to look through the clear wall at the crocodiles in the adjacent river. Most guests fly in. All-inclusive rates from US$370 per person.

**E Bwatherongi Bandas**, book through the warden, T064-20613, or **Kenya Wildlife Service**, T020-600 800, www.kws.org. There are 4 self-catering *bandas* near the park HQ within the park, each has 1 double and 1 single bed and en suite bathroom, but they are very basic and have no kitchen, only an outside BBQ area that overlooks the Bwatherongi River. Bring everything you may need including water, firewood, food and bed linen.

**E Murera Bandas**, just outside the New Murera Gate, reservations **Kenya Wildlife Service** as above. 4 self-catering *bandas* with 2 bedrooms, each with 1 double and 1 single bed, and en suite bathroom. BBQ area rather than a kitchen, and again you need to bring everything with you.

**Chogoria village** *p219*
**E Meru Mount Kenya Lodge**, just inside the park at the Chogoria Gate, 25 km from Chogoria on the lower slopes of the mountain (road is hard going; a 4WD is essential and if it's very wet even a 4WD won't make it). Reservations: **UNIGLOBE Let's Go Travel**, Nairobi, T020-444 7151, www.lets-go-travel.net. Reasonable *bandas* with hot showers and log fires, each sleeps 2-3 people and has a dining area and kitchen. There is also an additional cottage that can sleep 4. Bedding is supplied, but other than that you need to be fully self sufficient, and

the only electricity is supplied by a generator for a short time in the evening. This is at an altitude of around 3000 m where the dense forests and bamboo on the mountain end and the moorlands begin so obviously it can be very cold at night.

**Embu**
**E Isaac Walton Inn**, T068-20128/9. This is the best of the budget hotels in Embu, situated about 2 km north of town on the road to Meru. It is an old colonial hotel apparently named after an English angler because of the proximity of good fishing spots in the mountain streams nearby. The inn is set in lovely tropical gardens with a comfortable lounge with a log-burning fire, the 42 rooms are basic and gloomy but all have bathrooms with hot water and a balcony. The price includes breakfast and there is a good bar and restaurant. Friendly and the staff are helpful.
**F Highway Court Hotel**, next door to the BP petrol station, T068-20046. Large, modern concrete block with simple rooms with hot showers and TV, and excellent views over the town from the roof, restaurant, rates include a cooked breakfast, good security, but the ground floor bar is lively and can be very noisy.

## ⊙ Transport

**Meru** *p217*
The main bus and *matatu* area is behind the mosque on Mosque Hill Rd, reached from the road going past Barclays Bank. There are several daily buses to and from Meru and **Nairobi** and **Kensilver & Akamba Bus Services** are cheap and reliable. The journey to Nairobi takes about 4 hrs, to **Chogoria** about 1 hr, to **Embu** about 2½ hrs, and to **Thika** about 3 hrs. *Matatus* cover the same route and north to **Isiolo** take about 45 mins and depart from the main stand near the market and opposite the Shell petrol station.

**Chogoria village** *p219*
**Embu**
The road from Nairobi to Embu has a very good surface but is very busy. *Matatus* are frequent, or instead take the **Kensilver** or **Akamba** bus **(Nairobi** to **Meru**, via Embu). Journey to Nairobi takes 1½ hrs.

## ❶ Directory

**Meru** *p217*
**Banks** Barclays Bank, Tom Mboya St, has an ATM and exchanges cash and TCs. Money can also be changed at **Standard Chartered Bank**, Moi Av, and **Kenya Commercial Bank**, Njuri Ncheke St. **Internet** Cafe Candy Tom Mboya St. **Post office** Near Town Hall, with telephone, internet and fax, and Western Union money-transfer services.

**Chogoria village** *p219*
**Embu**
**Banks** Barclays Bank is to the south of town and has an ATM; and nearby is the **Kenya Commercial Bank** across the road from the bus and *matatu* stage. **Internet** At the post office. **Post office** Towards the north of town on Embu/Meru Rd.

# Contents

## Southern Kenya

### At a glance

◉ **Getting around** The best way
to explore the parks is to opt for
a fly-in or drive-in safari.

◉ **Time required** 2-3 nights each in
Amboseli and Tsavo East/West from
either Nairobi or the coast.

☼ **Weather** Fine and sunny most
of the year with clear views and
moderate temperatures.

✕ **When not to go** Can be visited
year round but the dirt roads in
the parks can become difficult
in the wet.

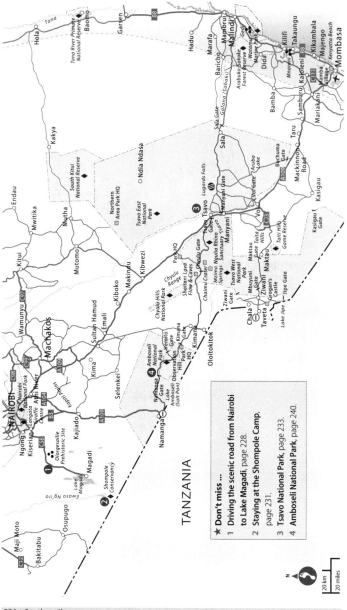

TANZANIA

★ Don't miss ...

1 Driving the scenic road from Nairobi to Lake Magadi, page 228.

2 Staying at the Shompole Camp, page 231.

3 Tsavo National Park, page 233.

4 Amboseli National Park, page 240.

20 km
20 miles

N

Southern Kenya is one of the most visited regions of the country. The major game parks in the region are a big draw: Tsavo West and Tsavo East, on either side of the Nairobi–Mombasa road, make up the largest park in the country, and Amboseli National Park, which is also very popular. Amboseli is probably most famous for its photographs of elephants with snow-capped Kilimanjaro in the background; a picture that, above all, says 'come to Africa'. Another reason for their popularity are their closeness to the coast; visitors to this region can go on safari and also spend some time on the beach.

There are many points of interest off the Nairobi–Mombasa road leading to the coast. This is one of the most important thoroughfares in the East Africa region as it runs the length of the country to Nairobi and then to Uganda, where it continues on to Kampala. Hundreds of trucks ply this road each day carrying goods imported through the Mombasa port into the interior of the continent. The Masai Mara Game Reserve in southwest Kenya, contiguous with the Serengeti National Park in Tanzania, is normally accessed via the town of Narok and is therefore included in the Rift Valley section, see page 140.

# South from Nairobi

*The road from Nairobi to Mombasa is in a reasonable condition and parts of it have been recently resurfaced. The only rough bit is the last 100 km or so before Mombasa, which is a steady hill where the tar routinely gets chewed up by heavy trucks heading to Nairobi from Mombasa's port. An alternative from driving from Nairobi to the coast is taking the many frequent flights, which take little more than an hour and thanks to strong competition among the airlines on this route, are very affordable. If you've got lots of time, you can also take the (very slow) train. Another road heads due south to Lake Magadi via the prehistoric site at Olorgesailie.* ▶▶ *For listings, see pages 230-232.*

## Nairobi to Lake Magadi ◉ ▶▶ *pp230-232.*

The C58 is a good tarmacked road that runs from Nairobi to Lake Magadi, which is 77 km from the city and makes for an easy day excursion. To get to it take the Langata Road out past Wilson Airport and Nairobi National Park. Soon after the park entrance, take a left fork that leads through the village of Kiserian and then it climbs up the Ngong Hills before descending to the floor of the Rift Valley. *Matatus* run up and down this road and Nairobi tour operators can arrange an excursion out here.

### Olorgesailie prehistoric site → *Colour map 1, A6.*
① *On the C58, 65 km southwest of Nairobi, www.museums.or.ke, daily 0930-1800, US$5.75, children (under 18) US$2.90.*
A trip to this important prehistoric site can be combined with a visit to Lake Magadi. The site covers an area of 21 ha, and is the largest archaeological site in Kenya. It was discovered in 1919 by geologist JW Gregory and later in the 1940s excavated by Kenya's most famous archaeologists, Mary and Louis Leakey. A team from the Smithsonian Institute in the USA continues to work here. In 1947 it was given national heritage status.

It is believed that a lake covered the present site of the mountain in prehistoric times, and that various mammals, including elephants, hippos, crocodiles and giraffes, lived near or in the lake. The abundant presence of game attracted hunters to this area. These early hunters are believed to have fashioned stone tools and axes. Fossilized remains of prehistoric animals, some gigantic compared to their descendants, and an abundance of Acheulean hand axes and other stone tools were uncovered here. A small, raised wooden walkway has been built around the display of prehistoric animal remains and tools, enabling the fossils to be exhibited where they were found; a guide is on hand to take you around.

### Lake Magadi → *Colour map 1, A4.*
Some 30 km further south of Olorgesailie, and located at the base of the Rift Valley is Lake Magadi, a vision in pink. As you approach the lake, the views are splendid and you will probably see Masai grazing their cattle. At an altitude of 580 m, this is the second-lowest of the Rift Valley lakes. It is 32 km long and 3 km wide and is the most alkaline of all the Kenyan Rift Valley lakes. The highly alkaline water, with its accumulated minerals and salts, makes the surrounding soils near the lakes alkaline. This has the knock-on effect of turning ivory and bones into fossils. The high rate of evaporation is the only way by which water escapes from the lake. Several hot springs, mostly at the southern end of the lake, bring to the surface a continual supply of *magadi* (soda), which evaporates forming a

crust of sodium carbonate. It is only 110 km from Nairobi but the climate – semi-desert with temperatures around 38°C – is very different to that of the capital. A soda ash factory has been built on the lakeshore, and the town of Magadi has grown up around this, which has a Total petrol station and a bank. There is an abundance of birdlife – in particular lesser flamingos, ibis and African spoonbills. The final scenes of the movie *The Constant Gardener*, based on John le Carre's novel, were filmed on the shoreline of the lake, when in fact the location in the story was Lake Turkana.

**Getting there**  It is fairly remote but accessible for those with their own transport. Main road access to Magadi is directly from Nairobi by bus, *matatu* or private transport, via Kiserian. The railway line, which serves the factory, does not take passengers, but there are twice-daily *matatus* and buses (No 125) that reach Magadi town.

## Mombasa road ●●❶ ▶ *pp230-232.*

The Mombasa road starts as a continuation of the Uhuru Highway (A109) in Nairobi, passing one of the city's drive-in cinemas and a number of housing estates around Athi River. The route passes through the **Kapitiei Plains**. Most of this area contains large-scale cattle ranches with herds of gazelle and antelope. It is along here that you turn right for Kajiado, see page 240. The next section of the route is through semi-arid country broken by the **Ukambani Hills**. The road up this long steep slope is poor, as years of heavy trucks making the laborious climb have dug deep ruts into the road. Just south of the road, by the railway line, is **Kima**, meaning 'mincemeat' in Kiswahili. Kima was so named after a British Railway Police Assistant Superintendent who was eaten by a lion in 1900. Charles Ryall, using himself as bait, was trying to ambush a lion which had been attacking railway staff and passengers. Unfortunately the ambush went horribly wrong when he fell asleep on the job.

Further on is the town of **Sultan Hamud**. It sprung up during the making of the railway at Mile 250 where it was visited by the then ruler of Zanzibar and named after him. It has hardly changed since that time and is a pleasant enough place to stop off for a drink and a snack. Just south of **Emali** you can head down to **Amboseli National Park**, see page 240 for details of the route down the park and the park itself.

If you continue on the Mombasa road you will pass through Masai country, which is primarily featureless scrubland. There is a lodge at **Kiboko** that is about a third of the way through the journey (160 km from Nairobi) and a good place to stop off for some refreshment, see Sleeping page 231. Another good place to break your journey is at **Makindu**, about 40 km from Kiboko where a Sikh temple of the Guru Nanak faith, built in 1926, offers free accommodation and food for travellers (donations gratefully received). Slightly further along the road (about 12 km in the direction of Mombasa) is the **Makindu Handicrafts Co-operative** where people hand-carve figures, for the tourist market. The cooperative society was established in 1981 by a few individuals, whose number steadily grew to now include over 120 members, few of whom are women. The variety in designs is impressive, including very unique pieces like crocodiles carved out of tree roots. The Akamba community is renowned for their skills in woodcarving. Locally available woods like itula, mango and olive are used, and within the grounds is a tree nursery that provides these woods.

The road continues its route passing into more lush pastures with a proliferation of the wonderful and rather grotesque baobabs. At this stage the Chyulu Hills are visible to the south. The main trading centre at **Kibwezi** is the most important region in the country for sisal growing. Honey production is also much in evidence and you are likely to be offered some from sellers at the side of the road. Try before you buy to check its quality as sometimes it is adulterated with sugar. From Kibwezi, the road passes through heavily cultivated land to the boundary of Akamba country at **Mtito Andei** – meaning 'vulture forest' – about halfway between Nairobi and Mombasa. There are petrol stations, a few places to eat and a curio shop.

From here the road runs through the centre of the parks **Tsavo West** and **Tsavo East** for around 80 km, see page 233 for details. Many years ago, herds of elephants could be seen crossing the road in the grasslands making progress along this route slow, but this occurs less frequently these days as there are fewer elephants. You may spot zebra though from the road.

### Voi → Colour map 1, A6. Phone code: 043.

The capital of this region, Voi is a rapidly developing industrial and commercial centre. According to local history the name of town comes from a slave trader called Chief Kivoi who settled near the Voi River about 400 years ago. The town started to grow at the end of the 19th century when the Kenya–Uganda railway was constructed. This was the first upcountry railhead where passengers would make an overnight stop, but this is no longer offered as you can dine, sleep and breakfast on the train. It has a couple of petrol stations, a bank with an ATM, a post office, a market and supermarkets, and busy bus and *matatu* stages. Voi Gate into Tsavo East National Park is around 8 km to the north of town. You can buy and top up your Smartcard at this gate.

### Voi to Mombasa

From Voi the road runs through the **Taru Desert** for another 150 km down to Mombasa. This area is an arid, scorched wilderness and there is little sign of life. You will see several small quarries. These supply many of the hotels on the coast with natural stone tiles used in bathrooms and patios. The next small settlement is **Mackinnon Road** with the Sayyid Baghali Shah Mosque as its only landmark. Some 30 km along the route you come to **Samburu**, a small town with no tourist facilities.

Another 30 km brings you to the busy market centre of **Mariakani**, a place of palm groves and an atmosphere quite different from upcountry Kenya. If you take the road to the right, the A107, then turn left at the junction with the A106, it leads to the **Shimba Hills**, which can also be reached from the coastal road south of Mombasa.

For the next 90 km the scenery becomes progressively more tropical, the heat increases, as does the humidity and the landscape changes to coconut palms, papaya and other coastal vegetation.

---

## ◉ South from Nairobi listings

*For Sleeping and Eating price codes and other relevant information, see Essentials pages 34-38.*

## ◉ Sleeping

**Olorgesailie prehistoric site** *p228*
**F Museum Bandas**, reservations through the **National Museums of Kenya**, Nairobi

T020-374 2161, www.museums.or.ke. There are 8 simple *bandas* here with shared showers, toilets, fireplace and picnic shelter but you need to bring all bedding and food and drink. You can also camp. It's quite peaceful and there are small antelope in the area if you go for a walk, but it gets very hot.

## Lake Magadi *p228*

**L Shompole**, www.shompole.com, is south of Lake Magadi on the Ewaso Ng'iro River and in the 140-sq-km Shompole Conservancy. From Magadi drive 35 km on a dirt road (4WD required after Magadi), the camp is 10 km after the bridge, there are signs. Alternatively fly in. Established in 2002, this is a fairly new wildlife conservancy and there are already lion, giraffe, zebra, wildebeest, buffalo and elephant within the boundaries making the additional US$45 daily conservancy fee worthwhile. This is a very elegant and stylish with fantastic views. As it is so hot in this region, the lodge cleverly uses channels of water throughout as a cooling system, and each of the 6 airy, spacious Arabian-style tents have their own plunge pool, his and hers compost toilets and wonderful showers that are more like small waterfalls. Built of local wood and stone, the decor is modern and imaginative. Very good fresh food is served in the open-plan dining room and activities include local day trips, game walks and drives. There's also a luxury 2-bed house to rent. Rates from US$365 per person per night.

## Mombasa road *p229*
### Kiboko

**C Kiboko Guesthouse**, signposted to the left of the Hunter's Lodge (below) and 500 m off the main road, Kiboko, reservations **Kenya Wildlife Service**, Nairobi, T020-600 800, www.kws.org. This is a simple guesthouse with 3 bedrooms suitable for a family or group in the foothills of the Chyulu Hills, which is fully furnished with bedding and mosquito nets, kitchen equipment and stove, and a caretaker on site. There is no electricity but kerosene lamps are provided. There are pleasant nature trails in the vicinity.
**D Hunter's Lodge**, Nairobi side of Kiboko, behind a petrol station, T0722-926 685. The ramshackle gardens are pleasant with hundreds of species of birds, and wonderful views out over the dammed Kiboko River, where there's also a site beneath some acacia trees where you can camp (**F**). Everything is rather faded but the rooms are comfortable, the staff friendly, and there's reasonable food and a bar.

## Makindu

**F Sikh Temple**, in the centre of Makindu, the Sikh temple complex of the Guru Nanak faith offers free accommodation (donations gratefully received). Secure parking, very clean rooms, very good Indian food in the dining hall which you pay for, you must be well behaved and polite and alcohol is not allowed.

## Voi *p230*

The safari lodges listed here are outside of Tsavo East and Tsavo West and therefore park entry fees do not apply. For those accommodation options within the parks, which are much better for game viewing, see page 237. There are also a couple of board and lodgings in Voi for budget travellers but there is no guarantee you'll be able to hitch into the parks. Note that when you are booking an overnight (or more) safari from the coast, accommodation could be at the not unreasonable lodges around Voi, but you will not be staying in the parks themselves, which do of course draw the daily Kenya Wildlife Service's park entry fee to their rates. In the past travellers have complained that their safari from the resorts around Mombasa and Malindi have advertised themselves as over-nighting in Tsavo, when in fact accommodation is in a lodge off the Nairobi–Mombasa road (so subsequently cheaper without the park entry fees), so question you coastal resort/safari operator carefully about what you expect to be included in the price.
**B Ngutuni Lodge**, 5 km south of Voi and 5 km off the main road in the small Ngutuni Game Sanctuary that borders Tsavo East, reservations **Rex Resorts**, Mombasa, T041-222 2532, www.rexresorts.com. Very well-designed lodge built of thatch and giant wooden poles with terraces overlooking a waterhole, which is illuminated at night.

The 48 rooms have 1 double and 1 single bed and balconies, the food is excellent and rates include dinner and breakfast, and there's a bar and curio shop. Game drives are on offer around the sanctuary and as it's outside the park, also night drives.

**B Voi Wildlife Lodge**, on a 10-ha site on the boundary of the park, 5 km from the main road, reservations Nairobi, T020-375 4393, www.voiwildlifelodge.com. It has fine views of nearby volcanic outcrops and has been designed to blend into the surrounding environment, with 72 rooms, some designed for the disabled (walkways around the camp are wheelchair friendly), restaurant, 2 bars, 1 on stilts overlooking a waterhole, beauty spa, pool table, library, shop and swimming pool. Game drives into Tsavo East and West on offer.

**C Rock Side Camp**, 29 km south of Voi, on the opposite side of the Nairobi–Mombasa road to Tsavo East, clearly signposted from the village of Maunga and then 10 km from the road, reservations, Nairobi, T020-204 1445, www.westermannssafaricamp.com. Family-run, there are 16 cosy wooden *bandas* and 7 bungalows, all with en suite facilities, swimming pool, cocktail bar, restaurant, activities include walking and birdwatching and there have been 84 species spotted in a single morning here.

**D Red Elephant Safari Lodge**, 4 km from Voi and 700 m from the gate to Tsavo East, T043-30749, www.red-elephant-lodge.com. Tourist-friendly lodge right on the edge of the park, with 14 smallish but comfortable en suite rooms with mosquito nets, plus a few new thatched cottages with additional ceiling fans. The spacious main thatched building has colourful murals on the walls and zebra-striped furniture, swimming pool. Can organize game drives into the park, and game walks out of the park and there's African dancing around a fire in the evenings.

**D Sagala Lodge**, 15 km south of Voi and clearly signposted off the main road, reservations Mombasa T041-548 0070, www.blueskycorporate.com/Sagala_Lodge. In a pleasant garden setting this has 24 newly renovated *bandas* with wooden beds and mosquito nets and nice bathrooms, plus a small swimming pool, restaurant and bar with outside tables under acacia trees, and can organize game drives into the park. Over 150 species of bird has been recorded in the gardens and there are plenty of walks.

**E Tsavo Park Hotel**, near the bus stand, T043-30050, tsavoh@africaonline.co.ke. A modern block with faded en suite rooms, with satellite TV, mosquito nets, and some have balconies. The restaurant is reasonable and serves simple fare like steak or chicken and chips, and rates include breakfast.

**F Distarr Hotel**, between the bus stand and the railway station, T043-30277. Basic but clean en suite rooms, friendly staff, very good restaurant where the vegetable curries and fresh juices are excellent.

## ⊖ Transport

**Voi** *p230*

There are buses coming and going all day long between **Mombasa** and **Nairobi**. There are also buses that go through Voi between Mombasa, the border town of **Taveta** and on to **Moshi** in Tanzania.

## ① Directory

**Voi** *p230*

**Banks** Kenya Commercial Bank, on the right on the way into town just past the railway track. **Post office** A little further up the same road near the *matatu* stage.

# Tsavo National Park

→ *Phone code: 043. Colour map 1, B5/6, C5/6.*
*Tsavo is the largest game park in Kenya, and its beautiful landscape and proximity to the coast make it a popular safari destination. It offers tremendous views with diverse habitats ranging from mountains, river forest, plains, lakes and wooded grassland. Because of its open spaces, the animals are fairly easy to spot and elephants, covered in bright red dust, are often seen wandering along every horizon. Its vastness creates a special atmosphere and on these endless plains trampled by thousands of animals it is not difficult to imagine that this is once how all of East Africa looked liked.* ▸▸ *For listings, see pages 237-239.*

## Ins and outs

**Getting there**  There are no scheduled flights to either Tsavo East or West, although **Mombasa Air Safaris** (see page 265) will touch down on request and there are several airstrips suitable for chartered light aircraft.

**Getting around**  Both Tsavo East and West are fairly easily navigated with a good map as all tracks are clearly defined, and junctions are numbered. Bring all your own provisions into the park including petrol and water. You should be able to eat or drink at any of the lodges if you so desire. There is a shop at Voi Gate in the east selling (warm) beers, sodas, bread and some vegetables, and another shop in Tsavo West selling basic provisions.

## Background

This is the largest national park in Kenya at around 21,000 sq km. It lies in the southern part of the country, halfway between Mombasa and Nairobi and is bisected by the Mombasa–Nairobi railway and road link. For administrative purposes it has been split into two sections; **Tsavo East** (11,747 sq km) lying to the east of the Nairobi–Mombasa road/railway is the part of the park made famous by the 'Man-Eaters of Tsavo', and **Tsavo West** (9065 sq km). The Waliangulu and Kamba tribes used to hunt in this area before it was gazetted. The remoteness of much of the park means it has had serious problems with poaching in the past. As a consequence, much of the northern area (about two thirds of Tsavo East) used to be off-limits to the public in an attempt to halt poaching here, which had decimated the rhino population from 8000 in 1970 to around 100 in 1990. Recent anti-poaching laws have been particularly successful in Tsavo; the number of rhinos and elephants are increasing and the northern area of Tsavo East is once again open to the public. In 2007, the Kenya Wildlife Service did a census of the elephant population in Tsavo and the number was 11,696.

The first European to visit this part of Kenya was Doctor Krapf, who journeyed on foot and crossed the Tsavo River in 1849 on his way to Kitui. Captain Lugards, the explorer, also passed through this area – the rapids on the Galana River are named after him.

## Tsavo East ▸▸ *pp237-239.*

Tsavo East is the much less-visited side of the park where you will be able to see the wildlife without the usual hordes of other tourists. It mainly consists of vast plains of scrubland home to huge herds of elephants. The landscape is vast, and empty of any sign of humans, dotted with baobab trees.

## Ins and outs

ⓘ *Gates open 0630-1830. US$50, children US$25, vehicle US$4.50 per day.*

The park HQ is at Voi Gate (where you can obtain and reload Smartcards) just north of Voi on the Nairobi–Mombasa road, where there is a small educational centre. Other gates off the main road are Manyani Gate, 25 km north of Voi, and Buchuma Gate at the extreme southeast corner of Tsavo East. It is also possible to enter the park on the C103 road from Malindi via Sala Gate on the eastern boundary of the park. This route, which runs alongside the Galana River between Manyani Gate and Sala Gate, may be impassable during the rains.

## Sights

Wildlife includes all of the Big Five, plus zebra, giraffe, impala, gazelle, eland and cheetah, and there are over 500 bird species. The **Kanderi Swamp**, not far from Voi Gate, has the most wildlife in the area. The main attraction is the **Aruba Dam** built across the Voi River where many animals and birds congregate. **Mudanda Rock**, about 30 km north of Voi, is a 1.6-km long outcrop of rock that towers above a natural dam and at times during the dry season draws hundreds of elephants. The **Yatta Plateau**, at about 290 km long is the world's largest lava flow. The **Lugards Falls** on the Galana River, 40 km northeast of Voi are pretty spectacular. They are a series of rapids rather than true falls. The rocks have been sculpted into fascinating shapes by the rapid water flow channelled into a gorge so narrow that it is possible to stand with legs spanning the cleft, overlooking the falls.

## ① Tsavo East National Park

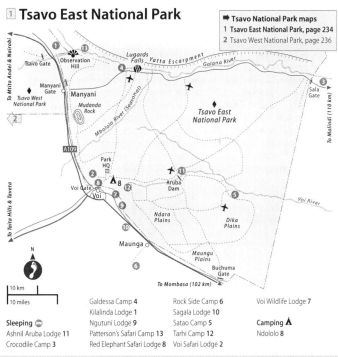

➡ **Tsavo National Park maps**
1 Tsavo East National Park, page 234
2 Tsavo West National Park, page 236

Galdessa Camp **4**
Kilalinda Lodge **1**
Ngutuni Lodge **9**
Patterson's Safari Camp **13**
Red Elephant Safari Lodge **8**

Rock Side Camp **6**
Sagala Lodge **10**
Satao Camp **5**
Tarhi Camp **12**
Voi Safari Lodge **2**

Voi Wildlife Lodge **7**

**Camping** ▲
Ndololo **8**

**Sleeping** 🛏
Ashnil Aruba Lodge **11**
Crocodile Camp **3**

Tsavo West is the more developed part of the park combining easy access, good facilities and stunning views over the tall grass and woodland scenery. The area is made up from recent volcano lava flows, which absorb rainwater that reappears as the crystal-clear Mzima Springs 40 km away, and supports a vast quantity and diversity of plant and animal life.

## Ins and outs

ⓘ *Gates open 0630-1830. Adults US$50, children US$25, vehicle US$4.50 per day. Smartcards can be reloaded (but not obtained) at the Mtito Andei Gate.*

There are several entrance gates into Tsavo West. Two are on the Nairobi–Mombasa road: Tsavo Gate, 320 km from Nairobi and 5 km north of Voi, and Mtito Andei Gate, 30 km north of Tsavo Gate, 240 km south of Nairobi and 249 km north of Mombasa. Buses from Nairobi to Mombasa pass near both, and hitching to these gates is fairly easy, but since walking inside the park is not allowed, visitors without vehicles may have a very long wait. Chyulu Gate in the northwest corner of the park is used by vehicles coming into Tsavo West from Amboseli National Park. 4WD and high-clearance vehicles are required for this route, especially in wet weather. Other entries are at Ziwani Gate, Jipe Gate and Kasigau Gate all to the south of the park. Buses also run between Voi and Taveta on the Tanzanian border (and then on to Moshi) through the south of the park via Maktau and Mbuyuni gates.

## Sights

The main attractions at Tsavo West are the watering holes by **Kilaguni** and **Ngulia** lodges that entice a huge array of wildlife particularly in the dry season. During the autumn the areas around **Ngulia Lodge** are a stopover for hundreds of thousands of birds from Europe in their annual migration. Not far from the **Kilaguni Lodge** is the **Mzima Springs**, a favourite haunt of hippos and crocodiles. There is an underwater viewing chamber, but the hippos have obviously decided against being watched by moving to the other side of the pool. Also around the lodges are the spectacular **Shaitani lava flow** and cones, as well as caves that are well worth visiting. You will need to bring a good torch. **Chaimu Crater** to the south of **Kilaguni Lodge** can be climbed and although there is little danger of animals here, it is best to be careful. At the extreme southwest of the park, bordering Tanzania, is the beautiful **Lake Jipe**, see page 243, which is fed by underground flows from Mount Kilimanjaro. Here are found pygmy geese and the black heron along with many other species of bird. Wildlife you are likely to spot include hyrax, agama lizards, dwarf mongooses, marabou storks, baboons, antelope, buffalo, zebra, giraffe, jackals and hyenas, crocodiles, hippos, leopards, lions and cheetahs. If you're very lucky you might see wild dogs. There are some black rhino although most have been moved to the **Ngulia Rhino Sanctuary** ⓘ *daily 1600-1800*, which is close to the Mzima Springs and is a fenced area of 62 sq km containing about 60 rhinos.

## Chyulu Hills National Park

This was established in 1983 as an extension to Tsavo West. Previously a game conservation area, the park is virtually untouched by humans. The long mountain range is home to lion, giraffe, zebra and oryx. Described as being the youngest mountain range in the world, it is made up of intermingled volcanic cones and lava flows that are considered only to be around 500 years old. Many of the cones are covered with grass and there are extensive forests. There is no permanent water supply in this mountain range except for a small spring at Ngungani. Kilimanjaro is clearly visible from the crest of the Chyulu Hills.

## 2 Tsavo West National Park

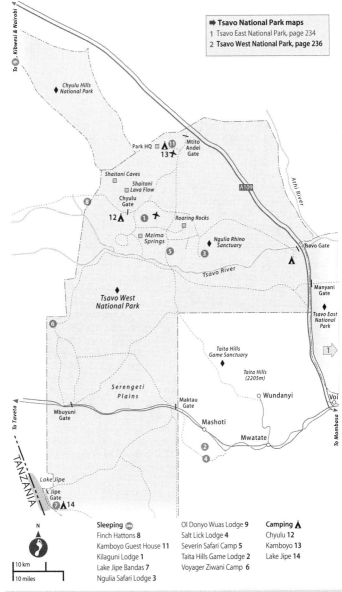

**Tsavo National Park maps**
1 Tsavo East National Park, page 234
2 Tsavo West National Park, page 236

To 9, Kibwesi & Nairobi

Chyulu Hills National Park

Park HQ

Mtito Andei Gate

Shaitani Caves

Shaitani Lava Flow

Chyulu Gate

A109

Athi River

Roaring Rocks

Mzima Springs

Ngulia Rhino Sanctuary

Tsavo Gate

Tsavo River

Manyani Gate

Tsavo West National Park

Tsavo East National Park

Taita Hills Game Sanctuary

Taita Hills (2205m)

Wundanyi

Serengeti Plains

Maktau Gate

Mashoti

Mwatate

Voi

To Taveta

To Mombasa

TANZANIA

Mbuyuni Gate

Lake Jipe

Jipe Gate

N

10 km
10 miles

### Sleeping
Finch Hattons **8**
Kamboyo Guest House **11**
Kilaguni Lodge **1**
Lake Jipe Bandas **7**
Ngulia Safari Lodge **3**

Ol Donyo Wuas Lodge **9**
Salt Lick Lodge **4**
Severin Safari Camp **5**
Taita Hills Game Lodge **2**
Voyager Ziwani Camp **6**

### Camping
Chyulu **12**
Kamboyo **13**
Lake Jipe **14**

## Taita Hills Game Sanctuary

In the south Tsavo West more or less surrounds the privately run Taita Hills Game Sanctuary which is actually south of the Taita Hills about 15 km west of Mwatate. There is a wide variety of game present here including lion, cheetah, elephant and plains game. Prolific bird life includes the extremely rare Taita Falcon, a bird recorded in early Egyptian hieroglyphics. **Mount Vuria** at 2205 m is the highest point in the Taitas, and from the summit there are excellent views of the plains of Tsavo below. The Taita are in fact three groups of hills, the **Dabida**, **Sagalla** and **Kasigau**. The Chyulu Hills can be seen if it is not misty. Road access to Taita Hills is on the road from Voi to Taveta. You'll need your own transport, or to be part of a safari, to reach this region.

## ◉ Tsavo National Park listings

*For Sleeping and Eating price codes and other relevant information, see Essentials pages 34-38.*

## ◉ Sleeping

**Tsavo East** *p233, map p234*
**L Galdessa Camp**, reservations **Galdessa Camp**, Ukunda, T040-320 2630, www.gald essa.com. 10 km upstream from Lugards Falls on the Galana River is 12 *bandas* with river frontage. The camp is divided into down-stream and upstream camps, with their own central facilities that can also be booked for exclusive use. The central mess areas house dining areas, bars, and large, comfortable lounges. Price includes full board (excluding alcohol), game drives, and walking safaris.
**L Kilalinda Lodge**, reservations **Private Wilderness**, Nairobi, T020-882 598, www.kilalinda.com. The 6 luxury cottages overlook the river, and the largest has its own plunge pool and jacuzzi. Facilities include central split-level bar, lounge, dining room, library and swimming pool. The highlight is the twin Victorian bath tubs in a private *boma* with open roof. Game drives in both Tsavo East and West national parks, fishing, game walks and fly camping on offer.
**B Ashnil Aruba Lodge**, reservations, **Ashnil Hotels**, Nairobi, T020-556 946, www.ashnil hotels.com. Newly opened in 2008, each of the 40 partly canvas rooms have wide terraces overlooking the Aruba Dam and safari-style decor and 2 have disabled facilities. There's a curio shop, ice-cream parlour, restaurant

and bar, rates are full board, and in the evening are wildlife and cultural talks and African dancing shows. An affordable option aimed at overnight visitors from the coast.
**B Crocodile Camp**, 3 km from the Sala Gate and usually accessed from Malindi on the C103, reservations **African Safari Club**, UK T+44 (0)20-8466 0014, www.africansafari club.com. Overlooking the Galana River in an exceptionally fertile area. There are fixed tents on a solid base or wooden bungalows with veranda and chairs, all covered by *makuti* thatched roofs. All have twin beds, a private shower and wc, a/c and hot water. Meals are served in the thatched dining room and there is a cosy bar and small swimming pool. This is principally used by guests on safari from the African Safari Club package resorts on the coast but it does accept independent bookings.
**B Voi Safari Lodge**, reservations, Mombasa, T041-471 861, www.safari-hotels.com. Slightly cheaper than the lodges of equivalent standard in West Tsavo and much less crowded, with 52 rooms, each with 2 beds, but they are starting to look dated and are overdue for a refurbishment. There's a swimming pool, the animal hide by the waterhole gives very good close-up views at eye level and baboons and rock hyrax wander through the hotel and gardens. Not recommended for the unfit or elderly as there are lots of steps between the buildings.
**C Patterson's Safari Camp**, on the Athi River in the north of the park, 8 km from the Tsavo Gate, reservations Nairobi T020-202 1674,

www.pattersonsafaricamp.com. There are
20 spacious and shady en suite tents, some
sleeping 4 people, with nice views over the
sludgy brown river, which attracts a lot of
game. The name derives from railway worker
John Patterson who shot the 'man-eaters'
of Tsavo when the railway was being built.
There's a pleasant thatched bar and
restaurant and a bonfire is lit in the evening.
**C Satao Camp**, reservations **Southern Cross
Safaris**, Mombasa T041-243 4600, www.satao
camp.com. Permanent tented camp with
20 double tents, 2 with disabled facilities,
constructed of sisal and *boroti* poles topped
with a *makuti* roof, very nice bathrooms with
stone features and hot showers. Overlooks
a waterhole with resident hippo, where
elephant, lion, zebra, etc drink at night. Lovely
thatched bar and restaurant with atmospheric
lighting, very good food, safari chairs out front
around a bonfire. Game drives and sundowner
trips into the bush on offer, although many
animals come right into the camp. Well
organized and professional, very good value.
**C Tarhi Camp**, 12 km from Voi Gate,
reservations, Mombasa, T041-548 6378,
www.camp-tarhi.de. Not in as scenic
a location as some of the other lodges,
but an affordable option within the park,
this German-run tented camp has simple
permanent tents each with toilet, shower
and fan, and there's a rustic bar and a mess
tent for meals. Rates are US$60 per person
full board and US$50 per person half board,
children are half price. You can arrive here in
a normal car, and then go on game drives in
a 4WD from the camp for US$20 per person.

### Camping

**F Ndololo Campsite**, near Voi Gate,
about 7 km into the park, has water and
pit latrines and firewood is available. You
pay for camping at the gates.

### Tsavo West *p235, map p236*

**L Finch Hattons**, 65 km from the Mtito Andei
Gate, reservations Nairobi, T020-553 237/8,
www.finchhattons.com. Award-winning luxury
camp that oozes atmosphere, which
accommodates up to 50 people, in large safari
tents with twin beds, each with minibar,
wooden Swahili chest, bookshelves and an
antique writing desk, large deck balconies with
chairs, tables and daybed. Elegantly appointed
bar and restaurant and a comfortable private
lounge, extensive library of books and an
excellent range of classical music including
Denys Finch Hatton's favourite selection of
Mozart, swimming pool, dinner is very formal
with 6 courses, fine china and crystal glasses.
**B Kamboyo Guest House**, 8 km from the
Mtito Andei Gate, reservations **Kenya Wildlife
Service**, Nairobi, T020-600 800, www.kws.org.
Self-catering cottage with 3 rooms with
double beds and 1 room with a single bed,
10 people maximum, must be taken as a unit
for US$200 per night, towels, bed linen and
kitchen utensils are provided, you just need
to bring food, firewood and drinking water.
**B Kilaguni Lodge**, 20 km from the Mtito Andei
Gate, T045-622471, www.serena hotels.com.
Good-quality lodge from the Serena chain,
blends well into the landscape, 56 spacious
rooms, lots of wooden decks for game
viewing, decorated with wooden sculptures
of animals, a rock-hewn bar, swimming pool,
excellent buffet meals with a wide variety of
choice, rates are full board. This was the first
lodge to be built in any of Kenya's parks.
Mt Kilimanjaro can be seen on a clear day.
**B Ngulia Safari Lodge**, 55 km from the Mtito
Andei Gate, reservations, Mombasa, T041-471
861, www.safari-hotels.com. Slightly cheaper
than the others at about US$100 per person
full board, but still very good, with 52 rooms,
a swimming pool and in a good location.
The waterhole, again, is a big draw both
for the animals and tourists. Staff are very
knowledgeable on the wildlife and are
extremely helpful. The lodge overlooks the
Ngulia Rhino Sanctuary and rhinos can be
viewed through the binoculars that are set up
especially. The lodge is renowned as a haven
for bird lovers every year Oct-Dec, who come
to be involved in the bird 'ring' of migrating
birds escaping the harsh winter conditions of

the northern hemisphere. It is the only place in Kenya where this activity takes place.

**B Severin Safari Camp**, 50 km from Mtito Andei Gate, reservations Mombasa, T041-548 7365, www.severin-kenya.com. Thatched central area with good restaurant and bar, and a pleasant fire pit for bonfires with traditional safari chairs overlooking the plains, spacious octagonal tents with very high ceilings and mosquito nets under thatch with good views.

**B-C Voyager Ziwani Camp**, reservations Nairobi, T020-444 6651, www.heritage-east africa.com. A Heritage Group's Voyager resort, of good standard and aimed at families and 1st-time safari goers. At the western boundary of the park on the edge of a small, secluded dam on the Sante River, with full-size permanent tents and excellent food. Of the camp's 25 tents, 16 sit on the southern bank of the Sante River and 9 on the northern. Offers game drives and walks with highly qualified naturalists, and there is an Adventurer's Club for children. Rates vary depending on season.

**D Lake Jipe Bandas**, reservations through the Warden 045-22483, or **Kenya Wildlife Service**, Nairobi, T020-600 800, www.kws.org. In total they sleep 5 people, have a kitchen but no utensils and you need to bring your own firewood, drinking water, food and bedding. Come here completely self-sufficient. Cost is US$50, regardless of the number of people, payable at the park gates.

## Camping

There are also campsites (**E**) close to each of the gates at Tsavo: **Kamboyo Campsite** 8 km from the Mtito Andei Gate, and **Chyulu Campsite** 1 km from the Chyulu Gate. There are no facilities but water and pit latrines so you will need to be completely self-sufficient. Another campsite is available on the shores of Lake Jipe. Campers share the outdoor cooking area and ablutions block with guests at the **Lake Jipe Bandas** (see above).

## Chyulu Hills National Park p235

**L Ol Donyo Wuas Lodge**, in the Chyulu Hills, www.oldonyowuas.com, reservations **Bush**

**and Beyond/Bush Homes of East Africa**, Nairobi, T020-600 457, www.bush-and-beyond.com and www.bush-homes.co.ke. 7 individual 2- or 4-bedroomed enormous luxury thatched cottages, some with private swimming pools, and a beautiful, central dining room. All cottages have en suite bathrooms, lounge with an open fireplace and a veranda with panoramic views of the plains and Mt Kilimanjaro and there is also the option of sleeping outside on the roof. All-inclusive of food, drinks, day and night game drives, and guided bush walks. You can also go horse riding or mountain biking with armed guards. Most guests fly in using **Safarilink** (page 30).

## Taita Hills Game Sanctuary p237

The 2 Sarova-run lodges here are quite close together, but they are both rather odd-looking structures, given that they advertize themselves as game lodges.

**C Salt Lick Lodge**, outside of the park in the Taita Hills, reservations **Sarova Hotels**, Nairobi T020-276 7000, www.sarova hotels.com. This is noted for its strange design, basically a group of 96 rooms in huts on elevated stilts that are connected by open-air bridges over a number of water-holes. All rooms have a balcony. The lodge is resplendent with African wooden tables and batiks and rugs. The area is lit by floodlights for game viewing at night, and there is an underground tunnel and chamber allowing guests to watch wildlife safely at ground level. Tour packages offered range from 2-4 days and generally include transport from Nairobi or Mombasa, sanctuary fees, game-drives and full-board accommodation.

**C Taita Hills Game Lodge**, reservations **Sarova Hotels**, Nairobi T020-2767000, www.sarovahotels.com. This is a rather unusual stone building covered with ivy, with 62 ordinary but comfortable rooms with balconies and wicker furniture, but the decor in the public areas is a little old fashioned. Rates include sanctuary fees and all buffet meals, there's a bar and enormous stone fireplace, plus tennis courts and a pool.

# Amboseli and the Tanzanian border

*Directly south of Nairobi, the southern part of Kenya is dominated by views of Africa's tallest mountain, Kilimanjaro, with its snow-capped peak. It's best appreciated from the Amboseli National Park, where preferably a few accommodating elephants will amble across the foreground when you take a photo. A steady stream of safari vehicles ply the Nairobi–Namanga road on their way to either Amboseli or Arusha in Tanzania, which is the springboard town for Tanzania's northern circuit parks including the Serengeti and Ngorongoro Crater. Many people on upmarket holidays may visit parks in both southern Kenya and northern Tanzania, and for independent budget travellers, the journey from Nairobi to Arusha can be easily done by public transport or there are shuttle services. Once in Arusha, camping and lodge safaris to the northern parks can be arranged; the cheapest and most popular being a three-day safari with one night in the Serengeti and one night near the Ngorongoro Crater. Another option is to climb Mount Kilimanjaro, and climbs can be organized in Moshi, 88 km to the east of Arusha. Remember you do not need to buy another visa on your return to Kenya if you have only been to Tanzania.* ▸▸ *For listings, see pages 244-246.*

## Nairobi to Tanzania 🚌🚐 ▸▸ pp244-246.

### Kajiado → *Colour map 1, B4.*
The road to Kajiado (A104) forks right off the Mombasa highway (A109) shortly after the southern boundary of Nairobi National Park, just east of the Athi River crossing the Athi Plains. Kijiado is the administrative headquarters of southern Masai-land at the southwestern corner of the Kapitiei Plains, which run between Machakos and Kajiado. The town is in the middle of bleak grasslands that show little sign of the abundance of zebra, wildebeest and giraffe that used to roam here. The town is typically Masai and there are many indicators of their preoccupation with cattle.

### Namanga → *Colour map 1, B4. Phone code: 045.*
Namanga is the Kenyan border town on the A104, see page 244 for border crossing information. It is the nearest town to Amboseli National Park, and is a convenient stopover between Arusha and Nairobi. Arusha is 130 km to the south and the drive from Nairobi to Arusha via Namanga takes about five hours. The road to Nairobi (A104) is in good condition and there is a petrol station in Namanga, as well as shops selling crafts, and lots of Masai street hawkers selling beaded jewellery and red blankets. Prices are high but negotiable.

## Amboseli National Park 🚌🚐🚗 ▸▸ pp244-246. Colour map 1, B4/5.

ⓘ *Gates are open 0600-1900 (no entry after 1815). Park entry fee is US$60, children US$30, vehicle US$4.70 per day by Smartcard.*

Amboseli's biggest draw is its location, with Mount Kilimanjaro providing a stunning backdrop. The whole park is dominated by Africa's highest mountain and at dusk or dawn the cloud cover breaks to reveal the dazzling spectacle of this snow-capped mountain. The downside is that its popularity (it has long been one of the most visited parks in Kenya) and the decades of tourism have left well-worn trails, and much off-road driving has made the park look increasingly dusty and rather bleak. Efforts are being made to remedy this with new roads being built to improve access and a tough policy on off-road driving.

## Ins and outs

The main route into Amboseli is along the C103 from Namanga, on the Nairobi–Arusha (Tanzania) road. From Namanga to the park is 75 km down an appalling road and there are no petrol stations. The whole journey from Nairobi to Amboseli takes about four hours. It is also possible to enter via the C103 from the Chyulu Gate in Tsavo West National Park. Iremito Gate can be accessed from a road that joins the C102 road from Sultan Hamud on the main Nairobi–Mombasa road. There is a daily direct flight by **Air Kenya** from Wilson airport in Nairobi. Buses from the capital reach Namanga but there is no public transport from there to the park gates. The park tracks are signposted and the maps are good. Both Kilimanjaro and Observation Hill serve as permanent reference points. When rains come harder than usual, some of the roads may be flooded, among them the main access to the Ol Tukai lodges from the Namanga road. In this case you will have to turn right towards Observation Hill and drive round the flooded area to the west.

## Background

This park was first established as a natural reserve in 1948, and in 1961 all 3260 sq km of it were handed to the Masai elders of Kajiado District Council to run with an annual grant of £8500. After years of the destructive effects of cattle grazing and tourists on the area, 392 sq km of the reserve were designated as a national park in 1973, after which the Masai were no longer allowed to use the land for grazing. The late 1980s saw the start of an environmental conservation programme to halt erosion.

## Sights

Amboseli is in a semi-arid part of the country and is usually hot and dry. The land is a mixture of open plains, savannah scattered with areas of beautiful yellow-barked acacia woodland, swamps and marshland and clutches of thornbush growing amidst lava

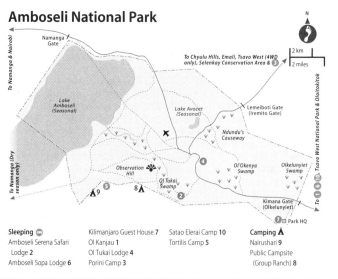

# Amboseli National Park

**Sleeping**
Amboseli Serena Safari Lodge **2**
Amboseli Sopa Lodge **6**
Kilimanjaro Guest House **7**
Ol Kanjau **1**
Ol Tukai Lodge **4**
Porini Camp **3**
Satao Elerai Camp **10**
Tortilis Camp **5**

**Camping** ▲
Nairushari **9**
Public Campsite (Group Ranch) **8**

## Ewart Grogan

Born in Britain in 1874, Ewart Grogan was the first man to walk from the Cape to Cairo – a three-and-a-half year journey that won him the hand of his bride.

In 1896 Ewart sailed for Cape Town, where he was given the task of running a wagon-load of ammunition up to Bulawayo in Southern Rhodesia. He then became Cecil Rhodes's personal escort, when he learnt of Rhodes' vision of 'civilizing' the African continent by building a railway and telegraph line from the Cape to Cairo. After a serious bout of blackwater fever he went back to England, where he met Gertrude Watt. They fell in love and discussed marriage, but Grogan had little future and no resources, so he returned to Africa and walked from the Cape to Cairo, to both prove his worth to Gertrude's father and to survey the route for Rhodes' railway and telegraph line. He was only 25 when he set off. From Cairo he returned to England, and presented the Union Jack, which he had carried with him throughout the journey, to Queen Victoria. Following the publication of his book in 1900, From the Cape to Cairo, Grogan became the youngest man ever to address the Royal Geographical Society and he and Gertrude were married later that year. Grogan returned to Africa a prosperous man and acquired 190,000 acres of land around Taveta in Kenya, which he developed for sisal and citrus production. He built his grand house in the 1930s, and although now in ruins, Grogan's Castle can still be seen on a high point near Taveta overlooking thousands of acres of flourishing sisal plantations. Gertrude died in 1943, and Grogan built a children's hospital in Nairobi in her memory called Gertrude's (www.gerties.org), which today is one of East Africa's most important children's hospitals. Ewart died in 1967 aged 92.

debris. To the west of the reserve close to Namanga is the massif of Oldoinyo Orok at 2524 m. The main wildlife you are likely to see here are herbivores such as buffalo, Thomson's and Grant's gazelle, Coke's hartebeest, warthog, gnu, impala, giraffe, zebra and lots of baboons. One of the most spectacular sites is the large herd of elephants here. The elephant population of the greater Amboseli Basin at the base of Mount Kilimanjaro now numbers 1000 animals in over 50 matriarchal families and associated bull groups. The Amboseli elephants have perhaps the oldest and most intact social structure of any elephant population in Africa. They are also the best known and well studied. You may also be able to see the very rare black rhino that has nearly been poached out of existence. There are a few predators, including lions, leopards, cheetahs, hyenas and jackals. Birdlife is also abundant especially near the swamps and seasonal lakes.

There have been environmental changes over recent years due to erratic rainfall. Lake Amboseli, which had almost totally dried up, reappeared during 1992-1993. The return of water to the lake flooded large parts of the park including the area around the lodges. Since then, flamingos have returned, and the whole park is far greener.

## Excursions

**Selenkay Conservation Area**, 17 km north of Amboseli National Park, has been established with local communities in mind. This 70-sq-km area has been developed in a joint venture with a Kenyan company, **Porini Ecotourism** Ltd ⓘ *www.porini.com*, and the Masai people. Porini, as well as meaning 'in the wilds' in Kiswahili is also an acronym for

Protection Of Resources (Indigenous and Natural) for Income. Roads have been created using local labour and a camp has been constructed (see Sleeping, below). Money raised from the entrance fees and rent are paid directly to the Masai. Profits are used to fund community projects such as schools and water supplies. Employment opportunities have also been provided for the local Masai people as game rangers, trackers and camp staff. Where once species migrating from Amboseli were killed or driven away by the local people, wildlife conservation is now encouraged. As a result of the establishment of the Conservation Area, wildlife numbers have recovered significantly in recent years and elephants are now seen frequently after an absence of nearly 20 years. The animals are truly wild and tend to behave more naturally than those in the parks, which are often habituated to the presence of vehicles.

## Along the Tanzanian border

### Oloitokitok and Taveta → *Colour map 1, B5.*

Oloitokitok is a busy Masai town between the parks off the main road that runs from Amboseli in the southeast through to the Kimana Gate of Tsavo West. It has a busy thriving atmosphere and the best views of any town in the area of Mount Kilimanjaro. The town has a branch of **Kenya Commercial Bank** and a post office, and there are market days on Tuesday and Saturday.

Taveta is a small town on the Tanzanian border next to Tsavo West National Park and is surrounded by sisal estates. It is fairly remote and inaccessible thanks to the bad road, but there is a bank and hospital, and it's also a border crossing, see 244. Taveta is actually on a piece of land that juts into Tanzania. The irregular shape of the border here was created in 1881 when Queen Victoria gave Mount Kilimanjaro to her grandson, then the Crown Prince of Prussia and later Kaiser Wilhelm II of Germany, as a wedding present. Consequently, the border was adjusted so that Kilimanjaro fell within the boundaries of the German colony of Tanganyika instead of the British protectorate of Kenya.

### Lake Chala → *Colour map 1, C5.*

Lake Chala is just 8 km north of Taveta, part of the lake being in Kenya and part being in Tanzania. This deep-water crater lake is about 4 sq km and is totally clear with steep walls and filled and drained by underground streams. It is a tranquil, beautiful place to explore by foot and camping is possible, though you will need to bring all your own supplies. Unfortunately, although the lake used to be popular for swimming, this is no longer recommended since a fatal crocodile attack on an English woman in March 2002. Aside from plenty of fish, there are also monitor lizards, baboons, monkeys and common snakes.

**Grogan's Castle** is an extraordinary construction on an isolated hill quite near the main road. It was built in the 1930s by Ewart Grogan (see box, page 242) as a resort for the sisal estate managers in the area. It has now fallen into disrepair, but retains spectacular views over Kilimanjaro and Lake Jipe.

### Lake Jipe → *Colour map 1, C5.*

Lake Jipe straddles Kenya and Tanzania, fed from streams on the Tanzanian side and from Mount Kilimanjaro. There are a number of small fishing villages around the Kenyan side, and its southeast shores lie inside Tsavo West National Park. Again, this is a peaceful place

# Border essentials: Kenya–Tanzania

## Namanga

Immigration and customs at the border are quick and efficient. Visas for both Kenya and Tanzania can be bought with US dollars, UK pounds and euros in cash, and the border is open 24 hours. If you are on a safari, or using one of the daily shuttle bus services between Nairobi and Arusha (see page 105) than the drivers/guides will assist with all border procedures. Remember you don't need to get another visa to return to Kenya if you've only been to Tanzania. Arusha is another two hours' drive, or 111 km from the border.

You are advised to take great care if changing money on the black market (which is illegal in both Kenya and Tanzania), as there are many scams practised at the border. It is important to have a rough idea of the current exchange rates for Kenyan and Tanzanian shillings, or wait until you get to a bank in either Nairobi or Arusha.

## Taveta

The border crossing leads to the Tanzanian town of **Moshi**, which is 41 km from Taveta. Buses between Moshi and Mombasa cross here. In Tanzania, 14 km from the border at Himo, the road joins the B1 south to Dar es Salaam, but you'll have to go into Moshi first to get transport.

to stop off where you will be able to see hippos and crocodiles, and plenty of birdlife. A good portion of the lake has become choked with papyrus, which looks nice and is also used by the local people for thatching their houses, but has reduced the fishing on the lake to negligible levels. You can hire a boat to take you round the lake, but there are some vicious mosquitoes in this area, so be warned. There are some *bandas* on the lakeshore run by Kenyan Wildlife Service but they are accessed from Tsavo West and you will need to pay park entry fees.

## ◉ Amboseli and the Tanzanian border listings

*For Sleeping and Eating price codes and other relevant information, see Essentials pages 34-38.*

## 🛏 Sleeping

### Namanga *p240*
**E-F Namanga River Lodge**, no phone.
This is a very simple lodge and campsite in a beautiful setting in wonderful gardens with plenty of shady trees to pitch tents under, or accommodation is in prefabricated wooden huts in the garden. Toilets and (warm) showers are communal. It has an excellent bar and restaurant, for both Kenyan and Western dishes, but choice depends on what

ingredients they have. This is primarily used by the cheaper safari operators to save on a night's camping within Amboseli.

**Amboseli National Park** *p240, map p241*
**L Ol Kanjau**, www.olkanjau.com, reservations
Bush and Beyond/ Bush Homes of East Africa, Nairobi, T020-600 457, www.bush-and-beyond.com and www.bush-homes.co.ke. The name means elephants in the Masai language and this is hosted by American naturalists Michael and Judith Rainy, who are working to add wildlife conservation to the traditional pastoral economy of the local community and have

been active in Kenya since 1968. A traditional seasonal safari-style tented camp situated just outside Amboseli on the Kisongo Masai group ranch, with just 6 tents, this is an intimate camp and in a good location to spot elephants. Game drives and bush walks with the Masai are on offer. Closed Apr, May and Nov.

**L Satao Elerai Camp**, 14 km southeast of Kimana Gate, reservations **Southern Cross Safaris**, Mombasa T041-243 4600, www.sataoelerai.com. Set on community land outside the park, this offers game walks and night drives in addition to game drives in the park, and you can walk with the local Masai as they graze their cattle. Accommodation is in 14 tents and suites, which are nicely designed, incorporate lots of acacia wood, and have stone bathrooms and wide verandas. Very good dinners are taken outside under the stars and there are superb views of Kilimanjaro.

**L Tortilis Camp**, www.tortilis.com, reservations **Cheli and Peacock**, Nairobi, T020-603 054, www.chelipeacock.com. 8 twin and 9 double bed luxury tents with en suite bathrooms, raised up on a wooden deck and sheltered by *makuti* roofs, large verandas, excellent views of the plains and Kilimanjaro, was listed in the 2006 *Condé Nast Traveller Gold Awards*. Activities include game drives and visits to a Masai village and there's a swimming pool.

**A Amboseli Serena Safari Lodge**, T045-622 361, www.serenahotels.com. A very attractive design, drawing on elements of Masai traditional dwellings, blending into the landscape, with 96 rooms that were completely refurbished in 2007, and now have hand-painted murals on the walls and wide terraces, and there's a swimming pool. One of the nicest place to stay in the park and near the Enkongo Narok Swamp, which means there is always plenty of wildlife to see. Activities include game drives, sundowners on Obervation Hill and visits to Masai *manyattas*.

**A Porini Camp**, in the Selenkay Conservation Area, reservations **Gamewatchers Safaris**, Nairobi, T020-712 3129, www.porini.com. Small and exclusive camp with 9 spacious tents, in a spot once favoured by big-game hunters. No permanent structures like a bar, restaurant or swimming pool, but the tents have en suite showers and toilets, meals are taken under the shade of an acacia tree and after dinner guests sit around a campfire. The camp is staffed by members of the local Masai community and there are very good walking safaris conducted here as well as game drives into Amboseli. Rates include all meals, some alcoholic drinks, activities and park entry fees.

**B Amboseli Sopa Lodge**, just outside the park on the road to Oloitokitok on the border with Tanzania, reservations T020-336 088, Nairobi, www.sopa lodges.com. Attractive lodge set in mature wooded gardens, pleasant bar area from where you can sometimes spot honey badgers and hyenas. 83 rooms in cottage-style accommodation in well-decorated thatched huts, meals are taken in the African-themed dining room or outside on a BBQ patio, very large swimming pool, airstrip, and game drives on offer.

**B Ol Tukai Lodge**, near the **Amboseli Serena Lodge**, reservations, Nairobi T020-444 5514, www.oltukailodge.com. This is a large lodge with 88 rooms in *bandas* that occupy one of the finest viewing points in the park and is set in well-laid-out gardens. Swimming pool, good value and good food, game drives and Masai dancing in the evening are on offer.

**C Kilimanjaro Guest House**, inside the park, 2 km from Kimana Gate, reservations **Kenya Wildlife Service**, Nairobi, T020-600 800, www.kws.org. 3 bedrooms; 1 with double bed and the others with single beds, bed linen and towels provided, all kitchen utensils provided plus gas cooker, and electricity is provided by a generator from 1900 to 2200. US$150 per night.

## Camping

The campsites in Amboseli National Park are run by Masai communities. Although they are technically just outside of the park boundary, they can only be accessed from within the park itself. The public campsite in Amboseli is sometimes referred to as the Group Ranch. It is quite large but popular with low-budget camping safari companies so that it can get rather crowded and noisy at times. This site is just outside of the park boundary, southwest of Observation Hill. There are pit toilets here and a water supply that is not always reliable, so water has to be brought from one of the lodges at times. The special **Nairushari Campsite** is used by higher-budget camping safari companies, located in a secluded site through the southwest corner of the park. There is firewood here, but bring your own food and water.

## ❷ Eating

**Amboseli National Park** *p240, map p241*
If you intend to go camping or use the *bandas*, you will need to bring your own supplies of most things, although there is a kiosk at the campsite selling drinks. Most of the lodges allow non-residents to use their facilities and the **Amboseli Serena Safari Lodge** is a nice place to stop off for a cold drink towards the end of the day.

## ❸ Transport

**Kajiado** *p240*
Plenty of buses and *matatus* to **Nairobi** and **Namanga** run through Kajiado.

**Namanga** *p240*
The bus to **Nairobi** takes 2½ hrs and costs US$3. The shuttle bus between Nairobi and **Arusha** also goes through Namanga (see page 105).

**Amboseli National Park** *p240, map p241*
There is a daily flight between **Nairobi**'s Wilson Airport and Amboseli with **Air Kenya**, T020-605 745, www.airkenya.com. It costs US$72 each way, and leaves Nairobi at 0730, arrives at Amboseli at 0810, leaves Amboseli at 0820 and arrives back in Nairobi at 0900.

# Contents

## Footprint features

## Border crossings

# The coast

## At a glance

◉ **Getting around** All-inclusive package holidays with local day and overnight tours; bus, *matatu*, or self-drive along the coast road.

◉ **Time required** 1-2 weeks with 1-2 nights in a nearby game park.

☼ **Weather** Warm, sunny and balmy most of the year.

✕ **When not to go** During the rainy season in Apr-Jun days are overcast and muggy and it rains in the afternoon.

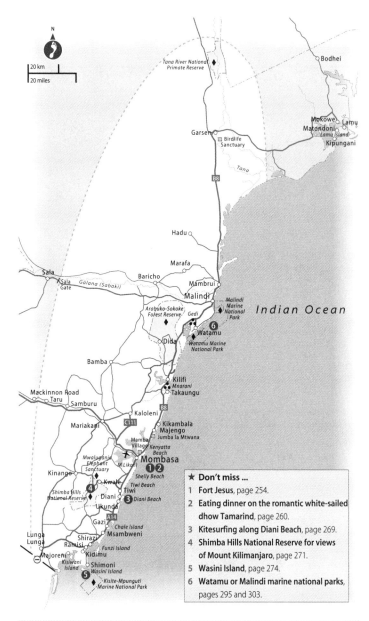

★ **Don't miss ...**

1 Fort Jesus, page 254.

2 Eating dinner on the romantic white-sailed dhow Tamarind, page 260.

3 Kitesurfing along Diani Beach, page 269.

4 Shimba Hills National Reserve for views of Mount Kilimanjaro, page 271.

5 Wasini Island, page 274.

6 Watamu or Malindi marine national parks, pages 295 and 303.

This coastal belt possesses a unique climate, a different type of people and a separate cultural history from the rest of the country. Along with the coast of Tanzania, the Swahili culture and Kiswahili language has its origins on the coast.

Built on a 15-sq-km island, and linked to the mainland by causeways and a rickety old ferry, Mombasa is Kenya's second biggest city and is East Africa's main port. It has a history dating back several hundreds of years, when the Persians, Arabs, Indians and Chinese visited the East African coast to trade in slaves, skins, ivory and spices.

Today, there's a long line of top-class beachside hotels to the south of the Mombasa's Old Town centred around Diani Beach, and to the north all the way up to Malindi. More than half of the country's international hotels are based along the coast served by direct flights from Europe. Most have been constructed from thatch and local materials and are well spaced out, so despite the coast's popularity as a beach holiday destination, it never gets overly crowded even during the high seasons. The beaches are of fine white sand and there are plenty of activities on offer including diving, snorkelling, windsurfing and jet skiing. There are marine national parks aplenty off the coast protecting the important marine life of the Indian Ocean, which can be experienced by *dhow*, glass-bottomed boat, or in a closer encounter, through a mask. Here the colourful coral reefs teem with fish, dolphins and turtles, and the aqua blue Indian Ocean provides near perfect visibility. Away from the beach there are a number of other attractions in the dense coastal forests and undulating hills, and a safari to one of the parks can easily be combined with down time on the beach.

## Ins and outs

### Getting there and around

The gateway to the coast of Kenya is Mombasa, although some visitors fly directly to Malindi or Lamu and there are daily scheduled services between these and Nairobi. The coastal highway runs north of Mombasa all the way to Kenya's northern frontier. Driving your own car or hired car as far as Malindi is very easy, and there are regular buses and *matatus*. Many hotels and resorts in this area have Mombasa shuttles or can arrange vehicle transfers. Private taxis from Mombasa will also take you to the north coast beaches for an agreed fare. Services are less regular north of Malindi, although there are daily buses to Lamu. To the south of Mombasa, the Likoni car ferry links the city with the coastal road that runs to the border with Tanzania. Once off the ferry there are regular *matatus* to Ukunda, the village at the turn-off for the beach road to the resorts along Diani Beach, where you can swap *matatus* or take a taxi. Again many of the southern resorts arrange shuttle services between Mombasa and the beach. Larger buses run daily between Mombasa, Moshi and Dar es Salaam in Tanzania, crossing the border at the extreme south of the coast road at Lunga Lunga. Another slower option for reaching the coast is to take the overnight train from Nairobi to Mombasa that runs three times a week. Many people book week-long package holidays to the resorts, but independent travellers may want to consider hiring a car to explore the coast as the roads from the southern tip of Diani Beach to Malindi are good and most of the resorts accept walk-in guests (often for discounted rates) if they have room, although this would be inadvisable in high season.

### Best time to visit

The climate on the coast is markedly different to that in Nairobi and the Kenyan Highlands, and if driving down the main Nairobi–Mombasa road, you will feel the rise in temperature and humidity as you get nearer to the coast. The average temperature is 28-30°C, and days are long and sunny just about all year round. Despite this, there is a down season on the coast during the rainy season from April to June, when it is often overcast and muggy, and many of the resorts and hotels offer discounts and some even close altogether out of season. If you can put up with a few afternoon showers, this is not a bad time to visit, and you are likely to have the beach to yourself, but on the downside, many other facilities such as restaurants and watersports centres also close. By contrast, during high season, especially around Christmas and New Year, the beaches are very busy with European package-holiday makers and room rates are at their premium.

# Mombasa

→ *Colour map 2, C1. Phone code: 041. Population: 707,000.*
*With a history going back 2000 years, Mombasa is the oldest town in Kenya. Although the town is centred on an island about 4 km long and 7 km wide, it has now begun to sprawl on to the mainland. It owes its development to its location, for the island forms an ideal natural deep-water harbour. Today goods are sent from the port to not only Kenya but to Uganda, Burundi, Rwanda and Sudan.*

*Mombasa has large communities of Indian and Arabic origin. It has the greatest concentration of Muslims in Kenya and their influence on the culture is strong. There are some ancient, Arab-inspired houses with elaborately carved doorways in narrow streets and passages, and a few other worthy distractions such as Fort Jesus and the city's most famous landmark: two pairs of crossed concrete elephant tusks created as a ceremonial arch to commemorate the coronation of Elizabeth II in 1952. Despite these, Mombasa is not a terribly attractive place and rubbish here is quite a problem, as is the traffic and pollution. Most visitors do not stay in the town itself – the city's hotels are not especially nice – and instead stay in one of the beachside locations to the north or south of Mombasa and visit on a day trip. It is now linked by causeways to the mainland at three points as well as by the Likoni Ferry.*
▶▶ *For listings, see pages 259-267.*

## Ins and outs

### Getting there
Mombasa is easily accessible and **Moi International Airport** ① *T041-433 221, www.kenyaairports.com*, is 10 km west of the city centre on the mainland. There are several direct charter flights from Europe bringing people out on package holidays, as well as several daily scheduled flights from Nairobi on **Kenya Airways**, **Fly 540**, and **Air Kenya**. Shop around but generally flights are good value; from US$110 return with Fly 540 for example. **Kenya Airways** code-shares with Tanzania's **Precision Air**, and there are now flights between Mombasa, Zanzibar and Dar es Salaam. **Mombasa Air Safaris** links Mombasa to airstrips in the Masai Mara and Amboseli. Arriving at Moi International from Nairobi is quite a pleasant experience as you emerge into the balmy sunny weather. There are desks for the car-hire companies, and stands for various taxi firms that offer transfers into town, and further afield to the north and south-coast beaches. For those arriving on international flights, visas are processed quickly at immigration.

The overnight train from Nairobi runs three times a week (see page 65) and there are several bus services a day with various different companies. Although on the coast, there are no boat links to anywhere else in Kenya or to neighbouring countries, and travelling by *dhow* is illegal for foreigners, but cruise ships pull into the port from time to time and there is the option of seeing Mombasa from the water on the *Tamarind dhow* (see page 260). ▶▶ *See Transport, page 265.*

### Getting around
The city is bisected by two main roads: Moi Avenue, which runs from the industrial area to the west of the island, and then becomes Nkrumah Avenue to Fort Jesus in the east, and Digo Road that crosses it in the centre of the city around the Old Town. Numerous *matatus* run up and down Digo Road going to the Likoni Ferry to the south and Nyali

Beach and other points in the north. Taxis can be found all over town parked on street corners. *Tuk-tuks* are beginning to feature on the city's streets and are considerably cheaper than regular taxis. You can walk around the centre of Mombasa but the heat and humidity will tire you out quickly if you are too energetic. The traffic fumes are also particularly bad. Moi International Airport is located on the mainland about 10 km out of the centre of town. To get from the airport to the centre of town, you will need to take a taxi, which should cost in the region of US$10-12 depending on the time of day. Inside the airport are several taxi and shuttle bus desks that can arrange not only lifts into town but direct shuttles to most of the beach resorts. Prices are clearly marked on their boards.

### Tourist information
There's no official tourist office as such but there is a clutch of tour operators along Moi Avenue that can give out information and display a variety of leaflets. They will of course want to book you on to something.

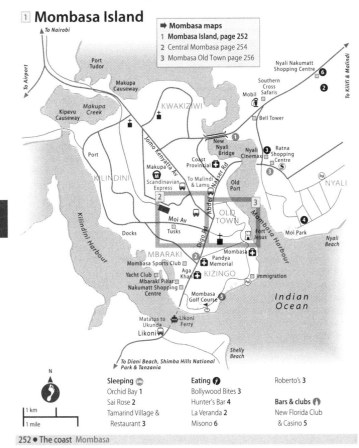

## 1 Mombasa Island

➡ Mombasa maps
1 Mombasa Island, page 252
2 Central Mombasa page 254
3 Mombasa Old Town page 256

N

1 km
1 mile

**Sleeping** 
Orchid Bay 1
Sai Rose 2
Tamarind Village &
  Restaurant 3

**Eating** 
Bollywood Bites 3
Hunter's Bar 4
La Veranda 2
Misono 6

Roberto's 3

**Bars & clubs** 
New Florida Club
  & Casino 5

## Safety

Although there's nowhere in the city centre that is considered a no-go area as such, petty theft does occur so don't flash valuables or walk down dark alleyways. Be particularly wary on the crowded Likoni Ferry. Also by contrast to Nairobi and other towns where streets empty after 1800, on the coast, and because of climatic conditions, many businesses close for a siesta in the middle of the day. As such the city stays awake longer, and the streets are still busy in the early evening and shops stay open later. Nevertheless, when they do close and people go home, do not wander the streets and take a taxi.

## Background

The seasonal monsoon wind known as the Kazkazi blows down the coast from the northeast between October and April, as it has done for thousands of years bringing trade to Mombasa. Between May and September this monsoon wind becomes the Kuzi, when it turns through 180° and blows back up the coast towards the Arabian Gulf. The Kazkazi and the Kuzi winds were the key to the foreign exploitation of Kenya and the rest of East Africa for thousands of years: the earliest known reference to Mombasa dates from AD 150 when the Roman geographer Ptolemy placed the town on his map of the world. Roman, Arabic and Far Eastern seafarers took advantage of the port and were regular visitors, and the port provided the town with the basis of economic development and it expanded steadily.

By the 16th century Mombasa was the most important town on the east coast of Africa with a population estimated at 10,000. A wealthy settlement, it was captured by the Portuguese who were trying to break the Arab trading monopoly, particularly in the lucrative merchandising of spices. The town first fell to the Portuguese under the command of Dom Francisco in 1505. He ransacked the town and burnt it to the ground. It was rebuilt and returned to its former glory before it was ransacked again in 1528. However, the Portuguese did not stay and, having again looted and razed the town, they left.

The building of Fort Jesus in 1593, the stationing of a permanent garrison there, and the installation of their own nominee from Malindi as Sultan, represented the first major attempt to secure Mombasa permanently. However, an uprising by the townspeople in 1631 led to the massacre of all the Portuguese. This led to yet another Portuguese fleet returning to try to recapture the town. In 1632 the leaders of the revolt retreated to the mainland leaving the island to the Europeans. Portuguese rule lasted less than 100 years and they were expelled by the Omanis in 1698. The Omanis also held Zanzibar and were heavily involved in the slave trade. Their rule was supplanted by the British in 1873.

The British efforts to stamp out the slave trade, and anxiety about German presence in what is now Tanzania, led in 1896 to the beginning of the construction of the railway that was to link Uganda to the sea. The first rail was laid at Mombasa Railway Station on 13 May 1896 and the railhead reached Port Florence (Kisumu) on Lake Victoria on 20 December 1901, having ascended the Great Rift Valley western wall and crested the Mau Summit at some 2700 m above sea level, making it the highest metre-gauge railway in the world. One of the railway camps that was established before the construction of the line across the Rift Valley was at Nairobi. This town grew so rapidly that by 1907 it was large enough for the administrative quarters to move inland. The climate of Nairobi was considered to be healthier than the coast, and because of its elevation was too high for malaria-bearing mosquitoes to survive. Meanwhile, with the railway, the importance of the port of Mombasa increased rapidly and it became known as the Gateway to East Africa, serving Kenya, Uganda, Rwanda and Burundi.

In more recent history, Mombasa was the scene of a terrorist attack in 2002 when a hotel on one of the northern beaches, popular with Israelis and the only Israeli-owned hotel in the Mombasa area, was car bombed by suicide bombers, leaving 10 Kenyans and three Israeli holidaymakers dead. At the same time an Israeli plane was fired at as it was taking off from Mombasa Airport. Although the attacks to this day still haven't been confirmed as the work of al-Qaeda, if they were, it would have been their first attack on Israelis, despite their alleged hostility towards Israel.

## Sights

### Fort Jesus
ⓘ Nkrumah Rd, T041-312 839, www.museums.or.ke, US$11.50, children (under 18) US$5.75, daily 0930-1800, guides are available for a tip or buy the information booklet at the entrance.
Mombasa Old Town's major attraction, Fort Jesus dominates the entrance to the Old Harbour and is positioned so that, even when under siege, it was possible to bring supplies in from the sea. There's nothing to see as such in the harbour itself – there may be a few boats but long gone are the days when ocean-going *dhows* docked here. The Portuguese built the fort to protect their trade route to India and their interests in East

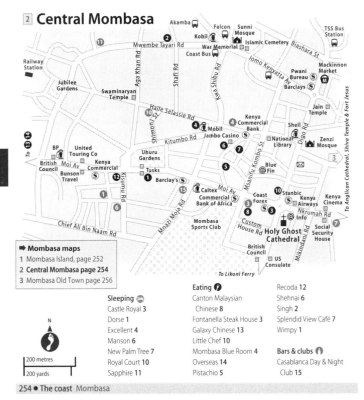

## 2 Central Mombasa

➡ Mombasa maps
1 Mombasa Island, page 252
2 Central Mombasa page 254
3 Mombasa Old Town page 256

**Sleeping**
Castle Royal 3
Dorse 1
Excellent 4
Manson 6
New Palm Tree 7
Royal Court 10
Sapphire 11

**Eating**
Canton Malaysian Chinese 8
Fontanella Steak House 3
Galaxy Chinese 13
Little Chef 10
Mombasa Blue Room 4
Overseas 14
Pistachio 5

Recoda 12
Shehnai 6
Singh 2
Splendid View Café 7
Wimpy 1

**Bars & clubs**
Casablanca Day & Night
Club 15

Africa and it was designed by Italian architect Jao batisto Cairato. The fort was his last assignment as chief architect for Portuguese possession in the east. Today it's hailed as one of the best examples of 16th-century Portuguese military architecture. It's believed that since the Portuguese sailed under the flag of the Order of Christ, Jesus was an obvious choice of name.

Despite this apparently secure position the Portuguese lost possession of the fort in 1698 following an uprising by the townspeople who had formed an alliance with the Omanis. The fort had been under siege for 15 months before it finally fell. The British took control of the fort in 1825 and it served as a prison from then until 1958, when it was restored and converted into a museum.

At the main gate are six cannons from the British ship the *Pegasus* and the German ship the *SS Konigsberg*. The walls of the fort are particularly impressive being nearly 3 m thick at the base, though the fort feels much smaller inside than it looks from the outside. Look out for what is effectively the oldest graffiti in Mombasa, inscribed by early Portuguese sentries. In the late 18th century the Omanis built a house in the northwest corner of the fort in what is known as the **San Felipe Bastion**. The Omanis also razed the walls of the fort, built turrets and equipped it with improved guns and other weaponry to increase its defensive capabilities. Since then the Omani House has served various purposes including being the prison warden's house, and today it houses a small exhibition of Omani jewellery and artefacts. You can climb up on to the flat roof for good views of Mombasa. Close to the Omani house you'll see one of the trolleys that used to be the mode of transport around town. Nearby is a ruined church, a huge well and cistern, and an excavated grave complete with skeleton. The eastern wall of the fort includes the Omani Audience Hall and the Passage of the Arches, a passage cut through the coral to give access to the sea.

The **museum** is situated in the southern part of the fort in the old barracks. Exhibits include a fair amount of pottery as well as other interesting odds and ends donated from private collections or dug up from sites along the coast. Also displayed are finds from the Portuguese frigate Santo Antonio de Tanna which sank near the fort during the siege in 1698, and the far end of the hall is devoted to the fascinating culture and traditions of the nine coastal Mijikenda tribes, including a map of sacred forests. The diversity of the exhibits is a good illustration of the wide variety of influences that this coast was subject to over the centuries.

## Old Town

While Mombasa's Old town doesn't quite have the medieval charm of Lamu or Zanzibar, it's still an interesting area to wander around, preferably early morning or late afternoon (out of the midday sun). The Old Town is not in fact that old, as most buildings are little more than 100 years old, though their foundations and some walls go back many centuries, and you'll get a clearer idea to the age of the town from its 20-odd mosques. The earliest settlement was probably around Mzizima Road, from where pottery dating from the 11th-16th centuries has been discovered but there's no other evidence left of this early settlement. However, the Old Town does have a few exceptional houses characteristic of Swahili coastal architecture, with fretwork balconies and ornately carved doors, which were once considered a reflection of the wealth and status of the family; the wealthier the merchant of the house was the bigger and more elaborate his front door. Sadly, many of these old houses have been destroyed but there are now preservation orders on the remaining doors and balconies, so further losses should hopefully be prevented.

Ndia Kuu (Great Way) Leading from Fort Jesus into the Old Town, this road is one of the oldest in Mombasa; it existed during the Portuguese period and formed the main street of their settlement. Today some of the road's older houses have been restored and now serve as souvenir shops to visitors to the fort. Further north **Mzizima Road** was the main route between the Portuguese town and the original Arab/Shirazi town. One of the older buildings on the island is **Leven House** located just off the top end of Ndia Kuu. This was built around the beginning of the 19th century and has served many different purposes since then. It was originally occupied by a wealthy trading family and later was the headquarters of the British East Africa Company. It also housed a German Diplomatic Mission and more recently has been used by the Customs Department. Among its most famous visitors were the explorers and missionaries Burton, Jackson and Ludwig Krapf. In front of Leven House are the Leven steps – here a tunnel has been carved through to the water's edge where there is a freshwater well. Burton actually mentions climbing up through this tunnel but you do not need to follow his example; there are steps nearby. Close to the Leven Steps and the Fish Market is **New Burhani Bohra Mosque**, with a tall minaret, built in 1902, and is the third mosque to have been built on this site. On Mbarak Ali Hinawy Street, to the east of Ndia Kuu, close to the Old Port is **Mandhry Mosque**, built of coral rubble and finished with lime plaster with a white minaret. This is thought to be the oldest mosque on the island dating from around 1570 and originally was only one storey but another two storeys were added in 1988 and 1992 because of the need of a madrasa and women's prayer gallery. To the west of here, there are many more mosques and elderly

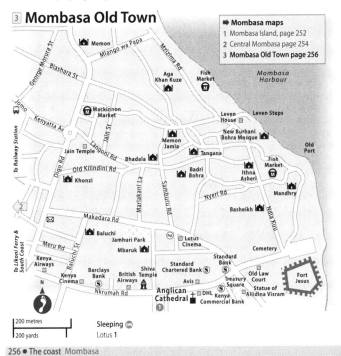

### ③ Mombasa Old Town

➡ **Mombasa maps**
1 Mombasa Island, page 252
2 Central Mombasa page 254
3 **Mombasa Old Town page 256**

Sleeping 🛏
Lotus 1

200 metres
200 yards

houses in the cramped winding alleyways ways linking the Old Town to Digo Road, which are wonderfully lively, with market traders selling everything from *kangas* and cell phone accessories to baobab seeds and fried taro roots. It's not a very big area and most of these lanes eventually lead to a main road, so it's not easy to get lost. On Langoni Road, the Jain Temple has an intricate icing-sugar exterior in dozens of pastel shades. It was built in 1963 and was the first Jain Temple to be built outside India. Jainism is a Hindu religion closely related to Buddhism, and inside are ornamental painted figurines of deities in niches, each with a drain so they can be easily cleaned and rinsed off. You may be permitted to go inside (mornings only) but ensure you remove shoes and anything made of leather as the Jain faith is strictly vegetarian.

## Nkrumah Road and around

At the eastern end of Nkrumah Road near Fort Jesus is the administrative centre of the British colonial period. The main buildings surround **Treasury Square**, with the handsome **Treasury** itself on the east side. In the square is a bronze statue of Allidina Visram, born in 1851 in Cutch in India. In 1863, at the age of 12, he arrived in Mombasa and became a prosperous merchant and planter, encouraging education and prominent in public life. He began trading in cloves and ivory, but when the building of the Uganda railway started, he opened up shops to supply food and other necessities to the workers of the railway. When the railway was finished, he had over 100 shops in Kenya and Uganda. He died in 1916.

The **Old Law Court** on Nkrumah Road dates from the beginning of the 20th century, and is well worth a visit, as it is now a library and also a gallery where there are often historic photograph exhibitions. It houses the collections of some scholars who have studied the Swahili Coast. Near the Law Court on Treasury Square is another building of approximately the same age. This was the **District Administration Headquarters**. The roof is tiled and there is a first-floor balcony.

Proceeding west from Treasury Square, on the left is the **Anglican Cathedral**, built in 1903 and with a plaque to mark 150 years of Christianity in Mombasa, celebrated in 1994. The cathedral itself is a mixture of European and Mediterranean influences, whitewashed with Moorish arches, slender windows, a dome reminiscent of an Islamic mosque, with a cross, and two smaller towers topped with crosses. On the right, just behind the main road and set in lovely gardens with ponds, is the spectacular, modern, Hindu **Shiva Temple**, which is topped with a gold spire and guarded by statues of lions and the Hindu god Ganesh with its elephant head.

Before the intersection with Moi Avenue is the **Holy Ghost Cathedral**, an elegant structure of concrete rendered in grey cement. Cool and airy inside, it has a fine curved ceiling of cream and blue, *fleur de lis* designs and stained-glass windows.

## Moi Avenue and around

This is Mombasa's main road with a two-lane carriageway and is about 4 km long and runs from east to west from Digo Road to the port area at Kilindini. Along it are many shops that the tourist will want to visit including souvenir shops travel agencies and tour operators offices. The **Tusks** are found on Moi Avenue and were built in 1952 to commemorate a visit by Queen Elizabeth (Princess Elizabeth as she was then). They are actually rather disappointing close up. There are curio shops for about 50 yards in both directions – the goods are not very good quality and are rather expensive, although do look out for the fabulous beaded sandals.

Near the Tusks are **Uhuru Gardens**. It is difficult to get in from Moi Avenue as curio kiosks block most of the entrance. Inside are some handsome trees, a fountain (not working), a café, and a brass cannon worn smooth from serving as a makeshift seat.

To the north of Moi Avenue, on the corner of Haile Selassie and Aga Khan is the **Swaminaryan Temple**, an exotic confection in powder blue and pink, and in front of the Railway Station, the neglected **Jubilee Gardens**, which were laid out to mark the 60th anniversary of Queen Victoria's reign in 1897. Finally, there is the **War Memorial** on Jomo Kenyatta near the bus company offices, with bronze statues dedicated to the African and Arab soldiers who served with the East African Rifles in the First World War.

## Kizingo

Kizingo area, in the southern part of the island around the lighthouse and Mombasa Golf Club, is considered to be one of the prime residential areas of the city. It has some very fine buildings whose style has been called **Coast Colonial**. These buildings are spacious and airy with wide balconies and shutters designed to take advantage of every breeze. Hardwoods were used and many of the building materials were imported from Europe and Asia. Along Mama Ngina Drive it is possible to look over the cliffs that rise above Kilindini Channel and out towards the sea.

## Mbaraki

To the south of the island at Mbaraki just to the west of the Likoni Ferry roundabout is the **Mbaraki Pillar**, which is an 8-m-tall coral stone hollow pillar that is tapered and leans at a slight angle and stands next to a small mosque, which was rebuilt in 1988. It's thought to be about 300 years old but not much is known about it. Theories suggest it might be a tomb, or a house built for a powerful spirit, or even a navigational mark and lighthouse. Old Portuguese maps show that there was an anchorage at the Mbaraki Creek and perhaps the pillar was a shipping mark indicating the entrance and as it has vertical window slits on all sides, maybe a lantern was placed at the top.

## Nyali

To the northwest of the island, Nyali is across the New Nyali Bridge, which was built in 2002 to replace an older one, which along with the Makupa and Kipevu causeways is one of the three road crossings on to the island. It was in this area that newly freed slaves settled, and a bell tower is erected in their memory, which can be seen at the junction of the main road north and Nyali Road. Today, Nyali is one of the wealthier suburbs of Mombasa, dominated by large houses where many of Mombasa's expat community live. There are a number of good restaurants here including the excellent Tamarind as well as the Ratna Shopping Centre, the Nyali Cinemax Centre, and the Nyali Nakumatt Complex, which has a number of shops, restaurants and a very large branch of **Nakumatt** supermarket. Only a few kilometres to the north of Nyali along the main coast road begins the strip of north coast hotels and restaurants.

## ⊙ Mombasa listings

*For Sleeping and Eating price codes and other relevant information, see Essentials pages 34-38.*

## ⊝ Sleeping

**Mombasa** *p250, map p252, p254, p256*
There is no upmarket accommodation in Mombasa and very little reason to stay in the city itself. It is much better to stay at a far more attractive beach hotel and visit Mombasa Old Town for the day.

**B Tamarind Village**, adjacent to the **Tamarind Restaurant**, Nyali, T041-474 600, www.tamarind.co.ke. This is a collection of 1- to 3-bedroom self-catering apartments (you can also order food from the restaurant) in a Swahili-style whitewashed building with turrets and curved archways in a lovely waterside setting, with 2 swimming pools, a squash court, gym and pleasant gardens. Each spacious, light apartment has Swahili furnishings, a/c, kitchenette, veranda and satellite TV.

**C Orchid Bay**, Nyali, immediately after you cross Nyali Bridge turn left at the petrol station and then follow the road back under the bridge, T041-473 238, www.orchidbay hotel.741.com. An attractive fairly new Moorish-style block with 42 rooms with a/c, hot water, TV, and patios or balconies with good views back across to Mombasa Island, set in lush tropical gardens right next to the water, though there's no beach. Secure parking, restaurant and pleasant mosaic swimming pool. Popular local conference venue.

**C Royal Court Hotel**, Haile Selassie Rd, T041-222 3379, www.royalcourt mombasa.co.ke. Spacious and luxuriant entrance hall decorated in Swahili style, central position, 8-storey modern hotel with modern en suite rooms, a/c, electronic door locks and balconies. Good rooftop bar/restaurant (see Eating), downstairs bar and

casino, and a swimming pool. Well run and offers good value.

**D Castle Royal Hotel**, T041-222 2682, www.680-hotel.co.ke. Lovely white colonial building and historic hotel built in 1909 that was completely refurbished and reopened in 2005 after lying derelict for several years. All 60 double, single and family rooms have nice modern furniture, cool tiled floors, satellite TV, electric safes, a/c, high-speed internet, sound proofing and the front ones have balconies. Very good terrace restaurant and bar (see Eating). Recommended as the best place to stay in the city centre.

**D Hotel Sai Rose**, Nyerere Av, T041-222 0932, www.sairosehotel.com. Next to the Ex-Telcom House this odd-looking narrow building has a spacious reception area and restaurant and 23 self-contained rooms, curiously some of which are in the basement. It's worth paying a little extra for the upstairs executive rooms, some of which have Swahili-style decor, fridges and a/c.

**D Lotus**, Cathedral Lane off Nkrumah Rd, close to Fort Jesus, T041-231 3207, www.lotushotelkenya.com. Recently renovated, this has a charming central courtyard shaded by tropical plants and a lovely atmosphere with wood panels and Oriental arches, single, double or triple rooms, all have a/c and hot water. There is a good bar and restaurant that serves buffet lunches. Recommended.

**D Sapphire Hotel**, Mwembe Tayari Rd, T041-494 893. In a handy location for the railway station, this has 110 comfortable modern rooms with marble decor, a/c, balconies and satellite TV, although saying that it hasn't been maintained very well. **Mehfil** restaurant, terrace BBQ, buffet lunch, also has a swimming pool and a gym.

**E Excellent Hotel**, Haile Selassie Rd, T041-222 7683. In a central location, just a short walk from the railway station or a moderate walk to bus terminals, spacious rooms have fans and bathrooms with lots of hot water. Friendly staff, well run, clean with good security, rooftop bar and the price includes breakfast. One of the best budget options and deservedly popular.

**E Hotel Dorse**, Kwashibu Rd, T041-222 252, hoteldorse@africaonline.co.ke. Very modern block, all 34 rooms have a/c, bathroom, phone and TV, secure parking around the side, nothing unique but high quality for the area, everything is very new and fresh, standard hotel dining room and conference hall.

**E Manson Hotel**, Kisumu Rd, T041-222 2419. Located in a fairly quiet residential area, some of the 80 rather dark rooms in this modern hotel have fans, others a/c, all rooms have hot water and mosquito nets. Restaurant, TV lounge with pool table, reasonable value and a cooked breakfast is included.

**E New Palm Tree**, Nkrumah Rd, T041-315 272. Rather striking whitewashed old building, reception area has a high ceiling and gallery with comfy sofas, simple, quiet but rather faded hotel, fans, bathrooms but no hot water, there is a cosy relaxed bar and the restaurant serves basic dishes.

## ❼ Eating

**Mombasa** *p250, map p252, p254, p256*
There are a number of eating places to choose from apart from hotel restaurants. With its large Indian population there is a lot of excellent Indian food as well as fresh fish and shellfish. At the budget end of the scale there are numerous canteens around the city centre that sell sausage or chicken and chips, samosas and pies, especially popular during the day with office workers. Also look out for the outdoor stalls selling Swahili snacks, which are all over the place especially in the Old Town, along Haile Selassie Road, and to the southeast of the island along Mama Ngina Drive. At these you might get egg

chapatti, as the name suggests, a chapatti cooked with an egg inside it, *kachri bateta*, a potato, tomato, chutney and chilli mix, *mshikaki*, grilled beef or mutton kebabs served with chapattis and a bit of salad, and *mogo* (roasted cassava), *makai* (maize meal) or *guvaji* (sweet potatoes). Also look out for fresh coconut juice.

**♔♔♔ Hunter's Bar**, near the **Tamarind** in Nyali, T041-231 1156. Open 1200-1500,1800-late, closed Tue. Secluded international restaurant popular with Nyali's expats, in a rather attractive Mediterranean style with a bar and tables arranged around a well-manicured courtyard offering a wide variety of seafood and meat dishes, but its speciality is its mouth-watering steaks. Other popular items offered include game meat, chicken Kiev and even apple pie.

**♔♔♔ Roberto's**, in the Nyali Cinemax, Nyali, T041-471 110. Daily 1000-2300. Traditional Italian trattoria with murals of Italian village life on the walls and one of the most extensive Italian winelists in Kenya. The long menu uses imported ingredients and features Italian classic cuisine and is strong on interesting fish dishes, jumbo prawns and wood-fired pizzas. Desserts include tiramisu and ice-cream with a shot of espresso coffee.

**♔♔♔ Shehnai**, Fatemi House, Maungano St, T041-222 2847. Open 1200-1400, 1900-2230, closed Mon. Superb cuisine, specialities are *mughlai* and tandoori dishes, very professionally run where the quality and taste of food is paramount, elegant furniture, soothing music, pleasant decor, although no alcohol, but there is a terrace bar at the **Jambo Casino** a few doors along if you want to have a drink before or after. Recommended.

**♔♔♔ Tamarind**, Silo Rd, Nyali, T041-474 600-2, www.tamarind.com, www.tamarind dhow.com. Daily 1230-1430, 1900-2230. This beautiful restaurant has marvellous views overlooking a creek that flows into the ocean, and the Moorish design of the building is well thought out, cool and spacious with high arches, while the food and service are both excellent. It specializes in seafood. It also offers cruises around Tudor Creek on the 2 luxurious *Nawalikher* and *Babulkher*, *dhows* where you can sip *dawa* cocktails (vodka, lime, honey and crushed ice) and eat lobster, whilst watching the moon rise over Mombasa Old Town and Fort Jesus, and listening to the strains of a traditional Swahili band. The set meals on the *dhow* include seafood hors d'oeuvres to start, followed by grilled lobster or seafood in coconut sauce. There are 2 sailings a day for lunch (US$40) and dinner (US$70). The lunchtime option is exclusive to package-day tours, while the evening option departs at 1830. Reservations essential. This is a memorable eating experience and thoroughly recommended for any visitor to the coast.

††††-†† **Misono**, at the Nakumatt Shopping Centre, Nyali, T041-471 454. Mon-Sat 1230-1430, 1900-2230. Restaurant offering not too expensive and authentic sushi, sashimi and tepanyaki dishes, the chefs are well trained and offer an authentic 'show' while cooking, the decor has a Japanese feel and diners receive a Japanese greeting at the door accompanied by the sound of a 'bong'.

††††-† **Castle Terrace**, at the **Castle Royal Hotel**, T041-222 0373. Daily 0600-1000, 1230-1500, 1900-2300, all day for snacks and drinks. Lovely refurbished terrace but rather unfortunately it looks straight at the traffic on Moi Av. Nevertheless this is a social place for a drink and the food is very good. Inventive menu, steaks and grills, some pasta, African specials such as 1 kg of fillet beef served with *ugali*, seafood platters for 2, sandwiches and ice cream. Recommended.

†† **Bollywood Bites**, at the **Nyali Cinemax** in Nyali opposite Ratna Sq, on the way to the **Tamarind**, T041-470 000. Mon-Sat 1800-2300, Sun 1200-1500, 1800-2300. Authentic vegetarian Indian cuisine, modern restaurant uniquely decorated in a Bollywood theme,

a wide selection of mughlai and tandoori dishes, specialities include Indian ice cream, *kulfi*, Indian milkshake, *faluda*, and freshly squeezed juice. Go and see a Bollywood movie at the cinema and eat here for rather a different night out.

†† **Canton Malaysian Chinese**, in the car park behind the Castle Hotel, T041-222 7977. Daily 1100-1500, 1800-2300. An upstairs formal restaurant, though the decor is rather plain, bar with some wine and spirits, good food including crispy duck with pancakes and deep-fried crab claws, good choices for vegetarian and lychee for dessert.

†† **Galaxy Chinese Restaurant**, Archbishop Makarios St, T041-231 1256. Daily 1100-1430, 1800-2300. Popular Chinese restaurant and is probably one of the best in town. It has especially good seafood dishes including excellent ginger crab and a good range of 'sizzling' dishes. Good service and refreshing a/c. There are other branches on the north and south coasts.

†† **La Veranda**, Mwea Tabere St, behind the **Nakumatt Shopping Centre**, Nyali, T041-548 5452. Daily 0900-late. Good traditional Italian restaurant and bar, home-made pasta with a variety of sauces, pizza oven, homely atmosphere, wide range of drinks including Italian wines.

†† **Overseas**, Moi Av just west of the Tusks, T041-227 801. Daily 1100-2200. Popular Chinese and Korean with a bar, it is family-run, friendly and the food is pretty cheap and good and it's particularly known for its seafood. Look out for the red lanterns hanging outside. It is next door to a Chinese herbal clinic.

†† **Rooftop Restaurant**, in the **Royal Court Hotel**, Haile Selassie Rd, T041-222 3379. Daily 1130-1430, 1730-late. High-quality food in balcony restaurant with great views of Mombasa's rooftops with pleasant decor of green plants and blue and white linen, with a good range of continental dishes, predominately Italian, plus some creamy Indian curries and tandoori dishes.

The casino and bar on the ground floor of the hotel is open until 0600.

☗ **Books First** is an excellent chain of bookshops. There are branches at the **Nakumatt Complex** near the Likoni Ferry, and at the **Nyali Shopping Centre**. They also double up as very good cafés for coffees, pizza, snacks, some Indian and Mexican dishes and offer internet access.

☗ **Fontanella Steak House**, on corner of Moi Av and Digo Rd. Mon-Sat 0900-1800. Nice relaxing courtyard workers' café off the street surrounded by plants, red and white checked tablecloths, attentive service, popular meeting place, very large menu with daily specials, everything from chicken masala, *nyama choma* and fried liver to simple fare such as ice cream, fresh juice and plenty of cold beer.

☗ **Little Chef**, Digo Rd. Centrally located, very busy canteen open all day until 2300, African food, burgers, chicken and chips on plastic tables, no booze, popular at lunchtime.

☗ **Mombasa Blue Room Restaurant**, Haile Selassie Rd, T041-222 4021, www.blueroom online.com. Daily 0900-2200. Established in 1952, this excellent bright, clean, and bustling cafeteria seats over 140 people and is somewhat of a Mombasa institution. A family-run, a/c self-service restaurant, it offers Indian snacks, like samoosas, bhajia, kebabs, as well as fish and chips, chicken, burgers and pizzas, and everything is homemade. The delicious ice cream is made with filtered water; in fact they produce ice cream that is suitable for people with diabetes. It also doubles up as a DVD hire shop, and has the nicest and quickest internet café in town. Popular with locals and a good place to meet people. Recommended.

☗ **Pistachio Ice-Cream and Coffee Bar**, Msanifu Kombo St. Open 0800-1700. Wonderful ice cream and fruit juices, home-made cakes and excellent coffees, it serves snacks and you can also have proper meals – including a buffet lunch, pleasant decor, well-run. Thoroughly recommended.

☗ **Recoda**, Moi Av near the Tusks, T041-222 3629. Daily 1830-2400. This canteen serves traditional Swahili cuisine and is one of the oldest restaurants in Mombasa (it opened in 1942). The food is basic but cheap with large portions, and it's only open in the evenings and closed during Ramadan. The menu features dishes such as fish with coconut rice and puréed beans, *mahamri* (a staple bread), and *mshikaki* (a type of kebab).

☗ **Singh**, Mwembe Tayari Rd, T041-493 283. Open 1200-1430, 1900-2230, closed Mon. Good modern a/c restaurant with chunky furniture run by the Sikh Temple. Although the menu is not very extensive the food is authentic, freshly prepared and tasty, in particular the butter chicken is excellent and there's a good choice for vegetarians. Serves alcohol.

☗ **Splendid View Café**, Maungano Rd. Mon-Sat 1100-2230. Very good, cheap Indian meals, plus some prawns and steaks – huge portions. Nice variety of dishes for US$4-10 in a clean canteen environment, look out for the daily lunchtime specials.

☗ **Wimpy**, next to the **Tusks**. Standard burgers and shakes, Wimpy breakfasts are not that bad if you are looking for a traditional fry-up.

## 🜚 Bars and clubs

**Mombasa** *p250, map p252, p254, p256*
**Casablanca Day and Night Club**, Mnazi Moja Rd, T0722-847 792, www.casablanca mombasa.com. Daily 24 hrs. A huge venue on 2 floors with several bars, 2 dance floors, restaurant, varied music from 1970s disco to Kenyan rap and hip hop, exotic floor shows, sports on giant TVs in the afternoons. It's popular but it can get crowded so watch your valuables and be aware that it's working girls' territory.

**New Florida Club and Casino**, Mama Ngina Drive, T041-220 9036, www.floridaclubs

kenya.com. Disco from 2100 daily, casino and bars 24 hrs. A branch of Nairobi's raucous Florida clubs, in huge premises, with several bars and dance floors, on the waterfront with ocean views, cabaret live shows at midnight, also casino and restaurant serving *nyama choma* and other snacks. Again gets absolutely packed and men will get a lot of attention from prostitutes.

## 🎭 Entertainment

**Mombasa** *p250, map p252, p254, p256*
**Golden Key Casino**, at the Tamarind Restaurant, Nyali, T041-471 071, www.tamarind.co.ke. Daily 1800-0400. Mombasa's most sophisticated and elegant casino in a lovely setting on the roof of the restaurant with great night time views of Mombasa Island from the terrace with a full range of gaming tables and modern slot machines, cocktails and snacks.
**Lotus Cinema**, Makadara Rd, and the **Kenya**, opposite the Social Security House on Moi Av, both have fairly up-to-date Hollywood and Bollywood movies.
**Nyali Cinemax**, located in Nyali opposite Ratna Square, T041-470 000, www.nyali cinemax.com. This is an ultra-modern a/c cinema that plays the latest box-office releases. There is also the **Scorpian Sports Bar** here, a couple of restaurants, a casino and a 10-pin bowling alley and a casino.

## 🛍 Shopping

**Mombasa** *p250, map p252, p254, p256*
The souvenirs that you will find in Mombasa are wooden carvings including Makonde carvings from Tanzania, soapstone carvings and chess sets, baskets, batiks and jewellery. There are lots of stalls in and around the market and around the junction of Digo Rd and Jomo Kenyatta Av. There are also lots

more along Msanifu Kombo St; along Moi Av from the Castle Hotel and down to the roundabout with Nyerere Av; and around Fort Jesus. For *kikois*, *kangas* and other material or fabric go to Biashara St, which runs off Digo St parallel to Jomo Kenyatta Av. The Indian tailors here can also make up clothes to order from the cloth. Avoid buying seashells. As a result of killing the crabs, molluscs and other sealife that live inside the shells to sell them to tourists, populations have declined dramatically and many are seriously threatened. Vendors may tell you they have a licence, but don't encourage this trade.

### Markets
**Mackinnon Market** is a lively, bustling and colourful market on Digo Rd and was named after Dr W Mackinnon, a colonial administrator at the turn of the 20th century. The main section of the market is situated in an enormous shed but numerous stalls have spilled out on to the streets. Apart from an excellent range of exotic fresh fruit and vegetables, you will be able to buy baskets, jewellery and other souvenirs. If you are prepared to haggle and bargain in a good-natured manner you can usually bring the price down quite considerably.

### Shopping centres
In Nyali is the **Ratna Shopping Centre**, the **Nyali Cinemax Centre**, and the **Nyali Nakumatt Shopping Centre**, which has a number of shops, restaurants and a very large branch of **Nakumatt** supermarket. There is also another vast branch of **Nakumatt**, with a number of other shops and cafés near to the Likoni Ferry.

Out of town on the road to the airport is the **Akamba Handicraft Cooperative**, off Port-Reitz Rd, Changamwe, T041-343 4396, www.akambahandicraftcoop.com. Daily 0800-1730. This sells a vast range of curios from animal statues and decorated spoons to walking sticks and wooden bowls. It was established in 1963 with 100 carvers and now promotes and distributes the work of about 3000 carvers. They are presently establishing a nursery of fast-growing neem wood trees to provide renewable resources of wood for the carvers (ebony now is very rare). The showroom is a popular stop for tourists as they are bussed in and out of the airport, or on city tours, you can watch the carvers at work, and reasonably low prices are fixed and 80% goes to the carver, while 20% goes to the cooperative.

## ▲▲ Activities and tours

**Mombasa** *p250, map p252, p254, p256*
### Sports clubs
**Mombasa Golf Club**, Mama Nginga Dr, T041-228 531. This 9-hole course was established in 1911 and sits on top of coral cliffs with good ocean views. Day membership is available and clubs and caddies can be hired.
**Mombasa Sports Club**, Mnazi Mosi Rd, T041-222 4226, www.mombasa sportsclub.co.ke. There's an old colonial saying that you can't put more than 3 Englishmen in a foreign country without them forming a club, and this is the country's oldest sporting club. Established in 1896, the same year the building of the Uganda Railway started, it hosted celebrations of Queen Victoria's Jubilee in 1897. There are facilities here for cricket, squash, tennis, basketball and football, among other sports, and there's a gym.

### Tour operators
Mombasa's tour operators act as booking agents for the beach hotels and most can also organize day or overnight safaris to the parks close to the coast such as Tsavo or Simba Hills, as well as tours of the city and other local attractions. For example, expect to pay around US$35 for a ½-day city tour,

US$75 combined with lunch on the Tamarind Dhow (see page 260), US$110 for a day trip up to Malindi and the Gedi Ruins, and US$130 for a day tip to Tsavo East. Some also offer car hire and transfers to the beach. For more Mombasa-based tour operators, visit
**Kenya Association of Tour Operators**, www.katokenya.org.
**African Quest Safaris**, Palli House, Nyerere Rd, T041-227 052, www.africanquest.co.ke. City tours and day trips to attractions on the north coast, plus longer safaris.
**African Route Safaris**, 2nd floor, Old Cannon Towers, Moi Av, T041-230 322, www.african routesafaris.com. Offers 1- to 2-night safaris to Tsavo East and 3-night trips to Tsavo and Amboseli, plus ½-day city tour and full-day Gedi Ruins tour.
**Bunson Travel Service**, Southern House, Moi Av, T041-231 1331, www.bunsonkenya.com. A good, reliable, well-established travel and tour agent. Flight and rail bookings, safaris and hotel bookings, and day tours to Shimba Hills, Gedi Ruins, Wasini Island and overnight trips to Tsavo.
**Distance Car Hire and Tours**, Wimpy Building, next to the Tusks, Moi Av, T041-222 2869, www.distancetours.com. 1- to 4-day tours to Tsavo, and a longer 6-day safari from Mombasa to the Masai Mara, Nakuru and Tsavo. Also can arrange tours of Tanzania's northern circuit from Mombasa.
**Kenya One Tours**, Nkrumah Rd, T041-202 2311, www.kenyaonetours.com. Good all-round operator offering safaris across the country, plus day trips from Mombasa, overnight safaris to Tsavo and Shimba Hills and fly-in safaris from Mombasa to the Masai Mara.
**Ketty Tours, Travels & Safaris**, Ketty Plaza, Moi Av, T041-231 2204, www.kettysafari.com. Combined Tsavo East, Tsavo West and Amboseli 4-day safaris, city tours, and day trips to Shimba Hills and Malindi and the Gedi Ruins.
**Pollman Tours and Safaris**, Taveta Rd, Shimanzi, T041-210 6000, www.poll

mans.com. General park excursions and safaris starting in Nairobi and finishing in Mombasa, has a large fleet of vehicles.
**Southern Cross Safaris**, Nyali Bridge Rd, T041-475 074, www.southerncrosssafaris.com. Established award-winning operator with over 40 years' experience, runs a daily trip to its own camp in Tsavo East, **Satao Camp**, has a fleet of safari vehicles and its own plane, is a specialist for safaris for disabled clients and agents for beach resorts. It also runs the excellent www.kenyalastminute.com, where you can pick up some bargain last-minute holidays to Kenya. Highly recommended.
**Special Lofty Safaris**, Nkrumah Rd, T041-222 0241, www.lofty-tours.com. City tours, Mombasa by night tours, half-day trips to Shimba Hills, and 1- to 3-day safaris to Tsavo.
**United Touring Company (UTC)**, UTC Building, Moi Av, T041-222 9834, www.utc.co.ke. Another professional operator offering safaris across Kenya and beach hotel reservations.

## ⊖ Transport

**Mombasa** *p250, map p252, p254, p256*
**Air**
**Moi International Airport** is on the mainland about 10 km out of the centre of town, T041-433 211, www.kenya airports.com. Airport tax for domestic flights is US$4 but this is included in the price of scheduled airline tickets and is only payable on charter flights. Some of the airlines are now flying between Mombasa and Tanzania, but remember you will need to show a yellow fever vaccination certificate on arrival in Tanzania. **Mombasa Air Safaris**, links Mombasa to airstrips in the parks and reserves.

**Air Kenya** has 1 daily flight to **Nairobi**'s Wilson Airport (1 hr 5 mins) that departs at 1105. In Nairobi you can link on to their scheduled services to the airstrips in the

parks and reserves. **Fly 540** has 5 daily flights to **Nairobi** (1 hr) from US$69 1 way, at least 2 daily flights to **Malindi** (15 mins) from only US$30 1 way, and 1 daily flight to **Zanzibar** (45 mins) in Tanzania, which from US$99 1 way is especially good value. **Kenya Airways** has about 10 flights a day to **Nairobi** (1 hr) between 0600 and 2300. They don't fly directly to Malindi or Lamu, so you'll have to back track via Nairobi or take another airline. **Kenya Airways** code shares with Tanzania's **Precision Air**, and there are now flights to **Zanzibar** and **Dar es Salaam** on Tue, Thu, Fri and Sun. **Mombasa Air Safari** uses small planes and operates a daily scheduled 'Beach to Bush' service between Mombasa, and the airstrip at Diani Beach, to **Amboseli**, **Tsavo**, and the **Masai Mara**. It also has daily scheduled flights to **Malindi** and **Lamu**.

**Airline offices** **Air Kenya**, Wilson Airport, Nairobi, T020-605 745, www.airkenya.com. **Fly 540**, T041-343 4822, www.fly 40.com. **Kenya Airways**, Wilson Airport, T041-350 5500, town office, Electricity House, Nkrumah Rd, www.kenya-airways.com. **Mombasa Air Safari**, Moi International Airport, T041-343 3061, www.mombasaairsafari.com.

**Bus**
On all buses seats can be booked and there is no overcrowding with standing passengers anymore. There are lots of bus companies that go to **Nairobi** and their kiosks are on Jomo Kenyatta Av opposite the Islamic Cemetery and near the market. They usually leave early morning and evening, take 9-11 hrs and cost about US$15. **Akamba Bus**, T041-349 0269, www.akambabus.com, is on Jomo Kenyatta Av. Buses and *matatus* depart for **Malindi** frequently throughout the day and take about 1½ hrs. They leave Mombasa when full from Abdel Nasser Rd outside the New People's Hotel. There are daily buses to **Lamu**, which also pick up in **Malindi**,

7 hrs, US$10, and the **Pwani Tawakal Bus Company**, T041-222 975, http://pwani tawakal.com, is recommended for the Lamu service, which has 3 daily departures between 0600-0800. The bus will take you to the Mokowe Jetty on the mainland from where you get a ferry across to Lamu (see page 322).

The bus service to Lamu has been targeted by bandits in past years, with some fatalities, and for many years the service was not recommended. However, there has not been an incident for quite some time and it is reasonably regarded to be safe. Despite this, armed escorts get on the bus on the last stretch of the road to Lamu at either Garsen or Witu. Heading south to **Tanzania**, **Scandinavian Express**, is a very good Tanzanian bus company, Arrow Plaza, Jomo Kenyatta Av, T041-490 975, www.scandinaviagroup.com. It runs a daily service at 0800, which takes about 4 hrs to **Tanga**, US$13 and 10 hrs to **Dar es Salaam**, US$23. There is an identical daily service in the opposite direction that departs Dar es Salaam also at 0800. Other buses to Tanzania also go from Jomo Kenyatta Av. The border is at **Lunga Lunga**, see page 275 for border-crossing information. If not going all the way to Dar es Salaam, then from Tanga there are bus connections on to **Moshi** and **Arusha**.

### Car hire
**Avis**, airport, T041-432486, Nkrumah Rd, T041-222 0465, www.avis.com.
**Budget**, airport, T041-343 3211, Associated Motors Complex, Kenyatta Av, T041-249 0047, www.budget-kenya.com.
**Distance Car Hire and Tours**, Wimpy Building, next to the Tusks, Moi Av, T041-222 2869, www.distancetours.com.
**Europcar**, Makena House, Nkrumah Rd, T041-311 994, www.europcar.com.
**Hertz**, airport, T041-434 4020, www.hertz.com.

**Special Lofty Safaris**, Nkrumah Rd, T041-222 0241, www.lofty-tours.com.

### Ferry
The Likoni Ferry docks at the southeast of the island. The two 24-hr ferries cross simultaneously and depart about every 15 mins from about 0400-0100, and every hour in the middle of the night and are free for pedestrians and cyclists (cars US$0.60 and motorbikes US$0.30). There is always a throng of people waiting to board or disembark from the boat – keep your hands tightly on your possessions and beware of pickpockets and thieves. The waters are said to contain sharks although this is debatable. *Matatus* to the ferry leave from outside the post office on Digo Rd – ask for Likoni. In fact it is possible to get a *matatu* to the Likoni ferry from just about anywhere in the city even if the taxi drivers tell you otherwise. When the ferry docks, the *matatus* for Ukunda (the turn-off to Diani Beach) are located at the top of the slipway from the ferry.

### Taxi
Taxis leave from **Moi International Airport** to local destinations. Prices are fixed and are posted up on boards and vary depending on whether you choose a small private car or minibus. Into town expect to pay around US$10, to **Nyali Beach** about US$20, to **Shanzu Beach** about U$35, and to **Diani Beach**, which includes the crossing of the Likoni Ferry, about US$60.

You can also organize shuttles from Mombasa's Moi International Airport to all the north coast resorts through the resorts themselves or with the taxi companies in the arrivals hall.

### Train
**Mombasa Railway Station**, T041-433 211, is at the end of Haile Selassie Av at Jubilee Sq. There are services 3 times a week between

Mombasa and Nairobi. See page 106 for full details. The train is notoriously late so don't book onward travel on the same day as the arrival of the train.

## ⊕ Directory

**Mombasa** *p250, map p252, p254, p256*
**Banks** There are many banks on Nkrumah Av and Moi Av with ATMs. The 3 branches of **Barclays Bank**, Digo Rd, Moi Av, and Nkrumah Av, have efficient foreign-exchange facilities and will give cash advances off cards. **Courier companies** DHL, Nkrumah Av, T041-222 3933, www.dhl.com. **Currency exchange** Pwani Bureau de Change, opposite Mackinnon Market on Digo Rd, is fast and efficient and good rates are offered, while **Coast Forex Bureau** is on the corner of Moi Av and Digo Rd on the opposite corner to the Stanbic Bank. **Internet** There are many cybercafés or small businesses offering email and internet access in Mombasa. However, access is compromised by frequent interruptions to the power supply. The best are the **Info Café**, Ambalal House, opposite the Kenya Airways office on Nkrumah Av, which also serves snacks and juices, and the internet café at the back of the **Mombasa Blue Room Restaurant**, Haile Selassie Rd. **Blue Fin Cyber Cafe**, Meru Rd, also sells fresh sugarcane juice. **Books First** is an excellent chain of bookshops that also double up as internet cafés, and there are branches at the Nakumatt Complex near the Likoni Ferry, and at the Nyali Shopping Centre. **Cultural centres** Alliance Française, Freed Building, Moi Av, T041-340 079, www.amba france-ke.org. **British Council**, Jubilee Insurance Building, Moi Av just west of the Tusks, T041-222 3076, www.british council.org. **Immigration** The visa office is on Mama Ngina Rd next to the police station, T041-231 1745. **Medical services** Aga Khan Hospital, Vanga Rd, T041-222 7710, www.agakhanhospitals.org. **Mombasa Hospital**, Mama Ngina Rd, T041-231 2191, www.mombasahospital.com. **Pandya Memorial Hospital**, Dedan Kimathi St, T041-231 3577, www.pandyahospital.org. **Coast Provincial General Hospital**, Kisauni Rd, T041-231 4201. There are plenty of well-stocked pharmacies in the city centre. **Post office** Digo St, Mon-Fri 0800-1800, Sat 0900-1200.

# South coast

*The beaches on the south coast are some of the best in the world. The sand – coral that has been pounded by the waves over the centuries – is fine and very white. There are a few well-developed areas, but you don't need to go far to find a quiet spot. The most popular beach is Diani – it is also the most built up and not surprisingly is now the most expensive. However, most of the buildings are well designed and local materials have been used so they do not intrude too much. The hotels all have their own restaurants and bars and most of them arrange regular evening entertainment such as traditional African dancers and singers or acrobats. They also organize watersports and day trips to sights in the region including Mombasa city tours, and day trips to Wasini Island and the Kisite-Mpunguti Marine National Park, as well as longer overnight safaris to some of the parks, so it is feasible to stay in one hotel for your entire holiday, and take organized local excursions from there. ▸▸ For listings, see pages 276-286.*

## Ins and outs

Once across the Likoni Ferry the A14 heads south on a reasonably good tarred road. It runs about 300 m parallel to the coast, although you cannot see the sea from the road. The turn-off to Tiwi Beach is about 20 km south of the ferry and the turn-off to Diani Beach is at Ukunda about 25 km. There are plenty of *matatus* running up and down between the township of Likoni where the ferry docks and Ukunda, but these are less frequent south of Ukunda. About 12 km from Likoni is the turn-off to the right to Kwale and the Shimba Hills National Reserve and Mwaluganje Elephant Sanctuary.

## Likoni and Shelley Beach ▸▸ *Colour map 2, C1.*

→ *Phone code: 040.*

Likoni is a sprawling (and none too clean with piles of unsightly rubbish everywhere) township on the southern side of the Likoni Ferry and is effectively a creek-side suburb of Mombasa. The road that leads from the ferry is lined with market stalls. Shelley Beach just to the east of the ferry is the closest beach to Mombasa, and can be visited for a day trip if you are staying in the town and are not too bothered by the proximity of the urban sprawl. However, it is narrow and uninviting and swimming here can be problematic due to excessive seaweed and there is the need to watch carefully over your belongings.

## Tiwi Beach ◉ ▸▸ *pp276-286. Colour map 2, C1.*

→ *Phone code: 040.*

The next resort, Tiwi Beach, is about 20 km from Likoni Ferry and 3 km off the main coastal road down a very bumpy track (turn left at the supermarket). Never walk down this road as muggings can occur. This beach is wider than that at Shelley but not as nice as Diani and for a number of years was particularly popular with families and with budget travellers. Its popularity has waned in recent years however in favour of the hotels at Diani, and **Twiga Lodge**, once a firm favourite on the backpacker circuit through East Africa, is a shadow of its former self.

However, the beach is ideal for children; the waves are smaller than those at Diani, and hundreds of rock pools are exposed when the tide is out, all with plenty of marine life in them. There is also some quite good snorkelling here and it is possible to scuba dive too. However, it is prone to large amounts of seaweed in April and May. If you walk up the beach in the direction of Shelley Beach for about 1.5 km you come to 'Pool of Africa', a rock pool in the shape of the African continent where you can swim, and even dive through a small tunnel to another pool aptly named **Madagascar**. Before you go exploring on the beach and reef check up on the tides (local people will be able to advise) and set out with plenty of time. It is very easy to get cut off when the tide comes in and it turns quite rapidly. Also be sure you have a good pair of thick rubber-soled shoes to protect your feet against the coral and sea urchins. It is possible to walk south to Diani Beach at low tide, but again it is important to ensure you check the times of the tides to avoid getting stranded.

---

## Diani Beach ⬤⬤⬤⬤▲⬤⬤ ⟩⟩ pp276-286. Colour map 2, C1.

→ *Phone code: 040.*

The beach itself is the longest commercially used beach in Kenya with about 20 km of dazzling white sand, coconut trees, clear sea and a coral reef that is exposed at low tide. It has acquired a whole string of hotels over the years, although most of these have been sensitively built, often out of thatch and local materials. Diani is the place to come if you want a traditional beach holiday; the climate and scenery are marvellous, accommodation and food is of a very high standard, and activities on offer include windsurfing, kitesurfing, sailing, snorkelling and scuba-diving. You can also go waterskiing or parascending, or hire a bike or motorbike and there is the additional option of combining time on the beach with a safari to one of the closer national parks and game reserves inland. Increasingly, a number of shopping centres have mushroomed on the 'strip' geared towards tourists, as well as numerous informal souvenir stalls, and other facilities include the golf course and casino at the Leisure Lodge, a number of independent restaurants and nightclubs outside the confines of the resorts, and many of the resorts have added wellness spas and/or fitness facilities to their ever growing list of things to do.

Diani is mostly geared to big-spending package tourists from Europe, which generates some disadvantages: intrusive beach touts or 'beach boys' that hound visitors trying to sell curios, camel rides along the beach or trips on glass-bottomed boats, as well as offering themselves as models for photos (some of the Masai who come round are not Masai at all but are of other tribes). Most of the goods are poor quality and hugely overpriced, although you can try bargaining the quoted prices down. Additionally, over the years Diani has gained a bit of a reputation as a bit of a pick-up place for European female tourists looking for sex with Kenyan men. Even if no payment for 'company' is exchanged, there are many hopeful young men in the area that seek to befriend a European woman in the hope of a passage to Europe.

## Getting there

From Likoni the A14, the main Kenya–Tanzania coastal road goes south and all the turnings off are well signposted. For Diani, go as far as Ukunda village (25 km) where there is the turning off to the smaller road that runs along Diani beach. At the T-junction, some hotels are to the left, while all the others are to the right. The hotels and other facilities surrounding this junction are commonly referred to as the Diani 'strip'. Most of the large resorts at Diani will collect you from Mombasa's Moi International Airport or the train station for a charge of around US$35 per person, and transfers are usually included in package holiday rates. *Matatus* run frequently from Likoni to the south coast.

## Sights

It is worth going out to the reef at low tide at least once when the very top is exposed to look at the myriad of fish. You'll need to take a boat if you want to go out to the main reef, although you should be able to wade out to the sand bank which is not too far. Of course this depends on the tides. At full moon and new moon there are **spring tides**, which means very high high tides and very low low tides, while in between there will be **neap**

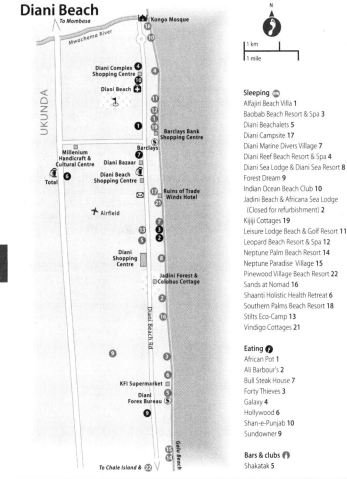

**Diani Beach**

N

1 km
1 mile

**Sleeping**
Alfajiri Beach Villa **1**
Baobab Beach Resort & Spa **3**
Diani Beachalets **5**
Diani Campsite **17**
Diani Marine Divers Village **7**
Diani Reef Beach Resort & Spa **4**
Diani Sea Lodge & Diani Sea Resort **8**
Forest Dream **9**
Indian Ocean Beach Club **10**
Jadini Beach & Africana Sea Lodge
  (Closed for refurbishment) **2**
Kijiji Cottages **19**
Leisure Lodge Beach & Golf Resort **11**
Leopard Beach Resort & Spa **12**
Neptune Palm Beach Resort **14**
Neptune Paradise Village **15**
Pinewood Village Beach Resort **22**
Sands at Nomad **16**
Shaanti Holistic Health Retreat **6**
Southern Palms Beach Resort **18**
Stilts Eco-Camp **13**
Vindigo Cottages **21**

**Eating**
African Pot **1**
Ali Barbour's **2**
Bull Steak House **7**
Forty Thieves **3**
Galaxy **4**
Hollywood **6**
Shan-e-Punjab **10**
Sundowner **9**

**Bars & clubs**
Shakatak **5**

**tides** with low highs and high lows. Wind and kite surfers can go out for longer at neap tides, while those wanting huge waves will do better at high tide.

At the far north of Diani beach just past the **Indian Ocean Beach Club**, is the **Kongo Mosque** (also known as the Diani Persian Mosque). It is rather a strange place, very run-down but not really a ruin, and still has some ritual significance. The mosque is believed to date from the 15th century and is the only remaining building from a settlement of the Shirazi people who used to live here. There are a number of entrances and you should be able to push one of the doors open and have a look inside.

### Jadini Forest
① *T040-320 3519, www.colobustrust.org, Mon-Sat 0800-1300, 1400-1700, US$7.50, children under 12 free.*
This is a small patch of the forest that straddles the main beach road and used to cover the whole of this coastal area. It is great for birdwatching, and many species of butterflies occupy the clutches of hardwood trees, but it's especially good for spotting primates. The forest is home to troops of baboon, a large population of vervet monkey and the endangered Angolan black and white colobus monkey. There are only an estimated 2000 colobus in Kenya, 400 of which are at Diani. Local group the **Colobus Trust** is devoted to the conservation of these rare primates and their habitat. Many of the primate species of this area are threatened both by traffic on the main coastal road, and by hand-feeding by tourists, which encourages anti-social and unnatural behaviour. The **Colobus Trust** works to build aerial bridges, known as 'colobridges' across the roads to prevent traffic casualties, and works to educate tourists against feeding monkeys. Another major problem is that the creatures get electrocuted on the many un-insulated power lines around Diani. The main electricity lines can carry up to 22,000 volts, which can be fatal, whilst the domestic power lines, which carry around 240 volts, can severely stun an animal and cause loss of a limb and/or secondary infections. Trees that allow access to the power lines have been cut back so the monkeys have reduced contact with them and the trust sends a team out weekly to keep vegetation trimmed. It has also been involved with rehabilitating vervet monkeys that were kept as pets and re-releasing them back into the wild at Shimba Hills. It has a centre called Colobus Cottage with plenty of information, nature trails, and can give good advice on local wildlife. It also offers a one-hour guided primate walk.

---

### Shimba Hills National Reserve ● ⇢ *pp276-286. Colour map 2, C1.*
① *US$25, children US$10, car US$4.30.*
This small reserve, 56 km southwest of Mombasa, is very easy to access on a day trip from the coast as it is less than an hour's drive from Diani Beach. The 300 sq km are covered with stands of coastal rainforest, rolling grasslands and scrubland. Due to strong sea breezes, the hills are much cooler than the rest of the coast making it a very pleasant climate. The rainforest itself is totally unspoilt and opens out into rolling downs and gentle hills and the flora ranges from baobab trees on the lower slopes nearer the coast to deciduous forests on the hills and vestigial rainforest along the watercourses. Two of Kenya's exquisite orchids are found here.

### Ins and outs
The main route to Shimba Hills and Mwaluganje is through the small town of Kwale, on the C106, which branches off the main A14 coast road 12 km south of the Likoni ferry. The

main gate is 3 km beyond Kwale. The road is well tarred as far as Kwale. It is also possible to enter the park through the Kivunoni (eastern) Gate, which is located about 1 km south of the C106 3 km from Kwale. It is possible to take a half-day trip from Mombasa and Diani for around US$50 through one of the tour operators or resorts.

## Sights

There are a number of Roan antelope, waterbuck, reedbuck, hyena, warthog, giraffe, leopard, baboon and bush pig in the reserve. The altitude and the damp atmosphere also attract countless butterflies and birds around the grassy hills and on the edges of the forest. However, it is famed for being the only place in Kenya where you might see the Sable antelope found in the same habitats as several large herds of buffalo. There are also about 300 elephant in the reserve who favour the refreshing fruit of the borassus palm, which is abundant here, and close-range elephant viewing is virtually guaranteed. The best place to see the wildlife is near the spectacular **Sheldrick Falls** and on the **Lango Plains** close to Giriama Point. Picnic sites on either side of the escarpment provide an entrancing view of the Indian Ocean to the east, and on a clear day, the imposing mass of Mount Kilimanjaro rising behind the Taita Hills to the west.

Adjacent is the **Mwaluganje Elephant Sanctuary** set up to provide access for the elephants between the Shimba Hills and the Mwaluganje Forest Reserve, and it protects 2500 ha of their traditional migratory route. The sanctuary is an innovative concept due to the fact that the local cultures, the Duruma and Digo people, have become involved along with other local landowners, the Kwale County Council, local politicians and the Kenya Wildlife Service, and a fee is payable to the local community from every visitor to the reserve. This has helped to build school classrooms and improved the water supply in the region. There is only one tented camp in the sanctuary and you can visit here either on a day or overnight trip arranged with the resorts on the coast.

---

## South of Diani ⊜▲▲ ➔ *pp276-286.*

### Chale Island ➔ *Colour map 2, C1.*

About 10 km at the southern end of Diani is a small bay and Chale Island, which lies about 600 m offshore and measures just 1.2 km long and 800 m wide. Chale refers to the name of an old warrior of the Digo tribe who is buried on the island, and on certain days of the year his descendants still come to celebrate religious rituals. During February and March, giant turtles lay their eggs on the beaches. When they are hatched, the baby turtles are helped back to sea by the local people and staff at the only hotel on the island, which is centred around a particularly fine half-moon shaped white-sand beach. Despite being off-shore, the forest behind the hotel is home to some wildlife including vervet monkeys and baboons and good birdlife. There are also some inland mangrove forests situated on lakes fed by the tides.

### Gazi ➔ *Colour map 2, C1.*

Gazi is a village at the southern end of Diani, once significantly more important than it is now as it was once the district's administrative centre. Here you will see the **House of Sheik Mbaruk bin Rashid**. There are said to be the bodies of eight men and eight women buried in the foundations of the house to give the building strength. He was also notorious for torturing people, and suffocating them on the fumes of burning chillies. In the Mazrui Rebellion of 1895 Mbaruk was seen arming his men with German rifles and flying the German flag. British troops did eventually defeat him and he ended his days in exile in German East Africa (Tanzania). The rather run-down house is now used as a school. It once had a very finely carved door but this has been moved to the Fort Jesus Museum. Ask directions for Gazi as it is not signposted on the main road.

# South coast

## Msambweni → Colour map 2, C1.

About 50 km south of Likoni is the village of Msambweni which is home to what is one of the best hospitals on the coast as well as a famous leprosarium. The beach is really lovely with coral rag-rock cliffs and there are some ruins in this area that are believed to have been a slave detention camp. **Funzi Island** is a private island located just off the coast from here at the mouth of the Ramisi River where there is a luxury lodge, and again like Chale Island it is blessed with swaying palms, mangrove forests and sugar-white beaches.

## Shimoni → Colour map 2, C1. Phone code: 040.

This is a small fishing village about 75 km south of Likoni whose name means 'Place of the Hole' and is derived from the method of entry to the system of **Slave caves** ① *to the west of the village, nominal entry fee (collected directly by the local people to help pay for the dispensary and educate the children), daily 0830-1030, 1330-1730.* 'Shimo' means cave in Kiswahili and the vast network opens directly on to the beach. There are several caves, once joined together and reputed to extend some 5 km inland. Due to silting, the floor has risen, blocking off access to the further caves, and what you now see is only the main entrance cavern. The next cavern, immediately behind this one, which is now only accessible via a hole in the roof of the cave, has a spring of completely fresh water in it. It is said that the caves were used by slave traders to hide the slaves, before they were shipped out to the slave market on Zanzibar. The other story associated with these caves is that they were used as a secret place of refuge by the

Sleeping
Betty's Camp **1**
Coral Cove Cottages **5**
Funzi Keys **7**
Maweni & Capricho Beach Cottages **4**
Msambweni Beach House **11**
Mwazaro Mangrove Lodge **9**
Pemba Channel Lodge & Fishing Club **10**
Sable Bandas **13**
Sand Island Cottages **14**
Sands at Chale Island **2**
Sheshe Baharini Beach **6**
Shimba Lodge **15**
Shimoni Gardens **3**
Shimoni Reef Lodge **12**
Tiwi Beach Resort **8**
Travellers Mwaluganje Elephant Camp **16**

Digo people during their intermittent battles with various marauding tribes, including the Masai, through the ages. Archaeological findings indicate that these coral caves, with their lovely stalactites, have been inhabited for several centuries. Today they are home to a thriving population of bats.

To reach the caves take the path that begins opposite the jetty and walk up through the forest. When you get to the entrance take a ladder down through a hole in the ground. Immediately opposite the entrance to the cave are the remains of the Imperial East Africa Company's old headquarters. It is now unfortunately a ruin.

Shimoni is best known as the take-off point for snorkelling excursions into the Kisite-Mpunguti Marine National Park and Wasini Island (see below) and for deep-sea fishing trips into the Pemba Channel, which is a 35-mile stretch of the ocean that separates Tanzania's island of Pemba from the mainland. It reaches depths of 823 m, and is home to three varieties of marlin – black, blue and striped – as well as sailfish, spearfish, swordfish, yellowfin tuna, tiger shark, mako shark and virtually every game fish popular with anglers. A gentle north current runs through the channel, acting much like a scaled-down version of the Gulf Stream, which is forced up by the lip in the north of the channel, also referred to locally as the Sea Mountain, which creates rips and eddies that bring nutrients to the surface that concentrate the fish in a very tight area. The fishing season is usually from August to the end of March. See under Activities and tours (page 285) for fishing operators.

## Kisite-Mpunguti Marine National Park and Wasini Island → *Colour map 2, C1.*
ⓘ *US$20, children US$10.*

To the far south is this marine park, which has superb coral gardens and lots of sea life. It covers 39 sq km on the southernmost part of the Kenyan coastline and is managed and protected by the Kenya Wildlife Service. The small islands dotting the coastline have old established trees including baobabs with their thick gnarled trunks and the coral seas of turquoise and dark green stretch away. Mountains rising straight up in the south over the ocean mark the Tanzanian/Kenyan border. Kisite-Mpunguti is a flat little marine park, an atoll, with a dead coral shelf in the middle rising up off it like a table. Unremarkable on the surface, what is truly amazing is what is in the waters around it: it is said to be the best snorkelling in Kenya. The protected areas have a high diversity of marine life with fringing reef, channels, islands and offshore reefs. Hard and soft corals are a common feature. Green and Hawksbill turtles and seven species of dolphins are present and are both sighted by visitors on a virtually daily basis. Humpback whales are sighted regularly on their yearly migration in October/November, sometimes as early as July. This stretch of the coastline is also a birdwatchers' paradise. Every morning, visitors are bussed in from the coastal resorts and the little convoy of *dhows* string out in a line and drop anchor. The water is pure, warm and turquoise in colour, and is so salt-saturated that it is difficult to swim in initially, as it seems to suspend you. There are thousands of fish, in a dazzling array of sizes, shapes and colours, just below the surface. There are also several dive spots here, and the reefs are excellent for drift diving. The bottom is a combination of sand flats and reef outgrowths. Sting rays and turtles are commonly seen, as are parrot fish, trumpet fish, bat fish, grouper, Napoleon wrasse, clown fish and Spanish dancers. One of the better reefs is **Nyulli Reef**, which lies at 30 m and drops to over 80 m. This reef is spectacularly long and a large quantity of large pelagics as well as reef fish are found here. This is also home to a family of very large groupers up to 68 kg in size.

# Border essentials: Kenya–Tanzania

## Lunga Lunga

About 95 km south of Mombasa, Lunga Lunga is the nearest village (5 km) to the border with Tanzania and can be reached by bus from Mombasa. Formalities at the border are fairly efficient, and visas for Tanzania and Kenya can be purchased. Remember you'll need to produce a yellow fever vaccination certificate to enter Tanzania. There are informal money changers on both sides of the border, where you may need to swap a small amount of Kenyan shillings into Tanzanian shillings (or vice versa) to cover yourself until you reach the next bank. These are in Tanga and Dar es Salaam, though for the latter you'll need enough money for transport from the bus station to the city centre and bear in mind the **Scandinavian Express** bus arrives in Dar es Salaam at 1800.

**Transport** Buses between Mombasa and Dar es Salaam or Tanga go daily in both directions taking about 10 hours to Dar and four hours to Tanga.

Wasini Island falls within the Kisite-Mpunguti Marine National Park. It is a wonderful place, 1 km wide and 6 km long, totally undeveloped with no cars, no mains electricity and no running water. There is no reliable freshwater supply on the island, only rainwater. Some of the proceeds of the tourist trade have been used to build large culverts where they can store rainwater. A small village on the island includes the remains of an Arab settlement. There are also the ruins of 18th- and 19th-century houses as well as a pillar tomb with Chinese porcelain insets that have, so far, survived. The beach is worth exploring as you might well find bits of pottery and glass. Also interesting are the dead coral gardens behind the village, which you can explore from a boardwalk. They are above the sea although during the spring tide they are covered as they are linked to the sea 30 m below through a series of caverns. Some of the coral formations are said to resemble animal shapes (they call one the elephant). There's also a good variety of birds including brown-headed parrots, sunbirds, palmnut vultures and African fish eagles, and animals include monitor lizards, Sykes monkeys and wild goats.

Most people visit the park on a tour. They depart daily from all the hotels along the north coast, Mombasa and Diani Beach. Included is transport, boat tours with snorkelling and lunch at the **Wasini Island Restaurant** (better known as **Charlie Claw's**). The day begins with collection from the hotels and a transfer to Shimoni. Then guests go snorkelling by *dhow*, or glass-bottomed boats are available for those who do not wish to swim. There is no shade or protection from the burning sun and wearing a shirt/long sleeved T-shirt whilst snorkelling is a wise precaution. Masks and snorkels are available but fins are not permitted to minimize damage to the reef. Lunch at **Charlie Claw's** includes steamed crabs in ginger with claws the size of your fist, along with fresh lime and baked coconut rinds for dipping in salt, followed by barbequed fish and rice steamed in coconut, and a fresh fruit platter and *sim sim* (ginger spiced coffee with balls of sugared sesame seed). This goes down well with cold Kenyan beer, but the wise drink water first. This restaurant has been going for 25 years. There is not much of a beach on Wasini Island, as it gets covered by the incoming tide, so the afternoon is spent lazing away on day beds in the restaurant gardens, or there are optional visits to the Wasini Village, the Shimoni Caves or diving. Prices for the full day trip are around US$100 from the north coast and

US$90 from the south, although these prices come down depending on the season. All the hotels and resorts can book this excursion.

## ◉ South coast listings

*For Sleeping and Eating price codes and other relevant information, see Essentials pages 34-38.*

## ● Sleeping

Hotel prices vary with the season. Low is Apr-Jun; mid is Jul-Nov; high is Dec-Mar. There's a wide choice of accommodation along the beach and a number of all-inclusive resorts where rates include all meals, usually buffets, and some watersports, which are favoured by package holidaymakers on 1- to 2-week stays. Nevertheless most of these accept direct bookings, and out of the high season, walk-in guests. A family or group may want to consider renting a good-value cottage or villa where you can cook for yourself. If you are self-catering at Tiwi Beach, it's a good idea to pick up a few provisions at the large branch of **Nakumatt** supermarket near the Likoni Ferry in Mombasa. At Tiwi itself, there is only a small shop for basic provisions at the turn-off to the beach. The next shops are at Ukunda and Diani further south.

**Tiwi Beach** *p268, map p273*
**C Sheshe Baharini Beach Hotel**, reservations, Nairobi, T020-856 2025, www.sheshebeach.com. A fairly upmarket place with 24 cool, spacious rooms with a/c and ceiling fans, patios or balconies, some with 4-poster beds, 4 of which overlook the beach, while the rest are located in the gardens or by the swimming pool. There are 2 bars and a good restaurant for seafood, which also has a pizza oven and a fairly good selection of wine. Trips on a glass-bottomed boat can be arranged and you can walk along the beach to the mangrove forest at the mouth of the Mwachema River.
**C Tiwi Beach Resort**, T040-330 0190, www.tiwibeachresort.com. An attractive

thatched resort with 210 rooms, all with queen-size bed and 1 single bed, a/c, TV, wooden floors, arranged in 2-storey blocks with either balcony or patio. Of the 3 restaurants, the Indian one **Shere e Punjab**, is among the best on the coast. There are several bars and cafés, business centre, all watersports can be arranged, rates are half board. It has an exceptional swimming pool, 250 m long, connected by channels and slides.
**C-D Coral Cove Cottages**, T040-320 5195, www.coralcove.tiwibeach.com. 9 self-catering *bandas* that vary in price – the 6 most expensive 2-bedroom cottages have bathrooms and cost about US$100 per night. All are attractively decorated. It is a lovely location, a beautiful white-sand beach, with swaying palm trees in a private cove. A personal cook/house-help/laundry-man/ woman can be hired for an additional cost, and local people come round daily selling fish and vegetables. Excellent value.
**D Maweni and Capricho Beach Cottages**, T040-330 0012, www.mawenibeach.com. Located on a small cliff overlooking the beach, which is about 5 mins' walk away down a flight of steps, there are 26 simple but comfortable 1- to 3-bed thatched self-catering cottages, either sea-facing or in the tropical gardens where there's a small swimming pool. If you don't want to cook yourself, you can hire a cook or eat simple seafood dishes in the **Dhow Restaurant**.
**D Sand Island Cottages**, T040-330 0043, www.sandislandtiwi.com. Quiet and a little remote, 1- to 3-bed self-catering low-rise thatched cottages in a grove of palms, 30 m back from the beach, similar set-up to the Coral Cove Cottages above, in that you can hire a cook/maid at extra cost and local people do the rounds with fish and vegetables. Snorkelling equipment available.

**Diani Beach** *p269, map p270*

There are plenty of all-inclusive large beachside resorts along the Diani 'strip', and most allow non-guests (for a fee) in for the day to use the facilities such as swimming pools and sun loungers. 2 of these, south of the Diani Shopping Centre, Jadini Beach Hotel and Africana Sea Lodge, managed by **Alliance Hotels** (www.alliancehotels.com), were at the time of writing closed for a complete refurbishment. If you are self-catering at Diani, there are plenty of supermarkets and local people come round the self-catering resorts each morning with a delicious selection of fish and seafood, and sometimes fruit and vegetables, for sale strapped to the back of their bicycles. Surprisingly for this inclusive stretch of prime holiday coastline, there are also a couple of good options for backpackers and campers.

**L Alfajiri Beach Villa**, T0733-630 491, www.alfajirivillas.com. An exclusive retreat aimed at families or groups, 3 beautiful Italian-owned double-storey thatched villas with wide verandas and balconies. Each has 2-4 en suite bedrooms with additional rooms under the *makuti* roof for children, vast beds swathed in mosquito nets, decorated with exquisite objet d'art from around the world, and rim-flow pools almost on the beach. Mediterranean-influenced food with olive oils, parma ham and cheeses flown in weekly from Europe. With 20 staff, Alfajiri was listed in 2005 by *Harpers and Queen* magazine as one of the world's top 100 places to stay. Very stylish but at a price, full board rates start from US$850 per person, half for children. Included is a vehicle for excursions, butlers and trained nannies for children. Closed Apr-Jul.

**A Baobab Beach Resort & Spa**, T040-320 2623, www.baobab-beach-resort.com, on the cliff at the southern end (to get to the beach you have to climb down the steep steps). This is a large recently renovated and extended resort popular with German package holiday-makers, with almost 300 a/c rooms with views over the gardens, ocean or the 3 swimming pools. Open-air disco, several bars and restaurants, fitness centre and spa, loads of activities from bicycle hire to windsurfing. Rates are full board and meals are mostly buffets, but there is the option to eat in the à la carte restaurant for additional cost.

**A Diani Reef Beach Resort and Spa**, T040-320 2723, www.dianireef.com. Refurbished in 2005, a super luxurious and comfortable hotel with 300 m of beach frontage, all the 300 rooms are a/c with satellite TV, mini bars, internet, and safes. The hotel has a full range of facilities including a craft shop, 5 bars, 6 restaurants, 2 swimming pools, kids' club, casino and disco, floodlit tennis courts, squash courts, a diving school, golf-putting course, and landscaped lagoons with boating facilities and sun bathing islands. The spa has a gym, steam rooms, jet baths, saunas, treatments, etc.

**A Shaanti Holistic Health Retreat**, T040-320 2064, www.shaantihhr.com. This is a new Ayurvedic sanctuary with just 8 sea-facing a/c rooms with attractive stone bathrooms and patios arranged in a long white block. Facilities include various beauty treatments and massages, yoga on a large yoga terrace under thatch overlooking the beach, jacuzzi, swimming pool, open-air bubble baths, and a meditation room where you can listen to soothing music on headphones. It has a good vegetarian restaurant in a thatched wooden tower and is also the location of the **Buddha on the Beach** restaurant (see under Eating).

**B Indian Ocean Beach Club**, T040-320 3730, www.jacarandahotels.com. Moorish-style arched main building with smaller *makuta* thatched-roof buildings in secluded 10-ha grounds with old coconut and baobab trees. 100 rooms with a/c, fans, phones, 3 restaurants, 3 bars including the **Bahari Beach Bar**, which is reputed to have the best view on Diani Beach. Facilities include a 200 m swimming pool and 3 smaller pools and tennis courts, and wind-surfing, sailing, snorkelling, scuba-diving, glass-bottomed boat trips and deep-sea fishing can be arranged.

**B Leisure Lodge Beach & Golf Resort**, T040-320 3624, www.leisurelodge resort.com. Over 200 rooms in standard hotel block with balconies or in villas clustered around private pools, many restaurants, casino, several swimming pools, tennis courts, health club, dive school and windsurfing school. The 18-hole, 72-par championship golf course, home to the Diani Beach Masters, is recognized as 1 of the best golf courses in East Africa.

**B Leopard Beach Resort & Spa**, T040-320 2721, www.leopardbeachresort.com. A popular newly refurbished luxury resort, set amidst 10 ha of lush tropical gardens, with 70 standard rooms, 20 superior garden rooms, 48 sea-facing rooms, plus some private cottages and villas. Several restaurants and bars, boutiques, diving, disco and live music, and swimming pool. The luxurious spa is set in a lovely patch of peaceful forest where massages, etc. can be taken outside. Closed end Apr to mid-Jun.

**B Pinewood Village Beach Resort**, T040-3203131, www.pinewood-village.com. Excellent accommodation in 58 newly renovated rooms and suites incorporating Swahili-style and home-made furniture set in cottages on Galu Beach, almost as far south as Chale Island and therefore at one of the quietest stretches of beach. Each has a/c, minibar, balcony/terrace, and internet and the more expensive suites have additional living rooms and kitchens with their own chef for private dining. Facilities include several restaurants and bars, an attractive swimming pool, gym and spa, a dive base, tennis court and gift shop. A popular venue for weddings.

**B The Sands at Nomad**, T040-320 3643, www.thesandsatnomad.com. This used to be a standard package resort but recently went under a complete refurbishment and now markets itself as a boutique hotel. The 37 stylish rooms and suites are decorated in Swahili style, and have a/c and minibars, and some have jacuzzis and 4-poster beds. The **Nomad Beach Bar and Restaurant** is one of the most popular along the 'strip', and

there's an additional sushi bar, plus a lovely 5-m deep pool surrounded by established overhanging trees, a spa, an internet café and watersports centre. Dive operators **Diving the Crab** and **H2O Extreme** have outlets here (see under Activities and tours), hence the deepness of the pool as it's used for practice dives.

**B Southern Palms Beach Resort**, T040-320 3721, www.southernpalmskenya.com. Quality resort with over 300 rooms arranged in 4-storey blocks with thatched roofs, with a/c, DVD players, minbars, and 4-poster beds, the additional 'day-bed' can be used by children or there are adjoining rooms. Facilities include 4 restaurants, 5 bars, hair and beauty centre, internet café and there are plenty of activities and entertainment on offer. The highlight here is the vast area of interconnecting swimming pools with 2 swim-up bars.

**B-C Forest Dream**, near **Baobab Beach Resort & Spa**, T040-320 3224, www.forest dreamcottages.com. 7 large 3- to 6-bed cottages with kitchen, cook and cleaner, ideal for groups and families of 4-12 people, some have jacuzzis and a/c, all set in established gardens and each cottage is quite private, though they are some walk from the beach. Very hi-tech swimming pool with underwater music, massage jets, a nice waterslide and a waterfall that cascades from a huge rock.

**C Diani Sea Lodge and Diani Sea Resort**, T040-322 114. dianisea@africaonline.co.ke. 2 large slightly faded all-inclusive resorts next to each other on the beach popular with German visitors. The rooms in the Lodge are in cottages and have balconies or terraces and a/c, but are simple and small. Better are the a/c rooms at the Resort, which are arranged in blocks with fridge, TV, and balcony. Both have swimming pools, mini-golf, kids' playgrounds and tennis courts. Diving and watersports can be arranged.

**C Neptune Palm Beach Resort**, T040-320 2350, www.neptunehotels.com. Together with its sister hotel (below) these are the most southerly of the large hotels, more than

2 km south of **Baobab Beach Resort & Spa** and actually on Galu Beach. 60 newly refurbished en suite rooms with balconies, set in attractive large gardens, all-inclusive rates, watersports available. Shared facilities with the Paradise Village below.

**C Neptune Paradise Village**, T040-320 2350, www.neptunehotels.com. 258 rooms set in 10 ha of gardens, organized in 2-storey cottages with 4 rooms in each, 2 restaurants serving buffet meals and 2 à la carte restaurants, several bars, rates include all meals. Watersports available, and there's a kiddie's club and a very large swimming pool.

**C-D Diani Marine Divers Village**, just to the north of **Forty Thieves restaurant**, T040-320 2367, www.dianimarine.com. A small, friendly place with a combination of rooms including a simple permanent tent under thatch on a wooden deck that sleeps 4, a self-catering honeymoon cottage with additional hot-tub on the roof, and 2 4-bedroom self-catering villas where a cook can be hired. All rooms are spacious and airy, with large Swahili-style beds with mosquito nets and overhead fans. The Village offers breakfast and in the vicinity there are many restaurants. The dive centre is based here and most people stay on a dive package (see under Activities and tours).

**D Kijiji Cottages**, T040-330 0035, www.kijiji cottages.com. These are some of nicest cottages in the Diani area, well looked after, rates include a cleaner, and for an additional expense, a cook. They have 2-3 spacious en suite bedrooms, broad terraces and are set in gardens, the sea-facing ones cost a little more. There's also an attractive swimming pool.

**D-E Diani Beachalets**, T040-320 3180, www.dianibeachalets.com. A range of chalets from fully equipped houses with bathrooms and kitchens suitable for families or groups, to cheap backpackers' *bandas* with shared facilities, the larger units overlook the beach. Tennis court but no pool or restaurant so you will have to stock up before you get here, although there is a supermarket in walking distance, fishermen come round in the mornings with fresh seafood and you can

buy cold beers at reception. This is one of the cheapest options on the south coast and accommodation can work out as little as US$9 per person sharing.

**D-E Vindigo Cottages**, T040-320 2192, www.vindigocottages.com. These 7 simple self-catering *bandas*, sleeping 2-8 people work out very cheap if shared by a family or group, and the *banda* sleeping 8 is only US$100 a night. All cottages are basically equipped with bed linen, mosquito nets, crockery, cutlery and saucepans but no towels. Set in 4 ha of gardens, a little way away from any other development, giving the cottages a more secluded feel than many other places in Diani.

**E-F Diani Campsite**, T040-320 3192, www.dianicampsite.com. Located near the now defunct ruins of the former Trade Winds Hotel, this self-catering resort has been tidied up in recent years and now offers 10 simple thatched *bandas* with kitchens, and a grassy campsite with a 'camphouse' with cookers, fridges and lockers, plus clean washing facilities and tents can be hired. There's a restaurant and bar where you can order simple seafood meals and pizzas and the beach is a short stroll away.

**E-F Stilts Eco-Camp**, T0722-523 278, stilts@barboursafaris.com. On the opposite side of the main road from the Ali Barbour's Restaurant in a lush tract of forest inhabited by monkeys and bushbabies, here are a clutch of basic cheap tree *bandas*, which as the name suggests are built on stilts, with beds, mosquito nets and balconies and a campsite, all with shared toilets and showers with solar-heated water. There's a pub and restaurant, which has day beds for lazing around, and the beach is a 5-min walk away.

## Shimba Hills National Reserve *p271*

**B Shimba Lodge**, reservations **Aberdare Safari Hotels**, T040-222 9608, www.aberdaresafarihotels.com. A well-designed timber lodge overlooking a waterhole illuminated at night for viewing, which offers similar 'cabin' accommodation

to that of Treetops in the Aberdares National Park, with small wooden rooms with shared bathrooms and verandas looking straight into the forest. A 100-m boardwalk has been constructed at tree level giving good views of the forest canopy and you can walk to the Sheldrick's Falls where there is a natural pool for swimming. The dining room is open air, there is a pleasant bar and several secluded decks for game viewing well into the night. There's an excellent opportunity to spot elephant, forest antelope, maybe leopard and bushbaby, and optional early-morning game drives into the park offer the opportunity to see Shimba's famous Sable antelope. Half-board rates are in the region of US$240 for a double, children under 5 are not permitted. Day and overnight excursions can be arranged through the Mombasa tour operators or from the coastal resorts.
**D-E Sable Bandas**, Kenya Wildlife Service, Nairobi, T020-600 800, www.kws.org. Located 3 km from the main gate to the reserve, this has 4 *bandas* with 2 double beds in each with linen and towels, shared showers and toilets, solar power, shared kitchen with gas cooker and tap (not drinking) water. There's also a well-maintained and peaceful campsite here with excellent views over the surrounding forested areas. Drinking water, firewood and food must be brought; US$35 per person in the *bandas* and US$10 per person camping.

## Mwaluganje Elephant Sanctuary
**B Travellers Mwaluganje Elephant Camp**, reservations through the **Traveller's Beach Hotel & Club** in Bamburi on Mombasa's north coast, T041-548 5121, www.travellers beach.com. Set on a small hill overlooking a waterhole in the Elephant Sanctuary, there are 20 tents, each with 2 beds, though there is room for a 3rd bed to be added, bathroom and private veranda with views over a well-used elephant trail. Again, excursions here are usually arranged from Mombasa and the coastal resorts and include transfers, entry fees, meals and game drives.

## Chale Island *p272, map p273*
**L The Sands at Chale Island**, T040-3330 0269, www.thesandsatchaleisland.com. Luxury all-inclusive resort, with 55 rooms centred around a beautiful white crescent-shaped sandy beach, comprising roomy and elegant tented bungalows, or apartments and penthouses in round multi-storey blocks topped with thatch, and a couple of water suites that are actually built over the ocean on stilts and reached by boardwalks, all furnished with African/Arabic antiques. The 2 restaurants offer local and international cuisine, diving and deep-sea fishing are on offer and there's a swimming pool, spa and gym.

## Msambweni *p273, map p273*
**L Funzi Keys**, Funzi Island, south of Msambweni, T0733-900 446, www.thefunzi keys.com. Very exclusive tented camp situated on a beautifully secluded island, furnished to a very high standard. 10 spacious cottages set along the high-water line and constructed of stone and thatch with large netted windows and hand-carved king-sized 4-poster beds, a perfect honeymoon venue. Facilities for many watersports are available and included in the price, as are all meals, drinks (except champagne) and transport. Rates are US$240-690 per person depending on season. This is a very special place and the management report that some guests have been in tears on departure. Closed Apr-Jul.
**A Msambweni Beach House**, on Msambweni Beach, reservations Nairobi, T020-357 7093, www.msambweni-house.com. Set in a commanding position on a small cliff with great ocean views, this is a super luxury family-run establishment with 6 spacious rooms in the main house with lovely all-white decor and Swahili furniture, in front of which is a stunning 25-m infinity swimming pool, plus 2 private villas with their own pool, jacuzzi cook and butler. Excellent cuisine including some French and Belgium dishes as well as seafood.

**Shimoni** *p273, map p273*

**B Pemba Channel Lodge and Fishing Club**, T0722-205 020, www.pembachannel lodge.com, www.pembachannel.com. Just 6 simple white *bandas* set in tropical gardens, with many trees indigenous to the Shimoni area. Each *banda* has a small veranda – all with sea views and there's a pool. The Clubhouse has an attractive, homely lounge filled with wicker sofas and overstuffed cushions, marlin trophies and fishing photos adorn the walls. There is a great camaraderie amongst the fishermen around the very 'Hemingway-esque' bar at the end of the day.

**C Betty's Camp**, near the jetty, T0722-434 709, www.bettys-camp.com. A small simple and a little over-priced place with no beach as such but overlooking the ocean with either tented rooms under thatch with own shower/toilet or en suite rooms within the main house, can accommodate 10-12 people in total, swimming pool, poolside terrace restaurant and bar open to all with a good range of seafood, can arrange fishing and trips to Wasini Island.

**C Shimoni Reef Lodge**, reservations, Mombasa, T041-471 771, www.shimonireef lodge.com. Wonderful location, overlooking Wasini Island, high standards catering almost exclusively to keen anglers, 10 open-plan cottages with ocean views and private verandas, each is on 2 levels and sleeps 4 people. There is a sea water swimming pool made up of multi levels that is good for kids, an open-air terrace restaurant overlooking the ocean where seafood is a speciality, and fishing, diving and snorkelling are on offer.

**C-D Mwazaro Mangrove Lodge**, T0722-711 476 (mob), www.keniabeach.de. About 8 km north of Shimoni, there is a sign to Mwazaro Beach, turn right there and the camp is another 1 km. Run by a friendly German man Hans, accommodation is in either thatched *bandas* on the beach with sand floors and lit by hurricane lamps, or en suite rooms in the main coral-rag house with solar and wind-powered electricity. The restaurant serves excellent affordable Swahili-style food,

there's a comfy lounge and bar where you can play chess or backgammon, and tea is served all day. A guide will take you on an interactive tour to a local fishing village or on a boat tour to a nearby mangrove forest. You can also negotiate to camp here. A lovely remote, laid-back spot and a far cry from the larger holiday resorts.

**D Shimoni Gardens**, 2 km west of the village, T0727-247 100, www.shimoni gardens.com. A quiet spot, not quite on the beach but not far away nestled in a patch of jungley forest, there are 16 small, clean en suite whitewashed thatched cottages, and 6 simple rooms built of reed and thatch with shared facilities, set in nice gardens full of palms and flowering shrubs. There's a small restaurant for basic meals and beers, and they run their own *dhows* to Wasini Island for the snorkelling excursion.

## 🍴 Eating

**Diani Beach** *p269, map p270*
Most of the large resorts have buffet meals, particularly for all-inclusive guests, and although these vary in quality, they are usually of a fairly high standard. Some also have individual specialist restaurants, which are also open to non-guests. The best choice is probably in the **Leisure Lodge Beach & Golf Resort**, which has both the upmarket Cascada's Mediterranean restaurant and the Fisherman's Cove seafood restaurant, and the **Diani Reef Beach Resort & Spa**, which has the Sake Oriental Japanese restaurant and the very good Fins, which again specializes in seafood. There are also a number of individual places along the Diani 'strip'. All offer very good fish and seafood and you can rely on it being very fresh. If you are on holiday on the south coast and have the cash to splash, ensure you visit both the **Tamarind** in Mombasa (page260) and **Ali Barbour's** (below).

**Ali Barbour's**, just north of the Diani Shopping Centre, T040-320 2033. Open daily from 1900. Diani's most popular restaurant, which is set in an underground cave that has various chambers that go 10 m below ground level, a stone floor has been fitted and a sliding roof that comes across if the weather is bad. Lights have been set in niches in the walls and it's very atmospheric. It does excellent seafood including an expensive but expansive platter, as well as French food. If staying on Diani Beach they will provide free transport. A very unique experience and most people who holiday in Diani visit. Casual, but beachwear is not permitted.

**♥♥♥ Buddha on the Beach**, at **The Shaanti Holistic Health Retreat**, T040-320 2064, www.shaantihhr.com. Daily 1200-1400, 1800-2300. A fairly new seafood restaurant with a small but excellent menu of inventive dishes such as lobster medallions grilled in honey and soy sauce, whole crab steamed in chilli and ginger, and Cajun blackened red snapper. There's an extensive winelist and tables are set in an attractive whitewashed thatched building overlooking the beach. On Fri and Sat 1800-2000, they run an oyster bar on the beach and serve fresh Kilifi oysters with a glass of wine.

**♥♥♥ Forty Thieves**, next door to **Ali Barbour's**, and under the same management, T040-320 3003. Daily 0900-late. Lively bar and restaurant open all day from breakfast serving good food and snacks, the steamed crab and Swahili prawns with coconut rice are especially good and the comfortable lounge-style tables are set under thatch right next to the beach where you can kick off your shoes in the sand. It's also a popular night spot and meeting place for many of the local residents who affectionately call it 'Forties', with pool tables, live entertainment, satellite TV, and discos on Wed, Fri and Sat nights. Also good live music and buffet lunch on a Sun. Provides free transport in the evening.

**♥♥♥ Nomads Beach Bar & Restaurant**, at **The Sands at Nomads**, T040-320 3643. Open 0900-late. Right on the beach on wooden decks and under canvas with good service and atmosphere. It does a very popular Sun buffet lunch with live jazz, which is good

value, and the à la carte menu features pizzas, excellent and imaginative pastas, risottos, seafood and grills.

**♥♥♥ Shan-e-Punjab**, Diani Complex Shopping Centre, opposite **Diani Reef Beach Resort & Spa**, T040-320 2116. Daily 1000-2400. Good-value Indian dishes, specializes in Punjab and tandoori cuisine, tikka and masala with a full range of seafood, more expensive continental dishes available, open-air beer garden and cocktail menu, provides free transport from the hotels.

**♥♥ Bull Steak House**, behind the petrol station just north of the **Diani Beach Shopping Centre**. Daily 1200-late. Informal restaurant and bar under a conical thatched roof, plus rooftop terrace, popular with Germans for the very large steaks from 250 gram fillets to 1 kg T-bones, good cuts of prime Angus beef, and also offers a German bratwurst that's a metre long!

**♥♥ Galaxy**, opposite **Diani Reef Beach Resort & Spa**, T040-300 018. Daily 1100-1430, 1800-2300. Part of a chain that also has branches in Mombasa and Bamburi Beach, this offers tasty Chinese cuisine, a small menu but with quality items such as grilled lobster, roast duck, and ginger crab, and is set on a nice open terrace surrounded by lush tropical gardens. Offers free pick-ups from the hotels.

**♥♥ Sundowner**, a 5-min walk from the **Diani Beach Chalets**, T040-320 2138. Serves excellent Kenyan food and local beers at low prices, one of the best-value places to eat, curries, grilled and fried fish, very good English breakfasts, sometimes has seafood such as lobster, simple decor in outside thatched bar and restaurant but nice atmosphere.

**♥ African Pot**, near the **Barclay's Bank Shopping Centre**, T040-320 3890. Daily 1000-late. Good value, tasty local food, served in the traditional way in (as the name suggests) big earthenware pots, such as *nyama choma* (charcoaled meat), masala curries, *chipati*, *matoke*, *ugali* and pilau rice, all washed down with cold Tusker beer. Good place for a group to share dishes

**Hollywood**, Ukunda opposite the **Total** petrol station, T040-320 2562. Daily 0900-2300. A rather odd combination of tasty Kenyan and German food at good prices, including chicken stew, fish and chips and the like, and German items like bratwurst and schnitzel, plus fresh juices (the mango is delicious), beer and some wines. Tables are set on a pleasant terrace bedecked with plants.

## Bars, clubs and entertainment

**Diani Beach** *p269, map p270*
Most of the large resorts put on some kind of evening entertainment for guests, which in Kenya is referred to as 'animation' and is usually a troupe of male dancers putting on a display of acrobatics (at which Kenyans seem to be uncannily good), or perhaps traditional drumming or Masai dancing. Almost all the resorts have nightclubs and many have discos on the beach, which are of varying quality and in the family resorts usually feature lots of children running around. Along the Diani Beach Rd there are also a couple of independent nightclubs. **Shakatak**, www.shakatak-kenya.com, on the opposite side of the road and just south of Ali Barbour's, is the biggest is nightclub, which is German-run with a restaurant and beer garden. It's very popular, expect to queue to get in during high season, with a large dance floor and floor shows that start daily at 2100, and although it's a little seedy and prostitutes abound, it can be a lot of fun. The website (which is in German) very generously explains that in Kenya, men over 40 go to nightclubs! They make their ice from mineral water and there are plenty of taxis outside.

Probably the nicest place to go dancing is **Forty Thieves**, next door to **Ali Barbour's** (see under Eating), which has pool tables, live entertainment, satellite TV, and on Wed, Fri and Sat nights the restaurant tables are pushed back for a disco.

There's a **Casino**, located in the **Leisure Lodge Beach & Golf Resort**, which is open

daily from 1200-0300 and has many slot machines, a few gaming tables and a bar.

## Shopping

**Diani Beach** *p269, map p270*
**Curios**
There are many curio stalls dotted along Diani Beach Rd, and they are usually grouped near the entrance to the resorts. Additionally 'beach boys' wander around selling items, who you'll have to be assertive with to leave you alone as they can be fairly aggressive with their sales tactics. There are also several upmarket curio shops in the shopping centres (see below).

**Food**
If you are self-catering it is worth buying most of your supplies in Mombasa where it is cheaper. Try the large **Nakumatt** supermarket just near the Likoni Ferry; it sells everything imaginable. There are a number of places closer to the beach. At the small village of **Ukunda** on the main road at the Diani turn-off, where you can get most things from stalls or small local shops. On Diani Beach Rd itself, there are now 4 shopping centres: opposite Diani Reef Beach Resort and Spa is **Diani Complex**, the smallest of the 4, while further south the **Barclays Bank Shopping Centre** is next to Barclays Bank and has a small supermarket, a shop selling booze, an internet café and a couple of top-end curio shops that among other items sell *kikoys* and the beautiful beaded leather sandals that are made on the coast. **Diani Shopping Centre** and **Diani Beach Shopping Centre** are close to each other to the north of Diani Beach post office. Unfortunately the latter was almost destroyed in a fire in late 2007, so it remains to be seen if it will re-open again. The **Muthaiga Mini Market** in Diani Shopping Centre is a very well-stocked supermarket with many chilled items and imported goods and there is also a shop here for the Kikoy Company. There's another good supermarket just up from the Diani Beachalets that also

sells booze. For fresh fruit, vegetables and fish you will be able to buy off the vendors who come round all the self-catering places with their stock on their bicycles.

## 🔺 Activities and tours

**Diani Beach** *p269, map p270*
Most of the resorts will help organize *dhow* and glass-bottomed boat trips, safaris and diving.

### Deep-sea fishing
Expect to pay in the region of US$600-700 per boat per day including all equipment for 4-6 people, and trips go out to the Pemba Channel off-shore from Shimoni (see page 285).
**Blue Marlin Fishing Club**, to the south of the beach close to the Neptune hotels, T040-320 2799, www.bluemarlinfishingclub.com.
**Fisherman's Paradise**, also near the Neptune hotels, T0728-705 447, www.fishermansparadise-kenya.nl.

### Golf
**Leisure Lodge Beach & Golf Resort**,
T040-320 3624, www.golfinginkenya.com. This attractive 18-hole championship course is open to all guests of Diani Beach hotels and resorts. Expect to pay in the region of US$70 for 18 holes with club hire and for keen golfers, there are weekly packages. The par 72 course has 85 bunkers and a large lake which is home to a resident crocodile who is inexplicably named Colin, and golfers may spot monkeys around the course. There's a club bar and restaurant, lessons available in English, German or Italian, and caddies and golf carts can be hired. To play the course men must have a handicap of at least 28 and ladies 36, or a playing certificate from a recognized club. Beginners welcome on the driving range. The course is home to the Diani Beach Masters.

### Tour operators
There are several tour agencies, mainly in and around the shopping centres, otherwise all the large resorts organize local tours and activities. The popular day trip for snorkelling by *dhow* in Kisite-Mpunguti Marine National Park and lunch on Wasini Island (see page 274) includes transport to and from the north beach and south beach hotels, snorkelling equipment, marine reserve entrance fees, soft drinks, beer, wine and lunch. The times of pick-ups vary depending on how far away you are, but they are generally fairly early to get to the *dhows* at Shimoni by around 0900.
**Adventure Tours & Safaris**, Barclays Bank Shopping Centre, T040-320 3759, www.kenya-wildlife-safaris.com. Day trips plus overnight and longer to Tsavo and other parks.
**DM Tours & Safaris**, Diani Shopping Centre, T040-320 4015, www.dmtours.net. Day tours, and longer safaris including a 3-day Tsavo and Amboseli combination.
**Malibu Tours & Safaris**, Diani Shopping Centre, T040-320 3164. A large fleet of taxis and other vehicles and can arrange day trips and safaris.
**Pilli Pipa Dhow Safaris**, Colliers Centre, near Barclays Bank Shopping Centre, T040-320 3599, www.pillipipa.com. Operates the excursion to Wasini and also offers diving.
**The Diani Beach Safari Company**, Diani Beach Shopping Centre, T040-320 4012, www.dianitours.com. Wasini Island, Mombasa, city tours, Shimba Hills day trips and overnight stays to Tsavo.
**Wasini Island Restaurant**, T040-320 2331, www.wasini-island.com. This company owns the famous Charlie Claw's restaurant on Wasini Island, and offers that day trip as well as diving.

### Watersports
There is a wealth of watersports on offer along the beach. With warm water and cross- and side-shore winds, Diani has good conditions for wind- and kitesurfing along the wide uncrowded beach and the flat water inside the reef is perfect for beginners. Windsurfers cost around US$50 for a half a day, while kitesurfing gear costs in the region

of US$90 per half day, and hourly and daily instruction for both is available. Snorkelling of course can be done by simply walking into the sea, or from *dhows*. There are over 30 dive sites within a 20-25 minute boat trip from Diani Beach, which with 15-30 m depths, offer excellent visibility and a diverse amount of marine life. There are also 2 wrecks for experienced divers to explore – the *HMS Hildasay* sank in 1945, while the *MV Funguro* sank in 2002 and both lie at a depth of just over 20 m. Expect to pay in the region of US$55 for an individual dive and US$470 for a 4-5 day PADI Open Water course. As well as below, Pilli Pipa Dhow Safaris and Wasini Island Restaurant above also offer diving.

**Aqualand**, Pinewood Village, T040-320 2720, www.southerncrossscuba.com. Watersports centre at Galu Beach offering kite- and windsurfing courses, sailing, kayaking, jet-skiing, banana boats, diving and snorkelling. A very professional company with a whole range of activities on offer and now have other branches known as **Ocean**, in the Diani Reef Beach Resort & Spa, and **Sx Scuba**, in the Indian Ocean Beach Club. Aqualand is also the base for the **East African Whale Shark Trust** (www.giantsharks.org). There has recently been an increase of whale shark numbers in Kenyan waters and the trust was established in 2005 to raise awareness about protection of whale sharks, and is involved in collecting and analyzing data on the local whale shark population.

**Barakuda Diving**, www.barakuda.50megs. com. Has a dive centre at **Tiwi Beach Resort** and at some of the resorts north of Mombasa.

**Diani Marine**, T040-320 2367, www.diani marine.com. A well-established operator with over 25 years' experience at Diani with several dive packages and also a unique 'bubble maker', which is a special pool for introductory dives for children over 8. Clients can stay in the Diver's Village (see under Sleeping).

**Diving The Crab**, at **The Sands at Nomad**, T040-320 3400, www.divingthecrab.com. Established operator with over 20 years' experience on the Kenya coast with a very comprehensive website, has over 150 sets of dive equipment and cylinders, 8 custom-built dive boats, and 10 PADI instructors.

**H2O Extreme**, offices at **Leisure Lodge Golf & Beach Resort**, **Leopard Beach Resort & Spa**, and **The Sands at Nomad**, T0721-495 876, www.h2o-extreme.com. A professionally run wind- and kitesurfing school that rents out equipment to experienced surfers. Also hires out pedalos and sea kayaks.

### Shimoni *p273, map p273*

**Pemba Big Game Fishing Club**, T0722-205 020, www.pembachannel.com. Can arrange fishing in the Pemba Channel and has 3 fully equipped boats, and liveaboard, which can sleep up to 10 people and frequently does a multi-day run to Pemba Island in Tanzania. The fishing club has a reputation as Africa's premier marlin destination and has attracted many illustrious guests.

**Sea Adventures**, reservations Mombasa, T020-217 0208, www.bigame.com. Run by experienced skippers Pat and Simon Hemphill, this offers deep-sea fishing charters into the Pemba Channel plus 4- to 8-day safaris to Pemba Island for small groups of up to 4 people. It also takes children over 8 years old and Simon's son and daughter both caught their first marlin under the age of 11.

## ⊖ Transport

### Diani Beach *p269, map p270*
**Air**

A small airfield at Ukunda is used for small planes – usually charters for safaris. **Mombasa Air Safari** (see page 265) will touch down here on request to pick up passengers for its flights between the coast and the parks.

### Bus and matatus

For **Diani** by *matatu* you have to change at Ukunda village. The fare from Likoni to **Ukunda** costs about US$1 and from from Ukunda to Diani US$0.40. There is also a large fleet of brightly coloured *tuk-tuks* operating between Ukunda and all along the beach road that you simply flag down, if the drivers themselves do not drive right up to you. These cost little more than a US$1 for any journey and take up to 3 people. There used to be a number of places along the beach to hire cars, but the *tuk-tuks* have replaced the need for car hire. Rather amusingly the Diani *tuk-tuks* have wobbly arms and hands that wave at you as they drive along and some even have giant hats on their ro

## ❶ Directory

**Diani Beach** *p269, map p270*
**Banks** All the banks have ATMs and foreign-exchange facilities. **Kenya** Commercial Bank, main road in Ukunda, **Barclays Bank of Kenya**, Diani Beach, at the head of the road to Ukunda. **Diani Forex Bureau**, in a white building near Diani Beachalets. **Internet** Good but expensive café in the **Barclays Bank Shopping Centre** and many of the hotels offer access. **Medical services** Diani **Beach Hospital**, south of **Diani Complex Shopping Centre**, T040-320 2435, www.dianibeachhospital.com. This is a private, modern hospital and 24-hr pharmacy with very high standards and is used to dealing with European patients. Since early 2008, it has been offering a growing list of cosmetic procedures to holiday-makers. **Post office** Opposite the ruins of the **Trade Winds Hotel**.

# North coast

*There is a whole string of beaches along the north coast including Nyali, Kenyatta, Bamburi and Shanzu, with lots of hotels on the seashore immediately north of Mombasa. North of Mtwapa Creek are Kikambala and Vipingo beaches. The major attractions of Watamu Marine Park, Malindi and Lamu are further north. At these latter places there is much more choice for the budget traveller and anyone who wants to avoid the package tours. There are major historical sites at Kilifi, Malindi and Lamu. The north coast is also the location of the Malindi Marine Biosphere Reserve. This strip along the coast is 30 km long and 5 km wide and was gazetted in 1968, and covers an area of 213 sq km. It lies about 80 km north of Mombasa, and includes the Malindi Marine Park, the Watamu Marine Park and Mida Creek. The vegetation includes mangrove, palms, marine plants and various forms of algae that are home to crabs, corals, molluscs, cowrie and marine worms. Coral viewing is popular here, as are boat trips and watersports.* ▸▸ *For listings, see pages 304-318.*

## Mombasa to Kilifi ●◗⨍⋔▲◖ ▸▸ *pp304-318.*

### Nyali, Kenyatta and Bamburi beaches → *Colour map 2, C2. Phone code: 041.*

Nyali, Kenyatta and Bamburi beaches are well developed and there are lots of hotels. Most of them cater for package tours from Europe and usually each hotel caters for a particular nationality. None of them are cheap. All have facilities such as swimming pools, tennis courts, watersports and they tend to look after their guests very well, organizing all sorts of activities and trips. Here the coast is lined with pristine palm-fringed beaches and the offshore reefs. Both outer and inner reef walls offer world-class diving with spectacular coral gardens and drop-offs, and Kenya's best wreck diving on the *MV Dania* (see box, page 290).

**Mombasa Marine National Park** (10 sq km) was established in 1986 for the protection of the area's coral reefs. It can be accessed by snorkelling or glass-bottomed boat trips from the resorts along the beaches and there are also good diving sites.

**Mamba Village** ⓘ *Links Rd, Nyali, behind Nyali Beach and the hotels, US$9.50, children US$5, daily 0800-1830, feeding is at 1700,* is the biggest crocodile farm in Kenya and is a habitat for over 10,000 crocodiles of all ages and sizes from newborns to huge fully grown adults. A film explains some of the conservation efforts as well as the financial side of the venture. However it's fairly run down now and the pools where the crocodiles live are rather dank and the display of 'deformed' crocodiles is not a pleasant sight. Of more interest is the small adjacent **Botanical Garden** and **Aquarium**.

**Wild Waters** ⓘ *Links Rd, Nyali, Next to the Mamba Village, T041-470 408, www.wildwaterskenya.com, US$22, children (under 18) US$10, Mon-Fri 1100-2200, Sat-Sun 1000-2200, water slides close at 1800,* a new water park, is set in manicured gardens and features 11 slides for adults, another five for children, and each is named after a Kenyan river. A 300-m 'lazy river' encircles the whole complex and other facilities include fairground rides, bouncy castles, a video game arcade and a food court. There are also a couple of bars here that stay open late.

**Bombolulu Workshops and Cultural Centre** ⓘ *about 4 km north of Nyali Bridge on the Malindi road, T041-447 4077, US$6.50, Mon-Sat 0800-1700, the shop stays open until 1800,* is where you might want to do some souvenir shopping and there's a selection of wooden carvings, leather products, textiles and jewellery. Founded in 1969, the crafts are produced by a team of 150 local handicapped people (mostly polio victims) and are generally of reasonable quality and good value. There is also a cultural centre with eight traditional homesteads from different ethnic groups, where guides demonstrate traditional dance, music and theatre. You can do a tour of the workshops and Swahili food is available in the Ziga restaurant.

### Haller Wildlife Park
ⓘ *8 km north of Nyali Bridge on the Malindi Rd, T041-548 5901, daily 0800-1700, adults US$9, children US$4.50.*

This park started out life as the Bamburi cement factory, which began quarrying coral to make lime for the cement around Mombasa in the 1950s. When quarrying stopped in 1971 an effort was made to reclaim the land by reforestation and a nature trail was created. The reclamation scheme was ahead of its time and it attracted the attention of ecologists from all over the world. The nature park has been renamed Haller Wildlife Park after the Swiss agronomist who turned the lunar quarry landscape into luxuriant tropical forest. Part of the process included the introduction of hundreds of thousands of millipedes that helped convert the infertile sand into soil, able to support the forest in which the centre is now situated.

There are all manner of things to do and see including a fish farm producing tilapia, a luxuriant palm garden, 3.6 km of forest trails with exercise points and equipment along which you can either walk, jog or cycle, a crocodile farm, a butterfly pavilion and a reptile house. Visitors have the unique opportunity of close-up contact with the variety of animal species, such as various antelope, monkeys, warthog, giant tortoises and lots of different birds. Tours are in English, French, German, Italian or Swahili. You can watch the hippos being fed daily at 1600, and can feed a number of Rothschild giraffes from an elevated

# North coast

**Sleeping**
Bahari Beach **1**
Boko Boko **4**
Coral Beach **3**
Fisherman's Leisure Inn **1**
Flamingo Beach **3**
Indiana Beach Apartment **2**
Kenya Bay **2**
Le Soleil Beach Club **5**
Mombasa Beach **1**
Neptune Beach Resort **2**
Nyali Beach **1**
Reef Hotel Kenya **1**
Serena Beach & Spa **3**
Severin Sea Lodge **2**
Shanzu Beach & Paradise Beach **3**
Sun n' Sand Beach Resort **5**
Traveller's Beach & Club **2**
Vasco de Gama **3**
Voyager Beach Resort **1**

**Eating**
Gold Chopsticks **4**
Il Covo **2**
Moorings Floating Seafood Restaurant **1**
Porini Seychellois **3**
Trekkers **9**
Yul's **2**

**Bars & clubs**
Casaurina Nomad **6**
Castaways **5**
Pirates Beach **7**
Tembo Disco **8**

# Footprint Mini Atlas
# **Kenya**

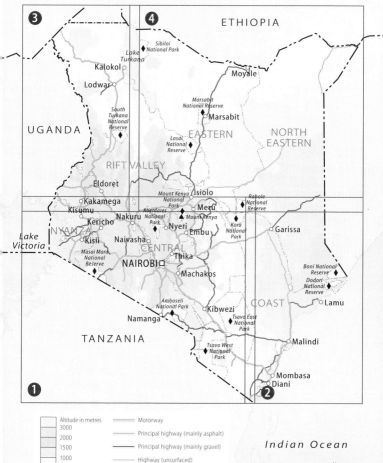

**❸** **❹** ETHIOPIA

Sibiloi
National Park ◆

Lake
Turkana

Kalokol ○

Lodwar ○                                    Moyale ○

South
Turkana
National
Reserve ◆                    Marsabit
National Reserve ◆
○ Marsabit

UGANDA                        EASTERN                    NORTH
EASTERN

Losai
National
Reserve ◆

RIFT VALLEY

Eldoret ○

Mount Kenya ○ Isiolo          Rahole
○ Kakamega   National          National
Park  ○ Meru          Reserve ◆
Kisumu ○          Aberdares ▲
Kericho ○  Nakuru ○ National  Mount Kenya          Garissa ○
NYANZA          Park ○ Nyeri          Kora
Kisii ○  Naivasha ○          ○ Embu          National
Park ◆
Masai Mara          CENTRAL
National          Thika ○
Reserve ◆          NAIROBI ☐                              Boni National
Reserve ◆
○ Machakos                              Dodori
National
Reserve ◆
Amboseli                                          COAST          ○ Lamu
National Park ◆  ○ Kibwezi
Namanga ○          Tsavo East
National
Park

TANZANIA                     Tsavo West ◆          ○ Malindi
National
Park

○ Mombasa
**❶**                              ○ Diani
**❷**

Lake
Victoria

---

Altitude in metres
3000
2000
1500
1000
500
200
100
0

Neighbouring
country

═══ Motorway

───── Principal highway (mainly asphalt)

───── Principal highway (mainly gravel)

----- Highway (unsurfaced)

─·─·─ Provincial road (partly-surfaced)

········ Secondary road, track

───── Railway

*Indian Ocean*

N

100 km
100 miles

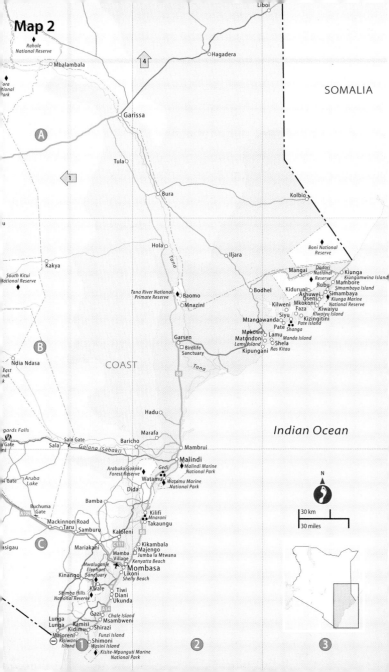

# Map 2

Rahole National Reserve

...ora National Park

Mbalambala

Liboi

Hagadera

**SOMALIA**

Garissa

○ A

Tula

← 1

Bura

Kolbio

u

Hola

Iljara

Boni National Reserve

Kakya

*Tana*

Mangai

Dadori National Reserve

Kiunga
Kiungamwina Island

South Kitui National Reserve

Tana River National Primate Reserve

Baomo

Mnazini

Bodhei

Kidurini

Rubu

Mambore

Simambaya Island

Ashuwei

Simambaya

Oseni

Kiunga Marine National Reserve

Kilweni

Mkokoni

Kiwaiyu

Siyu

Faza

Kiwaiyu Island

○ B

Ndia Ndasa

East ...nal ...k

**COAST**

Garsen

Birdlife Sanctuary

*Tana*

Mtangawanda

Pate

Kizingitini

Pate Island

Shanga

Mokowe

Matondoni

Lamu

Lamu Island

Manda Island

Shela

Kipungani

Ras Kitau

Hadu

Marafa

*Indian Ocean*

...gards Falls

...Gate

Sala Gate

Sala

*Galana (Sabaki)*

Baricho

Mambrui

...ni

Gedi

Malindi

Malindi Marine National Park

...i Gate

Aruba Lake

Arabuko-Sokoke Forest Reserve

Watamu

Watamu Marine National Park

Buchuma Gate

Dida

Bamba

Mackinnon Road

Taru

Samburu

Kilifi

Mnarani

Takaungu

N

...sigau

○ C

Mariakani

Kaloleni

Kikambala

Majengo

Jumba la Mtwana

30 km

30 miles

Mamba Village

Kenyatta Beach

Kinango

Mwaluganje Elephant Sanctuary

Mombasa

Likoni

Shelly Beach

Kwale

Tiwi

Diani

Ukunda

Shimba Hills National Reserve

Lunga Lunga

Gazi

Chale Island

Kinondo

Kidimu

Msambweni

Majoreni

Shirazi

Kisiwani

Shimoni

Funzi Island

○ 1

Wasini Island

○ 2

○ 3

Kisite-Mpunguti Marine National Park

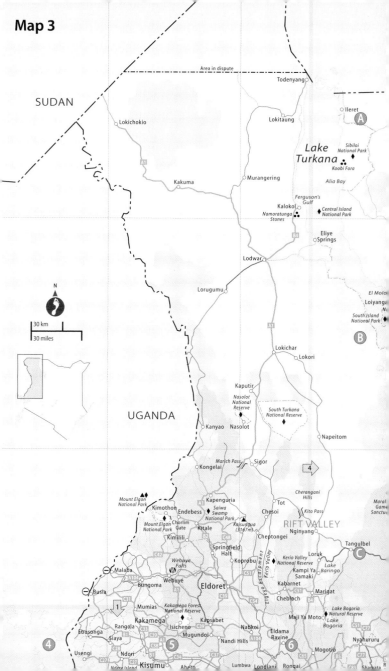

**Map 3**

SUDAN

*Area in dispute*

Todenyang

Lokichokio

Lokitaung

Ileret

**A**

*Lake Turkana*

Sibiloi National Park

Koobi Fora

Kakuma

Murangering

Alia Bay

Ferguson's Gulf

Kalokol

Central Island National Park

Namoratunga Stones

Eliye Springs

Lodwar

Lorugumu

El Molo

Loiyanga

South Island National Park

**B**

Lokichar

Lokori

Kaputir

Nasolot National Reserve

South Turkana National Reserve

Napeitom

**UGANDA**

Kanyao

Nasolot

Marich Pass

Sigor

4

Kongelai

Cherangani Hills

Maral Game Sanctu

Mount Elgon National Park

Kapenguria

Saiwa Swamp National Park

Tot

Chesoi

Kito Pass

**RIFT VALLEY**

Kimothon

Endebess

Chorlim Gate

Kaisuggua (3167m)

Nginyang

Tangulbel

**C**

Mount Elgon National Park

Kitale

Cheptongei

Kimilili

Springfield Halt

Koprobu

Kerio Valley National Reserve

Loruk

Lake Baringo

Kampi Ya Samaki

Malaba

Webuye Falls

Kabarnet

Busia

Bungoma

Webuye

**Eldoret**

Nabkoi

Chebloch

Marigat

Maji Ya Moto

Lake Bogoria Natural Reserve

Lake Bogoria

Mumias

Kakamega Forest National Reserve

Kapsabet

**4**

Ebusonga

Rangala

**1**

Kakamega

Isicheno

Mugundoi

Nandi Hills

Eldama Ravine

**6**

Mogotio

Nyahururu

Siaya

Ndori

**5**

Ahero

Lumbwa

Longlani

Rongai

Usengi

*Ndere Island*

**Kisumu**

30 km

30 miles

N

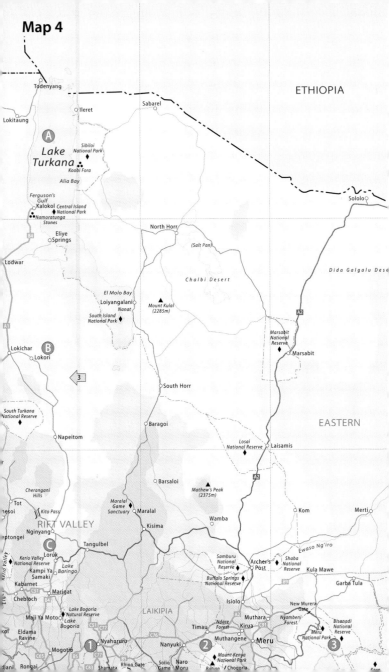

# Map 4

ETHIOPIA

Todenyang

Lokitaung

Ileret

Sabarel

Ⓐ
Lake
Turkana

Sibiloi
National Park
Koobi Fora

Sololo

Alia Bay

Ferguson's
Gulf
Kalokol    Central Island
National Park
Namoratunga
Stones

North Horr

*(Salt Pan)*

*Dida Galgalu Dese*

B4

Eliye
Springs

*Chalbi Desert*

Lodwar

El Molo Bay
Loiyangalani
Nanat

Mount Kulal
(2285m)

South Island
National Park

A2

A1

Marsabit
National
Reserve

Lokichar    Ⓑ
Lokori

Marsabit

3

South Horr

EASTERN

South Turkana
National Reserve

Baragoi

Napeitom

Losai
National Reserve

Laisamis

Cherangani
Hills

Kito Pass

Barsaloi

Mathew's Peak
(2375m)

A2

nesoi

Tot

RIFT VALLEY

Maralal
Game
Sanctuary    Maralal

Kisima

Wamba

Kom

Merti

ptongei

Nginyang    Ⓒ
Loruk

Tangulbel

Ewaso Ng'iro

*Kerio Valley*
Kerio Valley
National Reserve
Kampi Ya
Samaki

Lake
Baringo

Samburu
National
Reserve

Archer's
Post

Shaba
National
Reserve

Kula Mawe

Kabarnet

Marigat

Buffalo Springs
National Reserve

Chebloch

Lake Bogoria
Natural Reserve

Isiolo

Garba Tula

Maji Ya Moto

Lake
Bogoria

New Murera
Gate

Eldama
Ravine

Mogotio

C51  C7

Nyahururu

Timau

Muthara

Kirua

Ndare
Forest

Nyambeni
Forest

Bisanadi
National
Reserve

LAIKIPIA

Muthangene

Meru

Meru
National Park

kol

Rongai

C63

B5

⓵
Shamata

Rhino Gate

Nanyuki

⓶
Muthangene

Naro
Moru

Solio
Game

Mount Kenya
National Park

C91

⓷

Eldani

Njani

Mogotio

Naro Moru

Batian  /Chogoria

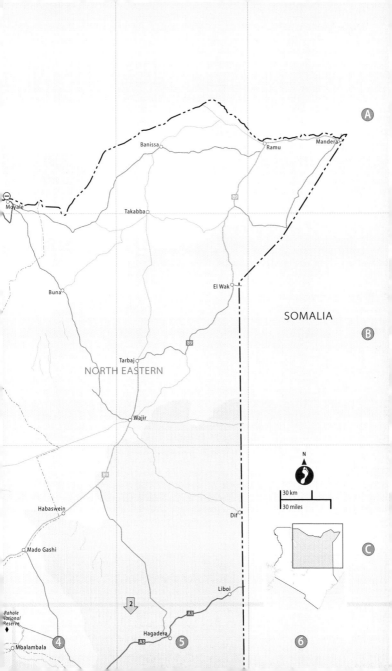

# Index

## Owen and Mzee

One of the newer residents of the Haller Wildlife Park is Owen the hippo. Just before Christmas in 2004, the Sabaki River to the north of Malindi flooded after heavy rains and washed a number of hippo into the sea, which local people tried to coax back. Then the tsunami hit on Boxing Day making the sea swell dramatically and temporarily the hippo were forgotten as people were absorbed with rescuing local fisherman. The next day the hippo all made it back to the mainland except for Owen who was stranded on a reef. He was less than a year old at the time. After a remarkable rescue by the Kenya Wildlife Service that was watched by hundreds of people he was brought to Haller Wildlife Park. His story is made even more remarkable as when he was released into an enclosure already occupied by some giant tortoises, he was adopted by one of them named Mzee (meaning 'old man' in Kiswahili) who is believed to be about 130 years old. Owen arrived exhausted, confused and extremely frightened and immediately ran to Mzee and cowered behind him as he would have done with his mother. Within days the tortoise and the hippo were eating and sleeping together, and the hippo licked the tortoise's face and followed him everywhere. Owen and Mzee remained inseparable until 2007 when Owen was removed to another enclosure with another hippo. A number of children's books have been written about them, and they have their own website: www.owenandmzee.com.

platform at 1100 and 1500 daily. Children in particular will thoroughly enjoy this excursion. Finally the **Whistling Pines** restaurant is an excellent place for lunch.

### Mtwapa and Shanzu Beach

Mtwapa is a small, bustling, chaotic and extremely friendly town, and is the main service point for Shanzu Beach. The main settlement is just north of the creek, which is busy with boats serving the big-game fishing industry. The beach itself is sheltered and bordered by palms and glass-bottomed boat rides out to the reefs are on offer. There are a number of resorts, most interlinked with one another so guests can use all the facilities.

**Ngomongo Villages** ① *10 km north of the Nyali Bridge and 1 km east of the main Mombasa–Malindi road, clearly signposted, T041-548 7063, www.ngomongo.com, daily 0900-1700, US$9, children US$4.50,* set in 6.5 ha of another reclaimed quarry in Shanzu, might be described as a theme park of traditional rural Kenyan lifestyles. There are nine villages, one for each of the tribes represented, complete with hut, cultivated crops, domestic and wild animals, village witch doctor and villagers. Visitors can walk around the site to see anything from subsistence farming methods to Akamba wood carving. There is an emphasis on participation, thus you can plant a tree or try many of the activities yourself, such as maize pounding or harpoon fishing whilst trying to balance on a raft. There is also a market selling jewellery and other ethnic items, and the **Kienyenji Restaurant**, built in traditional style, serves a range of African dishes and you can sample the local beer. This won an award from the United Nations Education Programme in 2001.

**Jumba la Mtwana** ① *www.museums.or.ke, daily 0930-1800, US$7.50, children (under 18) US$3; you can buy a short guidebook to the site or hire a guide,* is a national monument about 15 km from Mombasa and 1 km north of the Mtwapa Creek. The name means

## On the sea bed

The 80-m ship *MV Dania* spent 45 years plying the waters off the African coast, mainly as a live cattle transporter. In 2002 her life on the waves ended as she was sunk below the ocean just north of Mombasa. But the Dania has a new life as one of Africa's finest wreck dives and Mombasa's newest reefs, and the cattle pens and cabins already have become home to all kinds of sea life. The ship now lies in around 30 m of water just off Bamburi Beach and when she was sunk landed perfectly upright. She was fully prepared for sinking and had her engines removed and hull cleaned to minimise any environmental impact. The interior was fully cleared for safe penetration by divers, and all potentially dangerous objects, such as wiring and doors were removed, as have all but three of the original brass portholes, allowing divers and marine life to move freely in and out of the control room and the hull with ease. Many artificial reefs have been created around the world from wrecks; some as a result of natural disaster and some, as in Dania's case, intentionally. A variety of materials, ranging from military tanks to naval ships, have been used and over the years, extensive research has been carried out to monitor and quantify the success of these artificial reefs. The result has been that artificial reefs develop into thriving coral communities, almost indistinguishable from their natural counterparts. The solid structure that an artificial reef provides facilitates the attachment of algae, sponges, benthic organisms and gorgonia to its surface, organisms that would otherwise float around aimlessly, which are vital for coral production. Over time the vessel slowly transforms into a functioning reef; coral is produced, sea turtles and pelagic fish seek refuge amongst the protective overhangs, and as the reef matures it attracts larger sharks, groupers and moray eels. Artificial reefs also enhance the development of rare coral species that are not often found in natural reefs. In addition to the environmental aspect that artificial reefs bring, coral reefs, both natural and artificial, are also taking on an increasingly important role in supplying compounds for use in medicines. AZT is used in the treatment of HIV-infected patients and its chemical composition is derived from that of a Caribbean reef sponge. Furthermore, 50% of all new cancer drug research is conducted upon marine organisms.

With thanks to Bruce Phillips from **Buccaneer Diving**, www.buccaneer diving.com.

the 'house of the slave' and may have been a slave-trading settlement in the 15th century, although it was not mentioned in this capacity in either Arab or Portuguese sources. It is a lovely setting, close to the beach with shade provided by baobabs. To reach the site ask to be dropped off at the sign about 1 km beyond Mtwapa Bridge and from there it is a walk of about 3 km. However, you will probably be offered a lift as you walk down the track. Many of the houses have been rebuilt and undergone frequent changes and it has been suggested that Jumba la Mtwana could have been a meeting place for pilgrims on their way to Mecca. The site is one of Kenya's least-known sites and has only fairly recently been excavated. It is now run by the National Museums of Kenya. Within the site, which is spread over several hectares, there are three mosques, a number of tombs and eight houses. You will notice that architecturally they look little different from the houses of today in the area. This is due to it being such a successful design, there has been no need to change it. The people appear to have been very concerned with ablutions for there are many remains showing evidence of cisterns, water jars, latrines and other washing and toilet facilities. Building with coral rag (broken pieces of coral) was something reserved for the more privileged members of the community, and it is their houses that have survived. Those that belonged to the poorer people would have been built of mud and thatch.

## Kikambala Beach ⬤𝟂 ⤻ pp304-318. Colour map 2, C2.

→ Phone code: 041.

Beyond Mtwapa, and 27 km north of Mombasa, the last feasible beach to be reached from Mombasa on a day trip is Kikambala Beach. The turn-off is 8 km north of Mtwapa and the beach is 3 km from the main road. Backed by palms and clutches of thick forest, this is an 11-km long stretch of reef-protected white beach where the sand is so fine in places it squeaks underfoot. There are only a few resorts here, making it much less busy than the strip immediately north of Mombasa. In fact this is the location of the Israeli-managed Paradise Hotel that was bombed by terrorists in 2002, and it's never really recovered from the subsequent tourist slump. If you go for an isolated walk you may notice shells of abandoned once-fashionable holiday cottages with emerald moss growing on the interior walls. Nevertheless, Sun 'n' Sand remains popular and is one of the largest resorts on the north coast. The disadvantage here is that it's very flat in this area, which means the sea goes out for nearly a kilometre so swimming is only feasible at high tide and it's not the best destination for watersports. On either side of the road for about 40 km beyond Kikambala lie vast sisal estates.

# Kilifi

To Malindi

Kobil
Masjid-ul-Noor
Kaya Gardens
Agip
Kenya Commercial
Top-Life Gardens
Coast Rd
Old Ferry
Jetty
Kilifi Creek
Mnarani Ruins
Old Ferry Rd
To Bridge Toll Booth & Mombasa

N
500 metres
500 yards

**Sleeping** ⬤
Baobab Lodge Resort 1
Dhows Inn 3
Kilifi Bay Beach Resort 2
Mnarani Beach Club 6

## Kilifi ⬤⬤⬤ ⤻ pp304-318. Colour map 2, C2.

→ Phone code: 041.

The town of Kilifi is situated to the north of the Kilifi Creek, 60 km north of Mombasa, while Mnarani village is to the south. In the time of the Portuguese, the main town was located to the south of the creek at Mnarani. This popular boating and sailing centre is in an absolutely glorious location – the shore slopes steeply down to the water's edge and the view from the bridge is spectacular. The town has an interesting mix of people with quite a number of resident expatriates. The main industry in the town is the cashew nut factory which employs about 1500 people. To the south there are the Mnarani Ruins. It is an easy-going town with an attractive beach, which is fairly untroubled by the hassle of beach boys associated with some of the beaches closer to Mombasa.

**Mnarani Ruins** ① *www.museums.or.ke, 0930-1800, US$7.50, children (under 18) US$3.*
These were first excavated in the 1950s and it was the place of one of the ancient Swahili city-states that are found along this coast. It is believed that the town was inhabited from the latter half of the 14th century until about the early 17th century, when it was ransacked and destroyed by a group of Galla tribesmen. The inhabitants of the town are thought to have locked themselves into the Great Mosque as they were attacked.

The ruins include one of the deepest wells (70 m) along the coast, two mosques, part of the town wall and city gates and a group of tombs including a pillar tomb decorated with engravings of a wealthy sharif. Note the tomb of the doctor, which is easily the most ornate. At the ruins of the larger or **Great Mosque** can be seen the *mihrab* (which points towards Mecca) surrounded by carved inscriptions. There are many niches in the walls. To the left of the entrance, the smaller mosque is believed to date from the 16th century. There is a huge baobab tree nearby with a circumference of over 15 m. The ruins are best known for the inscriptions carved into them – many of them remaining untranslated. However, in general they are much smaller and less impressive than the ones at Gedi.

To get to the ruins, turn left off the main road to the south of the creek (signposted Mnarani Ruins) and go through Mnarani village. Turn right when you reach the tarmacked road and stop when you can see the creek. There is a signposted path to the left, and the ruins are a few hundred metres down this path and then a climb of about 100 steps. You also get a wonderful view of the creek from the ruins.

---

## Arabuko-Sokoke Forest Reserve ‣ *Colour map 2, C2.*

① *The main gate is on the Malindi Rd on the left if heading from Mombasa, 1.5 km before the turnoff to Watamu and Gedi, T042-32462, sokoke@africaonline.co.ke, open 0630-1800, US$25, children US$10.*
Don't expect tropical rainforest as you approach the Arabuko-Sokoke Forest Reserve – from the road the only discernible difference is that the scrub disappears and the trees are closer together. The forest runs for about 40 km north from Kilifi and is 20 km wide at its widest point. It is home to many species of rare bird and is the most important bird-conservation project in Kenya. There are over 40 km of rough driving tracks and a network of walking paths to explore and well-trained and knowledgeable local guides are available to take visitors on educational walks. A well-equipped visitor centre is open daily for information.

Over 260 species of bird have been identified in the forest, and Clarke's weaver is endemic to this area: the 16-cm Sokoke Scops owl is only found here and in a small area in eastern Tanzania, in the Usambara Mountains. The reserve also contains rare species of amphibian, butterfly and plant. It is said to be the largest-surviving stretch of coastal forest in East Africa and covers an area of 400 sq km. The forest is home to rare mammals too, such as the very small Zanzibar duiker (only 35 cm high and usually seen in pairs), the Sokoke bushy-tailed mongoose and the rare golden-rumped elephant shrew. There are four endemic plant species and five endemic butterfly species. The forest was gazetted as a Forest Reserve in 1943 and managed by the Forest Department until 1991, when the Kenya Wildlife Service became a partner in its management and opened it up for tourists. Kenya Forest Research Institute and the National Museums of Kenya joined the management team more recently and in recent years projects such as butterfly pupae production and bee keeping have been started in an effort to help local people make a legitimate living from the forest. Local farmers harvest butterfly pupae, for sale to the Kipepeo project in Gede, and for live export to overseas exhibitions. Efforts to prevent the forest being cut down completely are being made, but the constant needs for fuel and land in a country where the population is increasing so rapidly makes this difficult.

## Mida Creek

There is good birdwatching at Mida Creek, which covers 32 sq km of tidal inlet that stretches inland for about 6 km, and it is a key stopover site for migrating birds. It offers the ideal resting and feeding location for birds migrating from Europe, Asia and the Middle East to eastern and southern Africa. The birds refuel on the variety of invertebrate food items buried in the muddy sandflats at low tide and roost on the exposed sandbanks and on the mangroves at high tide. Young corals and fish also start their lives in these nutrient-rich waters, before the tides sweep them into the Indian Ocean. To reach the head of the creek, leave the Mombasa–Malindi road opposite the entrance to the Arabuko-Sokoke Forest and make your way down to the creek's shores. The creek is composed of extensive mudflats and mangrove forests that attract a wide variety of flora and fauna. The best time for birdwatching is the incoming tide, when all creatures are busy feeding. A telescope is very useful. You are likely to see crab plovers with their distinctive crab-crunching bills, curlews, sandpipers, stints, terns, spoonbills and flamingos. There is a suspended walkway that leads 260 m through a progression of mangrove species and a bird hide here. You can also visit by boat on organized excursions from the resorts.

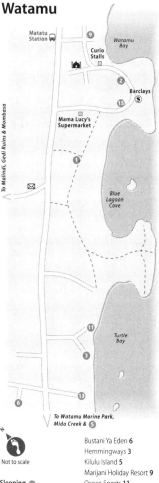

**Watamu**

Matatu Station
Watamu Bay
Curio Stalls
Barclays
Mama Lucy's Supermarket
Blue Lagoon Cove
Turtle Bay
To Malindi, Gedi Ruins & Mombasa
To Watamu Marine Park, Mida Creek &

N
Not to scale

**Sleeping**
Aquarius Beach Resort 1
Ascot Residence 2
Bustani Ya Eden 6
Hemmingways 3
Kilulu Island 5
Marijani Holiday Resort 9
Ocean Sports 11
Turtle Bay Beach Club 13
Villa Veronica 15

## Watamu 🌊☀️⛰️🍴🌙 ➤ pp304-318.
Colour map 2,C2.

### Watamu Village ➤ Phone code: 042.

In recent years this small fishing village has been seeing some fairly rapid tourist development and is certainly feeling the impact. The atmosphere is mixed, but Watamu still maintains quite a lot of traditional village charm and remains reasonably hassle free, despite the proximity of the tourist hotels. The village has several small supermarkets, a number

# Turtle watch

Watamu Turtle Watch was formed in 1997 to continue and further develop the marine turtle conservation efforts of a local naturalist Barbara Simpson, which she had been undertaking in the area since the 1970s. Watamu has a small but nationally important nesting population of sea turtles, with 60 nests a year. There is a nest protection programme, which works in cooperation with local people and Kenya Wildlife Services to protect all nests laid on Watamu and Malindi beaches. Daily patrols check for nesting turtles and tracks in the sand that indicate new nests. Nests are allowed to incubate in situ unless they have been laid in an area threatened by sea wash, in which case they are carefully relocated to a safe area. Watamu Turtle Watch is also involved in a project to encourage fishermen to release, rather than slaughter, turtles that get accidentally caught in their fishing gears. For more information about visit www.watamu turtles.com. There are placements on offer for volunteers.

of curio and souvenir dealers, a butchers, fishmongers and a post office. Watamu is known for its spectacular coral reef, and the coast splits into three bays: Watamu, Blue Lagoon and Turtle Bay, divided by eroded rocky headlands. Each bay becomes a broad white strand at low tide, and it is possible to walk across to the small offshore islands. Like the southern resorts, Watamu is inundated with seaweed at certain times, but the sand is usually clear from December to April. Most resorts are south of Watamu, on the road that runs down to the Kenya Wildlife Services HQ. The setting is attractive, and Turtle Bay is quite good for snorkelling (but watch out for speed boats ferrying fishermen to the large game boats). The water is much clearer here than at Malindi during the wet season. The most exciting way to the reef, 2 km offshore, is to go in a glass-bottomed boat, and at low tide, and especially Spring low tide, a number of eroded corals protrude from the surface, which resemble giant Swiss cheeses. Due to the high concentration of plankton in the sea around Watamu, the marine life is superb and it's also an excellent place for scuba-diving. In particular manta rays and whale sharks are common. Watamu is also a good place to hire bikes as an alternative way of exploring the surrounding area, including the Gedi Ruins. There are a number of shops in the village, with reasonable rates.

## Bio-Ken Snake Farm → *Phone code: 042.*
① *T042-32303, www.bio-ken.com, daily 0900-1200 and 1400-1700, US$10.*
Some 3 km north of the village is a research centre primarily dealing with reptiles, especially snakes and snake-bite venom. Bio-Ken is a registered international advisor on the handling of snake-bite victims and holds snake-bite seminars attended by experts from all over the world. There are over 200 snakes at the farm and a variety of species. Bio-Ken also offers a free 'remove-a-snake' service for people in the Watamu area. Any snakes removed from a property are relocated or brought back to the farm depending on the species. It also runs a snake-spotting day safari with a picnic lunch for visitors to show snakes and reptiles in their natural habitat. The project was established by the late James Ashe, who was appointed Curator of Herpetology at the National Museum of Kenya in Nairobi in 1964. There are about 127 different snake species in Kenya. Of these only 18 have caused human fatalities and only another 6 could kill. Another 10 could cause a lot of pain and the remaining 93 or so are non-venomous and not dangerous.

# A viewer's guide

**Manta Place** This dive site is one of the most distant and it takes about 45 minutes to reach by boat. The chances of seeing manta rays and whale sharks are high, and there are a very large number of moray eels. Depth varies between 15 and 24 m.

**Black Coral** This location is only suitable for experienced divers. At a depth of 30-40 m is the famous black coral. Its appearance is very unobtrusive and only a few divers recognize it. Another attraction is the blue and golden *cucumaia* or sea cucumber, which is very rare, plus huge basket sponges reaching up to 1.5 m in height. This whole reef is overgrown with whip wire corals.

**Shakwe Wreck** During a storm in 1990 the 25-m fishing trawler Shakwe capsized and sank. She lies at a depth of only 12 m, almost undamaged on her starboard side, but within a short period of time her hull has become overgrown with small coral heads in which there are many small crabs of different kinds. A shoal of batfish has established its home here, and there are large groupers, stingrays, and octopus. Only the wheelhouse of the wreck is accessible. The wreck is an ideal destination for beginners.

**Soldierfish Place** This dive site is only suitable for experienced divers due to its depths of 30-40 m. This spot is covered with many soft corals that provide shelter for hundreds of soldier fish, nudibranchs, groupers, stingrays and many other coral fish.

**Canyon, Canyon North, Deep Place and Brain Coral** These four dive areas are located on the northern reef and drop from 10 to about 27 m from where they turn into sandy bottom. In the Canyon the reef rises again after a 25-m-wide ditch. In this channel, where you sometimes experience a current, reef sharks or large stingrays can be spotted. The Brain Coral is a very old coral hill, now partly collapsing, which hosts a diversity of coral fish. All these dive locations are suitable for beginners.

**South Reef, Canyon East, Dolphin Corner and Lion Fish** These dive spots are also found on the outer reef and the descents are from 10 to 30 m and then end in sandy ground. As the name suggests, the Lion Fish is inhabited by a large number of various lionfish. At Dolphin Corner you may see dolphins with a bit of luck. On all these dive areas beginners can dive on the reef top.

## Watamu Marine Park → *Phone code: 042.*

ⓘ *www.kws.go.ke, US$20, children US$10.*

Along this coast close to Watamu village there is an excellent marine park that has been made a total exclusion zone. Obviously this change of status met with mixed feelings by some fishermen, but they seem to have adapted well, and the influx of tourists has increased the income of the village. The park headquarters are some way south of Watamu at the end of the peninsula that guards the entrance to the creek. Unfortunately the road goes a little inland, hiding views of the sea. The park covers 30 km of coastline, with a fringing reef along its entirety, as well as numerous patch reefs. The fringing reef forms several lagoons, some of which are rich in coral and fish species, while part of the beach within the park is a key turtle-nesting ground. It also encompasses Mida Creek, a diverse and rich ecosystem consisting of mangroves, coral, crustacea, fish and turtles. There are approximately 700 species of fish in the marine park and there are estimated to be over 100 species of stony coral. You go out in a glass-bottomed boat to the protected area and some of the hundreds of fishes come to the boat to be fed. The boats may seem rather expensive but really are well worth it. Trips can be arranged at any of the resorts, or else at the entrance to the actual park. You can also swim or snorkel amongst the fish, which is a wonderful experience and there are lots of shells and live corals that are a splendid range of colours. The water temperature ranges from 20-30°C. If you are short of time, try the islands just offshore from **Hemingways**.

## Gedi Ruins ›› Colour map 2, C2.

ⓘ www.museums.or.ke, 0930-1800, US$7.50, children US$3.60. If you come by matatu you will have to walk the last 1 km.

The Gedi Ruins are about 4 km north of Watamu and are signposted from the village of Gedi. This is one of Kenya's most important archaeological sites and is believed to contain the ruins of a city that once had a population of about 2500. It was populated in the latter half of the 13th century, and the size of some of the buildings, in particular the mosque, suggests that this was a fairly wealthy town for some time. However, it is not mentioned in any Arabic or Swahili writings and was apparently unknown to the Portuguese although they maintained a strong presence in Malindi just 15 km away. It is believed that this was because it was set away from the sea, deep in the forest. Possibly as a result of an attack from marauding tribesmen of the Oromo or Galla tribe, the city was abandoned at some time during the 16th century. Lack of water may have also been a contributing factor as wells over 50-m deep dried out. It was later reinhabited but never regained the economic position that it once had held. It was finally abandoned in the early 17th century and the ruins were rediscovered in 1884. The site was declared a national monument in 1948 and has been excavated since then. It has been well preserved.

There is a beautifully designed **museum** that includes a restaurant and library. Visitors are made to feel welcome, you can buy a guidebook and map of the site at the entrance gate and there are also informative guides.

The site was originally surrounded by an inner and outer wall (surprisingly thin). The most interesting buildings and features are concentrated around the entrance gate, although there are others. Most that remain are within the inner wall although there are some between the two walls. Coral rag and lime were used in all the buildings and some had decorations carved into the wall plaster. You can still see the remains of the bathrooms – complete with deep bath, basin and squat toilet. There are a large number of wells in the site, some exceptionally deep. The main buildings that remain are a sultan's palace, a mosque and a number of houses and tombs, a water system and a prison. Other finds include pieces of Chinese porcelain from the Ming Dynasty, beads from India and stoneware from Persia – some are displayed in the museum, others in Fort Jesus, Mombasa.

The **palace** can be entered through a rather grand arched doorway, which brings you into the reception court and then a hall. This is the most impressive building on the site. Off this hall there are a number of smaller rooms – including the bathrooms. You can also see the remains of the kitchen area that contains a small well.

The **Great Mosque** probably dates from the mid-15th century, and is the largest of the seven on this site. It is believed that substantial rebuilding was undertaken more recently. The mihrab, which indicates the direction of Mecca, was built of stone (rather than wood) and has survived well. As you leave, note the carved spearhead above the northeast doorway.

A great deal of trade seems to have been established here – silk and porcelain were exchanged for skins and, most importantly, ivory. China was keen to exploit this market and in 1414 a giraffe was given to the Chinese Emperor and shipped from Malindi. It apparently survived the trip. There was also trade with European countries and a Venetian glass bead has been found here too.

In all there are 14 houses on the complex that have so far been excavated. Each one is named after something that was found at its site – for example House of Scissors, House of Ivory Box. There is also one named after a picture of a *dhow* that is on the wall. In the houses you will again be able to see the old-style bathrooms. Deep pits were dug for sewage, capped when full and then used for fertilizer. Such techniques are still used in the Old Town district in Malindi.

The tombs are located to the right of the entrance gate and one of them is of particular interest to archaeologists as it actually has a date engraved on it – the Islamic year 802 which is equal to the year AD 1399. This is known as the Date Tomb and has enabled other parts of the site to be dated with more accuracy. There is also a tomb with a design that is common along the Swahili Coast – that of a fluted pillar. Pillar tombs are found all along the coast and were used for men with position and influence.

The site is in very pleasant surroundings – it is green and shady but can get very hot (cool drinks are available at the entrance). There are a spectacular variety of trees including combretum, tamarind, baobab, wild ficus and sterculia, a smooth-barked tree inhabited by palm nut vultures and monkeys because snakes cannot climb up the trunk. You may hear a buzzing noise. This is an insect that lives only for three or four days until it literally blows itself to pieces! There are usually monkeys in the trees above that are filled with the noise of many different types of birds.

It is in fact also a wildlife sanctuary and is home to the magnificent, and now sadly rare, black and white colobus monkey. This monkey has suffered at the hands of poachers for their splendid coats but a few remain and you may see some here. Also in the sanctuary are the golden-rumped elephant shrew (only seen at dawn and dusk) and various birds such as the harrier hawk and palm tree vulture.

## Kipepeo Project
ⓘ *Just inside the entrance to the ruins, T042-32380, www.kipepeo.org, 0800-1700, US$1.50.*
This is a community-based butterfly farm established in 1994, which has trained local farmers living on the edge of the Arabuko-Sokoke Forest Reserve, see page 292, to rear butterfly pupae for export overseas. It also produces silk cloth and honey from other insects. The project aims to link forest conservation with income generation for local communities and at present is the only butterfly farm in Africa of this kind. The project has led to a large increase in household incomes of those participating in the project and, since butterflies are shortlived and hard to breed abroad, the market is quite reliable. *Kipepeo* is Kiswahili for butterfly.

## Malindi ⬤🅐🅝🅞🔺🅑🅖 ⇥ *pp304-318. Colour map 2, C2.*

→ *Phone code: 042. Population: 81,000.*
Malindi is the second largest coastal town in Kenya after Mombasa. It has a pleasant laid-back atmosphere compared to Mombasa, and retains a village feel, especially along the shore road. The streets are also cleaner and the people much friendlier. In the narrow streets of the Old Town are bazaars and shops selling antique furniture and textiles. The

beach is excellent and popular and, although seaweed can be a problem (especially before the Spring equinox), it is less so than on the beaches around Mombasa. A great attraction is the Malindi Marine Park, with clear water and brilliantly coloured fish. It is also one of the few places on the East African coast where the rollers come crashing into the shore, there is a break in the reef, and it is possible to surf.

## Ins and outs

**Getting there** **Malindi Airport** ⓘ *T042-31201, www.kenyaairports.com*, is 2.5 km from the centre of town and is served by four airlines, as well as by chartered planes for safaris. A taxi to the centre costs about US$7 and the resorts to the south will be about US$12. There are also bus/*matatu* services from Mombasa daily. ►► *See Transport, page 317.*

**Getting around** You can either organize day trips through the hotels, or else try the public transport in the way of *tuk-tuks* and *boda bodas*. Both these are surprisingly efficient, cheap and easy to find in Malindi at any time of day or night. The main parts of town are relatively safe, even at night, but exercise caution away from the main tourist areas, however, and take a taxi if going further afield.

**Tourist information** ⓘ *Lamu Rd, T042-20747, malindi@tourism.go.ke, Mon-Fri 0800-1600.* Although this tourist office closes out of season, it is relatively helpful and the staff friendly.

## Background

The earliest known reference to Malindi is found in Chinese geography in a piece published in 1060 written by a scholar who died in AD 863. The first accurate description of the town is believed to have been written by **Prince Abu al-Fida**, who lived from 1273 to 1331. Archaeological evidence supports the theory that the town of Malindi was founded by Arabs in the 13th century. In any event, locals claim that there was a big Chinese trading influence. This belief is supported by the fact that many of the local people still retain traces of Chinese features.

In 1498 **Vasco da Gama**, having rounded the Cape of Good Hope, stopped off at various ports along the coast. At Mombasa he was not made welcome – indeed attempts were made to sink his ships. At Malindi he found a much warmer reception. The good relations between Malindi and the Portuguese continued throughout the 16th century. The town was governed by Arabs, who were the wealthiest group. The wealth came from the trade with India and the supply of agricultural produce grown in the surrounding plantations.

The town went into a period of decline in the 16th century and in 1593 the Portuguese administration was transferred from Malindi to Mombasa. Although Malindi continued to suffer as Mombasa expanded and took more trade, the town's prosperity did improve during this period and the use of slaves was an important factor. In the first year of resettlement in 1861 there were 1000 slaves working for just 50 Arabs. Malindi had a bad reputation for its treatment of slaves.

The period under the **Imperial British East Africa Company** (IBEAC) began in 1887 when the Company acquired a 50-year lease from the Sultan of Zanzibar for territories in East Africa. The company administered the area, collected taxes and had rights over minerals found. Bell Smith was sent to the town as officer for the Company and he began to lobby for the abolition of the slave trade. From around 1890, slaves who wished and were able to, could buy their freedom. For those who could not, the company offered jobs, or found paid employment. Relatively few took up the opportunity and the process was a gradual one. With the Protectorate government abolishing the status of slavery in 1907, merchandise trade developed, and in the early 20th century the most important exports were rubber, grain, ivory, hides and horns.

During the second half of the British period the foundations were laid for what is now Malindi's most important industry – tourism. The first hotel, **Brady's Palm Beach Hotel**, opened in 1932, and famous visitors included Ernest Hemingway in 1934. In the 1960s, Malindi became a popular place to live for the European population, many of whom were retired farmers from the highlands. The first charter flight from Europe flew to the Kenyan coast in 1972, when there were just five hotels in Malindi, but by 1976 the hotel bed capacity in the town had tripled and hotels had been built at Watamu Beach. Malindi became very popular with Europeans, especially Germans and Italians and the latter are today estimated to own some 3000 properties and businesses in the area such as private villas, restaurants and nightclubs, which have not been altogether welcomed by the local people. As a result it is in Malindi that you will find some of the finest espresso coffee, Parmesan and hams to be found in Kenya, but the combination of these European trappings and the old Swahili town gives Malindi a somewhat Jekyll and Hyde character and may not be everybody's cup of tea. Indeed the Italian attachment to this town that baffles both visitors and locals is so strong that at the height of recent violence in the country over the 2007 elections, the Italians demanded that their government drop the adverse travel advisory against Kenya, and while most of the towns in Kenya were still reeling from the effects of this recent chaos, Malindi had almost fully recovered its tourist industry only three weeks after the skirmishes. On the downside, there are also rumours of a mafia presence in Malindi and in 2004, there was a high-profile drugs bust when Kenyan police seized a consignment of

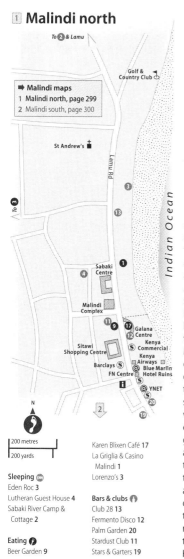

## 1 Malindi north

To 2 & Lamu

Golf & Country Club

➡ **Malindi maps**
1 Malindi north, page 299
2 Malindi south, page 300

St Andrew's

Lamu Rd

Indian Ocean

Sabaki Centre

Malindi Complex

Galana Centre
Kenya Commercial
Sitawi Shopping Centre
Kenya Airways
Barclays
Blue Marlin
FN Centre Hotel Ruins
YNET

N

200 metres
200 yards

**Sleeping**
Eden Roc 3
Lutheran Guest House 4
Sabaki River Camp & Cottage 2

**Eating**
Beer Garden 9

Karen Blixen Café 17
La Griglia & Casino Malindi 1
Lorenzo's 3

**Bars & clubs**
Club 28 13
Fermento Disco 12
Palm Garden 20
Stardust Club 11
Stars & Garters 19

US$6 million worth of cocaine destined for Europe from a private villa and two Italians and five Kenyans were arrested. Additionally, sex tourism in Kenya is at its most acute and brazen in Malindi, which sits very uncomfortably on the traditional Muslim coast.

## Sights

Although the history of the town dates back to the 12th century there are few remains of the ancient town. Two remains that are worth seeing, in the oldest part of the town, clustered around the jetty, are the **Jami Mosque** and two striking **Pillar Tombs**. These are

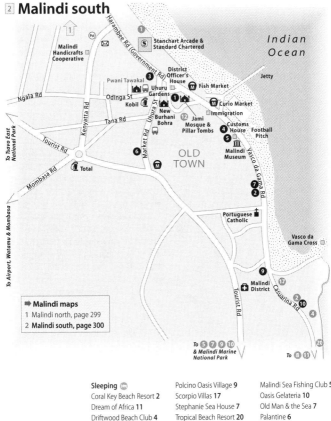

### 2 Malindi south

*Indian Ocean*

Malindi Handicrafts Cooperative

Harambee Rd (Government Rd)

Stanchart Arcade & Standard Chartered

Pwani Tawakal

District Officer's House

Jetty

Ngala Rd

Odinga St

Kobil

Uhuru Gardens

Fish Market

Kenyatta Rd

Tana Rd

New Burhani Bohra

Jami Mosque & Pillar Tombs

Curio Market

Immigration

To Tsavo East National Park

Tourist Rd

Market Rd

Uhuru Rd

Customs House

OLD TOWN

Malindi Museum

Football Pitch

Mombasa Rd

Total

Vasco da Gama Rd

To Airport, Watamu & Mombasa

Portuguese Catholic

Vasco da Gama Cross

Malindi District

Tourist Rd

Casuarina Rd

**Malindi maps**
1 Malindi north, page 299
2 **Malindi south, page 300**

To ⑤⑦⑨⑩ & Malindi Marine National Park

To ⑧⑪

N

200 metres
200 yards

**Sleeping**
Coral Key Beach Resort **2**
Dream of Africa **11**
Driftwood Beach Club **4**
Kilili Baharini **5**
Lawfords **1**
Malindi Bandas & Campsite (KWS) **10**
Malindi Beach Club **8**
Ozi's B&B **12**

Polcino Oasis Village **9**
Scorpio Villas **17**
Stephanie Sea House **7**
Tropical Beach Resort **20**

**Eating**
Baby Marrow **9**
Bahari Fast Food **1**
Baobab Café **2**
I Love Pizza **4**

Malindi Sea Fishing Club **5**
Oasis Gelateria **10**
Old Man & the Sea **7**
Palantine **6**

## Swahili culture

The coastal region is the centre of this distinct and ancient civilization. The Swahili are not a tribe as such – they are joined together by culture and language – Kiswahili – which is the most widely spoken language in East Africa. It is one of the Bantu languages and was originally most important as a trading language. It contains words derived from Arabic and Indian as well as English and Portuguese.

The Swahili civilization emerged from the meeting of East Africa, Islam, the classical world and eastern civilizations. Traders, as well as immigrants, from Asia and Arabia have had a gradual influence on the coast, shaping society, religion, language as well as literature and architecture. These traders arrived at the ports of the east coast by the northeast monsoon winds, which occur in March and April (the Kaskazi wind) and left around September on the southerly wind (the Kusi wind). Inevitably some stayed or were left behind and there was intermarriage between the immigrants and the indigenous people.

Slavery was important to the coastal region and was not entirely an alien phenomenon. Long before slaves were being rounded up from the interior and shipped overseas, there was an important although rather different 'slave trade'. This involved a family 'lending' a member of the family (usually a child) to another richer family or trader in exchange for food and other goods. That child would then live with the family and work for them – essentially as a slave – until the debt had been paid off. However, as with bonded child labourers in India today, the rates of interest demanded often ensured that the debt could never be paid off and the person would remain effectively a slave. Later slavery became an important part of trade and commerce and the old system was replaced with something much more direct. Many slaves were rounded up from the interior (some of them 'sold' by tribal chiefs and village elders) and taken to the coast. Here they would either be sold overseas to Arabia via Zanzibar or put to work on the plantations that were found all along the coast. Successive measures by the British formally ended the slave trade by 1907 although it did continue underground for many years. When slaves were released they were gradually absorbed into the Swahili culture, but when their history was known it was almost impossible to be rid of the stigma associated with being a slave.

thought to date from the 14th century. **Malindi Curios Dealers Associations** have a huge **market** here. Behind the Jami Mosque lies a maze of small streets that form the Old Town district. The oldest surviving buildings are the mosques of which there are nine (including the Jami Mosque) that date from before 1500. Contemporary accounts from the 14th century remark on two-storeyed houses with carved wooden balconies and flat roofs constructed from mangrove poles, coral and zinc mortar. None of these have survived. The smaller dwellings had timber and latticed walls covered with mud and mortar and woven palm frond roofs, called *makuti*. The density of the housing and the materials made old Malindi very venerable to fire, and periodic conflagrations (the most recent in 1965) destroyed all the older dwellings. The mosques survived by virtue of having walls of coral blocks and mortar.

The two buildings of note from the British period are the **District Officers' House** in front of Uhuru Gardens, and the **Customs House** behind the jetty. Both have verandas,

## Fireworks at Malindi

In 1498 Vasco da Gama, sailing north up the East African coast had met with a hostile reception both in Sofala (now in Mozambique) and Mombasa. He needed to establish good relations with a town at the coast so that he could load fresh water and victuals and engage an experienced mariner to guide his fleet to the Indies. The bales of cotton cloth and strings of beads the fleet had brought with them to trade had proved useless – the coastal people had gold from Sofola, ivory from the interior, silk from the east.

Vasco da Gama decided to present some unusual items to the King of Malindi – a jar of marmalade, a set of decorated porcelain dishes and a candied peach in a silver bowl. He then invited the king and his people to witness a firework display on the shore. The king had a brass throne with a scarlet canopy brought down to the shore and with a court of horn players, flautists and drummers gazed out to the San Gabriel and da Gama's fleet. In quick succession the ship's canons fired shells into the air which burst over the King and his townsfolk on the shore. It was spectacular and exciting, the king was impressed and the Portuguese had an ally for their conquest of the mainland.

and neither is in particularly good repair, but the District Officers' House is a handsome and imposing structure.

There are a couple of monuments that date from the Portuguese period, in particular the **Vasco da Gama Cross**, which is situated on the promontory at the southern end of the bay. It is one of the oldest remaining monuments in Africa and was built in 1498 by the great Portuguese explorer, Vasco da Gama, as a sign of appreciation for the welcome he was given by the Sultan of Malindi, and to assist in navigation. The actual cross is the original and is made of stone from Lisbon. You can reach it by turning down Mnarani Road. The small **Catholic church** close to the cross is also believed to date from the Portuguese period and is thought to be the same one that St Francis Xavier visited in 1542 when he stopped off at Malindi to bury two soldiers on his way to India. It is one of the oldest Catholic churches in Africa still in use today and the walls are original, although the thatched roof has been replaced many times.

**Malindi Museum** ① *close to the Customs House on Vasco Da Gama Rd, T042-31479, www.museums.or.ke, daily 0930-1800, US$7.50, children US$4.* This is one of Kenya's newest museums housed in an attractive 19th-century former house of an Indian trader. It was opened in 2004 and has a library on the top floor, where you can browse through local books of the region. The building was originally constructed in 1891, and in more recent years it has served as the office for Kenya Wildlife Service and is now a National Monument that was lovingly restored by National Museums of Kenya thanks to funding from the German Embassy. The house is on three floors with cool high rooms, intricate staircases and wooden shutters. There are several very interesting exhibits and everything is very clearly labelled. These include some sacred wooden carved grave posts of the gohu people, which are traditionally used as a link between the living and the dead. Sacrifices are made to them in preparation for harvesting and planting. There are a few boards about Vasco de Gama and his arrival on the coast in the 15th century, and a room of posters dedicated to 'Discover Islam' with information about how Muslim men and women live their lives. On the ground floor are some interesting early photographs of Mombasa, with corresponding modern photos on what the various areas look like today.

Also on display is a strange-looking coelacanth, a prehistoric fish that was once thought to be long extinct, but in recent years a few have been found around the coasts of east and southern Africa as well as Indonesia. The massive 1.7 m fish was caught at a depth of about 185 m off the coast of Malindi in 1991 and it has fleshy limb-like fins that move like our arms and legs. Scientists believe it could be a specimen that was part of a chain of creatures that evolved and moved to live on land some 360 million years ago. It was identified as an adult female coelacanth, and amazingly was found to be carrying 17 tennis-ball sized eggs, which would suggest that these rare fish are breeding along the Kenyan coast. There is a football pitch opposite the museum where you can watch teams of teenagers in respective coloured T-shirts play in the late afternoon.

## Around Malindi ● ➤ pp304-318.

### Malindi Marine National Park
① *Kenya Wildlife Service headquarters, Causuarina Point, T042-20845, www.kws.org, daily 0600-1800, US$20, children US$10.*
Situated within the Malindi Marine Biosphere Reserve is this small marine national park. Gazetted in 1968 this is an area of only 6 sq km that offers wonderful diving and snorkelling on the coral reefs off Casuarina Point. This park is popular and with good reason. The water is brilliantly clear, and the fish are a dazzling array of colours. There are two main reefs with a sandy section of sea bed dividing them. You can hire all the equipment that you will need and a boat here for around US$15, but it is advisable to check your mask and snorkel before accepting. The fish are very tame as they have been habituated by being fed on bread provided by the boatman. If you see any shells be sure to leave them there for the next visitor – the shell population has suffered very severely from the increase in tourism. Try and go at low tide as the calmer the sea, the better; also be sure to take some sort of footwear that you can wear in the water. You may also be taken to one of the sand bars just off the reef so take plenty of sun protection. Most of the resorts organize this excursion, many of which seem to have arrangements with local glass-bottomed boat owners, as does the Kenya Wildlife Services headquarters.

### Tana River National Primate Reserve → *Colour map 1, B2.*
① *T046-2035, www.kws.org, daily 0600-1800, US$20, children US$10.*
Situated 120 km north of Malindi on the Tana River between Hola and Garsen, the Tana River National Primate Reserve (TRNPR) is a highly diversified riverine forest that has at least seven different types of primate. It was gazetted in 1976 to protect the lower Tana riverine forests and two highly endangered primates, the crested mangabey and the Tana River red colobus monkey and this is the sole habitat of these endangered primates. A number of other animals roam here including elephant, hippo, baboon, gazelle, duiker, lesser kudu, oryx, river hog, giraffe, lion, waterbuck, bush squirrel and crocodile. The TRNPR is located on the lower reaches of the meandering course of the Tana River, covering an area of 171 km of forest, dry woodland and savanna habitat on the east and west of the river. The forest here is of high diversity with nearly 300 tree species recorded. There is a research station for study of the primates. It is possible to go boating down the swirling Tana River. This reserve has been under threat by human demands for its resources. Clearing and cultivation have been problematic, along with the damage resulting from the pastoralists bringing their animals here for water.

## Baobab trees

These huge trees have enormous girths, which enable them to survive during long dry patches. They live for up to 2000 years. You will see some extremely large ones – at Ukunda there is one with a girth of 22 m, which has been given 'presidential protection' to safeguard it. During droughts people open up the pods and grind the seeds to make what is known as 'hunger flour'.

The legend has it that when God first planted them they kept walking around and would not stay still. So He decided to replant them upside-down which is why they look as if they have the roots sticking up into the air.

The reserve is accessible via the Malindi–Garissa road. There are buses running between Lamu and Garissa, and some of them detour to Mnazini village just to the south of the reserve, from where it is possible to walk north along the river (there is a small boat ferry just before Baomo Village). However, most people visit as guests of the **Delta Dunes Camp**, the upmarket lodge on the Tana River, see Sleeping, page 311.

## To the Lamu Archipelago

After leaving Malindi you cross the Sabaki River, and then the turning for the village of **Mambrui**. This village is believed to be about 600 years old and all that remains of the ancient Arab City is a mosque, a Koran school and a pillar tomb, which has insets of Ming porcelain. Further on you will eventually pass **Garsen**, a small town at the crossing of the Tana River where you can get petrol and drinks. Just south of Garsen on the Tana River there is a **Birdlife Sanctuary**, home to many herons. From here the road turns back towards the coast and Witu, another small old town. As you drive in this area you may see people of the Orma tribe as well as Somalis, for this is getting close to the border. Both groups are pastoralists, and you will see the cattle that represent their wealth. Finally, about five hours after leaving Malindi, you will get to **Mokowe** and you will see the Makanda channel, which separates Lamu from the mainland. Here there is a small café and if you are in your own vehicle you can park it up here and arrange and pay for an *askari* to look after your car whilst you visit Lamu. This is also where the buses stop.

## ◉ North coast listings

*For Sleeping and Eating price codes and other relevant information, see Essentials pages 34-38.*

## ◉ Sleeping

Excluding Easter, low season on the coast is usually 1 Apr-30 Jun, when many of the hotels discount their rates considerably. If you are staying in one of the big hotels then the chances are that you will eat there. If you wish to try other places, you will usually need to have your own transport or else take a taxi.

**Nyali, Kenyatta and Bamburi beaches**
*p287, map p288*

There are more than 30 almost back-to-back beach resorts along the 6 km or so strip of coast immediately north of Mombasa. None of them are cheap and budget travellers have a better choice of accommodation south of Mombasa on Diani Beach.

**A Voyager Beach Resort**, Nyali Beach, reservations through **Heritage Hotels**, Nairobi, T020-444 6651, www.heritage-east africa.com. Completely renovated in 2007, this is a large resort with over 200 a/c comfortable rooms, some with sea views, set in spacious grounds, although the beach here is at its narrowest at Nyali. **Barakuda Diving** has a base here, and a full range of watersports is on offer including daily *dhow* and glass-bottom boat trips and they have a fully equipped boat for fishing, plus 3 swimming pools, several restaurants and bars and a kids' club. Good all round family resort.

**B Bahari Beach Hotel**, Nyali Beach, T041-547 2822, www.baharibeach.net. Set in gardens, the 100 rooms are in whitewashed thatched blocks with a/c, balconies or terraces, there's a large pool, but only a narrow beach that is covered at high tide. Fairly good-value rates are all inclusive of buffet meals, sodas and beer, and facilities include watersports, a PADI dive centre and tennis courts.

**B Mombasa Beach Hotel**, Nyali Beach, reservations, Nairobi T020-244 173, www.safari-hotels.com. Although in a block built in 1969, this is a pleasant hotel, up on a cliff looking over the beach and the sea, fully renovated in 2006. The 152 rooms have a/c and balconies, and it's very well managed with business facilities, tennis courts, 2 swimming pools, 1 of which is down at the beach, watersports, bars and restaurants.

**B Nyali Beach Hotel**, Nyali Beach, T041-471 551, www.nyalibeach.co.ke. This opened in 1946 and was the first hotel to be built on the mainland outside of Mombasa though obviously it has been refurbished and extended many times since then. It now has 170 rooms with a/c, minibar, satellite TV and balconies or terraces set in 8 ha of gardens. Facilities include 6 restaurants, 5 bars, nightclub, tennis courts, 2 swimming pools and evening entertainment. A kitesurfing centre is based here and 2 free beginners' scuba lessons are included in the room rates.

**B Severin Sea Lodge**, Bamburi Beach, T041-548 5001/2, www.severin-kenya.com. This consists of about 180 imaginatively designed *makuti* thatched rondavels all of which are a/c and very comfortable.

Facilities include 2 swimming pools, tennis courts, watersports and massages are available. There is a choice of international restaurants including the **Imani Dhow**, which as the name suggests is set in a *dhow* but it's not in the water.

**B Traveller's Beach Hotel & Club**, Bamburi Beach, T041-548 5121, www.travellers beach.com. A consistently popular resort with lots of fun activities, friendly professional staff and a relaxed holiday atmosphere, although the 128 rooms could do with a refurb. Facilities include a gym, spa, indoor and outdoor games, 4 swimming pools, 1 of which you can swim in to reception, watersports, the excellent **Sher-e-Punjab** Indian restaurant (see under Eating), plus an Italian and buffet restaurants. It also runs the tented camp in the **Mwaluganje Elephant Sanctuary** (see page 272).

**B-C Reef Hotel Kenya**, Nyali Beach, T041-471 771, www.reefhotelkenya.com. Recently renovated, the 160 rooms all have a/c, TV and balconies. Facilities include 3 swimming pools, tennis court, jacuzzi, and 3 restaurants serving mediocre buffet meals. There is a lively nightlife here with several bars, a disco and shows and there's a dive centre and they rent out sea kayaks and windsurfers. Fairly ordinary, but reasonably priced from US$145 for a double including all meals.

**C Neptune Beach Resort**, Bamburi Beach, T041-548 5701, www.neptunehotels.com. Newly refurbished in not very classy cane and floral decor this is the sister resort to the Neptune resorts to the south of Mombasa and is a very similar set up with the usual resort facilities such as pool, shops, beauty treatments, hairdresser, kids' club and TV room. Most of the 78 a/c rooms have ocean views. Has a nice informal atmosphere and good value rates are all-inclusive of buffet meals and some drinks.

**D Fisherman's Leisure Inn**, Nyali Beach, T041-547 1274, www.fishermans.visit-kenya.com. Very clean and great value, 5 mins from the beach by walking through the **Nyali Reef Hotel**, choice of double hotel rooms or

2-bedroom apartments with kitchenette, all with a/c and TV. Also has a decent restaurant, a bar with billiards table, swimming pool and a jacuzzi. Rates start at US$60.

**D Indiana Beach Apartment Hotel**, Bamburi Beach, T041-548 5895, www.indianabeach kenya.com. Unremarkable and simply furnished, the 39 rooms are in a boring white concrete block with balconies, and have a/c, minibar and TV, and some have kitchenettes. But on the plus side there's a pleasant thatched restaurant and bar almost on the beach, a good Indian restaurant, 3 swimming pools, a PADI dive school and a gym.

**D Kenya Bay Hotel**, Bamburi Beach, T041-548 7600, www.kenyabay.com. A friendly, laid back and traditionally built hotel with reception under *makuti* thatch, popular with a number of nationalities, the 106 comfortable a/c rooms are in 3-storey blocks with balconies or terraces, and there are some spacious communal areas with stone floors and Swahili-style furnishings. PADI dive school, jet-skis can be hired, pool, 3 restaurants, 2 bars and a disco, and Masai dancing and acrobats in the evening.

## Mtwapa and Shanzu Beach *p289, map p288*

### Shanzu Beach

With the exception of the **Serena**, the hotels at Shanzu Beach are managed by the UK-based **African Safari Club**, T+44(0)845-345 0014, www.africansafariclub.com, are very similar and are only available for package holidaymakers from the UK. These are the **Coral Beach**, **Vasco de Gama**, **Shanzu** and **Paradise Beach**, and **Flamingo Beach**. They are all in a long line next to each other, guests are free to use facilities at all of them regardless of which one they are staying at and there is a central watersports centre. Rates are all-inclusive and include flights from Gatwick with 2nd and 3rd weeks coming down in price considerably. They also have hotels in Kilifi and Watamu.

**A Serena Beach Hotel & Spa**, reservations Nairobi, T020-354 8771, www.serena

hotels.com. A very pleasant luxury hotel carefully designed to resemble Swahili architecture with about 120 rooms in double-storey cottages with carved balconies arranged in winding lanes full of lush vegetation. There's a nice Persian water garden with restaurant, ice cream shop and a number of boutiques, a decent-sized pool with swim-up bar, and a wide beach frontage. It's superior to some of the other resorts and popular with a broad range of nationalities.

## Kikambala Beach *p291, map p288*

These are the last stretch of resorts before you reach Kilifi.

**B Sun 'n' Sand Beach Resort**, T041-32408, www.sunnsand.info. This is an expansive resort set on 7 ha with 200 m of beach frontage and popular with European package holidaymakers, although the 300 rooms set in 4-storey blocks are well overdue for refurbishment. It has a good range of facilities including 5 restaurants, many bars, nightly entertainment, a business centre and conference facilities, 3 swimming pools, 1 of which has a 100-m slide. Rates are all-inclusive and include 1 pool scuba lesson.

**C Le Soleil Beach Club**, reservations, Nairobi, T020-203 7784, www.lesoleilkenya.co.ke. The 82 standard and 29 family rooms here are pleasantly furnished and have a/c and TV. Rates are half board, but you can upgrade to all-inclusive from a not unreasonable US$14 per person per day. There's a large pool with swim-up bar, a roof-top sundeck, several restaurants and bars, 1 of which sells seafood by weight and is cooked over a wood-burning grill. Plenty of activities and entertainment.

**D Boko Boko**, off the main road before the village of Kikambala, about 7 km north of the Mtwapa Bridge, www.bokoboko-kenya.de. This is a German/Kenyan enterprise with 3 simple but spacious cottages set in a peaceful verdant patch of jungle that is full of small mammals, butterflies and birds, surrounded by the *shambas* of the local Giriama people. The beach is about a 2.5-km walk or bike ride away, there's a swimming pool, fish pond with some interesting aquatic life, and it's home to 4 giant tortoises. It's also home to the excellent **Porini Seychellois Restaurant**, see under Eating.

### Kilifi *p291, map p291*
**L Kenya Holiday Villas**, reservations UK, T+44 (0)1256-881909, www.kenyaholiday villas.com, has a number of luxury private villas in the Kilifi area, each of a very high standard with Moorish architecture and have staff to cook and clean and their own pool and they can sleep 4-8 people. For families or groups these make a pleasant alternative to the resorts.
**A Kilifi Bay Beach Resort**, Coast Rd, about 6 km out of Kilifi, T041-522 511, www.mada hotels.com. Well designed by an Italian and the best place to stay in Kilifi, the complex accommodates guests in 50 thatched cottages with private balconies. Activities include windsurfing, canoes, snorkelling and diving, bicycles can be hired and free massages are on offer. It has well-tended surroundings, located on cliffs with path down to beach, and there are 2 swimming pools, restaurants and bars.
**C Baobab Lodge Resort**, Coast Rd, about 3 km out of Kilifi, T041-522 570, www.mada hotels.com. Also managed by **Mada Hotels** and much cheaper than the Kilifi Bay (above), located on a bluff with good ocean views but not much of a beach, although there's a large shaded swimming pool with swim-up bar and pleasant tree-filled gardens. The 30 a/c rooms are either in a double-storey block or spacious rondavels, and there are 2 bars and a restaurant, evening entertainment and again bicycles can be hired and free massages are on offer.
**C Mnarani Beach Club**, south side of Kilifi Creek, reservations South Africa, T+27 (0)12-4251000, www.mddm.co.uk/mnarani. Overlooking Kilifi Creek, this hotel is among the oldest in the country. It has been beautifully restored, with 84 guest bedrooms in natural wood finishes and smaller creek cottages. All rooms have a/c, mosquito nets and phones. It

is set in marvellous gardens and has wonderful views, facilities include watersports (sailing, windsurfing and waterskiing), a bar, and restaurant overlooking the creek, a swimming pool, a beauty therapist and evening entertainment. Children are not permitted. The restaurant is open to non guests and is of a very high standard, with superb seafood, excellent atmosphere and speciality nights.
**E Dhows Inn**, south side of the creek on the new road leading to the bridge, T041-522 028. Small hotel with rooms set in thatched blocks in the pleasant garden, with bathrooms and mosquito nets, clean and fairly basic but good value, and there is a popular bar and restaurant. However, theft has been a problem here in the past.

### Watamu *p293, map p293*
There are a number of resort hotels and unlike further south, a few options for budget accommodation. Again, as an alternative to the resorts, families or groups of friends may want to consider renting a house or cottage, many of which are very nice near the beach and sometimes have a pool. Visit www.discoverwatamu.com under holiday lets. You can eat at all the big hotels, which do various set menus and buffets.
**L Kilulu Island**, 3 km south of Watamu, reservations, Germany T+49 (0)40-330 000, www.vladi-private-islands.de. A super luxury villa with 3 elegant bedrooms, a large lounge with satellite TV, private bar, separate dining room, guest bath, covered sun terrace and a private swimming pool with marvellous views of the ocean and private beach. You can arrange all meals with the cook, or dine at one of the nearby hotels. US$2477 per day for 6-8 people all-inclusive, with staff.
**A Hemmingways**, about 1 km south of Watamu, T042-32624, www.heming ways.co.ke. A member of the **Small Luxury Hotels of the World** group, this is Watamu's famous fishing club and there's an enormous stuffed marlin over the reception desk. Very stylish a/c rooms, the ones in the new block are exceptionally spacious and have great sea

views, while the individually designed suites have additional lounges and dining rooms. The food is very good and overseen by an internationally acclaimed head chef and fishermen can get their catch prepared to their liking. As well as fishing, other water-sports can be arranged and there's a pool and spa, but not much for children to do.

**B Ocean Sports**, next door to **Hemmingways**, T042-322 88, www.ocean sports.net. This has recently had a complete refurbishment and has a series of thatched cottages set in gardens with sunny blue and white decor, plus a 3-bed self-catering unit sleeping 8, and a very attractive campsite (**F**) with good shared ablutions, a BBQ and tents for hire. There is a large bar and restaurant and all the other usual facilities and an especially nice large wooden deck overlooking the beach, where Sun lunch is a huge buffet, popular with expatriates and particularly good value. Activities include big-game fishing, diving, snorkelling, tennis and squash. Friendly atmosphere and well recommended.

**B Turtle Bay Beach Club**, just to the south of Ocean Sports, T042-32003, www.turtle bay.co.ke. A good value and fun all-round family all-inclusive resort popular with British guests, with 145 rooms in 4 ha of grounds, plenty of food and drink on offer as well as lots of activities and entertainment, and it looks after guests very well. Facilities include bike rental, tennis, diving, kids' club, Kiswahili lessons, tuition for windsurfing and sailing, and an enormous swimming pool.

**C-D Aquarius Beach Resort**, T042-32069, www.aquariuswatamu.com. Despite the name, not on the beach but a fairly pleasant Italian-run resort with 54 a/c rooms in thatched buildings set around a large swimming pool and tropical gardens and it has an additional restaurant and bar actually on the beach. Italian food, rents out bikes and can arrange deep-sea fishing. Out of high season rates are good value.

**D Ascot Residence Hotel**, T042-32326, www.ascotresidence.com. Not on the beach, but good central location in the village, with comfortable and spacious rooms in white-washed blocks with *makuti* thatched roofs, a bar, tennis courts, pizzeria, grill, and boutique. Civilized and friendly Italian management, and clientele include many retired Italians. The highlight here is the dolphin-shaped swimming pool. Excellent value.

**E Bustani Ya Eden**, to the east of Turtle Bay Rd, T042-32262. Just 6 small, very pleasant chalets available at a very good rate for 2 sharing a room, s/c, hot and cold water, fans, 300 m to beach, speciality African and seafood restaurant, a friendly Dutch/Kenyan couple run the place.

**E Marijani Holiday Resort**, to the north of the village, T042-32448, www.marijani-holiday-resort.com. An exceptionally friendly Kenyan/German enterprise 100 m from the beach offering spacious rooms with nets, fans, hot water and large 4-poster beds. Some cottages have a kitchen so you can choose bed and breakfast, or self catering, and dinner can be arranged with notice. It's set in lovely well-established gardens, which are home to parrots, tortoises, cats and dogs. Bicycles and surfboards can be rented.

**F Villa Veronica**, T042-32083. Among the better of the basic board and lodgings in Watamu, with clean rooms arranged around a shady courtyard, with en suite bathrooms and mosquito nets. It's a friendly family-run place, and the price includes breakfast, but thanks to the bar around the corner, can be noisy and sometimes has power problems.

## Malindi *p297, maps p299 and p300*

Tourism in Malindi is very seasonal, being packed into the periods of European holiday: Jun-Aug, Christmas and New Year and, to a certain extent, Easter. Outside these months you should bargain and can often pay as little as a third of the high-season rate.

There are a clutch of basic local lodgings in the town centre near the bus stand. Most charge little more than US$5 for a bed with or without bathroom but are mostly run-down and pretty grim. They often suffer from having more mosquitoes and being hotter as they do not get the sea breezes. They can also be noisy. Far better to stay near the beach. Most of the large resorts permit day visitors for a fee to use the pool and beach.

**L Dream of Africa**, Silversands Beach, 3 km south of Malindi, T042-20444, www.plan hotel.com. On the same property as the **Malindi Beach Club** (below), this super luxury and stylish lodge opened in 2005 and has consistently had good reports, with 35 spacious rooms with a/c, internet, satellite TV and jacuzzis in striking terracotta and white low-rise buildings within an easy stroll to the beach. There's a restaurant, 2 bars, pool, and watersports are available to guests at the **Tropical Beach Resort** (below), which is under the same management.

**L Kilili Baharini**, 4 km south of Malindi, T042-20169, www.kililibaharini.com. Exclusive luxury hotel in thatched *banda* style, 27 vast and exquisitely decorated rooms, almost entirely white with some antique furniture, several swimming pools, restaurants, bars, a/c, Italian-run Wellness Centre using expensive Italian products, the food is Italian too. Very stylish.

**A Lawfords**, Harambee Rd, T042-21265, www.lawfordsresort.com. This was for many years Malindi's most popular hotel that opened in 1936 and closed in 2003, and Ernest Hemmingway was once a guest. In 2006, it reopened as a luxury resort, and now has 60 suites and 10 3-storey villas with very elegant furnishings and works of art on the wall, a/c, Wi-Fi, TV and DVD player and minibars, all set in magnificent gardens full of flowering shrubs and baobab trees. There are 2 superb restaurants serving Mediterranean cuisine, several bars including a whiskey and cigar bar with leather furniture and books, 2 vast swimming pools, 1 in the shape of Africa, and a luxury spa.

**A Malindi Beach Club**, Silversands Beach, 3 km south of Malindi, T042-20444, www.planhotel.com. A very exclusive boutique hotel with 23 beautifully decorated rooms spread across 8 Arab/African style 2-level villas set in marvellous colourful gardens on a private beach. Each has a wide balcony or terrace with day beds, a/c, satellite TV and minibar. There's a romantic restaurant with Moorish arches, 2 bars, 2 swimming pools and again watersports are available at the **Tropical Beach Resort**.

**B Tropical Beach Resort**, Casuarina Rd, 3 km south of Malindi, T042-20442, www.plan hotel.com. Originally 2 resorts, now joined as 1 all-inclusive place catering largely for package tours, set in established gardens with lots of *makuti* thatched buildings with over 140 rooms with high standard furnishings in either Swahili-style or with a colonial feel. The good facilities include swimming pool, dive school, watersports centre, bars, buffet restaurant, and a disco on the beach.

**C Coral Key Beach Resort**, Casuarina Rd, 2 km south of town, T042-30717, www.coral keymalindi.com. Very attractive layout; the 150 a/c rooms have wide verandas with comfortable furniture. Facilities include 5 swimming pools, tennis, beach bar, restaurant and pizzeria, boutique, and there's a popular disco on Fri night open to all. Italian managed, rates drop significantly in low season.

**C Driftwood Beach Club**, Casuarina Rd, 3 km south of town, T042-20155, www.drift woodclub.com. 1 of the older hotels in Malindi, this has managed to retain a clubby but informal character. It has a range of a/c rooms, and 2 2-bed cottages that share their own pool and are ideal for 2 families, breakfast is included in the price. Facilities include what is probably the best restaurant in Malindi (the seafood in particular is spectacular), watersports including fishing, diving and windsurfing, and a squash court. Temporary membership is very cheap, so a lot of people drop in to use the facilities and the atmosphere in the pub is friendly, often boozy, and ex-pat orientated.

**C Scorpio Villas**, Casuarina Rd, 2 km from town, T042-20194, www.scorpiovillas.co.ke. An excellently Italian-managed complex with friendly service, the 25 villas are set in magnificent gardens, 3 swimming pools, a restaurant and bar and the beach is very close. The cottages are furnished with enormous Zanzibar beds and day couches on the terraces and balconies. Rates are bed and breakfast, full board or half board, and drop significantly during low season.

**C Stephanie Sea House**, Casuarina Point, close to the Kenya Wildlife Service HQ, 6 km south from Malindi, T042-20720, www.stephanieseahouse.com. Run by Italians, with mostly Italian guests, the 50 thatched simply furnished cottages are set in tropical gardens with Lamu-style furnishings, a swimming pool and restaurant, mostly Italian food but once a week a Swahili dinner is held next to the pool, watersports can be arranged.

**C-D Eden Roc**, Lamu Rd, T042-20480, www.edenrockenya.com. On a clifftop overlooking the bay in 9 ha of generous grounds containing lily ponds, this is a large hotel that was opened in 1957 by German big-game hunters, although it has been renovated and extended many times since then, and still tends to cater to German package tours. The 150 en suite rooms vary in price depending on whether they have a/c or fans, and if rates are bed and breakfast or half board, but they start at an affordable US$70. It has its own beach, although it's a long walk through the gardens and the sea is 100 m away, plus 4 swimming pools, tennis courts, watersports, open-air disco and business centre.

**D Polcino Oasis Village**, on Silver Sands Beach, 3 km south of town, T042-31995, www.holidays-kenya.com. Constructed in a 'U' shape with white walls and *makuti* roofs, this has a disco, a large 25-m swimming pool, 60 1- to 3-bed apartments with kitchenettes, plus 24 en suite hotel rooms, an internet café, bar, and restaurant serving seafood, Italian and Indian dishes. Good value for groups or families of 4 when rates work out at about US$20 per person.

**E Malindi Bandas and Campsite (KWS)**, Casuaria Point, adjacent to Malindi Marine Park, the *bandas* must be booked in advance with the warden T042-20845, or **Kenya Wildlife Service**, Nairobi, T020-600 800, www.kws.org. Run by the Kenya Wildlife Service, there are 4 simple *bandas* sleeping 2 with linen, towels and mosquito nets, a camping area with washing block, and a communal cooking area under thatch, which has a stove, fridge, electric kettle, utensils and crockery but you must bring all food. *Bandas* are US$35, while camping is US$5 per person.

**E-F Sabaki River Camp & Cottage**, about 8 km north of Malindi, T0722-861 072, www.sabakirivercampandcottage.com. Head north from Malindi, cross the bridge over the river, then immediately turn right to go through the village. Ask here for directions to the home of Rodgers Karabu, which is about 1 km further on. The cottage is on a hill overlooking the mouth of Sabaki River, where thousands of birds, including flamingos, gather, and this region has been earmarked as an important bird site for Kenya. Only 2 rooms, they are large and have en suite bathrooms, no electricity and lanterns are used, basic meals can be arranged for US$12 a day. The campsite is located on a breezy dune under cashew nut trees 150 m from the cottage, washing and drinking water is provided in tanks, shower, flush toilet, fireplace and cooking grill. Rooms cost US$30 and camping costs US$7. Good value in scenic location and very different to the huge resorts.

**F Lutheran Guest House**, north of the town off the Lamu Rd, behind Sabaki Centre, T042-30098. Good value and popular, a range of rooms here including singles and doubles with or without bathroom, and 2 clean self-contained cottages, which have ceiling fans and mosquito nets, and are set in a pretty patch of garden. No alcohol is allowed on the premises.

**F Ozi's B&B**, T042-20218, ozi@swiftmalindi. com. Situated overlooking the beach very close to the jetty, this hotel has a range of 16 rooms with nets and ceiling fans and mostly with shared bathrooms, ask for a front-facing room for ocean views. It is simple, but clean and good value and is one of the most popular of the budget hotels; the price includes a very good breakfast. Downside is you maybe woken during the night by the calls to prayer from the nearby mosque. Special offer is washing 5 items of clothing per day for free!

### Tana River National Primate Reserve *p303*

**L Delta Dunes**, reservations T0727-464 763, www.tanadelta.org. This is a small and remote exclusive camp with just 6 large airy cottages built of mangroves, thatch and driftwood situated in groves of indigenous trees on top of dunes with good ocean views. Situated on the estuary of the Tana River it is a 3-hr drive from Malindi. Meals are enjoyed in a mess tent, which is home to a resident family of genet cats. Expeditions down the river to the local villages can be arranged, or a 3-hr excursion to the **Tana River Primate Reserve**. It is expensive but you will be very well looked after and the food is excellent. You can be picked up from the nearby airstrip or from Malindi, and will be taken there by 4WD.

## ● Eating

You are not restricted to eating at your hotel and there are a number of other places to try, though you will need a car or taxi in the evening. There are also a number of good restaurants in the resorts where non-staying guests are welcome.

### Nyali, Kenyatta and Bamburi beaches *p287, map p288*

**¶¶¶ Il Covo**, between **Traveller's Beach Hotel & Club** and **Kenya Bay Hotel**, Bamburi Beach, T041-548 7481, www.ilcovo.net. Daily 1100-2400. Open until late when it turns into a very popular disco, this is set on 2 storeys with broad wooden decks and good ocean views. There's a variety of cuisine such as the Italian restaurant and pizzeria, a sushi and tepanyaki bar, and it also does seafood and grills and a good choice of cocktails. Offers free transport from/to the local hotels.

**¶¶¶ Mvita Grill**, **Nyali Beach Hotel**, Nyali Beach, T041-471 987. Tue-Sun 1900-2400. An established and atmospheric award-winning gourmet restaurant overlooking the beach, with chandeliers and candle-lit tables, and excellent professional service. With a leaning towards seafood, the dishes are delicately presented, sorbet is offered between courses and there's a good wine list.

**¶¶¶ Sher-e-Punjab**, **Traveller's Beach Hotel & Club**, Bamburi Beach, T041-493 283. Tue-Sun 1200-1430, 1900-2230. An excellent Indian with an established reputation and relaxed atmosphere, with a long menu of jalfrezi, korma, tikka and biryani dishes and plenty of choices for vegetarians. At Sun lunchtime there's a good-value buffet.

**¶¶ Gold Chopsticks**, on the main road close to the entrance of **Haller Wildlife Park**, T041-548 5496. Daily 1100-1430, 1800-2300. Very popular Chinese restaurant with an impressive fountain in the middle of it with especially good seafood dishes including excellent ginger crab and a good range of 'sizzling' dishes. Good service, and refreshing a/c. This is the north-coast branch of the Galaxy Chinese restaurant, which also has branches in Mombasa and on Diani Beach.

**¶¶ Yul's**, next to the **Bamburi Beach Hotel**, T041-203 9284. Daily 0900-2300. Popular thatched bar/restaurant under the palms right on the beach with an excellent variety of good food including seafood grilled over charcoal – try the seafood platter or red snapper in garlic butter – plus pizza, giant burgers, salad, steak, Indian curry and imported Italian coffee. They also make their own ice cream, which is drizzled with flavoured sauces and decorated with fresh fruit. Finally, they also offer watersports such as windsurfing and jet skis, so this is a pleasant place to spend an afternoon.

### Mtwapa and Shanzu Beach *p289, map p288*

**¶¶¶ The Moorings Floating Seafood Restaurant**, on the north side of Mtwapa Creek to the left of the bridge, T041-548 5045, www.themoorings.co.ke. Tue-Sun 1000-

2400. A magical floating wooden deck and a marvellous spot to watch the sun sink over the mangroves and baobab trees along Mtwapa Creek and the tables are atmospherically candlelit after dark. It has a fairly short menu but offers excellently prepared seafood, plus steak, chicken and pasta, and has a well-stocked bar with long cocktail list, and a boutique selling *kikoy* items, accessories, shoes and beachwear.

🍴 **Trekkers**, next to the **Ngomongo Villages**, Shanzu Beach, T041-206 8504. This is an outdoor entertainment complex and restaurant that offers a range of international cuisine and seafood, as well as *nyama choma* that you can watch being grilled, plus a sports bar with an enormous TV screen, and in the evening it turns into an open-air disco with a stage and good lighting. Sun is family day with kids' entertainment like face-painting, popcorn and ice cream.

### Kikambala Beach *p291, map p288*

🍴 **Porini Seychellois Restaurant**, off the main road before the village of Kikambala, about 7 km north of the Mtwapa Bridge, T0733-728 435, www.porini-kenya.com. Daily 1200-2230. Set in an open-plan thatched building surrounded by a stunning tropical garden (porini means 'bush' in Kiswahili) where giant tortoises roam, this is a unique restaurant specializing in Seychellois cuisine. The staff wear Seychelles traditional dress and assist diners with washing their hands in clay pots of warm lime water before a feast of spicy grilled meat and chicken, whole fish baked in coconut milk and Creole jumbo prawns, served with fragrant rice and cassava. You can also stay here at the **Boko Boko** cottages (see page 306).

### Malindi *p297, maps p299 and p300*

Most of the restaurants in the hotels are open to non-residents; their set menus and buffets can be good value.

🍴 **Baby Marrow**, south of town near the hotels. Daily 1100-1400, 1800-2300. Located under the arms of an enormous tree and under a thatched roof, this is very intimate with huge lampshades, terrace and lovely atmosphere, rustic decor with chunky wooden furniture, all lit up at night by delicate lights in the garden out front, very good continental food and service. Recommended.

🍴 **La Griglia**, at the **Malindi Casino**, Lamu Rd, T042-30878. Upmarket restaurant and cocktail bar at the back of the casino with an attractive gold and maroon decor, outdoor tables under palm trees and Lamu-style furniture. It specializes in Italian food, grills and seafood and there's a good range of gooey chocolate desserts.

🍴 **Lorenzo's Restaurant**, at the **Mwembe Resort**, west of town, 900 m off the main road, T042-30573. Daily 1900-2230. Set in the grounds of an upmarket Italian timeshare resort, this offers superb Italian cuisine and seafood. The nicely dressed tables are set under a terracotta roof with open walls overlooking the swimming pool and manmade waterfalls in tropical gardens.

🍴 **The Old Man and the Sea**, beachfront, north of the Portuguese chapel, T042-31106. Daily 1200-1430, 1900-2300. Very stylish and the best place to eat in town, named after the Hemmingway book, romantic, set in a lovingly restored low Arabic house with stone seats and arches, only a few tables so reservations are essential, impeccable service and gourmet food. Starters include lobster pâté and smoked sailfish, followed by whole crab, or the recommended Indian Ocean seafood platter.

🍴 **Baobab Café**, T042-31699. Daily 0800-2300. On the sea front with good views, close to the Portuguese church, this has red and white checked tablecloths and friendly staff and a wide ranging menu. You can have breakfast here, snacks and a beer or fruit juice, as well as full meals such as chicken or fish curry, though the quality of the main dishes is inconsistent.

🍴 **Driftwood Beach Club**, Casuarina Rd, 3 km south of town, T042-20155, www.drift woodclub.com. Daily 1230-1430, 1930-2200.

This is a nice way to spend a lazy day, you can eat here and for a small fee use the pool and sun loungers. The excellent restaurant has a set menu, an à la carte menu, a Fri night BBQ next to the pool and a great curry buffet at Sun lunchtime and serves snacks at the bar.

¶¶ **I Love Pizza**, Vasco da Gama Rd, T042-20672. Daily 1200-1500, 1830-2330. A good-value and established Italian restaurant that has been going since 1982, serving pizza, pasta, seafood dishes and other food. Located in an atmospheric Arab house, lobsters, crabs, giant prawns combine themselves very well with *pappardelle* or spaghetti, rice or *trenette*.

¶¶ **Malindi Sea Fishing Club**, beachfront, near the Malindi Museum, T042-30550. Daily 1200-2030. Comfortable club decor including giant stuffed fish on the wall, bar, and excellent views out over the ocean. Serves grills, seafood including a very good prawn curry, plus cheaper burgers and chicken and chips. Members congregate here for lunch and sundowners.

¶ **Bahari Fast Food Restaurant**, close to the Juma Mosque. Popular local café with excellent chapattis, beef stew, good value, very busy at breakfast and lunch, closed in the evenings.

¶ **Beer Garden**, opposite Galana Centre, north of the shopping centre. Daily 0900-late. Good for snacks like burgers or chicken and chips and plenty of cold beer, this open-air bar is popular in the evenings with a mainly German clientele.

¶ **Karen Blixen Café**, Galana Centre, Lamu Rd. Daily 0800-1800. Imaginatively designed with photos of Karen Blixen and Denys Finch-Hatton on the walls and tables under umbrellas in the courtyard, this popular café sells sandwiches, juices, good Italian coffees, and some light meals at lunchtime.

¶ **Oasis Gelateria**, next door to the **Coral Key Beach Resort**, Silversands Beach. Daily 0800-2300, shorter hours in low season. Snack bar serving sandwiches and basic meals like omelette and chips, good coffee and delicious fresh mango juice, but it's best known for its 40+ flavours of ice cream

and is popular with Kenyan families.

¶ **Palantine**, opposite the main market. Local basic canteen open 24 hrs selling Swahili food and chai (tea), and here you can get the likes of *ugali*, omelette and chips, pilau rice, or filling chapattis with *maharagwe* (beans) or *na machicha* (a kind of spinach).

## ♪ Bars and clubs

### Mombasa to Kilifi *p283*
There are a string of large nightclubs along the north coast, popular with both holidaymakers and locals. These can be fun but men must be prepared to be hounded by prostitutes. Some may close during the week in low season.

### Nyali, Kenyatta and Bamburi beaches
*p287, map p288*
**Castaways**, next to the **Bamburi Beach Hotel**, Bamburi Beach. Daily 1000-late. A popular laid-back expat-run bar overlooking the beach with pool tables and giant TV screens for crucial sports events, plays European pop music, and has karaoke every Sat night. The restaurant serves Western dishes and seafood and has good ocean views.

**Mamba International Night Club**, at the **Mamba Village** behind Nyali Beach, T041-547 5180. Daily 1700-late. This has a rather staggering 13 bars and can hold thousands of people under an enormous conical shaped *makuti* thatched roof. There's a laser show on weekend nights and music is a mixture of rap, reggae, commercial disco and African music and live bands or DJ 'spin-offs' feature on Fri nights.

**Pirates Beach Bar**, just to the south of **Traveller's Beach Hotel & Club**, Bamburi Beach, T041-548 7119. Daily 1900-late. This is another large venue with 5 bars, dance floor on the beach, pool tables, giant TV screens, and a restaurant serving basic grills and seafood, which offers snacks like burgers and kebabs late at night. There are also some swimming pools and curly water slides here open 0900-1700.

**Tembo Disco**, on the Mombasa–Malindi road near the entrance of the **Haller Wildlife Park**, T041-548 5074, www.tembo.net. This is another large establishment set in a series of *makuti* thatched buildings with a 24-hr beer garden and *nyama choma* and seafood restaurant and a disco from 2100 to about 0500 if the demand is there, which it certainly is in high season. There are 7 bars in total and a pool lounge where regular competitions are held. The newest additions to the complex are a pole-dancing club called **Lollipop** and some 'guest rooms' – use your imagination.

### Mtwapa and Shanzu Beach *p289, map p288*

**Casaurina Nomad**, on the Mombasa–Malindi road, 500 m on the right after crossing the Mtwapa bridge, T041-548 7515, www.casaurina.com. This is open 24 hrs and the restaurant serves up English fry-ups from early morning and burgers, steaks, fried chicken, *nyama choma* and snacks later in the day and night. There's a large open air dance floor with good lighting and mixed music, several bars, pool tables and entertainment such as acrobats or traditional dancing, and it's a popular local venue for events such as talent shows and beauty contests.

### Malindi *p297, maps p299 and p300*

Most of the large resorts have discos and there is also occasionally live music – ask around. There is a particularly dense crop of bars and discos in the northern part of town around the **Galana Shopping Centre** where it's easy enough to walk from one to the next until you find one that suits. They make for a lively night out in high season. See also Eating.

**Casino Malindi**, Lamu Rd, T042-30878, www.casinomalindi.com. Daily 0900-0500. Fairly upmarket Italian-owned casino with a/c, pleasant cocktail bar and restaurant, with slot machines and gaming tables. Open until 0500 in season. Casino chips can be bought in euro and US$, and it accepts credit cards.

**Club 28**, near **Eden Roc Hotel**, T042-20480. Daily in season 2200-late. Not for the timid, this small, hot and sweaty club heaves with prostitutes so expect a lot of unwanted attention and has indoor and outdoor bars and a grill for fried chicken and *nyama choma*.

**Fermento Disco Bar**, Galana Centre, T042-31780. Wed, Fri, Sat out of season, more nights in season if there is the demand. Serves Italian food and grills, and has a very large disco with karaoke and occasional live music, opens at 2200 and things gets underway at about 2300. The rather steep entry fee of US$15 includes the first drink.

**Palm Garden**, Lamu Rd, T042-20115. Daily 1200-late. You can sit in the shade of thatched *bandas* and the food is adequate – curries, chicken, seafood and so on – and it is very good value. There is also a lively bar, with pool tables that has live music at the weekends but again is notorious as a hangout for prostitutes.

**Stardust Club**, Lamu Rd, T042-20388. Daily 2100-late. In a big white building opposite the Galana Centre, this starts fairly late in the evenings but is nevertheless very popular and is open until at least 0400 in season, and Sat is the big night. There are 2 dance floors, the outside one has some palm trees in the middle of it and some elevated comfortable lounge areas.

**Stars and Garters**, opposite Kenya Commercial Bank. Daily 1800-late. Grills, seafood, good coffee and ice cream, thatched informal bar, big screen TV for watching sport, especially English football and gets busy when there is an important match on. Turns into a disco on weekend nights.

## O Shopping

### Watamu *p293, map p293*

There's a clutch of curio stalls in the village near the mosque and a supermarket called **Mama Lucy's**.

**Malindi** *p297, maps p299 and p300*
**Handicrafts**
There are numerous craft stalls at the Malindi curio market near the jetty. In general the quality is reasonably good as are the prices – although you must expect to haggle. During the low season when there are not many tourists about, you may pick up some good bargains. There are also a number of quality shops on the roads lining the Uhuru Gardens, and the back streets around here selling very good cloths and items such as bags, clothes and cushions made from *kikoys*. Many of these also sell Swahili antiques, presumably to decorate the Italian villas in the area.
**Malindi Handicrafts Cooperative** off Kenyatta Rd, T042-30248, www.malindi handicrafts.org. Daily 0830-1800. This was established in 1986 and currently represents over 1500 artists in the region and is now among the largest producers of crafts in Kenya. You can visit a number of workshops behind the shop. There is an excellent selection of crafts here, though there is no bargaining in the shop itself, but you can talk to the carvers themselves and have something custom-made. The cooperative has sponsorship from the EU among other interested parties. They are currently involved in a program that encourages not using rare traditional hardwoods such as ebony for carvings but to instead use fast growing wood from trees such as acacia, palm and mango, and the World Wildlife Federation (WWF) has recently installed an experimental solar-powered kiln at the site to be used to harden these woods, which have a high water content; hence their ability to grow fast.

**Shopping centres**
**Galana Centre** has the **Karen Blixen Café**, the **Fremento** nightclub, a bureau de change and a supermarket.

## ▲ Activities and tours

**Nyali, Kenyatta and Bamburi beaches**
*p287, map p288*
**Bike the Coast**, based at Mombasa Go-Kart (see below), T041-222 4055, www.bikethe coast.com. This is offers enjoyable off-road scenic guided mountain bike tours around the north coast through local villages and plantations over distances from 20 to 30 km and taking 1½-2½ hrs. Bikes, helmets, gloves and drinking water are provided.
**Mombasa Go-Kart**, on the Mombasa– Malindi Rd, 12 km north of Mombasa, www.mombasa-gokart.com. Tue-Sun 1600-2200. This is a 500-m bendy floodlit go-kart track. 10 mins cost around US$15.
**Nyali Golf and Country Club**, across the road from Mamba Village, T041-472 613, www.nyaligolf.co.ke. Some 64 ha of land were set aside for this golf clubs construction, and in 1956 the first 9 holes were completed, with the 2nd 9 completed in 1980. Playing golf here is said to be challenging as the winds influence playing conditions. Green fees are about US$40.
**Peponi Divers**, **Bahari Beach Hotel**, Nyali Beach, T0722-412 302, www.peponidivers.ch. Single dives, half- or full-day trips and PADI courses and picks up from all the nearby hotels. English, French and German speaking.
**Prosurf Kenya**, at **Nyali Beach Hotel**, Nyali Beach, the **Severin Sea Lodge**, Bamburi Beach and also at the **Serena Beach Hotel & Spa** on Shanzu Beach, T0733-622 882, www.prosurfkenya.com. These are watersports centres with a good range of equipment including canoes and catamarans and can organize diving. The one at Nyali beach has instructors and equipment for both kite and windsurfing, while the others just have windsurfing.

**Mtwapa and Shanzu Beach** *p289, map p288*
**Kenya Marineland**, about 500 m north of the bridge over Mtwapa Creek, turn right along a dirt track for 1.5 km, T041-548 5248.

Here there is a small snake and reptile park, an aquarium and a souvenir shop but most people come here for the daily excursion by *dhow* up the Mtwapa Creek. This is usually booked through the beach resorts and it's touristy, but affords excellent views of the mangrove-lined creek and includes a BBQ lunch and the opportunity for snorkelling. The crew entertain on board with acrobatics and rope climbing and there are some friendly women who do henna tattoos and hair braiding. The *dhow* usually departs about 0930 and is back by about 1600 and costs in the region of US$90 per person. There are also occasional 3-hr sunset cruises.
**Vipingo Ridge Golf Club** At the time of writing 2 new 18-hole, 72-par golf courses were being built on the north coast on a 162-ha plot near Vipingo, north of the Mtwapa Creek. For progress visit www.vipingoridge.com.

**Watamu** *p293, map p293*
If you happen to be in Watamu in Oct, look out for the Wildman Kenya Triathlon based at the **Turtle Bay Beach Club**. This attracts some 200 participants and is open to amateurs and involves a 1.8-km swim in the ocean, a 68-km bike ride, and a 12-km run with the last 1.5 km along the beach. For more information visit www.wildflowerkenya.com.
**Aqua Ventures**, at **Ocean Sports**, T042-32420, www.diveinkenya.com. A PADI Resort centre; single dives start from US$40.
**Blue Fin Diving**, next to the **Blue Bay Village**, timeshare resort, T042-32099, www.bluefin diving.com. An established operator with 6 diving boats, 3 Bauer air compressors and 100 diving tanks (INT and DIN), which is represented in 21 resorts in Watamu and Malindi. A 4-day PADI Open Water course is US$425, while 2 dives for experienced divers costs US$100.
**Hemingways Fishing Centre**, Hemingway's **Hotel**, T042-32624, www.hemingways.co.ke.

Organizes deep-sea fishing for big game fish in season, which is usually the beginning of Jul to mid-Apr with Aug being especially good for black marlin. Fully equipped boats cater for 4-6 people.

**Malindi** *p297, maps p299 and p300*
**Deep-sea fishing**
**Kingfisher**, T042-20123, www.kenyasport fishing.net. Offers 7-hr or 10-hr day deep-sea fishing trips for 2-4 people in one of their 6 fully equipped boats and operates out of the **Malindi Sea Fishing Club**, south of the jetty, which also has a notice board for fishermen.

**Golf**
**Malindi Golf and Country Club**, north end of town, right fork off Lamu Rd, T042-20404. Very unusual 11-hole and 15-tee course spread out on 54 ha. Inexpensive daily membership is available, as well as club hire and caddies. Facilities include tennis and squash.

**Scuba-diving**
Most of the resorts can organize watersports, and **Blue Fin Diving**, is represented at many of them (see Watamu, above).

● **Transport**

You can organize shuttles from Mombasa's Moi International Airport to all the North Coast resorts through the resorts themselves or with the taxi companies in the arrivals hall (see page 266).

**Kilifi** *p286, map p291*
Kilifi is about 50 km from **Mombasa**, and 45 km from **Malindi**. The buses that go between the 2 towns do pick people up here although only if there is space as they may be full. It might be easier to get a *matatu*. **Tana Express** and **Tawfiq** have booking offices near the bus station.

**Watamu** *p293, map p293*
Watamu is about 50 km north of **Kilifi**, and 3 km off the main road. From Watamu to **Malindi**, the 15 km, takes about 30 mins, there are plenty of *matatus* and it costs about US$1.

**Malindi** *p297, maps p299 and p300*
### Air
Malindi Airport is 2.5 km from the centre of town, T042-31201, www.kenyaairports.com, and is served by 4 airlines, and by chartered planes for safaris.

**Air Kenya**, has 1 daily flight between Malindi and **Nairobi** that departs Nairobi at 1530, arrives in Malindi at 1730, departs at 1745 and arrives in Nairobi at 1855.

**Fly 540**, has 1-2 daily flights between Malindi and **Nairobi** (1 hr 15 mins) from US$79 1 way, and at least 2 daily flights between Mombasa and Malindi (15 mins) from US$30 1 way.

**Kenya Airways**, has daily flights between Malindi, Nairobi and Lamu. The flight departs **Nairobi** at 1100, arrives in Malindi at 1215, departs at 1240 and arrives in **Lamu** at 1315. It then departs Lamu at 1340, arrives at Malindi at 1410, and departs for Nairobi at 1440, where it arrives at 1555. It is a popular route so be sure to book well ahead and confirm your seat.

**Mombasa Air Safari**, has daily flights between Malindi, **Mombasa** and **Lamu**. The flight departs Mombasa at 0800, arrives at Malindi at 0845, departs at 0845 and arrives in Lamu at 0915. On the return leg it departs Lamu at 1700, arrives in Malindi at 1730, departs at 1750, and arrives in Mombasa at 1810.

**Airline offices**  Air Kenya, Wilson Airport, Nairobi, T020-605 745, www.airkenya.com. **Fly 540**, Mombasa, T041-343 4822, www.fly540.com. **Kenya Airways**, on Lamu Rd opposite Barclays Bank, T042-20237, at the airport, T042-20192, www.kenya-

airways.com. **Mombasa Air Safari**, Moi International Airport, T041-343 3061, www.mombasa airsafari.com.

### Bus
There are plenty of buses between Malindi and **Mombasa**. The bus companies all have offices in Malindi around the bus station, but booking is not usually necessary. They mostly leave early in the morning and take about 2½-3 hrs. Non-stop *matatus* are faster, and take under 2 hrs. They leave when full throughout the day.

The bus to **Lamu** takes about 5 hrs and costs about US$8. They leave in the morning between 0800 and 1000. These buses will usually have come from Mombasa. **Pwani Tawakal Bus Company**, T042-31832, http://pwanitawakal.com, is recommended for the **Lamu** service and they have 3 services a day in both directions; the office is opposite the Kobil petrol station near the market. Try and buy the ticket the day before you want to travel to guarantee a seat. The bus will take you to the jetty on the mainland from where you get a ferry across to Lamu (see page 325).

**Safety**  In the 1990s, there were security problems, including fatalities, with armed bandits known locally as *shifta* hijacking and robbing vehicles on the road to Lamu. However there hasn't been an incident for a number of years and these days it is considered safe to travel by bus from Malindi to Lamu, though on the last stretch of road towards Lamu, armed guards hop on the buses.

### Tuk-tuks and boda bodas
All over Malindi are cheap *tuk-tuks* that cost no more than US$2 from 1 end of town to the other. There are also plenty of bicycle taxis known as *boda bodas* with a single seat on the back that will cost no more than US$1.

There used to be car-hire companies in Malindi, and indeed bicycle hire, but with the introduction of what is excellent public transport, they have become defunct.

## ❶ Directory

### Nyali, Kenyatta and Bamburi beaches
*p287, map p288*
**Banks** There are a few shopping centres along the Mombasa–Malindi road between Nyali and Shanzu beaches and each have banks with ATMs. These include the **Planet Centre** and **Nova Centre** near the entrance to Haller Park, the **Ocean View Plaza** just to the north of **Pirates Beach Bar** and there's a **Barclays Bank** close to the entrance of **Traveller's Beach Hotel & Club**.

### Kilifi *p291, map p291*
**Banks** There are 2 banks in Kilifi, which are open Mon-Fri 0830-1300 and Sat 0830-1130. The Kenya Commercial Bank has an ATM. **Post office** Next to the market.

### Watamu *p293, map p293*
**Banks** There are no banks in Watamu but the big resorts will change money, although the rate will not be very good. The nearest ATMs are in Malindi.

### Malindi *p297, maps p299 and p300*
**Banks** There are a number of banks in Malindi. **Barclays** is on the main coastal road (the Lamu road) opposite the (closed) **Blue Marlin Hotel** and is open Mon-Fri 9000-1500, and Sat 0900-1100. It has an ATM. There is also a **Standard Chartered Bank**, just to the south of here. **Kenya Commercial Bank** is also on Lamu Rd on the opposite side to Barclays. There are several forex bureaus in town including one in the **Galana Centre** and **Dollar**, next to the **Standard Chartered Bank**. **Immigration** Opposite the curio market T042-20149. **Internet Intercommunications**, and **YNet**, both on Lamu Rd, offer email access, as does the post office, but the fastest connection is at the **Book Cafe**, in the FN Centre on Lamu Rd, which also sells a good range of books and serves cold drinks and ice cream. **Medical services** Malindi District Hospital, Tourist St, T042-20490. **Buhani Pharmacy**, Uhuru St, near Uhuru Gardens. **Post office** Opposite the police station on Kenyatta Rd and is open Mon-Fri 0800-1700, Sat 0900-1200. **Tidal information** Posted at Customs and Excise, near the jetty.

# Contents

## Footprint features

# Lamu Archipelago

## At a glance

⊖ **Getting around** On foot or by donkey and *dhow*. There are no cars.

◉ **Time required** At least 4 nights to explore Lamu Town and enjoy the beach; longer for the adventurous to explore other islands.

☼ **Weather** Mildly tropical with average temperatures of 30-35°C, but tempered by the sea breeze.

✖ **When not to go** Can be visited year round; there are only short afternoon showers in the rainy season.

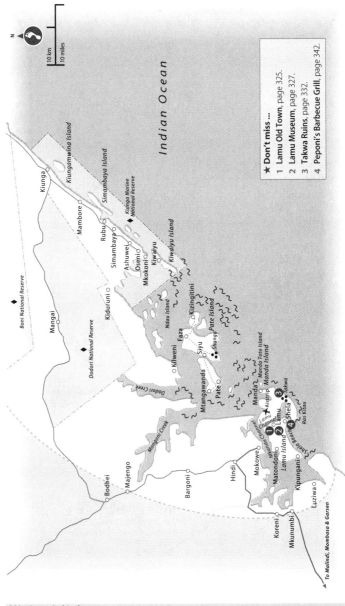

Indian Ocean

★ Don't miss ...
1 Lamu Old Town, page 325.
2 Lamu Museum, page 327.
3 Takwa Ruins, page 332.
4 Peponi's Barbecue Grill, page 342.

Boni National Reserve

Dodori National Reserve

Kiunga

Mambore

Kiungamwina Island

Simambaya Island

Rubu

Simambaya

Ashuwei

Osenio

Mkokoni

Kiunga Marine
National Reserve

Kiwaiyu Island

Kiwaiyu

Kiduruni

Ndau Island

Mangai

Kizingitini

Dodori Creek

Kilweni

Faza

Pate Island

Shunga

Mtangawanda

Siyu

Pate

Manda Toto Island

Mongoni Creek

Manda

Manda Island

Airstrip

Takwa

Majengo

Mokowe

Lamu Channel

Lamu

Lamu Island

Sheila

Shela Beach

Ras Kitau

Bodhei

Hindi

Matondoni

Mwamba Kuu channel

Bargoni

Kipungani

Luziwa

Koreni

Mkunumbi

To Malindi, Mombasa & Garsen

N

10 km
10 miles

In the extreme north are the intriguing islands of Lamu, which make for a fascinating excursion into the old Swahili way of life. Here visitors can experience the coast's cultural heritage at its most evocative and it is often said that Lamu is similar to how Zanzibar in Tanzania was 30 years ago, before the onset of mass tourism.

The old town of Lamu, known locally as Mkomani, was declared a UNESCO World Heritage Site in 2001 for its cultural importance and for being the oldest, best-preserved and still-functioning Swahili settlement on the East African coast. And yet, it is one of the most cosmopolitan few square miles of Kenya, where you are as likely to bump into stockbrokers from Wall Street and Hugh Grant lookalikes from London as you are Aussie backpackers.

In Lamu town, Shela and the small settlements on the other islands, the alleyways are barely wide enough to pass an oncoming donkey, and the whitewashed walls and Arabic arches contribute to some of the most elegant architecture on the continent. Without the sounds of traffic, the atmosphere is pleasantly peaceful interrupted only by the low rumblings of electric juicers in the waterfront cafés and the infectious chatter of Kiswahili. The evenings are enchanting, when the dimly lit alleyways are full of warm shadows and fragrant hues. The islands have some wonderful deserted beaches, very atmospheric places to stay and seafood to die for. Whilst embracing tourism, the people of Lamu want to retain the islands' mystic, religious sanctity and cloak of romance, and it should not be forgotten that they belong to another, older Africa. Lamu really is a paradise; it is so serene and beautiful that you are likely to want to stay forever.

Dhows make the short hop between islands. Manda Island is quite close to Lamu Island, Pate Island is about 20 km away, and Kiwayu Island is 50 km away.

## Ins and outs

### Getting there

Air Kenya, Fly 540, Kenya Airways, and **Mombasa Air Safaris** have flights to the **Manda Island airstrip** ① *T042-632 018, www.kenyaairports.com*. Flying to Lamu is a fantastic way to get a handle on the geography of Kenya's coast: tarmacked roads become dirt tracks criss-crossing each other and leading to tiny rural settlements shrouded in palmy forest, sand spits stretch tentacles out into the blue Indian Ocean, and after less than an hour the island of Lamu comes into view. Planes lands on the airstrip on Manda Island, just to the north. This is a delightfully simple airport with just a few benches set under *makuti* thatch for waiting passengers and a hand-drawn luggage trolley that takes bags down to the waiting boats to take you across the Lamu Channel. Some of the more expensive hotels will ferry you and your luggage over from the airstrip, otherwise there is always the motorized ferry and *dhows* to meet the planes at the jetty that will take you across for a few shillings.

The road to Lamu is tarmac to Malindi, a rough track to Garsen then a further 20 km of tarmac after which there is a good graded coral and sand section to Mokowe. Buses to Lamu go fairly regularly but the route is popular so you should book in advance. The trip takes about four to five hours from Malindi and costs US$8. They leave in the morning at between 0800 and 1000, and will have come from Mombasa first with departures approximately two hours earlier, which cost US$10. If possible sit on the left side of the bus (in the shade) and keep your eyes open for wildlife. In previous years, these buses have been targeted by armed robbers, and consequently armed guards ride on the bus for the last few kilometres to Lamu. However, there hasn't been an incident for a number of years and the buses are regarded as safe these days. The bus will take you as far as the jetty at Mokowe on the mainland from where you get a ferry, about 7 km, taking about 40 minutes, across to Lamu. All the bus companies put their passengers on the same boat and there's plenty of help with your luggage. The bus trip to and from Lamu is long, so ensure you have enough water, although every time the buses stop in the tiny settlements along the way, hawkers are waiting to throw hands through the windows with drinks, bananas and other snacks. If you are in your own vehicle it is also possible to park it up at the Mokowe jetty, which is effectively Lamu's nearest car park, but you will have to pay an *askari* to look after your car. ▸▸ *See Transport, page 343.*

### Getting around

There are no vehicles on the island except for the District Commissioner's Land Rover, a tractor owned by the town council and an ambulance at the hospital, and on Manda Island there's a fire engine at the airstrip. Donkeys, *dhows* and bicycles dominate and everywhere is walkable. The two main thoroughfares in Lamu town are the waterfront, also known as Kenyatta Road, and the Main Street, which is one block back from the waterfront, also known as Harambee Avenue. The maze of streets mean that it is easy to get lost; just bear in mind that Harambee Avenue runs parallel to the waterfront and the all the streets leading into town from the shore slope uphill slightly.

### Safety

Safety is not a major problem in Lamu, however, there have been a number of incidents over the last few years. Avoid walking around alone after dark in secluded areas of town and don't go to remote parts of the island unless you are with a group. On the beach, stay within shouting distance of other people. The increase in tourism has led to an inevitable

# Lamu's houses

Most of Lamu's houses were built in the 18th century and were constructed out of local materials, with cut coral-rag blocks for the walls, wooden floors supported by mangrove poles and intricately carved shutters for windows. They were traditionally built in an oblong shape around a small open courtyard with two to three storeys and flat roofs covered with *makuti* thatch. It was required that a father give his daughters their own living quarters when they married, so he would add another storey to the house or build an adjoining house. When this was across a street, a bridge would be built between the two houses to allow the women to move between them without being seen from the street. In some of the grander houses the ground floor was occupied by slaves or used as warehouses or workshops, and the family members lived above. To keep them private, the outer walls only had slits for ventilation and all the light came in through the inner courtyard. The main entrance was through a porch with stone seats, a *baraza*, on either side and a wooden carved door, which led into an inner porch and the courtyard. The men of the family would also handle business matters in this area, keeping such things away from the women who resided in the deeper areas of the home. Staircases started at the front door but because of the narrowness of the houses they twisted and turned in many directions before reaching their final destination within the house. Slaves would sleep under the staircases. A *sabule* (guest room) was typically at the top of a staircase, separate from the main family staircase, and had its own bathroom.

In the absence of guests (usually visiting kin or trading partners), the head of the family would often sleep in the *sabule*, particularly when his wife had close female kin staying with her. The living rooms on the main family floor traditionally faced north and towards Mecca and there were no separate rooms as such for sleeping, with beds simply put in curtained alcoves. However, one room was put aside for the husband and wife and the very young children to sleep, and was usually set up a step higher than the rest of the rooms; in some of the grander houses they were very cool and spacious with wall niches to display pieces of pottery. The kitchen was usually on one of the upper floors, firstly so the smoke wouldn't blow into the sleeping or living areas, and secondly so women could prepare food away from visitors. There was also a room that was specifically set aside for childbirth, and was additionally used for the laying out of corpses, and for the seclusion of widows.

rise in the number of touts or 'beach boys'. If they accompany you to your hotel, a substantial 'commission' (30%) will be added to your daily rate. To avoid using their services, try and be firm with them that you don't want their services or carry your own bags to a waterfront restaurant first, have a drink and look for accommodation later. You will have no problem finding a room. Also be aware that while the presence of touts can be annoying and they can be pretty persistent, they also elicit some aggressive attitudes in some visitors, which does not always bode so well among the local people. In short, some travellers complain bitterly about them, while others actually make firm friends and enjoy their additional helpful local knowledge and services (*dhow* trips for example). It's just a case of your personal attitude and patience on how to deal with the touts.

## Tourist office

**Lamu Tourist Information Centre** ⓘ *on the harbour front to the north of the landing jetty, north of the Donkey Sanctuary, T042-633 132, lamu@tourism.go.ke*, and next door the **Lamu Tour Guides Association**. Both have friendly staff, and can organize walking tours of the town and *dhow* trips to islands. Both are closed on Sundays and public holidays. A three-hour walking tour of the town costs in the region of US$20 for one to three people.

## Background

The town of Lamu was founded in the 14th century, although there were people living on the island long before this. Throughout the years, and as recently as the 1960s, the island has been a popular hide-out for refugees fleeing the mainland.

The original settlement of Lamu was located to the south of the town, and is said to be marked by Hidabu hill. There was also another settlement between the 13th and 15th centuries to the north of the present town. By the 15th century it was a thriving port, one of the many that dotted the coast of East Africa. However, in 1505 it surrendered to the Portuguese, began paying tributes, and for the next 150 years was subservient to them and to the sultanate of the town of Pate on the nearby island, part of the Omani Dynasty that ruled much of the East African coast.

By the end of the 17th century, Lamu had become a republic ruled by a council of elders called the Yumbe, who were in principle responsible to Oman. In fact the Yumbe were largely able to determine their own affairs, and this period has been called Lamu's Golden Age. It was the period when many of the buildings were constructed and Lamu's celebrated architectural style evolved. The town became a thriving centre of literature and scholarly study and there were a number of poets who lived here. Arts and crafts flourished and trade expanded. The main products exported through Lamu were mangrove poles, ivory, rhino horn, hippo teeth, shark fins, cowrie shells, coconuts, cotton, mangoes, tamarind, *sim sim* (oil), charcoal and cashews. Rivalries between the various trading settlements in the region came to a head when Lamu finally defeated Pate in the battle of Shela in 1813. However, after 1840 Lamu found itself dominated by Zanzibar, which had been developed to become the dominant power along the East African coast. At a local level there were factions and splits within the town's population – in particular rivalries between different clans and other interest groups.

New products were developed for export including *bêche de mer* (a seafood), mats, bags, turtle shell, leather, rubber and sorghum. Despite this, toward the end of the 19th century Lamu began a slow economic decline as Mombasa and Zanzibar took over in importance as trading centres. The end of the slave trade dealt a blow to Lamu as the production of mangrove poles and grains for export depended on slave labour. Additionally, communications between the interior and Mombasa were infinitely better than those with Lamu, especially after the building of the Uganda Railway.

The airstrip on Manda Island was established in the early 1960s and the first visitors as such were white settlers on day tours who reputedly flew in for the day with packed lunches as there were no hotels. Then, as places to stay started to open their doors in the early 1970s, it became known as an exotic, remote and self-contained destination and began to attract hippies and other non-conformists drawn by its undisturbed traditional culture. Since then budget hotels have become popular with backpackers, and today there are also numerous top-end places to stay and some luxury villas to rent. Some people argue that Lamu's popularity and increased tourism will ultimately undermine the

## Alley cat

With their long necks and saucer like eyes, narrow bodies and straight legs, the cats of Lamu are the only cats on earth to bear the same physiques as the cats depicted in Egyptian hieroglyphics. One popular theory suggests that these cats may be the only remaining descendant of a breed of cats that were once found in ancient Egypt and now extinct in North Africa.

Traders may have carried the cats to Lamu on *dhows* hundreds of years ago. Other breeds of cat have since been brought to the island, and as a result the local gene pool has been distilled, yet the distinctive-looking Lamu cats still survive among the winding streets. There is a cat clinic to the north of the Donkey Sanctuary where a resident vet treats injured animals.

unique value system and culture of this Swahili settlement. Indeed there is a sign posted for the benefit of tourists at the airport: "Please remember that Lamu is a conservative Muslim town with a heritage of peace and goodwill. This is our home. Please tread gently here for our children are watching. Please respect this, and enjoy the unique atmosphere of our enduring yet fragile culture". Nevertheless, it cannot be argued that in recent decades the tourist trade has helped improve Lamu's economic prospects greatly.

## Lamu Island ⊜❼◓❸❻ ⤻ *pp335-344.*

→ *Phone code: 042. Colour map 2, B3.*

Lamu Island is 16 km by 7 km, with a third covered by sand dunes. The best beach on the island stretches for 12 km at Shela. Elsewhere, the coast of the island is covered with crawling mangroves attracting a number of birds. It is possible to walk all over the island, and there are many tracks into the interior. Alternatively, *dhows* make the short hop between Lamu Town and Shela and Mantondoni.

### Lamu Town

The town dates back to the 14th century although most of the buildings are actually 18th century, built in Lamu's Golden Age. The streets are very narrow, and the buildings on each side are two or three storeys high and as the houses face inwards, privacy is carefully guarded. The streets are set in a rough grid pattern running off the main street called **Harambee Avenue**, which runs parallel to the waterfront and used to open out to the sea, although building from the mid-1800s onwards has cut it off from the quayside. The narrow waterfront stretches the length of the town where cannons still point seaward. Touts offer *dhow* rides and white billowing sails occupy every inch of shoreline. The smaller ones serve as local taxis for Manda or the nearby Shela Beach, and the large ocean-going vessels are stacked high with mangrove poles and sand. Muscled sailors with *kikois* hoisted around their waists heave wooden carts from the docks or slumber on deck amongst charcoal burners and grain sacks.

Carved doors are one of the attractions for which Lamu has become known. This artesanal skill continues to be taught, and at the north end of the harbour you can see them being made in workshops by craftsmen and apprentices. There are over 20 mosques on the island, but they don't have minarets and mostly they are usually not very grand affairs and some are little different from other buildings. You can usually pick

# Lamu town

To Mwenye Alawi Mosque & Dhow Boatyard

Wood-carving Workshops

Jumaa

Mwana Mshamu

N'nayaye

Lamu Social Hall

Cat Clinic

Swahili House Museum

Mu ū

Lamu Tour Guides Association

Utukuni

MKOMANI

Whetstone

M'na Lalo

Donkey Sanctuary

Sheikh Mohamed bin Ali

Mwana Hadie Famau Tomb

Mpya

Bohora

Lamu Museum

Jetty

KCB

Standard Chartered

Pwani

Pwani Tawakal

House of Liwali Sud bin Hamad

Fort

District Commissioner's Office

Jetty

GARDENI

To Pillar Tomb

German Post Office Museum

Muslim Academy

Air Kenya

Riyadha

TSS

Lamu Book Centre

Ismaili Mosque (Ruin)

Lamu Harbour

LANGONI

Rope Walk

To Shela

Harambee Av (Usita wa Mui/Main St)

Kenyatta Rd

(Promenade)

Kenyatta Rd (Promenade)

Dhow Moorings

100 metres
100 yards

## Sleeping
Amu House **3**
Baytil Ajaib **14**
Casuarina Rest House **4**
Hapa Hapa **5**
Jannat House **8**
Kipepeo Guest House **16**
Lamu Archipelago Villas **6**
Lamu House **13**
Lamu Palace **7**
Petley's Inn **9**
Pole Pole **10**
Stone House **15**
Sunsail **2**
Wildebeest **1**
Yumbe House **11**
Yumbe Villa **12**

## Eating
Bush Gardens **2**
Coconut Juice Café **3**
Hapa Hapa **4**
New Minnaa **5**
New Star **6**
Olympic **7**
Seafront Café **1**
Whispers **10**

them out by the pile of sandals outside the doors during prayer time. You will need to seek permission before entering to look around.

The oldest mosque in Lamu is believed to be the **Pwani Mosque**, near the fort, which dates back to 1370, and today is just a crumbling ruin though an Arabic inscription can still be seen on one of the walls. The **Jumaa** (or Friday) **Mosque** is at the north end of town and is the second oldest in Lamu, dating from 1511. Then comes the **M'na Lalo Mosque** (1753), more or less in the centre of town, just a little to the north of the museum and set back from Harambee Avenue. This mosque was built in Lamu's Golden Age, and it was followed by **Muru Mosque** (1821) on Harambee Avenue, **Utukuni Mosque** (1823), well into the interior part of the town, and **Mpya Mosque** (1845), in the town centre. **Mwana Mshamu Mosque** (1855) is in the northwest area of the town; **Sheikh Mohamed bin Ali Mosque** (1875), in the town centre, and the **N'nayaye Mosque** (1880) on the northwest fringe of town. Two mosques have been built in the 20th century, the **Riyadha Mosque** (1901), to the south of the town, which is the main centre for the Maulidi Festival (see box page 329), and the **Bohora Mosque** (1920), which is fairly central, just inland of Harambee Avenue. The **Mwenye Alawi Mosque** (1850) at the north end of Main Street was originally for women, but it has since been taken over by the men. The small Ismaili community did have their own **Ismaili Mosque**, on the Kenyatta Road at the south end of town, but this is now in ruins. Adjacent to the Riyadha Mosque is the **Muslim Academy**, funded by Saudi Arabia, and which attracts students from all over the world.

The excellent **Lamu Museum** ⓘ *Kenyatta Rd, www.museums.or.ke, daily 0930-1800, US$7.50, children (under 18) US$3.60*, is run by the National Museums of Kenya and plays an important role in the conservation of old Lamu. It's set in a beautiful whitewashed house built in 1891, which was where the British colonial administrators lived before Independence. Before that, it had housed Queen Victoria's consul – one Captain Jack Haggard, brother of the more celebrated author of King Solomon's Mines. It has a fine carved wooden door inlaid with brass studs, the ground floor has a good bookshop and the entrance has some photographs of Lamu taken by French photographer Guillain in the period 1846-1849, as well as a large aerial photo of Lamu Town. In a lobby to the right is a Swahili kitchen with pestles and mortars and vermicelli presses. Also on the ground floor are examples of decorative 18th-century *Kidaka* plasterwork, carved Lamu throne chairs with wicker seats and elaborately carved Lamu headboards. To the rear are displays on the archaeological excavations of the Takwa Ruins (see page 338) on Manda Island, and at Siya and Shanga on Pate Island (see page 332). On the first floor, the balcony has a display of large earthenware pottery. The balcony room has photographs and models of seagoing vessels, mostly *dhows*, and the various types and styles in use. Just behind the balcony room is a display of musical instruments used in festivals and celebrations, including drums, cymbals, rattles and leg rattles. The most celebrated exhibits are the two **Siwa horns**. These are in the shape of elephant tusks, with the mouthpiece on the side. The Lamu horn is made of brass, the horn from nearby Pate is of ivory. They date from the 17th century, are elaborately decorated, and were blown on special occasions such as enthronements or weddings. Local tribes are featured in a side room, and there are displays on the **Oroma** from around Witu, Garsen and southwest of Lamu; the **Pokot** from west of the Tana River, and the **Boni** from the north of Lamu. The jewellery includes nose rings, earrings, anklets and necklaces in bead designs and in silver. There are some illustrations of hand and feet painting, in henna, in black and red. The two end rooms are examples of typical Swahili bridal rooms with furniture and dresses on display.

**Swahili House Museum** ① *inland from the museum, www.museums.or.ke, daily 0930-1800, US$7.50, children (under 18) US$3.60.* This is a traditional and fully restored 18th-century Swahili house with period furniture and, although it's quite small, it is interesting and the guides are great. There are three areas on the main floor, and a centre aisle has beds off to the left and right. The beds are wooden with rope and raffia forming the base. The main room has a particularly fine **kikanda** plaster screen on the wall; at one time, all of Lamu's houses were plastered white with this limestone wash as it represented purity. Although historically, when people had slaves in the homes, the areas where the slaves slept weren't plastered. Furnishings include a clock with an octagonal frame and a pointed pendulum case, a style found all along the East African coast. In the kitchen is an *mbuzi* (coconut grinder) and a *fumbu*, a straw implement resembling a large sock, which is used for squeezing the coconut juice from the shredded fruit. There is also a large wooden pestle and mortar, a pasta maker, a water boiler and a flour-grinding stone, as well as other pots and pans. Outside are a well and a garden with frangipani.

The construction of the **Lamu Fort** ① *Harambee Av, www.museums.or.ke, daily 0930-1800, US$7.50, children (under 18) US$3.60,* began in 1813 shortly after Lamu's victory at the Battle of Shela and was completed in 1821. The battle was an attempt by the people of Pate, allied with the Mazrui clan from Oman in Mombasa, to subjugate Lamu, but the attempt failed totally, and victory at Shela signaled the rise of Lamu as the leading power in the archipelago. The fort used to sit on the water's edge, as did Harambee Avenue, but over time another row of houses was built on discarded rubbish, which put the fort 70 m back from the water and the waterfront at where it is today. The construction is of coral blocks, covered with mortar that has a yellowy-orange hue marked by black patches and inside is a central courtyard surrounded by internal walkways and awnings. It is possible to walk round the battlements, and they afford a good view of the nearby area. It initially served as a barracks for a garrison of soldiers sent by the Sultan of Oman to protect Lamu. Their presence must have been protective as merchants built houses nearby that date from the same period. Between 1910 and 1984 it served as a prison both under the colonial and Kenyan governments. Now it has a not very good exhibition on the environment, a shop and a library, plus a pleasant café overlooking the busy square at the entrance, which is the best vantage point to look at the fort given the hefty entrance fee for non-residents. It's generally used as a community hall for the local people.

In the southwest part of town is a fluted **Pillar Tomb**, thought to date from the 14th century, though it's in danger of collapse. It can be reached by going south, turning inland just after the Halwa Shop, towards the Riyadha Mosque, and continuing on.

Another tomb is the **Mwana Hadie Famau Tomb**, a local woman believed to have lived here in the 15th or 16th century. This is situated a little inland from the museum. The tomb had four pillars at the corners with inset porcelain bowls and probably a central pillar as well. Legend has it a hermit took up residence in the hollow interior of the tomb, and became a nuisance by grabbing the ankles of passing women at night-time. The solution was to wall up the tomb while the hermit was not at home.

Behind the fort is the **House of Liwali Sud bin Hamad**, a fine example of Swahili architecture. A Liwali was a governor appointed by the Sultan of Zanzibar. It is still possible to appreciate how it looked when it was a single dwelling, though it is subdivided now.

On Main Street, just next to the **New Star** restaurant, is the site of the offices of the German East Africa Company. Originally the Germans thought that Lamu would make a suitable secure base for their expansion into the interior (much in the same way as the British used Zanzibar). The agreement regarding British and German 'spheres of influence'

# Maulidi

Maulidi is the prophet Mohammed's birthday, and this religious festival has its origins in Egypt from the eighth century. The unique Lamu version is believed to have been developed by Habib Swaleh Jamal Lely, an Arab from the Comoros Islands who came to Lamu in 1866 and established the Riyadha mosque. It attracts pilgrims from Zanzibar, Somalia, Uganda, and the Comoros Islands, when the population of Lamu doubles. Maulidi celebrations take different forms and are normally held in early June. The main religious celebrations take place in and around the Riyadha Mosque, when the central square outside the mosque is partitioned into areas for men and women for traditional dancing accompanied by drumming groups. The best known of these dances is the Goma, which involves lines of men standing together holding long walking sticks known as Bakora. Swaying to the rhythm of the drums, the men extend the sticks forward or interlink them among their drums. More solemn are the all-night prayer vigils, when the townspeople gather around the mosque for group prayer. On the last day of Maulidi, the men gather at the town cemetery and, following prayers, begin a procession into town. The colourful, energetic procession winds along the seafront towards the centre of town, with the crowds singing and dancing.

During the festival there are also a number of sporting events. These include a donkey race along the waterfront, running the length of the town. For the donkey jockeys, victory in this annual race is a much-coveted title. The race attracts most of the townspeople, who gather along the waterfront or anchor offshore in *dhows* to watch the action. Other events include a swimming race, a cross-country race and football matches. There's also a *bao* competition in the large open square in front of Lamu's fort. *Bao* is probably the oldest-known board game in human history, with archaeological evidence suggesting that the game has been played throughout Africa and the Middle East for thousands of years. The game is based around a basic board of four lines of holes, and involves beads, seeds or stones being placed in the holes, and each player then moving these objects around the board by following a simple set order. The winner is the one who places theirs in a set pattern before the other can.

The annual three-day Lamu Cultural Festival usually held at the end of November is a similar (though not religious) event and has gained in popularity since it was established in 2001. Like Maulidi, there are *dhow*, donkey and swimming races plus performances by Taarab musicians, Kiswahili poetry competitions, traditional handicrafts and henna painting are demonstrated and there is a mock Swahili bridal ceremony and a Swahili food bazaar.

in 1886 caused the Germans to turn their attention to Bagamoya, although they opened a post office in Lamu in 1888, which closed three years later. The site is now the missable **German Post Office Museum** ① *Harambee Av, daily 0930-1800, small entrance fee*, which has a few faded photographs from the era and not much else. Towards the rear of the town is the **whetstone** for sharpening knives, said to have been imported from Oman as local stone was not suitable.

**Donkey Sanctuary**, in the northern part of the town close to the waterfront. This is run by the International Donkey Sanctuary ① *based in the UK, http://drupal.thedonkeysanctuary.*

*org.uk*, a charity concerned with the welfare of donkeys worldwide. In 2008 it celebrated its 21st anniversary in Lamu on 4 July – dubbed by one employee as Independence Day for the donkeys of Lamu. There are an estimated 2200 donkeys on the island, which are used in agriculture but also in carrying household provisions and building materials. They generally plod around town on their own and in theory each is owned by someone, although how donkey and owner stay connected is somewhat mystifying. The founder of the trust, Dr Elizabeth Svendsen, first visited Lamu in 1985 while on holiday, and after seeing the poor condition of the working donkeys, established the sanctuary and clinic here in 1987. There is a small enclosure that anyone can visit where sick donkeys receive free care, and the donkeys that roam the town can find fodder and water. It's rather endearing here to see a donkey with a cartoon-like criss-cross bandage somewhere on it covering a minor wound. The twice-yearly de-worming programme on Lamu and the surrounding islands has contributed hugely to the better health of the donkeys, and primitive practices of bleeding a donkey or burning them with hot irons to treat illness is thankfully much reduced. The donkey awards in March/April are organized by the Lamu Donkey Sanctuary in conjunction with the Kenya Society for the Protection and Care of Animals (KSPCA) to promote animal welfare. Prizes are given for the best-cared-for donkey, and a surprising number of local people turn out to proudly parade their well-groomed beasts of burden.

## Matondoni Village
This is a village of mud and thatched huts of a few hundred people on the western side of the island, about 8 km from town, where you can see *dhows* being built and repaired on the beach. The easiest way to get there is to hire a *dhow* between a group – you will have to negotiate the price and can expect to pay around US$30-40 for the boat. Alternatively you can hire a donkey – ask at your hotel. A third option is to walk, although you should leave early as it gets very hot. The walk will take a couple of hours and is quite complicated. You want to turn-off the main street roughly opposite **Petley's** and keep walking west inland. Ask for directions from there; you want to keep going in the same direction of the telephone wires which go to Matondoni – if you follow these you should get there eventually.

## Shela
Sticking out on the southeastern tip of Lamu, this village is a smaller duplicate of Lamu town and is the upmarket end of the island. It is a tangle of narrow, sandy lanes, tall stone houses, some smaller thatched dwellings, and a spacious square ringed with a few market stalls and small shops. Here in the cool of the evenings the elders gather to talk and women come out to shop. Also look out for boys washing donkeys on the beach at low tide. In the town are a number of old buildings including several wonderfully restored houses that you can rent (at a price). The people of Shela were originally from the island of Manda and speak a dialect of Swahili that is quite different to that spoken in Lamu. The **Friday Mosque** was built in 1829 and is noted for its slender, conical minaret. The 12-km Shela Beach starts a five-minute walk from the village. Shela is just 3 km or a 40-minute walk from Lamu, go down to the end of the harbour and then along the beach. If you don't want to walk you can catch a *dhow* taxi.

## Southern shores
The southern shores have the best beach, which begins just to the south of Shela – 12 km of almost deserted white sand that backs onto the sand dunes. As there is no reef the waves get fairly big. Here you can stroll for miles along the deserted shoreline littered

## Shela stash

In 1915 a man called Albert Deeming was convicted of the murder of a woman and two children in Melbourne, Australia. He was sentenced to death but before his execution he prepared a document detailing the whereabouts of 50 kilos of gold bars buried on Lamu Island.

In 1901, Deeming had boarded the bullion train from Pretoria to Laurenco-Marques, shot two guards and forced a third to open the bullion compartments. Grabbing as many bars as he could carry he jumped the train and made his way to the coast. At Delgoa Bay, he sailed by *dhow* to Lamu, but locals were suspicious, and he hid the gold at a small European graveyard at Shela, in the grave of William Searle, a British sailor.

Deeming's belongings were eventually returned to his relatives in South Africa, and one of them made a visit to Lamu in 1919, but was unable to locate the grave.

In 1947 the documents passed to a Kenyan farmer, who with a couple of companions travelled to Lamu and found the Shela graveyard. Four graves were marked, but none of them had the name of William Searle. Convinced that this must be the graveyard described by Deeming they began probing the sands. They located a solid object and removed the covering of sand. It was a gravestone with a well-weathered crack. Deeming's instructions were that the gold was in a small wooden box at the head of the grave, at a depth of two feet. Despite extensive excavations they found nothing. They were curious over the fact that an area of sand appeared less compacted than that of its surroundings. Also, when they examined the gravestone, it had some cracks that looked quite recent. They made discreet enquiries in Lamu Town. Four weeks earlier a party of three Australians from Melbourne had visited Lamu and had spent two days at the Shela sand dunes.

with pansy shells, otherwise known as sand dollars, where foamy waves sweep bare feet and cormorants attempt balancing acts on the sea breeze.

## Manda Island ⊙ ➤ *pp335-344. Colour map 2, B3.*

This island is just to the north of Lamu and has the airstrip on it. It is very easy to get to and is a popular day trip to see the ruins at Takwa. The island is about the size of Lamu but has only a small permanent population – partly because of a shortage of fresh water and thus cultivable land. About a fifth of the island is made up of sand dunes and sandy flat land with just thorn bushes and palms. Another three fifths of the island are mangrove swamps and muddy creeks. The island is separated from the mainland by the narrow Mkanda Channel and the main port is **Ras Kilimdini**, which is located on the northern side of the island.

### Ins and outs

Access to Manda Island and the towns is by way of motorized ferry to the airstrip as well as by *dhow*. However *dhow* is the easiest as it will take you closer to the ruins, otherwise you will have to walk across the island. The *dhow* will cost about US$30-40 for a group of four to five people. See page 343 about organizing a *dhow* from Lamu. It takes about 1½ hours and is dependent on the tides. You may have to wade ashore through the mangrove swamp.

## New Year's Day dhow race

The people of Lamu are fiercely proud of their maritime tradition and there is an annual *dhow* race on New Year's Day at Shela Beach. This event is an important event on the island, and winning the race is a great honour among *dhow* captains. Like the annual donkey race, it brings the island to life and the shorelines throng with supporters. Individual *dhows* are brightly decorated, and festivities on race day last well into the night. Local captains and their crews compete on a course that tests their skills and prowess, and race day is one of showmanship and celebration. Until recently *dhows* were built entirely without nails – sewn with coconut cord and pegged by wooden dowels. All *dhows* have eyes painted on the bows for protection and to see dangerous rocks. A poignant, well-used Kiswahili proverb, 'You cannot turn the wind, so turn the sail', originates from the sailors of Lamu.

### Sights

The **Takwa Ruins** ① *www.museums.or.ke, daily 0930-1800, US$7.50, children (under 18) US$3.60,* are ruins of another ancient Swahili town that is believed to have prospered from the 15th to the 17th centuries, with a population of 2000 to 3000 people. It was abandoned in favour of the town of Shela on Lamu, probably because salt water contaminated most of the town's supplies of fresh water. The ruins consist of the remains of a wall that surrounded the town, about 100 houses, a mosque and a tomb dated from 1683. As with many of the other sites on the coast, the remains include ablution facilities. The houses face north towards Mecca as does the main street. There is a mosque at the end of the street that is thought to have been built on the site of an old tomb. The other feature of the ruins is the pillar tomb, which is situated just outside the town walls. The ruins have been cleared but little excavation has been done here. The creek that Takwa is located on almost cuts the island in half during high tide.

### Pate Island ●● ▶▶ *pp335-344. Colour map 2, B3.*

Pate Island is about three times the size of Lamu and located about 20 km to the northeast. Unlike both Lamu and Manda, it does not have a large area taken up by dunes. The island is divided into two parts – indeed it may have once been two islands, but the channel dividing them is so shallow that only the smallest boats can go down it. The land is very low lying and the towns are situated on shallow inlets that can only be reached at high tide. The only deep-water landing point is at **Ras Mtangawanda** in the west of the island, but as it is not a sheltered harbour it has never had a major settlement. Although it is fairly easily accessible it does not receive many visitors.

### Ins and outs

To get Pate Island, there's a motorized public ferry that departs usually daily from the Lamu jetty about one hour before high tide – you'll need to check locally when this is. The reason for this is the Mkanda Channel is only accessible by boat at high tide. The ferry not only carries passengers but goods from Lamu to Pate, so it's a long and uncomfortable ride and you may find yourself wedged between boxes and many other people. You will also need plenty of food and water. However they do pull a blue tarpaulin over the boat to protect against the sun. After two to three hours, it stops at the near on deserted Mtangwanda on Pate Island, which is the nearest point to Pate Town. It takes about an hour to walk to Pate Town from here. After a further four to five hours the ferry stops at Faza, and then goes on to Kizingitini, which takes about another hour. Again you'll have to check locally when the ferry returns from these places on its run back to Lamu as times are determined by when it is high tide in the Mkanda Channel. Sometimes much smaller *dhows* link the points on Pate Island but again are dependent on the tides. Generally, when visiting Pate Island the best thing to do is to get off the ferry at Mtangwanda, walk to Pate Town, and then walk through Siyu to Faza from where you will be able to get the ferry back to Lamu. Alternatively a group can organize a *dhow* in Lamu to explore for a few days, but there is nowhere to stay as such though camping is possible if you have a tent.

## Pate Town

The town of Pate is only accessible from the sea at the right tide – and you will have to walk from the ferry's landing place at Mtangwanda. It is in the southwest corner of the island and is one of the old Swahili towns that dot the coast. The town shows strong Arabic and Indian influences, and was once most famous for the silk that was produced here. The old stone houses are crumbling and tobacco has been planted amongst the ruins. The main ruins are those of **Nabahani**, which are found just outside the town. Although they have not yet been excavated you should be able to make out the town walls, houses, mosques and tombs.

The age of the town is disputed – the earliest remains that have been found are from the 13th century – although according to some accounts the town dates back to the eighth century. The town was reasonably prosperous up to 1600, although by the time the Portuguese first arrived it had begun to decline. The Portuguese did not have much success and by the 17th century had withdrawn to Mombasa. The final decline of Pate was the war with Lamu. There had been an ongoing dispute between the two islands. Over the years the port at Pate silted up, so Lamu was used instead by the bigger *dhows*, and the tensions increased. The situation reached a climax in 1813 when the army from Pate was defeated at Shela and the town went into a decline from which it has never recovered.

## Siyu

The channel that Siyu is sited on is so silted up that only the smallest boats can reach Siyu. It is therefore necessary to approach the town by foot – either from Pate (about 8 km) or from Faza (about 10 km). Unless you are happy to get lost and therefore walk for hours, you would be advised to take a guide, as the route (particularly from Pate) is complicated. Siyu is a stone-built town dating from about the 15th century. It became most well known as a centre for Islamic scholarship and is believed to have been an important cultural centre during the 17th and 18th centuries. At one time is said to have had 30,000 inhabitants. Today there are probably fewer than 4000 people living in the town and the inhabited part of the town is slightly apart from the ancient ruined area. A creek separates the residential area from the **fort**, built by Seyyed Said, believed to date from the mid-19th century when the town was occupied by forces of the Sultan of Zanzibar. The fort has some impressive canons and has been partly renovated. The town is fairly dilapidated and outside the town are coconut plantations. It is a small fishing village that has a thriving crafts industry – you will be able to see leather goods being made, and doors, furniture and jewellery.

About one hour's walk from Siyu there are the **Shanga Ruins**, but they are almost impossible to find without the help of a local guide. Ask around in Siyu for someone to show you the way. There have been excavations in recent years and they show signs of unearthing impressive remains. There are buildings from the 13th and 14th century and many artefacts have been found dating back to the eighth and ninth centuries. There is a pillar tomb, a large mosque, a smaller second mosque, about 130 houses and a palace. The whole town was walled with five access gates and outside the wall is a cemetery containing well over 300 tombs. If you are visiting the islands by *dhow* and would rather not walk you can ask your boatman to take you to Shanga direct.

## Faza

Faza is about 18 km from Pate Town, and 10 km northeast of Siyu. Although the town of Faza is believed to date from the 13th century and possibly as early as the eighth century, there is little in the way of ruins left here. Today it's a ramshackle place of mud thatched huts crammed together and piles of rubbish everywhere. In 1990, there was a huge fire that destroyed most of the houses in the town so the huts are the replacement. However, the town is important in that it is the district headquarters of Pate Island and some of the mainland. It therefore has a number of modern facilities that are not found elsewhere on the island – such as post office, school, telephone exchange, a police station (where the police force has nothing to do) and some simple shops and restaurants.

The original town is believed to have been completely destroyed in the 13th century by the nearby town of Pate, rebuilt, and destroyed again in the late 16th century this time by the Portuguese. It was again rebuilt and joined forces with the Portuguese against Pate. However, its significance declined until recently when, being the district headquarters, it resumed its position of importance.

Close to where the ferries anchor are the ruins of the **Kunjanja Mosque**. Although no more than a pile of rubble, you can still see some the Mihrab, which points to Mecca and which is a beautiful example with fine carvings. There are some splendid Arabic inscriptions above the entrance. Outside the town there is the tomb of Amir Hamad, the commander of the Sultan of Zanzibar's army who was killed here, in action, in 1844. Faza makes an interesting place to walk around. From Faza you could, if you wanted, walk on to the other villages on the island, all within 40 minutes of Faza: Kisingitini, Bajumwali, Tundwa, and the closest, Nyambogi.

## Kiunga Marine National Reserve ●● ▸▸ *pp335-344. Colour map 2, B3.*

In the far northern part of the Kenyan coast, stretching from Boteler Islands to 20 km north of Kiunga, this marine national reserve, opened in 1979, has a reputation for having some of the best coral reefs interspersed with limestone islands in Kenya, but it suffers from being impossibly remote. Sadly, this area has suffered from the problems to the north in Somalia, and so there have been virtually no visitors in recent years. It is 250 sq km from the northeast coastal border of mainland Kenya to the Pate Island. The park has a chain of about 50 calcareous offshore islands and coral reefs running for some 60 km parallel to the coastline off the northern most coast of Kenya and adjacent to Dodori and Boni National Reserves on the mainland. Composed of old, eroded coral, the islands mainly lie inland around 2 km offshore and inshore of the fringing reef. They vary in size from a few hundred square metres to 100 ha or more. Leatherback turtles, dugongs and nesting migratory sea birds are to be found here. Dugongs resemble large sea lions and have been almost hunted to extinction, making them one of the rarest sea mammals. They give birth to live pups that suckle on teats situated high on the female's chest wall. They are believed to be the origin of sailor's mermaid sightings as it was thought that they had 'breasts'. The coastal area is made up of scrubland and mangroves surrounded by microscopic marine plants and dugong grass. The coral here is extensive. As you would expect, there is a good variety of marine birds with colonies of various gulls and terns.

**Kiwayu Island** is located on the far northeast of the Lamu Archipelago and is part of the reserve. The Island itself is 19 km long and roughly 1.5 km wide. There are lots of caves and coves to explore, and there two villages on the island, **Kiwayu** and **Chandani**. The highlight here is the 10-km-long virgin beach and the spectacular snorkelling on the unspoilt coral reefs. There is an airstrip that serves the two luxury lodges, see page 344, which can also organize *dhow* and speed-boat launches from Lamu.

## Dodori and Boni national reserves

Dodori and Boni national reserves are in the far north of the Kenyan coast close to the Somali border. Gazetted in 1976 they cover an area of 2590 sq km. Dodori National Reserve is in Coastal Province and is 877 sq km extending from northeast Lamu District up to Kiunga. It is named after the river ending in the Indian Ocean at Dodori Creek, a breeding place for dugongs. The vegetation consists of mangrove swamp, lowland dry forest, marshy glades and groundwater forest and is bisected by the Dodori River. Dodori Reserve was established to protect an antelope called the Lamu topi, as this area is a major breeding ground. There are also a few elephant, buffalo, giraffe, duikers and lesser kudu in the reserve. In addition the area is rich in birdlife. Pelicans are particularly common here. Boni National Reserve is one of the large, remote parks in the northeast of the country, contiguous with the Somali border down to the coast in Northeastern Province. It is 1340 sq km, and contains the only coastal lowland groundwater forest in Kenya. The diversity of the vegetation consist of coastal and riverine forests, mangroves, swampy grasslands and savannah. Away from the rivers and channels, impenetrable thornbush is scattered with gigantic baobabs. Unfortunately there is little information about what wildlife is in the reserve, and given that it borders Somali, the antelope here may well have been targeted by poachers for meat.

To reach the reserves, from Mokowe opposite Lamu take the road D568 inland and turn right at Bodhei. This track leads to Kiunga, on the northern limit of the Kenyan coast, passing between both reserves. Along the road, at the town of Mangai, a track allows for wildlife observation at both banks of Dodori River. Once in Kiunga, the road to Mkokoni borders the coast and provides access to some waterholes amongst the bush. However, the area is only passable in the dry season. The easiest access is by sea, especially if you wish to watch the sea wildlife at Dodori. You can travel by boat or *dhow* to Dodori Creek and from there sail the channels and mangroves. However, there are no camp sites or facilities at these reserves and given its proximity to the Somali border, most parts of this national reserve have been out of bounds to tourists for a while. If you want to go up here be sure to check with the local authorities and tour agencies before departure.

## ⊙ Lamu archipelago listings

*For Sleeping and Eating price codes and other relevant information, see Essentials pages 34-38.*

## ⊜ Sleeping

Price varies with the season. Peak periods are Dec and Jan for upmarket travellers,

and Jul-Sep for families and budget travellers. At other times, there's plenty of scope for negotiation, especially if you plan to stay for more than 1 or 2 days. If you are planning to stay here for a longer holiday and are in a family or group then it is worth renting a house (with staff). Many are holiday homes of Kenya residents and offer high-quality accommodation at a very modest price. People post details of houses to rent on notice board at the museum or visit www.lamuretreats.com or www.kenya safarihomes.com. At the lower end of the price range, the hotels in Lamu tend to be hot and suffer from frequent problems with the water supply (expect cold buckets), but nevertheless are still mostly housed in traditional and atmospheric old houses.

## Lamu Island *p325, map p326*

### Lamu Town *p325, map p326*

**B Baytil Ajaib**, to the west of the Donkey Sanctuary, T042-632 033, www.baytil ajaib.com. A recently and immaculately restored house with 4 spacious en suite rooms, or a group can rent it singularly. With verandas and an open courtyard on each floor supported by gracious columns and arches, where there are comfortable sitting areas with day beds piled with cushions and Swahili and other African artefacts on display. The name means 'House of Wonder' and there are great views over the town and the Lamu Channel. Rates are bed and breakfast or ½ board and you can discuss menus with the chef.

**B Lamu House**, near the Lamu Social Hall, T042-633 491, www.lamuhouse.com. 2 upmarket houses near the waterfront and the most luxurious place to stay in Lamu Town with 5 beautiful and stylish rooms, each decorated with lattice windows, dressing rooms and private terraces, and a lovely whitewashed courtyard with a refreshing plunge pool and day beds. Rates include breakfast and a free *kikoy*, lunch and dinner are US$25 each and the service is excellent. Can organize day trips or dinner on their *dhow*.

**C Lamu Palace Hotel**, T042-633 104, islands@africaonline.co.ke. Located on the harbour front at the south end of town, now managed with **Petley's Inn**. Set in an imposing 3-storey block, this has 22 a/c rooms and is very attractively decorated.

The pleasant patio restaurant has average and bland buffet set meals, but the à la carte seafood is very good. It's possible to negotiate a better rate off season, Oct-May, and it's one of few places that sells alcohol in Lamu. Friendly and helpful set up and can organize *dhow* excursions.

**C Petley's Inn**, Kenyatta Rd, reservations through Lamu Palace, above. A historic hotel founded by an Englishman called Percy Petley in 1962 who fell in love with Lamu whilst recovering from a safari accident. The hotel has 11 rooms and a swimming pool on the 1st floor. The rooms are very pleasant, in traditional Swahili style, the 2 front rooms have a private terrace. The restaurant no longer exists, but the 2 bars survive and remain popular, and it's one of the few places that serves chilled beers.

**C Wildebeest**, T042-632261, www.wilde beeste.com. Several lovely traditional apartments in 2 houses, sleeping between 2-7 people (the floor-level beds are draped with mosquito nets), each has a small kitchen. There are fantastic stone terraces dotted at various levels with comfortable day beds for lounging, steep stone steps around courtyard gardens and, *makuti* roofs. Downstairs is an art shop and gallery. Larger apartments are around US$130, so for groups the cost per person is very reasonable, rates include a house boy.

**C-D Stone House Hotel**, near the Swahili House Museum, T042-633 544, www.stone househotellamu.com. This is a quiet friendly and good-value option where the small interior coral-walled garden at the entrance provides a nice welcome, and it's one of the best preserved of Lamu's 18th-century houses. It has 10 simple en suite rooms and 4 sharing a bathroom, with Swahili furniture and 4-poster beds, mosquito nets and fans and a reliable source of (cold) water. The small rooftop restaurant has good views and serves seafood and Swahili dishes, as well as cold drinks and fresh juices.

**D Amu House**, T042-633 420, a few streets behind the **Standard Chartered Bank**. This very central and a charming place, owned by an American woman, is a reworked 18th-century Swahili house with plaster carvings and niches, pretty Swahili furniture and canopy beds, some rooms have a veranda. Breakfast included but other meals are only available on request.

**D Jannat House**, north end of town, near Mwana Mshamu mosque, T042-633 414, www.jannathouse.com. This dates from the 18th century and was built as a merchant´s house. The 16 rooms have Swahili furniture, warm (not hot) water and mosquito nets, and it offers Kiswahili language courses. Good food in pleasant garden atmosphere and is one of the few hotels with a swimming pool. Rates are bed and breakfast or ½ board, expect pay in the region of US$80 for a double but this drops considerably in low season.

**D Kipepeo Guest House**, on the waterfront to the north of Lamu House, T042-633 569, www.kipepeo-lamu.com. Opened in 2005, this imposing white 4-storey block run by a German woman has 7 simple but comfortable doubles, with or without tiled bathrooms, and offers some of the best views of the Lamu Channel from the rooftop terrace. You can self-cater in the kitchen or breakfast is available for US$3. Groups can hire a whole floor (with the kitchen) and fit in as many as they like to a maximum of 13 from about US$120.

**D-E Sunsail Hotel**, on the waterfront near the District Commissioner's Office, T042-632 065, sunsailhotel2004@hotmail.com. 18 double rooms in a fully restored 100-year-old building that was once the sugar depot, with whitewashed walls and an impressive large carved front door. Smart rooms with fans and Lamu beds, tiled bathrooms, restaurant under thatch on the roof with new windows and views of the busy jetty, big discounts during low season, very friendly management.

**E Yumbe House**, near the Swahili House Museum, T/F042-633 101. This is a basic but wonderful hotel full of atmosphere and excellent value and is consistently popular with backpackers. It's a traditional house of 4 storeys and is airy and spacious, clean, friendly, has a good water supply and

the price includes breakfast. The garden courtyard is especially pretty.

**E Yumbe Villa**, located near the fort, see Yumbe House, above, for contact details. This is the annex of Yumbe House where you'll stay if that's full and is another traditional house with Zidaka niches in the ground floor walls, and clean and tidy rooms with traditional Lamu beds, mosquito nets, en suite shower and toilet, some have fans and fridges.

**F Casuarina Rest House**, above the Kenya Airways office near the Lamu Museum, T042-633 123. Another popular budget option in a great location on the waterfront, with 10 clean and spacious rooms, 6 have their own bathroom while 4 have shared bathrooms, mosquito nets and fans in a building that used to be the Police Station and it's well run and friendly. There is a large rooftop area and breakfast is included, and they claim that they do not give commission to touts, so go alone.

**F Hapa Hapa**, to the rear of the **Hapa Hapa** restaurant on Main St. Fairly simple but spacious, with clean shared bathroom, some rooms look out over the Lamu Channel, no fans though so ask for one of the top rooms, which catch the sea breezes.

**F Lamu Archipelago Villas**, on waterfront at southern end, T042-633 247. Good location, 12 rooms in an imposing white building, some with their own bathrooms, includes breakfast, fans, nets, efficiently run, though rooms are a little grubbier than others in town.

**F Pole Pole**, just inland, north end of town, T042-633 344. This is one of the highest buildings in Lamu, with good views from the roof, but is quite run down now. It offers very basic board and lodgings with beds that are falling apart, mosquito nets and fans, some of the 15 rooms have bathrooms with cold water although water cannot be relied upon. Nevertheless cheap from about a negotiable US$8.

## Shela p330

In recent years there has been much restoration work going on in Shela (left to its own devices Shela would probably be far more dilapidated than it is today), and there are now some wonderful places to stay. By comparison, Lamu town is definitely the poorer cousin. Some of the houses are now very luxurious and are popular with wealthy Europeans: Princess Caroline of Monaco for example owns a house in Shela.

**L Shela House**, T042-633 419, www.shela house.com. This is a collection of 4 luxury houses in the village: **Shela House**, **Beach House**, **Garden House** and **Palm House**. The decor is very luxurious with lots of dark wood and cream walls, floors and furniture, and each house has 3 staff including a cook and must be booked for a minimum of 3 nights (7 nights in high season). You can self-cater or full-board meals are an additional US$70 per person per day, US$35 for children under 12. **Shela House** (from US$650 per night) is built on 3 floors around an open courtyard, the house well and an ancient gardenia. The entrance hall leads into the courtyard, edged by a *baraza* sitting and eating area, the upper rooms comprise 5 en suite bedrooms, nursery room and a day room and terrace; there are also hammocks on the rooftop. **Beach House** (from US$1300 per night) is a large house with 4 double and 1 triple en suite bedrooms, an infinity, fresh-water swimming pool, bar area and low comfortable *baraza* seats. Up the 1st flight of stairs is a large dining and living room, leading on to a terrace. **Garden House** (from US$300 per night) has a ground-floor dining and seating area, a double bedroom and a children's twin on the 1st floor and a top-floor master bedroom with a shaded rooftop *baraza* and open terrace with sun beds. **Palm House** (from US$650 per night) is designed around an open courtyard, with 2 doubles and 1 twin bedroom, all en suite with private balconies. There is a panoramic view from the covered rooftop, with a bar, sun beds and *baraza* lounging area.

**A Johori House**, reservations through **Kenya Safari Homes**, Nairobi, T020-890 699, www.kenyasafarihomes.com. Another well-restored 18th-century house, sleeping up to

6 on 3 floors, with excellent views. The top floor features a covered rooftop with hammocks and day beds. There is a lovely outside area for al fresco dining, fully equipped kitchen, and staff includes houseboy and cook. Other similar houses for rent in the village are **Kisimani House** and **Mnarani House**, which both sleep 8, and **Jasmine House** which sleeps 7. Rates start from around US$300 per night depending on season but shared among a group they represent good value.

**A Kijani House Hotel**, on water's edge between **Peponi's** and Shela Beach, T042-633 235, www.kijani-lamu.com. Here are 10 en suite rooms in a collection of restored old Swahili houses, with fine gardens, traditional furniture, white archways, verandas, 2 small swimming pools, seafood, Swahili dishes, and a touch of Italian cuisine in the Kijani restaurant, excellent standards. Room rates are bed and breakfast, half or full board and include boat transfers from the airport. Offers fishing, snorkelling and guided tours of Lamu town. Closed May-June.

**A Kizingo**, T0733-954 770, www.kizingo.com. This is a small peaceful eco lodge situated at the end of Shela Beach with 8 thatched cottages set well apart from each other, with verandas with hammocks and unrivalled sea views. Room rates include all meals as well as afternoon tea with homemade cake and boat transfers from Manda Island. Fine wines from South Africa, Chile and Italy and cocktails are extra. Supports a local turtle conservation project, and activities include visiting the turtles laying their eggs on the beach, fishing, snorkelling, and bird and bush walks or guests can hire bikes to explore the local villages. Closed May-Jun.

**B Peponi's**, Shela Beach, T042-633 4213, www.peponi-lamu.com. Facing the channel that runs between Lamu and Manda, this is a really wonderful setting with about 500 m of private beach. The hotel is made up of a series of cottages each with a veranda and full facilities. There is an excellent restaurant (see under Eating, below) as well as a bar. The hotel provides full watersports facilities, probably the best and most extensive on the island and organizes excursions. Very efficiently run and booking well ahead is advised. Closed mid-Apr to end of Jun.

**B-C Baitil Aman Guesthouse**, in the middle of the village, T042-633 022, www.baitil aman.com. Newly opened in 2006, this 18th-century house took over 7 years to restore and now features some particularly fine examples of Zidaka niches in the walls and some splendid carved wooden doors. There are just 8 en suite rooms with mosquito nets, fans and outdoor seating areas. Rates are bed and breakfast, dinner is US$20 extra per person, which is served in the dining room or on Swahili mats on the rooftop terrace. The name means 'House of Peace'.

**C Banana House**, in the village, 50 m back from the beach, T042-632 044, www.banana house-lamu.com. This is run by a friendly Dutch woman as a holistic place to stay, it offers daily yoga sessions and guests are required to wash their feet in a small pool before entering the house barefooted. There are 6 en suite rooms, plus 1 more for children that shares a bathroom with parents, a 2nd-floor restaurant, attractive sitting areas with hammocks and day beds and 1 lounge area has an interesting wall embedded with hundreds of coloured bottles.

**C Fatumu's Tower**, in the village, T042-632 213, www.fatumastower.com. Another nicely restored house, this has 5 en suite doubles plus a ground floor 3 bedroom family apartment, furnished in local antiques and fabrics, with several balconies and terraces for relaxing and a small plunge pool with a waterfall in the garden. On the 1st floor is a bright white yoga hall, which lets light in through slit windows, where yoga classes are held in the early evening and massages are available. You can either self-cater, a cook is provided, or lunch and dinner are US$20/25 respectively.

**C Shella Royal House**, in the village, T0722-698 059, www.shellaroyalhouse.com. Here there are 2 houses, 1 with 3 storeys and 1 with 4 storeys, with 13 spacious and airy rooms, all but 1 are en suite, with

traditional furnishings and whitewashed walls, and a lovely roof terrace with day beds for relaxing. Rates are half board and Swahili dinners feature plenty of fish and seafood. They also have a *dhow* for excursions, some tents and can arrange overnight camping trips to the other islands.

**D-E Stop Over Guest House**, on the beach, reservations through **Lamu Homes**, Nairobi T020-444 7397, www.lamuhomes.com. Newly renovated and locally owned, 5 clean rooms, simply furnished with fans and mosquito nets and have good views of the sea and plenty of sea breezes. The 3 rooms on the 1st floor can be rented as an apartment with access to kitchen facilities on the same floor. On the ground floor is a restaurant serving Swahili dishes, fresh juices, soft drinks and seafood.

**E Shela Bahari Guest House**, on the beach, close to Peponi's, T042-632 046. A similar set up to the nearby **Stop Over** with spacious rooms, big beds, nets, fans, Swahili furniture, the rooms open out on to a broad balcony that is right above the water at high tide, and the ones at the back without a view are cheaper. The top room here is the best and very private with its own balcony and hammock and there's a small restaurant where you can discuss what you want for dinner beforehand.

**E Shela Pwani Guest House**, very close to **Peponi's** and the jetty, above the shop selling *kikoys*, T042-633 540. Has 4 double rooms and 1 triple, the top double room is the best, though all have bathrooms (cold water), fans and mosquito nets, set in an old house with some nice traditional plasterwork and well managed. There is a small dining room downstairs, where it is possible to organize meals that include seafood and Swahili dishes and the rooftop terrace has fine views.

## Southern shores p330

**L Kipungani Explorer**, reservations **Heritage Hotels**, Nairobi, T020-444 6651, www.heritage-eastafrica.com. The 1st of Heritage Group's highest standard 'Explorer' resorts, this lodge, with just 14 *makuti* thatched cottages made from local palm leaf mats, is located at the southern tip of Lamu Island. All are extremely spacious and comfortable and each has a veranda. It organizes various excursions and snorkelling trips, and there is a sea-water swimming pool, good restaurant and bar where non-guests can visit for lunch. Boats to get there depart from **Peponi's**. The property has an extremely close bond with the people of neighbouring Kipungani Village, who will show you their ancient boat-building and mat-weaving techniques, or take you fishing or prawn-netting in the remote Dadori Nature Reserve. Rates are full board and include boat transfers from Manda Island. Closed mid-Mar to 1st July.

## Other islands

### Manda Island *p331*
There is no fresh water on Manda Island; it is brought over from Lamu daily. Consequently water is used carefully at the lodges and water conservation is encouraged.
**L Manda Bay**, T042-633 475, www.manda bay.com. An exclusive resort offering water sports and *dhow* safaris, all the buildings are constructed with local materials in traditional coastal style, with palm-thatch roofs and woven matting covering the floors. 16 spacious and comfortable cottages with their own bathrooms and verandas. Meals, seafood and Italian, are relaxed and casual, served in the dining room, on the beach, or on a *dhow*. Rates are full board and include soft drinks, beer and wine. Closed mid-May to mid-July.
**C-D Diamond Village**, T0720-015001, www.diamondbeachvillage.com. Very comfortable and affordable *bandas* on the beach with thatched roofs, 1 for families that sleeps 4-8 people, and the others with a double bed downstairs and a single bed mounted in the roof, each has a front porch and en suite shower and sink. Because of the lack of water, toilets are pit latrines. There is also a rather unique treehouse in the arms of a baobab tree, which has a wooden deck all the way around the trunk. Very good food in the open-air restaurant. A rather special feature of the lodge are the giant clam shells that act as bird baths and attract a colourful array of birds at both dawn and dusk.
**F Camping**, is available at a pretty site close to the Takwa Ruins, though there are no facilities and you will need to be completely self sufficient. Bring plenty of water as none is available on the island.

### Pate Island *p332*
Every few years a lodging house opens in Faza, but the lack of visitors forces them to close sooner or later. Private accommodation, though, is easy to find and you can ask around to stay at a family house and people may also approach you. Again in Siyu it is possible to rent rooms in local houses – there are no formal guesthouses. It's possible you may get offered food by your hosts and other than that there are only basic provisions available from small shops and stalls.

### Kiunga Marine National Reserve *p334*
**L Kiwayu Safari Village**, to the north of Lamu on the Kiwayu Peninsula, in a beautiful bay on the mainland opposite Kiwayu Island, reservations, Nairobi, T020-600 107, www.kiw ayu.com. Nestled among the dunes overlooking a sheltered lagoon, here there are 18 luxurious, traditional-style thatched *bandas*, a restaurant, bar and shop. The hotel has a fleet of deep-sea fishing vessels and game fishing, boat trips into the mangrove swamps and waterskiing are on offer, and the beach is wonderful. The food is excellent and non-seafood dishes are available on request. The honeymoon suite is so intimate and secluded it's a boat ride away on the opposite beach nestled amongst some baobab trees. Closes for 2 months from mid-Apr during low season.
**L Mike's Camp Kiwayu**, on Kiwayu Island, reservations Nairobi, T020-512 213, www.mikescampkiwayu.com. Formerly known as Munira Island Camp, this camp is totally eco-friendly running on solar and wind power, the water is brought in by a team of

donkeys from a nearby well. 7 comfortable and spacious *bandas*, built of *makuti* and *jambies* (local matting made from palm fronds), each with panoramic ocean views. Rates are US$250 per person full board, food is predominantly seafood and is served in a communal mess tent. Game fishing on a deep-sea fishing boat, diving, waterskiing and windsurfing are available and you can walk to the 2 simple villages on the island or explore the nearby mangrove creek.

## Eating

### Lamu Island *p325, map p326*
You will find lots of yoghurt, pancakes, fruit salads, and milk shakes as well as good-value seafood. If you are looking for the traditional food that you find in upcountry Kenya, such as *ugali*, beans, curries, chicken and chips, there are a number of places that do these, mainly on Harambee Av – particularly in the southern end of town. One of the highlights of eating in Lamu is the availability of fresh and cheap fruit juices and a pint of juice goes for little more than KSh50. They are made to order as attested to by the constant rumblings of electric blenders in the restaurants. There's a wide variety of fruit including orange, mango, lime, pineapple, pawpaw, avocado, banana, tamarind and coconut. They do tend to add sugar so you must tell them beforehand if you want your juices natural. Restaurants close fairly early, usually about 2100, so if you want a beer after dinner the only choices are the terrace bar at the **Lamu Palace Hotel** and the downstairs and rooftop bar at **Petley's**. In Shela, you can get a single malt on the terrace at Peponi's, and elsewhere on the island the **Kipungani Explorer**, and the **Kizingo** resorts have bars. Bear in mind that Lamu is a predominantly Muslim society, so during Ramadan – the month of fasting – many of the restaurants and cafés will remain closed all day until after sunset and it is considered highly

impolite to eat and drink (and smoke) in public until after dark. Stomach upsets are fairly common so stick to bottled water and avoid ice. If you are self-catering, the fresh produce market near the fort has everything you may need including fresh seafood, though the catch comes in early in the morning so get there before 0900.

### Lamu Town *p325, map p326*
**Lamu Palace Hotel**, southern end of waterfront, T042-633 104. Daily 0800-2300. This is a pleasant restaurant looking out over the waterfront with some tables on a very attractive terrace surrounded by plants, serving seafood, grills, Indian food, and alcohol including wine. Set meals at dinner are rather bland but presented nicely; the à la carte dishes although more expensive are far superior. Towards the back of the restaurant is an extremely comfortable bar and lounge area.
**Bush Gardens**, on the waterfront near the fort. Daily 0700-2100. This is a very good seafood restaurant and specialities include lobster cooked in coconut sauce, poached monster crab, jumbo prawns and oysters, good fresh juices, cheaper briyanis and stews, it is friendly but service can be extremely slow, especially when full. Tables are set outside under *makuti* thatched roofs.
**Hapa Hapa Restaurant**, on the waterfront close to Bush Gardens (above). Daily 0800-2100. One of the most popular restaurants with tourists, this has a long menu of pasta and pizza, good fruit juices and snacks, lots of fish including an overloaded seafood platter and jumbo prawns, occasionally barracuda, shark and tuna on the menu. Very simple decor under thatch but a lively place with excellent food. Breakfasts are good here too; try the banana or mango pancakes with honey.
**Stone House Hotel**, near the Swahili House Museum, T042-633 544, www.stone househotellamu.com. This small but lovely rooftop restaurant is open to non-hotel guests and has enchanting views of the narrow alleyways and Lamu's *makuti* rooftops. Tables are set in open Arabian

archways. With low lighting and sea breezes it's quite romantic. There's a short but neat menu of pasta, seafood and Swahili dishes and vegetarians are catered for.

**Whispers**, Harambee Av, T042-633 355. Daily 0900-2100, may close in the afternoon if it's quiet, though it stays open during Ramadan. Set in a lovely coral rag-built house with tables outside in the beautiful tropical garden courtyard, this is a high-quality café with juices, cappuccino, ice cream, spaghetti, pizzas, sandwiches, homemade cakes and serves wine.

**Coconut Juice Café**, Harambee Av, southern end. Daily 0800-2000. This is a 2-storey cafeteria and as the name suggests, serves specialist juices that are freshly made, with combinations of lime, peanut, avocado, papaya, mango, coconut and banana, and you can also ask them to blend them with their homemade yoghurt. Also serves basic local and fairly greasy meat and fish dishes.

**New Minnaa**, just off Harambee Av, to the southern end. Upstairs daytime cafeteria, very popular with local people and cheap with clean plastic tables that are continuously cleared, and serves local stews, biryanis, fried fish, chapattis and local specialities like *mkata wa nyama* (a kind of pizza) or *maharagwe* (beans in coconut sauce). If you are hankering after Nairobi-style chicken and chips, this is the place to come.

**New Star Restaurant**, Harambee Av, southern end, near the German Post Office Museum. Another cheap local canteen serving dishes like rice and beans, *ugali* and beef stews but under a tatty *makuti* roof and in a fairly grubby environment. It does open very early for breakfast though, from 0530.

**Olympic Restaurant**, south of the town also on the waterfront. Daily from 0800. A *makuti*-roofed eating area with only a handful of tables, to find it look out for the blackboard of specials outside but worthwhile for the excellent cheap food. If you're lucky and prepared to wait for about an hour you might get grilled red snapper with tamarind sauce and coconut rice, prawn biryani or crab served with fresh limes and salad. Also good juices and fruit pancakes for breakfast. Very friendly.

**Seafront Cafe**, on the waterfront east of the German Post Office Museum. Daily 0800-2200. Another *makuti*-thatched tourist restaurant that stays open later than most, and with shorter waiting times for food, this sells the usual fare including good fish curries with coconut rice, an excellent crab soup and seafood salads served with a chapatti plus juices and milkshakes. Ask about the catch of the day.

### Shela *p330*

**Barbecue Grill**, at **Peponi's**, T042-633 421-3, www.peponi-lamu.com. Daily 1200-1600, 1900-late. Excellent and open to non-residents, the food is of a very high standard, is probably the best on the island. The beautiful dining room has cool white arches and Swahili copper pots and furniture or there are tables on the terrace shrouded with bougainvillea. Service is excellent and discreet. Superb seafood, including oysters, lobster and crab and the giant prawns cooked in chilli and lime are to die for. Alternatively choose the Swahili menu, which is a variety of dishes served on a copper platter to share. The friendly bar serves a full range of alcohol including cocktails and international spirits and is popular with Shela's expat community.

**Stop Over Restaurant**, at the hotel of the same name. Serves simple, basic but good-value food, including pancakes for breakfast, grills and some seafood such as fantastic grilled prawns with coconut rice, fresh fruit juices, and it also has a great location right on the beach, which is just as well as food takes a long time to appear.

## ▲ Activities and tours

### Lamu Island *p325, map p326*
Watersports can be organized from **Peponi's** in Shela (see Sleeping) and include wind-surfing (with instruction), waterskiing,

snorkelling, sailing, and scuba diving (Nov-Mar). They also have their own fully equipped boat for deep-sea fishing and offer day trips with a picnic lunch and drinks from US$200 for 4 people.

Taking a *dhow* trip is almost obligatory and drifting though the mangroves is a wonderful way to experience the islands. Take your time to shop around and find a *dhow* captain you like. Prices vary, and expect to haggle hard, but generally it's around US$8 per person for half a day and US$12 for a full day per person for groups of 4-5 people. The boats aren't big enough for more than 5. If you are a solo traveller, ask around the budget hotels to see if you can tag along with another group. There are a number of options, but whatever you arrange, make sure you know exactly how much you'll be paying and what that will include, and don't hand over any money until the day of departure except perhaps a small advance for food or a deposit to hire snorkelling equipment. The most popular trips are the slow sail across to Manda Island with a barbeque lunch on the beach there, and perhaps a visit to the Takwa Ruins or a sail down the Lamu Channel to the southwest corner of Manda Island around Kinyika Rock to snorkel on the reefs. *Dhows* can be hired for trips to Pate, and full-moon trips can also be arranged. During the day, take a hat and sunscreen, as there is rarely any shade on the *dhows*. Also remember, *dhows* without motors are dependent on the tides, so departure and return times are obviously arranged around the tide times.

Around both Lamu and Shela you may be approached by ladies, usually in the restaurants, who offer to do henna tattoos on your hands and feet.

## O Shopping

**Lamu Town** *p325, map p326*
### Books
The museum has a very good collection of books on Lamu, its history and culture.

Lamu Book Centre has a reasonable selection as well as the local newspapers, and there are a couple of second-hand book stalls along the waterfront.

### Souvenirs
Boys walk around selling hand-built model *dhows*, which are not too easy to carry around so get them at the end of the trip. Other items to buy include carved chests, cloth, especially *kikoys*, jewellery (silver in particular), plus all manner of carved wooden curios. There are a few stalls on the waterfront and some shops, silversmiths and tailors along Harambee Av, and to the north of town are some wood-carving workshops where you'll see mostly chests and furniture being made, including the distinctive 4-poster beds. You can get things made for you but be prepared to bargain, and there is the question of getting it home. **Baraka**, Harambee Av, T042-633 264. This is Lamu's best and most beautiful gallery adjoining the **Whispers Restaurant** that sells high-quality but expensive carvings, Lamu chests, jewellery, and clothing, and there are pieces on display from across Africa. **Wildebeest**, see page 336, sells contemporary paintings as well as wall hangings made from goat hair and other fabrics. The gallery is on the ground floor and the workshop on the 2nd floor.

## ⊖ Transport

**Lamu Island** *p325, map p326*
### Air
**Air Kenya**, has a daily flight between Lamu and **Nairobi**, which departs Nairobi at 1530, arrives in Lamu at 1640, departs again at 1710, and arrives back in Nairobi at 1855, 1 way from US$142. For the Lamu flight, Air Kenya baggage allowance is just 15 kg. **Fly 540**, has 1 daily flight between **Nairobi** and Lamu, which departs Nairobi at 1040, arrives in Lamu at 1240, departs again at 1255 and arrives back in Nairobi at 1440. 1 way from US$139. **Kenya Airways**, flies between

Nairobi, and Lamu daily with a stop in **Malindi**. Flights depart Nairobi at 1100, arrive in Lamu at 1310, depart Lamu 1410, arrive Malindi 1340, depart Malindi at 1440, and arrive back in Nairobi at 1550.

**Mombasa Air Safari**, has daily flights between **Mombasa**, **Malindi** and Lamu. The flight departs Mombasa at 0800, arrives at Malindi at 0840, departs again at 0845 and arrives in Lamu at 0915. On the return leg it departs Lamu at 1700, arrives in Malindi at 1730, departs Malindi at 1750, and arrives in Mombasa at 1810. Check-in time is 30 mins before take off from the Manda airstrip. Allow plenty of extra time to arrange a boat transfer or *dhow* taxi to get to Manda, the crossing itself takes about 15 mins from Lamu town and about 30 mins from Shela.

**Airline offices** Air Kenya, Baraka House, T042-633 445, near the Whispers Restaurant, or reservations at Wilson Airport, Nairobi, T020-605 745, www.airkenya.com. **Fly 540**, ABC Place, Westlands, Nairobi, T020-445 3252, www.fly540.com. **Kenya Airways**, on the waterfront, on the ground floor of Casuarina Rest House, T042-632 040, www.kenya-airways.com. **Mombasa Air Safari**, Moi International Airport, Mombasa, T041-343 3061, www.mombasaairsafari.com.

**Bus**
The **Pwani Tawakal Bus Company**, on Main St near the fort in Lamu, T0722-550 111, T042-633 380, http://pwanitawakal.com, has 3 services a day in each direction between Lamu and **Malindi/Mombasa**. The buses stay overnight at **Mokowe** and return to Malindi and Mombasa from 0700. Allow plenty of extra time for the ferry from the main jetty to Mokowe and you need to be at the jetty before sunrise, but there are boats waiting to connect with the buses from 0600 and plenty of people waiting for them.

**Pate Island** *p332*
For details about getting to Pate from Lamu by ferry and *dhow*, see page 343.

**Kiunga Marine National Reserve** *p334*
The 2 luxury camps here are usually accessed by private air charter from Nairobi's Wilson Airport to the Kiwayu airstrip. Alternatively the lodges can arrange slow *dhow* transfers or much quicker speedboat transfers (about 2 hrs) from Lamu. A cheaper option to get here is to get a group of 5 or 6 together and charter a *dhow*. This should include food and water as well as snorkelling gear and should work out at around US$70-80 per day. The journey is dependent on the winds and the tides and so be prepared for the journey in each direction to be anything between 8 and 36 hrs. For sleeping the only option is to sleep on the *dhow* or camp on the beach.

## ❶ Directory

**Lamu Island** *p325, map p326*
**Banks** There are 2 banks on the island, **Standard Chartered** and **Kenya Commercial Bank (KCB)**, both on the waterfront, south of the Lamu Museum, which have ATMs and can change foreign currency and TCs, and accept Visa cards for cash withdrawals (but not Mastercard), although service can be very slow, open 0900-1500 on weekdays, and 0900-1100 on Sat. **Internet** It is possible to email from the post office and in the past there have been internet cafés, but they have never lasted long as internet connection is sporadic on Lamu and is often down. Nevertheless, keep your eyes peeled for new spots. **Medical services** Lamu District Hospital, T042-633 425, located in the southern end of the town to the south and inland from the fort, which does malaria tests but other than that is poorly equipped and busy so anyone with serious medical conditions should try to get to Mombasa. **Immigration** At the District Commissioner's Office near the jetty. **Post office** Just to the south of the jetty, Mon-Fri 0800-1230 and 1400-1700; Sat 0900-1200. There are some card phones outside and phone cards can be bought inside, though they sometimes run out.

# Contents

## Footprint features

## Border crossing

## At a glance

⊜ **Getting around** Self-drive
(a 4WD is essential); tours; flights
to Samburu, Buffalo Springs and
Shaba game reserves. Public
transport is very limited.

⊛ **Time required** To get to Lake
Turkana and back allow at least
1 week; 2 nights in a lodge in
Samburu.

☽ **Weather** Mostly very hot
with temperatures that can be
in excess of 40°C.

⊗ **When not to go** Can be visited
year round but the climate is harsh.

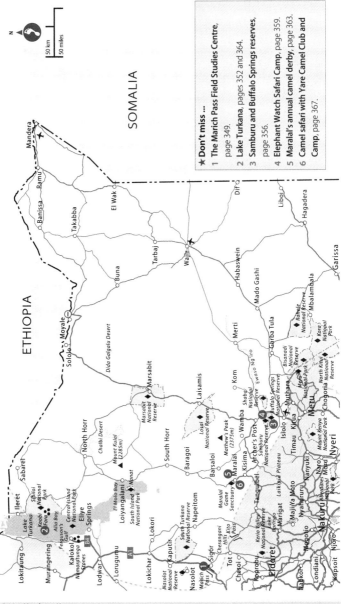

★ **Don't miss ...**
1 The Marich Pass Field Studies Centre, page 349.
2 Lake Turkana, pages 352 and 364.
3 Samburu and Buffalo Springs reserves, page 356.
4 Elephant Watch Safari Camp, page 359.
5 Maralal's annual camel derby, page 363.
6 Camel safari with Yare Camel Club and Camp, page 367.

ETHIOPIA

SOMALIA

This is a vast area of forested and barren mountains, deserts and scrubland occasionally broken by oases of vegetation and the huge Lake Turkana. Northern Kenya accounts for almost half of the country and yet only a fraction of the population live here. The people who do inhabit the area – the Samburu, Rendille, Boran, Gabbra, Turkana and Somali – are semi-nomadic peoples that cross between their villages in the region using ancient migration routes, existing as they have done for generations, hardly affected by the modern world. The main reason tourists come to Northern Kenya is to see the wonders of Lake Turkana – the Jade Sea – and, in spite of the barren environment, there are also plenty of national parks. Just north of Isiolo you will find Samburu, Buffalo Springs and Shaba national reserves, all three along the banks of the magical life-giving Ewaso Ng'iro River and which jointly cover an area of some 300 sq km. Further north still are the less-visited parks at Maralal, Losai and Marsabit. Travelling in the northern regions can be rough and uncomfortable; the roads are far from good, distances between places are vast, there are very few facilities, and it's a long way from the comfort of the game lodges and beach hotels in the rest of the country. Unfortunately, these days there are also increasing safety issues in the region, as well as an 18-year-long refugee crisis, which has given rise to conditions of acute poverty (see page 350).

## Ins and out

The main road through Northern Kenya is the A2 – or Trans-East African Highway – that passes through Isiolo, Marsabit and on to Moyale at the Ethiopian border (see page 372 for border crossing information). From Isiolo it is obligatory to travel in a convoy on this road, which is in a terrible condition and a 4WD is essential. In the extreme north, there are very few defined roads around Lake Turkana. The eastern and western shores of the lake are accessed completely separately, and are physically separated by the vast uncrossable Suguta Valley south of the lake. The eastern shore is reached via Maralal and Marsabit with the central point of access being the small oasis town of Loiyangalani. The western shore is accessed via Kitale and the central point of access is Lodwar. There are airstrips on both shores for chartered aircraft. Turkana and much of the north is best visited as part of a professionally organized safari. Most operators offer an eight- to nine-day tour heading up the Rift Valley to stop at Lake Baringo going on to Maralal and then to Lake Turkana via Baragoi and South Horr. The return journey goes via Samburu National Reserve and Buffalo Springs National Reserve. Some go via the Marsabit National Reserve crossing the Chalbi Desert. Most use open-sided 4WD trucks, not built for comfort but they are sturdy and reliable. If you have a bit more money to spend, some companies arrange flying safaris, and there is a scattering of upmarket lodges. See page 100 for tour operators specializing in the region; Gametrackers are particularly recommended. Driving yourself is a possibility if you are experienced in wilderness driving (a 4WD is imperative), though this is not exactly trouble free. You will need to bring a number of tools in case of breakdown or getting stuck in the sand, such as a jack, sand ladders, a shovel and a rope, and a GPS is a good idea. You'll need plenty of petrol too, as it is in particularly short supply. Driving at night is not only foolish, but illegal.

This barren region is in sharp contrast to the green, fertile land of the Central Highlands. Much of Northern Kenya is desert scrub where only the hardiest of vegetation is able to survive and recent droughts in the last decade or so have exacerbated the already formidable conditions and the nomadic people and their herds continue to suffer. The plains routinely reach dangerously hot temperatures by midday of 50°C with no hint of wind.

# Kitale to Lake Turkana

*If you are coming up into Northern Kenya from Kitale, you travel a glorious route through the highlands, close to the Saiwa Swamp National Park (see page 181). Continuing through the northern gorges of the Cherangani Hills will bring you to the desert plains through the Marich Pass. This is a dramatic deep rocky cleft at an altitude of 3000 m carved by the Moruny River between the heavily wooded Cherangani Hills, opening out to the arid plains of the Lake Turkana basin below. The views are incredible, looking down onto the plains from the lush highlands. At intervals the road passes close to the Morun River, and at two points crosses it. The first glimpse of Lake Turkana, at the end of the road, doesn't disappoint.* ▸▸ *For listings, see pages 354-355.*

## Ins and outs

The Marich Pass is about 70 km from Kitale. The most direct route is going north along the tarmacked A1 road, which goes via Kapenguria towards Lodwar and Lokichokio and on to the Sudanese border in the extreme northwest of the country. You can also reach it from Eldoret or Kabarnet via Iten and then on through the upper Kerio Valley joining the Kitale–Lodwar road near Kapenguria. The third way is via the unmade road from Lake Baringo through the Kito Pass, across the Kerio Valley to Tot, although this route involves travelling a track through the northern face of the Cherangani Hills that becomes impassable after heavy rains, when the streams flood the road. This route is only manageable with a 4WD. Just north of the pass is a police post where a convoy of vehicles collects with armed guards to continue north to Lodwar – mostly trucks carrying relief supplies to the refugee camps and famine-stricken areas. Note the road is surfaced all the way to Lodwar, but the heavy traffic has completely broken up the tarmac north of the Marich Pass so it's now a long and uncomfortable ride of about eight hours between Kitale and Lodwar by bus or *matatu*. Once through the pass the road levels out into the endless scrub where you'll see nothing but a few lonely Turkana goat herders.

## Marich Pass Field Studies Centre ● ▸▸ *pp354-355*.

The centre itself is off the main Kitale–Lodwar road to the north. It is clearly signposted 1 km north of the Sigor–Tot junction at Marich Pass. The centre (see also Sleeping, page 354), is a lovely spot on the banks of the Moruny River and Pokot guides can be hired to explore the region. The centre is primarily an education establishment, catering for school and university groups on academic field-study courses, but tourists and independent travellers are also welcome to stay. The compound comprises 12 ha of virgin forest leased from the Pokot County Country. Around 4 ha have been used to build the centre on the banks of the Moruny River and there are bush trails through the forest. Baboons, vervet monkeys and monitor lizards are permanent residents and are easily viewed, elephants and antelopes visit occasionally and the forests are full of birds. The centre has been built using local labour and traditional materials and a percentage of its takings are donated to the local development fund. **Pokot guides**, many of whom are English speaking, are used for all walks and treks in the region. There is a strong eco-tourism ethos. There are a variety of excursions including treks to visit local villages giving travellers an insight into Pokot culture. Further away, three-day trips to climb Mount Sekerr can be organized, or you can explore the Cherangani Hills to the south over several days.

# Travel warning

Draw a line across the map of Kenya starting at Kitale in the west, through Lake Baringo and Isiolo, all the way to the Tana River Delta in the east. The area above this line is referred to as Northern Kenya. These days, it is generally known as a lawless place. The pastoralists in the region are largely nomadic and depend on livestock (cattle, sheep, goats and camels) for their livelihood. They rely on access to pasture and water and such resources are scarce and under increasing pressure and the region has witnessed a lean period of droughts over the last decade. Violent conflicts involving pastoralists associated with competition for these basic resources have become widespread and severe, and in some areas herdsman have lost up to 80% of their herds through drought.

Added to this, there is a presence of gangs of armed bandits, mostly cattle rustlers, who are capable of attacking and destroying entire villages and their occupants, and robbing vehicles on the main roads throughout the region. Because of Kenya's porous borders with Sudan and Somalia they have been able to get automatic weapons, and a vicious cycle of revenge killings has emerged. Since 2005, incidents of road banditry along the Isiolo–Marsabit–Moyale road have increased, and vehicles including those ferrying relief food have been attacked on the Wajir–El Wak–Mandera road.

The problems in Sudan and Somalia, and the influx of refugees into Kenya from these countries, have also contributed to the tension and increased pressure on resources. The recent deterioration in the situation in Somalia caused an estimated 65,000 Somalis to flood into Kenya by the end of 2008, and new arrivals are expected during 2009. The camps, which were built from 1992 for 90,000 people, now house 250,000. The United Nations has identified Northern Kenya as a 'rapidly developing emergency' with an estimated 1.4 million people currently receiving food aid.

There is a high military presence in the north, vehicles usually travel in convoys and are in some cases are escorted by armed guards, road blocks are common and vehicle searches are a part of everyday life. Anyone travelling here should exercise extreme caution and get local on-the-ground advice. In particular, the area north of Isiolo into the far northeast towards the Somali border, including the town of Garissa, has a combination of dangerous desert travel, overcrowded refugee camps and frequent bandit raids, which make this region very risky for travellers. The national reserves of Samburu, Buffalo Springs and Shaba are not affected by these safety issues.

# Cherangani Hills

These wild, thickly forested hills are miles away from the popular tourist circuit with fine mountain landscapes. They are the fourth highest mountain range in Kenya and include rolling hills as well as dramatic mountain peaks, and forms the highest, most breathtaking and spectacular escarpments of the Rift Valley. Unlike most of Kenya's mountains and ranges, the Cherangani Hills are not volcanic in origin. They are centred upon a forested escarpment and surrounded on three sides by sheer cliff faces. They are criss-crossed by walking paths, and ease of direction and undemanding slopes make this excellent country for relaxing hill walking. The paths cross open farmland, pass through sheltered valleys and wind their way up to forested peaks. All the main routes cross the 3000 m contour, with decreased oxygen supplies. Car engine performance may be adversely affected by the altitude, and it is essential to carry extra supplies of fuel as consumption is heavy. There are two approaches, from the Kapenguria–Marich Pass road, past a terrifying deep valley, or through the Kito Pass and up the Tot Escarpment. The main road is known as the Cherangani Highway, and is one of the most terrifying and challenging roads in Kenya. Grave mounds are concealed on top of the Kaisungur Range, venerated and closely guarded by the local people. There are occasional sightings of the lammergeyers here, drifting on the thermal currents. The highlands are malaria free, but the lowlands are not.

## Mount Sekerr and Mount Koh

Mount Sekerr, also known as Mtelo Mountain or Sigogowa, is a few kilometres from the Study Centre and is a fairly easy climb over a couple of days. Climbing Mount Sekerr starts from the thornbush covered plains of Turkana to the lush upper reaches inhabited by the Pokot people. As you ascend the flora changes from woodlands to heathland near the summit. The views from the top (3326 m) are great looking down on to lush green forest glades and in the far distance the open thorn bush-covered plains of Turkana. Mount Sekerr is located to the north of the Cherangani Hills, an area where gold-panning is widespread.

Mount Koh, 2608 m, is very steep, with almost vertical rock rising for 300 m from a northerly spur of the Cheranganis. Should you feel inclined to climb it there are footpaths almost all the way, with just a couple of rough areas where scrambling is required. There are wonderful views overlooking the Weiwei Valley. The Marich Pass Field Studies Centre is a good local base and Pokot guides can be arranged from here.

## Elgeyo Escarpment

The Elgeyo Escarpment rises to over 1830 m and presents one of the most astonishing panoramic views in the Rift Valley. About 1000 m below the sheer cliff face south of the village of **Tot**, stretches the hazy scrublands extending as far as the eye can see north to Turkana and Pokot. This region is not easy to access: you'll need a 4WD and calm nerves to drive up the escarpment road. It is probably easier to walk from Tot (about 25 km).

The Elgeyo Escarpment has been inhabited for centuries. The **Marakwet**, who live here, arrived around 1000 years ago and claim they took over existing irrigation systems, which zigzag all over the escarpment and Cherangani Hills. The waterways make this area a lush land of agriculture with back-to-back *shambas* (small farms) everywhere.

## South Turkana National Reserve ►► *Colour map 3, B6.*

ⓘ *50 km north of the Marich Pass to the east of the main A1 road.*

This is remote, rarely visited and has no tourist facilities or roads, though the main road passes its western boundary. The Kerio River borders the reserve to the southeast and it is covered in dense thorn bush and riverine forest that make up its 1000 sq km area. The local Turkana kill wild animals for food unlike the other groups in this region, meaning there is little game left in the reserve, though elephant migrate through here to the Kerio Valley.

## Nasolot National Reserve ►► *Colour map 3, B5/6.*

ⓘ *Marich Pass Field Studies Centre is 30 km away and offers half-day tours.*

Nasolot National Reserve lies on the Kitale–Lodwar road and was gazetted in 1979. Because of its remote location and limited game resources, Nasolot receives very few visitors. It covers 92 sq km, ranging in altitude from 750-1500 m, and the boundary to the east is the seasonal Weiwei River. The habitat is predominantly thicket and dry bushland, with many succulents and acacias bordering the seasonal streams and rivers that criss-cross the reserve. There are elephants in the reserve but they are well camouflaged by the flora, though you are quite likely to spot their dung. Other mammals include the greater and lesser kudu, warthog and bushbuck. The birdlife is rich and varied and includes the white-crested turacos, Abyssinian ground hornbills, superb starlings and Abyssinian rollers.

A good road bisects the reserve and leads to the Turkwell Dam, a hydroelectric dam at the head of a gorge harnessing the waters of the Turkwell River. The dammed waters have formed a large artificial lake that stretches westwards between the hills, home to a large variety of birdlife. There are no formal camping facilities at Nasolot, though camping is permitted virtually anywhere in the reserve.

## Lodwar ●● ▸ pp354-355. Colour map 3, B6.

→ *Phone code: 054.*

The only town of any size in the northwest of the region is Lodwar, the administrative centre of the Turkana District. Historically it was an important colonial outpost where frequent Ethiopian raids were countered. Jomo Kenyatta was held here briefly in 1959 whilst in detention. It has been said that Kenyatta was taken to Lodwar so that the Mau Mau would be unable to rescue him given the distance and the fierce nature of the Turkana tribesmen. It is not nearly so isolated as in the past due to the opening of the surfaced road from the highlands and an airstrip, but it is still very much a backwater town. Poverty is very acute and many of the Turkana residents are under-nourished. Take good care of your possessions and be prepared for aggressive begging. There is a branch of **Kenya Commercial Bank** with an ATM (though do not rely on it taking TCs), a post office, a small supermarket and a Kobil petrol station in town. The local people are persistent in attempts to sell their crafts, but it is generally done in a friendly spirit. You can buy large, beautiful baskets made by local women.

North of Lodwar the A1 continues the 130 km to Kakuma on a good road that the UN has recently tarred. This is the site of a very large refugee camp that was set up in 1992, predominantly to house refugees from southern Sudan. The Lokichokio border is another 188 km further on. Now the civil war has ended in Sudan, people are starting to trickle back, but at its height it accommodated 70,000 people.

## Lake Turkana (western shore) ●● ▸ pp354-355. Colour map 3, A6.

The largest lake in the country, Lake Turkana runs about 250 km from the Ethiopian border in a long thin body of water that is never more than 50 km wide. It stretches into the Ethiopian Highlands where the Omo River enters its waters. Giant Nile perch are reported to grow from 90-180 kg in the lake, but Nile tilapia are a more commercial option as they are more palatable and are either dried or frozen before being marketed all over Kenya. There is also a profusion of birdlife including many European migratory species.

Count Sammuel Teleki Von Szek is believed to have been the first white man to see the lake in 1888. In honour of his patron, Von Szek named it Lake Rudolf, after the Austrian Archduke. President Jomo Kenyatta changed the name to Lake Turkana in 1975. This lake used to be far larger than it is today. Around 10,000 years ago it is believed the water level of the lake was about 150 m higher and considered to be one of the sources of the Nile. At that time it supported a far greater number and diversity of plant and animal life. Now a combination of factors including evaporation and major irrigation projects in southern Ethiopia have brought the water level to its lowest in memory. As a result, the water is far more alkaline than in the past. The lake still supports a huge number of hippos and the largest population of Nile crocodiles in the world, estimated to be 20,000-strong.

Do not be fooled by the lake's calm appearance, the waters are highly unpredictable; storms build up out of nowhere and are not to be dismissed lightly as they are capable of sinking all but the most sturdy craft. The climate up here is extraordinary. It can easily reach 50°C during the day with not a cloud in sight, then out of nowhere a storm will break whipping up a squall on Lake Turkana. For most of the year the area is dry, but when the rains do come, the rivers and ravines become torrential waterways sweeping over the parched plains. It is quite a sight, and it can leave you stranded until the water levels drop.

### Ins and outs
Seeing the western side of Lake Turkana by road involves a long rough trip. It is best to spend one or two nights at Marich Pass and access the lake from there. It is possible to get a *matatu* from Kitale to Marich Pass via Kapenguria. At Marich Pass transport on to Lodwar passes through around midday. It is then possible to get a *matatu* from Lodwar to Kalokol, of which there are about four daily. From Kalokol it is a one-hour walk or 4 km to the lake

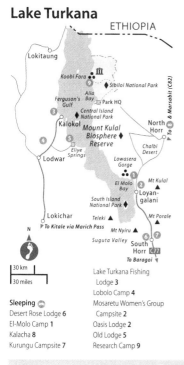

## Lake Turkana

Lake Turkana Fishing Lodge 3
Lobolo Camp 4
Mosaretu Women's Group Campsite 2
Oasis Lodge 2
Old Lodge 1
Research Camp 9

**Sleeping** 🛌
Desert Rose Lodge 6
El-Molo Camp 1
Kalacha 8
Kurungu Campsite 7

and you will need to walk out to the abandoned fish-processing plant. The local boys will offer to be your guide. You are advised to walk either in the early morning or evening as it gets extremely hot. Plenty of water and a good sense of direction are both vital. For access to the lake from the eastern side, see page 362.

### Kalokol
Only 58 km from Lodwar, this is a small, simple town lying just a few kilometres from the lakeshore and with quite oppressive heat. From this side of the lake it is possible to access Central Island National Park. Getting water supplies in the dry season poses major problems here and the women walk 3 km to extract water from the riverbed. Although you can drink the lake water after boiling it, it is brackish and tastes unpleasant. Note that there is nowhere to stay here and only a few very basic food stalls.

### Ferguson's Gulf
Some 4 km beyond Kalokol, this is the most accessible part of the Lake Turkana although not the most attractive. However, the lake is fringed with acacias, doum palms

and grass, in contrast to the moonscape appearance with a mass of volcanic lava around Teleki's Volcano at the south of the lake. There are loads of birds, particularly flamingos, and it is the only place in Kenya where, in the springtime, black-tailed godwits and spotted redshanks can be seen. Birds of prey can also be spotted, and the number of hippos and crocodiles make swimming exciting. If you intend to swim, ask the local people where to go. En route to or from Kalokol look out for the standing stones of **Namoratunga**, which have a spiritual meaning to the Turkana. Although they are only 50 m from the road they are hard to spot and resemble sacks of charcoal. There are 10 cylindrical stones about 1 m high, although some have fallen over. Nothing is known about them; the Turkana themselves don't know what their original purpose was. In the past the lakeshore may have come right up to the stones. The name is derived from a Turkana legend that some visitors came across a group of dancers at the site and laughed at them, turning the dancers to stone.

## Eliye Springs

Eliye Springs are a far more pleasant place to see the lake from and under the palm trees the springs themselves bubble up warm water. However, you will need a vehicle to get here. There is a small village nearby where you can get some food and drink and no doubt some of the local people will want to sell you their handicrafts. The turn-off for Eliye springs is about halfway along the Lodwar–Kalokol road. As it is 70 km from Lodwar, your best bet would be to base yourself there and travel up to the Springs. The last 10 km is very sandy.

## Central Island National Park

This was established as a 5-sq-km national park in 1983 in order to protect the breeding grounds of the Nile crocodile. Formed as a result of volcanic activity, the island is an old volcano with three immense crater lakes that lie in the basins of a series of volcanic vents. Researchers suspect that there is still a tiny active volcano situated on the tip of the island. The crater lakes are connected through subterranean ducts with the main lake, and are renowned for the differing shades of jade, green and blue at various times of the day. The island is a favourite haunt for breeding crocodiles as well as migratory and resident birds. If you arrive around April-May, you can witness crocodiles hatching and sprinting off down to one of the lakes. The island has black lava sand beaches. It was designated as a UNESCO World Heritage Site in 1997 and is approximately a 45-minute boat ride from Ferguson's Gulf. It is possible to negotiate with a local fisherman to take you out on his craft, but remember that the lake's unpredictable squalls are a real danger, and there are crocodiles.

## ◉ Kitale to Lake Turkana listings

*For Sleeping and Eating price codes and other relevant information, see Essentials pages 34-38.*

## ◉ Sleeping

You will need a room with both a fan and mosquito protection to get any sleep.

**Marich Pass Field Studies Centre** *p349*
**D-F Marich Pass Field Studies Centre**,
www.gg.rhul.ac.uk/MarichPass. Here there

are 19 African *bandas* sleeping 2-3 people with or without bathrooms, and 4 larger cottages that sleep up to 6. There are also larger dormitories housing 5-25 people and you can camp. The ablution block, about 140 m from the *bandas*, has toilets and cold showers. Hot bucket showers can be arranged. Facilities include firewood, a laundry service and fresh, pure drinking water from the well. There is a restaurant offering a buffet of fresh locally grown produce prepared in both African and Western style, and a small bar serves beer and cold sodas (no spirits). Plenty of walks with Pokot guides can be arranged here (see page 350).

### Lodwar p352
Lodwar has only a couple of basic board and lodgings places.

**F Nawoitorong Guest House & Conference Centre**, just outside of town to the south, 2 km off the main road. The centre was set up to support single mothers and drought victims but will take travellers of both sexes. Clean dormitories, well-maintained showers and toilets, mosquito nets. There are also *bandas* sleeping 2-4, some with small kitchens. Breakfast and dinner are provided with notice. Camping is allowed in the grounds.

**F Turkwel Hotel**, in the centre of town near the bus stand, T054-21201. Best in town, rooms come with a net, fan and bathroom, for slightly more you can hire a larger self-contained cottage with a full breakfast included in the price. The restaurant serves some Western dishes like simple chicken and chips and the bar is popular with Lingala music playing into the small hours, which can get quite noisy.

### Lake Turkana (western shore) p352, map p353
**L Lobolo Camp, Bush and Beyond/ Bush Homes**, Nairobi, T020-600 457, www.bush-and-beyond.com and www.bush-homes.co.ke. Quality camping with 6 individually designed tents overlooking the lake, with showers and short-drop toilets, boats can be hired for US$250 per day for fishing and trips to

Central Island, closed Apr. The camp is hosted by the Sheuermans who are very knowledgeable about the region.

**Lake Turkana Fishing Lodge**, is on a spit at the mouth of Ferguson's Gulf surrounded by water on 3 sides and access is by boat across the gulf to its sandy beach. However, it's presently closed. You could camp here but there are no facilities.

**Old Lodge**, Eliye Springs. Follow the main sandy road straight to the lake, where the palm leaves are on the road. This used to be a fishing lodge but it is now closed down. You can still negotiate with the local people to camp here but you will have to be completely self sufficient as facilities are virtually non-existent.

## ⊖ Transport

### Lodwar p352
Buses go between here and **Kitale** daily, taking around 8 hrs. There are also a few *matatus* that work the route, though whether they reach their final destination depends on the number of passengers. The bus leaves from Kitale at 1500 and leaves Lodwar for Kitale at 0700. It is wise to take water and food for the trip as breakdowns and delays are common. Book your seat on the return to Kitale the night before as the bus gets very full.

### Lake Turkana (western shore) p352, map p353
Occasional *matatus* go between **Lodwar** and Kalokol and take 1½ hrs. The petrol station at Lodwar is the last place to buy fuel and food on the way to the lake.

# Isiolo and around

*Isiolo is an interesting little frontier town, very different from the rest of the Central Province towns around Mount Kenya. It is a small town north of Meru inhabited mostly by the descendants of Somali people who were resettled there after the First World War. It is also the nearest town to explore the national reserves at Samburu, Buffalo Springs and Shaba, all grouped together 40 km to the north. These national parks are the most accessible of the northern wildlife sanctuaries.*
▶▶ *For listings, see pages 359-361.*

## Isiolo ●●●● ▶▶ *pp359-361. Colour map 4, C2.*

→ *Phone code: 064.*

There's a busy goat, cattle and camel market here, in addition to the fruit and vegetable market, though security problems with nomadic bandit groups operating to the north up to the Ethiopian border have disrupted livestock raising, leading to a fall in prosperity. Petrol is available and there is a branch of Barclays Bank (no ATM) and a post office (the last town to have these facilities until you reach either Maralal or Marsabit). It is also the last place to have a good supply of provisions. The social life in the town revolves around drinking and chewing *miraa*. George Adamson who was later to become internationally famous along with his wife, Joy, for hand-rearing Elsa, the lioness featured in *Born Free*, was a game warden in Isiolo prior to becoming a celebrity. The town is also closest to the entrance of the Lewa Wildlife Conservancy, situated about 15 km to the southwest, see page 213.

### Ins and outs

For travelling to Lake Turkana's eastern shores the best route is likely to be from Isiolo, but for any travel north from here, vehicles need to collect at the police post 3 km north of town to form a convoy, which is then accompanied by armed guards. However, *matatus* still cover the short distance to Archer's Post (below).

### Archer's Post

About one hour's drive north of Isiolo (35 km), this is a very small and hot outpost bordered by the Samburu and Buffalo Springs National Reserve to the west and the Shaba National Reserve to the east. It was named after a British colonial administrator Geoffrey Archer, who was posted here in 1911. There are a couple of small shops and cafés, as well as curio sellers hoping to catch the traffic into the reserves. The Samburu people inhabit this region and you are very likely to see some magnificently dressed and adorned people in Archer's Post, especially the warriors with their intricate hairstyles, ochre painted skin and purple robes. Always ask if you can take photographs and you may be permitted for a small fee.

## Samburu, Buffalo Springs and Shaba ●●●● ▶▶ *pp359-361. Colour map 4, C2/3.*

ⓘ *www.kws.org, daily 0630-1830, entry to each reserve is US$20, children US$10 per day, plus vehicle US$4.50.*

Just north of Isiolo and around 325 km north of Nairobi, are the Samburu, Buffalo Springs and Shaba national reserves, some of the more remote and least visited of Kenya's game parks. They are located in Kenya's hot and arid northern region, and when you see a camel train walking single file along a dry riverbed, you know you're in a pretty parched area.

The three reserves cover around 300 sq km in total and are separated by the Ewaso Nyiro River, which provides water for the animals including the local goats and sheep, and some relief from the equatorial sun. They are some of the most pleasant national parks in Kenya, are not too crowded, and are usually visited on a combined safari of all three. There are a number of lodges and campsites in the reserves, but think carefully when to go – daytime temperatures regularly reach 40°C between January and October, even when it rains.

### Ins and outs
A couple of hours drive north of Nanyuki, they are accessible by road via Isiolo and Archer's Post. There are airstrips in both Samburu and Buffalo Springs reserves. Samburu and Buffalo Springs are contiguous reserves, while the separate Shaba, which is often also included in safari itineraries in this region, is a short drive to the east. At Archer's Post the entrance to Shaba is at the right side, while the main gate to Samburu, Archer's Post Gate, is found 5 km on the left. Feasibly it is walkable, but very hot, there are safety concerns and you are unlikely to encounter any traffic that will give you a lift. Samburu also has another gate at its western end, but it is seldom used. Access to Buffalo Springs is either through Samburu or 20 km north of Isiolo, where there is a detour left leading to Isiolo Gate, formerly known as Ngare Mara Gate. Some 10 km ahead, 3.5 km before Archer's Post, a second detour leads to the Buffalo Springs Gate. Most people visit on an organized safari.

### Samburu
This national park was opened in 1965 in the hot, arid lowland area just to the north of Mount Kenya. Vegetation is made up of narrow stretch of palms and woodland along the Ewaso Ng'iro River, away from this is acacia woodland and hot, dusty scrubland. This

# Samburu & Buffalo Springs National Reserves

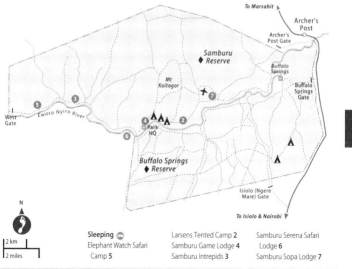

| | |
|---|---|
| **Sleeping** | Larsens Tented Camp **2** | Samburu Serena Safari |
| Elephant Watch Safari | Samburu Game Lodge **4** | Lodge **6** |
| Camp **5** | Samburu Intrepids **3** | Samburu Sopa Lodge **7** |

desolate landscape is the face of the less hospitable Africa, but is the preferred habitat for some mammals well adapted to this harsh environment, some of them rarely seen in milder climates. Among these are Grevy's zebra, reticulated giraffe and Beisa Oryx, whose natural habitat is north of the equator. There are also elephant, cheetah, vervet monkey, and hippo and crocodile habituate the river. The long-necked gerenuk, also known as the 'giraffe-necked antelope', is an unusual animal that spends much of its time on its hind legs reaching up to the withered bushes. Leopards are regularly spotted. The birdlife is unusually numerous in this park, and large flocks of guinea-fowl can be seen in the afternoons coming to drink at the riverbanks. Doves, sandgrouse and the pygmy falcon are frequently seen. The area north of the Ewaso Nyiro River is very attractive with plains and low hills that are rocky in places. The dry watercourses are fringed with acacias, and the blue-grey mountains fringe the view in silhouette. After a downpour the arid countryside turns green overnight, and soon flowers and sweet smelling grasses are abundant.

One of the highlights of the area are the 'Sarara Singing Wells'. Samburu warriors bring their cattle to these watering holes on a daily basis during the dry season. Some of the wells are up to 10 m deep. The warriors strip off, descend to form a human chain and chant traditional Samburu songs as they pass water up by hand for the cattle.

## Buffalo Springs

Buffalo Springs is south of the river from Samburu, and a bridge over the Ewaso Ng'iro River linking the two reserves was built in 1964. Elephant, zebra, giraffe, oryx, cheetah and crocodile can be found in the riverine forest of acacia and doum palm. In the park is a crater, made when an Italian bomber mistook buffalo for targets in the Second World War. It is now a spring and is reportedly safe to swim in. Unlike Samburu, Buffalo Springs has populations of the common zebra as well as the Grevy's zebra – it's an unexplained phenomenon why the common zebra is not found on the north side of the river.

## Shaba National Reserve

To the east of Archer's Post is Shaba National Reserve, which is to the south of the Ewaso Ng'iro River. It is home to a number of gerenuk, gazelle, oryx, zebra, giraffe, cheetah, leopard and lion, which roam around acacia woodlands, bushlands and grasslands. Shaba got its name from the volcanic rock cone in the reserve. The riverine areas are dominated by acacia and doum palms. The martial eagle can often be spotted here, alert for its prey the guinea-fowl, or the occasional dik-dik. Joy and George Adamson (see box, page 220) who hand-reared lions and leopards and returned them to the wild, had a campsite in Shaba Reserve. Joy's last project was the release of Penny the leopard, who subsequently mated and reared a cub in the eastern part of the reserve. It was here that Joy was murdered in 1980, and there is a simple memorial plaque commemorating Joy's life and work erected by Isiolo County Council at her campsite under the shade of umbrella acacias, adjacent to a swamp in eastern Shaba. The reserve was the location of some parts of *Out of Africa* and *Born Free*, and also the US TV show *Survivor Africa* in 2001.

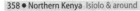

*For Sleeping and Eating price codes and other relevant information, see Essentials pages 34-38.*

## ● Sleeping

### Isiolo *p356*

Plenty of board and lodgings, but those preferring more comfort should move on.

**D Gaddisa Lodge**, 3 km east of town, follow the road past the post office, T0724-201 115, www.gaddisa.com. Set in spacious grounds behind a stone wall and gate, this offers secure parking and has a very large refreshing swimming pool, restaurant and bar, and simple en suite rooms have large beds and mosquito nets. Good drinking water comes from a well and rates include breakfast and dinner. Run by a Dutch woman who can arrange guided excursions to local villages.

**E Bowmen**, Kanisani Rd, T064-2389. The best bet in town, a little expensive but good value. Well furnished with a bar, TV room, pool table, simple restaurant, friendly staff, secure parking, and hot water mornings and evenings.

**E-F Rangeland Hotel**, 10 km south of town on the Nanyuki/Meru road, T064-2340, www.rangeland.co.ke. This is a curious set-up, which is predominantly a local country *nyama choma* spot, accompanied by loud music and a conference venue. It also has 3 thatched basic garden cottages, and camping is permitted with a cold shower and toilet. There's also a bar and children's play area in a pleasant garden setting with acacia trees.

**F Jamhuri Guest House**, 1 block back from the main road, near the livestock market, T064-2065. This is one of the better cheap hotels. The clean rooms have mosquito nets and the communal showers have hot water. You are ensured a warm welcome by the hosts. Small, clean restaurant attached.

**F Mocharo Lodge**, 2 streets southwest of the Total petrol station, T064-2385. Best of the cheaper hotels, obliging staff, rooms functional and clean with mosquito nets, hot water (although the supply can be erratic). Secure parking, moderate food.

### Samburu *p357, map p357*

**L Elephant Watch Safari Camp**, west of **Samburu Intrepids**, on the banks of the Ewaso Ng'iro River, reservations Nairobi T020-891 112, www.elephantwatch safaris.com. Eco-friendly camp with 6 tents draped with colourful cloth and unusual furniture including huge sofas, woven local mats and special beds and furniture made from fallen trees. The bathrooms are built around trees. Very good gourmet food. The whole area is lit by torches at night. This camp is owned by Iain and Oria Douglas-Hamilton, who have been involved in elephant conservation for over 40 years. They wrote the books *Among the Elephants* and *Battle for the Elephants* and Dr Iain Douglas-Hamilton is the founder and president of the

Kenya's premier *Safari* destination

WILDERNESS LODGES
KENYA

KEEKOROK·LARSENS CAMP
SAMBURU GAME LODGE

(+254 020) 532329 | sales@wildernesslodges.co.ke | www.discoverwilderness.com

registered charity, **Save the Elephants**, and has without doubt played a leading role in stopping elephant poaching in Kenya. The BBC has recently filmed a series in Samburu called *Living With Elephants* about the Douglas-Hamiltons. Highly recommended.

**L Larsens Tented Camp**, reservations **Wilderness Lodges**, Nairobi, T020-650 392, www.wildernesslodges.co.ke. By the river, 20 tents with en suite bathrooms, the dining tent is open and tables are adorned with silver and fine china. Rebuilt in 2005, and a swimming pool and spa were added in 2006. No children under 10.There is an animal-viewing platform in a tree. Very elegant colonial style, highly recommended.

**A Samburu Intrepids**, reservations **Heritage Hotels,** Nairobi, T020-444 6651, www.heritage-eastafrica.com. 27 luxurious tents overlooking Ewaso Ng'iro River, with large 4-poster beds and en suite bathrooms. Swimming pool, activities include camel safaris and visits to Samburu villages. Education is a focus and there are special safaris for children and nightly talks and slide shows on wildlife and culture in the lounge.

**B Samburu Game Lodge** reservations **Wilderness Lodges**, PO Box 42788-GPO 00100, Nairobi, T020-532 329, www.discover wilderness.com. This, the first lodge in the reserve, built in 1963, was renovated to very high standards in 2006, situated on the bend of the river. A wonderful place to stop off for a drink at the **Crocodile Bar** even if you don't stay. Relaxed atmosphere in a beautiful setting, swimming pool, shop, open-sided dining area, a wide range of accommodation along the river bank in 61 cottages and *bandas*, each with 4-poster beds with mosquito nets, 1 with wheelchair access.

**B Samburu Serena Safari Lodge**, lodge T064-30800, reservations Nairobi T020-284 2333, www.serena hotels.com. Located at the south bank of the river, west of **Samburu Game Lodge**. This lodge is outside the reserve, though it must be accessed from the inside. Facilities include swimming pool, restaurant and bar, and leopard bait. The verandas in front of the 62 rooms allow for the observation of crocodiles in the river. Both here and at **Samburu**, it is a good idea not to leave the floodlit paths after dusk, as leopards drop by.

**B Samburu Sopa Lodge**, reservations Nairobi T020-375 0235, www.sopa lodges.com. A fairly new set-up in the middle of the park on a raised hill with good views, the 60 2-bedroomed cottages have verandas, and the public areas are nicely decorated in Samburu colours, local stones and natural materials. Swimming pool, game drives, visits to Samburu villages and wildlife talks on offer.

## Camping

**F Kenya Wildlife Service**, Nairobi, T020-600 800, www.kws.org. The Samburu campsites are scattered along the Ewaso Ng'iro River near the Samburu Game Lodge and the West Gate. All sites are flat, cleared spaces under trees with limited facilities. Those nearer to the lodge tend to be more secure. At **Butterfly Public Campsite**, it is possible to walk to the lodge for a cold drink and a look at the crocs. This is not advisable after 1900 as the lodge gates are locked and leopard bait is laid. Another site is the **Vervet Campsite**, also near the lodge and popular with camping safari companies. In all the campsites baboons can be a real nuisance, so guard your belongings.

### Buffalo Springs *p358, map p357*
There is no formal accommodation in Buffalo Springs and most people stay at the lodges in Samburu and visit on game drives.

### Shaba National Reserve *p358*
**B Sarova Shaba Lodge**, reservations, Nairobi T020-271 4444, www.sarova.co.ke/shaba. The luxury lodging facility of the Sarova group is the only accommodation in Shaba. It offers 85 rooms, restaurant, bar, petrol station, a magnificent swimming pool that curves around a natural rock formation, and a game viewing deck from which you can watch and feed crocodiles. Inspired by the *Survivor TV* show that was filmed in Shaba, the lodge runs adventure-style team-building courses.

## Camping

**F Kenya Wildlife Service**, Nairobi,
T020-600 800, www.kws.org. There are
in theory 3 campsites in Shaba but they
have no facilities.

## 🍴 Eating

### Isiolo *p356*

🍴 **The Bomen Restaurant**. Has the widest
choice and the best food and is also the best
bet for a beer in the evening, has a pool table
and there's a *nyama choma* spot outside.
🍴 **Roots Restaurant**, on the main road
opposite the Caltex petrol station. The best
of the cheap restaurants, simple fare includes
*nyama choma*, some Somalian dishes, it has a
fully stocked bar and a TV for watching sport.

## 🚌 Transport

### Isiolo *p356*

**Akamba** runs 2 buses daily (0700 and 2000),
6 hrs, to **Nairobi**, stopping at **Nanyuki**, **Nyeri**
and other towns and many *matatus* link the
towns on this route. Regular *matatus* run to
**Meru** and other nearby Central Province towns
on the eastern side of Mt Kenya.

**Babie Coach**, a converted Isuzu truck, runs
between **Maralal** and Isiolo via **Archer's Post**

and **Wamba**, leaving each town on
alternate daysat 1100-1300 depending
on passenger numbers and takes 5-8 hrs.
If you are driving this route yourself, ensure
you have enough fuel to get to Maralal,
217 km away.

Isiolo is an important transport hub for
travel north to **Marsabit** and **Moyale**, and
northeast to **Wajir** and the very remote town
of **Mandera** close to both the Somali and
Ethiopian border in Kenya's far northeast,
although travel to north eastern Kenya is
currently advised against on grounds of
safety. It is possible to arrange a lift on a
truck (you may have to travel in the back on
top of the cargo) to **Marsabit** (8 hrs) and
**Moyale** (12 hrs from Marsabit). It is a hot,
dusty journey. Trucks leave in convoy at
0530 from the police post

### Samburu *p357, map p357*

*Matatus* run the 57 km from **Isiolo** to
**Archer's Post** (only trucks from Isiolo
go further north – see above).

**Air Kenya**, Wilson Airport, Nairobi,
T020-605 745, www.airkenya.com,
has daily flights between Samburu and
**Nairobi**, US$98 1 way, departs Nairobi
0915, arrives in Samburu 1030, departs
at 1110, arrives in Nairobi 1215.
It sometimes also stops at **Meru**,
lengthening journey time.

# Isiolo to Lake Turkana

*Exploring the lake from the east is far more exciting than the west, and you pass through a number of national reserves. Driving here takes skills and nerves of steel and you will need a 4WD vehicle. Few of the roads are surfaced, and the main A2 road is tricky to say the least. Avoid the rainy season as some routes become impassable. Some public transport is available, though it is not as easy as on the west. The following route is taken: north from Isiolo to Archer's Post on the A2 road, also known as the Trans-East-African Highway, then looping west along the C79 to Wamba and Maralal, before travelling north along the secondary road to Baragoi, South Horr and the eastern side of Lake Turkana including the remote Sibiloi National Park.* ⟫ *For listings, see pages 366-368.*

## Ins and outs

The **Babie Coach** (see page 361), a converted Isuzu truck, runs up and down between Maralal and Isiolo every other day and there may be the odd *matatu*. There are also buses and *matatus* running between Maralal and Nyahururu where you can hop on to a bus to Nairobi. But Maralal is really the end of the road as far as public transport is concerned and nothing else except trucks head north from here to South Horr. Without your own transport, going north to the lake or Marsabit requires putting the word out (and paying) and waiting, possibly for several days, for a lift.

## Wamba and the Mathew's Mountains ● ⟫ *pp366-368. Colour map 4, C2.*

Wamba is a small town 90 km northwest of Isiolo and 55 km from the Samburu National Reserve. Northeast of Wamba are the Mathew's Mountains, where the peaks are covered in cycads and podocarpus forest. The best view of the mountain is to be seen from the road going up to **Kitich Camp**. The highest peak in the range is Mount Warges at 2688 m. Other peaks are Mathew's peak at 2374 m, Mathew's South Peak at 2284 m, Lolokwe at 1852 m, Lesiolo at 2475 m and Poror at 2581 m. These mountains offer pleasant walking opportunities in the shade but views tend to be restricted by the flora. The Ngeng River has a couple of big rock pools suitable for swimming. Guides and *askaris* are needed to visit this area. Wamba is a useful place to stock up on fresh meat and other provisions. Near Wamba, in lush forest at the southern end of the Mathew's Mountains, are two luxury lodges (see Sleeping, page 366).

## Maralal ● ⟫ *pp366-368. Colour map 4, C1.*

→ *Phone code: 065*

High up in the hills, Maralal looks down onto the Lerochi Plateau, 240 km from Meru and 160 km from Nyahururu. Long before the British administrators moved in, this was a spiritual site for the Samburu. The town with two wide tree-lined dusty streets and ramshackle wooden shops has a 'Wild-West' atmosphere. Only a few visitors come to Maralal on their way to Turkana or for camel trekking at **Yare Safari Club and Camp**. Many rural Turkana and Samburu people who have lost their livestock through drought have moved into the town, and the poverty (and begging) can be rather disturbing. There is also the small **Maralal Game Sanctuary** that can be accessed from the **Maralal Safari Lodge**. It covers the cedar-clad hillside above the town and in the thorn scrub lower down

# Maralal International Camel Derby

The annual Maralal International Camel Derby has been operating since 1990, and from 1998 the event has been coupled with the Kenya Amateur Cycling Association Race, which offers rating points in the international cycling circuit for winning participants. These races are held over the first weekend of August each year, beginning with the Amateur Camel Race on the Saturday morning, followed by a Semi Professional Camel Race on the Saturday afternoon, and the Professional Camel Derby on the Sunday. The camel races can be hilarious events for amateurs, and an exciting one for professionals, and no matter what your experience, you can join in. All proceeds go to charity. The derby is centred at Yare Club and Camp. Yare Safaris, www.yaresafaris.com, usually arrange transport to and from Nairobi for the weekend. The amateur/novice camel and cycling events are over 12 km and run round Maralal town once, starting and ending outside Yare Club, and take about one hour to complete. There is a small entry fee in addition to hiring the camel and handler, which is about US$30. In the amateur race the handler accompanies the rider and runs alongside the camel, but not so in the semi-professional race, when the rider must have sufficient experience to handle a camel independently over the distance.

The professional Camel Derby is over 42 km and goes through the town and surroundings, again starting and ending outside Yare Club, and it takes three to four hours to complete. Apart from having lots of fun, the aim of the derby has also been to promote an interest in better camel breeding among the people of northeastern Kenya and for them to understand the benefits that such animals can bring to these desert and arid land inhabitants. The Kenyan national herd of over one million animals is rapidly growing, and there is an ongoing overflow from Somalia, which has estimated herds of 5.6 million camels, many of which have filtered into Kenya.

there are a few impala, eland, buffalo, baboon, warthog and zebra, and seasonally elephant pass through. Much of this wildlife can be seen from the comfortable terrace of the lodge and the only permanent water in the sanctuary is a small waterhole just a few metres away. There used to be many Grevy's zebra in the hills on the route from Isiolo but unfortunately most of these have been poached out in the last decade or so. Maralal was until his death in 2003 home to Wilfred Thesiger, explorer and travel writer, who spent a number of years here in his later life looking after orphaned children.

The town itself has a few basic amenities, and if you are heading north Maralal is the last town with a bank. Both the Kenya Commercial Bank and the post office are near the market and bus station, and there are also several petrol stations in town. Traditionally garbed Samburu are still very much in evidence here, brightening up the surroundings with their skins, blankets, beads and hair styles. You can buy Samburu handicrafts, like the colourful necklaces made of thousands of beads, as well as sandals made of tyres at the lively market.

## Baragoi 😊 ▸▸ pp366-368. Colour map 4, B2.

This next settlement on the route up to the eastern shores of Lake Turkana lies on the Elbarta Plains. From Maralal the road climbs into the mountains and is awful in parts, particularly as there are a fair few steep climbs and descents. It takes from three to six hours depending on conditions. About 40 km before Baragoi the scenery changes dramatically as the road drops off the pine clad mountainous ridge down to a lunar landscape of solidified lava rocks on the desert floor, where it is blisteringly hot.

Baragoi is a small settlement in this wilderness area. The locals jokingly say that the road is the 'International dividing line' between the Samburu and Turkana, and you will notice the design differences in their homesteads – the dome shape of the Turkana and the flatter wider Samburu *manyattas*. Livestock is paramount in this region and you may notice that some of the herders are armed to protect their flocks from rustlers. The nearby Baragoi secondary school produces an amiable bunch of English speakers, knowledgeable about the area. There are a few general stores here and you should be able to get petrol (sold out of barrels). However, at present there is no electricity or running water in Baragoi and local people rely on digging wells for water in a nearby dry riverbed that skirts the town.

## South Horr ☺ ▸▸ *pp366-368. Colour map 4, B2.*

The nearest village to the southern end of Lake Turkana. The village itself is set in a beautiful canyon and is an oasis of green between two extinct volcanoes (Mount Nyiru and Mount Porale). The Samburu regard Mount Nyiru as being a place sacred to N'kai, their god, at the flat top of the mountain and take their cattle there to graze during the dry season where there is a plentiful supply of water. If you want to climb the mountain, the shortest approach is via Tum, and an early morning start allows the ascent to be made in the mountain's shadow. On the summit a great pile of rocks marks the grave of a famous *laibon*, and there are excellent views of Lake Turkana and the Sugutu Valley. There are some great walks in the mountain forests all around you and you could either hike through (it's a good idea to take a guide) or go on a camel trek, best arranged from the **Desert Rose Lodge** in Baragoi (see Sleeping, page 367). There is no fuel for sale in South Horr.

## Lake Turkana (eastern shore) ☺ ▸▸ *pp366-368. Colour map 4, A1/B1.*

The region around the eastern shores of Lake Turkana has been made into one of Kenya's four biosphere reserves, the 7000-sq-km **Mount Kulal Biosphere Reserve**. The area includes many different types of environments ranging from mountain forest about 2400 m above sea level to desert with grasslands, dry evergreen forest, woodlands, bushlands and saltbush scrublands in between. It covers most of Lake Turkana, its volcanic southern shores, the **South Island National Park**, and the **Chalbi Desert**. The latter is a shimmering and seemingly endless expanse of sand stretching for 300 km to the south of North Horr to the shore of the lake of which it was once part. Even today, perhaps once in every decade, in one of the torrential downpours that occur during a rare rainy season, it will again come into flood to form a vast but shallow lake.

### Loyangalani

One of the biggest villages on the eastern lake shore, Loyangalani is a collection of huts, with thatched grass and galvanized-iron roofs. There is a life-giving spring here but the surrounds are flat stony plains scattered with the bleached bones of livestock carcasses. This is home to the dwindling numbers of El Molo people, a group of hardy fishermen. Believed to be of Cushitic origin from the northeast, this is Kenya's smallest ethnic group (according to ethnologists the 'pure' El Molo only number about 40-50, whereas others have traces of Samburu or Turkana ancestery). They are believed to have lived to the north of Lake Turkana, but were driven south by other warring tribesmen, seriously depleting their numbers in the process. They took refuge from their enemies by living on the small offshore islands. However, some of the small communities now live along the shoreline. An El Molo village overlooks the bay, perched above it on a hillside. The water level of Lake Turkana is declining at a rate of 30 cm per annum, in a region where the annual rainfall is estimated to be only 50-60 mm. The lake is estimated to be 150 m lower than in the last century. This dramatic change in the lake's water level is attributed in part to the increased volume of water withdrawn for irrigation purposes from the River Omo by the Ethiopians.

The barren lava beds at the southern end of Lake Turkana peter out into the waters of the lake itself. The high salinity and soda mean nothing much grows around the shores.

## South Island

South Island is 39 sq km and was established as a national park in 1983 again for the protection of the Nile crocodile's breeding ground. South Island is also home to several species of venomous snakes, including vipers, puff adders and cobras. It is also an important breeding ground for hippos and is home to a flock of feral goats. The terrain of South Island is rugged, access is difficult and there is no permanent human settlement on the island, making it one of Kenya's most inhospitable parks. Only well-equipped travellers should consider making the trip out to the island. To get there from the mainland, you will need to hire a boat and guide from Loiyangalani, but be aware that few local fishermen venture there and it's a 30-km round trip by boat.

## Teleki and Mount Kulal

There are two outstanding volcanoes in the reserve, **Teleki**, that bounds the southern end of the lake, and **Mount Kulal**, that stands at 2285 m high, an extraordinary much-eroded tertiary volcanic mountain with its ridge running parallel to Lake Turkana, 24 km to the east. Both mountains are a pretty straightforward climb if you are suitably equipped. Mount Kulal is covered by thick lush green forest in marked contrast to the desolate lava moonscape of the southern shores of Lake Turkana. Its ridge runs in a north-south direction, with deep gorges radiating to the east and west. **El Kajarta**, a great gorge with vertical walls rising over 300 m, located to the southeast of Kulal, appears to almost split the mountain in two. El Kajarta Gorge can be accessed with difficulty around the east side of the mountain.

## Sibiloi National Park

Lying on the eastern shores of Lake Turkana in the far north of Kenya, just 30 km to the border with Ethiopia, it is one of the less well known of Kenya's national parks, despite its large size of 2575 sq km. It is now designated a World Heritage Site athough it has no tourist facilities because of its isolated geographical location.

The landscape is relatively verdant lakeside terrain with grassy plains with yellow spear grass and doum palms, extending to dry semi-desert. Within the national park is **Central Island**, which contains the world's largest crocodile population of about 12,000. Despite the fact that this park is windblown and arid, it has a surprising variety of wildlife including the reticulated giraffe, Grevy's zebra, Grant's gazelle, oryx, hartebeest, topi, ostrich, gerenuk, lion and cheetah, although these are rarely seen. Birdlife is prolific with over 350 recorded species of bird. Sibiloi National Park extends well into Lake Turkana in the process encompassing a large portion of Lake Turkana's huge population of Nile crocodile.

Within the park stands a petrified forest, which serves as a reminder that seven million years ago, this area was lush and densely populated. The national park was originally established by the National Museum of Kenya to protect the unique prehistoric archaeological sites. In 1960-1970s the Leakeys made many remarkable fossil finds of humans from 10,000-12,000 years ago. These finds included *Homo Habilis* and *Homo Erectus*, which dated man's origin to three million years ago. **Koobi Fora palaeontological site** is located here, as is a museum near the park's headquarters which houses the remains of prehistoric elephants among other things. This is generally unstaffed and only open when there are researchers in the area, but there are some simple *bandas* to sleep in. Over 4000 fossil specimens have been found in this area. Important finds include the homanid remains, the shell of a giant tortoise believed to be over three million years old, the fossilized remains of the elephant's forebear – the behemoth with massive tusks, and crocodile jaws measuring over 1.5 m (which equates to an overall length of over 14 m). The discovery of these fossils has resulted in a greater understanding of the environment one to three million years ago.

Sibiloi is very remote and only fully equipped expeditions should attempt the drive there. The two main routes to the park headquarters at Alia Bay are from Loyangalani and from Marsabit. It is about 120 km from Loyangalani along an unpaved trail through the desert to North Horr and then northwest to Alia Bay, the park HQ. This is only passable by 4WD. Alia Bay is Sibiloi Park's Headquarters with some official buildings, an airstrip and a campsite. The campsite is located beside a dry river bed about 4 km from the airstrip. You will need to bring all your own supplies, and it must be stressed that sufficient supplies of fuel and water and spare tyres must be carried by any travellers who visit this area.

## ◉ Isiolo to Lake Turkana listings

*For Sleeping and Eating price codes and other relevant information, see Essentials pages 34-38.*

## ◉ Sleeping

### Wamba and the Mathew's Mountains *p362*

**L Kitich Camp**, 34 km northwest of Wamba on a rough road towards the village of Parsaloi, alternatively fly in, reservations www.kitichcamp.com or **Bush and Beyond/Bush Homes of East Africa**, Nairobi, T020-600 457, www.bush-and-beyond.com and www.bush-homes.co.ke. 6 twin-bed tents with bush showers and long-drop loos in an attractive setting beside a seasonal river, game walks, bird watching and a natural pool nearby suitable for swimming. The camp is hosted by Giulio Bertolli, who left Italy over 30 years ago to live in Kenya. Very good food and 3-course meals are traditional Tuscany cuisine, the olive oil still comes from the owner's farm in Tuscany, house wines are included, bar and sitting room with fireplace. Kitich means 'place of happiness' in Samburu.

**L Sarara Tented Camp**, north of Wamba in the Mathew's Mountains, reservations **Bush and Beyond/Bush Homes of East Africa Ltd**, Nairobi, T020-600 457, www.bush-and-beyond.com and www.bush-homes.co.ke. This is the first tourist lodge to be wholly owned and run by the local Samburu people, with the assistance of the Lewa Wildlife Conservancy. It is on the Namunyak Wildlife Conservation Trust, an area of 75,000 ha, home to the Samburu. Namunyak means 'place of peace'. The conservancy was set up in 1995 to promote wildlife conservation and to assist the local community to benefit from tourism, in return for protecting the wildlife species living on their land. This has been hugely successful – after the severe ivory poaching crisis of the mid 1970s and early 1980s, there were no recorded elephants remaining in the Mathew's Mountains by 1985; today there are several hundred. The tented camp has 5 luxury tents, each with its own flush loo and open-air bush shower. The lounge/dining *banda* overlooks a natural swimming pool and waterhole with views of the mountains. You can get here by chartering a plane from **Tropic Air** in Nanyuki (see page 210).

**F Saudia Lodge**, off the main street in Wamba, offering sound food and lodging in a family-run establishment, very simple rooms with shared facilities, the only place to stay in town.

### Maralal *p362*

**B Maralal Safari Lodge**, in the Maralal Game Sanctuary, about 3 km out of town towards Baragoi, T065-2060, www.angelfire.com/jazz/maralal. A classy country retreat with en suite cottages with verandas, main bar and restaurant, swimming pool, terraces for game viewing and birdwatching, and there is also a souvenir shop. The lodge is by a waterhole, which attracts a wide range of wildlife, and it is a nice place to go and have a beer (you don't need to be staying to eat or drink here). Rates are in the region of US$230 for a double, full board.

**E-F Yare Camel Club and Camp**, 3 km out of town on the road towards Isiolo, T065-62295, www.yaresafaris.co.ke. The Isiolo–Maralal bus will drop you at their gate. Quiet place, though it can get raucous in the evening once the bar gets going. The camping facilities are excellent, with lots of toilets and showers. US$3 a night for the pitch and there are also 14 charming *bandas*, all s/c (only cold water) and roomy for US$22. There's also a games room with a dart boards, table tennis and a pool table. Tours in a high-sided safari truck can be arranged and the 12-day Lake Turkana tour is an excellent way to see Northern Kenya and includes 2 days of camel trekking for US$1300 per person all inclusive of meals and pickups/drop-offs in Nairobi. Shorter camel treks can be arranged from the camp for US$45 per person per day including camels, Moran or Samburu guides, food and tents.

**F Impala Lodge**, opposite the *matatu* stage, near the main roundabout in town, T065-63292. Quiet and clean local board and lodgings, rooms don't have bathrooms but there is hot water in the shared showers, and you can park here.

### Baragoi *p363*

**L Desert Rose Lodge**, reservations Nairobi, T020-386 4831, T0722-322 745 (mob), www.desertrosekenya.com. To get here, turn left 18 km to the north of Baragoi and it's 15 km along a very steep sandy track (4WD only). Alternatively, the lodge has an airstrip and they can arrange car charters. On the southern slopes of Mt Nyiru, this is a remote and secluded lodge with 5 sympathetically designed luxury guesthouses, a notable feature being the open-air en suite bathrooms. Fantastic views, a stunning rock swimming pool, bar and restaurant and wooden decks. There are a number of walks around the lodge and leopards can sometimes be spotted as well as abundant birds, nearby is a unique waterfall that provides a rock slide. Profits from the lodge have been used to build the local primary school and medical centre. A typical 4-day package here including return flights from Nairobi, a scenic flight from the lodge, camel trekking, accommodation, all meals and drinks costs in the region of US$3900 per person but comes down considerably for a group of up to 5 people. They can also organize tailor-made camel trekking from 2 days to 1 week. On top of all this, the lodge has its own workshop for making unique and stylish wooden furniture, including wooden wash stands and bath tubs, you can commission a piece and they can arrange for shipping home.

### South Horr *p364*

**F Kurungu Campsite**. About 7 km north of South Horr, to the right of the road, this is in a nice sheltered spot surrounded by trees, and is run by the local Samburu who may put on a display of dancing if you're prepared to pay and can sell you trinkets. Bucket showers, long-drop loos and firewood is available, you need to pay extra for an *askari* for security.

## Lake Turkana (eastern shore) *p364, map p353*
### Chalbi Desert
**B Kalacha**, www.kalacha.org. This is situated in the Chalbi Desert, on the edge of a permanent oasis and the only way to get here is by air charter arranged by **Tropic Air** in Nanuyki (see page 210). Kalacha Camp has been set up as a community-based project for the Gabbra people of this area, providing them with a further source of income. The oasis provides water for vast numbers of their livestock, including cattle, sheep, donkeys and camels. A very simple camp, built using local materials, including *dhom* palm trunks for the poles, and leaves woven into mats which have been used for the roofs and walls. The 4 *bandas* have twin beds, flush toilet and cold shower. The mess area is a circular building designed around a kidney-shaped swimming pool. You need to bring your own food and drink, including plenty of drinking water, but the 4 members of staff will help prepare meals and there's a fridge run on paraffin. Rates are from US$110 per person per day.

### Loyangalani
These places to stay used to be on the lakeshore but are now some metres back given that the lake has shrunk in recent years.
**B Oasis Lodge**, on the lakeshore, reservations, Nairobi, T020-884 258, www.oasis-lodge.com. Primarily a fishing lodge, German-run, with 24 wooden cottages with electricity, fairly run down now, but very good meals based on fresh fish from the lake. Non-residents are charged an entrance fee to use the facilities, restaurant and bar and well worth it for a dip in the swimming pool. Can organize boat trips to South Island National Park and sport fishing for tiger fish, tilapia and the giant Nile Perch. It can arrange flights from Nairobi.
**F El-Molo Camp**, located next to **Oasis Lodge**. A scruffy campsite but it does have a swimming pool, showers and long-drop loos. You'll need to hire an *askari* to watch your vehicle. Gametrackers also have a campsite in the region but you can only stay there if you are on one of its (recommended) tours.
**F Mosaretu Women's Group Campsite**, also adjacent to **Oasis Lodge**, www.mosaretu.org. This is a community campsite run by a women's group comprising over 50 members, and stands for El MOlo, SAmburu, REndile and TUrkana. It's a pleasant fenced spot in a clutch of palm trees where you can camp or there are 4 simple thatch and reed *bandas* with mattresses and mosquito nets, plus toilets and showers, and a simple kitchen. You may be able to negotiate with the women to cook you fish from the lake.

### Sibiloi National Park
**F Research Camp**, reservations, Nairobi T020-374 2161, www.museums.or.ke. This is located on the Koobi Fora spit in the lake and has 4 dormitories as basic accommodation primarily for researchers, or you can camp. It is run by the National Museums of Kenya and can be booked through them in Nairobi. These are equipped with beds, bedding, mosquito nets and towels, and there's 3 flush toilets and 3 showers and a dining/research *banda*. You need to bring all food and drink but you can cook here over a fire.

# Isiolo to Moyale

*Travelling north on the Trans-East-African Highway from Isiolo the A2 heads north through very dry country to Marsabit and beyond to Moyale on the Ethiopian border. From Isiolo all the way through to Moyale, vehicles travel in an armed convoy , which departs at 0530 from the police post 3 km to the north of Isiolo. The next fuel is at Marsabit, 277 km away. In Isiolo and at a couple of police barriers along the way, you have to sign a log book which records all traffic moving on the road. This is a government policy to reduce gun trafficking and cattle rustling, but also a good safety net in that, should your vehicle not have reached the next village before nightfall, a search party could be sent out. There is no public transport, so without your own vehicle the only option is to hitch a ride on a truck.* ▸▸ *For listings, see page 372.*

## Losai National Reserve ▸▸ *Colour map 4, B/C2.*

The road travels through this reserve, with the majority of reserve located west of the road. This is 1800 sq km of thorny bushland situated in the Losai Mountains southwest of and adjacent to Marsabit National Reserve and about 175 km north of Mount Kenya, in Northern Kenya. The reserve was gazetted in 1976 to give protection to elephant, greater and lesser kudu, lion and a few black rhino, but none of these remain now thanks to poaching. In fact, rather amusingly, the Kenya Wildlife Services website claims the reserve these days is home to cobras, pythons, grasshoppers, bees, beetles and scorpions! Despite these intriguing attractions, it is unlikely tourism will develop in the near future as the lava plateau with scattered volcanic plugs is virtually impenetrable even with a 4WD.

## Marsabit ⬤⬤ ▸▸ *p372. Colour map 4, B3.*

Rising to 1000 m above the surrounding plains, Marsabit is permanently green. The hills around the town are thickly forested making a nice change to the desert that surrounds the area. Marsabit is in Kenya's Eastern Province 560 km north of Nairobi and 280 km from Isiolo. This is also the administrative capital of the district and a major trading centre. There are three petrol stations and a branch of Kenya Commercial Bank, but don't rely on it being open as it sometimes it runs out of cash given the difficult journey up here. There are three streets in Marsabit, with low slung concrete buildings painted in vivid green or blue or dirty white, and one general store selling all manner of oddments from car spare parts to cables, pipes, flour and sugar. There are a number of mechanics in town (for very good reason); just ask around. The main inhabitants of the town are the Rendille, who dress in elaborate beaded necklaces and sport wonderful hairstyles. They are nomadic people keeping to their traditional customs and only visiting the town to trade. There is also a fairly large population of Burji people, who mainly arrived in Northern Kenya from Ethiopia during the famines there in the 1970s. Marsabit National Reserve is nearby. During periods of drought Marsabit has had no running water or electricity. Like Northeast Kenya, the region has witnessed security problems in recent years.

## Marsabit National Reserve ⬤ ▸▸ *p372. Colour map 4, B3.*

ⓘ *www.kws.org, daily 0630-1800, park entry per day US$20 adults, US$10 children, US$3.50 per vehicle.*

# Crossing Kenya's 'badlands'

Despite the Trans-East-African Highway (A2) being a vital transport link to land-locked Ethiopia, it's in diabolical condition. In the dry season it's very rocky and bumpy and badly corrugated in patches, and in the wet it becomes a quagmire as the top soil, known locally as 'black cotton', becomes very slippery and it's easy to get a vehicle stuck in the mud. It has been tarred in the past, three times apparently, but the heavy trucks soon chew it up again and if it rains debris is washed away from the surface. At the time of writing the government had announced they were in negotiations with the Chinese to re-tar the road. This may be in exchange for oil exploration in Northern Kenya, which has long been rumoured to have oil reserves. The Chinese are presently tapping into oil resources all over Africa. For many years, local people have attributed the poverty and the lack of infrastructure in the northern region of Kenya to the poor state of this road.

From Isiolo and Archer's Post to Marsabit the road passes through hundreds of kilometres of flat desert landscape of red volcanic rock and sand with the occasional tortured tree jutting incongruously out of the sand as if in defiance of nature's attempt to wipe out life in this wasteland. You may see nomadic pastoralists driving their herds from water-source to water-source, picking at the sparse vegetation along the way. As you approach Marsabit, the sight of mist-covered Mount Marsabit, or Saku, as it's called locally, rises above the horizon of this empty desert, and the closer you get to the town, the vegetation becomes greener and the air cooler.

About 250 km north of Marsabit, Moyale is on the Kenyan–Ethiopian border. From the relative elevation at Marsabit the horrendously rough road flattens out again, and travels through an extraordinary landscape. The sight of the Marsabit Mountain falls away and the road falls again on to an unearthly flat plain that widens out far as the eye can see. This is the Dida Galgalu Desert; the name reputedly means 'the plains of darkness' in the Borana language. It features a desolate landscape of shimmering mirages, heat, a searing wind, the odd termite mound, black rocks the size of footballs scattered on the ground, and is devoid of vegetation and water. The black rock attracts the sun, which in turn causes a fierce heat to radiate from the ground. The 'road' itself becomes two barely visible lines and huge rocks are scattered across it from time to time. Quite astonishingly – what do these people and their animals eat and drink? – the stick figures of lonely Gabra herders and their charges can be seen on the horizons. The last 100 km to Moyale is much easier as you will have left the hard rock, the road goes over flat sand and thorn bush vegetation starts lining the road. A ridge of hills appears in time, marking the border with Ethiopia and the road turns eastward to run parallel with the hills. Eventually the road, which by now consists of fine red dust, turns north again through a narrow pass between the hills, and the clutch of tin shacks, which is Moyale, appears. On arrival, you sign the arrivals book at the police barrier and then cross the dusty river bed into Ethiopia, from where it is gloriously smooth tar all the way to Addis Ababa, 770 km away.

Marsabit National Reserve covers 2088 sq km and contains the cloud-capped Mount Marsabit, undoubtedly the most attractive of North Kenya's extinct volcanic mountains. It is a large massif covered with lush, verdant growth that offers a welcome change from the

## Ahmed the Elephant

Marsabit National Reserve used to be famous for its large stocks of elephants, but these have sadly become severely depleted. They included the famous Ahmed, the bull-elephant who was born in 1919 and whose long 3-m-long pointed tusks weighed over 45 kg each and reached the ground. These magnificent tusks added to his legendary status, but they also put his life in grave danger as a target for ivory hunters. The general public developed a deep concern for his safety and during 1972-1973, some 5000 letters calling for Ahmed's protection were sent to the East African Wildlife Society – the body that was in charge of the parks before the Kenya Wildlife Services was formed in 1990. This resulted in President Jomo Kenyatta designating Ahmed as a national monument, and according him 24-hour armed protection. Ahmed died in 1974 of natural causes aged 55 years, and when he died he was 3 m tall at the shoulder, and weighed approximately 5000 kg. His preserved remains can now be seen in the Nairobi National Museum and you can stand next to him for a photo.

desert that surrounds it. Its altitude stretches from 420 m, where thorny bushland dominates the scenery, to 1700 m above sea level. There are several craters in the forest. The upper reaches are covered in forest, merging into acacia grasslands. The mountain is covered in a thick mist that dissipates by midday, after which it becomes warm and sunny.

A number of birds are found here including 52 different types of bird of prey and it houses a wide variety of animals such as elephant, greater kudu, various species of monkey, baboon, hyena, aard-wolf, caracal, and the reticulated giraffe though it is difficult to see much through the thick forest. It's also home to a large number of snakes including giant cobras. The volcanic craters are a special feature of Mount Marsabit, several of which contain freshwater lakes. **Gof Sokorte Guda** (Paradise Lake) is a wonderful spot to observe elephant and buffalo in the late afternoon, when they congregate for water. Within the park's boundary is a 'singing well' where the Borana bring their camels and goats to drink. Athletic young men in loin cloths throw up buckets to their neighbours and so on up the human chain to the drinking trough above. This fluid and elegant motion of water accompanied by rhythmic singing of the Borana gives rise to the name. To visit the park you need to be in your own 4WD.

## Moyale ●● ↦ *p372. Colour map 4, A4.*

→ *Phone code: 0185.*

To get here, vehicles must join the convoy that collects at Marsabit's police barrier near the Esso petrol station at 0530 in the morning. About 250 km north of Marsabit, Moyale is on the Kenyan-Ethiopian border, and the larger and more prosperous part of the town is in Ethiopia, where the basic hotels and restaurants are considered to be better than the Kenyan side. This is where you'll have your first introduction to *injera*, Ethiopia's flat, pancake-like, sour bread that's eaten with just about any meal. This is a small town with a post office, basic shops and a police station, and it has only recently been supplied with (sporadic) electricity. It is developing slowly and there is now a bank here and two petrol stations.

# Border essentials: Kenya–Ethiopia

## Moyale

There have been differing reports on the time at which the Kenyan side of the border closes, either at 1800 or 1600, so get there before 1600. The Ethiopian border is closed all day Sunday, as well as on public and religious holidays. It is possible to cross freely during daytime hours into Ethiopian Moyale to do some shopping, or even stay in the Ethiopian part of the town overnight, leaving the car behind on the Kenyan side, prior to completing the border formalities. Driving is on the right in Ethiopia.

## ◉ Isiolo to Moyale listings

*For Sleeping and Eating price codes and other relevant information, see Essentials pages 34-38.*

## 🛏 Sleeping

### Marsabit *p369*

There is no formal accommodation in Marsabit, but locals rent out very basic rooms to truck drivers, usually a simple bed in a tin shack with mud floors. Several of these mostly unnamed board and lodgings can be found on the main road near the Shell petrol station. Overlanders should ask around town for Henry.
**F Henry's Place**, south side of town, to the west of the main road. The camp is down the back of a construction yard, past the cows and barns and has hot showers, clean long-drop toilets, flat ground for camping, plenty of room for vehicles, good drinking water, can organize beers and costs US$5 per person. Henry makes bread for the Marsabit shops, so you can also arrange basic food here.

### Marsabit National Reserve *p369*
**Marsabit Lodge**. This is wonderfully situated in front of the crater lake, Gof Sokorte Dik, within the Marsabit National Reserve, and has 24 rooms, but it's presently closed.

### Camping
**F Kenya Wildlife Services**, Nairobi, T020-600 800, www.kws.org. There is a site near the main gate of the national park, but there are no facilities. If you can organize a ranger to go with you, you can also camp on the rim of

Paradise Lake, which is beautiful but can be very cold.

### Moyale *p371*
There is hardly any choice on the Kenyan side of Moyale, and water rarely runs through the pipes. It's best to cross over into the Ethiopian side if at all possible, where there is a better choice of basic board and lodgings.
**F Barissah**, on the main road. You can rent a bed for the night in an unlockable room with a dirt floor for less than US$2, there are no showers, but you can have a bucket wash, and get chapattis and warm tea in the evening.
**F Medina Hotel**, central but a bit off the main road. Very simple concrete rooms with bucket baths, dirty toilets, no restaurant, but can organize *askaris* to watch vehicles.

## ⊖ Transport

### Marsabit *p369*
Trucks and private vehicles travel in convoy, with armed guards, usually passing through during the afternoon or early evening in either direction. The journey to **Moyale** can take up to 9 hrs but the roads become virtually impassable when it rains.

### Moyale *p371*
Convoys leave for the south at around 0800 and trucks congregate near the police barrier. Daily buses depart from the Ethiopian side towards **Addis Ababa**.

# Northeast Kenya

*The most remote part of the country is the northeast, a vast wilderness with almost no sign that humans have ever been here. Part of the attraction is the immense scale and vast emptiness of this remote wilderness. Endless blue skies and flat landscapes produce a sense of solitude that is hard to experience anywhere else. The landscape is made up of tracts of desert and semi-desert barely broken by settlements and with almost no public transport. Its inaccessibility combined with security problems around the Somali border make this area unappealing to even the most intrepid travellers – no tour companies operate in this region.*

*Grouped together adjacent to Meru National Park (see page 218) are a chain of reserves: Bisanadi National Reserve, Kora National Park and North Kitui National Reserve. Rahole National Reserve is north of Kora National Park.* ➤➤ *There are no facilities for visitors in any of these reserves.*

## Background

Physically, the area is very flat with two important rivers flowing through, the Tana River and the Ewaso Ng'iro. As you would expect, it is around these waterways that settlement is greatest and the national parks are based. The **Tana River Primate National Reserve** is based near Garsen though it is hard to reach. It was set up to protect the red colobus and crested mangabey monkeys (both endangered species). The reserve is more easily accessed from the coast, north of Malindi, so details are given on page 303.

The majority of people living in this area are Somali and before the creation of country boundaries pastoralists roamed the area freely. In fact in colonial days, the area was known as Somali country. As countries in the region gained independence, Somalis unsuccessfully tried to claim this area as part of Somalia. Shortly after, the area was closed to visitors by the Kenyan authorities who wished to drill for oil. Years of neglect and almost no development leave it one of the poorest areas of the country. These problems have been exacerbated more recently by the civil war in Somalia resulting in a huge influx of refugees into northeast Kenya. There are a number of refugee camps now set up for them (and for Somali-Kenyans who can no longer support their way of life in this barren area). Somalis are blamed for most of the poaching in the region.

## Bisanadi National Reserve ➤➤ *Colour map 3, C3.*

This is adjacent to the northeast boundary of Meru National Park and is about 600 sq km. The area is mainly thorny bushland and thicket merging into wooded grasslands with dense riverine forests of raffia palm along the watercourses. You are likely to see the same sort of wildlife as in Meru National Park as it acts as a dispersal area during the rains. It is a particularly good place to find elephant and buffalo in the wet season. Bisanadi National Reserve forms a protective screen to the east of Meru National Park, allowing the latter's wildlife more freedom of movement and at the same time restricting human encroachment. The reserve is underdeveloped, roads are virtually non-existent, and travelling to the reserve is difficult and is only possible in a 4WD from neighbouring Meru National Park or from the Tana River, at the reserve's south border. In any case and mainly due to the safety problems in the area access is restricted. If you want to arrange a visit, you will have to ask for a permit at **Kenya Wildlife Service's Headquarters** ① *T020-600 800, www.kws.org*, in Langata, Nairobi, next to Nairobi National Park.

## Kora National Park ›› *Colour map 4, C3.*

On one of Kenya's most important waterways, the Tana River, the Kora National Park is 125 km east of Mount Kenya in Coastal Province and covers 1787 sq km. It was gazetted in 1973 and was upgraded to a national park just three days before the death of George Adamson. Meru National Park and the Tana River mark its northern boundary for 65 km. The eastern boundary is the Mwitamyisi River. The land is mostly acacia bushland with riverine forests of doum palm and Tana River poplar. On Tana River are the spectacular Adamson's Falls, the Grand Falls and the Kora Rapids.

Rocky outcrops or *inselbergs* are a local feature. These are domed hills or hard rocks rising steeply from the surrounding area. Their cracks have filled with soil and a wide variety of shrubs, herbs and small wind-blown trees have become established in the crevices. The highest of the inselbergs is Mansumbi, 488 m, followed by Kumbulanwa, 450 m, and Kora Rock, 442 m. There is also a wide variety of animal species here including elephant, hippo, lion, leopard, cheetah, serval, caracal, wildcat, genet, spotted and striped hyena, and several types of antelope. The rivers hold lizards, snakes, tortoises and crocodiles. This area has had serious problems with poachers in recent years. George Adamson and two of his assistants were murdered here in 1989 by poachers. His Kora camp, Kampi ya Simba, is where George's grave is flanked by that of his brother Terence, and the one of the lion he called Boy.

## Rahole National Reserve ›› *Colour map 4, C3/4.*

Situated to the northeast of Kora National Park, this reserve is an enormous stretch of dry thorny bushland in the Garissa district of Northeastern Province about 150 km northeast of Mount Kenya. It is home to elephant, Grevy's zebra and beisa oryx. The reserve is located on the north bank of the Tana River at the western extreme of North Eastern Province. The reserve is a vast expanse of unspoiled wilderness, accessible only by 4WD vehicles, as tracks are few and far between in the park. Even where tracks do exist, they are extremely rough and in generally poor condition. Rahole, like neigbouring Kora National Reserve to the south and Bisanadi and North Kitui reserves further west, serve as protective areas for migrating animals from Meru National Park. The closest approaches to the reserve are at the south, near the Tana River. One track leads north-west from Garissa to the village of Mbalambala on the Tana near the eastern edges of both Kora National Park and Rahole. From Mbalambala, there is a road heading north into the eastern section of Rahole. Alternatively, there are tracks leading to the western sections of the reserve from the town of Garba Tula off the main Isiolo-Wajir road (B9). Again, if you want to arrange a visit, you will have to ask for a permit at **Kenya Wildlife Service's Headquarters** ① *T020-600 800, www.kws.org*, in Langata, Nairobi, next to Nairobi National Park.

## North Kitui National Reserve ›› *Colour map 3, C3.*

Adjacent to and southeast of Meru National Park is North Kitui National Reserve in Eastern Province. It measures 745 sq km and is mainly bushland and riverine forest. The Tana River runs through the reserve and you are likely to see crocodiles and hippos. There are no good roads leading to North Kitui National Reserve. The main route into the reserve would be from Meru National Park, across the Tana River, but bridging the Tana River is difficult if not impossible for vehicles.

## Garissa ▸▸ *Colour map 2, A1.*

This is the town in the northeast that is closest to Nairobi both geographically and culturally. It is on an alternative route back from Lamu to Nairobi. It is the administrative centre for the district, and there are shops for provisions, petrol and a bank. The heat is fierce and there is high humidity making it an unpleasant climate to stay in for long. The town is mostly populated by Somalis, as well as a few of the original riverine people. The Somalis claim that much of what was then known as the Northern Frontier District (NFD), had originally been part of Somalia following the redrawing of the border between Kenya and Italian Somaliland by the British in 1925, a fact much disputed by the Kenyans. The Laikipiak Masai lived in this area as far north as the Juba River and over the years have fought incessantly with the Somalis. Travellers are advised not to travel east of Garissa towards the Somali border, as there have been many incidents of armed robbery with fatalities by heavily armed *shiftas* (bandits) in recent years.

## Wajir ▸▸ *Colour map 4, B5.*

Some 300 km from Isiolo, along the most remote route in the country, the area is a vast scrubland that seems to go on forever. Due to security problems in this area following the Somali War, this unappealing journey is ill advised.

The town of Wajir itself is growing as many rural people have migrated their after a devastating famine hit this area hard in 2006 and many people lost their livestock. The population and atmosphere of the place has more Arab than African influences than Garissa. The settlement developed around wells that have been fought over by rival clans for generations, water being such a valuable commodity in this area. The Kolbio border post is less than 100 km north of here on the A3 where there is a reception centre for Somali refugees who routinely stream over the border into Kenya before being transferred to the massive refugee camp known as Dadaab 75 km from Kolbio towards Garissa. This particular camp has been in existence since 1992 and today houses an estimated population of 180,000 refugees. As you can imagine, with so many people trying to live in one place, it has seriously impacted the environment as fuel and building materials are in constant demand. Additionally, after four years of drought, there was massive flooding in 2006, which temporarily cut off the access road to the camp and more than 2000 homes were destroyed.

## Mandera ▸▸ *Colour map 4, A6.*

This is the furthest point in Kenya, 370 km northeast beyond Wajir on the Ethiopian, Somali and Kenyan border. The war has made this a particularly foolhardy expedition at the moment with marauding rival Somali clans. The main line of contact is on the private aircraft who fly in shipments of *miraa*. In the past, trade and communication with Somalia was more important than with Kenya as Mandera is far closer to Mogadishu, the capital of Somalia, than to Nairobi.

Until recently Mandera was a fairly small border town servicing the local community. Since the Somali civil war, it has become home to literally tens of thousands of Somalians putting an impossible strain on resources. The lack of water, always a problem, has become critical. Also, the stability of the place is severely tested by the prevailing conditions and deadly ethnic clashes are common in this region. *Miraa* (see page 219) is the big business in town. There is a post office, police station and bank.

# Contents

Background

# History

### Earliest times

There is evidence that the forefathers of *Homo sapiens* lived in this part of East Africa 10,000-12,000 years ago. In the 1960s Louis Leakey, a Kenyan-born European, and his wife Mary, began a series of archaeological expeditions in East Africa, particularly around Lake Turkana in the north. During these excavations they traced human biological and cultural development back from about 50,000 years to 1.8 million years ago. They discovered the skull and bones of a two million-year-old fossil, which they named *Homo habilis* and who they argued was an ancestor to modern man. Since the 1970s, Richard Leakey, son of Louis and Mary Leakey, has uncovered many more clues as to the origins of humankind and how they lived, unearthing some early Stone Age tools. These findings have increased our knowledge of the beginnings of earth, and establish the Rift Valley as the Cradle of Humankind. Many of the fossils are now in the National Museum of Nairobi. Little evidence exists as to what happened between the periods 1.8 million and 250,000 years ago except that *Homo erectus* stood upright and moved further afield, spreading out over much of Kenya and Tanzania.

More recently there have been two significant discoveries. In March 2001 it emerged that a team including Richard Leakey's wife Meave had found an almost complete skull of a previously unknown creature near Lamekwi River in the north. The skull of *Kenyanthropus platyops* has a flat face, much like modern humans and has been dated at between 3.2 million and 3.5 million years old. This is about the same time as the famous 'Lucy' – *Australopithecus afarensis* – found in Ethiopia in 1974, was living and suggests that modern humans evolved from one of several closely related ape-like ancestors of that period.

A potentially more remarkable find was also announced in 2001. Fourteen fragments of a six million-year-old 'Millennium Man' were discovered in the remote Tugen Hills west of Lake Baringo. The fossils from four bodies of *Orrorin tugenensis* are among the oldest remains of ape-like ancestors ever found, about twice as old as Lucy. They appear to be more human-like than could have been imagined for a creature that lived so long ago and could be the remains of the oldest known direct ancestor of humans.

In more recent times, from 5000-3000 BC Kenya was inhabited by hunter-gatherer groups, the forefathers of the Boni, Wata and Wariangulu people.

### Bantu expansion

Later still began an influx of peoples from all over Africa that lasted right up until about the 19th century. The first wave came from Ethiopia when the tall, lean Cushitic people gradually moved into Kenya over the second millennium BC settling around Lake Turkana in the north. These people practised mixed agriculture, keeping animals and planting crops. There is still evidence of irrigation systems and dams and wells built by them in the arid northern parts of Kenya. As the climate changed, getting hotter and drier, they were forced to move on to the hills above Lake Victoria.

The Eastern Cushitics, also pastoralists, moved into central Kenya around 3000 years ago. This group assimilated with other agricultural communities and spread across the land. The rest of Kenya's ancestors are said to have arrived between 500 BC and AD 500 with Bantu-speaking people arriving from West Africa and Nilotic speakers from Southern Sudan attracted by the rich grazing and plentiful farmland.

The Kenyan coast attracted people from other parts of the world as well as Africa. The first definite evidence of this is a description of Mombasa by the Greek Diogenes in AD 110 on his return to Egypt. He describes trading in cloth, tools, glass, brass, copper, iron, olives, weapons, ivory and rhinoceros horn at Mombasa. In AD 150 Ptolemy included details of this part of the coast in his Map of the World. It was to be another few centuries before the arrival of Islam on the coast and the beginning of its Golden Age.

Arab and Persian settlers developed trade routes extending across the Indian Ocean into China establishing commercial centres all along the East Africa coast. They greatly contributed to the arts and architecture of the region and built fine mosques, monuments and houses. Evidence of the prosperity of this period can be seen in the architecture in parts of Mombasa, Malindi and Lamu, and particularly in the intricate and elegant balconies outside some of the houses in the old part of Mombasa. All along this part of the coast, intermarriage between Arabs and Africans resulted in a harmonious partnership of African and Islamic influences personified in the Swahili people. This situation continued peacefully until the arrival of the Portuguese in the 16th century.

## Portuguese and Arab influence

Mombasa was known to be rich in both gold and ivory, making it a tempting target for the Portuguese. Vasco da Gama, in search of a sea route to India, arrived in Mombasa in 1498. He was unsuccessful in docking there at this time, but two years later ransacked the town. For many years the Portuguese returned to plunder Mombasa until finally they occupied the city. There followed 100 years of harsh colonial rule from their principal base at Fort Jesus overlooking the entrance to the old harbour. Arab resistance to Portuguese control of the Kenyan coast was strong, but they were unable to defeat the Portuguese who managed to keep their foothold in East Africa.

The end of Portuguese control began in 1696 with a siege of Fort Jesus. The struggle lasted for nearly 2½ years when the Arabs finally managed to scale the fortress walls. By 1720, the last Portuguese garrison had left the Kenyan coast. The Arabs remained in control of the East African coast until the arrival of the British and Germans in the late 19th century. In this period the coast did not prosper as there were destructive intrigues amongst rival Arab groups and this hampered commerce and development in their African territories.

## The Colonial period

The British influence in Kenya began quite casually in 1823 following negotiations between Captain Owen, a British Officer, and the Mazruis who ruled the island of Mombasa. The Mazruis asked for British protection from attack by other Omani interests in the area. Owen granted British protection in return for the Mazruis abolishing slavery. He sent to London and India for ratification of the treaty, posted his first officer together with an interpreter, four sailors and four marines and thus began the British occupation of Kenya. At this time, interest in Kenya was limited to the coast and then only as part of an evangelical desire to eliminate slavery. However, 50 years later attitudes towards the country changed.

In 1887 the Imperial British East Africa Company (IBEAC) founded its headquarters in Mombasa with the purpose of developing trade. From here it sent small groups of officials into the interior to negotiate with local tribesmen. One such officer Frederick Lugard made alliances with the Kikuyu en route to Uganda.

The final stage in British domination over Kenya was the development of the railway. The IBEAC and Lugard believed a railway was essential to keep its posts in the interior of Kenya supplied with essential goods, and also believed it was necessary in order to protect Britain's position in Uganda. Despite much opposition in London, the railway was built, commencing in 1901, at an eventual cost of £5 million (US$7.3 million).

Nairobi was created at the centre of operations as a convenient stopping point between Mombasa and Lake Victoria where a water supply was available. Despite problems, the railway reached Nairobi in 1899 and Port Florence (Kisumu) in 1901, and was the catalyst for British settlers moving into Kenya as well as for African resistance to the loss of their lands.

From 1895 to 1910 the government encouraged white settlers to cultivate land in the Central Highlands of the country around the railway, particularly the fertile Western Highlands. It was regarded as imperative to attract white settlers to increase trade and thus increase the usefulness of the railway. The Masai bitterly opposed being moved from their land but years of war combined with the effects of cholera, smallpox, rinderpest and famine had considerably weakened their resistance. The Masai were moved into two reserves on either side of the railway, but soon had to move out of the one to the north as the white settlers pressed for more land. Kikuyu land was also occupied by white settlers as they moved to occupy the highlands around the western side of Mount Kenya.

By 1915 there were 21,400 sq km set aside for about 1000 settlers. This number was increased after the Second World War with the Soldier Settlement Scheme. Initially the settlers grew crops and raised animals, basing their livelihood on wheat, wool, dairy and meat, but by 1914 it was clear that these had little potential as export goods so they changed to maize and coffee. Perhaps the most famous of the early settlers was Lord Delamere. He was important in early experimental agriculture and it was through his mistakes that many lessons were learnt about agriculture in the tropics. He tried out different wheat varieties until he developed one that was resistant to wheat rust. The 1920s saw the rapid expansion of settler agriculture – in particular coffee, sisal and maize – and the prices for these commodities rose, increasing settlers' optimism about their future.

However, when the prices plummeted in the Depression of the 1930s the weaknesses of the settler agriculture scheme were revealed. By 1930 over 50% by value of settler export was accounted for by coffee alone, making them very vulnerable when prices fell. Many settlers were heavily mortgaged and could not service their debts. About 20% of white farmers gave up their farms, while others left farming temporarily. Cultivated land on settler farms fell from 2690 sq km in 1930 to 2030 sq km in 1936.

About one-third of the colonial government's revenue was from duties on settlers' production and goods imported by the settlers. Therefore the government was also seriously affected by the fall in prices. In earlier years the government had shown its commitment to white agriculture by investment in infrastructure (for example railways and ports) and, because of its dependence on custom duties, it felt it could not simply abandon the settlers. Many of the settlers were saved by the colonial government who pumped about £1 million (US$1.46 million) into white agriculture with subsidies and rebates on exports and loans, and the formation of a Land Bank.

Following the Depression and the Second World War the numbers of settlers increased sharply so that by the 1950s the white population had reached about 80,000. As well as dairy farming, the main crops they grew were coffee, tea and maize. However, discontent among the African population over the loss of their traditional land to the settlers was growing. In order to increase the pool of African labour for white settler development (most Africans were unwilling to work for the Europeans voluntarily) taxes and other levies were imposed. Furthermore, Africans were prevented from growing coffee, the most lucrative crop, on the grounds that there was a risk of coffee berry disease with lots of small producers. Thus many Africans were forced to become farm labourers or to migrate to the towns in search of work to pay the taxes. By the 1940s the European farmers had prospered in cash-crop production.

As the number of Europeans moving into the country increased, so too did African resistance to the loss of their land and there was organized African political activity against the Europeans as early as 1922. The large number of Africans, particularly Kikuyu, moving into the growing capital Nairobi formed a political community supported by sections of the influential Asian community. This led to the formation of the East African Association, the first pan-Kenyan nationalist movement led by Harry Thuku. His arrest and the subsequent riots were the first challenge to the settlers and the colonial regime.

**Jomo Kenyatta**, an influential Kikuyu, led a campaign to bring Kikuyu land grievances to British notice. In 1932 he gave evidence to the Carter Land Commission in London which had been set up to adjudicate on land interests in Kenya, but without success. During the war years, all African political associations were banned and there was no voice for the interests of black Kenyans. At the end of the war, thousands of returning African soldiers began to demand rights, and discontent grew. Kenyatta had remained abroad travelling in Europe and the Soviet Union and returned in 1946 as a formidable statesman. In 1944 an African nationalist organization, the **Kenya African Union (KAU)** was formed to press for African access to settler occupied land. The KAU was primarily supported by the Kikuyu. In 1947 Kenyatta became president of KAU and was widely supported as the one man who could unite Kenya's various political and ethnic factions.

## Mau Mau era

At the same time as the KAU were looking for political change, a Kikuyu group, Mau Mau, began a campaign of violence. In the early 1950s the Mau Mau began terrorist activities, and several white settlers were killed as well as thousands of Africans thought to have collaborated with the colonial government.

The British authorities declared a state of emergency in 1952 in the face of the Mau Mau campaign and the Kikuyu were herded into 'protected villages' surrounded by barbed wire. People were forbidden to leave during the hours of darkness. From 1952 to 1956 the terrorist campaign waged against the colonial authority resulted in the deaths of 13,000 Africans and 32 European civilians. Over 20,000 Kikuyu were placed in detention camps before the Mau Mau finally were defeated. The British imprisoned Kenyatta in 1953 for seven years for alleged involvement in Mau Mau activities, and banned the KAU, though it is debatable as to whether Kenyatta had any influence over Mau Mau activities.

The cost of suppressing the Mau Mau, the force of the East African case, and world opinion, convinced the British government that preparation for Independence was the wisest course. The settlers were effectively abandoned, and were left with the prospect of making their own way under a majority-rule government. A number did sell up and leave, but many, encouraged by Kenyatta, stayed on to become Kenyan citizens.

The state of emergency was lifted in January 1960 and a transitional constitution was drafted allowing for the existence of political parties and ensuring Africans were in the majority in the Legislative Council. African members of the council subsequently formed the **Kenya African National Union (KANU)** with James Gichuru, a former president of KAU, as its acting head, and **Tom Mboya** and **Oginga Odinga**, two prominent Luos, part of the leadership. KANU won the majority of seats in the Legislative Council but refused to form an administration until the release of Kenyatta.

In 1961 Kenyatta became the president of KANU. KANU won a decisive victory in the 1963 elections, and Kenyatta became prime minister as Kenya gained internal self-government. Kenya became fully independent later that year, the country was declared a republic, and Kenyatta became president. Kenya retained strong links with the UK, particularly in the form of military assistance and financial loans to compensate European settlers for their land, some of which was redistributed among the African landless.

## Kenyatta

The two parties that had contested the 1963 elections with KANU were persuaded to join KANU and Kenya became a single-party state. In 1966 Odinga left KANU and formed a new party, the Kenya People's Union, with strong Luo support. Tom Mboya, was assassinated by a Kikuyu in 1969. There followed a series of riots in the west of the country by Luos, and Odinga was placed in detention where he remained for the next 15 months. At the next general election in 1969 only KANU members were allowed to contest seats, and two-thirds of the previous national assembly lost their seats.

The East African Community (EAC) comprising Kenya, Tanzania and Uganda, which ran many services in common such as the railways, the airline, post and telecommunications, began to come under strain. Kenya had pursued economic policies which relied on a strong private sector; Tanzania had adopted a socialist strategy after 1967; Uganda had collapsed into anarchy and turmoil under Amin. In 1977, Kenya unilaterally pulled out of the EAC, and in response Tanzania closed its borders with Kenya.

Kenyatta was able to increase Kenya's prosperity and stability through reassuring the settlers that they would have a future in the country and that they had an important role in its success at the same time as delivering his people limited land reform. Under Kenyatta's presidency, Kenya became one of the more successful newly independent countries.

## Moi

Kenyatta died in 1978 to be succeeded by Daniel arap Moi, his vice president. Moi began by relaxing some of the political repression of the latter years of Kenyatta's presidency. However, he was badly shaken by a coup attempt in 1982 that was only crushed after several days of mayhem, and a more repressive period was ushered in. Relations between Kenya and its neighbours began to improve in the 1980s and the three countries reached agreement on the distribution of assets and liabilities of the EAC by 1983. At this time the border between Kenya and Tanzania was reopened. In 1992 political parties (other than KANU) were allowed. Moi and KANU were returned (albeit without a majority of the popular vote) in the multiparty elections late in 1992. In the 1997 presidential elections Moi was again victorious, with an increased share of the vote. In the elections for the National Assembly KANU achieved a slender overall majority with 107 seats out of 210.

# Modern Kenya

## Politics

Daniel arap Moi was elected to the Presidency in October 1978 following the death of Jomo Kenyatta, and began a programme to reduce Kenya's corruption and release all political detainees. Moi, a Kalenjin, emphasized the need for a new style of government with greater regional representation of tribal groups. However, he did not fully live up to his promises of political freedom and Oginga Odinga (the prominent Luo who had been a voice of discontent in KANU under Kenyatta) and four other former KANU members who were critical of Moi's regime were barred from participating in the 1979 election. This led to an increase in protests against the government, mainly from Luos. Moi began to arrest dissidents, disband tribal societies and close the universities whenever there were demonstrations. This period also saw the strengthening of Kenya's armed forces.

On 1 August 1982 there was a coup attempt supported by a Luo-based section of the Kenyan Air Force supported by university students. Although things initially appeared to be touch-and-go, the coup was eventually crushed, resulting in an official death toll of 159. As a result of the coup attempt, many thousands of people were detained and the universities again closed. The constitution was changed to make Kenya officially a one-party state.

Moi decided to reassert his authority over KANU by calling an early election in which he stood unopposed. Inevitably he was re-elected but less than 50% of the electorate turned out to vote.

Subsequent measures have served to centralize power under the presidency, and to reduce the ability of the opposition to contest elections. The president acquired the power to to dismiss the attorney-general, the auditor-general and judges, while control of the civil service passed to the President's Office. Secret ballots were abandoned, and voters were required to queue behind the candidate of their choice. This severely reduced willingness to be seen voting against the government. Secret ballots were restored in 1990.

In 1990, Dr Robert Ouko, a Luo and Minister for Foreign Affairs and International Cooperation, was murdered. British police were asked to investigate, and named Nicholas Biwott, a Kalenjin and Minister for Energy, as being implicated in the killing. Biwott was dropped from the cabinet, but has subsequently returned.

International pressure in 1991 persuaded Moi to introduce a multi-party system. The opposition was fatally split, however, and in the 1992 elections Moi was returned as president with 36% of the popular vote. However, the opposition did secure 88 seats of the 188 contested, and the democratic process was significantly strengthened as a result.

The 1997 election was similar, with the opposition split, and Moi returned with 40% of the vote. In the Parliament the opposition made gains, with nine opposition parties securing 103 seats between them, while KANU obtained a slender overall majority with 107.

Moi was re-elected five times over 24 years. His term ended when the KANU candidate, Uhuru Kenyatta (the son of Jomo Kenyatta), who replaced him as head of the party, was beaten at the polls in a landslide victory in the 2002 election by Mwai Kibaki of the opposition party, the **National Rainbow Coalition** (**NARC**). Kibaki was previously vice-president (1978-1988) and held numerous cabinet positions. He pledged to attack corruption and established the Kenya Anti-Corruption Commission (KACC). As a result of this, the IMF resumed loans to Kenya over a three-year period. But some international donors estimate that US$1 billion has been lost to corruption through government departments between 2002-2005, and to date despite numerous investigations, no high-profile figures have been convicted in court on corruption charges. In 2003, the government also decided to grant immunity to Moi over corruption charges. However one of his successes has been to provide free education for primary school age children across Kenya, which saw nearly 1.7 million more pupils enroll in school by the end of 2004.

Kibaki instigated a constitutional referendum in 2005 calling for more presidential power with a lesser role for the Prime Minister and cabinet members. However, the final draft of the constitution retained sweeping powers for the Head of State. Some members of his own cabinet and the main opposition party mobilized a powerful campaign that resulted in a majority of 58% Kenyan voters rejecting the draft. As a consequence, Kibaki sacked and reappointed his entire cabinet and his popularity with the public plummeted.

Kibaki was sworn in on 30 December 2007 for his second presidential term after emerging winner of an election that was marked by accusations of fraud and widespread irregularities that led to civil unrest. His primary contender for President was Raila Odinga, son of Kenya's first vice-president under Kenyatta, who went to the polls for the 2007 election on the **Orange Democratic Movement** (ODM) ticket. The general and parliamentary election was held on 27 December 2007, which was declared a public holiday for people to vote. The day was peaceful and people formed orderly queues at the polling stations. The following day was also peaceful as votes were counted in the constituencies and early reports from these seemed to indicate that Ondinga was well in the lead and the ODM declared victory for him on 29 December. As the polling boxes were delivered and recounted at the Electoral Commission in Nairobi, it began to become apparent that the vote had swung towards Kibaki. A spokesman for the Electoral Commission appeared on television on December 30th and declared Kibaki the winner by about 230,000 votes though admitted that there seemed to be some discrepancy between the results counted at the constituencies and the recount in Nairobi. Odinga then claimed that at least 300,000 votes for Kibaki were falsely included in the total. Within minutes of the Commission's declaration of Kibaki's victory, rioting and violence, primarily directed against Kikuyus (Kibaki is a Kikuyu), broke out across Kenya. Most noticeably in Odinga's homeland of Nyanza Province in Western Kenya and in the slums of Nairobi, particularly Kibera, which is part of Odinga's Langata constituency. Later in January, the Rift Valley towns of Nakuru and Naivasha were seriously affected. There was some violence on the coast, but it wasn't ethnic fuelled; the people were simply demonstrating about the injustice of the election result. By the fifth day after the elections, the army and police were out on the streets, who also attacked and got attacked by demonstrators. By then there was a news blackout in Kenya, which presumably was a move by the government to try and stop the fuel of violence by not allowing news of events happening in other parts of the country to spread. Although the violence was triggered by the elections, long-standing grievances over unequal distribution of land, wealth and power are seen as the real reasons behind the demonstrations; mostly dubbed by the press as 'ethnic' clashes.

The worst of the chaos went on for about 10 days and peaked when about 30 people, including many children, were killed when a church was burnt down near Eldoret, although more incidents broke out sporadically until mid January in the Rift Valley towns. An estimated 700 people lost their lives, although some resources have put this number as high as 1500, and over 200,000 were displaced. Within hours of the crisis, many world leaders including Ghanaian president John Kufuor and South Africa's Arch Bishop Desmond Tutu flew in for emergency talks with Kibaki and Odinga. By mid-January, former Secretary General of the United Nations and now a member of the Global Elders, Kofi Annan arrived in Nairobi to broker peace talksi. Eventually, a power-sharing agreement was reached in February 2008, according to which Kibaki would remain President and Odinga would gain the new post of Prime Minister with both of them having equal decision making powers. A coalition government, with an equal number of ministers for both parties was named in April. Although it is not known which of the two legitimately won the election, this agreement seems to have worked, and a Truth, Justice and Reconciliation Commission has been established to investigate the events surrounding the 2007 election. As a positive sign, by-elections for five parliamentary seats held on 11 June 2008, passed peacefully.

## Economy

Kenya's economy remains heavily reliant on rain-fed agriculture and tourism revenues, leaving it vulnerable to cyclical booms and busts caused by the climate and internal stability. Income levels are modest for an African country although it's not as poor as some of its neighbours. GDP per capita has been about US$1700 per year since 2007.

The agricultural sector continues to dominate Kenya's economy, although only 15% of Kenya's total land area has sufficient fertility and rainfall to be farmed and only 7–8% can be classified as first-class land. Most families rely on agriculture for their livelihood, and 75% of the labour force is engaged in farming, but incomes in agriculture are low, and the sector generates only 23.8% of GDP. Kenya's chief exports are horticultural products such as flowers and vegetables destined for European supermarkets. In 2005, the combined value of these commodities was put at just over US$1000 million per annum, with Kenya's third largest export coffee coming in at around US$100 million per annum. Industry contributes 16.7% of output, but it must be remembered that there is little contribution from mining which boosts industrial output in many other African countries. Services is the largest sector at 59.5% of the GDP, and it contains tourism, which is Kenya's largest source of foreign exchange.

Kenya has been in receipt of structural adjustment loans from the World Bank. Foreign Aid receipts per head are about average for Africa – they would be higher if the international community were more confident about the government's intention to tackle corruption. Some US$5.9 billion of external debt is estimated at being outstanding. Debt service takes up 13.5% of export earnings and at present this is within Kenya's ability to service, providing export revenues can be maintained.

### Recent economic developments

Economic growth dropped from 7% in 2007 to around 4% in 2008 but is expected to improve again in 2009. In early 2008 inflation shot up briefly from 9.3% in 2007 to 25% because of increased food and fuel prices caused by the post-election crisis but is expected to return to single digits in 2009 on the back of improved food supplies, lower transport costs and easing global oil prices.

**Agriculture** The 2007 post-election violence briefly disrupted agriculture and tea and coffee production as well as affecting transport, manufacturing and construction. These are all back on track today although it will take some time for the stock market to fully recover and substantial foreign investment to be attracted to the country again.

**Tourism** The 2007 violence also affected tourism significantly, at a time when Kenya had recovered from a tourism slump caused by the 2002 terrorist attacks. Despite the absence of violence in the tourist areas like the game parks and on the strip of coastal resorts, during the crisis itself many tourists cut their holidays short and headed home. KLM for example sent an empty plane to pick up nationals from the Netherlands. Nevertheless, tourism is now recovering significantly, all adverse travel warnings for Kenya have been lifted, the Kenya Tourism has been aggressively marketing overseas, and in April 2008 Kenya won the Best Leisure Destination award at the World Travel Fair in Shanghai, China.

## Social conditions

Although there hasn't been a census in Kenya since 2001, the population in 2008 was estimated at around 38 million and it continues to grow rapidly at 2.7% a year. Most people live in the rural areas, with only a quarter in the towns. Overall population density is high by African standards, over double the average. Given that a large proportion of the country is arid, the pressure on the land in the fertile areas, particularly in the central highlands and around Lake Victoria, is intense.

Literacy rates are good at 85%, and noticeably better than the African average. Primary education runs for eight years with 95% enrolments and since 2004 primary education has been free. Secondary enrolments are fairly good, with almost 25% of children receiving education at this level, although this may increase soon as the government has plans to provide free secondary education too. Tertiary education opportunities are limited to about 2%, despite the fact that Kenya has expanded its university enrolments substantially since 1980.

Life expectancy at 56 years is better than the Africa average. Food availability in some areas, particularly in the arid north, which is also affected by routine droughts, means that about 30% of the population is considered to be malnourished, which gives cause for concern. Population per doctor is very high, but medical delivery is good, given the low income level. The fertility rate is at 4.7 children per woman is about average for Africa, as is the infant mortality rate, which is about 56 per 1000 births.

## Culture

Tribal identity is still important in Kenyan life though this is changing as more people move into towns and tribal groups become scattered. Polygamy is still practised, though it is not officially condoned. The custom of a man taking more than one wife is only recognized in the traditional systems, and not by official Kenyan family law. There is much resistance to Western censure of polygamy. However, the practice is dying under the twin influences of economic realities and social pressure. Few men can now afford to take more than one wife. Among the better off, it is frowned upon for anybody in public life as it causes embarrassment when mixing with the international community. The Christian churches strongly disapprove.

### People

Kenya has long been a meeting place of population movements from around the continent. This has resulted in there being as many as 40 different tribes living in Kenya, and many more sub-groups, with an estimated overall population of 38 million people. There are three main groupings based on the origins of these groups. The Bantu came from West Africa in a migration, the reasons for which are not clearly understood. The Nilotic peoples came from the northwest, mostly from the area that is now South Sudan. They were mainly pastoralists, and moved south in search of better grazing on more fertile land. Finally there is the Hamitic group, made up of a series of relatively small communities such as the Somali, Rendille, Boran, Ogaden and others, all pastoralists, who have spread into Kenya in the north and northeast from Ethiopia and Somalia.

Kikuyu (Bantu) Primarily based around Mount Kenya, this is the largest ethnic group with 22% of the total population. They are thought to have originated in East and Northeast

The administration of the Kikuyu was undertaken by a council of elders based on clans made up of family groups. Other important members of the community were witch doctors, medicine men and the blacksmiths. The Kikuyu god is believed to live on Mount Kenya and all Kikuyus build their homes with the door facing the mountain. In common with most tribes in Kenya, traditionally men and women go through a number of stages into adulthood including circumcision to mark the beginning of their adult life, athough it is almost unheard of for women to be circumcised today.

It is said the Kikuyu have adapted more successfully than any other tribe to the modern world. Kikuyu are prominent in many of Kenya's business and commercial activities. Those still farming in their homelands have adapted modern methods to their needs and benefit from cash crop production for export, particularly coffee and tea. They have a great advantage in that their traditional area is very fertile and close to the capital, Nairobi.

**Kalenjin (Nilotic)** Kalenjin is a name used by the British to describe a cluster of tribes; the Kipsigis, Nandi, Tugen, Elgeyo, Keiyo, Pokot, Marakwet, Sabaot, Nyangori, Sebei and Okiek, who speak the same language but with different dialects, and in total make up about 12% of Kenya's population. They mainly live in the western edge of the central Rift Valley and are thought to have migrated from southern Sudan about 2000 years ago. Most Kalenjin took up agriculture though they are traditionally pastoralists. Bee-keeping is common with honey being used to brew beer. Administration of the law is carried out at an informal gathering of the clan's elders. Witch doctors are generally women, which is unusual in Africa. In the modern world, the Kalenjin are renowned for their prowess as athletes and are often dubbed 'the running tribe' for their success in long distance running (see box, page 136).

**Kamba (Bantu)** The Kamba (more correctly the Akamba) traditionally lived in the area now known as Tsavo National Park. They comprise 11% of the total population. Originally hunters, the Kamba soon adopted a more sedentary lifestyle and developed as traders because of the relatively poor quality of their land. Ivory was a major trade item as were beer, honey, ornaments and iron weapons, which they traded with neighbouring Masai and Kikuyu for food. In common with most Bantu tribespeople, political power lies with clan elders.

The Kamba were well regarded by the British for their intelligence and fighting ability and they made up a large part of the East African contingent in the British Army during the First World War.

**Kisii (Bantu)** The Kisii (also known as Gusii) are based on the same name in the west, south of Kisumu. Traditional practices have been continued, with soothsayers and medicine men retaining significant influence, despite the nominal allegiance of most Kisii to Christianity. They occupy a relatively small area, and population densities are the highest anywhere in Kenya's countryside, with plot sizes becoming steadily smaller with the passing of each generation.

**Luo (Nilotic)** The Luo live in the west of the country on the shores of Lake Victoria, and are the third-largest ethnic group with 13% of the total population. They migrated from the Nile region of Sudan in around the 15th century. Originally the Luo were cattle herders but the devastating effects of rinderpest on their herds compelled them to diversify into fishing and subsistence agriculture. The Luo were also prominent in the struggle for independence and many of the country's leading politicians, including Tom Mboya and Oginga Odinga, were Luos. The Luos had a different coming-of-age ritual to other tribes in the region, which involves extracting the bottom four or six teeth, though this practice has fallen into disuse.

**Luyha (Bantu)** The Luhya are based around Kakamega town in Western Kenya, and make up 14% of the total population. They are Kenya's second largest grouping after the Kikuyu and the Luo. They are cultivators, and small farmers are the mainstay of sugar-cane growing in the west.

**Masai (Nilotic)** The Masai are probably the best-known tribe to people outside Kenya with their striking costume and reputation as fierce and proud warriors. They comprise 2% of Kenya's people. The Masai came to central Kenya from the Sudan around 1000 years ago, where they were the largest and one of the most important tribes. Their customs and practices were developed to reflect their nomadic lifestyle and many are still practised today, though change is beginning to be accepted. The traditional basic Masai diet is fresh and curdled milk carried in gourds. Blood tapped from the jugular vein of cattle is mixed with cattle urine and this provides a powerful stimulant. Cattle are rarely killed for meat as they represent the owners' wealth.

**Meru (Bantu)** Arrived to the northeast of Mount Kenya around the 14th century, following invasions by Somalis to the coast, this group is not homogenous being made up of seven different groups of people, accounting for 5% of Kenya's population. Some of the Meru were led by a chief known as the *mogwe* until 1974 when the chief converted to Christianity and ended the tradition. A group of tribal elders administer traditional justice along with a witch doctor known as a *njuri*, which is the only traditional judicial system recognised by Kenya.

The Meru occupy some of the country's richest farmland which is used to produce tea, coffee, pyrethrum, maize and potatoes. Another highly profitable crop grown by the Meru in this region is *miraa*, a mild stimulant particularly popular amongst Islamic communities and Somalis, see page 219.

**Swahili (Bantu)** The Swahili dwell along the coast, and make up less than 3% of the total population. Although they do not have a common heritage, they do share a common language, religion and culture. Ancestry is mainly a mixture of Arabic and African. Today the majority of coastal people are Muslims. The language is Kiswahili, which about 90 million people speak in East Africa.

**Turkana (Nilotic)** Like the Masai, this group has retained its rich and colourful dress and has a reputation as warriors. They comprise less than 1% of the total population. They are mainly based in the northwest part of Kenya living in the desert near the Ugandan border. This is the most isolated part of the country and as a consequence the Turkana have probably been affected less by the 20th century than any other tribe in Kenya.

The Turkana are pastoralists whose main diet consists of milk and blood. Cattle are important in Turkana culture, being herded by men. Camels, goats and sheep are also important and are looked after by boys and small girls. Recently some Turkana have begun fishing in the dry season.

The traditional dress of the Turkana is very eye-catching and is still fairly commonly worn. Men cover part of their hair with mud which is then painted blue and decorated with ostrich feathers. The main garment is a woollen blanket worn over one shoulder. Women wear a variety of beaded and metal adornments many of which signify different events in a woman's life. Women wear a half skirt of animal skins and a piece of black cloth. Both men and women sometimes insert a plug through the lower lip. Tattooing is still fairly common. Men are tattooed on the shoulders and upper arm each time they kill an enemy. Witch doctors and prophets are held in high regard.

## Music and dance

Most traditional Kenyan music and dance are centred on drums (ngomas), and there is a variety of drums used throughout the country that are played for people to dance to. Other instruments include reed flutes and basic stringed instruments, such as the nyatiti, which is similar to a medieval lyre and is usually played by a solo singer. Inland, the colonial period gave rise to Beni singing; very long narrative songs with strong elements of social commentary and political criticism. On the coast, the Swahili culture saw the growth of a unique style of music called Taarab, which fuses African percussion with Arabian rhythms and is performed by a large group of musicians playing violins, ouds and singing in Kiswahili. It was thought to have its origins from the 19th century when the Omanis traded on the coast. In modern times, these instruments are being replaced by electric guitars and keyboards but the scales of the notes are still distinctively Arabian. Most of the singers are female and the songs these days are very similar to the music that accompanies Bollywood movies. Since the 1970s pop music has been popular in Kenya, especially imported West African music such as makossa or highlife, or Congolese rumba, which are all very infectious and danceable. Today Congolese music (Lingala) is extremely popular and the type you are most likely to hear on matatus, in the streets, in bars and clubs, in fact anywhere and everywhere. Many of the musicians that play this music have actually relocated to Nairobi because of their success there. Also today, thanks to radio, young Kenyans are listening and dancing to, as well as playing, the same sort of chart topping music as their contemporaries in the rest of the world. Rap has become increasingly popular among young Kenyans, and there are several Kenya-based rap bands. Whilst the style of music is virtually indistinguishable from US-based rappers, the lyrics are most definitely Kenyan and have much to say about life in modern Kenya. Since the late 1990s, two young Kenyan musicians, Joseph Ogidi and Jahd Adonijah who call themselves Gidi Gidi Maji Maji, have become one of Kenya's most successful rap bands, not only in Kenya but in South Africa. Their style of music is a fusion of contemporary rap and African music in Dholuo, their mother tongue. One of their most famous songs is Unwogable (Unbeatable) a danceable and politically flammable song that became an anthem for opposition politics and reached its peak during the 2003 change of government in Kenya. The rise of Christianity greatly increased the popularity of gospel and choral music and many Kenyans sing in church each Sunday. Acrobatics have also become increasingly popular in Kenya. A growing number of young performers have taken to this art of traditional dance combined with modern gymnastic technique. In Nairobi's poorest suburbs, acrobatics has become a popular form of exercise, entertainment, and a low-cost and accessible form of performance art, and these acts are beginning to feature as entertainment in the tourist hotels.

## Art

Although Kenya has less formal art galleries than many other countries, it has an invaluable artistic wealth seen in the many curio and craft markets and shops. Going right back in time there are a few locations in the country with examples of rock art painted by early man when they still lived in caves. Many of Kenya's tribes have traditionally held a great significance on decoration of both functional objects such as pots and baskets, weapons, and musical instruments, and also the body. You only have to see a proud Masai or Samburu warrior wrapped in vivid robes and intricate jewellery to see evidence of how important adornment is in these societies. In fact the Samburu who pay a great deal of attention to their appearance with their ochre-stained skin and elaborate hairstyles, were named, perhaps a little scornfully, by the other tribes – Samburu means butterfly.

For the Masai, the use of decorative beading is very significant as it is used to emphasise social status and to record stages of initiation and passage. Wood carving all over Kenya was at first used for decoration of personal items, but today of course anything that might be attractive to tourists is carved out of wood; a lucrative trade that employs a number of talented carvers in Kenya. Some of the best carvers are found on the islands of Lamu, who produce excellent doors, brass inlaid boxes, picture frames and small replica *dhows*.

The Kisii of Western Kenya are also well known for their carving in stone, using local soapstone in various shades. Most are small items such as goblets, chess pieces or ash trays. Sisal baskets usually produced in Kikuyu areas are usually used as handbags, although their traditional use is being carried by Kikuyu women behind the head, with the strap across the forehead. Painting and drawing in the formal European sense was introduced in Africa by colonialism. Probably the best known artist in Kenya was Joy Adamson, who as well as being known for her work with the conservation of big cats (see box, page 220) she was also commissioned by the Kenya government to pay a series of portraits of Kenya's tribes in the 1940-1950s. Even today these are a great testament to the people of Kenya, especially as these days younger people are choosing not to follow their tribal traditions. Today Kenya has a number of young modern artists and the Nairobi galleries exhibit contemporary art, whilst the curio markets continue to find a steady stream of customers for crafts.

## Religion

The Constitution of Kenya guarantees freedom of worship and there are hundreds of religious denominations and sects in the country. The population in Kenya generally follows three major, modern religions: 38% is Protestant, 28% Roman Catholic, and 10% are Muslim. The remaining people are followers of tribal religions, plus a few Hindus and Sikhs. Most of the Christian population lives in western and central Kenya, while Islam is the main religion for most of the coastal communities and the Somali community. Islam arrived along the East African coast in the eighth century, as part of the trade routes from the Persian Gulf and Oman. Kenya's Christian churches are the outcome of early missionary activities, which assisted in the administrative of the country during colonial times. In Kenya today there are still many mission churches and many worldwide religious groups have a strong presence, including US-style evangelism, which has become very popular in Kenya in recent years. Although traditional beliefs and practices vary among Kenya's ethnic groups, they share many general characteristics. Almost all involve belief in an eternal creator. For example the Kikuyu's god is named *Ngai*, who is represented in the sun, moon, thunder and lightning, stars, rain, the rainbow and in large fig trees that serve as places of worship and sacrifice. In many traditional religions, ghosts of ancestral spirits are thought to return to seek revenge on the living so they too must be paid homage.

## Geography

Kenya is 580,367 sq km in area with the equator running right through the middle. Physically, the country is made up of a number of different zones. It lies between latitude 5° North and 4° 30' South and longitude 34° and 41° East. The Great Rift Valley runs from the north to the south of the country and in places is 65 km across, bounded by escarpments 600-900 m high. This is probably the most spectacularly beautiful part of the country, dotted with soda lakes teeming with flamingos. To the east of the Rift Valley lies the Kenya Highlands with Mount Kenya, an extinct volcano, which at 5199 m is Africa's second-highest mountain. This is the most fertile part of the country, particularly the lower slopes of the mountain range. Nairobi sits at the southern end of the Central Highlands. The north of Kenya is arid, bounded by Sudan and Ethiopia. To the west lies Uganda and the fertile shores around Lake Victoria. Further south, the land turns into savannah, and is mainly used for grazing.

The Indian Ocean coast to the east of the country runs for 480 km and there is a narrow strip of fertile land all along it. Beyond this, the land becomes scrubland and semi-arid. Somalia borders Kenya in the northeast, and this is also a fairly arid area.

## Climate

Kenya's different altitudes mean that the climate varies enormously around the country. Probably the most pleasant climate is in the Central Highlands and the Rift Valley, though the valley floor can become extremely hot and is relatively arid. Mount Kenya and Mount Elgon both become quite cool above 1750 m and the top of Mount Kenya is snow-covered. Mount Kenya and the Aberdares are the country's main water catchment areas. Western Kenya and the area around Lake Victoria is generally hot, around 30-34°C all year with high humidity and rainfall evenly spread throughout the year. Most rain here tends to fall in the early evening. The country is covered in semi-arid bushland and deserts throughout the north and east of the country. Temperatures can rise to 40°C during the day and fall to 20°C at night in the desert. Rainfall in this area is sparse, between 250 and 500 mm per annum.

The coastal belt is hot and humid all year round, though the heat is tempered by sea breezes. Rainfall varies from as little as 20 mm in February to 240 mm in May. The average temperature varies little throughout the year but is hottest in November and December, at about 30°C.

## Vegetation

Kenya is justifiably famous for its flora and fauna. In areas of abundant rainfall, the country is lush, supporting a huge range of plants, and the wide variety of geographical zones house a corresponding diversity of flora. The majority of the country is covered in savannah-type vegetation characterized by the acacia. The slopes of Mount Elgon and Mount Kenya are covered in thick evergreen temperate forest from about 1000 m to 2000 m; then to 3000 m the mountains are bamboo forest; above this level the mountains are covered with groundsel trees and giant lobelias. Mangroves are prolific in the coastal regions.

## Mammals

Practically everyone travelling around Kenya will come into contact with animals during their stay. Of course there is much more than the big game to see and you will undoubtedly travel through different habitats from the coast to the tropical rainforests but the mammals are on the top of most people's 'to see' lists.

Big Nine The 'big five' ('elephant, **lion, black rhino, buffalo** and **leopard**) was the term originally coined by hunters who wanted trophies from their safaris, but nowadays the **hippopotamus** is usually considered one of the big five, whereas the buffalo is far less of a 'trophy'. Equally photogenic and worthy to be included are **zebra, giraffe** and **cheetah**. Whether they are the Big Five or the Big Nine these are the animals that most people come to Africa to see, and, with the possible exception of the leopard, you have an excellent chance of seeing all of them.

They are all unmistakable and when seeing them for the first time in the wild you will find that they are amazingly familiar and recognisable. The only two that could possibly be confused are the leopard and the cheetah. The **leopard** is less likely to be seen as it is more nocturnal and more secretive in its habits than the cheetah. It frequently rests during the heat of the day on the lower branches of trees, and, as you drive round the parks, your best bet is to look for the animal's tail, which hangs down below the branches and can be quite easily spotted while the rest of the animal remains well concealed. If you are lucky you will see one with its kill, which it may have hauled up into the lower branches.

**Cheetahs** are often seen in family groups walking across the plains or resting in the shade. They are slimmer and longer legged than leopards, with a characteristic sway back. (If all else fails you can identify cheetahs by the accompanying minibuses.)

**Lions**, usually found in open savanna in Africa, are the second-largest carnivorous members of the cat family (after tigers). They live in prides or permanent family groups, numbering up to around 30 animals. The prides are usually composed of a group of inter-related females and their cubs, led by a dominant male, or occasionally, a group of males. There is no dominant lioness. They communicate with one another with a range of sounds that vary from roaring, grunting and growling to meowing. Roars, more common at night, can reach sound levels of over 110 decibels and be heard from distances of up to 8 km. The females do most of the hunting, while the males are mostly involved in protecting their pride from other lions and predators. Lions are very sociable except when eating, when aggressive fighting can break out. Although the female kill most of the prey the males are first to feed, followed by the lionesses, the cubs just getting the leftovers. (The main cause of cub death is starvation.) Lions augment their diet by scavenging prey killed by other predators.

**Elephants** are awe-inspiring and it is wonderful to watch a herd at a waterhole. Although they have suffered terribly from the activities of poachers in recent decades they are still readily seen in many of the game areas.

The other animals which have suffered badly in recent times are the two rhinos. The **white rhino** is now probably extinct in much of its former range in eastern Africa though it flourishes in places. The **black rhino** has also diminished in number in recent years.

The **buffalo** can be seen everywhere, sometimes in substantial herds in many areas. Beware: cut off from the herd, they can become bad-tempered and easily provoked.

The **hippo** is another animal that appears harmless, even comic (from a safe vantage point). During the day it rests in the water and you can get excellent views and interesting photographs, particularly if there are displaying males in the area. These Hippos will 'yawn' at each other and two animals will sometimes spar. At night the Hippo leaves the water and ranges very far afield to graze (a single adult animal needs up to 60 kg of grass every day). Should you meet a Hippo on land by day or night keep well away. If you get between it and its escape route to the water, it may well attack. These animals are now considered as dangerous as buffalos, once thought to be the most dangerous of all the big mammals.

In many ways the most stunning of the Big Nine is the **giraffe**. It may not be as magnificent as a full-grown Lion, nor as awe-inspiring as an Elephant, but its elegance is unsurpassed. To see a small party of giraffe galloping across the plains is seeing Africa as it has been for hundreds of years. Although the giraffe itself is unmistakable and easily identified, there are in fact several sub-species that differ from each other. Authorities, though, are not always agreed on the exact division into species and races, as there seems to be much overlap of the types. Extending from about the Tana River northwards and eastwards into Somalia and Ethiopia is the almost chestnut coloured **reticulated giraffe**, which is sometimes considered a separate species. Found further south than the reticulated giraffe the **common giraffe**, which has two forms, or races: one is the **Masai giraffe** which occurs in southwest Kenya (and Tanzania). This has a yellowish-buff coat with the characteristic patchwork of brownish markings with very jagged edges. In most animals there are only two horns, though occasionally animals are seen with three horns. The other form of the Common giraffe is known as **Rothschild's giraffe** and occurs west and north of the Masai giraffe as far west as the Nile. It is usually rather paler and heavier looking than the Masai giraffe and can have as many as five horns, though more commonly three. The lolloping gait is very distinctive and it produces this effect by the way it moves its legs at the gallop. A horse will move its fore and hind legs diagonally when galloping, but the giraffe moves both hind legs together and both fore legs together. It achieves this by swinging both hind legs forward and outside the fore legs. It is not a dumb and voiceless animal as many believe but can produce a low groaning noise and a variety of snorts.

The **zebra** is another easily recognized animal. It forms herds, often large ones, sometimes with antelope. As with giraffe, there is more than one sort of zebra in eastern Africa, and, again, the relationship between the types is complex, but they can be considered as two main types: **Grevy's zebra** and the **common** or **Burchell's zebra**.

**Larger antelope** The first animals that you will see on safari will almost certainly be antelope; these are by far the most numerous group to be seen on the plains. Although there are many different species, it is not difficult to distinguish between them. For identification purposes they can be divided into the larger ones which stand at about 120 cm or more at the shoulder, and the smaller ones under that height.

For the record, it is worth pointing out here that antelope are not 'deer', which do not occur in Africa, except in parts of the very north, but you will undoubtedly hear many people refer to them as such. There are many differences between the two groups. For example, deer have antlers, which are solid, bony, branching outgrowths from the skull and which are shed annually. Antelope, on the other hand, have horns, which are hollow, unbranched sheaths made of modified skin, rather like finger and toe nails. They are not shed seasonally and if a horn is lost it is not replaced.

The largest of all is the **eland** (*Taurotragus oryx*), which stands 175-183 cm at the shoulder.

Not quite as big, but still reaching 140-153 cm, is the **Greater Kudu** (*Tragelaphus strepsiceros*). Although nearly as tall as the Eland it is a much more slender and elegant animal altogether.

Its smaller relative, the **lesser kudu** (*Strepsiceros imberis*), looks quite similar, with similar horns, but stands only 99-102 cm high. It lacks the throat fringe of the bigger animal, but has two conspicuous white patches on the underside of the neck. It inhabits dense scrub and acacia thickets in semi-arid country, usually in pairs, sometimes with their young.

The **roan antelope** (*Hippotragus equinus*) is a rare species in Kenya. Roan associate in herds of up to 20 individuals with a very characteristic social structure. Amongst the females, the more dominant is the leader. There is only one adult bull in each herd, and the juvenile males are evicted at the age of about three years. All the female calves remain within the herd, and when it becomes too big, it divides into smaller groups of cows and their young, with once again only one adult bull. The young males evicted from the herd, form bachelor groups of up to about 12 individuals. Amongst these, the most dominant is the first one in line to join a new group of females. Roan are fairly courageous amongst antelopes. If threatened by predators, including lion, they will confront them, and lion have been known to be gored to death by the scimitar-shaped horns of a roan. Adults attain a mass of up to 270 kg and they can live to about 15 years.

Another large antelope with a black and white face is the **oryx** (*Oryx beisa*). This occurs in two distinct races, the **beisa oryx**, which is found north and west of the Tana River, and the **fringe-eared oryx**, which occurs south and east of this river. Both these animals stand 122 cm at the shoulder. They both also have very long straight (not curving) horns, present in both sexes, and which make identification of this animal quite easy. The two races may be distinguished by the long dark fringe of hair on the tips of the ears in the fringe-eared oryx, absent in the beisa oryx. The beisa oryx is found in herds in arid and semi desert country and the fringe-eared oryx, also in herds, in similar habitat, but also sometimes in less dry habitats.

**Common waterbuck** (*Kobus ellipsiprymnus*) are about 122-137 cm at the shoulder. The males have long curving horns which are heavily ringed. They are fairly common and widespread.

The **wildebeest** or **gnu** (*Connochaetes taurinus*) is well-known to many people from published photographs of the spectacular annual migration through Masai Mara. It is a big animal about 132 cm high, looking rather like an American bison from a distance, especially when you see the huge herds straggling across the plains. The impression is strengthened by its buffalo-like horns (in both sexes) and humped appearance. The general colour is greyish with a few darker stripes down the side. It has a noticeable beard and long mane.

The four remaining large antelope are fairly similar. Three of these four are **hartebeest** of various sorts and the fourth is called the **topi**. All four antelope have long, narrow horse-like faces and rather comical expressions. The shoulders are much higher than the rump giving them a very sloped back appearance, especially in the three hartebeest. Again all four have short, curved horns, carried by both sexes. In the three hartebeest the horns arise from a boney protuberance on the top of the head and curve outwards as well as backwards. One of the hartebeests, **Jackson's hartebeest** (*Alcelaphus buselaphus*) (about 132 cm) is similar in colour to the **topi** (*Damaliscus korrigum*) (about 122-127 cm) being a very rich dark rufous in colour. But the topi has dark patches on the tops of the legs, a coat with a rich satiny sheen to it, and more ordinary looking lyre-shaped horns. Of the other two hartebeest,

**Coke's hartebeest** (*Alcephalus buselaphus*) (about 122 cm), also called the **Kongoni**, is usually considered to be a race of Jackson's hartebeest, but is a very different colour being a more drab pale brown with a paler rump.

**Smaller antelope** The remaining common antelopes are a good deal smaller than those described above. The largest is the **impala** (*Aepyceros melampus*) which is 92-107 cm. Another two are **Grant's gazelle** (*Gazella granti*), about 81-99 cm, and **Thomson's gazelle** (*Gazella thomsoni*), about 64-69 cm. Thomson's gazelle can usually be distinguished from Grant's by the broad black band along the side between the rufous upper parts and white abdomen, but not invariably, as some forms of Grant's also have this dark lateral stripe. If in doubt, look for the white area on the buttocks which extends above the tail on to the rump in Grant's, but does not extend above the tail in Thomson's. The underparts are white. Thomson's gazelle, or 'Tommies', are among the most numerous animals that inhabit the plains of Kenya. You will see large herds of them often in association with other game. Grant's gazelle, occurs on dry grass plains, in various forms.

The last two of the common smaller antelopes are the **bushbuck** (*Tragelaphus scriptus*), about 76-92 cm, and the tiny **Kirk's dikdik** (*Rhynchotragus kirkii*) only 36-41 cm. Both are easily identified. Kirk's dikdik is so small it can hardly be mistaken for any other antelope. In colour it is a greyish brown, often washed with rufous. The legs are noticeably thin and stick-like, giving the animal a very fragile appearance. The snout is slightly elongated, and there is a tuft of hair on the top of the head. Only the male carries the very small straight horns.

Finally, mention must be made of a rare antelope that is fairly frequently seen in the Aberdare National Park. This is the **bongo** (*Boocercus euryceros*), a large and handsome 112-127 cm forest antelope.

**Other mammals** Although the antelope are undoubtedly the most numerous animals to be seen on the plains, there are others worth keeping an eye open for. Some of these are scavengers. They include the dog-like jackals, of which there are three main species, all being similar in size (about 86-96 cm in length and 41-46 cm at the shoulder). The **black-backed jackal** (*Canis mesomelas*), which is the most common and ranges throughout the area, is a rather foxy reddish fawn in colour with a noticeable black area on its back. This black part is sprinkled with a silvery white, which can make the back look silver in some lights. In general colour the **side-striped jackal** (*Canis adustus*) is greyish fawn and it has a variable and sometimes ill-defined stripe along the side. It is most likely to be seen around Lake Victoria. The other well known plains scavenger is the **spotted hyaena** (*Crocuta crocuta*). It is a fairly large animal, 69-91 cm high.

A favourite and common is the comical **warthog** (*Phacochoerus aethiopicus*). In suitable rocky areas, such as kopjes, look out for an animal that looks a bit like a large grey-brown guinea pig. This is the **rock hyrax** (*Heterohyrax brucei*), an engaging and fairly common animal that lives in communities in rocky places.

The most common and frequently seen of the monkey group are the baboons. The most widespread species is the **olive baboon** (*Papio anubis*), which occurs almost throughout the area. This is a large (127-142 cm), heavily built olive brown or greyish in colour. Adult males have a well-developed mane. In the eastern part of Kenya, including the coast, the olive baboon is replaced by the **yellow baboon** (*Papio cynocephalus*) (116-137 cm), which is a smaller and lighter animal than the olive baboon, with longer legs and almost no mane in the adult males. The tail in both species looks as if it is broken and hangs down in a loop. Baboons are basically terrestrial animals, although they can climb very well. In the wild they are often found in acacia grassland, often associated with rocks, and are sociable animals living in groups called troops. Females are very often seen with young clinging to them. In parts of East Africa they have become very used to the presence of man and can be a nuisance to campers. They will readily climb all over your vehicle hoping for a handout. Be careful, they have a very nasty bite.

The smaller monkey that makes a nuisance of itself is the **vervet or green monkey** (*Cercopithecus mitis*), which is the one that abounds at camp sites and often lodges. This has various forms, the commonest and most widespread having a black face framed with white across the forehead and cheeks. Its general colour is greyish tinged with a varying amount of yellow. The feet, hands and tip of the tail are black.

At dusk in Africa you will notice many bats. The most spectacular of them is the **straw-coloured fruit bat** (*Eidolon helvum*) which has a wing span of 76 cm.

### Birds

East Africa is one of the richest areas of birdlife in the world. The total number of species is in excess of 1,300, and it is possible, and not too difficult to see 100 different species in a day. You will find that a pair of binoculars is essential. The birds described here are the common ones and, with a little careful observation, you will soon find that you can identify them. They have been grouped according to the habitat.

Urban birds   The first birds that you will notice on arrival in any big city will almost certainly be the large numbers soaring overhead. Early in the morning the numbers are few, but as the temperature warms up, more and more are seen circling high above the buildings. Many of these will be **hooded vultures** (*Neophron monachus*) 66 cm, and **black kites** (*Milvus migrans*) 55 cm. They are both superficially similar, rather nondescript brownish birds. They are, however, easily distinguished by the shape and length of the tail. The tail of the hooded vulture is short and slightly rounded at the end, whereas the black kite (which incidentally is not black, but brown) has a long, narrow tail that looks either forked when the tail is closed or slightly concave at the end when spread. Also soaring overhead in some cities you will see the **marabou stork** (*Leptoptilos crumeniferus*) 152 cm. Although this bird is a stork it behaves like a vulture, in that it lives by scavenging. Overhead its large size, long and noticeable bill and trailing legs make it easily identified. The commonest crow in towns and cities is the **pied crow** (*Corvus albus*) 46 cm. This is a very handsome black bird with a white lower breast that joins up with a white collar round the back of the neck. It is a slender, shiny black bird with a grey neck. In gardens and parks there are a number of smaller birds to look out for. The **dark-capped or common bulbul** (*Pycnonotus barbatus*) 18 cm, can be heard all day with its cheerful call of "Come quick, doctor, quick". It is a brownish bird with a darker brown head and a slight crest. Below, the brown is paler fading to white on the belly, and under the tail it is bright yellow.

There are a large number of weaver birds to be seen, but identifying them is not always easy. Most of them are yellow and black in colour, and many of them live in large noisy colonies. Have a close look at their intricately-woven nests if you get the chance. The commonest one is probably the **black-headed weaver** (*Ploceus cucullatus*) 18 cm, which often builds its colonies in bamboo clumps. The male has a mainly black head and throat, but the back of the head is chestnut. The underparts are bright yellow, and the back and wings mottled black and greenish yellow. When the bird is perched, and seen from behind, the markings on the back form a v-shape.

**Birds of open plains** Along with the spectacular game, it is here that you will see many of the magnificent African birds. In particular, there are two large birds which you will see stalking across the grasslands. These are the **ostrich** (*Struthio camelus*) 2 m, and the **secretary bird** (*Sagittarius serpentarius*) 101 cm. The secretary bird is so called because the long plumes of its crest are supposed to resemble the old-time secretaries who carried their quill pens tucked behind their ears. The bird is often seen in pairs as it hunts for snakes, its main food source. The ostrich is sometimes seen singly, but also in family groups. There are other large terrestrial birds to look out for, and one of them, the **kori bustard** (*Otis kori*) 80 cm, like the secretary bird quarters the plains looking for snakes. It is quite a different shape, however, and can be distinguished by the thick-looking grey neck (caused by loose feathers). It is particularly common in Serengeti National Park and in the Masai Mara. The other large bird that you are likely to see on the open plains is the **ground hornbill** (*Bucorvus cafer*) 107 cm. When seen from afar, this looks just like a turkey but close up it is very distinctive and cannot really be mistaken for anything else. They are very often in pairs and the male has bare red skin around the eye and on the throat. In the female this skin is red and blue.

Soaring overhead on the plains you will see vultures and birds of prey. The commonest vulture in game areas is the **African white-backed vulture** (*Gyps africanus*) 81 cm. This is a largish, brown bird with a white lower back, with the characteristic bare head of its family. Because they are commonly seen circling overhead the white rump can be difficult to see. So look out for the other diagnostic characteristic – the broad white band on the leading edge of the undersurface of the wing. The **bateleur** (*Terathopius ecaudatus*) 61 cm, is a magnificent and strange-looking eagle. It is rarely seen perched, but is quite commonly seen soaring very high overhead. Its tail is so short that it sometimes appears tailless. This, its buoyant flight, and the black and white pattern of its underparts make it easy to identify.

Where there is game look out for the oxpeckers. The commonest one is the **red-billed oxpecker** (*Buphagus erythrorynchus*) 18 cm. These birds are actually members of the starling family although their behaviour is not like that of other starlings. They associate with game animals and cattle and spend their time clinging to, and climbing all over the animals while they hunt for ticks, which form their main food. There are other birds that associate with animals in a different way. For example the **cattle egret** (*Bubulcus ibis*) 51 cm, follows herds and feeds on the grasshoppers and other insects disturbed by the passing of the animals. Occasionally too, the cattle egret will perch on the back of a large animal, but this is quite different from the behaviour of oxpeckers. Cattle egrets are long-legged and long-billed white birds, most often seen in small flocks. In the breeding season they develop long buff feathers on the head, chest and back

**Birds of dry, open woodland** The two habitats of open plain and dry open woodland form a vast area of Africa and most of the game parks come into these categories. As well as being quintessentially African, this dry open woodland with acacia thorn trees is an extremely rewarding area for bird watching, it supports an enormous variety of species and it is relatively easy to see them.

The guinea fowls live in flocks and if you surprise a group on the road they will disappear into the bush in a panic. There is more than one sort of guinea fowl, but they are rather similar, being a slate grey with white spots.

The tops of the thorn trees are used as observation perches by a number of different species. Specially noticeable is the **red-billed hornbill** (*Tockus erythrorynchus*) 45 cm, which has blackish-brown back, with a white stripe down between the wings. The wings themselves are spotted with white. The underparts are white and the bill is long, curved and mainly red. As the bird flies into a tree the impression is of a black and white bird with a long red bill and a long tail. Another striking bird that perches on tree tops is the **white-bellied go-away bird** (*Corythaixoides leucogaster*) 51 cm. This gets its strange name from its call "Go-away, go-away". It is a basically grey bird with a very upright stance. The top of the head carries a long and conspicuous crest. The belly is white and the long tail has a black tip. It is usually seen in small family parties.

The strange-looking, brightly coloured bird **d'Arnaud's barbet** (*Trachyphonus darnaudii*) 15 cm, is common in the dry bush country. The impression you get is of a spotted bird, dark with pale spots above, and pale with dark spots below. It has a long, dark, heavily spotted tail. Its call and behaviour is very distinctive. A pair will sit facing each other with their tails raised over their backs wagging them from side to side, and bob at each other in a duet. All the while they utter a four-note call over and over again. "Do-do dee-dok". Another brightly coloured bird is the **lilac-breasted roller** (*Coracias caudata*) 41 cm, which is very easy to see as it perches on telegraph poles or wires, or on bare branches. The brilliant blue on its wings, head and underparts is very eye catching. Its throat and breast are a deep lilac and its tail has two elongated streamers. It is quite common in open bush country. Also often seen sitting on bare branches is the **drongo** (*Dicrurus adsimilis*) 24 cm, but this is an all-black bird. It is easily identified by its forked tail, which is "fish-tailed" at the end. It is usually solitary.

There are many different species of starling to be seen in eastern Africa, and most of them are beautifully coloured. Two of the most spectacular are the **golden-breasted starling** (*Cosmopsarus regius*) 32 cm, and the **superb starling** (*Spreo superbus*) 18 cm. Both are common, but the superb starling is the more widespread and is seen near habitation as well as in thorn bush country. Tsavo East is probably the best place to see the golden-breasted starling. Look out for the long tail of the golden-breasted starling, and the white under tail and the white breast band of the superb starling. Both are usually seen hopping about on the ground. Another long-tailed bird quite commonly seen in bush country is the **long-tailed fiscal** (*Lanius cabanisi*) 30 cm. Unlike the golden-breasted starling, however, it is a black and white bird that is usually seen perched on wires or bare branches. It can be identified by its very long all-black tail and mainly black upperparts, which are grey on the lower back and rump.

Finally look out for three birds, which though small are very noticeable. The **red-cheeked cordon-bleu** (*Uraeginthus bengalus*) 13 cm, is a lovely little blue bird with a brown back and bright red cheek patches. They are seen in pairs or family parties, and the females and young are somewhat duller in colour than the males. They are quite tame and you often see them round the game lodges. In the less dry grasslands you can see the beautiful red and black bishop birds. There are two species, both of which are quite brilliant in their colouring. The brightest is the **red bishop** (*Euplectes orix*) 13 cm, which has brown wings and tail, and noticeable scarlet feathers on its rump. The almost equally brilliant **black-winged bishop** (*Euplectes hordeaceus*) 14 cm, may be distinguished from the red bishop by its black wings and tail and rather less obvious red rump. Both species occur in long grass and cultivation, often, but not invariably, near water.

**Water and waterside birds** The inland waters form a very important habitat for both resident and migratory species. A lot can be seen from the shore, but it is especially fruitful to go out in a boat, when you will get quite close to, among others, the large and magnificent herons that occur here. The king of them all is the aptly named **goliath heron** (*Ardea goliath*) 144 cm, which is usually seen singly on mud banks and shores, both inland and on the coast. Its very large size is enough to distinguish it, but the smaller **purple heron** (*Ardea purpurea*)

Background Land & environment • 399

80 cm, which frequents similar habitat and is also widespread, may be mistaken for it at a distance. If in doubt, the colour on the top of the head (rufous in the goliath and black in the purple) will clinch it; also the purple is much more slender with a slender bill.

The flamingos are known to most people and will be readily identified. However, there are two different species that very often occur together. The **greater flamingo** (*Phoenicopterus ruber*) 142 cm, is the larger and paler bird and has a pink bill with a black tip. The **lesser flamingo** (*Phoenicopterus minor*) 101 cm, is deeper pink all over and has a deep carmine bill with a black tip. They both occur in large numbers in the soda lakes of Western Kenya. The magnificent **fish eagle** (*Haliaeetus vocifer*) 76 cm, has a distinctive colour pattern. It often perches on the tops of trees, where its dazzling white head and chest are easily seen. In flight this white and the white tail contrast with the black wings. It has a wild yelping call, which is usually uttered in flight. Try and watch the bird as it calls: it throws back its head over its back in a most unusual way.

There are several different kingfishers to be seen, but the most numerous is the black and white **pied kingfisher** (*Ceryle rudis*) 25 cm. This is easily recognized as it is the only black and white kingfisher all round the large lakes and also turns up at quite small bodies of water. It hovers over the water before plunging in to capture its prey.

## Marine wildlife

The fish and coral here are wonderful and can be observed without having to dive. Many of the fish do not have universally recognized English names, but one that does is the very common **scorpion** or **lion fish** (*Pterois*), which is probably the most spectacular fish you can see without going out in a boat. It is likely to be wherever there is live coral, and sometimes it gets trapped in the deeper pools of the dead reef by the retreating tide. It can be up to 26 cm long and is easily recognized by its peculiar fins and zebra stripes. Although it has poisonous dorsal spines it will not attack if left alone.

While most visitors naturally want to spend time diving and snorkelling on the live reef and watching the brilliant fish and many coloured living corals, do not bypass the smaller, humbler creatures that frequent dead as well as living coral. These can be seen on most of the beaches, but one of the best places is Tiwi beach by Twiga Lodge, see page 268. Here a vast area of dead coral is partly exposed at low tide and you can safely paddle. Be sure to wear shoes though, because there are many sea urchins. These **sea urchins** (*Echinoidea*) are usually found further out towards the edge of the reef, but can be found anywhere. There are two forms, the more common **short-needled sea urchin** and the much less common **long-needled** variety. Their spines are very sharp and treading on them is extremely painful. Look out also for the common **brittle stars** (*Ophiuroidea*), which frequent sandy hollows. They vary in size, but are usually 10 cm across. They are so called because the arms break off very readily, but grow again. These are not sea urchins, though they are related, and can safely be picked up for a closer look, but handle them carefully.

Other living creatures that can be seen crawling along in the shallows include the sea **slug** (*Nudibranchia*) and the **snake eel** (*Ophichthidae*). Both are quite common in sandy places. The unlovely sea slug is blackish brown and shaped a bit like the familiar garden slug, though much bigger. It often has grains of sand sticking to it. Don't be put off by the name of the snake eel, it is quite harmless. It looks a bit like a snake and has alternating light and dark bands on its body. What are beautiful, without doubt, are the **starfish** (*Asteroidea*), best seen by going out in a boat, but some can be seen nearer in shore.

The commonest shells are without doubt the **cowries**. Many dead ones can be found on the beach. The two most common are the **ringed cowrie** (*Cyprea annulus*) and the money cowrie (*Cypraea moneta*). Of these the ringed is especially plentiful and is a pretty grey and white shell with a golden ring. The money cowrie, once used as currency in Africa, varies in colour from greenish grey to pink according to its age. The big and beautiful **tiger cowrie** (*Cypraea tigris*) is also seen occasionally. They can be up to 8 cm in length. There is quite a lot of variation in colouring, but it is basically a very shiny shell with many dark round spots on, much more like a leopard than a tiger.

# Books

## History

**Anderson D**, *Histories of the Hanged: Britain's Dirty War in Kenya and the end of Empire*, covers the final years of the Mau Mau uprising and looks at the mistreatment of the Kikuyu people, who the British herded into concentration camps where many died.

**Fox J**, *White Mischief*, looks at the notorious 'Happy Valley', set in 1940s colonial Kenya and investigates the unsolved murder of Lord Erroll, aka Josslyn Hay.

**Hibbert C**, *Africa Explored: Europeans in the Dark Continent 1769-1889*, describes the exploits of the main explorers, including the search for the source of the Nile.

**Huxley E**, *Flame Trees of Thika*, stories of the lives of the early pioneers told through the eyes of a young girl growing up on a coffee farm.

**Kenyatta J**, *Facing Mount Kenya*, written in the colonial times before he became the first president of Kenya, this gives an interesting insight into the history and the culture of the Kikuyu people.

**Miller C**, *Lunatic Express*, highly readable history of East Africa, centring around the building of the railway.

**Monbiot G**, *No Man's Land*, tells how the nomadic tribes in Kenya and Tanzanian are being forced off their land by drought and the pressures of a modern world.

## Memoirs

**Adamson J**, *Born Free*, the classic tale of Elsa the lioness that was raised and set free by Joy and George Adamson in the 1960s. Joy wrote several more books about releasing big cats into the wild in Kenya.

**Blixen K**, *Out of Africa*, wonderfully written, impressions of the author's life in Kenya.

**Maathai W**, *Unbowed: A Memoir*, autobiography of 2004 Nobel Peace Prize winner Wangari Maathai, an extraordinary woman who has instigated the planting of some 30 million trees in Kenya (see page 190).

**Markham B**, *West with the Night*, marvellous autobiography of the woman who made the first solo east to west Atlantic flight.

**Patterson J**, *The Man-eaters of Tsavo*, adventurous account of how railway supervisor John Patterson tracked down and shot 2 man-eating lions that had been terrorizing workers during the building of the Uganda Railway.

## Fiction

**Hemingway E**, *Green Hills of Africa*, masterly short stories based on the author's African visits in 1933-1934.

**Le Carré J**, *The Constant Gardener*, a powerful story about a British diplomat in Nairobi whose wife is murdered while investigating a drugs trial scandal; later made into a popular movie.

**Mwangi M**, *Going Down River Road*, grim but entertaining story of African urban life.

# Footnotes

# Useful words and phrases

Here are some useful words and phrases in Kiswahili. Attempting a few words will be much appreciated by Kenyans.

| | |
|---|---|
| Good morning | *Habari ya asubuhi* |
| Good afternoon | *Habari ya mchana* |
| Good evening | *Habari ya jioni* |
| Good night | *Habari ya usiku* |
| Hello! | *Jambo!* |
| A respectful greeting to elders, actually meaning: "I hold your feet" | *Shikamoo* |
| Their reply: "I am delighted" | *Marahaba* |
| How are you? | *Habari yako?* |
| I am fine | *Nzuri / Sijambo* |
| I am not feeling good today | *Sijiziki vizuri leo* |
| How are things? | *Mambo?* |
| Good/cool/cool and crazy | *Safi / poa / poa kichizi* |
| See you later | *Tutaonana baadaye* |
| Welcome! | *Karibu! (Karibu tenai!)* |
| Goodbye | *Kwaheri* |
| Please | *Tafadhali* |
| Thank you | *Asante* |
| Sorry | *Pole* |
| Where can I get a taxi? | *Teksi iko wapi?* |
| Where is the bus station? | *Stendi ya basi iko wapi?* |
| When will we arrive? | *Tutafika lini?* |
| Can you show me the bus? | *Unaweza ukanioyesha basi?* |
| How much is the ticket? | *Tiketi ni bei gani?* |
| Is it safe walking here at night? | *Ni salama kutembea hapa usiku?* |
| I don't want to buy anything | *Sitaki kununua chochote* |
| I have already booked a safari | *Tayari nimeisha lipia safari* |
| I don't have money | *Sina hela* |
| I'm not single | *Nina mchumba / siko peke yangu* |
| Could you please leave me alone? | *Tafadhali, achana na mimi* |
| It is none of your business! | *Hayakuhusu!* |
| One | *moja* |
| Two | *mbili* |
| Three | *tatu* |
| Four | *nne* |
| Five | *tano* |
| Six | *sita* |
| Seven | *saba* |
| Eight | *nane* |
| Nine | *tisa* |
| Ten | *kumi* |

## Advertisers' index

# Acknowledgements

Firstly, grateful thanks must go to Michael Hodd for the enormous amount of work he put into compiling *Footprint East Africa*, which still forms the core of the *Kenya Handbook*.

Lizzie would like to thank Wendy Gore for use of her lovely cottage in peaceful Karen, and Graeme and Rosemary Thomson, also in Karen, for their exceptional hospitality. Also the staff at the Comfort Inn and the Boulevard Hotel downtown who are always very helpful. Other long-term, helpful friends in East Africa include Dougie at Karen Camp, and Bulawayo Bruce, Dutch Pete and Sparky. Thanks too to Karl-Heinz Straus from Kenya One Tours and Leanne Guild from South African-based Africa Travel Company, for providing useful snippets of information. Readers that wrote in with suggestions include Steven Teliszewski, Angie Zautner, Gabriel Gloeckler, Charlotta and Heribert Heck, Simon Lewis, and Anna Bryant. Thanks must also go to Footprint's Ria Gane for putting it all together.

# About the author

Originally from London, Lizzie has worked and lived in Africa for 14 years. Starting out on trips across the continent as a tour leader on overland trucks, she has sat with a gorilla, slept amongst elephants, fed a giraffe and swum with a hippo and is now something of an expert on border crossings and African beer. For Footprint she is author of the *South Africa, Namibia, Kenya* and *Tanzania* handbooks; she has written the only country guide to Nigeria and the first city guide to Johannesburg for Bradt; is author of the *AA Key Guide to South Africa, AA Spiral Guide to South Africa* and *Africa Overland*, a glossy look at the overland route from Nairobi to Cape Town, is co-author of the DK Eyewitness to Kenya, and has contributed to Turkey and Egypt for Rough Guides. She has written various online African destination guides for leading websites in the UK and US including Frommers, British Airways and www.worldtravelguide.net. When not on the road, Lizzie lives in Cape Town.

# Credits

**Footprint credits**

**Editor:** Ria Gane
**Map editor:** Sarah Sorensen
**Colour section:** Kassia Gawronski

**Managing Director:** Andy Riddle
**Commercial Director:** Patrick Dawson
**Publisher:** Alan Murphy
**Editorial:** Sara Chare, Nicola Gibbs, Jen Haddington, Alice Jell, Felicity Laughton,
**Cartography:** Robert Lunn, Kevin Feeney, Emma Bryers
**Cover design:** Robert Lunn
**Design:** Mytton Williams
**Sales and marketing:** Liz Harper, Zoë Jackson, Hannah Bonnell
**Advertising sales manager:** Renu Sibal
**Finance and administration:** Elizabeth Taylor

**Photography credits**
**Front cover:** Robert Harding
**Back cover:** Vera Bogaerts/Shutterstock

Manufactured in Italy by LegoPrint
Pulp from sustainable forests

**Footprint feedback**
We try as hard as we can to make each Footprint guide as up to date as possible but, of course, things always change. If you want to let us know about your experiences – good, bad or ugly – then don't delay, go to www.footprintbooks.com and send in your comments.

**Publishing information**
Footprint Kenya
2nd edition
© Footprint Handbooks Ltd
March 2009
ISBN: 978 1 906098 47 6
CIP DATA: A catalogue record for this book is available from the British Library

® Footprint Handbooks and the Footprint mark are a registered trademark of Footprint Handbooks Ltd

Published by Footprint
6 Riverside Court
Lower Bristol Road
Bath BA2 3DZ, UK
T +44 (0)1225 469141
F +44 (0)1225 469461
www.footprintbooks.com

Distributed in the USA by Globe Pequot Press, Guilford, Connecticut

Every effort has been made to ensure that the facts in this guidebook are accurate. However, travellers should still obtain advice from consulates, airlines, etc about travel and visa requirements before travelling. The authors and publishers cannot accept responsibility for any loss, injury or inconvenience however caused.